The Founding of a Nation

The Founding of a Nation

A HISTORY OF THE AMERICAN REVOLUTION 1763–1776

Merrill Jensen

Hackett Publishing Company, Inc.
Indianapolis/Cambridge

Printed in the United States of America
10 09 08 07 06 05 04   1 2 3 4 5 6 7

For further information, please address:

      Hackett Publishing Company, Inc.
      P.O. Box 44937
      Indianapolis, IN   46244-0937

      www.hackettpublishing.com

Cover photograph courtesy of Library of Congress, Prints and
    Photographs Division
Cover design by Abigail Coyle
Printed at Sheridan Books, Inc.

Library of Congress Cataloging-in-Publication Data

Jensen, Merrill.
    The founding of a nation : a history of the American Revolution,
1763–1776 / Merrill Jensen.
      p. cm.
    Originally published: New York : Oxford University Press, 1968.
    Includes bibliographical references and index.
    ISBN 0-87220-706-4 (alk. paper) — ISBN 0-87220-705-6 (pbk. : alk. paper)
      1. United States—History—Colonial period, ca. 1600–1775. 2. United
States—History—Revolution, 1775–1783—Causes. I. Title

E195.J4 2004
973.2'7—dc22

                 2003056880

Acknowledgments

In writing this book I have incurred a host of debts that mere words can only acknowledge, never repay. The obligations to the men of the Revolution who left diaries, letters, newspapers, and other documents for posterity to ponder over are obvious. So too are the obligations to the historians who have been writing about the American Revolution ever since it began. With some of them I have agreed, with others I have disagreed, but always I have learned from them.

The debt to librarians is beyond measuring. The staffs of such libraries as the Public Record Office in London, the Library of Congress in Washington, the Historical Society of Pennsylvania, the New York Public Library, the New-York Historical Society, and the Massachusetts Historical Society have been invariably helpful. One library, perhaps more than any other, has a call upon my gratitude: the Huntington Library. Some years ago, Dr. John E. Pomfret, the director, now retired, provided me with a fellowship, the facilities, and the ideal scholarly atmosphere which made it possible for me to get the writing of this book under way. I also owe very particular thanks to the staff of the library of the State Historical Society of Wisconsin, whose patience has been beyond compare.

Quotations from the Adams Papers are from the microfilm edition, by permission of the Massachusetts Historical Society.

Over the years the people who have at one time or another been members of my research seminar at the University of Wisconsin have taught me as much as I was ever able to teach them. In the course of weekly battles with words, wits, and facts there developed a community of scholars for whom I have great respect and to whom my gratitude is very great indeed. Citations to their research in the footnotes of this book give some small indication of their contributions. In addition certain former students have read and criticized portions of the manuscript. My thanks go therefore to Jackson Turner Main of the University of New York at Stony Brook; James Ferguson, Queens College, New York; Carl Ubbelohde, Case-Western Reserve University; and Joseph Ernst, York University, Toronto. My colleague, Norman Risjord, also read a large portion of the manuscript and offered many helpful suggestions. I am also grateful to William Abbott of the University of Virginia and Charles Mullett of the University of Missouri, who read the manuscript at the publisher's request.

For assistance in research I am deeply grateful to the Research Committee of the University of Wisconsin Graduate School, and also, since 1964, to the Trustees of the Estate of Senator William F. Vilas, and particularly for providing money for graduate students to work with me as research assistants. Among the former research assistants whose help has been indispensable are Roger Champagne of Northern Illinois University; Peter Barry, Wisconsin State University, Whitewater; Rupert Charles Loucks, University of Hartford; Stephen Patterson, University of New Brunswick; and Kenneth Bowling, University of Wisconsin. I owe a very particular debt to the two research assistants who have helped me see this book through its final stages: John Shaeffer of San Fernando Valley State College, and Robert Becker, a graduate student at the University of Wisconsin. Without their unflagging energy, meticulous attention to detail, and forthright criticisms of ideas and style (some of which I ignored as being too conservative), this book would have taken far longer than it has to complete.

Last, but by no means least, my gratitude and my admiration are due to Virginia Fiedler and Ellen Story who typed and re-typed page after page of the manuscript with meticulous care; and to my wife, Genevieve Jensen, who has read and re-read page proof and found errors missed by all others.

It should be needless to say so but the responsibility for everything between the two covers of this book is entirely mine, and I acknowledge it gladly.

Merrill Jensen

Madison, Wisconsin
June 1968

Symbols and a Note on Sources

Frequently cited sources with long titles, newspapers, the names of manuscript depositories, and the like, have been assigned symbols. The symbols are given in square brackets immediately after the title in the first full citation. A table of symbols, with the chapters and the numbers of notes in which the first full citations are given, appears on pages 705–7.

In quoting from eighteenth-century sources, spelling and capitalization have usually been modernized and abbreviations have been spelled out. Punctuation has been added or deleted when necessary to clarify meaning.

Contents

Introduction

After independence had been won many Americans looked back and sought to explain the history they had helped to make. Among those who did so were Dr. Benjamin Rush and John Adams. In 1787 Rush wrote that "there is nothing more common than to confound the terms of American Revolution with those of the late American war. The American war is over, but this is far from being the case with the American revolution. On the contrary, nothing but the first act of the great drama is closed." A quarter of a century later John Adams made the same distinction. "What do we mean by the Revolution? The War?" he asked Thomas Jefferson. He answered his own question by declaring that the war "was no part of the Revolution. It was only an effect and consequence of it." And to another friend he wrote that "a history of the first war of the United States is a very different thing from an history of the American Revolution."

While Rush and Adams agreed that the American Revolution and the war for independence were two quite separate events, they differed in their interpretation of the nature of the American Revolution. Rush looked upon it as a continuing process. "We have changed our forms of government," he said in 1786, "but it remains yet to effect a revolution of our principles, opinions, and manners so as to accommodate them to the forms of government we have adopted." On the other hand John Adams believed that the Revolution took place before 1776. He told Thomas Jefferson that his idea might be "peculiar, perhaps singular," but asserted that "the Revolution was in the minds of the people, and this was effected, from 1760–1775, in the course of fifteen years before a drop of blood was shed at Lexington." A bit later he wrote to another correspondent that "the revolution was in the minds and hearts of the people and in the union of the colonies, both of which were accomplished before hostilities commenced." Adams looked upon the accomplishment as something of a miracle, for the colonies were so different in so many ways that to unite them "was perhaps a singular example in the history of mankind. Thirteen clocks were made to strike together—a perfection of mechanism which no artist had ever before effected." To understand how it was done, he insisted repeatedly, "the records of the British government and the records of all the thirteen colonies and the pamphlets, newspapers, and handbills of both parties must be examined and the essence extracted before a correct history can be written of the American Revolution."

What "essence" can be extracted from such records? Historians have interpreted the origins of the war for independence in various ways. They have found its "cause" or "causes" in political and constitutional issues, in economic difficulties, in religious concerns, in intellectual forces, and the like. However, all too often the concern with "causes" leads historians to fasten upon a single explanation to the exclusion of others equally relevant, or to adopt abstractions that oversimplify complex events. No one understood this better than John Adams when he declared that "the principles of the American Revolution may be said to have been as various as the thirteen states that went through it, and in some sense almost as diversified as the individuals who acted in it. In some few principles, or perhaps in one single principle, they all united."

The primary concern of this book is not with a search for the "causes" or the "principles" of the war for independence; its purpose is to set forth as fully as possible the complex history of a period of time which ended when Americans declared their independence and proclaimed the foundation of a new nation which they named the United States of America. This book is a political history, and while political and constitutional theories, economic conditions, and social and religious tensions are a part of the story, the emphasis is on the deeds of men rather than on their motives and their rhetoric, on the actions of men on both sides of the Atlantic Ocean which ended in the most important political decision in American history—the decision to separate from the British Empire after more than a century and a half as a part of it.

To a certain extent, therefore, this book is an account of the extraordinary group of men who rose to power and led thirteen of Britain's New World colonies to declare their independence. It is also an account of other powerful American leaders who opposed independence but who, in the end, were forced to choose between loyalty to Britain and citizenship in a new nation.

And since the men who led the new nation after 1776 had their roots in and rose to power within their home colonies, this book is necessarily a history of thirteen separate colonies, although not all colonies have been treated equally, and some have been virtually ignored. It is a history further complicated by the fact that, while there was opposition to British policies in all the colonies, Americans disagreed about the means, the methods, and the ends of that opposition. Beyond this, several of the colonies were divided into "factions" or "parties" on domestic issues, and as American leaders jockeyed for popular support and political power, the question of opposition to Britain was sometimes subordinated to or even lost sight of in the course of local political battles.

The history of the period is therefore one of extraordinary intricacy. It is not the history of a united American people marching inexorably along the road to independence and the creation of a new nation. It is instead a history of a divided people, many of whom, if they had been free to choose, would have remained within the British Empire rather than risk their lives and fortunes in a struggle for independence and citizenship in a new nation.

Finally, this book is based on the assumption that both Benjamin Rush and John Adams were right in their interpretations of the American Revolution although it is limited to the revolution described by the latter. The "principles" of that revolution were indeed "various" and it is to setting forth a portion of that great variety that the following pages are devoted.

The Founding of a Nation

Part 1: The First Crisis

The first British Empire achieved its greatest triumph in the Treaty of Paris in 1763. Twenty years later a second Treaty of Paris marked the humiliating end of that empire when Britain acknowledged the independence of thirteen of her former colonies on the mainland of North America. Few if any men who gloried in the triumph of 1763 foresaw the collapse to come, although some of the issues that led to the war for American independence had roots in the war which preceded it.

The Treaty of 1763 ended the fourth war since 1689 in which Britain and France had been the major antagonists in a struggle for the domination of western Europe, and increasingly, for possession of colonial empires as far apart as India and North America. The Seven Years War, or the French and Indian War as the Americans were to call it, had an inglorious beginning in the American wilderness in the summer of 1754. The Ohio Company, a group of Virginia land speculators who were interested both in private profit and in the establishment of Virginia's claims to the lands of the Ohio Valley, began building a fort at the forks of the Ohio River. France, with a great chain of communications from the St. Lawrence River to the Gulf of Mexico farther to the west, was by then building a new chain in the hope of forever confining the English colonists east of the Appalachian Mountains.

In April 1754, French troops moved south from Lake Erie, seized the Ohio Company post and named it Fort Duquesne. That same month, Governor Robert Dinwiddie of Virginia, a member of the Ohio Company, sent a force of 200 men westward under the command of a twenty-two-year-old man utterly lacking in military experience. His name was George Washington. On the way, he learned of the French capture of the post at the forks of the Ohio, but was joined by some South Carolina troops and they pushed on, and in a surprise attack, killed and captured men of a French scouting party. The colonials then retreated to the Great Meadows where they entrenched themselves in a "fort" aptly named Necessity, and on 4 July 1754 they surrendered to a superior French force.

The undeclared war thus begun took an even more disastrous turn the next year. Britain sent out General Edward Braddock with two regiments of British regulars and with orders to secure the help of the colonies. Colonial governors quarreled with one another and with their legislatures but eventually Braddock was able to start west with his regulars and a motley collection of colonial militia. On 9 July 1755 a French and Indian force shattered Braddock's army only a few miles from Fort Duquesne. Braddock was killed, and only twenty-three of eighty-six officers and 459 of 1373 non-commissioned officers and privates escaped death or wounds. Those who could fled panic-stricken back across the mountains, leaving the French in undisputed control of the Ohio Valley.

In 1756 war began in Europe and Britain continued to suffer one disaster after another until William Pitt took charge. With an imperial disdain for the bookkeeper souls who cherished budgets and worried about taxes, he poured men and money into the war around the world, and triumph followed triumph. That he brought Britain to the verge of bankruptcy was for him an irrelevant detail. Pitt resigned before the end of the war but Britain rolled on to the victory capped by the Treaty of Paris. All of North America east of the Mississippi River, Canada with its 60,000 French inhabitants, the Spanish Floridas, and several islands in the West Indies became a part of the British Empire in the New World. France was left with only bits and pieces of her once great holdings in America and Asia, and she gave the unknown vastness of Louisiana to her hapless ally, Spain.

In 1763 Britain was on the very pinnacle of worldwide power and her old enemies were seemingly prostrate. But at the same time the nation was beset with political instability and was stumbling on the edge of bankruptcy. The agencies in charge of the empire were so enmeshed in conflicting jurisdictions and were staffed by so many incompetent men that it is a wonder that the administration of colonial affairs did not collapse completely. It fell to the ministry of George Grenville to attempt to bring order out of chaos and to establish governments for the vast new territories that had been added to the empire. In doing so, the Grenville ministry tried to subject the far-flung colonies to that centralized control which had always existed in theory but had seldom been achieved in practice. In making the attempt the Grenville ministry presented the American colonies with issues they could not ignore, issues with consequences neither American nor British leaders could foresee.

The colonies had always been the domain of the Crown, administered by royally appointed officials. Parliament had seldom interfered—except to pass the Acts of Trade and Navigation, laws relating to finance, and laws prohibiting or limiting certain colonial manufactures. The disputes between America and Britain before 1763 had been mainly disputes between royal officials and the colonial legislatures, and on the whole the latter had triumphed and achieved a remarkable degree of self-government. But after 1763, with the support of the new king, Parliament interfered directly in affairs that had long been handled by royal appointees. Above all, it interfered in an area the colonial legislatures had controlled so long that they regarded that control as an inalienable right: the levying of taxes and the direction of the expenditure of the money collected. The attempt by Parliament to raise money in the colonies by acts of Parliament, coupled with other restrictive legislation and administrative decisions, forced Americans, for the first time, to attempt a serious definition of their concepts of the power of Parliament over the colonies.

By 1766 many Americans were claiming the sole right of taxation for their own legislatures and some were denying the right of Parliament to pass any laws whatsoever for America. Independence, long a subject of idle speculation as a prospect in some dim future, suddenly became a specter on the near horizon for Americans who feared it, or perhaps a bright hope for others. Parliament answered all American arguments with a flat assertion of its absolute sovereignty over the whole empire when it declared that it had the power and right to legislate for America "in all cases whatsoever." Thus, only three years after Britain's sweeping victory over her enemies, the issue was squarely before her and her American colonies. The men who made the political decisions on both sides of the Atlantic refused to retreat from their diametrically opposed interpretations of the constitution of the empire, and in the end, turned from argument to the use of force.

The first crisis centered on the Stamp Act. The Americans achieved an unprecedented degree of unity in opposing it and in defeating its operation. But the crisis not only divided Americans and Britons; it also created sharp divisions among Americans themselves, which widened in the years ahead. There was thus no inevitable progression toward a declaration of independence after 1766, despite the clear presentation of the issues to Americans ten years before the event.

I

America in 1763

The horizons of British America seemed boundless in 1763. Gone was the century-old threat of encirclement and confinement to the seacoast by the French and Spanish and their Indian allies. True, the Indians remained and they continued to resist, but they could not withstand forever the onslaught of men armed with the conviction that destiny was on their side—and with superior weapons. The fur trade of Canada and the Great Lakes, long a French monopoly, was now open to British and American merchants, who rushed in to reap a golden harvest; and the vast lands of the Mississippi Valley excited the even more golden dreams of land speculators on both sides of the Atlantic.

Once the new territories acquired during the Seven Years War had been made a part of the empire, Britain could count at least thirty formal colonies in the New World: eighteen on the American mainland and twelve in the West Indies. In addition there were Newfoundland, British Honduras, British Guiana, a portion of the Virgin Islands, and the vast uncharted territory claimed by the Hudson's Bay Company. Some of the new possessions were given governments modeled on seventeenth-century colonial patterns. In order to attract settlers a legislature was established in West Florida in 1766 although the colony had but 2000 inhabitants. The tiny Virgin Islands were given a legislature in 1774. Some of the new colonies were ruled only by governors and councils, as were Quebec, East Florida, and Prince Edward Island, the last becoming a separate colony in 1769.

The colonies, new and old, ranged from Hudson Bay to the northern shores of South America, but the thirteen colonies extending from New

Hampshire on the north to Georgia on the south, were the economic heart and the political center of the far-flung empire in America. At the beginning of the eighteenth century these mainland colonies were militarily and economically weak links when compared to the prosperous West Indies, and they seemed strong only in the militant assertion of their political rights. They formed a narrow band of settlement along the seacoast, nowhere extending more than fifty miles inland. Nor was that band continuously occupied. There were a few scattered coastal settlements northeast of Massachusetts. To the south of Virginia was a tiny settlement in what was to become the northeastern part of North Carolina. There was little but wilderness between it and Charleston, South Carolina, and no one knew if that village of perhaps 100 houses could survive raids by the Spanish in Florida and by hostile Indians. Everywhere frontier settlements were under constant pressure from Indians, and in the North, from the French as well. During the wars between 1689 and 1713, French and Indian attacks had forced the abandonment of such settlements as Worcester in Massachusetts, and had all but wiped out others such as Schenectady, only a few miles from Albany in New York.

After a century of effort and the expenditure of untold lives and uncountable sums of money, and after prodigious labor by those who had survived, there were perhaps no more than 400,000 people in the mainland colonies when the Treaty of Utrecht was signed in 1713. And that number represented a doubling of what the population had been when the wars began in 1689.

In the decades of peace that followed the Treaty of Utrecht, the mainland colonies began the explosive expansion that did not end until Americans reached the shores of the Pacific Ocean early in the nineteenth century. Americans soon filled in the gaps along the Atlantic coast and began to push back the frontiers to the north, the west, and the southwest. By 1763 they had settled parts of the valleys within the Appalachian ranges and were beginning to move across the Alleghenies into the Ohio Valley. This expansion was by a population which grew with a rapidity that astonished Europeans and Americans alike. The number of people in a relatively small colony such as Connecticut, for instance, jumped from 130,000 to over 197,000 between 1756 and 1774. Men at the time commonly estimated that population doubled every twenty years. Whatever the rate, by 1775 there were probably 2,500,000 people in the thirteen mainland colonies.

At the outbreak of the war for independence, Virginia was the largest colony in numbers, in area, and, according to its neighbors, in pride and arrogance. Its 500,000 inhabitants, white and black, amounted to 20 per cent of the total population, a fact of great political and economic importance all too often forgotten today. Virginia with the other southern colonies accounted for at least half of the American people. Massachusetts was second in size with 360,000; Pennsylvania (with Delaware) was third with 300,000. New York with 182,000 was still one of the smaller colonies: even Connecticut had more, and only New Hampshire, Rhode Island, New Jersey, and Georgia had fewer inhabitants. Georgia with 33,000 was still little more than a frontier outpost.[1]

The rapid territorial expansion produced a new "region" in most colonies. By 1775 probably 25 per cent of the Americans lived in what the men of the time called the "backcountry." It was not a static but an ever changing, ever growing area of small farms and villages lying beyond the coastal settlements of the seventeenth century. Its far edge was always raw frontier where people hacked at the wilderness and fought off the Indians; sheltered behind it were what had once been frontiers but which were rapidly becoming settled societies with villages and cultivated farms. The colonies to the south of New York had the largest backcountries with perhaps 50 per cent of the people in Pennsylvania and South Carolina and 40 per cent of those of North Carolina living in them.[2]

Although most of the older Americans and the flood of eighteenth-century immigrants were, and wanted to be, farmers, the colonial cities grew ever more rapidly. They were cities in every sense of the word, with all the problems of any rapidly expanding urban area. By 1775 the seven largest cities probably did not contain more than 4 or 5 per cent of the American people, yet Philadelphia, with over 30,000 inhabitants, was among the four or five largest English-speaking cities in the British Empire. New York ranked second in the colonies with 20,000 and Boston third with 15,000. Behind them were Charleston (14,000), Newport (9100),

---

[1] Most estimates of colonial population are based on guesses rather than census reports. Officials used the number of houses, militia lists, tax lists, and the like to try to estimate population. The two basic sources for population figures are Evarts B. Greene and Virginia D. Harrington, *American Population Before the Federal Census of 1790* (New York, 1932), and Stella H. Sutherland, *Population Distribution in Colonial America* (New York, 1936). The latter work is important because it contains maps showing distribution of population and contains histories of population growth in various colonies. A summary set of figures based on these works is in Merrill Jensen, ed., *English Historical Documents* [EHD] (*American Colonial Documents to 1776*, London and New York, 1955), IX, 479–80.

[2] Carl Bridenbaugh, *Myths and Realities: Societies of the Colonial South* (Baton Rouge, 1952), 121, for estimates of the population of the southern backcountry.

and Baltimore (5900). The last, a village of only one hundred people in 1752, had boomed as the trading center of the growing backcountry of Maryland and Pennsylvania.

The vast increase in population came in part from large families. "The increase is prodigious," wrote a Scottish traveler in 1774–75. "It is no uncommon thing to see a mother of thirteen or fourteen years of age, and it is rare to see a maid unmarried at eighteen. They generally have many children, the country houses swarm with them." They marry young because of "the ease with which people can maintain a family," and this, he wrote, "is a very clear proof of a happy country." [3]

The economic opportunity that encouraged early marriages and large families also attracted an increasing number of immigrants from Europe. From the beginning the English colonies had been pictured as a land of opportunity, but it was not until after 1713 that non-English peoples began to come in great numbers. The migration in the seventeenth century had been mostly English, but the mixture had begun even then. Within a few years after Philadelphia was founded it contained not only English but also Welsh, Scots, Dutch, Swedes, Germans, Finns, Danes, Irish, and Negroes. New York was equally cosmopolitan. During the eighteenth century the migration was so great that by 1775 perhaps a third of the people had been born outside the colonies or at least were the children of immigrants.

There were three main groups of immigrants and many lesser ones. Largest in numbers were those brought by force: the Negroes. By 1775 there were at least 400,000 Negro slaves, amounting to about 17 per cent of the total population. The Germans were the next largest group, amounting to 10 per cent, and in Pennsylvania made up perhaps a third of the population. The Scots-Irish from northern Ireland came in numbers as great as the Germans, although no records were kept of them since they spoke English. They too amounted to probably 10 per cent of the people of the colonies and, like the Germans, were perhaps a third of the population of Pennsylvania.

Among the lesser groups were about 25,000 Swiss who migrated to the southern backcountry during the eighteenth century. Still smaller in numbers but of great importance were the French Huguenots who began fleeing France after the revocation of the Edict of Nantes in 1685. For the most part they settled in colonial cities where they became merchants or professional men, and many a prominent family of revolutionary times was

[3] Patrick M'Robert, "Tour Through Part of the North Provinces of America," *The Pennsylvania Magazine of History and Biography* [PMHB], LIX (1935), 171–72.

descended from such refugees: the Cabots, Bowdoins, and Reveres in Massachusetts, the Jays in New York, the Laurenses in Charleston. Jews too found their way to the relative freedom of America, and like the Huguenots tended to settle in the cities, where some became prominent merchants, as in Newport and Philadelphia. A goodly number of Highland Scots came after 1745, particularly to the backcountry of North Carolina. There were many Dutch in New York, which the Dutch had founded. There were Irish from southern Ireland, but how many came no one knows. And stretching in a great arc along the frontiers were the Indians. The colonists' only interest in the Indians was to keep peace with them if possible, to kill them if necessary, and at all times to push them from the lands they occupied as settlement expanded.

Despite this mixture of peoples and the fear of some older inhabitants that the newer immigrants would never fit into the established patterns of colonial life, most of them did. While laws might have to be translated into German, as in Pennsylvania, the laws remained English, as did other institutions of colonial society. Furthermore there were no quarrels among national groups serious enough to disrupt life anywhere, although one group might be contemptuous of another. Not even religious differences, and these were enormous in an age when each sect took its creed seriously, were enough to cause major difficulties. In fact, there were so many different sects that toleration was a virtual necessity. Furthermore, many sects settled on the frontiers where their mutual problems transcended their religious differences, and in colonies with established churches they could unite to demand religious freedom.

In time the new peoples and the older colonists began to merge into a people that caused a young Frenchman to ask: "What then is the American, this new man?" Crèvecœur then went on to answer his own question, perhaps romantically, but with an element of insight.

> He is either an European, or the descendant of an European, hence that strange mixture of blood, which you will find in no other country. . . . He is an American, who, leaving behind him all his ancient prejudices and manners, receives new ones from the new mode of life he has embraced, the new government he obeys, and the new rank he holds. He becomes an American by being received in the broad lap of our great *Alma Mater*. Here individuals of all nations are melted into a new race of men, whose labors and posterity will one day cause great changes in the world. Americans are the western pilgrims, who are carrying along with them that great mass of arts, sciences, vigor, and industry which began long since in the east; they will finish the

great circle. . . . The American is a new man, who acts upon new principles; he must therefore entertain new ideas, and form new opinions. From involuntary idleness, servile dependence, penury, and useless labor, he has passed to toils of a very different nature, rewarded by ample subsistence.—This is an American. . . .[4]

Whatever the difficulties of life in the New World, and there were far more than Crèvecœur admitted, it was still a land of opportunity for the many who came: far more opportunity than most of them could ever have had in the Old World. Men who could never have expected to own a square foot of Europe's soil might acquire many acres in America. Wages were far higher than in Europe. Class lines were not so sharply drawn and men could rise from poverty into higher ranks. For those who had suffered religious oppression the English colonies offered a freedom unheard of in most of Europe. And to those to whom political rights meant something, the acquisition of fifty acres of land or other property usually entitled a man to vote. Such opportunities, despite the horrors of the trip across the Atlantic, social discrimination in older areas of the colonies, and the rigors of life—whether in towns or on farms—had an impact on the people who came to America.

A German traveler in 1747 stated it well, although he disapproved of what he found. He wrote,

> Immigrants who in their native country (surrounded by thousands of their equals) were of no account whatever, as soon as they come here assume airs and play the master, to such a degree as to excite the utmost astonishment; continuing in this course, until others of their rank outrun them in the race. This is the case too, with the clergy in this country, and generally with persons who hold office. How they ever came to hold them is a matter inexplicable. This aspect of society is, as it were, the genius of the land and leads to a thousand issues, which could not be explained, but on the ground of its almighty influence.[5]

The overwhelming majority of the people were farmers—at least 90 per cent of them—and the economic life of the rest was largely dependent upon that fact. The principal business of the merchants in colonial cities was the exportation of farm products and the importation of goods which were paid for by such exports. Such had been the case ever since the first

[4] EHD, IX, 478–79.   [5] PMHB, XVI(1892), 120.

colonists had learned that there were no mines of gold and silver and that they must raise their own food or starve. The principal exports in 1772 indicate the importance of agriculture in colonial life. In that year the thirteen mainland colonies shipped 450,000 bushels of wheat; 1,233,000 bushels of corn; 167,000 barrels of rice; 784,000 pounds of indigo; and nearly 107,000,000 pounds of tobacco (which alone amounted to more than 20 per cent of the value of all the products shipped from the British colonies in the New World). In addition, there were lesser but not unimportant exports of other grains, vegetables, and horses and cattle.[6] Furthermore, by the 1760s, Americans had begun to process agricultural products. In 1772 nearly 57,000 tons of bread and flour were exported. Philadelphia "superfine" flour was the envy of colonial rivals and had set a standard recognized all about the rim of the Atlantic Ocean. The growth in livestock production was accompanied by the rise of a meat-packing business that shipped out 41,000 barrels of beef and pork in 1772. The rum distilleries, using molasses from the West Indies, produced more than 2,500,000 gallons of rum in the same year.

Americans had developed still other resources. From the beginning the vast forests of the Atlantic slope were a source of profit as well as material with which to build homes and ships, and by the 1760s forest products were significant in overseas trade. In 1772 Americans exported 50,000,000 feet of boards and planks, 49,000,000 shingles, 33,000,000 hoops and staves, and 185,000 barrels of pitch, tar, and turpentine. In the form of ships, Americans were by this time providing perhaps 30 per cent of the tonnage of the whole British Empire.

The sea too contained riches which had been developed to the point where 377,000 quintals of dried fish and 50,000 barrels of pickled fish were exported in 1772. On land, deposits of iron ore and wood from nearby forests made possible a small but important iron industry, which in 1772 produced nearly 5000 tons of pig iron and over 3000 tons of bar iron for export. Even then it is probable that most colonial iron was used in the colonies, where it was converted into tools, nails, pots, and pans by American "mechanicks."

Such statistics are only a rough, and in some ways misleading, guide to the ways Americans made a living. They show only the major exports and not the great diversity of things grown or made by farmers and artisans. There were no factories as the British knew them, yet many Americans

---

[6] EHD, IX, part III: "The Economic Development of the Colonies." The statistics are given in full, 389–411.

were manufacturers, or in the literal meaning of the word: makers of things by hand. Most farmers were of necessity carpenters and in their spare time turned out innumerable products such as shoes, nails, and wooden dishes, while their wives spun wool and flax and wove cloth. In the cities a growing number of artisans, some alone and some with apprentices, made hoes, axes, shoes and clothes, printed and bound books, turned out fine furniture, or created beautiful silver, as did Paul Revere. Most such products were used at home or sold in the communities where they were produced, but some of them found their way into trade with other colonies and the West Indies.

Statistics do not show the differences between colonies or between groups of colonies. The New Englanders had early turned to the sea and the forests and by the eve of the Revolution 50 per cent of the value of New England's exports consisted of lumber products and fish. New England merchants sent these around the Atlantic and to other colonies, and in addition their ships carried barreled beef and pork, vegetables, candles, soap, rum, shoes, nails, and the great variety of articles they imported from England. The middle colonies were known as the "bread colonies" because of their great wheat and corn crops. Early they turned to making bread and flour, and by the 1770s Pennsylvania was sending more than half of all that was exported from the mainland, more than twice as much as New York, her nearest rival. The southern colonies were the "staple colonies" because they had early concentrated on a single crop much prized in Europe, and were not competing with anything grown in Britain. In Virginia and Maryland the "staple" was tobacco, and in South Carolina it was rice, although indigo had been added as a second staple by the middle of the eighteenth century.

Important as these staples were, the picture was changing rapidly by 1763. The settlement of the southern backcountry by multitudes of small farmers who produced grain and livestock, the conversion of worn-out tobacco land in tidewater Virginia and Maryland to the production of grain, and the development of forest products, challenged and, in some cases outstripped, the northern colonies in areas that had once been theirs alone. In 1772 Virginia and Maryland exported 300,000 of the 450,000 bushels of wheat and 746,000 of the 1,233,000 bushels of corn shipped from the mainland. They were creeping up on second-place New York in the production of bread and flour, and they were third in the export of barreled beef and pork. The Carolinas and Georgia were exporting as much corn as all the middle colonies put together, and ranked second only to New England in beef and pork. The southern colonies were even challenging New England's longtime monopoly of pickled fish, for they shipped out 12,400 barrels in 1772 to New England's 29,000. In the case of dried fish, however, New England had no rivals: it shipped out all but 7000 of the 377,000 quintals in 1772.

Even more remarkable was the growth of the lumber industry in the south. Early in the eighteenth century, Britain had offered a bounty to encourage the production of naval stores. The hope was that New Englanders would be diverted from manufacturing if they were provided with a means of paying their debts to Britain. The New Englanders did not respond, but the southerners did vigorously. In 1772 New England exported only 14,000 barrels of pitch, tar, and turpentine, as compared with 130,000 barrels from the Carolinas and Georgia, and 28,000 barrels from Virginia and Maryland. New England still dominated in lumber exports, but she was facing rising competition from the south. She shipped 35,000,000 of the 50,000,000 feet of boards and planks in 1772, but only 21,000,000 of the 49,000,000 shingles. The five southern colonies together produced as many shingles as New England. In the business of making hoops and staves, while New England was shipping a third of all those exported in 1772, Virginia and Maryland were close behind, and also produced more than half the pig iron shipped from colonial ports. On the eve of the Revolution, the south was not only outstripping the north in population, but was well on the way to producing at least half of the economic wealth of the mainland colonies, if not already doing so.[7]

&

While the economic life of the colonies was based on agriculture and on forests and fisheries, its growth and prosperity were largely dependent on ocean-borne commerce to dispose of the great surpluses for which there was no home market. To meet the need and to profit from it was the role of American merchants. By 1763 they were a wealthy and powerful group which dominated the economic life of the seaport cities, and their power stretched far into the backcountry. Their ships crisscrossed the Atlantic, carrying the produce of America to Britain, the West Indies, Spain, Portugal, and the Mediterranean. They brought back many things, but most important, British manufactures, molasses, rum, salt, sugar, and cash and bills of exchange. These imports were sold to shopkeepers and individuals in home ports and carried to other colonies as well. The mechanisms of

[7] EHD, IX, 394–401.

trade were infinitely complex, and any great merchant needed agents in the seaports circling the Atlantic to buy and sell for him; he needed credit in Britain with manufacturers and suppliers; and he usually sold on credit to his American customers. All this, coupled with the chances of wind and weather, the rise and fall of prices at harbors months away, and the judgment, or lack of it, on the part of agents, meant that a successful merchant had to be a man of ingenuity, patience, and capital, and above all, be possessed of a large quantity of sheer luck.

Merchant ships seldom followed a simple "triangle" pattern; instead the routes were a maze dictated by rumors of good prices or bad, and by wind and weather. There were, however, certain routes defined by markets and by the needs of American customers. For one thing, Americans traded more and more with one another. Every conceivable product, from British manufactured goods to food, lumber, tools, rum, and American-made furniture, was shipped up and down the coast and to the West Indies, much of it in small boats but some in large ships. Merchants from colonial cities were always searching for profitable cargoes, not only in their home ports but also in others as well.

The trade that loomed largest in the economy of British America was that of the southern mainland colonies. The chief patterns of their commerce had been established early, for their staple crops—tobacco, rice, and indigo—could be shipped only to Britain or other British colonies. The Navigation Act of 1660 "enumerated" tobacco, and other items were added in later years, except that usually rice could be sent directly to southern Europe without first being shipped to Britain. The trade of the plantation colonies was therefore in large measure a direct trade with Britain. During the course of the eighteenth century the merchants of Boston, New York, and Philadelphia began carrying some of the enumerated products to Britain, but the bulk of it was still carried in British ships or in those of the producing colonies.

The trade patterns of the northern colonies were far more intricate. Because of soil, climate, and the inclination of the inhabitants, their agricultural products and fish competed directly with those of Britain and could not be sent there except in times of emergency or crop failure. The northern colonies did, of course, produce some things which went to England: hides, furs, whale oil, and the like, but these were not major items. Instead the surplus grain, lumber, flour, and bread of the mainland found its first and largest market in the West Indies. The islands concentrated on the production of sugar and to a lesser degree on coffee, indigo, dyewoods, and the like. So highly specialized were the great sugar plantations worked by slave labor that they produced neither enough food for their people nor sufficient lumber for their houses and for the barrels in which they shipped their products.

So close was the tie with the mainland that West Indians believed that starvation would set in if they were cut off from that source of supply for more than a few weeks. In return for food, livestock, and lumber, they sent back great quantities of molasses and rum, smaller amounts of sugar, cocoa, and dyewoods, cash in the form of bills of exchange drawn on accounts in London, and gold and silver coins that came into the West Indies from Spanish America. With the profits from this trade, mainland merchants paid for a large part of their imports from Britain, and the need for such profits is shown by the fact that in 1772 New England imported goods from Britain valued at £825,000, while she shipped back goods worth only £126,000.

The eighteenth century was not out of its teens before mainland merchants began to find the British West Indies totally inadequate, both as markets and as sources of supply. The burgeoning population of mainland farmers produced ever greater surpluses which the British islands could not begin to use. Furthermore, since those islands made much of their own molasses into rum, they could not supply the demands of the growing mainland distilleries. Therefore, mainland merchants turned more and more to the foreign West Indies. The French islands were legally opened to trade in 1717, and trade went on with Dutch, Danish, and Spanish possessions, whether legal or not. In the French islands molasses was largely a waste product, for French wine producers saw to it that there was no alcoholic competition from their colonies. As a result, molasses could be bought there more cheaply, and American food and lumber sold at a higher profit, than in the British islands.

Even so, the Caribbean area could not absorb all that the farmers, fishermen, and lumbermen of the mainland colonies produced in the expanding economy of the eighteenth century. Therefore, colonial merchants soon turned to Spain, Portugal, and the "Wine Islands" off the African coast. This trade began early in the century and exports of wheat, corn, flour, fish, lumber, rum, and rice increased steadily. It was an extremely profitable trade, for the Americans usually brought back only wine and salt, and the heavy balances in their favor were paid in cash and bills of exchange. On the eve of the Revolution this trade was equal in volume to that with the West Indies and was probably more profitable.

Despite the expansion of American trade around the periphery of the North Atlantic, Britain remained the center of the economic life of the colonies, although by 1775 only about half the total tonnage going in and out of American ports was to and from the mother country. The variety of goods imported from Britain was enormous, but cloth and wearing apparel bulked largest: in 1772 these two items amounted to £2,355,000 out of a total of £5,155,000 worth of goods imported from Britain. Imported iron-ware was valued at over £500,000, while foreign goods shipped to the col-onies through Britain came to more than £770,000. The "miscellaneous" items, ranging from medicines to hairpins, were valued at nearly £1,500,000.

The greatest problem of the American merchants, particularly in the northern colonies, was how to pay for such imports when they could not pay for them by direct exports. In 1772 the imports of northern colonies from Britain were valued at £1,677,000 but in return they shipped goods worth only £338,000. This was the essential fact that made the trade of the northern colonies with the southern mainland colonies, the West Indies, and southern Europe so vital. It was a complicated web of trade and finance, and northern merchants were convinced that any interference with it might result in disaster.

Yet most British policy-makers never understood this, and those who did either came to it too late or had too little influence on policy. The northern colonies never seemed as desirable to them as the plantation colonies, above all those in the West Indies, because they did not fit in with British theories of the proper role of colonies. Their farmers com-peted with those of England; their fishermen captured markets that might otherwise have been English; their shipbuilders competed with those of Britain; and their merchants acquired an ever larger share of the carrying trade of the empire. When policy-makers looked at the debts owed by northern merchants to Britain it seemed even worse. The plantation colo-nies usually shipped as much as or more in value to Britain than they bought from her, but the northern ones never did.

The statistics the British looked at were not as simple as they seemed. Northern merchants had to maintain their credit with British merchants and manufacturers and were far more apt to pay their debts than the tobacco planters of Virginia and Maryland. The planters were caught in an economic squeeze from which it seemed impossible to escape. Virtually all their tobacco went to England and Scotland, yet perhaps 90 per cent of it was re-exported. The toll of freight, insurance, taxes, handling charges, and middleman profits left very little for the man who actually grew the tobacco. By the 1760s the debts of some of the great planters were large and virtually hereditary. Not only this, but British merchants, and particularly the Scots, had established many small stores throughout Virginia and Maryland, with the result that multitudes of small farmers as well as large planters were involved in tangles of debt.[8]

The first direct interference with the trade of the northern colonies came in 1733 when Parliament, at the urging of West Indies planters, placed a prohibitive duty of six pence a gallon on foreign molasses brought into the English colonies, and duties on foreign sugar. The Molasses Act was not enforced, but if it had been the commerce of the mainland colonies would have suffered greatly. When an attempt at enforcement was actually made at the end of the Seven Years War, New Englanders were embittered. The reduction of the duty to three pence a gallon in 1764 gave them no relief, or so they said. Then in 1766, British merchants and manufacturers, who knew far more about the mechanics of trade than the politicians, forced Parliament to lower the duty to a penny a gallon and to apply it to both foreign and British molasses. The duty was at last low enough to make it cheaper to be honest than to smuggle, a fact soon reflected in the customs records. Furthermore, it demonstrated the rightness of the American argument that trade with the foreign West Indies was indispensable. Of the 4,800,000 gallons of molasses imported by the mainland colonies in 1772, only 100,000 gallons came from the British islands.[9]

The economic life of the mainland colonies had reached such a state of complexity that it was impossible for Britain to enforce the economic rules and theories of the seventeenth century, which even then, happily for both Britain and the colonies, had remained more in the realm of theory than of practice.

By 1763 the colonial economy was of so complex a nature that ancient theories no longer squared with reality. This was equally true of the colonies as political societies.[10] As opposed to imperial theory, the colonies had achieved virtual self-government. At the same time the explosive expansion of the colonies in population and area in the half-century before 1763 had created a multitude of internal problems. Indian relations, land

[8] Jacob M. Price, "The Rise of Glasgow in the Chesapeake Tobacco Trade, 1707–1775," *The William and Mary Quarterly* [WMQ], 3 ser. XI(1954).
[9] EHD, IX, 696–98, 407.
[10] Ibid. part II: "The Evolution of Colonial Governments" and the select bibliography of works on the subject.

granting, religion, finance, local government, and other matters produced internal tension, and in some colonies, outright rebellion. British policies after 1763 added fuel to fires already burning, and the result was not only growing antagonism to Britain, but also an intensification of antagonisms among Americans themselves.

The basic aim of British policy ever since 1660 had been to centralize control of the economic and political life of the colonies in the mother country. To achieve such centralization the Navigation Acts required that certain colonial products such as tobacco and sugar be shipped only to England or another colony, that all goods must be shipped in English or colonial ships, and that foreign manufactured goods must pass through England en route to English colonies. To administer such policies, various administrative boards were created, culminating in the appointment of the Board of Trade and Plantations in 1696. In time a bureaucracy of naval officers and customs officials was established in the colonies.

Legal procedures were also devised. Certain laws passed by colonial legislatures had to be sent to the Privy Council for approval before going into effect. Certain cases from colonial supreme courts could be appealed to the Privy Council for final decision. And in the hope of bringing about an even closer control of colonial affairs, the colonies were one by one converted into royal governments with governors, upper houses of legislatures, judges, and other officials appointed by the Crown. The result of this policy was that by 1763 there remained on the mainland only two corporation colonies, Connecticut and Rhode Island, and only three proprietary colonies, Pennsylvania, Delaware, and Maryland.

While the theory was one of centralization, in practice the colonies retained the self-government they had established by the eighteenth century. From the beginning the colonists had claimed a large measure of control over their internal affairs as a "right" of Englishmen. Above all, the colonies owed their self-government to the fact that one house of their legislatures was elected by the voters.

Whatever the policy and whatever the theoretical powers of royal governors and other officials, the carrying out of most British policies depended upon colonial legislators. Governors could not control troops because legislatures often refused to grant money unless they appointed the officers and even planned campaigns. Indian relations were in the charge of governors and yet here also they had to yield to the assemblies which provided the money. The result, reported the Privy Council in 1754, was that "the assembly have taken to themselves not only the management and disposal of the public money, but have also wrested from your Majesty's governor the nomination of all officers of government, the custody and direction of all military stores, the mustering and regulating of troops raised for your Majesty's service, and in short almost every other executive part of government." The report concerned New York, but it could have been made about almost any other colony.

ક્ષ

The structure of government in every colony was essentially the same, whether royal, proprietary, or corporation. At the head was a governor with executive authority, and a deputy or lieutenant governor who took over in the governor's absence or at his death. Governors were appointed by the Crown or proprietor and were elected only in Connecticut and Rhode Island. The second common feature was a council which acted as both an advisory body to the governor and as an upper house of the legislature. The proprietors appointed the councils in their colonies and the Crown those in the royal colonies, with the exception of Massachusetts, where the council was elected annually by the lower house and the outgoing council. In Connecticut and Rhode Island the councils were elected by the voters. The elective or lower houses of the colonial legislatures went by various names. In New England they were made up of representatives from the townships; in the other colonies, from the counties, the parishes, and from certain cities and boroughs. In every colony there was a supreme court, consisting of the governor and council, as in Virginia, or of separate appointive bodies, as in most colonies.

The two basic units of local government were the townships in New England and the counties in the colonies to the south. Town government was in large measure self-government, for the towns divided their lands, controlled schools and churches, levied town taxes, and elected town officials and representatives to the legislatures. By the eighteenth century local self-government, particularly in Massachusetts and Connecticut, was being limited by the county courts made up of justices of the peace appointed by the governor and council. The county courts had both judicial and civil functions. They had the power to lay out roads, build bridges, and supervise tax collections. The justices could fine town officers, appoint town officers when the voters did not, and approve or disapprove of town by-laws and regulations.

The county form of government, however, reached its fullest development outside New England, and above all in New York, Virginia, and

North Carolina. The governing body was the county court appointed by the governor and council. Its members were usually justices of the peace, for the county court was the principal judicial body of the county as well as the chief administrative agency. The court laid out roads, apportioned taxes, licensed taverns, made up lists of eligible voters, and in general, oversaw all matters affecting the county. Its executive officer was the sheriff, also appointed by the governor. The county courts thus ruled without any check upon their actions by the inhabitants, whose only political right, if they possessed enough property, was to vote for the county representatives in the colonial legislatures. In practice, even this right was limited by the fact that the county's political bosses were usually members of the county court, who saw to it that the representatives were either members of the court itself or men approved by it.

The pattern of colonial governments at all levels was well established while the colonies were still a narrow band of settlements lying along the seacoast. This was the area that was organized into townships and counties and given representation in the legislatures before the great explosion of population and expansion into the wilderness during the first half of the eighteenth century.

It was in this seacoast area too that planter and merchant aristocracies arose, aristocracies based on the possession of wealth in the form of land, slaves, ships, stores, and goods. By mid-eighteenth century the American aristocracies tended to be hereditary, but the way to the top was never closed to those who acquired wealth, no matter how poor or obscure their beginnings, or how dubious their methods of acquisition. And the rise of newly rich men to political and social power was rapid, unlike the situation in the mother country, where two or three generations of inherited wealth were usually needed before a family was accepted by the existing aristocracy. In the colonies most men were accepted as soon as they had acquired enough property to give them weight and power in their communities. Furthermore, the members of the colonial aristocracies, whether from old families or from new, were not merely planters or merchants or lawyers; most of them took part in the political life of the colonies as a matter of course and pursued political careers with such determination that most colonial governments were staffed by them from top to bottom. At the same time, local governments were often in the hands of their youthful relatives or political allies intently working their way up the ladder of political preferment.

The top of the ladder for many, both politically and socially, was a seat in the council of a royal colony, and Americans intrigued endlessly for what were usually lifetime appointments. The elective assemblies had consciously modeled themselves on the House of Commons, and councilors were not unaware that the body in which they sat had some resemblance to the House of Lords. With some exceptions, seats in the councils were usually held by the wealthier members of colonial society. British instructions to royal governors ensured this: governors were told to nominate "principal freeholders" and to "take good care that they be men of good life, well-affected to our government, of good estates, and of abilities suitable to their employments." Americans who possessed all the other qualifications but lacked the "good estates" were seldom appointed, and sometimes, a "good estate" was enough even if all the other qualifications were lacking.

Although the elected assemblies had steadily encroached on the authority of the councils, the councils were a powerful force in the government of the colonies. They were the second branch of the legislature and they could, and often did, refuse to approve bills passed by the elective branch. Even more important as a means of political influence was the council's role as an advisory body to the governor. In fact, with the governors, the councils served as the joint executives of the colonial governments. A royal governor had to have his council's approval for most executive actions, and in particular, for appointments to office. Hence appointments all the way from supreme court judges to local justices of the peace and militia officers passed in review before the councilors, and governors who hoped to succeed seldom ignored their advice and wishes. Thus a network of conciliar power and influence extended into the farthest reaches of most of the colonies, and it is not surprising that the elected assemblies were well stocked with friends, relatives, and protégés of councilors. Conciliar power and influence was also bolstered because the governors and councils in the royal colonies granted land. Ambitious men in a land-hungry society were well aware of this and were not inclined to give offense lightly.

Conciliar influence was further strengthened because many councilors acquired more than one office. In Massachusetts, Thomas Hutchinson was simultaneously lieutenant governor, chief justice, judge of a county court, and held a few minor offices in addition. His relatives were also provided with more than one office. Furthermore, the assembly elected Hutchinson to the council every year until 1766. As a councilor he was a member of the legislature and an adviser to the governor. Hutchinson was not unique in the colonies—he was only more successful than most political leaders. In addition, in the royal colonies, a few, and often inter-related, families managed to dominate the councils generation after generation, as in Virginia. And this was true even in Connecticut where the council was elected annually by the voters.[11]

The members of the colonial aristocracies, who occupied most of the important appointive offices in the colonies and most of the seats in the colonial legislatures, had an enormous social and psychological advantage. The age before the American Revolution was one in which the ordinary man paid respect to and followed the leadership of the "gentleman," the local squire, the wealthy merchant, the wealthy planter. No matter how "democratic" the suffrage might be, the voters were usually offered a choice on election day, when offered any choice at all, between men picked by the aristocratic leaders from among their own number, although occasionally those leaders decided to further the political career of a young man of obscure family.

In 1755 George Washington, at the age of twenty-three, was defeated when he first ran for the House of Burgesses in Frederick county. Washington was from a tidewater county but in Virginia a man could run in any county in which he owned land. Washington did not belong to one of the great families of the colony but he was a protégé of Lord Fairfax, one of the most prominent men in Virginia, and the leading man in Frederick county. Three years later plans were laid more carefully. Because of military duties, Washington himself could not attend the election and thank the voters as was customary, and Colonel James Wood, one of the leaders in county politics, took Washington's place at the polls. What followed was clear evidence that the county leaders had decided to replace the two incumbent burgesses with Washington and a nephew of Lord Fairfax.

As soon as the polls opened, Lord Fairfax, the greatest landowner in Virginia, county lieutenant, and chief magistrate of the county court, stepped up and voted for Washington and his own nephew. He was followed by the leading Episcopal clergyman, who voted likewise. So too did most of the other leading men in the county, including the only doctor and the Baptist and Presbyterian ministers. By the time such men had voted, the lesser voters understood what was wanted and followed suit, for few in the days of oral voting cared to offend men to whom they owed money or from whom they expected favors, or whose leadership they had long trusted and followed. Needless to say, Washington and Lord Fairfax's

[11] Leonard W. Labaree, *Conservatism in Early American History* (New York, 1948), chapter I.

nephew won in a walkaway.[12] In a similar fashion the "River gods" of western Massachusetts were able to dominate their counties and towns down to the outbreak of the war for independence.[13]

In addition to the deft manipulation of the machinery of politics, colonial leaders along the seacoast had other means to help them maintain their control of the colonial governments: the property qualification for voting and the refusal to grant representation in the legislatures to newly settled areas. If the laws were enforced, a good many inhabitants of the cities could not vote, although the property qualification had little effect in the backcountry, where land was easy to acquire. The refusal or slowness to grant the backcountry and the cities representation in any way proportionate to population limited their influence on political decisions, at least legally.

It is true, of course, that American society was far more democratic than that of Europe. There was widespread ownership of property and a far greater proportion of the population was entitled to vote than in any other part of the world. There seemed to be a feeling of equality, and Americans were not always as subservient to their "betters" as men were in the Old World.[14] British officials, travelers, and some Americans pointed to such behavior as a dangerous tendency toward democracy, if not democracy itself. However, such opinions are no more evidence of the existence of "democracy," or lack of it, in colonial America, than tabulations of the number of men who could vote. Whether the colonists had democracy or not is not as relevant as that many Americans were becoming more and more discontented with the way colonial governments operated, and by 1763, were beginning to make insistent demands for change.

The rapid growth of the cities had outstripped the capacity or the willingness of their governments to care for their needs. Charleston, South Carolina, was governed by the legislature of the colony. Philadelphia was ruled by a closed, self-perpetuating corporation so inadequate that the legislature of Pennsylvania had to intervene from time to time to care for the needs of that flourishing metropolis. New York had a more adequate government, but it too looked backward as often as forward. Boston was governed by a town meeting in which all voters, and often non-voters, took

12 Charles S. Sydnor, *Gentlemen Freeholders: Political Practices in Washington's Virginia* (Chapel Hill, 1952), 67–69.
13 Robert Taylor, *Western Massachusetts in the Revolution* (Providence, 1954), chapter II.
14 For a detailed analysis of the distribution of property and the nature of social classes, see Jackson Turner Main, *The Social Structure of Revolutionary America* (Princeton, 1965).

part. It was an unwieldy form of government and one unsuited to the needs of an urban center, but it was the delight of political manipulators and not abandoned until 1820.[15]

The rapidly expanding backcountry was a far more explosive problem in several colonies. The backcountry was settled mostly by small farmers, some of whom showed little love for the seacoast leaders. Most of those leaders in turn looked upon backcountry men as a rude and lawless rabble which should be denied all political influence. The property qualification for voting meant little in the backcountry, where land was easy to acquire. Those areas could gain political influence only if they could gain representation in the legislatures, and this most colonial legislatures were unwilling to give them. The legislatures were slow to organize new counties, and when they did, saw to it that they were never given enough representatives to endanger seacoast control. South Carolina refused to establish counties so that the backcountry had no local government, and almost no voice in the legislature. In Massachusetts, by contrast, each new township was usually given representation, but the trip to Boston was long and expensive and the men elected either did not attend legislative sessions or did not stay long enough to influence decisions. Some towns were so poor that they did not even bother to elect representatives. In addition, many backcountry areas, as in Massachusetts, were controlled by political leaders who were allies of the ruling political factions.

The causes of backcountry discontent varied from colony to colony. In some it was the lack of adequate local government, or counties so large that it was difficult for men to get to the county courts. Sometimes the county courts were corrupt. Many felt that the taxes were too heavy for frontier areas to pay. Some areas, needing credit, complained that the governments did not provide enough. As population moved beyond navigable rivers and beyond the mountains, the settlers demanded roads and bridges, and no matter what colonial governments might do, many settlers thought the efforts inadequate. There were religious grievances everywhere in the colonies, but they were more intense in the backcountry, which was settled by a great variety of sects; and in the colonies with a state church, members of other sects objected to paying taxes for its support and demanded religious freedom. Some of the grievances were serious and some were minor, but they added up to enough to produce outbursts of bitter feeling, and sometimes violent action in the years after 1763.

[15] On the cities and their problems, see Carl Bridenbaugh, *Cities in Revolt: Urban Life in America, 1743–1776* (New York, 1955).

The first challenge to eastern rule occurred in Pennsylvania, where the rapid growth of the backcountry created one of the sharpest cleavages in the colonies. The three old counties in the East and Philadelphia controlled the government, and they, for the most part, were in turn controlled by the Quakers. By 1763 the backcountry had filled up with Scots-Irish and Germans and it contained about half the population of the colony. Representation in the one-house legislature was so restricted that although eight backcountry counties were created by 1774, they had only thirteen representatives as contrasted with twenty-six from the East.

The main contention between the two sections was frontier defense. During the Seven Years War the Quaker-controlled assembly granted money reluctantly, and even when it did, insisted on taxing the Penn lands. The Penns demanded money for defense but refused to allow their lands to be taxed. The result of the deadlock was always too little money too late, and the frontiers were ravaged repeatedly. Just as the war ended in 1763, an Indian uprising threatened to wipe out every frontier settlement from Florida to the Great Lakes, and once more the Pennsylvania frontiersmen demanded help. The assembly refused to give it and the outraged frontiersmen killed some "tame" Indians under the protection of the government. When they were denounced by the governor they organized a large body of men and called themselves the Paxton Boys, the name of a frontier township that was a center of discontent. They then marched on Philadelphia to kill still other "tame" Indians lodged in barracks near the city.[16]

As the Paxton Boys neared Philadelphia at the end of January 1764, many citizens were convinced that the backwoodsmen were going to sack the city. Even the Quakers began to build fortifications and shoulder arms. Henry Muhlenberg, the German Lutheran leader who had little affection for either Quakers or frontiersmen, recorded in his diary that

> . . . it was a strange sight to the children on the streets. A whole troop of small boys followed a prominent Quaker down the street shouting in amazement, "Look, look! a Quaker carrying a musket on his shoulder!" Indeed, the older folks also looked upon it as a miraculous portent to see so many old and young Quakers arming themselves with flintlocks and daggers, or so-called murderous weapons! What heightened their amazement was this: that these pious sheep, who had such a tender conscience during the long Spanish, French,

[16] Brooke Hindle, "The March of the Paxton Boys," WMQ, 3 ser. III (1946). For a collection of some of the many pamphlets arising from this affair see John R. Dunbar, ed., *The Paxton Papers* (The Hague, 1957).

and Indian War, and would rather have died than lift a hand for defense against the most dangerous enemies, were now all of a sudden willing to put on horns of iron . . . and shoot and smite a small group of their poor, oppressed, driven, and suffering fellow inhabitants and citizens from the frontier! [17]

But in the end there was no fighting. A group of leading officials met the Paxton Boys at Germantown, and after hours of parleying, the frontiersmen agreed to return home. Two of their members stayed behind to prepare a long and eloquent statement of frontier grievances. They denounced the inequality of representation, the failure of the assembly to provide for defense, which they blamed on the Quakers, and they even accused James Pemberton, a Quaker leader, of being a spy for enemy Indians.[18] Once the assembly had recovered from its fright, it continued for the most part to ignore the demands of the frontier. The West did not make its weight felt until 1774–76, when it united with allies among the people of Philadelphia to bring about a real revolution in writing the first state constitution of Pennsylvania.

After the middle of the eighteenth century the South Carolina backcountry was settled so rapidly by people moving in from the north that by 1776 it contained about 50 per cent of the total and nearly 80 per cent of the white population of the colony. The settlers were a mixture of hardworking and ambitious, if crude and unlettered, people and the wildest kind of bandits. The region was separated from the rich low country around Charleston by fifty to one hundred miles of wilderness, yet the legislature refused to establish government of any kind despite repeated petitions from the settlers. It was true that they could vote if they wished to travel from a hundred to two hundred miles to the seacoast parishes, but they could not be sure to which parish they belonged because parish lines had not been run very far inland. The only court in the colony was in Charleston, which was too far away for most of the inhabitants of the backcountry to attend; and even when they did, justice was seldom their lot.

After 1763 more and more lawless men moved into the backcountry. They stole horses, burned houses, killed men, and raped women. In 1766 the frontiersmen once more petitioned: they were not represented in the legislature; there was no protection from Indians and robbers; there were no schools or churches; lands were taxed as heavily as the rich indigo and rice lands of the low country. Above all, the petition demanded the estab-

[17] EHD, IX, 612.
[18] "Remonstrance" of Matthew Smith and James Gibson, 13 Feb. 1764, ibid. 614–17.

lishment of law and order; yet the legislature, far more interested in the Stamp Act crisis, refused to act. By the spring of 1767 a reign of terror existed in the backcountry and desperate inhabitants organized Regulator associations to protect themselves, their property, and their families, and they proceeded to hang robbers and horse thieves on sight. The governor, Lord Charles Montagu, was shocked at such "lawlessness" and demanded that the legislature suppress it. At this point a long "Remonstrance" appeared in Charleston in the name of 4000 backcountry men, and it was backed up with the threat that an invasion of the low country would follow. The legislature moved with understandable speed and passed an act for the establishment of courts in the backcountry.

But the act had to be sent to Britain for approval, and the turmoil continued. Fortunately for the colony, Lord Montagu spent very little time in it. When he was there he arrested Regulator leaders and upon one occasion sent against them militia that included some of the very crooks and horse thieves against whom the Regulators were fighting. He could not induce the planters themselves to march. They were willing enough perhaps, but they simply did not dare leave unguarded the huge slave population of the low country. During Montagu's long absences the lieutenant governor, William Bull, a native Carolinian, was in charge. He understood the problems of the backcountry and sympathized; he pardoned Regulator leaders and offered rewards for horse thieves and robbers. When the first court act was vetoed in England, Bull helped push through a second bill, which was approved, and in 1772 courts were at last established. The Regulator movement in South Carolina ended without the kind of civil war that occurred in North Carolina, but it did not lead to any trust of the low country aristocracy or to very active support for the war for independence. From the backcountry's point of view, the legislature's resounding declarations about American rights and liberties were blatant hypocrisy, and the popular leader Christopher Gadsden was the most blatant hypocrite among its members.[19] "They would fetter and chain the back inhabitants," wrote Charles Woodmason, "could they get them in their clutches. And deprive them equally of their civil concerns as they do their spiritual. These are the Sons of Liberty!" [20]

The Regulator movement in North Carolina was far more widely known

[19] Two full accounts may be found in Richard J. Hooker, ed., *The Carolina Backcountry on the Eve of the Revolution: The Journal and Other Writings of Charles Woodmason, Anglican Itinerant* (Chapel Hill, 1953), and Richard M. Brown, *The South Carolina Regulators* (Cambridge, Mass., 1963). The latter pictures the legislature as far more sympathetic to backcountry needs than I do.
[20] Woodmason to the Bishop of London, 26 March 1771, Fulham Palace Archives: South Carolina, Library of Congress [LC] Transcripts.

at the time because the dramatic events culminating in the battle at Alamance Creek in May 1771 were widely reported and debated in the colonial newspapers. The backcountry of North Carolina contained some large land- and slave-owners but most of the people were small farmers. County governments were established, but some of the county courts were clearly corrupt, their members uniting with lawyers and land speculators to enrich themselves at the expense of the inhabitants. When men could not pay taxes and debts their property was sold for a fraction of its real worth, and usually to the officials themselves or to their friends. The sheriffs in particular were crooked. They collected taxes and then failed to turn them over to the colonial treasury. When William Tryon became governor in 1765 he tried to bring about legal reforms, and to make the sheriffs disgorge, but the various county court politicians controlled the legislature and united to block the governor's efforts.

Meanwhile the legislature ignored backcountry petitions for more representation, paper currency, lower taxes, and enforcement of laws limiting court fees. In desperation many backcountry men organized Regulator associations which began to attack the courts to prevent them from sitting, or at least to keep away the hated lawyers. The Regulators were violent men who observed no niceties. When Governor Tryon ordered their leaders seized, their followers stormed the jails and released them.

In 1768 Tryon led an armed force into the backcountry, but he managed to avoid an open fight by promising reforms. In the elections of 1769 the Regulators were strong enough to capture control of the lower house of the legislature. But no sooner did it meet than the governor dissolved it for adopting resolutions denouncing British policies. The Regulators then became even more violent. Judges and lawyers at county courts were beaten or driven out and local enemies of the Regulators were whipped and their houses and barns burned. Governor Tryon raised a small army from among the aristocracy and marched forth to battle. When Tryon's army met the Regulator forces, almost twice its size, at the Alamance on 16 May 1771, the two sides parleyed for hours, but finally the governor opened fire. The Regulators panicked and many of their leaders fled. Some were captured; one was executed on the spot and six more after a court-martial the next month.[21]

Thus ended the Regulator movement in North Carolina, but not the

[21] Anson County Petition, 9 Oct. 1769, EHD, IX, 604–9; John S. Bassett, "The Regulators of North Carolina (1765–1771)," American Historical Association, *Annual Report* (1894), and Bridenbaugh, *Myths and Realities*, "The Back Settlements," for two differing interpretations.

grievances that gave birth to it nor the hatred it spawned. The North Carolina Regulators, like those in South Carolina, took a dim view of the low-country leaders, who while shouting for liberty against Britain were willing to shoot their fellow citizens who demanded liberties for themselves. During the war some former Regulators were loyalist, for they had received more sympathy from Britain than from their fellow Americans. Others went into state politics to redress the grievances they had long felt. As for William Tryon, who left in the summer of 1771 to become governor of New York, a writer in Massachusetts, where there were expert name-callers, declared that Tryon "exhibits the character of a robber, a murderer, a hater of mankind, an infernal fiend, with a soul more dark and horrible than the midnight of hell." [22]

In New York the cause of trouble was the desire of tenants on some of the great estates to own the land they farmed. Beginning in the seventeenth century most of the readily available land extending up either side of the Hudson River had been given out to a few families. The manor of the Van Rensselaers amounted to a million acres, the Philipses had at least 400,000, the Livingstons, 160,000. Many of these great domains had been built up through fraud: by the extension of vague boundaries set forth in the original grants. Most of the manor lords refused to sell and demanded perpetual rents from tenants. The reason was simple enough. The Van Rensselaers, for instance, paid a total annual rent of fifty bushels of wheat for their million acres and extracted as much from a tenant on a single 100-acre farm. The landlord class and its merchant and lawyer allies in New York City dominated the government.

During the early part of the 1760s some tenants on the Philipse estate began buying land from Indians who claimed that the boundaries of the estate had been extended by fraud. The tenants then refused to pay rent to the landlord. The case was at once carried to the courts, which naturally supported the landlord, and the sheriff was ordered to evict the tenants. Other tenants on other estates followed the example set, and by the fall of 1765, while New York City was in the midst of the uproar over the Stamp Act, the tenants formed an organization with William Prendergast as their leader, which was to provide help for those refusing to pay rent and was also to prevent sheriffs from throwing them off the lands they claimed. By the spring of 1766 the "anti-rent" movement was widespread. The landlords denounced the "levellers," and the governor issued proclamations

[22] *Virginia Gazette* (Purdie and Dixon) [VG(PD)], 21 May 1772, from "Toleration" in the *Massachusetts Spy*.

against them. On one occasion several hundred tenants marched to the outskirts of New York City, hoping for support from the Sons of Liberty, but they got none.

When tenant-farmer leaders were jailed in upcountry towns, mobs released them, and on some occasions, men were killed. Finally, troops of the regular British army crushed the tenants' rebellion, and their leaders were brought to trial. William Prendergast was sentenced to death, the court ordering "that the prisoner be led back to the place whence he came and from thence shall be drawn on a hurdle to the place for execution, and then shall be hanged by the neck, and then shall be cut down alive, and his entrails and privy members shall be cut from his body, and shall be burned in his sight, and his head shall be cut off, and his body shall be divided into four parts and shall be disposed of at the King's pleasure."

In the end Prendergast escaped punishment, the governor having got a pardon for him by interceding with British authorities. Like discontented people in other colonies, many New York tenant-farmers took a dim view of the leaders of the revolutionary movement, as well they might, for John Morin Scott, a flaming leader of the Sons of Liberty at the beginning of the Stamp Act crisis, sat on the court that condemned Prendergast to death.[23]

The discontent in the American colonies was an integral part of the history of the time; to ignore it is to misunderstand the complexities of the history of the age. The amount varied in quality and quantity from colony to colony but did present a challenge to the established order in America. It was coming to a head at the very time that Britain sought to establish tighter economic and political control. The colonial aristocracies were thus faced with two simultaneous challenges to their rule: that of British policy, and that of their discontented fellow Americans. The discontent and the demands for change within America had an impact on resistance to British policies; helped shape the decisions of many leaders on the issue of independence; influenced the writing of the first state constitutions; and were a vital element in American politics once independence was won.

Aside from the disputes over political and social issues, there were, in some colonies, sharp rivalries among political factions for the control of governments. There were intercolonial rivalries over such matters as

[23] Irving Mark, *Agrarian Conflicts in Colonial New York*, 1711–1775 (New York, 1940), chapter V, "The Great Rebellion of 1766."

boundaries and schemes for expansion. There was a vast gap between the ideas and interests of southern planters and northern merchants. So real were such differences that an English traveler in 1759 thought that the colonies could never unite.

> Fire and water [declared the Reverend Andrew Burnaby] are not more heterogeneous than the different colonies in North America. Nothing can exceed the jealousy and emulation which they possess in regard to each other. . . . In short, such is the difference of character, of manners, of religion, of interest, of the different colonies, that I think . . . were they left to themselves, there would soon be a civil war from one end of the continent to the other; while the Indians and Negroes would, with better reason, impatiently watch the opportunity of exterminating them all together.[24]

So at odds were Americans with one another that more than one feared that civil war might be the outcome of independence, and forty years afterward John Adams still felt that the union of the colonies in 1776 was something of a miracle.

> The colonies had grown up under constitutions of government so different, there was so great a variety of religions, they were composed of so many different nations, their customs, manners, and habits had so little resemblance, and their intercourse had been so rare, and their knowledge of each other so imperfect, that to unite them in the same principles in theory and the same system of action, was certainly a very difficult enterprise. The complete accomplishment of it, in so short a time and by such simple means, was perhaps a singular example in the history of mankind. Thirteen clocks were made to strike together—a perfection of mechanism which no artist had ever before effected.[25]

What brought the thirteen clocks to strike at once, the thirteen colonies to unite in declaring independence? Some have sought the explanation in the growing "maturity" of the American people, or in a rising consciousness of "American nationality," which has been located in such diverse places as the frontier and the urban centers on the seacoast. Obviously the Revolution had deep roots: some ideas can be traced back at least as far as Magna Carta. Obviously too, Americans had achieved an economic and political society of such maturity that they resented outside interference

[24] Andrew Burnaby, *Travels Through North America* (New York, 1904), 152–53.
[25] John Adams to Hezekiah Niles, 13 Feb. 1818, C. F. Adams, ed., *The Works of John Adams* (10 vols., Boston, 1850–56), X, 283.

with their operation of it. Likewise, some of them at least had begun to look upon Americans as a different or a "new" people long before the troubles began in 1763. But it is also probable that in 1763 most influential Americans still thought of England as the mother country, were as deeply loyal to the Crown as most Britons, and regarded America as a part of a larger whole, the British Empire. Yet by 1776 enough Americans to constitute an effective political force were convinced that America should be an independent nation, and the Declaration of Independence presented a common front and defined a common loyalty to the new nation they called the United States of America.

However important such concepts as "maturity" or "nationalism" may seem as we look back, it is difficult to detect them as operative forces in the day-to-day politics of the time, even at the moment independence was declared. Once one goes behind the superficial word-screen of a common political language, unity is replaced by an amazing diversity of motive, thought, and local interests. The primary loyalty of most men was not yet given to the new nation they were founding; their "national feeling" was for the separate states of which they were citizens. And while some of their leaders might declaim that they were "Americans" first and that all Americans were one people, their political actions usually gave the lie to their oratorical flights.

Local political attachments were a basic political fact with which the architects of independence had to deal, and they knew it. Never once before 1776 were Americans united as to either the means or the ends of opposition to British policies. And yet, as John Adams insisted over and over again, the American Revolution "was in the minds of the people, and in the union of the colonies," and it took place before the war began.[26] It was brought about first of all by British policy, which began as a fumbling attempt to reorganize a ramshackle empire but which ended with a determination to impose the absolute will of Britain on America by armed force. This "revolution" and "union" were the work, too, of a small group of American leaders who, despite constant opposition from other American leaders, and often public indifference, won enough support to make independence possible.

Despite all their differences, Americans did have one thing they could unite upon as they faced Britain after 1763. They had a common political tradition and they talked and wrote a common language of political and

[26] To Thomas McKean, 26 Nov. 1815, ibid. X, 180.

constitutional theory. The tradition and the theory were in part their heritage from England, and in part the result of a century and a half of political debate and practice in America. Americans did not discover new ideas after 1763; they reformulated and reiterated ideas with which they had long been familiar. Ever since the seventeenth century they had modeled their legislatures on the House of Commons and claimed all its rights and privileges, including the sole right of laying taxes and controlling the expenditure of the money raised.

As individuals they had always insisted on the "rights of Englishmen" which their first charters gave to them, and by 1763 such rights were thought of as "natural rights" as well. Both as private men and as legislators, Americans after 1763 could and did appeal to their "ancient" traditions and rights as opposed to what they insisted was "new" in British policies.[27] Thus it was that the "lower classes" in the Boston town meeting and the planter aristocrats in the South Carolina Commons House of Assembly could understand one another on the level of political and constitutional theory, and seemingly stand side by side in opposition to Britain, although in fact they had little else in common.

It was this agreement on the high level of theory that misled British policy-makers before 1776, as it sometimes has men since then. The Americans in the several colonies were an exceedingly diverse lot of people on the level of practical politics, and remarkably independent in their relations with one another, but since they all sounded alike, Britain treated them as a common, unified mass of men. Never once did British leaders seem to realize that beneath the eloquent surface of political theorizing, westward of the Atlantic, there lay a complex of differing interests, passions, and loyalties; and because they failed to do so, they did much to defeat the policies they tried to enforce. It is the ultimate irony of the age that those British leaders were in fact, if in all ignorance, the most powerful allies of those Americans who wrote the Declaration of Independence.

[27] For a summary of the heritage from England see Merrill Jensen, "Commentary," in R. G. Adams, Political Ideas of the American Revolution (3rd ed., New York, 1958), 5–31. For a panoramic account of the whole British Empire in the middle of the eighteenth century, see the first eight volumes of Lawrence H. Gipson's The British Empire Before the American Revolution (13 vols., Caldwell, Idaho, and New York, 1936–67). Volume VIII brings the story to the end of the Seven Years War.

II

British Politics, Policies, and America, 1763–1765

The political and administrative center of the British Empire was in turmoil after the Seven Years War. Ministry followed ministry so rapidly that policy-making, colonial or domestic, was erratic and often a matter of chance.[1] Eventually the issue was reduced to whether or not the colonies should be forced to do what Britain ordered. Even then, expediency rather than conviction often governed because some politicians wavered from side to side as they calculated their chances of getting into office, or of staying there once in.

Parliament was controlled by an oligarchy of wealthy families collectively known as Whigs. The Tory party, which had supported the power of the Crown as opposed to the legislature at the end of the seventeenth century, and the Stuarts rather than the Hanoverians at the beginning of the eighteenth, had disintegrated. Tory remnants could still be found but the word "Tory" was used mostly by disappointed politicians to discredit their opponents in office.[2] The Whigs had united to bring a German prince to the throne as George I in 1714 and to kill off the Tory party. They then proceeded to fall upon one another, warring for office and the profits of

[1] Documents illustrating the colonial policies discussed in this chapter are in EHD, IX, 637–58. The bibliographies therein, pages 623–34, list the basic printed sources and the principal monographic works published before the end of 1954.

[2] The "Whig" interpretation of the nineteenth century to the effect that George III and a "Tory" party were engaged in overturning the "constitution" has been pretty much demolished during the twentieth century. Clarence W. Alvord in *The Mississippi Valley in British Politics* (2 vols., Cleveland, 1917) was one of the first to expose its fallacies. Sir Lewis Namier later elaborated Alvord's interpretation in *The Structure of Politics at Accession of George III* (2 vols., London, 1929) and in *England in the Age of the American Revolution* (London, 1930).

office. Few if any principles were involved that resembled those of political parties. Thus in 1762 the young king could write that while the age was one of even greater depravity than at the beginning of the century, he was still grateful that "government has now an advantage from the House of Commons having now no party distinctions. . . ." [3] Yet there were memories of past political issues and the political leaders in the 1760s played upon them to further their own ends—ends which George III believed to be corrupt and little concerned with the welfare of the nation.

There were four main Whig factions. The Old Whigs were led by the aged and wealthy Duke of Newcastle, who had been a patronage boss for decades. His sole political principle was that every man had his price. But he was not an effective leader, for the men he bought seldom felt any compulsion to stay bought if a better offer appeared. A second group was led by Earl Temple and his younger brother, George Grenville. A third faction, known to its enemies as the "Bloomsbury Gang," followed the Duke of Bedford. William Pitt, the "Great Commoner," had long presented himself to the public as its defender against the corrupt politicians and the image was idolized by the middle class, the London merchants, and the London mob, the last being a powerful force in times of political crisis. But the "Pittites" controlled relatively few votes, for Pitt was a man who could neither lead nor follow; yet his personal force and oratorical powers were so great that ministries tottered when he denounced them. Around the fringes of these four groups were lesser men whose only hope for office was attachment to one or another of the factions.

A fifth force in the government was that of the Crown. The king controlled a number of seats in the House of Commons and he normally had the support of many independent country gentlemen who were attached to no faction. There were a great number of appointive jobs at his disposal throughout Great Britain and in the colonies. He and he alone could grant titles to men without them, or promote men of rank to higher rank. During the reigns of George I and II, much of the Crown's patronage had been delegated to the Whig leaders, but George III soon began taking it back into his own hands. The monarch had in addition enormous social prestige. It meant much to the men of the eighteenth century whether a man saw the king in public, in private, or not at all. Political fortunes rose and fell with the king's smiles and frowns.

The all-important constitutional fact was that the king was the executive

[3] To Lord Bute, Feb. 1762, Romney Sedgwick, ed., *Letters from George III to Lord Bute 1756–1766* (London, 1939), 83.

head of the government and the ministers were his ministers and responsible to him, not to a political party or to Parliament. No ministry could go into office or stay in office without the acquiescence and support of the king. But the king often had to accept ministries of which he did not approve, either as a whole or in part, because the operation of the government depended upon a ministry which could win the support of a majority of Parliament for the passage of measures. Sometimes there was deadlock and sheer administrative anarchy; always there was political intrigue to patch together a combination that might work.

When George III became king in 1760, no one Whig faction controlled Parliament. Alliances between factions were therefore cemented with the spoils of office, titles, pensions, and sometimes outright bribery. Such alliances were never founded on trust and seldom on political principles, and treachery began as soon as one was formed. Such had been the alliance between the forces of the Duke of Newcastle and William Pitt in 1757, with Newcastle as the nominal head of the government and Pitt as a secretary of state. The two men despised each other, but Newcastle contented himself with handling the patronage while Pitt carried the Seven Years War toward a successful conclusion.

On 25 October 1760, George II died at the age of seventy-seven and was succeeded by his twenty-two-year-old grandson. The old king hated the boy as he had hated the boy's father and had been hated by them in return. Ever since the accession of George I in 1714, hatred between the monarch and his heir had existed, and was the outgrowth, among other things, of the political life of the times. Discontented politicians gathered around the heir to the throne, and he and his followers played politics to embarrass the reigning monarch and organized to take over the government upon his death. Thus the son of George II and his followers were waiting for the old king to die when the Prince of Wales died suddenly, leaving his thirteen-year-old son as heir and a large group of politicians with no place to turn.

The young boy was a retarded child and, given his ancestry, there seemed to be little hope for him. When he was born his father was still addicted to running about at night, breaking people's windows. The boy's mother had been picked out by George II for no other reason than that her family seemed free from insanity. Her father-in-law commented succinctly, "I did not think ingrafting my half-witted coxcomb upon a madwoman would mend the breed." The hapless child born to this couple was still unable to read at the age of eleven. For years he resisted the efforts of tutors to bring him out of what amounted to a coma. But he finally acquired a tutor who won his affection, and among other things, taught him to dislike and distrust every politician of the age. Lord Bute, a Scot, had few if any qualifications for public life, but the boy became utterly and pathetically dependent upon him, both emotionally and politically.[4] Bute's influence inevitably aroused distrust among political leaders, who appealed to the active dislike of many Englishmen for Scotland and its people and tried to persuade them that Bute was only ancient Stuart despotism in a new form.

During his first years as king, George III was not the ogre his American subjects thought him to be by 1776. His letters are those of a frightened child in a grown-up world he did not understand. He clung desperately to Bute, afraid to make decisions without his advice, and fearful of his disapproval, and it was natural for him to want to have the one man he trusted in the ministry. The two leading figures in it were Pitt and Newcastle, and it was easy to play off those jealous leaders against one another; within a short time Bute was in the cabinet.

Meanwhile the war was dividing Englishmen on an issue of policy and principle such as rarely faced them in the eighteenth century. The scattered and disorganized Tory element had long been opposed to entangling alliances on the continent of Europe, believing that England should concentrate on naval warfare and control of the seas. The Tories objected strongly, as did many others, to the vast sums paid Frederick the Great and other German princes to fight England's battles on land. Pitt, on the other hand, believed in the old Whig policy of Continental alliances, as well as in naval supremacy, and he was determined to carry on the war until French power was crushed forever. Young George III, backed by Bute and many members of the cabinet, soon determined to end the war and the enormous growth of the national debt.

Continuation of the war was the issue on which Pitt lost power, never really to regain it. France had made various proposals for peace but Pitt forced their rejection, and when news of a treaty between France and Spain leaked out in the summer of 1761, Pitt, suspecting that it was aimed at Britain, demanded war against Spain. The majority of the cabinet agreed with Bute and the king and rejected Pitt's demand. Pitt and his brother-in-law, Earl Temple, therefore resigned in October 1761. Pitt's

---

[4] Sedgwick's introduction to the *Letters from George III to Lord Bute* is a good short account of the early life of George III and of the political situation in England in 1760. See also Sir Lewis Namier, "King George III: A Study in Personality," *History Today*, III (1953), and J. H. Plumb, "George III," in *Men and Centuries* (Boston, 1963).

suspicions were proved right when the terms of the treaty were published, and less than three months after his resignation Britain declared war on Spain.

Meanwhile the dithering Newcastle continued as the nominal head of the ministry. In May 1762 he finally resigned after more than forty years in office, and Lord Bute took his place. The king, Bute, and others were determined to end the war in spite of Britain's resounding victories over Spain during the year. So anxious were they that they yielded territories and concessions to France and Spain that Britain might well have kept; certainly Britain won no friends in France or elsewhere by giving them up. The preliminaries of the peace were laid before Parliament at the end of November 1762. Pitt and his supporters attacked the terms but Parliament approved them by an overwhelming vote, and the war formally ended with the Treaty of Paris, 10 February 1763.[5]

Bute was ready to resign. He had neither talent nor taste for the rough and tumble of politics—such talents as he had were for backstairs intrigue—and he was despised by most of the men who supported him. By the spring of 1763 he was one of the most hated men in England. The London mob, which worshipped Pitt, howled at Bute and even attacked his carriage when he appeared on the streets. Scandalmongers hinted that he was more than a friend of the king's mother. Bute was a nervous wreck and finished politically, but before he resigned he arranged for a new ministry headed by George Grenville.

Meanwhile the young king was learning the political game, and he played it as it had been played since the beginning of the century. He did not subvert the constitution: he simply took back into his own hands the power and the patronage his grandfather and great-grandfather had delegated to the Whig politicians, and in the course of time he became a highly skillful practical politician. Year by year he built up a political following dependent upon him rather than on one or another of the Whig leaders. The "king's friends" consisted of politicians who preferred office to the political wilderness, if loyalty to an older leader meant the latter. But it should be remembered in all this that George III's aim was to create a stable administration, a workable executive. Throughout the eighteenth century, Britain fumbled in an effort to establish "an executive powerful enough to administer the laws of Parliament, but not strong enough to

[5] The most recent and detailed account of the war and the Treaty of Paris is to be found in volumes VI–VIII of Gipson's *The British Empire Before the American Revolution.*

endanger the liberties of Englishmen and the rights of Parliament." [6] During the first ten years of George III's rule, ministries supported only by minorities rose and fell as the king grew increasingly desperate for stability. By 1770 he had a following strong enough to put his own man, Lord North, at the head of the ministry and to keep him there for twelve years.

ॐ

George Grenville, who became head of the ministry as first lord of the treasury and chancellor of the exchequer in the spring of 1763, was a Whig of the Whigs, and devoted to the British constitution as he understood it. He came to the House of Commons for the first time in 1741 and he held the same seat until his death in 1770. He received his first post in a ministry in 1744 and thereafter held one office after another. He was long a follower of his brother Richard, Earl Temple, and of their brother-in-law William Pitt, but soon after the accession of George III, Bute won Grenville over. When Pitt and Temple resigned in October 1761, Grenville stayed on in office. In the Bute ministry he was first a secretary of state and then the first lord of the admiralty. When he succeeded Bute in the spring of 1763, he was known as a hard worker and as one of the few men in the House of Commons who understood finance.

Innumerable problems faced him. Britain had acquired great new territories in North America inhabited by Spaniards, Frenchmen, and hordes of hostile Indians. In Britain the problem of financing the national debt was so great that at times national bankruptcy seemed imminent. It was Grenville's task, in the midst of a postwar depression, to appease British taxpayers and yet pay the interest on the debt, to save money and yet keep enough hungry politicians on the payroll to maintain a majority in the House of Commons. Internal discontent was growing. The city of London and its mob constantly threatened to get out of hand. The "cider counties" of southern England threatened revolt against the cider tax of 1763. John Wilkes and his followers created a turmoil, and the attempt to suppress him and the printers seemed to many a real threat to English liberties.

At the same time Grenville was forced to deal with the colonial problems left in the wake of the Seven Years War. Upon him was to be placed the blame for the initiation of policies that led to the revolt and the independence of thirteen of the colonies on the North American mainland, yet

[6] John W. Wilkes, "British Politics Preceding the American Revolution," *The Huntington Library Quarterly*, XX (1957); Richard Pares, *King George III and the Politicians* (Oxford, 1953).

Grenville and the leaders who succeeded him, and the majorities who supported them, were not guilty of malevolence or of a desire to destroy the empire. However, they did suffer from a common failing among men: inability to predict the future. If guilt there was, it consisted of a lack of understanding of the complexities of the political and economic life of the colonies, a failure born partly of ignorance and partly of an unwillingness or an inability to learn. But Grenville was not alone in this among Englishmen, or even among some American leaders at the time. To Grenville it seemed that the Americans were unwilling to obey the laws; that they expected benefits from the mother country but were unwilling to yield anything in return.

It is sometimes said that Britain shifted from a "colonial" to an "imperial" policy after 1763, but this is hardly adequate to describe the day-to-day actions of those in power. Men such as Grenville seldom dealt in terms of broad theoretical propositions; in fact it is doubtful that they were capable of doing so. They were practical politicians who had budgets to meet, debts to pay, domestic turmoil to face, and the never-ending problem of satisfying job hunters so that the affairs of government could be carried on. They took no time to sit back and speculate; such theories as they had they inherited from a past stretching back to the beginning of English colonization. If there was any basic shift in policy after 1763 they were unaware of it.

It is also said that one of the reasons for the difficulties after 1763 was that the Grenville ministry adopted "new" policies, but this is at best a half-truth. Most of the so-called "new" policies were adopted during the Seven Years War, before Grenville came to power, and even those had roots running far back. The enforcement of the laws of trade had been a policy ever since the passage of the first Navigation Act in 1660. The idea of closer political control over the colonies was as old as that day in 1624 when Virginia became the first royal colony. During the Seven Years War certain new things were added. A commander in chief of all military forces in the colonies was appointed for the first time in 1755. The control of Indian affairs was taken from the colonies and given to the commander in chief and to royal officials, the Indian superintendents. At the same time William Pitt, as a wartime measure, began effective enforcement of the laws of trade for the first time. Finally, the crucial decision to leave a standing army in America in peacetime was made before Grenville came to power.[7]

---

[7] A detailed account of the British experience during the Seven Years War, and its relation to the colonial policies of the Grenville ministry, is to be found in George L.

Grenville, as head of the ministry between 1763 and 1765, was trying to carry out policies which he had inherited not only from previous ministries but also from previous generations. The one new thing he did try was to raise money in the colonies through direct taxation by Parliament. But even this policy was born of the decision to leave an army in the colonies, and had been talked of for years by colonial governors and by officials in Britain. The attempt to tax the colonies was disastrous, but in the beginning it had the support of politicians who were shortly to promote their own political fortunes by damning Grenville for making the attempt. Grenville, then, was trying to solve the problems left by an expensive war and to implement colonial policies of long standing. He was an innovator only if a literal-minded belief that laws should be enforced and old policies should be maintained makes a man such.

ट~

Grenville faced a host of problems in April 1763 and they had to be met almost simultaneously. The question of colonial policy was only one among many, but he took it up at once. He turned first to the enforcement of the Acts of Trade and Navigation. On the whole the colonies had accepted the Navigation Acts and the bulk of their trade flowed within the channels defined by them. But one law had been ignored from the day of its passage: the Molasses Act of 1733, which placed a duty of six pence a gallon on foreign molasses imported by the British colonies and duties on foreign rum and sugar. It was a law that made little economic sense, however much the British West Indies planters hoped it would rescue them from their economic plight—and even they profited by "naturalizing" foreign molasses and sugar and shipping them on as British. The merchants of the mainland colonies took such products from the British islands or carried them directly from the foreign islands and either bribed mainland customs officers or worked out devices that had the appearance of legality.

It was no secret on either side of the Atlantic that the law was a dead letter, but it was not until the Seven Years War that many British officials became convinced that Americans were smugglers by nature. The merchants of the northern mainland colonies believed that trade with the foreign West Indies was essential to their economic well-being. Furthermore,

Beer, *British Colonial Policy, 1754–1765* (New York, 1907), chapters IV–VII. O. M. Dickerson, *The Navigation Acts and the American Revolution* (Philadelphia, 1951), chapter III, "Evasion of the Navigation Acts," also discusses the question with emphasis on the role of the Navigation Acts which he argues were not a "cause" of the Revolution. For a more detailed account of the policies discussed in this chapter, see Bernhard Knollenberg, *Origin of the American Revolution: 1759–1766* (New York, 1960), and Gipson, *British Empire*, X, chapters IX–XII.

the French and other foreign islands were as dependent as the British islands upon supplies from the mainland colonies, and a trade that was profitable in peacetime was even more so during the Seven Years War. In 1756 the board of trade ordered colonial governors to embargo all vessels unless they were bound for another British colony. The order was futile, and in 1757 Parliament passed an act forbidding the export of all provisions except fish, rice, and roots to any place except Britain, Ireland, and other British colonies. The law was no more effective than the order to the governors.

French planters paid better prices and sold molasses cheaper than ever before. Enterprising colonial merchants, and Irish and British as well, often managed to secure French licenses to carry on the trade. Another device was to acquire a French prisoner or two and a pass from a colonial governor. Then, under the pretext of exchanging prisoners, cargoes could be carried to the French islands "legally." "Flag of truce" vessels soon became a racket. Governor William Denny of Pennsylvania sold a few passes for high prices, then began signing them in blank, and as the value depreciated issued more and more. Military officers complained bitterly. The British navy went into action and eventually stopped much of a trade that had made American provisions cheaper in French islands than in the British and had resulted in the shipment of French sugar to Britain itself as "British" sugar. Merchants also sent cargoes to the neutral Dutch islands, whence they could be transshipped to the French in neutral Dutch ships. Britain countered with the "Rule of 1756" to the effect that neutrals could not carry on a wartime trade which was denied them in peacetime. The navy began seizing Dutch ships, whereupon merchants turned to the Spanish colony of Santo Domingo. The port of Monte Christi, which had little trade before the war, soon had hundreds of vessels going in and out. In time the navy put a stop to this trade as well.

On the mainland, military commanders, under orders from William Pitt, tried to stiffen the spines of governors and customs officers. Writs of assistance were demanded of courts to enable customs officers to enter and search for suspected illegal cargoes. The colonists resisted, but by the end of the war, as a result of the prodding of the British government, the determination of British military commanders, and the activity of the British navy, the Molasses Act of 1733 was enforced fairly effectively.

But enforcement was possible only as a wartime measure, and there were many obstacles in the way of the successful prosecution of illegal traders. The capture of a vessel and cargo was only the first step. Cases had to be tried in either admiralty or colonial common law courts. It was virtually useless to try them in the latter, for few juries would convict a local citizen. Even the admiralty courts proved faulty during the war, for in colony after colony judges seized on technicalities to avoid prosecutions, or dismissed cases despite plain evidence of illegality. Few admiralty judges, however, equaled one in the Bahamas who engaged in illegal trade himself and took fees from Philadelphia merchants for releasing their vessels when cases involving them were brought before him. Even if prosecutions in admiralty courts were successful, the seizing officer could be sued for damages in the common law courts. It was a rare customs officer whose zeal for the service was such that he would carry out his duties at the expense of his own pocket. There were such, but there were many more who ignored law-breakers or who took bribes to eke out small incomes. Experience during the war therefore called British attention to the mainland colonies as never before, and left British officials with the conviction that reforms had to be made.

During the last months of the Bute ministry, Grenville, as first lord of the admiralty, had seen the effectiveness of the navy in checking illegal trade, and he was largely responsible for the law of 1763 stationing British naval vessels in American waters in peacetime.[8] The law gave naval officers the power to act as customs officials, thus adopting a practice already used in the waters around Britain, where smugglers, incidentally, could have taught their American cousins many tricks of the trade. By the autumn of 1763, naval vessels were cruising in American waters from Newfoundland to the West Indies, with their officers and crews on the alert for the profits to be gained from the capture and successful prosecution of illegal traders.

Colonial governors were ordered to help enforce the trade laws and, repeatedly, they were asked for reports on illegal traders. Almost to a man the governors reported that whatever might be true of other colonies, there was almost no illegal trade in their own. Francis Fauquier of Virginia declared that his colony was as free of it "as any country that trades at all; insomuch that the men of war stationed on our coast think it hardly worth watching." Of course ships from Lisbon did bring in chests of fruit as gifts to big tobacco shippers, and occasionally they brought in a small cask of wine. But such were usually gifts from the captain and not a part of a ship's cargo. There were New Englanders, however, who sneaked out tobacco to the other colonies without paying duties, but even they had been stopped by recent seizures.[9]

[8] 3 Geo. III, c. 22, Danby Pickering, ed., *The Statutes at Large* . . . [Pickering], XXV, 347–48, sec. 4.
[9] To secretary of state [SS], 20 Nov. 1764, British Public Record Office [PRO], Colonial Office [C.O.], 5/1345.

The much-maligned New Englanders had their defenders, or at least Massachusetts did. In 1761 Governor Francis Bernard reported that it was almost impossible to distinguish between British and foreign molasses coming into the colonies.[10] But when the investigation began in 1763, he was discreetly silent about molasses and asserted that nowhere were the Navigation Acts better enforced than in Massachusetts. It was true that small amounts of wine and Lisbon lemons came as ships' stores, but the lemons were necessary for the health of the sailors. Even the good health which the governor enjoyed was largely due to such "illegal" lemons. As for Portuguese wine, no distinction was made between wine from the mainland and from the islands, and he implied that none should be made for "the fish trade of New England is of too great consequence to old England to run any risk of checking it." [11] A year later he told the ministry that if it wanted to find illegal traders it should look to Connecticut and Rhode Island, which elected their governors. "In such governments, it is vain to expect that British laws should be carried into execution." He had even heard it said that the governor of Rhode Island had publicly asserted that "the Parliament of Great Britain had no more right to make laws for them than they had for the Mohawks. These two republics are the allies of Great Britain, and not the subjects." [12]

Thus governors denied the existence of illegal trade in their own colonies while pointing a finger at others. The ingenious disclaimers of the governors were intended to mislead, yet they were essentially right. The great bulk of colonial trade, even that with foreign possessions, was legal. It was not illegal to ship cargoes of lumber, provisions, and fish to the foreign West Indies and to southern Europe. The illegality consisted in not paying the six pence duty on each gallon of foreign molasses brought in. But the trade was so important that the governors of the northern colonies either chose to ignore violations or defended them, however feebly.

In England, Grenville as head of the treasury began an investigation. At once he attacked the old practice of giving major customs posts to men who stayed in England, collected the salaries, and hired poorly paid deputies to do the work in America. Grenville ordered such men to go to the colonies or resign their posts. There were immediate and outraged protests. Horace Walpole, who had lost his sinecure as a commissioner of the customs shortly before Grenville took office, pleaded for one of his former deputies

[10] To board of trade [BT], 17 May 1761, C.O. 5/891.
[11] Bernard to SS, 25 Oct. 1763, C.O. 5/755.
[12] To SS, 14 Dec. 1764, C.O. 5/755.

who had been collector of the port of Philadelphia for more than a quarter of a century, apparently without ever crossing the Atlantic. Grenville's reply was firm. The customs service in America collected between £1000 and £2000 a year, while the costs of collection were between £7000 and £8000. Officials must either go to America or resign.[13]

Some went but most resigned rather than face the American wilderness. Dukes and lesser men at once began demanding for friends and underlings the new jobs thus made available, and sometimes for unusual reasons. Lord Holland asked Grenville to give the comptroller's post in New York to an Irish actor named O'Bryen. The actor had eloped to New York with the daughter of Holland's brother, Lord Ilchester. "The keeping him there in credit," said Holland, "is all that can be done, whilst we, if possible, forget them here at home." [14]

The treasury investigation was completed by the fall of 1763. It was based on the proposition that customs revenues in the colonies had not kept up with the growth of trade because of connivance and fraud. Better regulations must be established or it would soon be impossible to remedy the defects. The treasury had done what it could by ordering customs officers to their posts in America, and it would appoint more officials where necessary. New instructions had been sent to customs officials to stop frauds, to make careful reports on trade, and to offer suggestions for improvement.

But the treasury alone could not stop illegal practices. It needed the help of other branches of government. The governors should be sent strict instructions; the commanders in chief of the army and navy in America should be directed to help and protect customs officers from desperate and lawless persons. The royal navy should be used as a "sea guard." Beyond this, parliamentary legislation was needed to provide better methods of trying cases in the courts. The admiralty courts in particular should be put on a uniform basis.

The Privy Council adopted this report and the various departments were ordered to co-operate.[15] In addition, the report served as a blueprint for the so-called "Sugar Act," which was far more comprehensive than its popular name implied. It contained three essential parts: it made changes in

[13] Walpole to Grenville, 7 Sept. 1763, W. J. Smith, ed., *The Grenville Papers* . . . [GP] (4 vols., London, 1852–53), II, 113–15; Grenville to Walpole, 8 Sept. 1763, Grenville Letter Books, I, Henry E. Huntington Library [HEHL].
[14] GP, II, 447.
[15] 4 Oct. 1763, EHD, IX, 637–39. For the origins of the report see Thomas C. Barrow, "Background to the Grenville Program, 1757–1763," WMQ, 3 ser. XXII (1965).

duties and added new ones on a variety of foreign goods imported into the colonies; it provided elaborate new procedures for the loading and unloading of goods; and it established new procedures for the trial of alleged lawbreakers in colonial courts.

The revenue features were presented to the House of Commons early in March 1764.[16] Within four days a bill was brought in and the House went to work. Facts and figures were called for, Americans in London were brought in for advice, various amendments were offered, and by 5 April the bill had been signed by George III. The preamble made clear that it was a revenue measure as well as a regulatory measure: "it is just and necessary that a revenue be raised . . . in America for defraying the expenses of defending, protecting, and securing the same. . . ."

The law imposed various import duties on foreign cloth, sugar, indigo, and coffee brought into the colonies. At the same time most of the drawbacks paid in England on foreign goods re-exported to the colonies were abolished. An entirely new duty was put on foreign wine, most of which had come directly to the colonies from southern Europe and the islands off the coast of Africa. The duty was £7 a tun (252 gallons) if brought directly, but only ten shillings if shipped through England.

The key to any real increase in revenue was of course molasses. The act of 1733 was made perpetual, but the duty on foreign molasses was reduced from six to three pence a gallon, while that on foreign refined sugar was increased, and the colonists were forbidden to import foreign rum or spirits.

Other economic features of the act were the addition of coffee, pimento, hides, coconuts, whale fins, raw silk, and potash and pearl ash to the list of enumerated articles that could be shipped only to Britain or to other British colonies, and a provision that no iron or lumber could be put on board a ship for Europe without giving bond that it would be landed in Great Britain.[17] The trade in coffee and pimento between the British West Indies and the mainland was hampered by additional duties if they were shipped to any place except Great Britain.

As a revenue measure, the law was a failure. The prohibition of the importation of foreign rum was meaningless except as an irritant to the Americans, for the foreign islands produced very little. The additions to

[16] 10 March 1764, House of Commons *Journals* [HCJ], XXIX, 934–35.
[17] This section of the act aroused so much opposition that the next year an act (5 Geo. III, c. 45, Pickering, XXVI, 440–41) allowed the exportation of iron and lumber to Ireland and of lumber to Europe south of Cape Finisterre.

the list of enumerated products made little difference. Only the wine duty and the molasses duty were productive of much revenue, but even so, they by no means brought in enough to in any way solve the budget problem of the British government. In fact, the principal product of the economic portions of the act was mounting irritation in the northern colonies.

Of far greater long-range significance were the sections that greatly elaborated the procedures and the paper work involved in the loading and unloading of sea-borne cargoes. The purpose was to prevent fraud, much of which began in the British West Indies, where many British planters and officials connived to evade the Molasses Act. To prevent the "naturalization" of foreign molasses, sugar, and rum in the British islands, the law required any ship loading such products to secure an affidavit from the owner or grower (sworn to before a justice of the peace) stating the quality and quantity of the goods and giving the name of the producing plantation. The affidavit then had to be given to a customs officer who would provide a certificate listing the contents of the shipment for the captain, and send a copy to the customs officer at the port of destination. When the captain arrived, he had to present the certificate and take an oath that his cargo was as listed. If he could not produce such a certificate, he had to pay the duties levied on foreign goods.

But the captain had to do even more. He could not load the goods, to begin with, until he produced a warrant or sufferance from a customs officer permitting him to do so. Once loaded, but before he sailed, he had to make out a cocket listing each package of goods on board and giving the names of the shipper and the consignee. If any of the goods were subject to duties on shipment, the cocket must also show when and where the duties were paid. Before the goods could be unloaded on arrival, the cocket had to be shown to a customs officer. If the captain did not have a cocket, or the cargo did not tally with it, all the goods were declared forfeit. The captain also had to secure a certificate showing that he had given bond, which he was to deliver along with his other papers on arrival at a British or a colonial port.

New restrictions were placed on ships leaving Britain for the colonies. The revenue act asserted that British and colonial ships had stopped off in Britain with goods "pretended to be destined to some foreign plantation," had then loaded goods for some British colony, and then "clandestinely landed in the British American dominions" with the whole cargo. To stop this practice a drastic step was taken. Thereafter no ship could clear from Britain for the colonies unless its whole cargo was put on board in Britain. If there were foreign goods, they had to be unloaded and reloaded.

One can only imagine what anguish the vast increase in paper work caused the tough sea captains of the Atlantic and their merchant employers. It meant a big increase in the cost of shipping, for the new documents required payment of additional fees to customs officials who made them out, and it meant an increase in the number of the officials to take care of the additional work. And some of the officials were not above taking advantage of the many technicalities in the law to harass Americans, smugglers and solid law-abiding citizens alike.

The new duties and the new methods for carrying on trade were irritating enough, but the new procedures for the trial of ships and goods seized by customs officers were such as to outrage American merchants who had never smuggled. There is little doubt that colonial courts, both admiralty and common law, had favored Americans accused of wrongdoing, and customs officers had more than once been victimized for doing their legitimate duty. Under the Navigation Acts, cases of fraud or evasion had to be tried in a colonial vice-admiralty court or in a common law court of the colony where the seizure of ships or goods had occurred. The Act of 1764 provided that this could still be done, but it also provided for the establishment of a new vice-admiralty court over all the colonies, and allowed the prosecutor or informer to take the case directly to this court if he chose. Such a court was soon established at Halifax in Nova Scotia, but it was so remote from the trading centers of the mainland colonies that it proved useless.

Americans denounced the new admiralty court at once, but their immediate concern was with the new procedures for trials. These hit and hit hard, for in operation there was often very little justice in them. To begin with, if a ship and/or cargo were seized and a violation of a law charged, the owner could not begin suit for recovery unless he first provided enough security to pay the costs of the trial. If he did not provide security, the goods and/or ship were declared forfeit. Second, the owner was in effect declared guilty of lawbreaking before the trial began. The customs officer did not have to provide evidence of fraud—the owner had to provide proof that he was innocent! Third, if the owner proved his innocence, he was not entitled to recover the costs of the suit or damages from the customs officer if the presiding judge issued a certificate to the effect that the officer had a "probable cause" for making the seizure. And if the customs officer or court released the goods and/or ship without bringing the case to trial, the owner could not collect more than two pence in damages, and the customs officer could not be fined more than one shilling.

The revenue act went so far as to tell colonial juries the verdicts they must render if cases were tried in common law courts in the colonies. In any suit against a customs officer enforcing the Act of 1764 or any other act of Parliament, the customs officer could plead the "general issue," citing the law under which he took action. If this was the case, the jury must find for the defendant. If the plaintiff suing a customs officer stopped a case before it came to trial, or the jury found against the plaintiff, the customs officer could collect treble the costs.[18] The result of these provisions was to free customs officers from virtually all responsibility for their actions, and many of them took advantage of the opportunity offered to line their pockets by making seizures without evidence and by using technicalities in the law. Small wonder that the Americans fought back.[19]

Two weeks after the passage of the Revenue Act of 1764, Parliament passed a second law interfering even more directly with the economic life of the colonies: the Currency Act. During the first half of the eighteenth century most of the colonies began to use paper money in some form or other. There was little or no gold and silver money in circulation and the colonies had long since outgrown the days when commodities and paper notes based on commodities, such as the tobacco notes of Virginia, could provide an adequate money supply. The gold, silver, and bills of exchange acquired in the West Indies trade circulated mostly among merchants and were used to pay their debts in Britain. There was also a need for private credit in a rapidly expanding economy, and several colonies met the demand by establishing "land banks." These were simply government loan offices which let out money on farm mortgages. The interest rates were low and the money was paid back in installments. In the middle colonies these government "banks" were well run, performed a real service for farmers, and were a profitable source of revenue. Pennsylvania's land bank

---

[18] The act is printed in part in EHD, IX, 644-48 and in full in Pickering, XXVI, 33-52. For two accounts with different emphases, see Dickerson, *Navigation Acts*, chapter VII, and Edmund S. and Helen M. Morgan, *The Stamp Act Crisis: Prologue to Revolution* (Chapel Hill, 1953), chapter III.

[19] The activities of customs officers are treated in detail in Dickerson, *Navigation Acts*, chapter IX, "Era of Customs Racketeering," and at various places in this volume.

was so successful that for a quarter-century before the Seven Years War the interest received on farm mortgages paid the expenses of the colonial government.

The money issued by colonial governments could be used to buy land and pay taxes and import duties; usually it was legal tender in the payment of private debts. Most colonial political battles over paper money concerned private debts. Some colonies, and particularly in New England and the Carolinas, tended to issue too much currency, or failed to collect it in taxes. The result was depreciation in terms of gold and silver and in terms of sterling money, and this aroused the opposition of creditors on both sides of the Atlantic.

British officials recognized that the colonies needed paper money, and until 1740 the board of trade approved land bank and currency issues. The board insisted, however, that the money have adequate backing and be redeemed at the times stated in the issuing laws, and not be re-issued indefinitely. Colonial governors were ordered not to sign paper money bills unless they included a clause suspending operation of the laws until approved by the Crown. But governors could be bullied, even after they were told in 1740 that they would lose their positions unless they obeyed orders.[20] During the 1740s the board of trade began opposing the use of paper money to pay private debts, and thus followed the lead of creditors, particularly in New England, where Rhode Island's excessive issues caused trouble, and where the Massachusetts land bank led to a bitter internal fight.

Administrative orders from London had no effect, so in 1751 Parliament passed an act regulating New England currency that wrote into law the old policies which the board of trade had been unable to enforce. Money in circulation must be redeemed according to the issuing laws, and old issues could not be re-extended. The governments could issue paper money from year to year to pay expenses if they levied taxes to pay it off within two years. But the key provision of the act was the prohibition of the use of paper money to pay private debts.[21]

At the beginning of the Seven Years War, as in previous wars, British officials abandoned attempts at restriction, for the colonies needed to issue paper money if they were to fight. However scornful the British were of colonial war efforts, the colonies did spend enormous sums. For instance,

[20] EHD, IX, 428–29.
[21] 24 Geo. II, c. 53, Pickering, XX, 306–7.

the average cost of government in Pennsylvania, and in New York, had been about £5000 a year in peacetime. During the war, New York issued £535,000 in paper money, and Pennsylvania, which usually had about £80,000 in circulation, issued £540,000. Virginia, which had never used such money (although it had tobacco notes in circulation), issued £440,000. The board of trade estimated that the colonies as a whole spent about £2,500,000 sterling beyond the ordinary costs of government. Of this amount, Parliament paid about half in cash subsidies.

Despite the size of their debts, the colonies were able to pay them off with astonishing rapidity. The grants from Parliament helped, but the colonial method of finance was the answer. It was an answer as baffling to English officials in the eighteenth century as it was to nineteenth-century financial historians, perhaps because it was so simple. Government debts consisted of paper money in circulation and the colonial governments paid their debts by levying taxes payable in the money they had issued.[22] The board of trade sent out inquiries in 1764, and in January 1766 it reported, without any apparent comprehension of how the colonies had done it, that of £2,515,038 in paper money issued by the mainland colonies since 1749, only £760,455 remained to be paid, and that it would be paid within four or five years.[23]

British opposition to American financial practices revived long before the war was over and the attack centered on Virginia, which had issued paper money for the first time in 1755. Such money could not be sent to Britain to pay sterling debts but it could be used to buy the bills of exchange with which such debts were usually paid. In 1749 Virginia had fixed a legal rate of exchange which declared that £125 in current money in Virginia was worth £100 sterling, a rate lower than it usually cost to buy a £100 bill of exchange. British creditors protested but no action was taken until 1755, when Virginia amended the law. The amendment allowed the local courts to settle suits for debt collections at a "just" rate of exchange, which presumably meant the market value of bills. Some courts, however, favored the local planters rather than the far-off creditors.

British merchants protested to the board of trade and it in turn demanded that Virginia guarantee the full sterling value of debts. In 1763

---

[22] E. James Ferguson, "Currency Finance: An Interpretation of Colonial Monetary Practices," WMQ, 3 ser. X (1953) is the best available account of such matters and includes a comprehensive critical bibliography of writings on the subject.
[23] The board of trade sent the letter 11 May 1764. The governors' replies are in C.O. 323/19.

when the board ordered Virginia to abolish the use of paper money in the payment of private debts, the House of Burgesses flatly refused. British merchants again appealed to the board of trade, but they were divided. London merchants who dealt mainly with individual Virginia planters demanded the complete abolition of paper money as legal tender for any debts. The Scottish merchants who had built up chains of small stores throughout Virginia, stores which received paper money in payment for goods, were more realistic. They did not want legal tender paper money abolished; they wanted it more carefully regulated so that its value would remain steady.

The board of trade ignored the explanations of the Scots and the Virginians, declared the experience of the middle colonies to be false, and denounced the history of paper money in America as one of iniquity and fraud. The only "honest" money was gold and silver. The Privy Council, as blind to economic reality as the board, sent the board's report to a Parliament equally unenlightened.[24]

The result was the Currency Act of 1764, which applied to all the colonies outside New England, where the Currency Act of 1751 still remained in force. The new act forbade the issuance of paper money which would be legal tender "in payment of any bargains, contracts, debts, dues, or demands whatsoever. . . ." Paper money then in circulation was not abolished but it could not be re-issued. Any governor who signed a bill contrary to the new act would be fined £1000 and forever removed from public office.[25] The law was more drastic than the Act of 1751 for its purpose was to wipe out paper money in the colonies south of New England, once their wartime issues had expired.

Men in colonies with well-managed currencies were outraged and colonists everywhere were convinced that the act was a major source of the hard times that followed the war. In fact, the law had little relation to the realities of colonial economic life, and its sweeping character denied any discretion to colonial governors or to the board of trade, which was soon to learn its mistake. It thus served, along with other measures, to add to the growing irritation of many Americans toward the mother country and to

[24] Report of the board of trade, 9 March 1764, W. L. Grant and James Munro, eds., Acts of the Privy Council of England. Colonial Series [APC:CS] (6 vols., London, 1908–12), IV, 623–31, 641–48. For Virginia's defense of paper money, see letter of the Virginia Committee of Correspondence to the Virginia agent in Britain, 16 June 1763, EHD, IX, 435–37. Joseph A. Ernst gives a scholarly account in "Genesis of the Currency Act of 1764: Virginia Paper Money and the Protection of British Investments," WMQ, 3 ser. XXII (1965).
[25] EHD, IX, 648–50.

convince some at least that they would always be sacrificed to the interests of selfish British merchants.[26]

While Parliament was legislating on matters of colonial trade and finance, the ministry was evolving a policy relating to western expansion—an area in which Britain had never had a policy. Prior to the Seven Years War, the colonial governments controlled Indian affairs, the fur trade, and land granting, and the Americans had pushed on toward the most western of the Appalachian ranges. But the acquisition of the whole of the great valley east of the Mississippi River created new problems. The evolution of a western policy by the British government was affected by many things: sheer ignorance of geography, the conflicts between colony and colony over boundaries and rival land claims, and conflicts among rival land speculators. British politics were involved, for many British politicians were as avid as any American for the riches men thought could be found in the Mississippi Valley. In the end, few if any of the men who promoted rival land schemes made money, but the significant fact is that they hoped to, and because they had political power they had influence in both British and colonial politics before the war and in the politics of the United States after 1776.[27]

Central was the fact that Virginia, by virtue of its royal charter, claimed the whole of the vast region north and west of the Appalachians. But the Virginians did not act until about the middle of the century, by which time the Pennsylvania fur traders had penetrated far into the region claimed by Virginia. In 1747 a group of Virginians, including the Washingtons and the Lees, organized the Ohio Company and appealed to the Crown for a land grant at the forks of the Ohio River, the key to future expansion in the Ohio and Mississippi valleys. Two years later they received a royal grant of 200,000 acres in the region south of present-day Pittsburgh. The Virginians made preparations for settlement while the Pennsylvania fur traders encouraged the Indians to kill off the settlers. But a far greater challenge was shortly at hand. Ever since the beginning of the century the French had been slowly extending their control over the net-

26 See Chapter XIII below for later changes in policy.
27 The pioneer study is Alvord's *Mississippi Valley in British Politics*. His views are challenged and sometimes revised by John R. Alden, *John Stuart and the Southern Colonial Frontier* (Ann Arbor, 1944), and by Jack M. Sosin, *Whitehall and the Wilderness: The Middle West in British Colonial Policy, 1760–1775* (Lincoln, Neb., 1961).

work of waterways stretching from the St. Lawrence through the Great Lakes to the mouth of the Mississippi. After the end of the War of the Austrian Succession in 1748, the French began building a chain of forts far to the east to block American expansion into the Ohio Valley.

By 1753 officials in Britain were convinced that another war was imminent and that Indian aid would be invaluable. The board of trade ordered colonial governors to meet and unite the colonies to help in the coming war, and to persuade the Indians to help as well. The Albany Congress in 1754 produced a plan of union that was rejected by every colonial legislature to which it was submitted and was ignored by the British. The next year partial control of the West was placed in the hands of British officials. General Edward Braddock came to America as commander in chief of all British and colonial military forces, and with instructions to appoint superintendents of Indian affairs. Sir William Johnson was appointed superintendent north of the Ohio. In 1756 Edmund Aitkin was named for the region south of the river; in 1762 he was succeeded by John Stuart. The superintendents took their positions seriously and reported in detail on fraudulent land grants, schemes of land companies, and the corrupt methods of fur traders. Repeatedly they warned of the danger of encroachment on Indian lands.

Pennsylvania took the first step in the direction of a new policy at the Treaty of Easton in October 1758. It promised the Indians that Pennsylvania would make no settlements within the colony west of the Alleghenies. But with the completion of the conquest of Canada in 1760, frontiersmen began moving westward once more, reoccupying homes from which they had fled, and pushing on beyond the mountains. Henry Bouquet, the commandant at Fort Pitt, realized that the onward push of settlers might mean Indian troubles, and in October 1761 he forbade all settlement west of the Alleghenies. The ordinary settlers ignored him, and protests came from others of more importance: the governor of Virginia objected, as did the Ohio Company.

The board of trade acted shortly thereafter. In December 1761 it forbade governors and other officers to grant lands within the colonies "which may interfere with the Indians bordering thereon. . . ." [28] The only way to acquire land was to apply to a governor who would forward the application to the board of trade for a final decision. By the end of 1761, therefore, Britain had taken over from the individual colonies the military

[28] 3 Dec. 1761, APC:CS, IV, 500.

protection of the frontiers, political relations with the Indians, and the purchase of Indian lands.

Within less than a month after Grenville took office in 1763, a great Indian uprising in the Ohio Valley very nearly wiped out the English and Americans west of the mountains. The Indians had ample grievances. The fur traders got the Indians drunk and then cheated them. Settlers constantly encroached on Indian lands, ignoring the proclamations of governors and generals. Instead of continuing to try to win the support of the Indians by the usual method of giving presents, General Jeffrey Amherst stopped the practice, partly to save money and partly because he had nothing but contempt for Indians.

The Indians of the Northwest organized a confederacy based on the understandable assumption that their only salvation lay in killing every white man west of the mountains. The Ottawa chief, Pontiac, after whom the rebellion was named, has a reputation ranging from that of a brilliant organizing genius to that of a "local villain" and a coward. In any case, Indian plans were so well laid and carried out that within two months the British military posts west of Fort Pitt, except Detroit, fell to the Indians, and fur traders and settlers were killed, captured, or driven back across the mountains. The British and the colonists were caught completely unprepared, and the frontier settlements of Virginia and Pennsylvania were wide open to attack.

Amherst was recalled to England. He left filled with contempt for Americans, red and white alike, and with his once great reputation badly battered. General Thomas Gage made plans to suppress the rebellion. Generals disobeyed his orders and colonial legislatures either refused support or gave it grudgingly and tardily, but by the close of 1764 Pontiac's Rebellion was at an end.[29]

Almost simultaneously with the outbreak of the rebellion, officials in England began planning a policy for the American West, and governments for the new territories acquired in the war. In May 1763 the secretary of state for the southern department, which was in charge of the colonies, outlined a policy for the board of trade. The board had been told repeatedly that encroachment on Indian lands would cause trouble and it proposed the immediate issuance of a royal proclamation reserving western

[29] Alvord, *Mississippi Valley*, I, 184–88, and in detail in Howard Peckham, *Pontiac and the Indian Uprising* (Princeton, 1947). A good brief account is in John R. Alden, *General Gage in America* (Baton Rouge, 1948), chapter VI.

lands to the Indians. Two months passed before anything was done, however. The Grenville ministry was still shaky, and complicated negotiations were going on to strengthen it. Then Egremont died and Lord Shelburne, president of the board of trade, resigned, while still other officials left for summer vacations. The result was that no policy was announced until the royal Proclamation of 1763 on 7 October.[30]

The document was a catchall which established new governments for Quebec, East and West Florida, and the West Indies island of Grenada. It annexed the Labrador coast and adjacent islands to Newfoundland, attached Prince Edward and Cape Breton Islands to the government of Nova Scotia, and defined the southern boundary of Georgia. To encourage settlement of the new mainland colonies, it announced that their governors would call representative legislatures as soon as circumstances warranted. Governors of both the new and the old colonies were instructed to grant lands without "fee or reward" and free of quitrents for ten years to any officers and soldiers of the British army and to naval officers living in America.

The proclamation then turned to the question of the Indians and their lands. The governors of the three new mainland colonies were forbidden to grant lands outside their boundaries, and the governors of the old colonies were told that they could not grant lands beyond the headwaters of the rivers flowing into the Atlantic Ocean. The lands beyond the "Boundary Line of 1763" were reserved to the Indians, and land purchases forbidden without "our especial leave and license." People in the region were ordered "forthwith to remove themselves from such settlements." Thereafter no private person could purchase lands within the area. If the Indians did wish to sell, the sale must be made at a public meeting conducted by the governor of the colony in which the lands lay, in the name of and for the Crown. The Indian trade was to be open to anyone who took out a license from the governor of the colony in which he lived, provided that he gave security to abide by whatever rules were provided "by ourselves or by our commissaries, to be appointed for this purpose. . . ."

So far as the older colonies were concerned, the Proclamation of 1763 legalized the controls that had evolved since 1755. The establishment of the boundary line of 1763 blocked at once the plans of land companies such as the Ohio Company of Virginia, which had a grant west of the line, and the schemes of new companies which planned to take up land in the

---

[30] For differing accounts see Alvord, *Mississippi Valley*, I, chapters VI and VII, and Sosin, *Whitehall*, chapter III. The proclamation is in EHD, IX, 640–43.

Ohio and Mississippi valleys. The whole region on which men had fastened such high hopes was now reserved to the despised Indians. Even if the Indians did choose to sell, lands were to be bought by and for the use of the Crown, whatever the charter claims of such colonies as Virginia. The Indian trade too was placed, however vaguely, in the hands of royal officials. So far as the actual settlers were concerned, the backwoodsmen west of the line ignored the proclamations of governors who dutifully told them to move. Occasionally British troops drove them east of the mountains but they always went back, and they brought still others with them.

The Proclamation of 1763 left much unsettled, all the way from the government of Quebec to the forgotten French settlers in the Illinois country. Land speculators were no more to be stopped than the frontiersmen, and the speculators produced "legal" opinions that no proclamation could anticipate. Hence, along with many other policies of the British government after 1763, the Proclamation of 1763 was to be so changed in practice that its author could not recognize it.[31]

As the various measures of the Grenville ministry appeared in 1763 and 1764, the colonies protested and grumbled and predicted dire consequences, but their grumbles were mere mutters compared with the roar of protest and violent action that greeted the next to the last of the colonial measures of the Grenville ministry before it fell in the summer of 1765. That measure was the Stamp Act, which became law on 22 March 1765. Like most other measures it was not a new idea but one that had been talked about for years. When General Edward Braddock arrived in Virginia in the spring of 1755, he asked a conference of colonial governors for money. They told him that it was hopeless to ask their legislatures and that the only solution was for Parliament to compel them to provide money; and Braddock supported the idea. The board of trade then proposed a stamp tax and additional duties on foreign West Indies products brought to the mainland colonies, but the proposal was killed by William Pitt.

As a result the successive commanders in chief were obliged to appeal to colonial governors who appealed in turn to their assemblies. Some colonies did much, others did little, but whatever they did, British officials always thought it too little and too late. William Pitt, however, followed the same policy with the colonies that he did with Frederick the Great: he promised, and Parliament paid the colonies large cash subsidies for their efforts

[31] See Chapter XII below.

in the war. It was left to the Grenville ministry to pass a stamp act with consequences that few people anticipated.[32]

The Stamp Act was the result, in part, of the conviction that Americans would never willingly pay for their own defense, and in part the result of the financial difficulties of the British government. By the end of 1763 the funded debt was estimated at over £129,500,000, with annual interest and other charges of £4,688,000.[33] The amount of money spent in the colonies was growing too. The House of Commons was told that at the end of 1763 that the regiments and garrisons stationed in America would cost at least £231,000 a year, and the artillery companies and their appendages at least another £23,000. Then there were the expenses of the new colonies, some of which Britain paid. The total amount that Parliament was expected to raise to be spent in America came to perhaps £350,000 a year.[34] The reform of the customs service and the new revenue from the act of 1764 might produce as much as £40,000 or £50,000 a year,[35] but this was not enough to satisfy British taxpayers.

Grenville began planning a stamp tax during the summer of 1763, and two men were assigned to prepare drafts. These were in his hands by October but no one in the government knew enough about the American legal documents to be taxed to be able to list them, much less describe them. Information had to be gathered first.

The resolutions which were the basis of the Revenue Act of 1764 called for the levying of the stamp tax on the colonies, but a delay of a year was requested so the colonies could be consulted. The colonies might have objections to such a tax, they might suggest some more satisfactory tax, or they might prefer to raise the money themselves in some other way. Grenville made it clear that he hoped that no one would question the "right" of Parliament to tax the colonies.

Parliament agreed and preparations began. Thomas Whately, whom Grenville had appointed secretary to the treasury, wrote to at least two of his friends in America, Jared Ingersoll in Connecticut and John Temple, surveyor of customs in the northern district, and asked them for advice. The secretary of state sent a circular letter to the colonial governors in August asking them for lists of legal papers used in their provinces. Meanwhile the colonial agents were busy. They reported to their employers, the

---

[32] Morgan, *Stamp Act Crisis*, chapter V is the most detailed study of the passage of the Stamp Act. My account owes much to it although my interpretation differs.
[33] HCJ, XXIX, 432, 760. For the British national debt in the eighteenth century see House of Commons, *Parliamentary Papers* (1868–69), XXXV.
[34] HCJ, XXIX, 681, 686–87.   [35] Beer, *British Colonial Policy*, 281–84.

legislatures in America, what Grenville had said. But the agents were puzzled as to what he meant. Some of them had a conference with him in May 1764 and asked how much money he expected from the colonies. Grenville did not know how much he wanted, or if he did he did not tell the agents. Instead, he told them that there were many difficulties in the way of the colonies' taxing themselves, and in effect he asked them to get the colonial assemblies to agree in advance to taxation by Parliament. He refused to give any details. He told them that everyone knew what a stamp tax was: England had had one for years and Massachusetts had adopted one in 1755. He did agree to consult with the agents before Parliament acted, if the colonies, in the meantime, would agree to the idea of a stamp tax. Protests from the colonies instead of agreement would have little effect.

The agents were little better off than before the conference and again they sent reports back to America. Far from assenting, the colonies protested and prepared petitions against a stamp tax, or any other taxation by Parliament, for that matter. Pamphlets were written and sent to England for publication. Colonial agents were told to get busy, and they did. The aid of English merchants trading to America was sought.

Again the colonial agents sought a conference with Grenville, and they delegated four men to talk to him in February 1765. Each of the four either owed a political debt to Grenville or hoped to gain something from him. Charles Garth, agent for South Carolina and a new member of Parliament, had just surrendered his sinecure post of king's agent for Georgia which Grenville had given him in 1763. Richard Jackson, agent for Pennsylvania, was a member of Parliament and also one of Grenville's own secretaries. Jared Ingersoll, special agent for Connecticut, was seeking the establishment of an admiralty court in Connecticut as a part of his campaign to take the business of supplying masts to the royal navy away from the powerful Wentworth family, the political bosses of New Hampshire. Benjamin Franklin, who had just arrived from Pennsylvania as special agent, had a royal appointment as one of the two deputy postmaster generals for North America, a post he had held since 1753. His son William Franklin had been appointed the royal governor of New Jersey in 1763. And Franklin was in England for the purpose of persuading the British government to take Pennsylvania away from the Penn family and convert it into a royal colony.

Therefore, although the four were opposed to the proposed stamp act, they were in no position to be forceful with a ministry to which they owed much and from which they hoped to gain even more. However, they did present the colonial arguments against taxation by Parliament. Grenville again told them that a stamp tax was the best way for the colonies to provide money, but that if they had anything better to offer he would adopt it. No one of the four objected to the main point: that the colonies should provide money. What they asked was that the colonies be allowed to do it themselves, which was "the method the people had been used to—that it would at least seem to be their own act and prevent that uneasiness and jealousy which otherwise we found would take place. . . ." Richard Jackson predicted that if the stamp tax were levied to pay royal governors and the army, the colonial assemblies would be "subverted" and never again be called into session.

Grenville vigorously denied that such an idea had ever entered his head. He then asked if they could agree among themselves on the amount each colony should raise. The agents made the obvious reply that they had neither the authority nor the materials with which to answer his question, as Grenville doubtless knew. He may have been devious and insincere, as has been asserted, but he must have known, if experience meant anything at all, that the colonists would not voluntarily contribute to the support of British troops, especially in peacetime. The colonies had done so during the war but as often in response to their own danger as to the requests of British officials. Granted that Grenville knew all this, his political maneuvering between March 1764 and the opening of Parliament in 1765 was skillful indeed. He had put Parliament on record in favor of a tax, and of having the right to tax, and then he had offered to let the colonies provide the money themselves, knowing that they would not.

The protests and petitions from the colonies only irritated the ministry. As early as the middle of September 1764 a letter from London to Philadelphia reported that the "late extraordinary proceedings of the Massachusetts government" had been laid before the ministry "who with great warmth have expressed their displeasure. They esteem it a very high insult on government. . . ." [36] The board of trade had received a copy of the letter written by a committee of the Massachusetts House of Representatives in June to the agent of the colony, Jasper Mauduit. It had also seen a copy of James Otis's pamphlet *The Rights of the British Colonies Asserted and Proved*, which accompanied the letter and which was reprinted in England, as well as a forthright address of the General Assembly of New

[36] Nicholas Waln to Richard Waln, 12 Sept. 1764, Waln Collection, Historical Society of Pennsylvania [HSP].

York to Governor Colden. The board was shocked. It reported to the king that "the acts and resolutions of the legislature of Great Britain . . . are treated with the most indecent respect, principles of the most dangerous nature and tendency openly avowed," and they are "calculated to raise groundless suspicions and distrust in the minds of your Majesty's good subjects in the colonies, and have the strongest tendency to subvert those principles of constitutional relation and dependence upon which the colonies were originally founded. . . ."[37]

Documents such as these were turned over to Parliament when it met 10 January 1765, and the members were so aroused that a stamp tax was a foregone conclusion. When Grenville introduced the subject on 6 February he argued that the colonies were virtually represented in Parliament, as were the people of England who could not vote. He cited various acts laying duties on America as precedents and declared that there could be no distinction between the power of legislation and the power of taxation. Even if members of the House of Commons could not understand such arguments, they could understand what followed. Grenville told them that the West Indies and mainland colonies collectively did not spend more than £75,000 a year on their governments and that they had a total debt of not more than £900,000, all of which would be paid off by 1769. For this reason he said, "it was but reasonable the colonies should contribute at least to take off that part of the burden from the mother country which concerned the protection and defense of themselves."[38]

In the debate that followed, no one denied that Parliament had the right to tax the colonies or that it was proper for them to contribute. The most ardent defenders of America argued only that a tax would be unfair or inexpedient, or that the colonies should be allowed to tax themselves. In the course of the debate two attitudes became clear, attitudes that were to harden in the years ahead. With a rhetorical flourish Charles Townshend asked: "Will these Americans, children planted by our care, nourished up by our indulgence until they are grown to a degree of strength and opulence, and protected by our arms, will they grudge to contribute their mite to relieve us from the heavy weight of that burden which we lie under?"

Colonel Isaac Barré, who had been a soldier in America during the Seven Years War, answered the query in words that won fame for himself

[37] 11 Dec. 1764, "Great Britain: Privy Council Papers," HEHL; APC:CS, IV, 692. See Chapter III below for the origin of the letter from Massachusetts.
[38] Garth to South Carolina Committee of Correspondence, 8 Feb. 1765, in Sir Lewis Namier, "Charles Garth, Agent for South Carolina," *The English Historical Review* [EHR], LIV (1939), 649–50.

in America and provided the name "Sons of Liberty" which Americans were to put to such potent use.

> They planted by your care? No! Your oppressions planted 'em in America. They fled from your tyranny to a then uncultivated and unhospitable country where they exposed themselves to almost all the hardships to which human nature is liable, and among others to the cruelties of a savage foe, the most subtle, and I take upon me to say, the most formidable of any people upon the face of God's earth. . . .
>
> They nourished by *your* indulgence? They grew by your neglect of 'em. As soon as you began to care about 'em, that care was exercised in sending persons to rule over 'em, in one department and another, who were perhaps the deputies of deputies to some member of this house, sent to spy out their liberty, to misrepresent their actions and to prey upon 'em; men whose behaviour on many occasions has caused the blood of those sons of liberty to recoil within them; men promoted to the highest seats of justice; some who to my knowledge were glad by going to a foreign country to escape being brought to the bar of a court of justice in their own.
>
> They protected by *your* arms? They have nobly taken up arms in your defence, have exerted a valour amidst their constant and laborious industry for the defence of a country, whose frontier while drenched in blood, its interior parts have yielded all its little savings to your emolument. And believe me, remember I this day told you so, that same spirit of freedom which actuated that people at first, will accompany them still.

At the end of Barré's speech "the whole house sat a while as amazed, intently looking and without answering a word," wrote Jared Ingersoll to the governor of Connecticut.[39]

Amazed though the Commons might have been, it turned down a motion to adjourn, and the next day it passed the fifty-five resolutions that were the basis of the Stamp Act. The bill was brought in on 13 February and read; and read a second time on the 15th. The colonial agents on the outside, and those who were members of Parliament, were ready with petitions from various colonial assemblies. Charles Garth had predicted correctly that "the power of Parliament was asserted and so universally agreed to, that no petition disputing it will be received." [40] The colonial agents who were members did try, one by one, but Parliament refused to hear

[39] Jared Ingersoll to Gov. Thomas Fitch of Connecticut, 11 Feb. 1765, EHD, IX, 650–55.
[40] To S. C. Comm. of Corres., 8 Feb. 1765, EHR, LIV, 650.

them.[41] It was useless to argue and the Stamp Act became law on 22 March 1765 when George III signed it.

The purpose of the act was set forth clearly in the preamble. The Revenue Act of 1764 granted several duties to be set aside for the expense of "defending, protecting, and securing the British colonies and plantations in America," but it was "just and necessary" that a further revenue be raised "towards defraying the said expenses. . . ." The act placed stamp duties on almost every form of paper used in the everyday life of the colonists: licenses and documents used in court and other legal proceedings; legal papers relating to the survey and conveyance of land and to the shipment of goods in and out of colonial ports; commissions appointing men to office; all private contracts; pamphlets, almanacs, and newspapers; and every individual advertisement in the newspapers.

The stamps were to be paid for in gold and silver money and the money raised was to be set aside in a separate fund to be disposed of by Parliament for use in the colonies. Violations of the act could be tried in admiralty courts as well as in common law courts.[42]

Plans were made at once to distribute the stamps. An American stamp office with five commissioners was set up in London. In America there were to be inspectors over various districts, with one distributor for each of the colonies. The job of distributor was lucrative, for each was to receive eight pounds sterling for every £100 of stamps sold. Grenville called in the colonial agents and told them that he would appoint natives of the colonies to be distributors and asked for their recommendations.

The agents had done their duty to their employers, the colonial assemblies, and had expressed their own opposition to the passage of the act. Now they eagerly recommended friends and even themselves for the jobs. Only three Americans who could take the posts were in England at the time: Jared Ingersoll of Connecticut, George Meserve of New Hampshire, and George Mercer of Virginia. Each was appointed agent for his native colony. Franklin secured the Pennsylvania appointment for his political ally in the Pennsylvania assembly, John Hughes. Andrew Oliver, brother-in-law of Thomas Hutchinson, and secretary of the province, judge, and councilor, was appointed for Massachusetts. Such men, and those who recommended them, had no conception of the "rage of the people" that was shortly to drive them from office in their native colonies, to ruin most of

41 Garth to S. C. Comm. of Corres., 17 Feb. 1765, ibid. 650–51.
42 EHD, IX, 655–56 in part, and in full in Pickering, XXVI, 179–204.

them politically, and to render uncertain for a time the future of even so agile a politician as Benjamin Franklin.

The Grenville ministry secured the adoption of one final colonial measure shortly before it fell from power in the summer of 1765—the Quartering Act—but the impetus came not from the ministry but from General Thomas Gage, commander of the British army in America. The idea of stationing British regulars in America in peacetime had been in the air throughout the Seven Years War. The origins of the idea are clouded in obscurity. Some leaders believed that the new areas acquired by the war, and inhabited by hostile Indians and potentially hostile Frenchmen and Spaniards, would have to be policed. Others were convinced that the colonial governments were incapable of maintaining order and keeping peace with the Indians, and that the only way to avoid expensive Indian wars was to have the army supervise Indian relations and the fur trade. George III, always concerned with the army, was anxious to maintain as many regiments as possible in peacetime if for no other reason than it provided him with patronage and hence political support. Officers, facing the grim prospect of half-pay, lobbied to keep their regiments in being. There were still others who had long been convinced that British regulars would be needed to keep the old colonies along the seaboard in "due subordination" to the mother country.[43]

Whatever the origins and motives there was no public discussion, and the decision was implemented casually in March 1763 when Parliament voted funds to maintain troops in America. William Pitt silenced the potential opposition of those who feared a standing army and those who objected to the additional patronage provided the Crown.

The decision, made with such apparent lightness, forebode ill for the future, although no one in Britain seemed to realize it at the time. The presence of the army in America was largely responsible for the attempt of Parliament to tax the colonies. It was responsible for the Quartering Act which led to endless brawls with colonial legislatures. And in the end, the use of the army in civil affairs convinced many Americans that they would be governed by military force unless they met force with force to maintain the liberties they insisted were rightfully theirs.

There had been troubles over the quartering of troops in America during

[43] John Shy, *Toward Lexington: The Role of the British Army in the Coming of the American Revolution* (Princeton, 1965), chapter II, "The Decision of 1763."

the Seven Years War, and the troubles continued afterward. General Gage soon found that the British Mutiny Act no more fitted American conditions than it fitted American ideas. In January 1765 he reported that ever since the peace, the difficulties "increase very fast." Americans denied that the Mutiny Act extended to America except for the clauses in it naming America. Americans tempted soldiers to desert, hid them, and bought their clothes and arms. Officers who captured deserters who had become indentured servants were seized, prosecuted, and fined. Officers had even been sent to jail for living in the quarters assigned to them. Others had been prosecuted for taking carriages while on the march. Gage said that such examples were rare but that the news was spreading and that it would soon be difficult to keep the soldiers in the service and to march and quarter them without "numberless prosecutions, or perhaps worse consequences."

Gage sent along proposed amendments to the Mutiny Act which had been prepared by his deputy quartermaster general. That official declared that since there were not enough public houses in America, justices of the peace and other magistrates should be "required" to quarter officers and soldiers in private homes; that the inhabitants should be required to supply food to the soldiers on the march at rates established by the Mutiny Act. When in barracks provided by the inhabitants, the soldiers should be provided with fire, candles, bedding, and utensils at public expense. And since beer and cider were scarce or high-priced in America, the act should provide an alternative of a "half a pint of rum mixed in a quart of water." Gage's subordinate predicted that such a law would be "received without murmur," but "if the minds of the people be once inflamed by the disputes I see ready to arise, the most moderate law that can be extended to this country, will be numbered among its greatest grievances." [44] The first of his predictions was completely wrong; the second was far more right than he dreamed it could be.

Gage's letters produced an immediate response and a bill was ordered brought into the House of Commons. But George III soon had second thoughts about quartering troops in private homes. He told George Grenville that Lord Halifax "appears to disregard the noise that may be made here in Parliament" by quartering soldiers in private homes in America. Grenville replied at midnight of the same day. He agreed that the proposal might cause difficulties and uneasiness "especially as the quartering of sol-

[44] Gage to Welbore Ellis, 22 Jan. and to SS, 23 Jan. 1765, Clarence E. Carter, ed., *The Correspondence of General Thomas Gage with the Secretaries of State 1763–1775* [Gage, *Corres.*] (2 vols., New Haven, 1931), II, 262–66; I, 47–49.

diers upon the people against their wills is declared by the Petition of Right to be contrary to law." [45]

Meanwhile the bill with the objectionable feature had been brought into Parliament on that very day.[46] Charles Garth, agent for South Carolina and member of Parliament, at once told the other colonial agents and also the London merchants trading to America. He did not tell them what to do but he hinted what he thought "their friends in America have a right to expect from them upon this occasion." The merchants promptly appointed a committee to meet every evening to plan ways to combat a measure "so oppressive in its tendency." [47] Others were interested as well, and George Grenville promised support. When Thomas Pownall, ex-governor of Massachusetts, and Benjamin Franklin offered to write a clause for billeting soldiers in America, Grenville replied: "I approve extremely . . . for I own I have always thought it very disagreeable to put it upon the footing it was proposed if it can be avoided. . . ." [48] Meanwhile, the merchants' committee agreed that Garth and Richard Glover, a London merchant and member of Parliament, should see Grenville. After a two-hour talk he promised to help alter the bill. Two days later, Welbore Ellis, the secretary at war, agreed to see Garth, who took along Franklin and Jared Ingersoll, "as gentlemen perfectly well acquainted with the northern colonies." In the course of the conference Ellis altered the bill to suit the Americans. The colonial agents and the London merchants approved, and the bill passed through Parliament without opposition.[49]

The Quartering Act,[50] as the Americans called it, authorized colonial civil officials to quarter troops in barracks belonging to the colonial governments. If they were inadequate, "then in such case only," troops were to be quartered in inns, livery stables, alehouses, victualing houses, and in the houses of retail sellers of wine, rum, brandy, and "strong water." If there was still not enough room, "in such and no other case, and upon no other account," governors and councils or any two justices of the peace could rent and equip "uninhabited houses, outhouses, barns, or other buildings, as shall be necessary. . . ." This section of the act made abundantly clear

[45] GP, III, 11–13.

[46] Joseph Redington and R. A. Roberts, eds., *Calendar of Home Office Papers of the Reign of George III. 1760–1776* [CHOP] (4 vols., London, 1878–99), I, 529, 534.

[47] Garth to S. C. Comm. of Corres., 5 April, 25 May 1765, EHR, LIV, 641–42.

[48] Grenville to Charles Jenkinson, 13 April and to Welbore Ellis, 27 April 1765, Grenville Letter Books, II, HEHL.

[49] Garth to S. C. Comm. of Corres., 25 May 1765, EHR, LIV, 641–42.

[50] EHD, IX, 656–58. See Shy, *Toward Lexington*, chapter IV, "The Problems of Peace," for an account of the background of the Quartering Act.

that there would be no quartering of troops in inhabited private houses. Nor did this section cause trouble in America.

What did cause trouble, and what brought about the ultimate defeat of the act, was the section relating to soldiers' supplies. When soldiers were quartered in inns, taverns, and alehouses, the proprietors were to provide certain items at established rates, payment to be made from the soldiers' subsistence money provided by Britain. But when quartered in public barracks or in uninhabited buildings, they were to be given firewood, candles, vinegar, salt, bedding, cooking utensils, and not more than five pints of beer or cider or half a pint of rum mixed with a quart of water, all at the expense of the colonial governments. Most colonial legislatures refused to pay, and within five years the law was a dead letter.[51]

The program of the Grenville ministry between 1763 and 1765 was concerned primarily with the economic life of the colonies, but it had political implications which were clear. It was supported by large majorities in Parliament. Only the Quartering Act met significant opposition and it was altered accordingly, for the original proposals went against a deeply ingrained English distrust of the military, a distrust which George Grenville himself shared.

But the Grenville ministry did not have to face the results of mounting colonial opposition which by the end of the year 1765 resulted in the effective nullification of an act of Parliament by the people of America. The Grenville ministry went out of office as a result of the political conditions in England, not because of its American policies.

[51] See Chapters VII and XIII below.

III

The Economics and the Politics of American Protest, 1763–1764

On the third of February 1763, contrary winds blew the *Nautilus,* bound for New York, into Virginia waters. The next day Governor Francis Fauquier sent special messengers to the other colonies with the news of the signing of the preliminaries of peace between Britain and France.[1] But the news brought no "peace" to the mainland colonies. Within a few months the outbreak of Pontiac's Rebellion devastated the frontiers of Pennsylvania and Virginia. The settlers who survived were bitter at the slowness of the two colonies to help British troops fight the Indians, and in Pennsylvania one result was the murder of some "tame" Indians and the march of the Paxton Boys on Philadelphia early in 1764. In the Carolinas, the discontent of the backcountry was growing and would soon lead to open rebellion against the government of North Carolina. Tenant-farmers in New York took the first steps that would result in violence in 1766. The South Carolina legislature was locked in a struggle with Governor Thomas Boone that brought public business to a standstill and was to end in driving the governor from the colony in 1764. Ever since 1761 the political leaders of the town of Boston had been engaged in a no-holds-barred fight against Thomas Hutchinson, the dominant political leader in Massachusetts. In Pennsylvania, Benjamin Franklin and Joseph Galloway, the non-Quaker leaders of the Quaker party, continued their fight against the proprietary party to convert Pennsylvania into a royal colony.

A depression was already under way and it spread rapidly. Virginia tobacco planters, great and small, were facing bankruptcy. Merchants in northern towns were complaining and their complaints grew louder

---

[1] To SS, 4 Feb. 1763, C.O. 5/1345. Fauquier was actually lieutenant governor. In this book the man who acted as governor is called governor whether he had the official title or not.

month by month. Unemployment in the cities was fertile ground for the seeds of riot that were shortly to produce a seemingly unmanageable crop.

The end of war in 1763, therefore, came to an America in which virtually every colony was engaged in some sort of political struggle, and as the news of the colonial measures of the Grenville ministry crossed the Atlantic, new causes of strife were added to an already turbulent political scene. Those measures were opposed by most of the colonies and by their legislatures, but the moment one goes behind legislative petitions to king and Parliament, the apparent unity of America disappears.

British policies were a divisive factor in the internal politics of most colonies. Even though the citizens of a colony might agree on opposition, and they did not always do so, they differed ever more sharply on the means to be used, and continued to differ until the Declaration of Independence. The history of the opposition to Britain between 1763 and 1776 is therefore not only the history of thirteen revolutionary movements but also the history of political struggles between groups in each of the thirteen colonies: groups using different methods and having different ends. It was something of a miracle that "thirteen clocks" were made to strike at once in the Declaration of Independence in July 1776.

Rumors of things to come appeared in colonial newspapers early in 1763. Only two weeks after the news of peace a report from London said that ten provincial regiments in the pay of the colonies would be kept in America in addition to fifteen regiments of regulars.[2] At the end of May, another rumor had it that sixteen regiments of regulars would be quartered in the colonies and that the colonies would have to pay for them. The writer went on to predict with some accuracy that "the money . . . will be levied by Act of Parliament, and arise on a Stamp duty, excise on rum distilled on the continent, and a duty on foreign sugar and molasses etc., by reducing the former duty on these last mentioned articles. . . ." This, declared the letter, "will be thought greatly to diminish even the appearance of the subject's liberty, since nothing seems to be more repugnant to the general principles of freedom than the subjecting a people to taxation by laws in the enactment of which they are not represented."[3] In the years to come Americans were to embroider and elaborate this statement of March 1763, but they were not to alter its essential argument.

By the end of May, Americans heard that British naval vessels would be

[2] *Newport Mercury* [NM], 14 Feb.
[3] Ibid. 30 May; *New Hampshire Gazette* [NHG], 27 May.

stationed in American waters [4] and within a few months the rumor was confirmed when the *Providence Gazette* printed a list of twenty-seven naval vessels which had arrived to help enforce the laws of trade.[5] By the end of the year, customs officials were advertising that smugglers of illicit cargoes of rum, sugar, and molasses must obey the law.[6] Appointments of new customs officials and the arrival of old ones who had come to America rather than give up their jobs were also mentioned.

Americans had no intention of submitting. In January 1764, John Temple offered £50 for news of a ship seized in Rhode Island but which "was in the night . . . got under sail and carried off by persons unknown, in violation of an express act of Parliament." [7] Meanwhile, the newspapers denounced the navy. "Every little master and commander . . . is appointed by license to detect smugglers" but he attacks "defenseless coasters" and "assumes all the importance of a commissioner of the Customs." "After all," said the writer, "I believe it would puzzle any reasonable person to define properly what smuggling is in North America." [8]

Something more was needed. Americans knew that the Molasses Act lapsed in 1763 and that it had been extended for only a year. They wanted it abolished, particularly if it was to be enforced. In October, newspapers in New York and Providence urged merchants to send memorials to England.[9] In November the Boston merchants, who had created a formal merchants' organization in April 1763, and who had been gathering materials to oppose the renewal of the Molasses Act, proposed joint action by the northern colonies.[10]

The merchants and the newspapers in 1763 talked about trade, not about constitutional questions, and they attacked the "selfish" British West Indies planters. The *Newport Mercury* exhorted the northern colonies to state their case to the board of trade and complained about the discrimination in favor of the West Indies. How can we pay our bills in England if "the employment of three fourths of our seamen and shipping is cut off? Of what use will our lands be, if the produce of them is prohibited exportation?" [11] The *Massachusetts Gazette* reprinted a defense of the trade of the northern colonies with the foreign islands from the London *Public Ledger*, which declared that the British planters wanted to force British subjects everywhere to buy sugar from them although they could produce only enough to supply Britain alone, and that the northern colo-

---

nies should be free to trade with the foreign colonies, for this would encourage British manufactures; otherwise the colonies would manufacture
for themselves.[12]

The Boston merchants incorporated such ideas and others in a "State of
Trade," in December 1763. It was a long, ingenious, and occasionally devious document, but an effective statement of a major problem of New England merchants. The British islands could not use all the fish, provisions,
and lumber produced in North America, nor supply the demand for rum
and molasses. Therefore trade with the foreign islands was indispensable,
the fishery being particularly dependent upon it. Good fish went to southern Europe and "refuse" fish to the West Indies, and the two could not be
separated until after the catch was cured. Stop the trade in "refuse" fish to
the foreign islands and the export of good fish to southern Europe would
also end. With molasses at twelve pence sterling a gallon, any tax on it
would stop the trade with the foreign islands. The result would be ruin for
the fishery and hard times for barrel-makers and farmers. Imports from
Britain would fall off, for it was the profits of the trade with the foreign
islands and southern Europe that paid for those imports. The Molasses
Act was secured by the British West Indies planters "with no other view
than to enrich themselves," but the idea that they can supply the needs of
northern colonies "is perfectly chimerical."

Copies were sent to merchants in the other northern colonies with letters asking for help "to defeat the iniquitous schemes of these overgrown
West Indians," and 250 copies were sent to merchants in Britain for use
there. The Boston merchants said that they were appealing to their legislature for aid, and that as individuals they were writing to correspondents in
England, but that since the trade of each colony was different, each colony
would have to use arguments adapted to its own circumstances.[13]

The memorials of the Boston merchants and of other seaport towns in
the colony were presented to the legislature late in December 1763 but

---

[12] 24 Nov. 1763.
[13] Charles M. Andrews, "The Boston Merchants and the Non-Importation Movement," Colonial Society of Massachusetts *Publications* [CSMP], XIX (1916–17),
159–67, and the "State of Trade," 379–90. An even more extended account of the
trade problems of the northern colonies was the widely reprinted "An Essay on the
Trade of the Northern Colonies." See PrG, 14 Jan.; *New York Mercury* [NYM], 6 Feb.;
and NM, 13 Feb. 1764. The author was Governor Stephen Hopkins. See David S.
Lovejoy, *Rhode Island Politics and the American Revolution, 1760–1776* (Providence,
1958), 32. The essay is reprinted in Merrill Jensen, ed., *Tracts of the American
Revolution, 1763–1776* (New York, 1967), 3–18.

party politics prevented Massachusetts from making an official protest against the renewal of the Molasses Act. Ever since 1760 Massachusetts had been the scene of a virulent political fight between a "faction" in Boston and the political machine, headed by Thomas Hutchinson, which controlled the government of the colony.

When Francis Bernard came as governor in August 1760, he reported that he expected a peaceful administration, that no disputable points of government remained to be settled, and that the people of Massachusetts were "better disposed to observe their compact with the Crown, than any other on the continent that I know." [14] He could not have been more wrong. Within three months he was embroiled in a fight that lasted until he left the colony forever in 1769, followed by a barrage of slander which to this day colors the accounts of his years in America.

The chief justice of the superior court died in September 1760 and there were several eager candidates, none more so than Colonel James Otis of Barnstable, speaker of the House of Representatives. He was a well-known lawyer with a wide following among the rural members of the legislature. He claimed that a former governor had promised him a place on the superior court whenever a vacancy occurred. Otis and his following had been loyal supporters of the "government party" and one reward had been the appointment of his son, James Otis, Jr., as king's advocate general of the vice-admiralty court in Boston. Otis, Jr., was thus the prosecutor of Massachusetts merchants accused of illegal trade.

The Otis family expected the new governor to make good on the promise of former-Governor William Shirley and asked Lieutenant Governor Thomas Hutchinson to intercede. But Bernard appointed Hutchinson himself chief justice in November, and the fight was on. The Otis family was furious and from then on, as long as his sanity lasted, James Otis, Jr., carried on a fight against Hutchinson and Bernard, a fight that is so entwined with rising opposition to British policies that it is impossible to separate one from the other.[15]

In 1760 Thomas Hutchinson was forty-nine years old, a man of wealth and education who was soon to publish the first volume of a history of

[14] To BT, 18 Aug., C.O. 5/891.
[15] Governor Bernard was convinced that the Otis family's opposition was the result of the failure of James Otis, Sr., to secure a place on the superior court. To SS, 22 Dec. 1766, EHD, IX, 733. This was also the view of at least one member of the popular party. See William Palfrey to John Wilkes, 23–30 Oct. 1770, CSMP, XXXIV, 419–20. Ellen E. Brennan, *Plural Office-Holding in Massachusetts, 1760–1780* (Chapel Hill, 1945), chapter I contains an excellent account of political control by the Hutchinson group. This and the following chapters owe much to Leslie M. Thomas, *Partisan*

Massachusetts that to this day marks him as a great historian. He had about him none of the unconventionality that had driven his great-great grandmother, Anne Hutchinson, from the colony in the 1630s. He went to Harvard, became a merchant, but turned more and more to politics. At the age of twenty-six he was elected a selectman of the town of Boston and a representative of the town in the colonial legislature. In 1746, at the age of thirty-five, he was elected speaker of the House of Representatives, an unusual honor in a political society where seniority rather than ability usually dictated political preferment. As a man of wealth he was opposed to paper money and to such schemes as the land bank in 1740, of which Samuel Adams's father was an important member. In 1748 and 1749 Hutchinson brought an end to paper money in Massachusetts. The colony received a large cash subsidy from Britain for its expenses in King George's War and Hutchinson persuaded the legislature to call in all old paper money and to give specie in return at the rate of eleven to one. It was a drastic act of deflation that delighted the merchants, who probably had most of the old paper in their hands, and infuriated the populace of Boston. The next year they refused to elect Hutchinson to the legislature and never thereafter did he hold an office through the direct vote of the people.

But he accumulated offices one by one. The House of Representatives promptly elected him to the council, the upper house of the legislature, and continued to do so annually until 1766. In 1752 the governor gave him two judgeships, those of probate and of common pleas in Suffolk county. Two years later he was a delegate to the Albany Congress. In 1758 the king appointed him lieutenant governor of the colony. In 1760 Bernard gave him the chief justiceship. Hutchinson was not only the chief officeholder in the colony, his relatives were also secure in other appointive jobs. Multiple office-holding was common in most colonies, but Hutchinson stood out in his many conspicuous posts and thus was an easy target for the "mob high eloquence" of James Otis. John Adams wrote in his diary: "Let us ask a few questions. Has not his honor the lieutenant governor discovered to the people, in innumerable instances, a very ambitious and avaricious disposition? Has not he grasped four of the most important offices in the province into his own hands?" And look at all the other important offices in the hands of his relatives. "Is not this amazing ascendancy of one family foundation, sufficient on which to erect a tyranny? Is it not enough

Politics in Massachusetts During Governor Bernard's Administration, 1760–1770 (Ph.D. Thesis, University of Wisconsin, 1960) which is the most detailed and most accurate study of Massachusetts politics during this period. Hereafter referred to as Thomas, Massachusetts.

to excite jealousies among the people?" [16] Oxenbridge Thacher and James Otis devoted themselves to doing just that with relentless energy from the day Hutchinson was appointed chief justice.

A realignment of political forces followed. James Otis, Sr., and some of the "country party" in eastern Massachusetts broke with the "government party" and joined the leaders of the Boston populace who had long been a minority in the legislature. For a time too they had the support of the Boston merchants, who were alarmed by British efforts to enforce the acts of trade in Massachusetts while leaving Rhode Islanders to do pretty much as they pleased. In the minds of Bostonians this amounted to "unfair" competition and they began a campaign to destroy the effectiveness of the customs service. They hired as one of their lawyers the man who had formerly prosecuted them for evasion, James Otis, Jr., and they soon had the help of Benjamin Barons.

Barons, a former London merchant, was appointed collector of the port of Boston, where he arrived in August 1760. He was eager to make money and he proposed to do as former collectors had done: ally himself with the Boston merchants rather than with his fellow customs officials. Within weeks he revealed to the merchants that the admiralty court had paid informers' fees from the colony's one-third share of the proceeds from smuggled goods seized and sold. The merchants prepared a petition and James Otis, as their lawyer, appeared before the legislature and persuaded it to order the provincial treasurer, Harrison Gray, to sue Charles Paxton, surveyor of the port, for the money "illegally" diverted from the provincial treasury. The case of *Gray* vs. *Paxton* dragged through the courts twice. Each time the lower court decided in favor of the treasurer, but the superior court, presided over by Thomas Hutchinson, finally decided in favor of the customs officer.

Meanwhile, the death of George II required the customs officers to apply for new writs of assistance since such writs were valid for only six months after the death of the sovereign in whose name they were issued. Ever since 1755 the Massachusetts superior court had issued writs of assistance empowering customs officers to search for smuggled goods, but when Thomas Lechmere, the surveyor general, requested a new writ in February 1761, the Boston merchants challenged their legality. Their attorneys were

[16] John Adams, 15 Aug. 1765, Lyman H. Butterfield, ed., *Diary and Autobiography of John Adams* (4 vols., Cambridge, Mass., 1961). Citations to Adams's diary will be to this edition and by date only. Citations to the autobiography will be to volume and page.

Oxenbridge Thacher and James Otis. The attorney for the Crown and Thacher argued for and against the existence of legal precedents, but Otis ignored such pedantic matters and took to higher ground. He declared that the writ asked for was "against the fundamental principles of law." An act of Parliament "against the constitution is void: an act against natural equity is void," and even if Parliament passed an act in the "very words" of the petition for a writ, "it would be void." The superior court delayed a decision until Chief Justice Hutchinson could find out the nature of writs issued in England. The information was received before the end of the year, and in December 1761 the superior court issued the writ that had been asked for in February.[17]

The campaign of legal harassment was carried on at other levels. Thomas Lechmere, surveyor general of customs, suspended Barons in June 1761 and Barons promptly began suits against his former colleagues, including the aged Lechmere whom he had jailed. The most revealing example of the Boston merchants' attitude was a case involving John Erving, a member of the council. One of Erving's ships was libeled in the vice-admiralty court for smuggling. In effect he admitted his guilt by paying a "fine" of £500, but no sooner had he recovered his ship and goods than he sued the seizing officer, George Craddock, for damages. The jury in the common law court awarded Erving nearly £600 and Craddock appealed the case to the superior court. There, despite the instructions of the judges, a jury again found for Erving. Craddock then appealed to England, and Erving finally gave in to avoid the expense, and quite likely, because he knew he would lose.[18]

The merchants and their lawyers were beaten again and again by Thomas Hutchinson and his allies in the superior court but they did succeed in disrupting the customs service and bringing it into disrepute. As for James Otis, he won great popularity among the people of Boston and in

[17] L. Kinvin Wroth and Hiller B. Zobel, eds., *Legal Papers of John Adams* (3 vols., Cambridge, Mass., 1965), II, 125, 127. The introduction and documents in this volume (pages 106–47) are the best account of the legal problems involved. See also Oliver M. Dickerson, "Writs of Assistance as a Cause of the Revolution" in Richard B. Morris, ed., *The Era of the American Revolution* (New York, 1939), and Joseph R. Frese, "James Otis and the Writs of Assistance," *The New England Quarterly* [NEQ], XXX (1957).

[18] Accounts of these quarrels, which vary even in such details as the spelling of proper names, may be found in Thomas, Massachusetts, chapter II; Beer, *British Colonial Policy*, 117–23; Thomas C. Barrow, *Trade and Empire: The British Customs Service in Colonial America, 1660–1775* (Cambridge, Mass., 1967), 169–72; and Gipson, *British Empire*, X, chapter VI.

the spring of 1761 they elected him one of their four representatives in the legislature. His father was re-elected speaker and swung his followers to the support of the Boston leaders. Thus was formed the "popular party." [19] James Otis and Oxenbridge Thacher, as its leaders, began a campaign in the newspapers and in the legislature against the iniquities of "multiple-office-holding," that is, against Thomas Hutchinson and his connections. Judges should not sit in the council, argued Otis and Thacher, because no man should be both a legislator and a judge. Judges were paid to study law, not to make it. But the popular party made no headway at first, Hutchinson and his friends continued to hold their many offices, and the majority of the House of Representatives continued to elect them to the council year after year.

However, the popular party did win a few minor victories. In 1762 it succeeded in removing Hutchinson's friend William Bollan as agent of the colony in England. Otis and Thacher stirred up the easily aroused religious antagonism against Anglicans, and Bollan was one. They hinted that Governor Bernard was "deep in the plot" to bring an Anglican bishop to the colonies. James Otis declared that many American Episcopalians were "very high in their religious and political principles." Thus did he inform a leading English dissenter, Jasper Mauduit, of his election to replace William Bollan as agent for Massachusetts and, added Otis, "I have the merit of a small share in your election." [20] Hutchinson was outraged and declared that "I never knew an instance of such mad proceedings." He tried to block the appointment of Jasper Mauduit in the council, but for once it failed to support him because of the "terror of election which is just at hand. . . ." [21] The popular party won a petty victory during the same session when the house cut the judges' salaries, but the house refused to pass an act excluding superior court judges from sitting as members of either the house or the council.

Otis and Thacher renewed their campaign against plural office-holding before the elections in the spring of 1763, but again they failed to win a majority of the house. Governor Bernard then tried to bring about a "coalition" by using the patronage. A judgeship fell vacant in Barnstable county and he offered the post to Colonel Otis, and another county job to

---

[19] The nature of the "popular parties" in various colonies is discussed in subsequent chapters.

[20] Rev. Jonathan Mayhew to Thomas Hollis, 6 April 1762, Massachusetts Historical Society *Collections* [MHSC], LXXIV, 30n; Otis to Jasper Mauduit, 23 April, ibid. 29–31.

[21] To William Bollan, 24 April, ibid. 32.

one of his sons. The Otises remained quiet until they had their commissions but they did not "stay bought." [22]

Such was the situation when the legislature met in December 1763 and faced the issue of British policy in the form of memorials from Massachusetts merchants asking for help in opposing the renewal of the Molasses Act. Party warfare rather than colonial policy governed what followed. In January, friends of Hutchinson in both houses chose him special agent to go to England with the memorials of the merchants. Governor Bernard then pointed to the fact that a lieutenant governor could not leave a colony without permission from the Crown. James Otis spread the rumor that Bernard was afraid Hutchinson would try to get the governorship if he went to England, and considering Hutchinson's record as a job-getter, Bernard might well have feared such an outcome. In any case, Hutchinson accepted the appointment, subject to permission to leave the colony.

At that point, Oxenbridge Thacher, who had not been in the house when Hutchinson was elected, told the house that it would be dangerous to the liberties of the people to send Hutchinson to England: he already had too many offices and was a friend of royal power. As a result, the house rescinded the election by a narrow vote, although the council refused to agree. The governor then prorogued the legislature which did not meet again until the end of May, and Massachusetts thus did nothing to satisfy its merchants except to send instructions to the agent, Jasper Mauduit, to oppose renewal of the Molasses Act, and even these did not reach him until after the passage of the Revenue Act of 1764.[23]

ϑ❧

Rhode Island too had its political brawls. Ever since Stephen Hopkins of Providence had been elected governor in 1755, Newport and its candidate Samuel Ward had tried to recapture control in each annual election. It was a political battle in which slander, corruption, and the use of force to keep voters from the polls were commonplace. But there was one issue on which the merchants of Providence and Newport could agree. They cared nothing for the fish of Massachusetts but were convinced that molasses was the very foundation of Rhode Island's economy. Hence, when the letter of the Boston merchants reached Newport, its merchants asked Governor Hopkins to call a special session of the legislature, and he did so at once.

In a three-day session at the end of January 1764, the legislature, with a unanimity unseen for years, prepared a defense of Rhode Island's trade

22 Thomas, Massachusetts, 113–17.   23 Ibid. 130.

with the foreign West Indies. It was a document well illustrating the complexities of New England trade in general, and of Rhode Island trade in particular. The petition declared that Rhode Island did not raise enough food for its 48,000 people, a third of whom lived in Newport and Providence. Rhode Island imported food and about £120,000 sterling worth of British manufactures, mostly from the other mainland colonies, but sent only about £5000 a year directly to Britain.

What kept Rhode Island going? Molasses from the foreign islands was "the engine in the hands of the merchant" with which the colony paid its bills. During 1763, said the petition, the 150 Rhode Island vessels in the West Indies trade brought back 14,000 hogsheads of molasses, and not more than 2500 of those were from the British islands. The 352 Rhode Island vessels in the coastwise trade carried the molasses to Massachusetts, New York, and Pennsylvania, to pay for British manufactures and to buy cargoes to take to the West Indies. They also carried it to the southern colonies to buy cargoes of rice and naval stores for shipment to Europe. Thirty distilleries converted the remainder into rum, most of which was used in the African slave trade. For thirty years Rhode Islanders had sent about eighteen ships a year to the African coast. There they purchased slaves, gold dust, and elephants' teeth. They sold the slaves in the British West Indies, the Carolinas, and Virginia for bills of exchange and various articles. By this trade alone Rhode Island was able to send at least £40,000 a year to Britain to pay its debts there. And some additional bills of exchange as well as molasses were gotten from the Dutch colonies. Therefore any tax at all on molasses at its current price of twelve pence a gallon would ruin Rhode Island, and even if it did not, there was not enough gold and silver to pay duties for a single year.[24] This memorial was sent to the colony's agent in England, while the *Massachusetts Gazette*, the official paper of the Massachusetts governor and council, sniffed that the way Rhode Islanders treated customs officers was "a very extraordinary method to meet with success in their applications home." [25]

The New York merchants were less concerned with molasses than those of Rhode Island, and had very little interest in fish, but they willingly followed Boston's lead in protesting against the renewal of the Molasses Act. New York was suffering from a depression. The merchants met in January

[24] PrG, 14 Jan.; NM, 30 Jan. 1764. The "Remonstrance" is in John R. Bartlett, ed., *Records of the Colony of Rhode Island and Providence Plantations* [RICR] (10 vols., Providence, 1856–65), VI, 378–83. For a detailed account see F. B. Wiener, "The Rhode Island Merchants and the Sugar Act," NEQ, III (1930).
[25] 16 Feb. 1764.

because, said the *New York Mercury*, "the state of commerce of this continent is of universal concern to its inhabitants; at present it is in a languishing condition; our debt in Europe increases; our power to pay it off decreases." [26] The legislature approved a merchant memorial and also agreed to pay the expenses of the New York colonial agent's "utmost opposition to the renewal or continuation of the said act." By then the legislature had received even more alarming news, for the agent reported that the British merchants trading to Virginia were demanding the extension of the New England Currency Act of 1751 to all the colonies.

New York's currency was well managed and the legislature declared that if such a law were passed, it would not only reflect on the credit, honor, and punctuality of the colony but would also "reduce it to a state of bankruptcy, as by the want of a proper medium of gold and silver" New York could not carry on its public business, "unless a paper currency be permitted to be issued on solid funds, and that such currency be allowed as a proper tender in all payments. . . ." The legislature appointed a committee to prepare a defense of New York's paper money and to instruct the agent to oppose any unfavorable legislation by Parliament.[27]

The New York merchants asked the Philadelphia merchants for support and they in turn requested the Pennsylvania legislature to order its agent in England to work with those of other colonies.[28] The assembly was too busy fighting with the governor to be bothered. Ever since the beginning of the Seven Years War it had been trying to tax the great landholdings of the Penn family, and deadlock after deadlock was the only result. Early in 1764 Governor John Penn, at the request of General Amherst, asked for troops to help suppress Pontiac's Rebellion. The assembly was willing to issue paper money to raise troops if it could tax proprietary as well as other lands. Governor Penn refused, and from January to May 1764, bills went back and forth while the Indians raided and the frontiersmen fumed, and finally the Paxton Boys marched on Philadelphia. Neither the assembly nor the governor had any sympathy for the frontiersmen; in their fright, however, they stopped wrangling long enough to persuade the Paxton Boys to return home. As soon as they had gone, their petitions were ignored, and governor and legislature had at each other once more. The assembly finally

26 23, 30 Jan., 13 Feb. 1764.
27 New York Assembly Journals [NYAJ], 19, 20 April; NYM, 14 May. Assembly journals not readily available in printed form will be cited by date only. For a list of such journals on microfilm, see *A Guide to the Microfilm Collection of Early State Records* (Washington, D.C., 1950, and *Supplement*, 1951).
28 Letter from Philadelphia, 22 Feb., NM, 2 April 1764.

gave in at the end of May, "protesting at the same time the violence done the constitution. . . ."

In the course of the fight the Pennsylvania assembly ignored not only the frontiersmen but the merchants of Philadelphia as well. The surrender to the governor was probably a move in a bigger game being played by Benjamin Franklin and Joseph Galloway, the leaders of the Quaker or antiproprietary party which controlled the assembly. In March the assembly blamed all the trouble on the governor and the proprietors and adopted twenty-six resolutions explaining why the king should convert Pennsylvania into a royal colony. Before the governor could answer, the assembly adjourned to "consult" its constituents, and in May it came back with petitions supporting the demand for a royal government. Two days after it met, the assembly elected Franklin speaker and then sent orders to the agent in England, Richard Jackson, to present a petition to the Crown asking for the change if he was sure that Pennsylvania could retain all the civil and religious privileges it enjoyed under the Penns.[29] Thus Pennsylvania, like Massachusetts, made no official protest against the renewal of the Molasses Act simply because its legislature was far more concerned with a local political fight.

ટ⁀

By the summer of 1764 Americans recognized that something far more important than molasses was at stake. The northern merchants and a few legislatures had no more than finished their protests than they heard that the Molasses Act had been renewed. Early in April a New Yorker heard from London that "you'll soon have a parcel of Marmadonian Ravens who will feed upon and rip up your very vitals such as officers of stamp duties, appraisers of lands, houses, furniture, etc. The Ministry are determined to make you pay for the peace which you like so well; the people here find so much fault with it that they are fearful to load them with any more taxes." [30]

Week by week more news arrived. By mid-May the parliamentary resolutions of 10 March, the basis of the Revenue Act of 1764, appeared in colonial newspapers. The rumors of a stamp tax which Americans had been

[29] The foregoing is based on the "Votes of Assembly" from January to May 1764 in *Pennsylvania Archives* [Pa. Ar.] (119 vols. in 9 series, Philadelphia and Harrisburg, 1852–1935), 8 ser. VII, passim. For a realistic appraisal of Franklin's politics see William S. Hanna, *Benjamin Franklin and Pennsylvania Politics* (Stanford, 1964), and for a more traditional interpretation see Theodore Thayer, *Pennsylvania Politics and the Growth of Democracy, 1740–1776* (Harrisburg, 1953).
[30] NYM, 2 April; NM, 16 April.

hearing since the spring of 1763 were at last confirmed.[31] The Revenue Act itself followed on the heels of the resolutions, but Americans did not at first realize the sweeping changes made in shipping and trial procedures. Their attention was fastened on the proposed stamp tax, on the threat that direct parliamentary taxation of the colonies would at last become a reality, and thus the constitutional issue was added to the economic grievances so loudly complained of. Could Parliament levy such a tax legally, or could internal taxes be levied only by colonial legislatures?

The first reply came from the Boston town meeting. The Revenue Act of 1764 was law and a stamp act was in prospect when the town met in May 1764 to elect representatives to the legislature. The town's instructions to its four representatives combined the continuing attack of the town's leaders on Thomas Hutchinson and his supporters with a theoretical statement of principles opposing parliamentary taxation of America, although the Boston leaders did not discover until a year later the political advantage of accusing the Hutchinsonians of being supporters, and even originators, of British legislation.

From May 1764 onward, the Boston town meeting played an ever more important role, not only within Massachusetts but in other colonies as well. The popular leaders of the town set forth their views in the newspapers and then carried them into the town meeting. From the town meeting they kept up constant pressure on the legislature, using the device of instructions. Voters in colonial America commonly wrote such instructions for their representatives, and legislatures had to consider them whether they liked them or not. Increasingly after 1763 such instructions were used to state far more radical views in opposition to British policies than most legislatures were willing to accept. No one used the device more effectively than the popular leaders of Boston. They were usually among Boston's four representatives, and they either wrote their own instructions or dictated their contents. The instructions were thus in a real sense political platforms and whether the legislature accepted or rejected them made little difference: they got widespread publicity. And rejection made it possible to denounce conservative-minded legislative majorities as foes of American liberty, enemies of the people, and the hireling tools of British power, as contrasted with the fervid patriotism of the popular leaders.

The instructions adopted on 24 May 1764 apparently were written by Samuel Adams,[32] who at the time had little prominence except as one of

[31] NM, 14 May.
[32] Draft, Samuel Adams Papers, New York Public Library [NYPL].

Boston's tax collectors whose accounts were sadly in arrears. The instructions began with a denunciation of plural office-holding. They then turned to the question of British policies. Surprise was expressed that the legislature had not instructed the colonial agent in time, although no newspaper reader in Boston could have been ignorant of the deadlock in the legislature which had delayed action. The representatives were told to secure a legislative petition for repeal of the Molasses Act. As for the future,

> if our trade may be taxed, why not our lands? Why not the produce of our lands and everything we possess or make use of? This we apprehend annihilates our charter right to govern and tax ourselves. It strikes at our British privileges, which, as we have never forfeited them, we hold in common with our fellow subjects who are natives of Britain. If taxes are laid upon us in any shape without ever having a legal representation where they are laid, are we not reduced from the character of free subjects to the miserable state of tributary slaves?

Boston's representatives were ordered to secure instructions to the colonial agent to remonstrate for all those rights and privileges "which justly belong to us either by charter or birth," but at the same time they were to set forth the unshaken loyalty of the province and the town of Boston, their "unrivalled exertions" in behalf of the government of the colony, and "its acknowledged dependence upon and subordination to Great Britain, and the ready submission of its merchants to all just and necessary regulations of trade. . . ." Finally, the representatives were to seek the support of the other northern colonies so that redress could be obtained by "united applications." [33] The instructions were a stirring political platform although, like other such platforms, as history they have deficiencies.

Six days later the legislature met for a short session of two weeks, the legislature being "at this busy season of the year in a great hurry. . . ." Near the close, Hutchinson, as chief justice, left to hold court in the eastern circuit, and several legislators left at the same time. With Hutchinson and some of his supporters out of the way, the Boston members had an unusual opportunity to control the house. They engaged in what Hutchinson called "the most injudicious conduct I ever knew the House of Representatives guilty of." In his opinion, the Boston leaders "care not for the consequences to the public, provided they can make themselves popular and conspicuous." [34]

[33] A *Report of the Record Commissioners of the City of Boston containing the Boston Town Records, 1759–1769* [BTR] (Boston, 1886), XVI, 121–22, and in part in EHD, IX, 663–64.
[34] Thomas Cushing to Jasper Mauduit, 22 June, and Thomas Hutchinson to ———, 11 July, MHSC, LXXIV, 160–64.

The house appointed a five-man committee of correspondence, three of whom—James Otis, Thomas Cushing, and Oxenbridge Thacher—were from Boston, and directed the committee to write to the other colonial legislatures and appeal for help to obtain the repeal of the Revenue Act and to prevent the passage of a stamp act. The house also appointed a six-man committee, including Otis, Cushing, and Thacher, to answer several letters from its agent in London. Jasper Mauduit had not been very vigorous and he had pleaded lack of instructions. The committee's reply denounced him. He was not an effective agent; his lack of instructions was no excuse; and above all he had no right to concede that Parliament could levy taxes upon "a people who are not represented in the House of Commons."

The committee scoffed at Grenville's delay of a stamp act as "any vast favor." It was simply a threat that Parliament would tax the colonies if they did not tax themselves. And the committee was contemptuous of the British argument that the acquisition of Canada would benefit the northern colonies. The colonies got along for a century without much help from England and they had gone to vast expense in the recent war. Now Britain was proposing to cut off their resources at the same time that she was planning to make them pay for the support of the British troops in the colonies. If the colonies were taxed without the consent of any Americans in Parliament, there would be no difference between Americans and the subjects of the most absolute prince. "If we are not represented, we are slaves." [35]

The idea of colonial representation in Parliament was James Otis's. During the session a document called "The Rights of the British Colonies" was twice read to the House of Representatives and then turned over to the committee to answer the agent. The house sent a copy to the agent along with the letter denouncing him and British policy. A few weeks later, James Otis's *The Rights of the British Colonies Asserted and Proved* was published in Boston. Otis began his confused and contradictory pamphlet boldly. All government originates in the will of God; in every society there must be a supreme, sovereign power; and in the order of nature, under God, comes the "power of a simple democracy." But he then went on to praise the British constitution as the best ever devised and to assert that Parliament had the power to legislate for the colonies and that the colonies had to obey its laws. Americans, however, had the same rights as their fellow subjects. He scorned colonial charters as the basis for those rights and

[35] Massachusetts House Journal [MHJ], 1, 8, 12, 13 June; Thomas, Massachusetts, 142–45. "The Rights of the British Colonies Asserted and Proved" is reprinted in Bernard Bailyn, ed., *Pamphlets of the American Revolution, 1750–1776*, I (Cambridge, Mass., 1965), 419–82.

insisted that colonial rights were based on the laws of God and nature, the common law, and acts of Parliament.

After asserting the uncontrollable power of Parliament, he got around it by appealing to a "higher law," as he had in his speech against writs of assistance in 1761. Acts of Parliament that were contrary to the "natural laws" of God were void. Therefore, he argued, "no part of his Majesty's dominions can be taxed without their consent." His solution was American representation in Parliament.

The pamphlet alarmed the British but it had little impact in America. Most American leaders, canny politicians that they were, had no intention of asking for representation in Parliament. It would destroy their soundest argument against parliamentary taxation, and they knew perfectly well that even if they were represented they would not have enough members of Parliament to have much influence.

The Massachusetts government as a whole had not protested officially against anything Britain had done or might do, and it was plain that the council disapproved of the house's action. Furthermore, Massachusetts merchants were far more interested in economics than in statements of political theory and they asked Governor Bernard to call a special session of the legislature. He agreed and it met in October 1764. This time the Hutchinson forces were there in strength and they had the support of the merchants.

The Boston representatives at once presented a petition asserting the "natural right" of the colonies to tax themselves and persuaded the house to adopt it. Hutchinson blocked it. He thought that the Revenue Act of 1764 was bad and he privately objected to the proposed stamp act, but as holder of many offices he was discreet. Furthermore, he was convinced that Parliament had a right to legislate for the colonies, however uneconomic or inexpedient the laws might be. Hutchinson insisted that the petition be based on economic grounds and that instead of talking about colonial "rights" they ought to talk about "privileges." Above all, the question of constitutionality should be ignored. With all his force he opposed the "very ill-judged petition" which "the lawyers upon the Boston seat" had written. Hutchinson had his way and both the house and council agreed to his formulation of a petition to the House of Commons, which he thought "a more decent one." It objected to the Revenue Act of 1764, to the new enforcement policies of the customs service, and to the proposed stamp act, all on economic grounds. Ignoring their defeat, the popular leaders wrote the colonial agent that the letter of the past June and Otis's *Rights of the British Colonies* expressed the sentiments of "the representative body of the people" far better than the official petition.[36]

છ

The Rhode Islanders met the threat of a stamp tax as smoothly as they had the renewal of the Molasses Act, and they made a new suggestion. The legislature met at Newport for one day in July and appointed Governor Hopkins and two others a committee of correspondence to confer with other colonial legislatures on measures to secure the repeal of or the lowering of the duties in the Revenue Act of 1764, and to prevent the levying of stamp duties. Beyond this the committee was instructed to oppose any taxes "which may be inconsistent with their rights and privileges as British subjects. . . ."[37]

When the legislature met in the fall, it adopted a petition to the king fulsomely declaring the loyalty and devotion of the colony. It then predicted ruin from the Revenue Act and deplored the new admiralty court at Halifax which would deprive the colonies of "that darling privilege, trials by juries, the unalienable birthright of every Englishman. . . ." The proposal for a stamp tax and "other internal taxes" would tend to deprive the colonies of equal freedom with the king's subjects in Britain "whose essential privilege it is, to be governed only by laws to which themselves have some way consented. . . ." Furthermore, duties of any kind would be bad because money was scarce. The petition ended by asking that the "freedom and the just rights" of the colonies be inviolate, that trade be restored, that the court of vice-admiralty have no more power than in Britain, and that the "colonists may not be taxed but by the consent of their own representatives, as your Majesty's other free subjects are."[38] On the whole, the petition was mild: while it stated colonial rights and asked for confirmation of them, it did not assert them. Such tact was likely born of the fact that while Rhode Island was a tiny colony, it had a big reputation that was very bad.

[36] Hutchinson to William Bollan, 7 Nov. 1764, MHSC, LXXIV, 167–68, n. 2, and Thomas Cushing to Jasper Mauduit, 17 Nov., ibid. 170–71. The petition is in Alden Bradford, ed., *Speeches of the Governors . . . 1765 to 1775 . . .* (Boston, 1818), 18–23. For the background see Thomas, Massachusetts, 148–54.
[37] RICR, VI, 403–4; NM, 6 Aug. 1764.
[38] RICR, VI, 414–16. Governor Hopkins wrote "The Rights of Colonies Examined" at the same time and the legislature ordered it printed and sent along with the petition. Ibid. 416–27.

ह‍े‍

The Pennsylvania assembly had ignored the request for help in protesting the renewal of the Molasses Act in the spring of 1764; its chief interest was in the movement for a royal government. Meanwhile politics became so heated that very few indeed could be bothered with matters beyond Pennsylvania. Newspapers, pamphlets, and broadsides were filled with charges and countercharges. Franklin was accused of stealing provincial funds while he was an agent in England. His henchman, John Hughes, later to be stamp distributor, was charged with stealing land warrants from the state house itself with the help of Joseph Galloway, who, in addition to other crimes, was reputed to have taken an office from an old man who needed it. Thus did the proprietary party wage its campaign.

The Quaker party gave as good as it got. Chief Justice William Allen, the patronage boss for the proprietors, was charged with subverting the supreme court itself in the interest of his masters. Israel Pemberton, the Quaker leader, who deserted his old friends to oppose the movement for a royal government, was accused of having an affair with a pregnant Indian squaw. There was also the story that as a schoolboy he had stolen marbles from his schoolmates and in later life had cheated his brothers of a part of their inheritance.

Churches and schools got into the fray and the College of Philadelphia, controlled by the Presbyterians, carried on the campaign against Franklin and the Quaker party in the classroom. Not all the political writing during the campaign was slander and personal abuse, but most of it was. If the propaganda was to be believed, there was not an honest man in Pennsylvania. In the fall election, both sides bought as many votes as they could. The vote in Philadelphia shocked the Quaker party, for both Franklin and Galloway lost their seats, and the "Presbyterian party" showed real strength for the first time. The Presbyterians had little use for the Penns, and even less for the Quakers; its leaders were convinced that Franklin's scheme for a royal government was nothing but a smokescreen to divert the minds of the frontiersmen from their just grievances. Despite the setbacks, the Quaker party won enough votes throughout the colony to retain control of the assembly.[39]

When the assembly met in September 1764 before the election, it could no longer avoid the issue of colonial policy. The speaker presented a letter from the Massachusetts committee of correspondence appointed in June. In it, Otis and Thacher reported what they had done and asked for

[39] Thayer, *Pennsylvania*, 95–105.

help in protesting past and future acts of Parliament. The assembly responded by sending some additional instructions to its agent Richard Jackson. It told him that the passage of a stamp act would have a "tendency" to deprive them of their rights as British subjects and of their rights under the Penn charter, which, among other things, gave them the "right of assessing their own taxes . . . the indubitable right of all the colonists as Englishmen." The assembly ignored James Otis's idea of representation in Parliament. Instead, it hinted at a plan it had in preparation whereby the colonies could supply funds in time of danger without "infringing the natural and legal rights of the colonies." The agent was to work for the repeal or amendment of the Revenue Act of 1764, and particularly for the repeal of that section prohibiting the export of lumber to Ireland and Europe.[40]

When the new assembly met in October after the election it once more had to consider British policy, for it had a letter from the Rhode Island committee of correspondence headed by Governor Hopkins. This letter was far more to the point than the one from Massachusetts. Not only were restrictions on trade and the proposed stamp act bad economically, they pointed to the servitude of the people. Parliament's claim to the right to tax the colonies, if carried into effect, "will leave us nothing to call our own." The colonies should unite in protest to try "to preserve everything they have worth preserving." Some method should be hit upon to collect the sentiments of all the colonies and to form "the substance of them all into one common defense of the whole. . . ."[41]

Governor Hopkins was hinting very broadly at the need for a union of the colonies, and well he might, for he had been with Franklin at the Albany Congress in 1754 when Franklin and others had created a plan of union. But the Franklin forces in the assembly now reversed themselves. Although in September they had told agent Jackson they were preparing a plan for contributing money for defense, in October, after reading the Rhode Island letter, they told him to forget the September instructions. The assembly said it could not form such a plan because of "the disjointed state and separate interests of the different colonies. . . ." Instead, he was to tell the ministry that Pennsylvania would do everything it could for defense, as it had before. As for taxes, only the separate assemblies could know what to tax and what not to tax. Taxes levied in any other way "where the people are not represented" and by those unacquainted with the colonies, would be "unequal, oppressive and unjust, and what we trust a British Parliament will never think to be right." Having made this brief bow in the direction of constitutional theory, the remainder of the new instructions

[40] Pa. Ar., 8 ser. VII, 5627–29, 5643–45.   [41] 8 Oct. 1764, ibid. 5675–76.

described in detail the bad economic effects of the Revenue Act of 1764 on Pennsylvania. They declared that Pennsylvania would soon be in desperate straits for money as a result of the drain of gold and silver to England and the eventual disappearance of paper money. As for heavy taxes, Pennsylvania simply could not pay them. It was true that wartime expenditures gave an appearance of prosperity but that was now gone, prices were falling, and debts were hard to pay, as every English merchant knew.[42]

This second set of instructions did not mention the proposed stamp act. It would seem that Franklin and his party had no intention of giving offense to Britain. On the same day the instructions were adopted, the assembly renewed the fight over the scheme for a royal government. The proprietary party made a desperate effort to undo what had been done. Motions to recall the petitions that had been sent, to instruct the agent not to present them, and even a final motion to adjourn for two weeks, were beaten down one by one. The triumphant majority then moved to elect a second agent to "assist" Richard Jackson.

It was no secret that the "assistant" was to be Benjamin Franklin. The proprietary party countered by presenting a petition asserting that three-fourths of the inhabitants opposed a royal government, and that if an assistant agent were to be sent, it should not be Franklin. The reasons were "weighty." Franklin had been the leader in promoting petitions for the change and he was not likely to be objective. His enmity for the proprietors was so great that they could not act together for the "public good," yet this was a time when the proprietors' help was needed to prevent further burdens from being laid on the province. Above all, both Franklin and his son held profitable offices by royal appointment and it was not likely that Franklin would "sacrifice his interests for the sake of the Province, which he must necessarily do, if he but seems to oppose the measures of the ministry. . . ." If Pennsylvania needed an additional agent, it should be a man of "unshaken resolution and fidelity. . . ." The majority ignored the petition and on the same day elected Franklin to go to England.[43] Within a short time he was there to play a role during the passage of the Stamp Act which convinced his enemies that the petition told less than half the truth.

In 1764 the popular leaders in Massachusetts were still certain that Thomas Hutchinson was a greater enemy than Parliament, and James Otis

[42] Ibid. 5678–82.   [43] Ibid. 5682–90.

was talking about representation in the House of Commons. The Rhode Islanders were predicting economic chaos and asking for a confirmation of privileges, while continuing the rankest kind of attacks on customs officials. The members of the Pennsylvania assembly stated that taxes should be levied only by colonial legislatures, but they placed most of their emphasis on the economic problems created by parliamentary legislation.

The most radical stand taken by any colonial legislature during 1764 was that of the New York assembly, a body dominated by the great landlords of the colony and their merchant and lawyer allies. For years the colony had been the scene of a political battle between two groups within the aristocracy led by two great families—the Livingstons and the De Lanceys. For more than a decade before 1760 the De Lanceys dominated the assembly and government offices. Their leader, James De Lancey, son of a Huguenot refugee who had married wealth, also married wealth and went into politics early. Attaching himself firmly to the royal governor, he was named to the council at the age of twenty-six, to the supreme court two years later, and then, at the age of thirty, was made chief justice. As such he presided over the trial of Peter Zenger, during which he disbarred two of the colony's leading lawyers. After George Clinton became governor in 1743, De Lancey reversed himself and became a "popular leader," and so powerful that he blocked virtually all New York aid during King George's War. When Clinton left in 1753, De Lancey added the job of lieutenant governor to his other posts, for he obtained the commission which Clinton had withheld for six years.

The new governor, Sir Danvers Osborne, committed suicide as soon as he arrived, and so from 1753 to 1755 De Lancey ruled the colony in name as well as fact. During that period he issued a charter to King's College as an Anglican institution, further embittering the Presbyterian Livingstons. He again acted as governor from 1757 to the summer of 1760, when he died. The long reign of the De Lanceys came to an end, for the new elections made necessary by the death of George II ended in a triumph for the Livingston family, who despite their vast wealth, had made little headway in the scramble for political jobs as long as James De Lancey lived. They won control of the assembly and held it for eight years, while the De Lanceys wandered in the political wilderness, once more posing as "popular leaders" in an effort to regain power.

While the great families might fight with each other for offices and prestige, they were in fundamental agreement on one thing: there must be no effective British interference within the colony. By the middle of the century they had wrested all real power from the royal governors. Above all, their purpose was the protection of their great land holdings, many of which had been acquired or extended by corrupt means, and on which they managed to evade the payment of quitrents and taxes. In achieving self-government, the aristocracy had talked much of natural rights and of the idea that government should be based upon the consent of the governed, although it had no intention of putting such principles into practice within the colony itself.

At the same time the factions had developed political institutions which were to threaten their power in the days ahead. Both sides appealed to the voters and by the 1740s they were holding mass meetings to nominate rival candidates. By the 1750s they were issuing what amounted to political platforms. The nominations and the platforms were of course managed by a few leaders and the acclamation of the multitude was but ratification of what had been prepared for them by their betters. Both the political theories used to oppose British interference and the devices adopted to fight one another were dangerous weapons which could be and were used against the aristocracy itself in the years after 1760.

The year 1760 also saw a further rise in the political fortunes of a man who, almost single-handedly, was a third force in New York politics: the seventy-two-year-old Cadwallader Colden who, as president of the council, became acting governor upon the death of De Lancey. Colden was born in Scotland in 1688. After studying medicine in London, he moved to Philadelphia in 1718 and then to New York, where he was appointed surveyor general of the colony in 1720, a post he held until 1776. In 1721 he was appointed to the council and in the years ahead he was the power behind certain governors. He was always regarded as a danger by the aristocracy for he was an ardent imperialist and an eager supporter of royal power in the colonies. For this the aristocracy might have forgiven him but what aroused their fear and hatred was the fact that year after year he wrote letters to British officials describing in accurate detail the corrupt means by which the New York landlords acquired and held onto vast tracts of land to the detriment of the colony and to the derogation of British power. Endless maneuvers to destroy his political influence always failed and the aristocracy's desperate hope that he would die was equally vain. He got his commission as lieutenant governor in 1761 and for the next fourteen years, except for periods when a full governor was in residence, he ruled the colony. Constantly he wrote to Britain cynically reporting on the low motives of greedy landlords and smuggling merchants who, he said, dictated the actions of the New York legislature.[44]

He was governor in 1764 when news of the proposed stamp act reached the colony. The assembly produced a statement of colonial rights such as even the Bostonians were not yet ready to adopt. In the spring it had supported merchant opposition to the renewal of the Molasses Act and expressed alarm at the proposed currency act. Both were laws when the assembly met again in September, and a stamp act was on the way. Furthermore, the great landlords were alarmed at rumors that Parliament would also tax American lands. When the assembly replied to Colden's opening speech it declared that it was depressed by the prospect of ruin as a result of the news from "home." It asked Colden to join in "an endeavor to secure that great badge of English liberty of being taxed only with our own consent," and pointed to the "many mischiefs" arising from the Revenue Act of 1764.

Colden returned a "soft" answer in which he said that it was not fitting to present such an address to him but that he would send it to more "proper judges." He reminded the assembly that the mother country had poured out blood and treasure in defense of the colonies and that in return they ought to help her and to express their sentiments "with gratitude and filial submission."

Privately, he wrote the board of trade that the assembly's address was "undutiful and indecent." For a while he thought of dissolving the legislature but the address was printed in the newspapers and Colden and the council decided that a dissolution would only "tend further to inflame the minds of the people. . . ."

Colden once more explained why there was such a "violent spirit" among the leaders: it was due to the fears of the great landlords. Three members of the assembly claimed over a million acres each, and several others over 200,000. Such grants had been acquired without a previous survey and without warrants and very little had been given in return. Much of the land was uncultivated. Not only this, but the landlords were daily adding to their holdings by suing and ruining poor families who had settled near them. And they controlled the assembly. Three manors had the right to

[44] See Carl Becker, *The History of Political Parties in the Province of New York, 1760–1776* (Madison, 1909), and Mark, *Agrarian Conflicts in Colonial New York.* For a detailed account of Colden's career to 1760 see S. B. Rolland, Cadwallader Colden: Colonial Politician and Imperial Statesman, 1718–1760 (Ph.D. Thesis, University of Wisconsin, 1952).

send representatives, with the result that the proprietors were hereditary members. Other great owners were so influential in their counties that they were perpetually re-elected. There were a few "common farmers" in the assembly but these were "men easily deluded, and led away with popular arguments of liberty and privileges."

The great landowners not only did not pay the quitrents which small landholders paid, their influence was such that they were freed from every other public tax on their land. Every horse, cow, ox, hog, and acre of the small landowner paid taxes while "millions of acres, the property of private persons, contribute nothing. . . ." But now, wrote Colden, they are worried because people in England have told them that land would be taxed. Therefore, "by every artifice [they] inflame the people's minds, with hopes thereby to deter a British Parliament." But, said Colden, if the owners of cultivated lands, who are the great majority, find that by taxation of all lands they can be free of unequal taxation, the board of trade can judge what an effect it will have "when they consider things as they really are." [45] The lieutenant governor was clearly not impressed by constitutional rhetoric. As far as he was concerned, it was a mask for the fears of the great men who hoped to avoid paying taxes in the future as they had in the past.

Whatever the motives, the New York legislators adopted a petition to the House of Commons. It told of the great services of the colony in past wars; declared a willingness to accept parliamentary regulation of trade, but claimed an exemption from all duties on trade; elaborated on the bad effects of the Revenue Act of 1764 and on the necessity of trade with foreign islands; protested against the admiralty courts while commenting on the "wisdom" of jury trials; and predicted the worst of results from the Currency Act of 1764. Of course the assembly claimed no "desire of independency upon the supreme power of Parliament. Of so extravagant a disregard to our own interests we cannot be guilty."

But all of this was prefaced by a ringing assertion of rights that was guaranteed to raise the hackles of British officialdom. Exemption from "ungranted, involuntary taxes" is "the grand principle of every free state," and is "the natural right of mankind. . . ." The New Yorkers declared that the people of the colony "nobly disdain the thought of claiming that exemption as *a Privilege*. They found it on a basis more honorable, solid,

[45] NYAJ, 11, 17 Sept.; Colden to BT, 20 Sept., E. B. O'Callaghan and B. Fernow, eds., *Documents Relative to the Colonial History of the State of New York* [NYCD] (15 vols., Albany, 1856–87), VII, 653–55.

and stable; they challenge it, and glory in it as their right." [46] Little wonder that the board of trade was horrified and that the best friends of the colonies in Parliament would not present the memorial.

Not even the House of Burgesses of Virginia, which yielded to no colonial assembly in the rhetorical capacity of its members, could match the New York petition; but it did act in December, the last colonial assembly to do so before the passage of the Stamp Act. Virginia too had its economic problems. The financing of the Seven Years War brought paper money to Virginia for the first time, and the heaviest taxes it had ever known. The fall of Fort Duquesne in November 1758 ended the immediate pressure, but other problems threatened early bankruptcy for some of the leading citizens, not to mention the hordes of small farmers. For all the diversity of crops and exports, tobacco was still the chief money crop. After a small crop in 1758 when a few lucky planters did well, the price of tobacco began to drop, and the trend was encouraged by merchants who united to force prices down. By 1763 tobacco was eighteen shillings a hundredweight and the next year, despite a small crop, planters could get only a little more than twelve shillings. Merchants, who were marking up their goods 200 per cent, reported that the tobacco trade was the best it had been in many years!

Thus, by 1764, with tobacco bringing only 25 per cent of what it had four years earlier, even the greatest families in the colony found it impossible to pay their debts. Byrds, Burwells, Carters, and Lees were no better off than the small farmers. Bills of exchange from the most prominent men in the colony were not honored in England. The county courts and the general court were so filled with debt cases that they could not keep up with their work. Prominent men who had never defaulted before were threatened with jail and hid from sheriffs, while lesser men resorted to tearing down the jails. Yet despite their debts, the Virginians continued to buy more and more goods from Britain, and British merchants continued to extend credit. [47]

The only answer seemed to be more paper money, although merchants on both sides of the Atlantic had been protesting against it since 1759. In 1762 Governor Francis Fauquier approved an issue, but he soon received

---

[46] NYAJ, 18 Oct.
[47] See David J. Mays, *Edmund Pendleton, 1721–1803* (2 vols., Cambridge, Mass., 1952), I, chapter IX, "The Decline of the Plantation System," upon which this section is based, and Fauquier to BT, 3 Nov. 1763, C.O. 5/1330.

orders from England to veto further issues and to insist that the House of Burgesses provide for payment of debts in sterling money. The house defended itself and insisted that merchant demands were "an instance of weakness or caprice." [48] When the governor called the burgesses to meet in January 1764, and asked for special troops to help suppress Pontiac's Rebellion, they replied in effect: no paper money, no troops. They urged the governor to use instead the Virginia militia, whose conduct and bravery they applauded.[49]

With that, the governor prorogued the house on 21 January, and it did not meet again until the end of October. By then the first part of the Grenville program was law. The Currency Act of 1764 and the renewed demand that merchants be allowed to collect debts in sterling, when the colony had no sterling, further irritated the hard-pressed gentlemen of Virginia. The session, of course, had to deal with such routine business as a bill to prevent hogs from running in the streets of Winchester. The town had been trying for ten years to secure such an act, and at last succeeded. George Washington was the author and sponsor of the law, which only got past the council as a water conservation measure.

The burgesses turned from such matters to a statement of their rights and grievances and took the lead in the public declaration of colonial rights, a leadership which they were to share only with the town of Boston during the next twelve years. They decided to send three memorials: one each to the king, lords, and commons. These were debated for a week in terms which the governor labeled "very warm and indecent," but the outcome was acceptable to the conservatives in the House of Burgesses and the council, or at least enough so to win a majority.

As in other colonies, constitutional arguments were combined with economic, particularly in the case of the proposed stamp act. The burgesses asked the king to protect them in their right to tax themselves, and they told the House of Lords flatly that it was a fundamental principle of the British constitution that a people could be taxed only by its own consent. The burgesses had possessed the right of taxing the people from the first establishment of regular government in the colony, and "they cannot now be deprived of a right they have so long enjoyed, and which they have never forfeited." The colony had contracted a debt of nearly a half million pounds during the late war; tobacco was in a low state; there was no specie

[48] 20 May 1763, *Journals of the House of Burgesses of Virginia* [JHB] (1761–65), 174. For a full defense, see the address to the governor, 28 May, ibid. 188–92.
[49] Ibid. 203–4, 212.

in the colony. The new trade regulations would make for an "extremely distressful" people and parliamentary taxation would "make them truly deplorable."

The House of Burgesses told the House of Commons firmly that it was "essential to British liberty that laws imposing taxes" should be enacted only by representatives chosen by the people. Such a privilege was "inherent" in the people who settled in America and could not be renounced or forfeited by their removal to the colonies. Furthermore, it had been confirmed by royal charters and governors' commissions. How Americans could be deprived of "that sacred birthright" they could not discern, nor could they discern how they could be taxed by Parliament "wherein they are not, and indeed cannot, constitutionally be represented."

Even if it were proper, such a tax would ruin Virginia with its war debt, its taxes, its expenses for Indian warfare, and the low price of tobacco. The colonies had been "principal means" of Britain's growth in wealth and prosperity, but if Americans were reduced to poverty they would manufacture for themselves.

The petition ended with a clear warning to the House of Commons that if it passed a measure "fitter for exiles driven from their native country" than for the prosperity of those who at all times had demonstrated a "due reverence to the mother kingdom," then "British patriots will never consent to the exercise of anticonstitutional power, which even in this remote corner may be dangerous in its example to the interior parts of the British Empire, and will certainly be detrimental to its commerce." [50]

Thus did the Virginia assembly declare itself on Tuesday the 18th of December 1764. Three days later it adjourned to meet on 1 May 1765 in a session that adopted the resolutions that set off the colonial revolt against the Stamp Act.

---

[50] 18 Dec. 1764, ibid. 302–4. The memorial to the House of Commons is reprinted in EHD, IX, 667–69.

IV

The Revolt Against the Stamp Act

The passage of the Stamp Act transformed American opposition to British policies. Only a few legislatures and some of the merchants in the northern colonies objected to the renewal of the Molasses Act, and to the new enforcement policies, and they did so on economic grounds. The merchants and planters in the southern colonies cared little for the fish and molasses trade and had no particular liking for northern merchants anyway, but the prospect of a stamp tax aroused their alarm and indignation. Beginning with the first House of Burgesses in Virginia in the seventeenth century, colonial legislatures had asserted that taxes should be levied only by representatives of the colonists' own choosing, and from the summer of 1764 onwards, the legislatures that did petition or send instructions declared that it was their right to levy their own taxes.

Colonial protests and petitions meant nothing to a Parliament bent on taxing the colonies. It refused to listen to colonial petitions, and assumed that it had the right to tax the colonies, or if not the right, the power, as the supreme legislature of the empire. The implications were clear, and from the southernmost West Indies legislature to Quebec there was opposition to the Stamp Act. The resolutions of the West Indies legislatures rang with all the clarity of those on the mainland, but the West Indies, unlike the mainland colonies, did not have a large enough population of free white men to make opposition effective.

The Stamp Act was law for less than five months and even during that short time it was a dead letter in the twelve most populous colonies. Yet it was of enormous importance in that it produced at least a surface unity among the colonies, for almost every political leader, whatever his political principles, was opposed. Nevertheless, the struggle within the colonies over methods of opposition wrecked the political careers of some men and made possible the political futures of others. The campaign against the act brought local communities to debate public affairs as never before. It gave local political leaders in towns and counties an opportunity to write sweeping statements of colonial rights in resolutions and in instructions to legislators. The formulation of and voting on these documents educated many people who had been politically indifferent, and also accustomed them to thinking in larger terms. Statements of opinion on the "grass roots" level became a powerful weapon in forcing colonial legislatures to take ever more radical steps in opposition to British policies. In addition, the mass meeting became a common method of action, in which all who cared could participate whether they had the right to vote or not. For many, this was little more than shouting approval of resolutions written by their "betters," but it gave them a taste for political action that they were not to lose.

The nullification of the Stamp Act was brought about by mob action or the threat of it. Even the most conservative colonial leaders realized that such action was necessary, and some of them encouraged and even joined the mobs; but many of them soon repented, for the mob, once started, was hard to control, much less to stop. And very shortly certain of the popular leaders began using the mobs to help carry on their fight against the dominant political machines within the colonies. Small wonder then, that from 1765 onward, some conservative American political leaders began to worry more about the danger of mobs than they did about British policies, whatever they might be.

The Stamp Act crisis brought colonial newspapers to the very head of the protest movement. Newspapers abandoned their politeness and became the chief means of formulating public opinion and of stating far more radical ideas than most legislatures were willing to adopt. Newspaper writers, taking the names of the dead great of history, expounded doctrines they would never have dared express in a public forum. It was they who raised for the first time what was to some Americans a promise and to others a threat: the idea that independence might be the ultimate outcome of the quarrel with Britain.

The British reaction to American opposition was a hardening of the attitudes of those in a position to shape colonial policy. American violence also did much to alienate the sympathies of British merchants and manufacturers who, more than any other single group, were responsible for the repeal of the Stamp Act. Few Americans realized that British merchants were entitled to such credit. So far as any Briton got credit, it was William Pitt, who in fact had scented a political issue rather late in the game. Most Americans thought that they had achieved the result themselves through economic pressure and direct action.

Finally, the Stamp Act brought about a clarification of the constitutional positions of both Parliament and the colonies. For the next ten years the Americans were to reiterate and embroider but not really alter their basic premise: Parliament had no constitutional right to tax the colonies. Taxation within the colonies was the province of each individual legislature. Parliament must of course regulate the trade of the whole empire, but aside from that the bond of empire was the king, not the Parliament. King and Parliament, on the other hand, never once abandoned the principle of the Declaratory Act of 1766: that Parliament could legislate for the colonies in all cases whatsoever. Parliament might not choose to, but it could do so at any time and in any circumstances it saw fit. There were leaders on both sides of the Atlantic who wanted to let the issue die, but others, for a variety of reasons, kept it alive and sharpened it in the years that followed. In the end, no compromise was possible and moderates on both sides of the Atlantic were swept aside when arms rather than argument became the final arbiter of constitutional theory.

જે⊷

The news of the actual passage of the Stamp Act reached the colonies in mid-April 1765.[1] Newspapers reported reactions ranging all the way from a Maryland planter who felt that "taxation" by London tobacco merchants was just as bad as taxation by Parliament,[2] to a New York writer who declared that the act would drain off all the gold and silver in the colony within two years.[3] Other newspapers denounced the colonial agents for not presenting colonial petitions before the Stamp Act became a money bill because they surely knew that Parliament never received petitions against money bills.[4]

The rumbling discontent was brought to a head and given a platform by the Virginia House of Burgesses in May 1765, although it is unlikely that a majority of its members had any intention of leading a colonial revolt against an act of Parliament. But then the majority had nothing to say for

[1] NYM, special supplement, 15 April, lists the duties; *South Carolina Gazette* (Peter Timothy) [SCG(T)], 13 April.
[2] *Maryland Gazette* [MdG], 4 July.   [3] NYG, 30 May.   [4] NM, 27 May.

it had headed for home to take care of farms and plantations before the event occurred.

When the house met on 1 May, it asked the governor to issue writs for special elections to fill vacancies. Among them was one from Louisa county, whose burgess, William Johnston, had resigned. The special election was held and on 20 May the new burgess arrived: he was Patrick Henry of Hanover county, twenty-nine years of age and already a lawyer of widespread fame. He was added to the committee on courts of justice and, as a new member of inconspicuous family, was doubtless expected to hold his peace among the great men of the colony.[5]

Although his family was not among the great, it was of importance in Hanover county. His father, John Henry, had migrated from Scotland and had become a member of the ruling clique of the county for he was a justice of the peace and hence a member of the county court, a colonel in the militia, and a vestryman of the established church. Furthermore, his uncle, the Reverend Patrick Henry, was an Anglican parson. Young Patrick Henry had something of an education, mostly at home, and then at fifteen he became a clerk in a crossroads store. At sixteen he and a brother opened a store of their own but they soon came to grief. At eighteen he married a girl with a small dowry and started farming with a few slaves and some land but within three years he was deeply in debt. At twenty-one he again started a country store, a venture as hopeless as the first.

At the age of twenty-four he turned to law and got a license to practice after only a few weeks' study. He was at once an astonishing success. During his first three years as a lawyer he acted in nearly 1200 suits and won most of them. His oratorical powers, which later won him the name of the Demosthenes of America, dazzled country juries. He won more than local fame in a case known as the "Parson's Cause."

In 1755 and again in 1758, when tobacco crops were short and prices high, the legislature passed acts allowing debts, taxes, and salaries, customarily paid in tobacco, to be settled at the rate of two pennies for each pound of tobacco due. Since 1696 Anglican clergymen had received salaries in tobacco and they were bitterly opposed to the Two Penny Act of 1758 which deprived them of a larger income. They held a convention and sent a delegate to England where the Privy Council vetoed the act in August 1759. Various clergymen in Virginia then started suits in county courts to recover what they had lost.

[5] JHB (1761–65), 315, 345. The only modern biography is the admiring one of Robert D. Meade, *Patrick Henry: Patriot in the Making* (Philadelphia, 1957).

The most famous case was that of the Reverend James Maury. His parish was in Louisa county, but, knowing that it was hopeless to bring suit in a county settled mostly by dissenters, he sued the collectors of parish levies in the Hanover county court in the spring of 1762. The case dragged on until December 1763, when the defendants hired a new lawyer, Patrick Henry, the son of the presiding justice, Colonel John Henry. Since the Two Penny Act had already been vetoed in England, the only question to be decided was the amount of back salary due. Maury had lost before the case was argued. He declared that the sheriff packed the jury, that having approached one or two gentlemen who refused to serve, he "made no further attempts to summon gentlemen." Instead he "went among the vulgar herd" and picked three or four "dissenters of that denomination called New Lights." Maury protested, but Patrick Henry insisted that "they were honest men and therefore unexceptionable."

Henry made a speech that had nothing to do with the evidence but much to do with exciting the jury and the audience and arousing antagonism against the established church. At the same time he voiced some extremely radical ideas on the subject of colonial rights. The law of 1758 was a good law he said, and it could not, "consistently with what he called the original compact between King and people, stipulating protection on the one hand and obedience on the other, be annulled." The king in disallowing the measure ceased being the father of his people and "degenerated into a tyrant and forfeits all right to his subjects' obedience." As for the Anglican clergymen, their only function in civil society was to enforce obedience to civil sanctions. They were no longer useful members of the state and ought to be "considered as enemies of the community," and as far as Maury was concerned, he deserved "to be punished with signal severity." If the jurymen did not want "to rivet the chains of bondage on their own necks," they should make an example of Maury as a warning to him and those like him who disputed the only authority that could make laws for Virginia, the legislature of the colony.

When Henry denounced the king, "the more sober part of the audience were struck with horror." Maury's lawyer cried treason, as did some of the audience, but the justices sat silent and at least one juror nodded approval. But law was law and the jury had to find for Maury; the jury was out less than five minutes and decided that he was entitled to one penny. After the court adjourned, if one can believe the defeated parson, Patrick Henry apologized for what he had said, "alleging that his sole view in engaging in the cause, and in saying what he had, was to render himself popular. You see, then, it is so clear a point in this person's opinion, that the ready road to popularity here, is, to trample under foot the interests of religion, the rights of the church, and the prerogative of the Crown." [6]

Patrick Henry did win popularity with the dissenters and the populace of Hanover and Louisa counties, and even with staid Anglican planters, who were disgusted with the clergy. Louisa county showed its gratitude by electing Henry to the House of Burgesses at the first opportunity. He appeared there on 20 May 1765 to take his seat, and he was soon to win far wider fame. In ten short days in his first session he became the leader of a group of young politicians in the house who were ready to challenge the old leaders of the colony. Discontent was growing; frontier inhabitants violated Indian treaties with impunity and killed Indians going through the colony with passes from the governor; debts owed to Britain and to one another made Virginians "peevish and ready to murmur at every occurrence." Circulating money was so scarce that the people were "really distressed" and the evil was "daily increasing" as the paper money was taken in, while gold and silver did not circulate at all. The private distress felt by every man "increases the general dissatisfaction at the duties laid by the late Stamp Act, which breaks out and shows itself at every trifling occasion." Thus the governor described the inflamed state of public opinion in the spring of 1765. Adding to the tension within the House of Burgesses itself were the rumors that John Robinson, speaker of the house and treasurer of the colony, had been embezzling public funds for years to aid himself and his friends. Richard Henry Lee had suspected as much as early as 1760 but his efforts at exposure had been blocked by the canny Robinson. In the May session of 1765 Robinson and his allies proposed the creation of a loan office or land bank in the hope that they could use one to cover up their peculations. The house passed the bill but it was rejected by the council. Thereafter many of the members left for home.[7]

Richard Henry Lee was not present at the session, possibly because Robinson had heard that Lee had applied for a post as stamp distributor and had threatened to expose him. However, Patrick Henry took the lead, and his strategy was superb. He waited until the session was almost at an end except for formalities. When he presented his resolutions on 29 May,

[6] James Maury to Rev. John Camm, 12 Dec. 1763, Ann Maury, ed., *Memoirs of a Huguenot Family* (New York, 1853), 418–24. Although Maury was a prejudiced witness his account rings true. See also preface, JHB (1761–65), which contains copies of the laws, and a discussion of the pamphlet debate on the church.
[7] Fauquier to Halifax, 14 June, C.O. 5/1345; JHB (1761–65). See Chapter VII below for the public exposure of Lee's application and of Robinson's embezzlement.

only thirty-nine of the 116 members were present. The conservative older leaders were shocked but were "overpowered by the young, hot, and giddy members." In the course of the debate Henry used some "very indecent language." Apparently he talked as he had to the "Parson's Cause" jury for he spoke of Caesar's having had his Brutus and Charles I his Cromwell and hoped that "some good American would stand up for his country. . . ." But when Speaker John Robinson cried that this was treason, Henry backed down and said "that if he had affronted the Speaker, or the house, he was ready to ask pardon, and he would show his loyalty to his majesty King George the third at the expense of the last drop of his blood, but what he had said must be attributed to the interest of his country's dying liberty which he had at heart, and the heat of passion might have led him to have said something more than he intended. . . ." [8]

The next day the house adopted his five resolutions, the last by a vote of only 20-19, while the largest vote for any of the others was only 22-17. At the end of the day Henry nonchalantly left for home. The next day the conservatives made an effort to strike all five resolutions from the journals but were able to remove only the fifth. The governor, who was convinced that none would have passed in a full house, then dissolved the legislature.

The resolutions asserted: (1) that the first settlers brought with them and transmitted to their posterity all the privileges and immunities at any time held by the people of Great Britain; (2) that the two royal charters gave them the privileges and immunities of natural-born subjects living in England; (3) that taxation by the people themselves or by their representatives was "the distinguishing characteristic of British freedom, without which the ancient constitution cannot exist"; and (4) that the people of Virginia have enjoyed the right of being governed by their own assembly in taxation and internal police and have never forfeited or surrendered it. The fifth resolution, rejected the day after Henry left, stated that the legislature of Virginia has "the only exclusive right and power to lay taxes and imposts upon the inhabitants of this colony," and that every attempt to vest such a power in any other person or persons "is illegal, unconstitutional, and unjust, and has a manifest tendency to destroy British as well as American liberty." [9]

[8] Fauquier to BT, 5 June, C.O. 5/1331; "Journal of a French Traveller in the Colonies, 1765," The American Historical Review [AHR], XXVI (1920-21), 745-46. This is the only known contemporary account of the speech. Years later Henry's biographers produced far more heroic versions. On the "thin" house see SCG(T), 26 Aug. 1765, which reprinted the story from New York.
[9] JHB (1761-65), 359-60; Fauquier to BT, 5 June, C.O. 5/1331. See also the introduction to the JHB (1761-65) and Morgan, Stamp Act Crisis, 88-98.

The governor heard that there were two other resolutions even "more virulent and inflammatory" which had not been presented because of the difficulty in passing the fifth one. Apparently he had heard correctly, for in less than a month the *Newport Mercury* printed six resolutions, omitting the third passed by the burgesses, but including the rejected fifth. The fifth and sixth reported as passed by the *Mercury* were indeed inflammatory. One proclaimed that Virginians did not have to obey any laws levying taxes except those passed by their own legislature, and the other asserted that anyone who denied the sole right of the legislature should be "deemed an enemy to this, his Majesty's colony." Within a few days the *Maryland Gazette* printed seven resolutions, including the four adopted, the one rejected, and the two "inflammatory" ones that had not been presented.[10] Henry and his supporters had learned what the popular leaders in other colonies already knew or were soon to learn: never let fact stand in the way of what you want the public to believe. The Virginia resolutions, true and false, were printed by newspapers from one end of America to the other except by the timid editor of the *Virginia Gazette*, who got no sympathy from brother publishers when he complained of the "lies" told about Virginia.[11] It mattered not that less than 20 per cent of the burgesses had voted for only four resolutions; no one cared except the unhappy governor and the conservative leaders of the colony. So far as the rest of America was concerned, Virginia had thrown a magnificent challenge into the teeth of Parliament and dared other legislatures to match it.

৪৯

The Virginia resolutions appeared in Massachusetts at a time when the Boston leaders were suffering defeats and were in a state of shock because of the behavior of James Otis.

Hutchinson had licked them in the fall of 1764 when the legislature had adopted his version of a petition to Parliament. Then, when the legislature met in January 1765, Otis deserted the other Boston leaders. He helped Governor Bernard elect the governor's friend Richard Jackson as associate agent with Dennys De Berdt, whom the house had elected to replace Jasper Mauduit as the agent of the house. Even more startling was Otis's vote to restore to Hutchinson the additional salary as chief justice that Otis had persuaded the house to deprive him of in 1762. All the shaken Boston leaders could do was to praise the Virginia petitions of December 1764 as

[10] EHD, IX, 669–70. The various versions of the resolutions are reprinted in Edmund S. Morgan, ed., *Prologue to Revolution: Sources and Documents on the Stamp Act Crisis, 1764–1766* (Chapel Hill, 1959), 46–50.
[11] MdG, 3 Oct. 1765, quoting the *Virginia Gazette* of 30 August.

compared with the weak and watery document sent from Massachusetts.[12]

Some weeks later Otis wrote a pamphlet reversing the stand he had taken in his pamphlet *The Rights of the British Colonies* in 1764. There were rumors that Britain would punish him for his stand, and it was said that he suffered a "failure of nerves." The occasion for his recantation was a pamphlet written by Martin Howard, Jr., of Newport. Howard was one of a group in Newport intriguing for the establishment of a royal government in Rhode Island, as Franklin and Galloway were doing in Pennsylvania. Governor Stephen Hopkins denounced the group in a speech to the legislature in the fall of 1764. Then, when Governor Hopkins published his *The Rights of Colonists* in December 1764, Howard attacked it in *A Letter from a Gentleman at Halifax to his friend in Rhode Island.* Howard attacked Otis as well and roundly defended the sovereignty of Parliament over the colonies.

In return, James Otis attacked Howard in two pamphlets, in one of which he called the "royalists" of Newport a "little dirty, drinking, drabbing, contaminated knot of thieves, beggars and transports, or the worthy descendants of such, collected from the four winds of the earth, and made up of Turks, Jews, and other Infidels, with a few renegado Christians and Catholics. . . ."

But, as Howard pointed out in reply, Otis did more than call names: he reversed the position he had taken in 1764 and had betrayed his whole party. And Otis had done so, for in his first pamphlet attacking Howard he declared that Parliament had "a just and equitable right, power and authority, to impose taxes on the colonies, internal and external, on lands as well as on trade. This is involved in the idea of a supreme legislative, or sovereign power of the state." Such taxes might be inexpedient or inequitable but Parliament had the power nevertheless. He went on to say that the colonies were represented in Parliament, in law if not in fact; that the supreme legislative power represented the whole community and that "this is the true reason why the dominions are justly bound by such acts of Parliament as name them."

Otis went even further in asserting the right of Parliament to tax the colonies and again insisted that they were represented. He even praised a pamphlet justifying the measures of the Grenville ministry and declared that when Parliament passed an act everyone must "humbly acquiesce," that Parliament should not be charged with improper and unreasonable proceedings. "The law of Parliament is, that Parliament cannot err." As for the Stamp Act, Otis declared that he would not say a word as to its expedi-

[12] *Boston Gazette* [BG], 25 March 1765; Thomas, *Massachusetts,* 155–56.

ence or utility for "I humbly, dutifully, and loyally presume . . . that the supreme legislative of Great Britain do, and must know infinitely better what they are about and intend, than any without doors." [13]

This second pamphlet was published 6 May 1765, a week before Boston met to elect its representatives. The delighted governor wrote that Otis "now repents in sack cloth and ashes" and would probably lose the election. The populace of the town was furious at its hero. The popular newspaper hinted openly that Otis had been bribed and that his political career was at an end, and more than a half-century later, John Adams remembered that Otis was called "a reprobate, an apostate, and a traitor in every street in Boston." [14] Otis, now doubly frightened, sought to save himself politically. The day before the town meeting he published a signed defense in the *Boston Gazette* denying that he had ever given up any rights or had been false to his "beloved constituents." He begged for but half an hour to talk to them at the meeting the next day, and said he cared not whether it was before or after the election. He ignored the pamphlets he had written.[15]

He was saved, as he said later, "by the song of a drunkard." In his personal attack on Martin Howard, published the week before, he had ended with the statement that "To crown all, he should be a delicate chanter of *Lillibulero*, and other songs ancient and modern." On the same day that he published his appeal to the voters in the *Boston Gazette*, the *Boston Evening Post* published a parody of *Lillibulero* in which Otis was raked from stem to stern. Such verses as

And Jemmy is a silly dog, and Jemmy is a tool;
And Jemmy is a stupid cur, and Jemmy is a fool;
And Jemmy is a madman, and Jemmy is an ass,
And Jemmy has a leaden head, and forehead spread with Brass.

convinced some of Otis's outraged followers that he had not sold them out. The next day he was re-elected, but he got the fewest votes among the four representatives.[16]

[13] Bailyn, ed., *Pamphlets*, I, 554–79, prints the first of Otis's pamphlets attacking Howard. Both pamphlets are printed in Charles F. Mullett, ed., *Some Political Writings of James Otis* (University of Missouri *Studies*, IV, Columbia, 1929). See also Ellen E. Brennan, "James Otis: Recreant and Patriot," NEQ, XII (1939).
[14] Bernard to John Pownall, 6 May 1765, Bernard Papers [BP], III, 287–89, Harvard University Library [HUL]; BG, 6 May 1765; John Adams to William Tudor, 11 March 1818, *Works*, X, 295–96.
[15] 13 May 1765.
[16] BTR, XVI, 141; BEP, 13 May. Otis was re-elected moderator of the meeting despite his troubles.

The popular party had not recovered from this nerve-wracking experience before the legislature met a few days later. By then of course the news of the passage of the Stamp Act and of Andrew Oliver's appointment as stamp distributor had arrived.[17] Governor Bernard told the legislature that although the Stamp Act might be "disagreeable" it should show "a respectful submission to the decrees of Parliament" because "there must be a supreme legislature. . . ." The Boston leaders at once began a campaign to prevent the re-election of Oliver and his brother-in-law Hutchinson to the council, but they failed as usual. Meanwhile the *Boston Gazette* trumpeted away at the Stamp Act, attacked the admiralty courts which would deprive Americans of their "darling privilege" of jury trial, and predicted even more admiralty courts with judges paid from American revenues. The *Gazette* predicted too that British troops would be quartered in American homes and that American lands would be taxed by Parliament.[18]

The Boston leaders then proposed that an intercolonial congress of American legislatures meet in New York. The move was so well supported that the "government party" could not block it. As the governor put it, "it was impossible to oppose this measure . . . and therefore the friends of government took the lead in it. . . ." [19] The house then elected three delegates, Oliver Partridge, Timothy Ruggles, and James Otis. "Two of the three are fast friends to government of Great Britain," reported the governor.[20]

When the legislature was prorogued in June, after less than a month, the Boston leaders had little to show for their efforts. Then within a few days the Virginia Stamp Act resolves were printed in Boston newspapers. Again the popular leaders were shocked, for James Otis, among others, declared the Virginia resolves to be treasonous. They suffered still another blow when Oxenbridge Thacher died in July. But the Virginia resolves were, as Governor Bernard said, "an alarm bell to the disaffected," and the popular newspaper soon "swarmed with libels of the most atrocious kind." [21] The *Boston Gazette* made the most of the opportunity. It praised the Virginia resolves and excoriated the "tame, pusillanimous, daubed, insipid thing, delicately touched up and called an address" sent by Massachusetts "to please the taste of the tools of corruption" in Britain. Those who asked for "prudence" in stating American rights were "ye hungry wolves, ye insatiable vultures, ye devouring monsters." Such men

[17] Abstracts of the resolves which were the basis of the Stamp Act were published in the *Boston Gazette* and the *Boston Evening Post* on 8 April.
[18] BG, 3 June.   [19] Bernard to BT, 8 July, C.O. 5/891.
[20] Thomas, Massachusetts, 173–74.   [21] Bernard to SS, 15 Aug., C.O. 5/755.

"have swelled with the proud hopes of one day striding over the backs" of their superiors and making them beasts of burden. Such "dirty sychophants" and "ministerial hacks" were traitors to America and to king and Parliament. Shortly thereafter the *Gazette* charged that the English measures had been proposed by Americans: by "mean mercenary hirelings or parricides among yourselves, who for a little filthy lucre would at any time betray every right, liberty, and privilege of their fellow subjects." [22]

Action followed. Early in the morning of 14 August effigies of Andrew Oliver and Lord Bute were hung on a tree. When the alarmed governor consulted the council it labeled such actions "boyish sport." He then ordered the sheriff to take down the effigies, but the sheriff did not dare. After sunset the effigies were carried to a new building erected by Andrew Oliver, which the mob tore down, carrying the wood to Fort Hill where "they made a burnt offering of the effigies for these sins of the people which had caused such heavy judgments as the Stamp Act, etc. to be laid upon them." The fuel was inadequate so they tore pickets from the fence around Oliver's nearby house. The house itself "received from the populace some small insults, such as breaking a few panes of glass in the windows of his kitchen." However, some of Oliver's friends in the house committed "indiscretions" which so "enraged the people," who had hitherto maintained "the utmost decorum," that they entered the lower part of the house "in multitudes." They did no damage, said this friendly account, and they took nothing away. Other accounts reported that the mob went into the wine cellar and consumed the contents. When Governor Bernard asked the colonel of the militia to call out his men, the colonel said it was useless, since probably all his drummers were in the mob. Thomas Hutchinson and the sheriff went to the riot only to have rocks thrown at them, and they ran from the scene. The forces of law and order in Boston were helpless and the riot ended about midnight, probably because after eighteen hours of activity, the members of the mob were worn out. [23]

The next day a frightened Andrew Oliver resigned as stamp distributor. The mob gathered again that night and marched to Hutchinson's house on hearing a rumor that "a certain honorable gentleman in high posts, had forwarded the stamp act by recommending it as an easy method of gulling the people of their liberty and property. . . ." Hutchinson refused to appear but "some reputable gentlemen" assured the mob that the rumor was false and it dispersed after breaking a few windows.

[22] BG, 8 July, 5, 12 Aug.
[23] BEP, 19 Aug.; BG, 19 Aug.; Bernard to SS, 15, 16 Aug., C.O. 5/755.

But Hutchinson was not to escape so easily. For four years the leaders of the Boston faction had been attacking him in the newspapers, the town meeting, and the legislature, and now they were accusing him of writing the Stamp Act. The charge was false but the populace that had listened to inflammatory denunciations for years believed it to be true. The mob had had great success with Oliver and had been backed by leading citizens. At least fifty "gentleman actors" in disguise were reportedly members. All sorts of rumors continued to float about, and on the night of 26 August, wrote Governor Bernard, "a great company of people gathered together crying liberty and property, which is the usual notice of their intention to plunder and pull down a house." They went first to the house rented by Charles Paxton, marshal of the admiralty court. Paxton had already left, and the owner of the house distracted the mob by inviting them to a tavern for a barrel of punch. "As soon as they had drinked the punch" they went to the house of the deputy register of the admiralty court, William Story, "tore it all to pieces," and then made a bonfire of the records of the admiralty court. Then they went to the house of Benjamin Hallowell, comptroller of the customs, and destroyed the interior of that elegant new mansion.

And then, as Hutchinson said, "the hellish crew fell upon my house with the rage of devils. . . ." Hutchinson wanted to stay and defy the mob but his daughter would not leave without him so they fled. The mob worked until daylight, "by which time one of the best finished houses in the province had nothing remaining but the bare walls and floors." Doors were split, furniture smashed, featherbeds thrown out, and all the clothing and pictures ruined or stolen. The books and the manuscripts which Hutchinson had been gathering for thirty years were destroyed or thrown in the streets, among them the manuscript of the second volume of his history of the colony. Money to the amount of £900 sterling was stolen, as was the family silver. The mob spent two hours tearing the cupola from the top of the house and were at work taking the slates from the roof when daylight stopped them. The next day the streets of Boston were littered with the debris, including the manuscript history, which luckily was saved.

There is no doubt that the mob had gotten out of hand. Even Hutchinson said that "the encouragers of the first mob never intended matters should go this length. . . ." [24] The leading people of Boston were hor-

[24] Thomas Hutchinson to Richard Jackson, 30 Aug., J. K. Hosmer, *The Life of Thomas Hutchinson* (Boston, 1896), 91–94; Bernard to SS, 31 Aug., C.O. 5/755 (printed, EHD, IX, 675–80); BG, 2 Sept.

rified at the "unparalleled outrage" and many of them now promised the governor that they would help provide a military guard to maintain order. The popular leaders, afraid of possible British retaliation, called a town meeting the next morning and voted "utter detestation of the extraordinary and violent proceedings of a number of persons unknown" and promised to help maintain order.[25] No one was taken in by such pious declarations, least of all Thomas Hutchinson.

The governor and council ordered the arrest of the mob leader, but no sooner had the sheriff done so than certain leading citizens persuaded him to release Ebenezer Mackintosh. They told him that if he did not, there would be no military guard in the town that night. The "gentlemen" were afraid that Mackintosh would reveal their part in the earlier riot, so he walked the streets of Boston a free man.[26] The popular leaders were determined that the attack on Hutchinson's house should be by "persons unknown," and many prominent men of the town shared their view.

ॐ

The Stamp Act was a dead letter in Massachusetts after Oliver's resignation on 15 August. And as the news spread to other colonies, violence spread with it. There were of course stamp distributors who did not wait for violence. George Meserve of New Hampshire arrived in Boston from England less than ten days after the attack on Hutchinson's house. He resigned before he went home to Portsmouth, and once there, resigned again in a public ceremony, and a third time in January 1766.[27] When James McEvers in New York heard of the Boston riots, he resigned, "being terrified by the suffering and ill usage the stamp officer met with at Boston and the threats he received at New York." [28] William Cox of New Jersey hurriedly followed suit a few days later.[29]

The Rhode Islanders did not let their enemies off so easily. The news of Oliver's resignation was followed by rumors that effigies would be hung in Newport on 27 August. Martin Howard, Jr., bravely but indiscreetly denounced the idea in the *Newport Mercury*, and the next morning his effigy, that of his friend Dr. Thomas Moffat, and of Augustus Johnston,

25 BTR, XVI, 152; BEP, 2 Sept.
26 P. O. Hutchinson, ed., *The Diary and Letters of His Excellency Thomas Hutchinson* . . . (2 vols., Boston, 1884–86), I, 70–71. For a sketch of Mackintosh see Chapter V below.
27 *Massachusetts Gazette* [MG], 12 Sept. 1765; NM, 28 Jan. 1766.
28 Colden to Sir William Johnson, 31 Aug. 1765, Emmett Collection no. 10,747, NYPL.
29 *Pennsylvania Gazette* [PG], 12 Sept. 1765, and 2 Jan. 1766 for a second resignation.

the stamp distributor, were paraded in the streets and hung on a gallows before the courthouse and were guarded by three leading merchants armed with clubs. One of the men left town at once and two went aboard the British naval vessel *Cygnet*, lying in the harbor, where they found John Robinson, collector of customs, who had no illusions about his own popularity. The governor, Samuel Ward, discreetly left town and stayed away until the trouble was over.

That afternoon the effigies were burned but efforts to start a riot were futile. The next day the four refugees returned and that evening John Robinson got into a brawl on the streets. There was soon a mob which wrecked the houses of Moffat and Howard, while Johnston escaped with minor damage by promising to resign as stamp distributor. Robinson and the others gathered once more on board the *Cygnet*, where Captain Leslie was willing to protect them although he was worried about an attack on the ship itself.

The next day the mob threatened to get out of hand in a different way. A young Irishman who had been in town only a few days boasted that he had been the mob's leader. The Newport gentlemen who had encouraged the mob and provided it with liquor were alarmed that their own part might be revealed. The sheriff promptly collared him and delivered him on board the *Cygnet*. The mob on shore then made such an uproar that the sheriff went out to the ship, told Captain Leslie that he had made a mistake, and took the young man ashore. There, on his promise to leave the colony at once, he was released. Instead, he turned up the next morning, again boasting of his leadership and threatening destruction of the houses of those who had seized him the day before unless they gave him presents. According to Captain Leslie, the frightened gentlemen of the town promised the Irishman clothes and money and the sheriff offered to lie down and let him walk on his neck. The gentlemen, aghast at the mob they had encouraged, now united to suppress it. They co-operated heartily with the former stamp distributor, who was also the attorney general of the colony, in jailing the mob leader who had turned upon them. But the result was that there was no stamp distributor for Rhode Island.[30]

Jared Ingersoll, distributor for Connecticut, was made of tougher stuff. He landed in Boston from England at the end of July, quite sure that the people of his colony would grumble but would submit. He had little reason

---

[30] NM, 2 Sept.; William Almy to Elisha Story, 29 Aug., EHD, IX, 674–75; letters of Captain Charles Leslie of the *Cygnet*, CHOP, I, 609–11; Morgan, *Stamp Act Crisis*, 144–50.

to suppose otherwise, for he was besieged by fellow citizens wanting posts as deputy distributors in their home towns. He was soon disillusioned. The Virginia Stamp Act resolves, the violence in Boston, and the Connecticut newspapers stirred up a people convinced they were paying quite enough taxes as it was. Ingersoll, who had been a reasonably popular man, suddenly found that his initials were those of "Judas Iscariot." His effigy was hung and burned everywhere in the colony, but he defended himself in the newspapers, and his friend, Governor Thomas Fitch, refused to convene the legislature so that it could elect delegates to the Stamp Act Congress.

Fitch and Ingersoll were leading citizens of western Connecticut, the more conservative part of the colony which controlled the government. Eastern Connecticut, however, had been a center of religious and economic discontent for years. Its leaders had organized the Susquehanna Company and tried to settle men in the upper Susquehanna Valley in Pennsylvania. They argued that Connecticut's charter extended over that area but they received no support from Governor Fitch and his followers in western Connecticut. The Stamp Act provided the people of eastern Connecticut with an issue they had long needed in their fight with the western part of the colony.

Governor Fitch finally called the legislature to meet at Hartford on 19 September, and Ingersoll left New Haven to lay his case before it. Meanwhile, the people of eastern Connecticut had organized as Sons of Liberty and sent three bodies of armed, mounted men to invade New Haven and force Ingersoll to resign. They caught Ingersoll at Wethersfield and silently and pointedly led him under a large tree. They parlayed for hours, eventually in a tavern, with Ingersoll squirming and arguing and refusing to resign. The crowds outside grew so large and threatening that finally Ingersoll read his resignation to the mob and yielded to the demand that he throw his hat in the air and cheer for "Liberty and Property." They then took him on to Hartford, where he read his resignation once more, cheered for liberty, and threw both his hat and wig in the air. At last, thoroughly humiliated, he was allowed to leave for home, while his friend Governor Fitch committed political suicide by taking the oath to uphold the Stamp Act.[31]

Marylanders showed no interest in the Grenville program until the passage of the Stamp Act. The new trade regulations had little effect on Maryland, and financially the government was in a unique position. Its paper

---

[31] NM, 26 Aug., 2 Sept.; *Connecticut Courant* [CC], 2, 23 Sept.; Lawrence H. Gipson, *Jared Ingersoll: A Study of American Loyalism in Relation to British Colonial Government* (New Haven, 1920), chapter VI.

money was on the point of retirement and the colony was left with a balance of £29,000 in Bank of England stock. But the Stamp Act changed indifference to sharp concern. By August 1765 towns in Maryland were hanging, whipping, and burning effigies and holding funerals for the Stamp Act. At Frederick Town the "lifeless body lay exposed to public ignominy" until it was thought fit to bury it in order to prevent "infection from its stench. . . ." A legislator suspected of applying for the post of distributor found it expedient to make a profuse public denial.[32] Marylanders soon turned on Zachariah Hood, their stamp distributor; when he refused to resign, they pulled his house down and he fled to New York.

There, under the cannon of Fort George, said the *Maryland Gazette*, "he remains, hid from the resentment of his countrymen, but not from the terrors of his conscience." [33] Hearing of this, the New York Sons of Liberty resolved that stamp officers from other colonies should not have refuge in New York. Hood fled to Long Island but a group of "volunteers" sought him out "both by land and by water." Hood pleaded with the fifty men, telling them of the sad state of his personal affairs. They listened "with as much tenderness as the case would admit" but insisted that he resign. He gave up promptly when they threatened to send him back to his fellow citizens in Maryland and the Baltimore Sons of Liberty thanked their New York brethren for bringing Hood "to a sense of his treachery to his country, and for causing him before a magistrate on his oath, to renounce the despicable employment." [34]

In Pennsylvania, as in Massachusetts, resistance was involved in party politics. Opinion was overwhelmingly against the Stamp Act, but an even bigger issue was the scheme for a royal government. Franklin, the leader of the Quaker party, was in England and he urged his party to submit. He sent a pamphlet vindicating the act to Thomas Wharton; he wrote Charles Thomson that the act would not be repealed; and he told his friend John Hughes, whom he had named stamp distributor, that he would be unpopular for a while but that the people would submit in time. When William Cox, whom Franklin had named distributor for New Jersey, resigned, Franklin told Hughes that his son should apply. Sir William Franklin in New Jersey asked for troops to help enforce the act and informed his father, who apparently did not disapprove. Franklin's attitude in the sum-

[32] MdG, 29 Aug., 5 Sept., 3 Oct. 1765; 30 Jan. 1766; NM, 30 Dec. 1765; 6 Jan. 1766.
[33] MdG, 3 Oct. 1765.   [31] Ibid. 30 Jan. 1766; NM, 30 Dec. 1766.

mer of 1765 seems clear enough. He wrote Hughes that "a firm loyalty to the Crown and faithful adherence to the government of this nation . . . will always be the wisest course for you and I to take, whatever may be the madness of the populace or their blind leaders. . . ." [35]

But the leader of the proprietary party, Chief Justice William Allen, was not blind; at least he thought he saw a chance to ruin Franklin and block his schemes. Many of the Quaker party refused to follow Franklin's urgings to loyalty, but Franklin's ally, Joseph Galloway, did. In the middle of August he published an essay signed "Americanus" in which he justified taxation of America by Parliament. It was useless, he wrote, to expect the colonial legislatures to raise money to help the mother country. The only alternative to parliamentary taxation was to create an American legislature with the power to tax, or if Americans preferred a common legislature with the mother country, they should petition for the right of sending members to Parliament. He applauded the call for the Stamp Act Congress, but meanwhile Americans should stop the "indecent reflections" in the newspapers, for "they tend to create in the minds of the weak and ignorant a spirit of disloyalty against the Crown and a hatred of the people of England." [36]

The revelation of Galloway's authorship provided political ammunition for the proprietary party. When the assembly met in September before the annual election, the proprietary party had its way. It sent opponents of the Stamp Act, including John Dickinson and George Bryan, to the Stamp Act Congress, and adopted a series of forthright resolutions against the Stamp Act and other British measures. They were ordered printed in the German and English newspapers of the city, but discreetly, were not sent to England officially.[37] William Allen told the assembly that Franklin was the greatest enemy to the repeal of the Stamp Act.

In the election that followed, the efforts of the proprietary party proved vain, for the image of it as the "Court Party" was firmly planted in the minds of the voters. The Quaker party's reputation as the "People's Party"

---

[35] Thayer, *Pennsylvania*, 113–15. The facts are from Thayer; the interpretation is mine. See Franklin to Thomson, 11 July, Thomson Papers, LC, and to Hughes, 9 Aug., Albert H. Smyth, ed., *The Writings of Benjamin Franklin* [*Writings* (S)], (10 vols., New York, 1905–7), IV, 391–93.

[36] *New York Journal* [NYJ], 15 Aug. 1765. This essay was reprinted in the same paper on 30 October as a "SUPPLEMENT EXTRAORDINARY," with Galloway identified as the author. In an answer a writer expressed his shock "that this assertor of American slavery, this reviler of American honor" had been re-elected to the Pennsylvania assembly.

[37] Pa. Ar., 8 ser. VII, 5769, 5779–80.

was largely the result of Franklin's vast charm and wit and supple political skill, however little, in reality, the reputation was deserved, and despite all its efforts the proprietary party could not undo it. Then, too, many of the voters apparently were convinced that the real issue was the question of royal government, not the Stamp Act, however much they might dislike it. Both sides tried to win votes. Governor Penn appealed to the Germans and Lutherans by incorporating their churches, but the more practical Quakers countered by paying the two-dollar naturalization fee for some 2600 Germans just before the election. The Quaker party won a sweeping victory, defeating even John Dickinson and George Bryan, who were away at the Stamp Act Congress. Joseph Galloway, despite the campaign against him, was re-elected after a year out of the assembly.[38]

When the new assembly met in October, not more than seven or eight proprietary men were left in it. The majority promptly re-elected Jackson and Franklin as joint agents and put Galloway on the committee of correspondence to write to them. In its first letter the committee instructed the agents to continue to work for the change in government. As for the Stamp Act, they were told to join other agents in presenting an address if the Stamp Act Congress sent one.[39]

As in Massachusetts, when defeated by the legislature, the opponents of the Stamp Act turned to a mob. A mass meeting had been held in the middle of September and a mob led by James Allen, son of the chief justice, and other gentlemen, had gone to the house of John Hughes. He was a sick man but stood them off with guns and told them that he could not resign a commission he had not received. Some of the mob then decided to tear down Franklin's house, but his friends surrounded it and prevented damage.[40]

The ships carrying the stamps arrived in Philadelphia on 5 October, after the triumph of the Quaker party in the election. All the ships in the harbor hung their colors at half-mast and the bells of the city were muffled and tolled all day. That afternoon thousands of inhabitants attended a mass meeting "to consider the proper ways and means for preventing that unconstitutional act of Parliament (the Stamp Act) being carried into execution." The leaders of the meeting, except for Charles Thomson, still loyal to Franklin, were of the proprietary party and included four sons of Chief Justice Allen, John Dickinson, Robert Morris, and others. A committee of seven such men went to Hughes and again demanded his resignation. He refused, but promised that he would not exe-

[38] Thayer, *Pennsylvania*, 119–20. [39] Pa. Ar., 8 ser. VII, 5790–94.
[40] Thayer, *Pennsylvania*, 118–19.

cute the act until it was complied with in the other colonies. When this news was brought back to the meeting, "the company were instantly transported with resentment, and it is impossible to say what lengths their rage might have carried them" if the delegation had not reported that Hughes was ill to "the point of death." The meeting then agreed to put the demand in writing and to give Hughes until Monday morning to reply. He still refused but again promised that he would not do anything to execute the Stamp Act. The stamps were put on board a British naval vessel, which kept them from exposure to the resentment of "an injured and enraged people." The *Pennsylvania Gazette* smugly reported that Pennsylvania had followed the example of "our fellow sufferers in the neighboring colonies" but without "any unnecessary acts of violence." [41]

ૐ

To the south of Virginia the colonies were so preoccupied with internal affairs that they made no protests against British policies until the Stamp Act. Then all of them except Georgia did so with vigor and effect. In October, 500 people met in Wilmington, North Carolina, and hanged and burned the effigy of William Houston, the stamp distributor. In November he came to town, whereupon several hundred people "with drums beating and colors flying," surrounded the house he was in. He promised that he would do nothing disagreeable, but that was not enough. He was taken to the courthouse, where he resigned. Then, placed in an armchair, he was carried around the courthouse and given three huzzas at every corner, then to his lodgings, where he was cheered again. Thereafter he was taken into the house "where was prepared the best liquors to be had," and treated "very genteely." [42]

In August the *Georgia Gazette* published Isaac Barré's "Sons of Liberty" speech, and some inhabitants of Savannah proposed to follow the methods of the northern colonies.[43] Their efforts were futile, for Georgia had a popular and forceful governor, Sir James Wright. He had troops and he was willing to use them, and in the end Georgia yielded. A letter at the end of the year regretfully reported that "the number of the Sons of Liberty are too few here to make any head against the other party, which is supported by the rangers of this province. . . ." [44]

South Carolinians had been too busy with other matters to concern

[41] PG, 10 Oct.; Thayer, *Pennsylvania*, 121. Hughes never formally resigned his post.
[42] PG, 2 Jan. 1766.
[43] *Georgia Gazette* [GG], 1 Aug., 31 Oct., 7 Nov. 1765.
[44] PG, 2 Jan., 3 Feb. 1766. See Kenneth Coleman, *The American Revolution in Georgia, 1763–1789* (Athens, 1958), chapter II.

themselves with British measures before the Stamp Act. They had finished a war with the Indians in 1761, and then began a brawl with the new governor, Thomas Boone, which lasted until they drove him from the colony in 1764. The political life of the colony centered in the Commons House of Assembly, made up almost exclusively of wealthy planters and merchants in and around Charleston. Unlike Virginians, most of the leading citizens scorned places on the council, which consisted largely of British-appointed officeholders such as the chief justice, the secretary, the admiralty judge, and the attorney general.

In December 1761 Thomas Boone came as governor. He had inherited property in the colony, had visited it twice before, and on his second trip had married a Carolina woman. His uncle, Joseph Boone, had been prominent in the early history of the colony. The promise of a happy administration was soon shattered. In the spring of 1762 Boone told a committee of the Commons House, which had long taken part in Indian affairs, that he was willing to treat them as private gentlemen but that he would not consult them on executive matters, and Indian affairs were such. The members were irked, but real trouble did not begin until September. The house, in examining the returns of a by-election, found that the church wardens had not taken the oath required by law before opening the polls. However, it was clear that the voters wanted Christopher Gadsden and the house approved his election and sent him to the governor to take the state oath. Boone refused to give it, told the Commons House that it had arrogantly ignored the law, and then dissolved the legislature.

A new election returned most of the same members, including Gadsden. An issue of principle was at stake and at once the house made the most of it: like the House of Commons in England, the Commons House of South Carolina was the sole judge of the qualifications of its own members. A committee, with Gadsden as a member, told Boone that his action was a breach of the privileges of the house, a "great violation of the freedom of elections, and having a manifest tendency to destroy the most essential and inviolable rights of the people." Boone replied that he was responsible only to the king and would do as he pleased. The house reiterated its position in an even longer statement, whereupon Boone verbally and rudely told the house that "forty more messages" would make no difference to him.

The house then voted to do no more business with the governor and instructed the committee of correspondence to send a full account of the dispute to the agent in England. When the house met in January 1763, enough men stayed away to prevent a quorum. Finally in September 1763, a quorum did appear but the fight was renewed at once. Sir John Colleton was elected in a special election and the house made a point of sending Gadsden and William Moultrie with him to the governor to take the oath. Boone ordered Gadsden and Moultrie out of his house and invited Sir John in. The Commons House declared itself outraged, ignored the governor's message asking for a tax bill, prepared a petition to the king demanding his removal, and then went home. Boone was beaten and in May 1764 he left for England with a woman who might have been a lady but was certainly not his wife. In England he appeared in a grim session before the board of trade, which declared that he had displayed "more zeal than prudence and in the process of it to have been actuated by a degree of passion and resentment inconsistent with good policy and unsuited to the dignity of his station." Boone resigned.[45]

The triumphant Commons was ready to do business with the popular lieutenant governor, William Bull, a native son. Business needed doing, since no taxes had been levied since 1762 and no debts had been paid. The Commons enacted tax bills for 1762 and 1763 but omitted any salary for ex-Governor Boone, who had been paid for only a few weeks at the end of 1761. The council amended the bill, adding £7000 for his salary. Here again was an issue of principle: the council could not amend a money bill. The Commons denounced the councilors as "placemen" who had "no natural tie or connection whatever with the Province," as compared with "the natural representatives" of the people. The council was forced to give in, for the Commons would have blocked all legislation if it had not.[46]

The legislature was in session when the Massachusetts invitation to the Stamp Act Congress arrived in July 1765. The Commons promptly chose Christopher Gadsden, Thomas Lynch, and John Rutledge to attend and provided £600 sterling to pay their expenses. Throughout the rest of the summer the *South Carolina Gazette* reported events in the northern colonies. Despite the news of northern violence, great merchants such as Henry Laurens, who disliked the Stamp Act intensely, still hoped that South Carolina would be free of "all riot and mobbing and every mark of tumult and sedition" and that it would obey the law until it could be repealed.[47]

[45] W. R. Smith, *South Carolina as a Royal Province, 1719–1776* (New York, 1903), 339–49; Lewis B. Namier, "Charles Garth and His Connections," EHR, LIV (1939), 462–69; Boone to BT, 29 March and 15 Sept. 1763, C.O. 5/377. Petition of the Commons House for Boone's removal is also in C.O. 5/377.
[46] South Carolina Commons House of Assembly Journal [SCHJ], 22–25 Aug., 22, 27 Sept., 3–4 Oct.; Bull to BT, 13 Sept., 8 Oct. 1764, C.O. 5/378; D. D. Wallace, *The History of South Carolina* (4 vols., New York, 1934), II, 40.
[47] SCHJ, 19, 26 July; Henry Laurens to Joseph Brown, 11 Oct., Laurens Letter Book, HSP. *The South Carolina Gazette* (T) printed resolutions, accounts of riots, effigy burnings, and resignations of stamp distributors in the North in full detail. See issues from 14 July to 5 October.

But the riots in Boston and Rhode Island were too attractive an example for many Charlestonians to ignore. Governor Bull blamed New England, which "vaunts its numbers and arrogates glory to itself in taking the lead of North America." Carolinians were quiet until the arrival of ships from the North and then "by the artifices of some spirits the minds of men here were so universally poisoned with the principles which were imbibed and propagated from Boston and Rhode Island" that they were determined to destroy the stamps and prevent the stamp officers from doing their duty.

The stamps arrived on 18 October. The governor placed them on a naval vessel in the harbor and then moved them to Fort Johnson and enlarged the garrison. During the next few days there were effigy burnings, riots, and a funeral of "American Liberty." The governor said that "although these very numerous assemblies of the people bore the appearance of common populace, yet there is great reason to apprehend they were animated and encouraged by some considerable men who stood behind the curtain." [48] Henry Laurens was contemptuous "of those Sons of Liberty as they style themselves" who did not "close the play in defense of liberty before they had most shamefully given the lie to their pretended patriotism" by acts of licentiousness, robbery, and burglary. [49]

The mob did not know where the stamps were and among other places it looked was in the house of Henry Laurens. At midnight on 23 October Laurens heard a "violent thumping and confused noise" at his doors and windows and then shouts of "LIBERTY, LIBERTY STAMPED PAPER. OPEN YOUR DOORS." Laurens opened a window and said he had no stamps but the mob refused to believe him. He then "accused them of cruelty to a poor sick woman far gone with child and produced Mrs. Laurens shrieking and wringing her hands. . . ." If any one of the mob had a grudge against him, Laurens said, he had a brace of pistols and would settle it then and there. But nothing would do except to let the mob search the house. Despite their disguises, Laurens said that he called at least nine of the mob by name and recognized at least an equal number of others. As a result the search was superficial, but they demanded "A Bible Oath" that he did not know where the stamps were. Laurens refused, "not failing to confirm my denials with Damns of equal weight with their own language. . . ." "Barbecue me," he told them, but swear oaths or speak ill of other men he would not. The mob wound up the affair by giving Laurens three cheers and retired calling, "God bless your honor, Good night

[48] To BT, 3 Nov., C.O. 5/378. Printed in EHD, IX, 680–83.
[49] To Stephen Brown, 22 Oct., Laurens Letter Book, HSP.

Colonel, We hope the poor lady will do well." Laurens professed amazement that "such a number of men, many of them heated with liquor, and all armed with cutlasses and clubs" did not do a penny's damage to his house and garden.[50]

All this was too much for Governor Bull, who was now convinced that the Stamp Act could not be enforced. On 28 October, George Saxby the inspector and Caleb Lloyd the distributor came to town from Fort Johnson, and before a crowd of perhaps 7000, declared that they would not act.[51]

ટ્સ

Virginia, which had set off the protest movement, saw the resignation of its own stamp officer on 31 October, the day before the Stamp Act became effective. The effigy of George Mercer was hung in various places in Virginia during the summer and fall[52] but he did not arrive from England and appear in Williamsburg until 30 October. Governor Fauquier had been expecting him for weeks and hoping desperately that he would not arrive during the sessions of the general court because "there is always a vast concourse of people then in town." Not only did people come from all over the colony for legal business, but merchants and others came because it was the usual time of the year to transact business, pay accounts, and buy and sell bills of exchange. Furthermore, there were rumors that parties would come from all over the colony to destroy the stamps. The court had no sooner met than it received memorials from two counties asking that new justices be appointed because their present justices would not act after 1 November. The governor and council refused to consider the idea because "in few counties there are gentlemen enough properly educated and qualified to execute the trust." They preferred that there be no courts at all rather than to fill them "with a meaner sort of people."

When Mercer arrived, a large crowd went in search of him. The governor said, "this concourse of people I shall call a mob did I not know it was chiefly, if not altogether, composed of gentlemen of property in the colony, some of them at the head of their respective counties. . . ." The men of the gentlemanly "mob" met Mercer on his way to the capitol and demanded his resignation. He evaded by saying that he must consult his friends and that he would let them know on Friday, 1 November. They

---

50 Laurens to Joseph Brown, 28 Oct., ibid.
51 George Saxby and Caleb Lloyd to William Bull, 29 Oct., C.O. 5/378; GG, 24 Oct.; PG, 2 Jan. 1766.
52 MdG, 12 Sept.

followed him to the coffee house, where the governor, council, and Speaker Robinson sat on the porch. The great men of the colony received Mercer warmly, while the mob muttered threats to "rush in." Governor Fauquier stepped forward boldly and the mob fell back. Mercer finally promised that he would give his decision the next day and then Fauquier took Mercer with him "through the thickest of the people who did not molest us, though there was some little murmurs."

In a long talk the governor told Mercer that "if he was afraid of his life, it was too tender a point to advise him." But if he was not, he should not listen to his father and brother "who were both frightened out of their senses for him." The next day Mercer resigned at the capitol and the following day, 1 November, the general court met. Neither lawyers nor their clients appeared at the bar. The governor asked Mercer if he could supply stamps so that the court could proceed according to law and Mercer replied that he could not. The governor then turned to the clerk and asked him if he could do business without stamps. The clerk said he could not. Fauquier then turned to his brother judges and asked them one by one if they thought the court should adjourn until 10 April, since they had no business. They solemnly agreed that it should. The carefully staged little play was almost upset by Mercer, who asked Fauquier if he would accept his resignation. "I was taken by surprise," said the governor; but he recovered quickly and said that he was unable to because he had not given the commission. And he had another reason which he did not think fit to give in public "for the Court was filled with people." If he accepted Mercer's resignation, he would have to appoint another and he was convinced that no one would accept. The comedy was thus played to the end, but it left Governor Fauquier in a gloomy mood. "The flame is spread through all the continent," he wrote, "and one colony supports another in their disobedience to superior powers." [53]

The people of the American colonies defeated the Stamp Act before it went into effect by mass meetings and riots entirely outside the law. While they were doing so, some of the colonial legislatures were preparing to make a united protest. As early as May 1764 the Boston town meeting suggested such united action and Governor Bernard had at once scented a plot "to lay a foundation for connecting the demagogues of the several

---

[53] Fauquier to BT, 2 Oct., 3 Nov., C.O. 5/1331; *Supplement Extraordinary to the Virginia Gazette for October 25, 1765*, under "Williamsburg, October 31."

governments in America to join together in opposition to all orders from Great Britain which don't square with their notions of the rights of the people." [54] Nothing came of the suggestion although various committees of correspondence were established. Then in June 1765 the Massachusetts House of Representatives formally proposed a congress. Bernard could not block the move but took credit for the appointment of Timothy Ruggles and Oliver Partridge to accompany James Otis to the meeting in New York in October.[55] When the Massachusetts delegates got to New York, they paid a call on old Governor Colden, who made no effort to hide his opinions of the congress. He "received them very coldly and told them that the meeting . . . was very unconstitutional, unprecedented, and unlawful, and that he should give them no kind of countenance or encouragement." [56]

Colden did not convene his legislature, so the New York legislative committee of correspondence simply nominated itself to attend. The New Hampshire legislature pleaded business of its own as a reason for not sending delegates. The governors of Virginia, North Carolina, and Georgia refused to summon their assemblies, in an effort to prevent action, but this kind of opposition did not stop the legislators in New Jersey and Delaware, who met informally and elected delegates.[57]

The twenty-seven delegates from nine colonies, who met in New York on 7 October 1765, were on the whole a conservative lot except for a few like Christopher Gadsden; while James Otis impressed one New Yorker as being "not riotous at all." The congress demonstrated its respectability by electing the conservative Timothy Ruggles of Massachusetts chairman. It then proceeded to debate until 19 October, when it adopted a declaration of rights and a statement of grievances. The congress adjourned on 24 October after adopting an address to the king, a memorial and petition to the House of Lords, and a petition to the House of Commons.

The declaration contained nothing new and was far more moderate than the petitions and resolutions that had been adopted by some of the colonial legislatures, by town and county meetings, by mass meetings of no legal standing, not to mention the resounding, if anonymous, proclamations in the newspapers. The declaration started with an acknowledgment of "allegiance" to the Crown and "all due subordination" to Parliament. It stated that the colonists were entitled to the "inherent rights and liberties" of the king's natural-born subjects in Great Britain, and that it was essen-

---

[54] To BT, 29 June 1764, C.O. 5/891.   [55] To BT, 8 July, C.O. 5/891.
[56] BEP, 14 Oct.   [57] Morgan, *Stamp Act Crisis*, 103.

tial to the freedom of a people and the undoubted right of Englishmen "that no taxes should be imposed on them, but with their own consent, given personally, or by their representatives." One thing the declaration did put an end to: the idea of colonial representation in Parliament. It stated "that the people of these colonies are not, and from their local circumstances, cannot be represented in the House of Commons in Great Britain." The only representatives of the people of the colonies are those chosen by themselves and "no taxes ever have been, or can be constitutionally imposed on them, but by their respective legislature." And since supplies to the Crown were free gifts of the people, it was unreasonable and inconsistent with the principles and spirit of the British constitution for the people of Great Britain to vote taxes on the American colonies.

The remainder of the declaration dealt with specific things. The right of trial by jury was an "inherent and invaluable" right of the colonists; the Stamp Act by imposing taxes, and the extension of the jurisdiction of the admiralty courts in that and other acts, had a "tendency to subvert the rights and liberties of the colonists." The duties on trade were a burden and the scarcity of specie made payment impossible. The profits of colonial trade centering in Britain contributed "very largely" to revenues there; the restrictions on trade would make it impossible for the colonies to purchase British manufactures. The declaration concluded with a statement that it was the right of colonists to petition the king and both houses of Parliament. In addition, the petitions to the king, Lords, and the Commons asked for repeal of the Stamp Act, limitation of the jurisdiction of the admiralty courts, and repeal of the various acts restricting American commerce.[58]

The declaration and petitions of the Stamp Act Congress were of little practical importance, for they were ignored in England and they did not reflect either opinion or action on the local level in America. The great significance of the Stamp Act Congress was that it was the first official meeting of delegates from colonial legislatures and as such it was a precedent for future action. The day after the Stamp Act Congress adjourned, the "freemen" of Essex county, New Jersey, professed allegiance to George III and the British constitution and then declared the Stamp Act "unconstitutional" and their determination to transmit their liberty and property to their posterity "in as full and ample manner as they received the same from their ancestors." They agreed to "discourage" the execution of the

---

[58] The declarations and petitions are printed in Morgan, *Prologue to Revolution*, 62–69, and the declarations in EHD, IX, 672–73.

act, and concluded by expressing their abhorrence of and contempt for anyone who accepted any office relating to the Stamp Act and "all and every stamp pimp, informer, favorer and encourager of the execution of the said act, and that they would have no communication with any such person, nor speak to them on any occasion, unless it be to inform them of their vileness." [59]

In December the "freemen" of Talbot county, Maryland, copied these resolutions and added some of their own.[60] The same month the "respectable populace" of New London, Connecticut, went much further. They started by resolving "that every form of government rightly founded, originates from the consent of the people," continued with assertions that the people set boundaries in all constitutions, and that when those boundaries are exceeded, "the people have a right to reassume the exercise of that authority which by nature they had before they delegated it to individuals." Taxes imposed upon English subjects without their consent were beyond the bounds of the constitution and the Stamp Act was such a tax. They then declared that it was the duty of every person in the colonies to oppose the execution of such acts, and if they could be relieved in no other way they should "reassume their natural rights and the authority the laws of nature and of God have vested them with." [61]

In the light of such radical statements, including the clear assertion of the right of revolution, it is evident that the Stamp Act Congress did not reflect the feelings of the more extreme Americans whose actions proved that they had no faith in petitions. Before the congress met, mob action had forced most of the stamp officers to resign, and after 1 November, Americans proceeded to nullify the Stamp Act by opening the ports of the colonies and forcing many officials and some of the courts to do business as if Parliament had never acted.

[59] NYM, 7 Nov. 1765.   [60] MdG, 10 Dec.
[61] MG, 19 Dec. 1765; reprinted, EHD, IX, 670–71.

V

The Nullification of the Stamp Act

On the first of November 1765 no stamps could be bought in the mainland colonies. Therefore if the Stamp Act was to be obeyed, actions at law from the supreme to the county courts, the sailing of ships in and out of ports, the borrowing of money and the payment of debts, the buying and selling of land, the printing of newspapers and pamphlets—all must stop. Some Americans were convinced that the law must be obeyed until it could be repealed. Others disagreed, for the resulting stoppage of business would be an acknowledgment of the validity of an act of Parliament. In every colony popular leaders insisted on defiance by continuing all the activities requiring the use of stamps. The question was raised in Boston in August a few days after Andrew Oliver resigned as stamp distributor. It was answered by another "question" from Rhode Island a little later: "What signify all our arguments against the Stamp Act, if we by it, in any instance, are turned out of or stopped in our ordinary way of transacting our affairs." The newspaper that printed the query had already answered it: the *Pennsylvania Gazette* was appearing without stamps.[1]

No group in America was more directly affected than the publishers of the twenty-four newspapers in the mainland colonies. It was fortunate for America, wrote David Ramsay in 1789, that the newspapers were subject to such heavy duties. "Printers," he said, "when uninfluenced by government, have generally arranged themselves on the side of liberty, nor are they less remarkable for attention to the profits of their profession. A stamp duty, which openly invaded the first, and threatened a great diminution of the

[1] BEP, 26 Aug. 1765; PG, 16 Jan. 1766.

last, provoked their united zealous opposition." [2] The sale of newspapers was only a small part of a publisher's business, for he printed and sold pamphlets, legal forms, almanacs, and even books. An important part of his revenue was money from advertising. All these things were taxed. There was a halfpenny duty on every copy of a newspaper or pamphlet published on "half a sheet" of paper, with higher rates for larger sizes. Every single newspaper advertisement had to pay a tax of two shillings. Since the stamps had to be paid for in sterling money, the pocketbook nerve of every publisher in America began to throb long before 1 November.

The publishers made various choices on the "fatal day." Some were like the publisher of the *Virginia Gazette,* who stopped his paper; he died shortly thereafter, but the *Gazette* reappeared early in March 1766 with an explanation by his successor that he was tired of doing no business for four months. William Bradford of the *Pennsylvania Journal* brought out an issue on 31 October bordered in black, with skulls, crossbones, and a coffin for decoration. What amounted to a headline read: "Expiring: In Hopes of Resurrection to Life Again." He explained that because of "the fatal tomorrow" he was stopping publication to "deliberate whether any method can be found to elude the chains forged for us, and escape the insupportable slavery. . . ." Meanwhile, he hoped that subscribers in arrears would pay their bills so that he could live. The issue concluded with the representation of a black coffin, followed by the lines: "The Last Remains of the Pennsylvania Journal, which departed this life, the 31st of October 1765, of a Stamp in her Vitals, Aged 23 Years." But the *Journal* did not die. Bradford issued his paper as usual, merely dropping his name as publisher until 19 December.

Many other publishers likewise defied the law. The Boston papers appeared regularly, either changing their names slightly or omitting the publishers' names. On 4 November the *New York Mercury* came out with "No Stamped Paper to be had" in place of its usual masthead. In October the *Maryland Gazette* appeared with the heading: "Expiring in uncertain Hopes of a Resurrection to Life Again." On 10 December the editor printed an issue as "An Apparition of the late Maryland Gazette, which is not Dead, but only Sleepeth." Surviving this bold venture, he took courage, and by February the paper was appearing as usual. [3]

The newspapers played a tremendous role in political life from the Stamp Act onward. Publishers from New Hampshire to Georgia exchanged

[2] David Ramsay, *The History of the American Revolution* (2 vols., Philadelphia, 1789), I, 61–62.
[3] See Arthur M. Schlesinger, Sr., "The Colonial Newspapers and the Stamp Act," NEQ, VIII (1935). Peter Timothy suspended publication of the *South Carolina*

papers and reprinted so liberally from one another that the readers of the
Virginia Gazette could often find out more about events in Boston than
they could about the affairs of their own colony. Some of the publishers
took part directly in the popular politics of the times. William Bradford of
the *Pennsylvania Journal* was an ardent Son of Liberty. John Holt of the
New York Gazette, or Weekly Post-Boy supported and was supported by
the Sons of Liberty. Benjamin Edes and John Gill, of the *Boston Gazette*,
were in the thick of popular politics, and Edes was a member of the inner
ring that directed mob actions in Boston.

The newspapers, far more than most pamphlets, appealed to the mass of
the people, stirred their emotions, and urged them to action. The newspapers expounded political ideas in language that made most pamphlets
and formal legislative resolutions look stuffy, indeed. Not until Thomas
Paine's *Common Sense* did a pamphlet appear with the popular appeal
many newspapers had had for a decade. Repeated suggestions by conservative Americans and British officials that publishers be tried for libel, if not
treason, were rejected, for no official body dared take any action which
might bring on a riot.

At the same time, mobs saw to it that "freedom of the press" was maintained when conservative-minded publishers got out of line or rejected
material that popular leaders wanted printed. The editors on the popular
side were triumphant over the defeat of the Stamp Act and became more
daring as time went on. It was with pardonable pride that the *New York
Journal* printed a poem in 1770 called "The Newspaper." It began:

> 'Tis truth (with deference to the college)
> Newspapers are the spring of knowledge,
> The general source throughout the nation,
> Of every modern conversation.
> What would this mighty people do,
> If there, alas! were nothing new.

and ended with the lines:

> Our services you can't express,
> The good we do you hardly guess;
> There's not a want of human kind,
> But we a remedy can find.[4]

Gazette for the duration of the Stamp Act but William Crouch began publishing
his *South Carolina Gazette and Country Journal* [SCG(C)] on 17 December 1765.
[4] NYJ, 19 April 1770. For an account of the role of the newspapers, see Arthur M.

ह≫

The merchants, like the publishers, resented the Stamp Act, and they too were divided as to what to do. In most colonies, merchants sent out as many ships as possible before 1 November. When they returned, the merchants pled the lack of stamps to escape the penalties. The ardor of zealous customs officers began to cool long before such ships came back and the threat of mob action encouraged them to ignore the letter of the law. After 1 November, some merchants wanted to carry on business; others felt they must not disobey the law. Most of them were also worried about the growing demand for home manufactures and the non-consumption of British goods. The importers and sellers of such goods were not interested in domestic manufactures, and even less so in non-consumption, however patriotic it might be.[5]

Merchants, however, could see some point in putting economic pressure on Britain by adopting temporary non-importation agreements, which also had the advantage of heading off talk of non-consumption. The New York merchants took the lead. On 31 October two hundred of them met and agreed that all orders for British goods would be accompanied by instructions to cancel the orders if the Stamp Act were not repealed, and they agreed that all previous orders should be cancelled as well. The merchants also declared that they would not sell commission goods shipped from Britain after 1 January 1766. To back up, and at the same time to put pressure on the importers, the retailers of the city signed an agreement not to buy goods shipped from Britain after 1 January 1766. The merchants of Albany soon adopted an agreement like that of New York.[6]

The news spread to Philadelphia, where on 7 November the merchants agreed to non-importation, and even had cancellation forms printed. They allowed certain exceptions such as bulky articles and dyestuffs and utensils for manufactures. They agreed to meet again on 1 May 1766 to see if continuance was necessary.[7] The Boston merchants were reluctant to follow, but after attacks on them in the popular party newspaper, and threats of non-consumption agreements, they adopted an agreement on 9 December,

Schlesinger, Sr., *Prelude to Independence: The Newspaper War on Britain, 1764–1776* (New York, 1958).
[5] From July to December 1765 the newspapers carried accounts of proposals for home manufactures and non-consumption of British goods.
[6] NYM, 28 Oct., 7 Nov. 1765; *New York Post-Boy*, 31 Oct., 7 Nov.; NM, 3 Feb. 1766.
[7] PG, 7, 14 Nov.; "The Papers of Charles Thomson," New-York Historical Society *Collections* [NYHSC] (1878), 6–7.

and Salem, Marblehead, Newburyport, and Plymouth followed soon after.[8]

With the adoption of non-importation agreements, many merchants had gone as far as they cared to go, for they felt it was too risky to defy the law. But the popular leaders wanted to go further. Wealthy merchants could survive a period of hardship far more easily than dock workers, sailors, and artisans. Furthermore, the popular leaders charged that the merchants were taking the opportunity to raise prices of scarce goods and to get rid of others that were difficult to sell. The popular leaders therefore demanded that the ports be opened in defiance of the law, and it was easy to gain the support of the poor and the unemployed to back up their demands, as was done in New York.

That city had escaped violence during the summer because of the hurried resignation of the New York stamp distributor, but literary violence increased. Songs, satires, and essays stirred the populace to action against the day when the stamps would arrive, and pointed the way to independence. If the welfare of the mother country required the sacrifice of the natural rights of the colonies, said one writer in June, "then the connection between them OUGHT TO CEASE; and sooner or later, must inevitably cease. . . ."[9] Early in September Holt's *Gazette* reprinted the tale that on "the 7th of February 1765, died of a cruel stamp on her vitals, Lady North American Liberty. She was descended from the ancient and honorable family of the Bulls." Her father, John Bull, married her to a gentleman called Toleration and gave her a large tract of land named North America. With it she received the promise that she and her children should enjoy all the liberties and immunities of the natural-born subjects of John Bull. Now she is dead but she has left a son whom she "prophetically named Independence and on him the hopes of all her disconsolate servants are placed for relief under their afflictions, when he shall come of age."[10]

On 21 September the only issue of *The Constitutional Courant* appeared on the streets of New York. On it was the snake device with the motto "Join or Die" which had been used by several newspapers prior to the Albany Congress in 1754. It was "Printed by ANDREW MARVEL, at the Sign of *the Bribe refused, on Constitution Hill, North-America.*" The two articles it contained were such violent attacks on the Stamp Act and its American abettors that the New York printers, discreetly, had re-

[8] BG, 25 Nov., 16 Dec.; *Boston Post-Boy*, 9, 16, 23 Dec.
[9] "Freeman," NYG, 6 June.   [10] Ibid. 5 Sept. Also in BEP, 19 Aug.; GG, 31 Oct.

fused to publish them. The paper was printed secretly in New Jersey, brought to New York, and sold on the streets by hawkers; it was slipped secretly into the bags of post-riders and carried to other colonies, where it was republished. The supporters of the Stamp Act were denounced as "a set of mushroom patriots," and "dastards." In denying the authority of Parliament, Americans can offend no one "but a set of the blackest villains . . . With them liberty is always treason, and an advocate of the people's rights, a sower of sedition." The choicest epithets were reserved for the stamp distributors who had not yet resigned: "Ye blots and stains on America! Ye vipers of human kind! Your names shall be blasted with infamy, the public execration shall pursue you while living, and your memories shall rot, when death has disabled you from propagating vassalage and misery any further: your crimes shall haunt you like spectres. . . ." As for native Americans who supported the Stamp Act, to call them parricides was not enough. "Parricides! 'tis too soft a term. Murder your fathers, rip up the bowels of your mothers, dash the infants you have begotten against the stones and be blameless; but enslave your country! entail vassalage, that worst of all human miseries, that sum of all wretchedness on millions! This, this is guilt, this calls for heaven's fiercest vengeance."

This rousing "call to arms" shocked men like Governor Colden, who soon learned how the mails had been used to spread the paper, but in the end he ignored it for fear of raising a mob if he tried to investigate.[11] Alarmed as some of the gentry were, they did not try to stop a mass meeting in mid-October, called by a newspaper notice to all who were friends of liberty and "not already slaves." When a ship carrying the stamps arrived from England on 23 October, it was greeted by a mob of two thousand. Governor Colden was determined to enforce the act. The stamps were put in the fort and its defenses strengthened, while tension grew day after day. On 31 October people appeared on the streets in mourning, and even the backgammon and dice boxes in the merchants' coffee houses were draped in black. That night three mobs went through the streets shouting "Liberty," breaking lamps and windows, and threatening to bury alive the commander of the fort, Major Thomas James.

The old governor was determined to defend the stamps. The next night the riot lasted until four in the morning. The mob took the governor's car-

[11] Colden to SS, 12 Oct., NYCD, VII, 767. The *Courant* was distributed as far away as Charleston. SCG(C), 11 Feb. 1766. It is reprinted in Albert Matthews, "The Snake Devices, 1754–1776, and the Constitutional Courant, 1765," CSMP, XI, (1906–7), 422–32.

riage and paraded it through the city. Then his effigy and that of the devil were hung on a gallows. Finally, effigies, gallows, and coach were taken and burned under the very muzzles of the guns of the fort, while the mob dared the soldiers to fire. No one gave the order, for the mob was ready and able to break in. Next, the *New York Mercury* reported, "the whole body proceeded with the greatest decency and good order" to the house of Major James. There they smashed the windows, tore down the shutters, broke down partitions, stole the silver, furniture, clothes, and books, and made away with more than nine casks of wine. And then, still unwearied, some of the mob wound up the night with a raid on the bawdy houses of the city.[12]

The next day Colden gave in. He announced that he would wait until the arrival of the new governor, Sir Henry Moore, who was expected at any moment. But the stamps were still in the fort and the mob demanded that they be burned. By 4 November there were rumors that armed men were coming from Connecticut to plunder the city. Colden tried to put the stamps on board a warship in the harbor but the commander refused to take them. Desperate consultations took place among the now frightened merchants of the city, Colden, General Gage, the mayor, and the council. The fifth of November was "Pope's Day" and they feared that the mob would break into the fort and burn the stamps as well as "the Pope." Colden at last delivered the stamps to the mayor and corporation of the city, breathing defiance to the last and declaring that he would not then have done so except "to prevent an effusion of blood and the calamities of a civil war. . . ." The next day Captain Montresor recorded in his journal, "Perfect tranquility," but that everyone blamed the lawyers as "hornets and firebrands of the Constitution. The planners and incendiaries of the present rupture." [13]

"Tranquility" did not last long. Many prominent men who had encouraged the mob were now frightened by their creation, and the mob was taken over by far more radical leaders who demanded that the port be opened. They called a great mass meeting at the end of November to instruct the city's delegates in the legislature. Large numbers of people, said the *New York Mercury*, felt that "the discontinuance of business itself, is a sort of admittance of the legality of the Stamp Act, and has a tendency to enforce it. . . ." They also had reason to believe that the "secret enemies

[12] NYM, 4 Nov.; "Journals of Capt. John Montresor," NYHSC (1881), 336–38. Montresor was an engineer in the British Army whose journal gives a remarkable picture of the times.
[13] Montresor, ibid. 339; Becker, *New York*, chapter II.

of liberty" hoped that "the necessities to which the people will be reduced by the cessation of business" would put the act into effect. "The great design of the late meeting, therefore, was to put business in motion again in the usual channels without stamps."

Handbills were put up throughout the city inviting everyone "of all ages, ranks, and conditions" to attend. The handbills were torn down repeatedly but the meeting could not be stopped. The alarmed conservatives, including some of the former leaders of the Sons of Liberty, then captured control of the meeting. They named their own men to draft an address which ignored the reason for calling the meeting: "it was defective in the grand point, it contained nothing to remove the present obstructions to business. . . ." The "real promoters" of the meeting had been caught off guard but they could still argue their case in the newspapers. Within a few days their own proposed instructions were in print. These declared the Stamp Act to be "the most open and violent attack that was ever made upon the rights of a free people" and demanded that the legislature take positive action "to prevent the Stamp Act from taking place in this government" by "giving a legislative sanction to the transacting business as usual without stamps." [14] The legislature, although thoroughly alarmed at the popular uproar, refused to do anything, and the New Yorkers had to wait until other colonies had opened their ports before New York's ships defied the law.

Virginia carried on trade without stamps from the beginning. Peter Randolph, the surveyor general of customs in the southern district, lived in Virginia. He advised the collectors to clear ships by giving them certificates stating that no stamps were available. He did this on 2 November and five days later Governor Fauquier approved.[15] The Rhode Islanders did likewise. They had been blasting away at the Stamp Act in newspapers and handbills ever since the Newport riots in August. In October a meeting in Newport voted that if the customs officials would not clear ships without stamps they would be driven out of town, and that if any merchant used stamps, he would meet with "our highest displeasure." A handbill posted on the Long Wharf said that if the stamp distributor should violate his oath "and send for the accursed stamp papers, and now bid you kiss his a–s," he should not be allowed to live. Do not let the commander of the ship of war in the harbor scare you, exhorted the handbill. "Indeed fear nothing but slavery, love your liberty, and fight for it like men who know the value of it." [16] The governor in effect backed up such threats by refusing to take

14 NYM, 2 Dec.   15 Morgan, *Stamp Act Crisis*, 159–60.   16 NM, 21 Oct.

the oath to enforce the Stamp Act, and in September the assembly supported him by passing a series of resolves against the Stamp Act far stronger than those of any other legislature. The Stamp Act was unconstitutional, Rhode Islanders did not have to obey it, and officials of the colony should do business without regard to it.[17] Meanwhile stamps arrived in Newport and Augustus Johnson, despite his resignation as distributor, stored them on the British naval vessel *Cygnet*. After 1 November the harbor rapidly filled with vessels and the threats against Collector John Robinson became so great that by the end of the month he was clearing vessels without stamps.[18]

In Massachusetts the effort to defy the Stamp Act was as usual complicated by the political fight. In September the Boston town meeting declared the Stamp Act unconstitutional and instructed its delegates in the legislature to follow a policy of passive resistance by refusing to join in measures to put the act into effect. It also took one of the most significant steps in the history of the times when it elected Samuel Adams to the legislature to replace Oxenbridge Thacher, who had died in July.[19]

When the legislature met on 25 September, Governor Bernard told it that "submission" to the Stamp Act was the only way to secure its repeal. By a narrow majority of one the house opposed submission, and the alarmed governor promptly adjourned the legislature to 23 October, saying that the county courts were in session and that many representatives could not attend until then. This was true enough, but the real point was that many of the absent assemblymen were supporters of the "government" party and Bernard wanted them on hand. Infuriated by the adjournment, the popular leaders of Boston stepped up their campaign. The *Boston Gazette* declared the Stamp Act unconstitutional and predicted the creation of a British civil list to make officials independent of the people and the taxation of American lands by Parliament if the Stamp Act were successful.[20] The country towns were asked to join Boston in instructing their delegates in opposition and some of them did so, notably Braintree.[21] John Adams claimed many years later that the instructions he drafted for Braintree were adopted by at least forty towns and that even Samuel

---

[17] RICR, VI, 451–52.   [18] Morgan, *Stamp Act Crisis*, 149–51.
[19] BTR, XVI, 152, 155–58.
[20] BG, 30 Sept., 7 Oct.; Bernard to BT, 28 Sept., BP, IV, 164–65.
[21] BEP, supplement, 28 Oct., for praise of Braintree and denunciation of Medford which adopted "loyal" resolves. Marblehead instructed its delegates not to submit to the Stamp Act but its criticism of "evil-minded people" in Boston for the riots in August caused some anguish in the capital. See BG, 14, 21 Oct.

Adams used some of them in the Boston instructions. Governor Bernard certainly regarded all such instructions as "seditious." [22]

In October the House of Representatives flatly rejected Bernard's suggestion of submission, and a few days later denied the right of Parliament to tax the colonies. Bernard said that the resolutions were written by a committee packed by "the Faction" and that they were pulled from the pocket of one of the writers for the *Boston Gazette*, "ready cut and dried." The house and council appointed a joint committee which proposed that all public offices remain open after 1 November. But in the end the legislature was unable to agree. Some thought it would be unwise to declare an act of Parliament illegal, while others feared that if they used the argument that no stamps were available, Bernard might offer them for use. Bernard saved them from their dilemma by proroguing the legislature until January.[23]

Bernard did not solve his own dilemma, for the port filled with ships after 1 November and unemployed sailors were added to the mob that threatened continuously. The frightened customs officers wanted no responsibility for making decisions. They asked John Temple, the surveyor general, what to do. He said that he had no orders from England but that if they did not know the meaning of an act of Parliament they should ask the legal officers of the colony. The customs officials then asked Andrew Oliver for stamped papers but he said that he had not received a commission, and that even if he had, he could not provide stamps. They then asked the governor, who said he had no authority to act, and when they appealed to the attorney general and to the advocate general of the admiralty court, these officers said to ask John Temple.

Comptroller Benjamin Hallowell and Collector William Sheaffe started on the round once more. What would happen to them if they did or did not clear vessels without stamps: would they be legally liable for damages either way? Temple sent them to the law officers, who stated that they might not be liable if they cleared vessels without stamps when none were available. They took this opinion to Temple, who sent them to the governor, who told them to ask the law officers. Round and round they went all through November as the popular demand for opening the ports

[22] *Autobiography*, III, 282–83; Bernard to BT, 17 Oct., C.O. 5/891.
[23] Thomas, *Massachusetts*, 204–14. The House of Representatives also appointed Dennys De Berdt as a special agent to work for repeal. See letter to De Berdt, 7 Nov. 1765, Arthur Lee Papers, I, HUL. Arthur Lee was chosen agent for the Massachusetts House of Representatives in 1770 (as was Benjamin Franklin), hence his papers contain a good deal of Massachusetts material.

became ever more violent. When Oliver got his official commission on 30 November he said he could not provide stamps. The attorney general, when appealed to again, suddenly developed such an attack of rheumatism in his right shoulder that he could not even write, so he refused to answer their questions.[24]

While the officials were passing the buck to one another, the Sons of Liberty were preparing to use force to open the customs house. There were rumors that it would be stormed on the night of 11 December, but the Sons of Liberty were not quite ready. On the 16th the *Boston Gazette* said that all the stamp men in North America had resigned with the sole exception of Andrew Oliver. What did he intend to do? Obviously his resignation in August was not enough. The same issue contained a declaration from Oliver that he would not act, but this did not satisfy the Sons of Liberty. They wrote Oliver demanding that he meet them under the Liberty Tree at twelve o'clock the next day and make a public resignation. "N. B. Provided you comply with the above, you shall be treated with the greatest politeness and humanity. If not——!"

The next morning a handbill invited one and all to attend. Oliver, desperately trying to maintain a little of his dignity, asked to resign at the Town House, but 2000 waiting people "desired he would come up under the Tree." And come he did and read a statement promising never to act in his office or to do anything directly or indirectly to enforce an act "which is so grievous to the people." That afternoon the two distraught customs men, still unable to place responsibility on higher officials, opened the customs house.[25]

Meanwhile the Philadelphia port was opened. The merchants there had adopted the device of getting clearance papers before November first and then had spent the month loading their ships and adding items to their pre-dated clearances. By the end of November the customs officials were openly issuing clearances without stamps, and early in December the surveyor general of the middle district advised officials in New York, New Jersey, Delaware, and Pennsylvania to clear vessels. He explained to them that it was dangerous indeed to have large seaports filling up with unemployed sailors. New York customs officials promptly opened their port when they heard from Philadelphia. They, like the merchants of Philadelphia, were afraid of the threatening mob reinforced by out-of-work sailors. The only person not alarmed was one commander of a British naval vessel in the harbor, who still tried to enforce the law.[26]

[24] Morgan, *Stamp Act Crisis*, 134–39.   [25] BG, 16, 23 Dec.
[26] Morgan, *Stamp Act Crisis*, 160–63.

An eager naval captain was indirectly responsible for opening the ports of North Carolina. In January, Captain Jacob Lobb of the *Viper* seized three ships entering Brunswick without stamped papers. The captain then asked the collector of the port to start a prosecution. Collector William Dry was a cautious man and consulted the attorney general, who told him that he could send the ships to the new admiralty court at Halifax, Nova Scotia, since the court was not open in North Carolina. The news spread and the merchants of Wilmington promptly wrote Dry that if he sent the ships the people of the country would come to town and "we leave you to judge how far our properties or yours may be secure." Three days later the "principal gentlemen, freeholders, and other inhabitants" of several counties met at Wilmington and formed an association. After expressing their loyalty to George III, "whom God preserve," but "preferring death to slavery," they solemnly united "in preventing entirely the operation of the Stamp Act." A thousand strong they marched on Brunswick, told Governor Tryon they meant no violence, and then formed a large circle, in the middle of which they placed Collector Dry and such other customs officials as they could find. The surrounded officials promptly agreed that they would not prosecute the captured vessels and promised not to enforce the Stamp Act. To make sure, the "committee" entered the customs house, seized the papers, and then sailed the vessels up the river to Wilmington.[27]

The port of Charleston was opened more quietly. In October a rousing election campaign was characterized by appeals to reject all "politicians," all narrow-minded and ambitious men, all men of "narrow fortunes," and to vote for those who would defend the constitutional liberties handed down by "our Forefathers." [28] A number of new men did appear in the Commons House as a result, and when the delegates to the Stamp Act Congress returned home in November, the house adopted its resolutions with only one dissenting vote. A dissolution would have been useless, said Governor Bull, for the "opinions so universally entertained on the Continent" had been sent to South Carolina from other colonies as well.[29]

But the governor opposed opening the port, and many great merchants such as Henry Laurens supported him. When Surveyor General Randolph appeared in January and advised that the port be opened as in the other colonies of his district, the Sons of Liberty made much of it. On 30 January a handbill applauding the Sons for past actions and urging them to use force to open the port was put up in the customs house. On the same day

[27] BG, 24 March; MdG, 10 April 1766.   [28] SCG(T), 28 Sept., 5 Oct. 1765.
[29] To BT, 17 Dec., C.O. 5/378.

Caleb Lloyd, the stamp distributor, again promised that he would not act, "voluntarily no doubt," commented Laurens cynically. "Commotions increase every hour," he added,[30] and well they might, for the harbor was filled with ships and more than a thousand sailors were wandering about the town. A few days later Governor Bull gave in and began issuing clearances, accompanied by certificates stating that no stamps were available.[31]

ड़॰

By the first of March 1766 colonial commerce was under way as usual except in Georgia. The qualified clearance papers, accompanied by certificates stating that no stamps were available, were accepted everywhere on the mainland, in the West Indies, and even in Britain itself. Only here and there did an occasional naval captain attempt to enforce the law. But even naval captains had to come in to port occasionally, and they soon lost their fervor. Here and there some vessels appeared with stamped papers and some merchants either used or said they would use stamps. When this happened, enthusiastic mobs took action that kept opposition to the Stamp Act very much alive, and provided a constant source of propaganda for the newspapers.

A captain from Halifax arrived in Philadelphia, reportedly carrying stamped papers. A committee investigated and found that he had a "cover," with three ninepenny stamps on it, wrapped around some letters. The cover was taken to a coffee house "and there publicly burnt." A few days later a piece of stamped parchment in Philadelphia "was purified by fire at the Coffee House in the presence of a full company, who all expressed their satisfaction therewith." [32] In Portsmouth, New Hampshire, when a captain arrived from Barbados carrying a "let-pass," "with the ignominious ensigns of Creole slavery" upon it, the Sons of Liberty "put it to a proper use, that shall serve to show posterity their abhorrence of a people who can tamely submit themselves to the yoke of servitude. . . ." [33] A Son of Liberty in Philadelphia wrote to the New York Sons expressing the "utmost grief and astonishment" that the Sons of New York would allow some of their merchants to send a stamped bond to Philadelphia. The New Yorkers promptly salvaged their honor by burning some stamped bonds and forcing the guilty to confess their sins on the Common.[34] When some stamped paper was discovered in Milford, Connecticut, the citizenry held a trial "without the consent or approbation of the

[30] Laurens to John S. Gervais, 29–31 Jan. 1766, Laurens Letter Book, HSP.
[31] Wallace, *South Carolina*, II, 70–71.   [32] PG, 19, 26 Dec. 1765.
[33] CC, 6 Jan. 1766.   [34] *Virginia Gazette* (Purdie) [VG(P)], 21 March 1766.

Court of Admiralty," found the stamped paper "guilty of slavery and imposition," and sentenced it to burning by the common hangman.[35]

In Virginia, despite the continuation of trade from 1 November onwards, certain merchants were willing to use stamped paper. In March some of them applied to the governor for stamped Mediterranean passes he had received from the admiralty, but they did it "in great secrecy out of fear of drawing the colony on their backs." [36] One merchant, Archibald Ritchie of Hobb's Hole, made so bold as to say publicly at the Richmond county court that he would clear his vessels with stamped paper and that he knew where to get it. "Enraged at the said Ritchie's matchless impudence," a meeting at Leeds Town on 27 February formed an association. After the usual profession of allegiance to George III and a declaration of Virginians' freedom from taxation except by their own consent, the association proclaimed that its signers would do everything they could, "paying no regard to danger or to death," to prevent the execution of the Stamp Act in Virginia. And if "any abandoned wretch shall be so lost to virtue and public good" as to use stamped paper, "we will with the utmost expedition, convince every such profligate that immediate danger and disgrace shall attend their prostitute purpose." The committee also prepared a statement for Ritchie and resolved that if he refused to sign it, "his person should be taken and stripped naked to his waist, tied to the tail of a cart, and drawn to the public pillory, where he should be fixed for one hour. . . ." If he still refused, they would bring him to Leeds Town to decide what further should be done.

The next day 400 men descended on Hobb's Hole, where they drew up in two lines on the main street. The committee found Ritchie, who asked for the appointment of a committee to "reason with him." They told him that the decision had been made and took him into the street. He argued that the terms were too severe, but the mob would have none of it. Hat in hand "and with an audible voice" he read the declaration prepared for him, which began, "sensible now of the high insult I offered this country," and wound up with a profuse statement that he would not use stamps unless they were authorized by the legislature of the colony.[37]

Nullification of the Stamp Act by opening colonial ports was a relatively easy matter because merchants were anxious to continue trade if it was

---

[35] CC, 10 Feb. 1766.   [36] Fauquier to SS, 12 March 1766, C.O. 5/1345.
[37] *Virginia Gazette* (Rind) [VG(R)], 16 May; MdG, 27 March.

safe, customs officials were afraid of mobs, and ordinary workers had no desire to lose their jobs. Opening the courts as a symbol of defiance was a far more complex matter. Courts everywhere stopped business on 1 November and the judges, particularly of the colonial supreme courts, were willing to keep them closed. But the bulk of the legal business of America centered in the county courts and to stop them was a far more drastic matter. Some men thought that the need for them was so great that the people would be forced to yield to the Stamp Act. Some feared anarchy and a complete disruption of society unless they were opened. Debtors in many a colony were happy indeed to have the courts closed, for so long as they were no debts could be collected. Creditors, on the other hand, wanted them open. Lawyers, as might be expected, were of mixed minds. They did not like the Stamp Act, but were hesitant about defying it; they were concerned about the loss of incomes, yet the Stamp Act would hit them badly if it were enforced.

From the start, popular leaders put pressure on the lawyers. Early in December a New York mass meeting sent a committee to see the lawyers of the city and within a few weeks the New York lawyers agreed to carry on.[38] The Philadelphia bar met the same month and likewise agreed to do business. As early as September some New Jersey lawyers met and resolved that they would not use stamps. At the same time they declared that the chief justice of the supreme court should not act as a stamp distributor if the governor appointed him.[39] When the New Jersey lawyers met later at New Brunswick in February 1766, hundreds of Sons of Liberty came too. They asked the lawyers to start doing business immediately and to use their influence to open the courts of the colony. The majority of the lawyers promised to resume business on 1 April and sent two spokesmen to the Sons of Liberty, and in "a solemn manner" promised that the lawyers themselves would join the Sons of Liberty if the Stamp Act were not suspended or repealed.[40]

Resolutions by lawyers might win a certain amount of popular support for their good intentions, but did not force them to practice what they professed, since most courts were not open. The real need was for the county courts to function, and some of them did. In December 1765 the justices of the Frederick county court in Maryland unanimously resolved to do business without stamps. When the clerk of the court refused, fearful of damages to himself, the justices put him in jail for contempt and he soon

[38] NYM, 9, 23 Dec. 1765.   [39] MdG, 10 Oct.
[40] VG(P), 7 March; NM, 3 March 1766.

changed his mind.[41] The Northampton county court in Pennsylvania opened in January and some New Jersey courts followed in February.[42] In Virginia although some leaders did not want to disobey a law of Parliament, they tried to keep a number of the courts open for at least some business.[43] On 11 February the Northampton county justices went the whole way and declared the Stamp Act unconstitutional and voted that the officers of the court could do business without suffering any penalties.[44]

The opening of the county courts in some of the colonies was evidence not only of popular feeling but also of the conservative fear that anarchy would result without them. But the opening of supreme courts was a different matter. Not only would it be difficult, but success would mean conspicuous defiance of Britain that no one could mistake. In Virginia, where the governor and council, as the general court, were the supreme court, nothing happened. Governor Fauquier adjourned the court on 1 November 1765, and he had dissolved the legislature in May 1765 and did not call it to meet again until November 1766. Therefore, no legislative demands could be made upon him. And while Virginians might use mobs to coerce unpopular merchants, none of them were ready to stage a march on Williamsburg, and in the end the Stamp Act was repealed before an issue could arise.

Marylanders had raised the question of doing business without stamps in the fall of 1765,[45] and their ports were open before the end of January 1766. But the supreme court and all other government offices were closed and stayed that way. Late in February a number of "the principal gentlemen" met at Baltimore and organized as the Sons of Liberty. They then asked the counties to send delegates to Annapolis to "oblige the several officers" there to operate without stamps. Hundreds of men appeared and voted to ask the chief justice and other provincial officials to open the court and other offices by 31 March if a majority of the supreme courts in the northern colonies were open by then. The meeting demanded answers in writing but the chief justice and some officials sent verbal replies. This was "deemed a great indignity offered the Sons of Liberty," and once more written answers were demanded. The chief justice replied that what he would do when the court met depended on the opinion that "I have as yet to form." But he promised to consult with his brother justices.

The meeting sent copies of the proceedings to all the counties in Mary-

---

[41] An Apparition of the Maryland Gazette [10? Dec. 1765].
[42] PG, 6 Feb.; Pennsylvania Journal [PJ], 27 Feb. 1766.
[43] Mays, Pendleton, I, 167–71.   [44] VG(P), 21 March.   [45] MdG, 24 Oct.

land and asked their Sons of Liberty to send at least twelve delegates from each county to a meeting at Annapolis on 31 March "to see the event of, or repeat, if necessary, the applications already made." [46] On the appointed day, Sons of Liberty from all over Maryland came to Annapolis, where the supreme court was sitting. A petition to open the court was read to the justices. At first they refused, but when an "immediate compliance was earnestly insisted for, and demanded, by the Sons of Liberty, with united hearts and voices," the court abandoned its reluctance and not only opened for business without stamps but directed the land office and the register's office to open as well. The triumphant Sons then unanimously declared their allegiance to George III, promised to help the civil power of the colony execute all laws passed by the legislature, and the laws and statutes of Britain as well! They resolved also to "suppress all riots, or unlawful assemblies, tending to the disturbance of the public tranquillity. . . ." [47] What the judges thought they discreetly kept to themselves.

As early as January 1766, reports reached other colonies that the chief justice of North Carolina, who had sworn he would use stamps, had been hauled from his bed by the Sons of Liberty and made to swear that he would do all in his power to prevent the Stamp Act from taking effect, and that he would continue to keep his court open. Whether the courts were really open or not is uncertain, for as late as the end of April it was reported in Virginia that the Sons of Liberty were determined to open the courts in North Carolina. [48] It is likely that debtors in North Carolina, as in other colonies, were of two minds about having courts open.

Chief Justice Shinner in South Carolina adjourned his court in November because of the lack of stamps. Shortly after the Charleston port was opened, "the popular clamor began to extend further demanding the courts of justice to proceed in civil causes." Before the chief justice was due to open court for the 1766 term, the lawyers of Charleston petitioned him to do business and declared that they could not be bound by a law which "annihilates our natural as well as constitutional rights." He would have none of it, so the lawyers persuaded Governor Bull to appoint three new associate justices. They joined with the other associate justice in outvoting the chief justice. Then the clerk of the court refused to act, and the associate justices asked the governor to suspend him. At first he refused, but when the Commons House twice demanded it, he agreed. The unofficial news of the repeal of the Stamp Act arrived 3 May and all government

[46] Ibid. 6 March.　　[47] Ibid. 3 April; PG, 10 April.
[48] CC, 6 Jan.; VG(P), 25 April.

offices opened, but the chief justice held out until July, when he was "officially" notified. By then he was the most unpopular man in the colony. The legislature continued the fight against him, and in 1767 a new governor suspended Shinner as ignorant of the law and unfit for his post.[49]

In New England the Rhode Island courts continued to operate without a break, backed by a guarantee of the legislature that it would indemnify all the officers of the colony who ignored the Stamp Act. The New Hampshire supreme court opened in February.[50] The conservative element in Connecticut managed to keep that colony's courts closed, a decision underlaid by a certain satisfaction that many of the debts owing outside the colony could not be collected in the meanwhile.[51]

The popular leaders in Boston were "warm to have the courts open," reported John Adams after a meeting of the Monday Night Club. The day after Oliver resigned a second time and the customs house opened (17 December), the town meeting sent James Otis, Jeremiah Gridley, and John Adams to the governor and council to demand that they open the courts by executive decree. The governor and the council evaded by saying that it was a matter of law and that they would not presume to tell the courts what to do. The town meeting promptly declared the answer unsatisfactory, and James Otis, as "John Hampden," took to the *Gazette* to continue the argument.[52]

The popular leaders then turned on the Suffolk county courts. Thomas Hutchinson was judge of probate and his friends warned him that he would be mobbed if he did not open the court. He took a leave of absence and the governor appointed Foster Hutchinson in his place. The *Boston Gazette* reported gleefully that Foster, unlike his brother, "had no scruples about the matter. . . ."[53] Foster Hutchinson was also one of the judges of the court of common pleas, a job he had acquired from his brother when the latter became lieutenant governor in 1758. Agents of the popular leaders put pressure on the judges and they discreetly opened the court of common pleas on 13 January.

Thomas Hutchinson was made of tougher stuff and as chief justice he was determined to obey a law he privately deplored. Although the superior court was not due to open until March, the popular leaders began a campaign to open all the courts in the colony by legislative action. Meanwhile

---

[49] Bull to BT, 8 May, C.O. 5/378; Wallace, *South Carolina*, II, 71–74.
[50] Morgan, *Stamp Act Crisis*, 176–77.   [51] Gipson, *Ingersoll*, 211–18.
[52] BG, 23, 30 Dec.; BTR, XVI, 158–60; John Adams, *Diary*, 23 Dec. 1765, 4 Jan. 1766.
[53] BG, 23 Dec. 1765; 6 Jan. 1766.

Hutchinson's friends were ever more alarmed for his safety. They told him he must open the court and proceed without stamps, resign as chief justice, or leave the colony. At first he offered to resign, but when he heard the names of men the governor might appoint in his place he refused. The governor and council advised him to leave the colony, but he stayed on to lead the fight in the legislature. He did so knowing full well, as he said, that "the town of Boston *determined* it must be done. That is now the common way of peoples expressing themselves there." [54]

The Boston leaders went to the legislature in mid-January armed with instructions to work for legislation opening the courts and calling for an investigation of the men in the colony "guilty" of furthering the Stamp Act. The house seemed agreeable at first for it began preparing acts to open the courts and to bar judges and other officials from sitting in the council. A few days later it resolved by a vote of 81 to 5 that the courts should be opened. Hutchinson then demonstrated his political finesse by persuading the council to ask the superior court judges for their opinion. The judges then neatly shifted responsibility to the lawyers. They told the council that they might open the courts if the lawyers demanded it. The council then rejected the house resolution.[55]

Once more the Boston leaders had been outwitted by Thomas Hutchinson and they were furious. As "Freeborn Armstrong," Otis blasted away in the *Gazette* at Hutchinson for blocking the house resolution, for his plural office-holding, and for "usurping" the position of president of the council, in which he and the other judges had no right to sit anyway. The governor and Hutchinson urged the council to take action against the printers and to ask the house to discipline Otis, but the council, afraid of mob action, refused to do more than defend Hutchinson in the newspapers.[56]

The Boston leaders had suffered another defeat and they knew it. They suffered a further defeat when the house reversed itself and turned down the bill to bar judges from the council by a ratio of three to one. All the popular leaders achieved in the end was the humiliation of Hutchinson's supporter Timothy Ruggles, who had presided over the Stamp Act Congress but who had refused to sign its petitions. The house censured him for "neglect of duty," and after promising that he could print his defense in the journals, refused to let him do so. The house also cut the salary of Andrew Oliver, secretary of the province. Bernard by this time had had

[54] BTR, XVI, 160–61; Hutchinson to William Cushing, 15 Jan. 1766, William Cushing Papers, Massachusetts Historical Society [MHS].
[55] Thomas, Massachusetts, 246–57.
[56] BG, 27 Jan., 3 Feb.; MG, 30 Jan.; Bernard to BT, 10 March C.O. 5/892.

enough, and on 21 February he adjourned the legislature to meet on 9 April.[57]

Despite his victory, Hutchinson felt that some gesture had to be made to public opinion. On 11 March the superior court met, although Hutchinson himself was absent, and heard a case which had been pending before the Stamp Act. After asking the lawyers present for their approval, the court adjourned until the middle of April, hoping in the meantime to hear of a decision from Parliament about the Stamp Act. Among the lawyers who approved was James Otis, who had been bewailing the sufferings of the people because of the closure of the courts, an approval that clearly indicated that he was more concerned with politics than with public distress.[58]

Another opportunity for political agitation was soon at hand. At the end of March the governor prorogued the legislature from 9 April to 23 April, and Otis at once took to the newspapers, arguing that this action was unconstitutional. He and the other Boston leaders now actually took the extreme step of trying to call a session to meet on 9 April in outright defiance of the governor's power under the charter. Bernard indignantly dissolved the legislature, and only a few men appeared.[59]

Before the May elections the news of the repeal of the Stamp Act reached Boston. The Boston leaders were at last on the brink of success. The spring elections gave them, for the first time, a majority in the House of Representatives. Thomas Hutchinson soon found that he had won a hollow victory in keeping his court closed.

ट~

Most American leaders realized from the beginning that all their resounding statements of constitutional rights would not stop the passage of the Stamp Act or its operation. It could be stopped only by means unknown to the "constitution," and they turned to mob action. To begin with, the "mobs" were encouraged and sometimes even led by the "better sort," sometimes in disguise and sometimes not, although most of the work was done by the "lower sort." This was well understood by the first historian of the Revolution, William Gordon, who wrote that it was a mistake to assume that the riots "were chargeable solely on the dregs of the colonies." In addition to the "rabble," the first mobs at least were made up of "independent freemen and freeholders"; and "merchants, assemblymen, magistrates, etc., united directly or indirectly in the riots, and without their

[57] Thomas, Massachusetts, 259–61.   [58] Ibid. 266–70.   [59] Ibid. 270–73.

influence and instigation the lower class of inhabitants would have been quiet; but great pains were taken to rouse them into action." [60] On the whole, the gentlemen who led or encouraged riots to force the resignation of stamp distributors were willing and even anxious to end violence at that point, but they found that mobs, once started, had a way of getting out of hand. Even more important, popular political leaders soon realized that mobs could be used for purposes of their own which often had nothing to do with opposition to British policies.

The name "Sons of Liberty" was widely used after the report of Barré's speech against the Stamp Act spread through the colonies.[61] At first there was no formal organization and the name was used by various groups, whether the purpose was the passage of resolutions or the tearing down of a house. By the end of 1765, however, the Sons of Liberty were well-organized action groups in several colonies, led by men who were willing to use force to achieve their ends when defeated in the realm of legal political action. In Charleston the organization was a political tool in the hands of Christopher Gadsden. In Philadelphia it was in essence a popular political party. The "principal gentlemen" of Maryland and Virginia usually called themselves "Sons of Liberty," but only occasionally did they do more than pass resolutions. The most important group was in New York City, and it came close to revolutionary action before the repeal of the Stamp Act.[62]

The Boston Sons of Liberty were the controllers rather than members of the mob. The North End and South End mobs had long been a part of Boston life. For years they had met on 5 November to celebrate Guy Fawkes' Day or "Pope's Day" by doing battle with one another. The fight in 1764 was unusually violent. Staves and clubs were used, heads were broken, a five-year-old boy was killed, and the captain of the North End mob was "senseless" for days thereafter. All the efforts of the town officials and the governor, who called out the militia, had failed to stop the brawl. The hero of the occasion was Ebenezer Mackintosh, shoemaker and fireman, and captain of the South End mob. Mackintosh got his start in 1760, at the age of twenty-three, when he became a member of one of the Boston fire companies. In that year Boston had a disastrous fire which revealed

---

[60] William Gordon, *The History of the Rise, Progress, and Establishment of the Independence of the United States of America* (4 vols., London, 1788), I, 199.

[61] Jared Ingersoll's report of Barré's speech, for instance, was printed in the *Georgia Gazette*, 1 Aug. 1765.

[62] Differing interpretations of the Sons of Liberty may be found in Morgan, *Stamp Act Crisis*, chapter XI, and Philip Davidson, *Propaganda and the American Revolution 1763–1783* (Chapel Hill, 1941), chapter IV.

that most of the members of the nine fire companies were too old to leg it to fires as they should, and they were replaced by younger men such as Mackintosh.[63]

Captain Mackintosh, as he was now known, was elected one of Boston's "sealers," or inspectors of leather, in the spring of 1765. In August he led the mob that wrecked houses and forced Oliver's resignation, and the attack on Hutchinson's house. His followers got out of hand in the latter riot and he was arrested for a brief time and then let go. He was both too popular and too dangerous to the men behind the scenes to risk offending him. Governor Bernard noted that during the August riots some of the North End mob joined with the South End and that "it was cried out that there was an union between the North End and South End." [64]

The idea that such a "union" might be useful attracted the popular leaders and they proceeded to bring it about. Ten days before "Pope's Day" in November 1765, two wealthy merchants entertained the leaders of the two mobs, and, wrote Governor Bernard, "reconciled them to one another, for other purposes I fear than burning a Pope." On the first of November this new "force" in Boston politics paraded. Captain Mackintosh, dressed in blue and red, wore a gold-laced hat and gilt gorget on his breast. A rattan cane hung at his wrist and he carried a speaking trumpet so that his commands could be heard. The "officers" under him also wore laced hats and carried wands. This time the members of the mob carried neither sticks nor staves.

On 5 November the now united mobs appeared before the Town House, where the legislature sat, with images of Popes, devils, and stamp men, and "publicly confirmed their union." On such occasions they usually collected money, but this time it "exceeded all expectation; many contributed from affection, much more from fear." The funds were so great that the "captains" invited two hundred to a tavern for a "public entertainment" and a "Union Feast"; not many gentlemen attended, and those who did, later "expressed a kind of shame for it."

The governor felt that he knew what the "union" meant at a time when the militia was refusing to obey him. "You may imagine," he wrote, "that the popular party is greatly elated with this accession of strength founded upon the ruins of the power of government." Some of them talk of this town being forever independent of the king's government; they even talk

[63] George P. Anderson, "Ebenezer Mackintosh: Stamp Act Rioter and Patriot," and "A Note on Ebenezer Mackintosh," CSMP, XXVI (1924–26).
[64] To John Pownall, 26 Nov. 1765, C.O. 5/891.

of turning out the governor himself "as they could do at Rhode Island or Connecticut." [65] And the popular party was in effect a "government," as Hutchinson described it the next spring. It ranged from the mob headed by Mackintosh, "partly legislative, partly executive," which burned effigies and tore down houses, on up through a controlling group of masons and carpenters, to a committee of merchants. For all matters of a general nature, such as opening the courts, the town meeting was the proper place. There "Otis with his mob-high eloquence, prevails in every motion, and the town first determine what is necessary to be done, and then apply either to the governor or council, or resolve that it is necessary the general court correct it; and it would be a very extraordinary resolve indeed that is not carried into execution. . . ." [66]

The steering committee of the mob called itself the Loyal Nine. It consisted of two small merchants, two braziers, a ship captain, a distiller, a painter, a jeweler, and a printer. The printer was Benjamin Edes, one of the two publishers of the *Boston Gazette*, the newspaper of the popular party. The Loyal Nine worked behind the scenes and planned the parades and the riots that Mackintosh led. In time its members called themselves the Sons of Liberty and achieved a kind of respectability by adding men like John Adams to their committees.[67] The mob controlled by the Loyal Nine was thus a part of the political apparatus of the popular party, but since the town meeting provided official backing, the Sons of Liberty, as an organization, never achieved the importance in Boston that it did in New York.

The mass meeting, with no legal standing and no effectiveness except through mob action, was the only means whereby the popular leaders in New York City could exercise any power. As in other colonies, the name Sons of Liberty was first used to describe any gathering, but shortly a secret political organization was formed, and for a time it functioned as the actual, if illegal, government of the city. At first mob action was encouraged by rising young lawyers like William Livingston and John Morin Scott to defeat the operation of the Stamp Act. Having done this, they wanted an end to violence, for their basic allegiance was to the aristocracy. The direction of the mobs therefore fell into the hands of far more radical leaders who could appeal to the mechanics and artisans of the city: men like Alexander McDougall, the son of a milkman; John Lamb, a maker of mathe-

[65] Ibid. For the events of 1 Nov. see BEP, 4 Nov., and for the "Union Feast" see BG, 18 Nov.
[66] Hutchinson to ——, 8 March 1766, Hosmer, *Hutchinson*, 103–4.
[67] Thomas, Massachusetts, 230–33.

matical instruments; Marinus Willet, a cabinetmaker; and Isaac Sears, a small merchant. After 1 November, these new leaders demanded the opening of the port, while the lawyers and merchants were content to wait for action by Parliament.[68] The Sons of Liberty kept up a continuous agitation in the newspapers, for few publishers dared reject their writings. They forced the resignation of the Maryland stamp distributor who had fled to New York, and forced the New York stamp distributor, James McEvers, to resign again, this time in public.[69] They sent emissaries to Philadelphia to aid the people there in putting pressure on John Hughes.

In New York City the mob was on the street night after night in pursuit of supposed supporters of the Stamp Act. It repeatedly demanded the burning of the stamps stored in the city and hanged and burned effigies of George Grenville, and of Admiral Colville, commander of the British navy in American waters. Late in December it polled the householders, asking them whether the stamps should be burned or sent back to England. The next night a mob threatened to burn the house of Captain Kennedy, commander of a naval vessel, who was still seizing vessels without stamps although customs officers were giving clearances.[70]

By the end of December the leaders of the New York Sons of Liberty had far more in mind than local agitation. Their city was the headquarters of General Thomas Gage, commander of the British army in America, and it seemed likely that Britain might eventually use the army to stop rioting in American cities and to enforce the Stamp Act. If Britain did, she had every reason to begin with New York. Therefore the New York Sons prepared to meet force with force. Any hope of success lay in obtaining help from other colonies and on 31 December two agents from New York appeared in New London, Connecticut, with a letter from "King" Isaac Sears, "a noted captain of the mob." The two men reported that New York was likely to be attacked first and asked for the help of the Connecticut Sons of Liberty.[71]

The people of eastern Connecticut were willing. They had sent hundreds of mounted men to force Ingersoll's resignation in September. Continuing to suspect him of readiness to act as stamp distributor, they had

---

[68] On New York see H. B. Dawson, *The Sons of Liberty in New York* (Poughkeepsie, 1859) and Herbert M. Morais, "The Sons of Liberty in New York," in Morris, *Era of the American Revolution.*
[69] NYG, 9 Dec. 1765; PG, 12 Dec. 1765.
[70] Montresor, NYHSC (1881), 26 Nov.–25 Dec., 340–43.
[71] "Narrative," enclosed in letter of Governor Bernard to SS, 19 Jan. 1766, Connecticut Historical Society *Collections* [CHSC], XVIII, 385–86.

recently invaded New Haven and demanded all his correspondence with Britain. He "delivered up with tears," and the letters were taken back to Pomfret in Windham county, where they were read to a large crowd on Christmas Day. The crowd then adopted resolutions to be published in the newspapers. They began with the usual protestations of loyalty to George III, proclaimed that "God and nature brought us into the world free men," denounced the Stamp Act and its abettors, and then turned on Ingersoll. He was, they declared, still plotting to overthrow his native country "by all the ways and means his malice and craft suggests, or his unbridled audacity can attempt. . . ." If he does not stop he will learn "by sad experience all the horrors of falling a defenseless prey into the hands of a free and enraged people; whose bosoms glow with the true spirit of British liberty; and account not their lives dear in the defense of freedom." [72]

Eastern Connecticut was therefore ripe for the proposals of the New York agents. A military alliance was agreed upon whereby hundreds of Connecticut people, fully armed, would come to the support of New York if it were attacked.[73] A copy of the "treaty" was sent to the Boston Sons of Liberty.[74] They circulated it through the colony and promised their support although apparently they did not sign a formal alliance. The *Boston Gazette* obligingly printed reports from New York that military force would be used on the mainland as it had been in Canada and the West Indies.[75] It seemed that rumor might become fact a few weeks later when colonial newspapers began printing excerpts from the circular letter sent by Secretary Conway in October, invariably to "the governor of a neighboring colony." The letter instructed the governors to use persuasion but if that did not halt "the folly and ignorance of some misguided people," the governors were to repel acts of "outrage and violence . . . by such a timely exertion of force, as that occasion may require," and to call on General Gage and Admiral Colville for the means of doing so.[76]

Armed with the promise of help from Connecticut, the New York Sons of Liberty now came out in the open. At a meeting on 7 January 1766 they resolved that they would go to the "last extremity" to prevent the Stamp

---

[72] NM, 23 Dec. 1765; 13 Jan. 1766.
[73] The "treaty" is printed in Gordon, *History*, I, 195–98. For a full account see Roger Champagne, "The Military Association of the Sons of Liberty," *The New-York Historical Society Quarterly* [NYHSQ], XLI (1957).
[74] Gordon, *History*, I, 198–99; Boston Sons of Liberty to John Adams, 5 Feb. 1766, Adams, *Works*, II, 183–84.
[75] BG, 13 Jan. 1766.
[76] For example in the BEP, 3 Feb., and VG(P), 7 March 1766. Conway's circular letter to the colonial governors, 24 Oct. 1765, is in CHSC, XVIII, 362–63.

Act's going into effect; that any person who used stamps would incur their "highest resentment" and be branded with "everlasting infamy"; promised to protect anyone who carried on business without stamps; agreed to attack the private characters of only those men who promoted the Stamp Act; and declared that they would help maintain peace and order in the city. A few weeks later the New York Sons met again, republished their resolves of 7 January, and added a sixth proclaiming the need of a union among the American colonies and offering their help to the neighboring colonies "to repel every attempt that may be made, to subvert or endanger the liberties of America." [77]

Action followed resolution. In February the New York Sons of Liberty appointed a committee of correspondence to write to kindred spirits in other colonies and urge the importance of forming organizations and an intercolonial union of the Sons of Liberty.[78] The Boston leaders sent similar letters throughout New England. The result was new meetings and new resolutions by groups calling themselves Sons of Liberty, and the organization of new groups where none had existed before, all the way from New Hampshire to Georgia. Local groups had local purposes, as we have seen. Lawyers were persuaded to do business, merchants not to use stamps and, as in Maryland, the supreme court of the colony to open.

Newspapers kept up an endless barrage of propaganda against suspected enemies of "the people." Occasionally there were lighter touches such as the story of the lady of Newport who, "though in the bloom of youth, and possessed of virtues and accomplishments really engaging, and sufficient to excite most pleasing expectations of happiness in the married state," declared that she would remain an old maid rather than have the Stamp Act in force in the colonies.[79] Not to be outdone, "several sons and daughters of liberty" in Connecticut, although married, "promised to suspend their usual endeavor to contribute towards the population of North America, till the Stamp Act is suspended or finally repealed." [80]

But most of the propaganda was far more grim, and the idea of armed resistance and intercolonial union spread. Albany, Oyster Bay, and Huntington, New York, agreed with the plans of the New York City Sons of Liberty.[81] County, town, and township meetings in New Jersey promised to come to the help of New York if needed.[82] The Providence and New-

[77] NYM, 24 Feb.   [78] VG(P), 7 March.   [79] NM, 23 Dec. 1765.
[80] Ibid. 20 Jan. 1766, and 14 April, for the Bristol "Daughters of Liberty" who considered rejecting the "addresses" of any males favoring the Stamp Act.
[81] NYM, 10 March; NM, 3 Feb. 1766.
[82] NYM, 14, 21 April, 12 May; NM, 17, 24 March; PG, 27 March, 3 April.

port Sons of Liberty agreed that union was necessary and appointed committees to correspond with other colonies.[83] In Connecticut, after many county meetings and resolutions, a colony-wide convention of the Sons of Liberty met at Hartford. It supported the idea of intercolonial union and then turned itself into a political convention to plan the overthrow of Governor Fitch and his party.[84] In Maryland and Virginia, Sons of Liberty met and promised their support to their "brethren" in other colonies.[85] By April 1766 the New York leaders were planning an intercolonial congress of the Sons of Liberty.[86]

Meanwhile the newspapers, which carried the reports of the growing organization, were filled with accounts of success and exhortations to even greater efforts. In February a rumor spread that Sons of Liberty throughout the continent had agreed on a day to burn all the stamps they could find. In Boston the effigies of Bute and Grenville were hung on a gallows with the devil handing a stamp to Bute and telling him to "force it." Bute said it could not be done but a placard on Grenville's effigy declared, "but we will force it on the Rebels." Eventually the effigies were taken to Boston Neck "attended by a vast multitude of people" and there burned "amidst the loud acclamations of the assembly," which afterward dispersed without riot or disorder.[87] Far to the south the Sons of Liberty in Charleston were reported successful in their ban on the shipment of rice to Georgia, where the people "tamely received the stamps." [88] Newspaper writers urged the Sons of Liberty to continue to demand the opening of government offices. Not until the courts are open "will the cause of Liberty be triumphant, and Tyranny lie gasping at her feet." [89] The Sons of Liberty were praised as the "only guardians and protectors of the rights and liberties of America" and urged to continue their union.[90]

The glowing picture of the Sons of Liberty presented by the newspapers was not accepted by many alarmed Americans who looked upon them as nothing but dangerous, and all too often drunken, mobs. Naturally they kept such opinions to themselves or wrote of them in private letters to friends whom they could trust. There is no doubt that the leaders often

[83] NM, 24, 31 March; BG, 24 March, 14 April. When the Portsmouth, New Hampshire, Sons of Liberty received a letter from the Sons of New York, Connecticut, and Boston, a thousand people gathered and voted support. NM, 3 March.
[84] CC, 3, 10, 24 Feb., 10, 24, 31 March; PG, 13 March, 3 April.
[85] MdG, 20 March; VG(P), 4 April.
[86] New York Committee to the Baltimore Committee, 3 April, Isaac Q. Leake, Memoir of the Life and Times of General John Lamb . . . (Albany, 1850), 19.
[87] BEP, 24 Feb.   [88] VG(P), 4 April.   [89] MdG, 20 Feb.
[90] NM, 17 March.

found the mobs hard to control. In New York, even children paraded at night carrying effigies and candles.[91] Mobs sometimes appeared on the streets in daytime, as upon the occasion when a British naval lieutenant said that John Holt of the *New York Gazette* ought to be sent to England and hanged "for the licentiousness of his paper." For three days mobs paraded the streets, threatening to murder the lieutenant, and order was not restored until General Gage provided the commanders of the naval vessels with extra arms.[92]

The behavior of the mobs in towns like New York and Boston tended to obscure for many Americans and most British the extraordinary effect of the Stamp Act crisis on America. In every sense it was a political "great awakening" which stirred Americans as nothing before in their history. It produced a fundamental clarification of the American conception of the constitutional relationship that should exist between the colonies and Great Britain. It sharpened political divisions that had long existed in some colonies and it led to the development of political parties or "factions" in others. Above all, it stirred thousands of men who had seldom concerned themselves before, to think of politics and to engage in political action, and it provided opportunities for young political leaders to achieve a position that could not have been theirs in a quieter political age. No one summed up better the impact of the Stamp Act on American thought and feeling than the young Massachusetts lawyer John Adams. At the end of 1765 he wrote in his diary:

> The year 1765 has been the most remarkable year of my life. That enormous engine, fabricated by the British Parliament, for battering down all the rights and liberties of America, I mean the Stamp Act, has raised and spread, through the whole continent a spirit that will be recorded to our honor with all future generations. In every colony, from Georgia to New Hampshire inclusively, the stamp distributors and inspectors have been compelled by the unconquerable rage of the people to renounce their offices. Such and so universal has been the resentment of the people, that every man who has dared to speak in favor of the stamps, or to soften the detestation in which they are held, how great soever his abilities and virtues had been esteemed before, or whatever his fortune, connections, and influence had been, has been seen to sink into universal contempt and ignominy.
>
> The people, even to the lowest ranks, have become more attentive

---

[91] Montresor, NYHSC (1881), 349.   [92] Ibid. 353–54; NYM, 24 March.

to their liberties, more inquisitive about them, and more determined to defend them, than they were ever before known or had occasion to be. Innumerable have been the monuments of wit, humor, sense, learning, spirit, patriotism, and heroism, erected in the several colonies, and provinces in the course of this year. Our presses have groaned, our pulpits have thundered, our legislatures have resolved, our towns have voted; the crown officers have everywhere trembled, and all their little tools and creatures been afraid to speak and ashamed to be seen.[93]

[93] *Diary*, 18 Dec. 1765.

VI

The First British Retreat: Repeal of the Stamp Act and Commercial Reform

The news of the fall of the Grenville ministry reached America in September 1765. Joyfully the *Boston Gazette* predicted that the new Rockingham ministry would repeal the Stamp Act, the Revenue Act of 1764, and allow free trade with the foreign West Indies.[1] The Grenville ministry had been falling ever since it took office, and by the spring of 1765 it was almost as unpopular in Britain as in America. Its troubles began almost at once with the Wilkes affair in the spring of 1763. In time John Wilkes became the hero of British and American radicals and the war cry of "Wilkes and Liberty" was to be heard on both sides of the Atlantic. Seldom in history has a man of so dubious a private character been so lionized. Born in 1727, educated at home and abroad, married to a wealthy older woman who took to the courts to defend herself against him, eager participant in the scandalous revels of a group of "monks" at an "abbey," Wilkes entered Parliament in 1757 as a protégé of William Pitt and Lord Temple. In 1762, backed by Lord Temple, Wilkes founded *The North Briton* to carry on the fight against the Bute ministry and its policy of peace with France.[2]

The publication was brilliant, unscrupulous, and enormously effective. It combined glowing defenses of liberty of the press with vicious attacks on such pro-ministerial writers as Dr. Samuel Johnson and the aged William Hogarth, although the latter had the final revenge in his great cartoon of Wilkes "drawn from the life." *The North Briton* implied that the king's

[1] BG, 16 Sept. 1765, supplement.
[2] Horace Bleackley, *Life of John Wilkes* (London, 1917) is a detailed biography and George Nobbe, *The North Briton: A Study in Political Propaganda* (New York, 1939) is a full study of the publication.

mother was the mistress of Lord Bute, and constantly it appealed to popular prejudice against the Scots. It reprinted an essay on Scottish "character"
which said of Scottish women that "pride is bred in their bones and their
flesh naturally abhors cleanliness. . . . To be chained in marriage with
one of them were to be tied to a dead carcass and cast in a stinking ditch."
Above all, *The North Briton* denounced the foreign policy of Bute and the
"betrayal" of England in the treaty of peace with France by "the Scottish
prime-minister of England."

John Wilkes rapidly became one of the most furiously hated and widely
applauded men in Britain, but he managed, amazingly, to avoid serious
trouble until the appearance of "No. 45," which was to be the subject of
endless toasts in America in the years ahead. On 19 April 1763, George III
praised the peace in a speech to Parliament. Four days later *The North
Briton* No. 45 described the speech as "the most abandoned piece of ministerial effrontery ever attempted to be imposed on mankind." It denounced Bute, called the ministers who wrote the speech "the foul dregs of
his power, the tools of corruption and despotism," and lamented that
the king had given the sanction of his name "to the most odious measures,
and to the most unjustifiable public declarations" ever to come from the
throne. The king is the first magistrate of the country but "he is responsible to his people for the due execution of the royal functions . . . equal
with the meanest of his subjects. . . ." His personal character "makes us
easy and happy" but he cannot escape the "general odium" caused by the
"favorite." "The prerogative of the crown is to exert the constitutional
powers entrusted to it in a way, not of blind favor and partiality, but of
wisdom and judgment. This is the spirit of our constitution. The people
too have their prerogative, and I hope, the fine words of Dryden will be
engraved on our hearts, 'Freedom is the English subject's Prerogative.'"

Number 45 was by no means the most scathing issue of *The North
Briton,* but George III had had enough, and the Grenville ministry acted.
Secretary of State Halifax issued a general search warrant, and more than
forty people were arrested before evidence could be obtained against
Wilkes. He was then arrested and put in the Tower of London and his
house ransacked for incriminating papers. His backer, Lord Temple, secured a writ of habeas corpus. Chief Justice Charles Pratt of the court of
common pleas, a friend of William Pitt, released Wilkes on the ground
that a member of the House of Commons was entitled to the privileges of
that body and could not be arrested except for treason, felony, or a breach

of the peace. He was guilty of none of these, said Pratt, and furthermore, general search warrants were illegal.

Wilkes was now a popular hero in London, but the ministry was not done with him. Wilkes promptly issued *The North Briton* in book form and privately printed a few copies of an obscene poem entitled *An Essay on Woman*. Government officers bribed the printer for a copy. The poem was taken up by the House of Lords, for it had been attributed to a bishop. The man who brought the charges against Wilkes was the notoriously immoral Lord Sandwich, new secretary of state in the Grenville ministry and onetime fellow "monk" with Wilkes in the lewd revels at Medmenham Abbey. Sandwich now piously denounced Wilkes, and the Lords unctuously declared *An Essay on Woman* to be a "most scandalous, obscene and impious libel," although it is entirely likely that most of the members thoroughly enjoyed it. On the same day the House of Commons voted that *The North Briton* No. 45 was a "false, scandalous and seditious libel" tending "to excite traitorous insurrections against his Majesty's government," and ordered it burned by the common hangman. The debates in the Commons were violent, and the next day Wilkes fought a duel with a fellow member, was wounded, and shortly thereafter left for Paris. He refused to return, pleading ill health; in January 1764 the House of Commons expelled him. Later on in the same year, when Wilkes did not appear for trial, the Court of King's Bench declared him an outlaw. Four years later he returned, to become the popular hero of London and of America.[3]

Wilkes as a symbol of liberty was almost completely the creation of his opponents, for in assaulting the man, they were attacking, whether they knew it or not, principles of the highest order: the idea that every Englishman's house is his castle, the freedom of the press, the privileges of members of a legislature, and the privilege of voters to elect whom they please. Men concerned with principles, as well as Wilkes's blindest followers, opposed the use of general search warrants, as James Otis had done in Massachusetts in his speech against the writs of assistance in 1761. The expulsion of Wilkes from the House of Commons raised an issue which American legislatures were as sensitive about as many a member of Parliament. The use of general search warrants to attack printers aroused alarm

[3] Bleackley, *Wilkes*, chapters VII–X. *North Briton*, No. 45, is reprinted in D. B. Horn and Mary Ransome, eds., *English Historical Documents, 1714–1783* (London and New York, 1957), X, 252–56. Justice Pratt's opinion is given on pages 256–57.

on both sides of the Atlantic. Despite this, the Grenville ministry brought more than 200 printers into court during 1764 for printing libelous stories. Whatever the justification, such indictments were attacks on "liberty" that helped bring the Grenville ministry into disrepute.

A growing depression added to its unpopularity. Grenville was at first greeted warmly by businessmen who hoped for a "businesslike" administration, but he was soon charged with causing the economic problems of the postwar years, particularly because of the restraints placed on American trade. A cider tax passed during the Bute ministry was so unpopular in the "cider" counties that troops were used to suppress riots. In London itself the mob rioted, defied the government, cheered Wilkes, and all these activities were approved, if not openly supported, by the officials of the city.

Meanwhile George III developed an abiding dislike of Grenville and his colleagues. The Duke of Bedford joined the ministry in the fall of 1763 and that haughty hereditary chieftain was almost openly contemptuous of the young king. George III, who was a highly moral man, despised Lord Sandwich, who came in with the Bedfords. Grenville himself lectured and bored the king to distraction. "When he has wearied me for two hours," said George, "he looks at his watch to see if he may not tire me for one hour more." Supposedly the king got to the point where he "had rather see the devil in my closet than George Grenville."

Grenville irritated the king in big things and small. When the king wanted to buy land near Buckingham Palace, Grenville would not let him have the money. Then in the spring of 1765 George III suffered what was apparently the first of his attacks of insanity. When he recovered he decided that a regency should be established in case of further illness. The ministry convinced him that his mother's name should not be listed among the regents because the House of Commons would reject it, but the opposition proposed her name and the Commons accepted it. George III was outraged at the ministry and at once proposed to get rid of it. In May the silk-weavers of London staged a riot against the Duke of Bedford, who opposed their demand for the exclusion of French silks from England. The mob, carrying black flags, followed the king's coach to the House of Lords, destroyed the coach of the Duke, wounded him, and then attacked his house, which was saved only by calling out troops.[4]

George III again tried to persuade Pitt to form a ministry, as he had

[4] W. E. H. Lecky, A History of England in the Eighteenth Century (2nd ed., 8 vols., London, 1879–90), III, contains a full and still valuable account of the events of this period. See also Charles R. Ritcheson, British Politics and the American Revolution (Norman, Okla., 1954), chapter I.

tried to do in the summer of 1763, but Pitt would not act without his brother-in-law Lord Temple. Temple, who had recently settled his quarrel with his brother George Grenville, would not join Pitt. Grenville and Bedford in their moment of triumph further humiliated the king. Grenville made him promise never to see Lord Bute privately and forced him to dismiss Bute's brother from his Scottish post. Bedford followed it up with a lecture on "unconstitutional" behavior, which so enraged the king that he wrote, "if I had not broken into a profuse sweat I should have been suffocated with indignation." Furious, he wished that he were a "private man that I might with my own arm defend my honor and freedom" against the "wretches." [5]

More determined than ever, George III turned to the Duke of Newcastle and the Old Whigs whom he had sworn he would never have in office again.[6] On 10 July he dismissed George Grenville, who considered himself blameless. In his last interview with the king, who refused to approve of anything the Grenville ministry had done, Grenville insisted that the plan of the new ministry "was a total subversion of every act" of his own, and he pled with the king to maintain the colonial policy of the past two years. He even threatened the king, "as he valued his own safety," not to permit anyone to advise him "to separate or draw the line between his British and American dominions: that his colonies was the richest jewel of his Crown" and "that if any man ventured to defeat the regulations laid down for the colonies, by a slackness in execution, he should look upon him as a criminal and the betrayer of his country." [7]

ε≫

The Old Whigs who took office in July 1765 were a mixed lot. There were a number of old leaders like the Duke of Newcastle, happy to dabble once more in patronage, along with several young men who had little experience and even less support in Parliament. The head of the new ministry was young Lord Rockingham whose large property holdings made him a respectable link between the old leaders and the young men whose motives and methods they distrusted. Rockingham himself was virtually incoherent and reputedly without intellect or knowledge, but he acquired a brilliant young Irishman, Edmund Burke, as private secretary. Another member, Charles Townshend, despised his colleagues. General Conway, who had

5 To Lord Bute, May 1765, *Letters*, 240–41; GP, III, 41; Lecky, *England*, III, 92–93.
6 Lecky, *England*, III, 91–92.
7 George Grenville, "Diary," 10 July 1765, GP, III, 211–17, and Grenville to Robert Nugent, 28 July, Grenville Letter Books, II, HEHL.

lost his army commission because he voted for Wilkes, was a secretary of state but had few qualifications except good intentions. Lord Northington, the chancellor, and Barrington, the secretary at war, were "king's men" and ready to knife their colleagues at a moment's notice. Weak and wobbly from the start, the ministry had few if any principles and no policy except to stay in office.

Such was the ministry that had to face the storm of protest blowing eastward from America. It did not know what to do, but the merchants and manufacturers of England, facing declining exports to and the non-payment of debts from America, felt that they did know. In desperation the Rockingham ministry turned to such men for support, although the elder statesmen among the Old Whigs felt that this was a contemptible move.

Weak and ever tottering to its fall, the Rockingham ministry managed to last for a year and twenty days, in the course of which it achieved some remarkable results. It persuaded the House of Commons to condemn general search warrants; it restored the positions of military officers who had lost rank when they voted against the Grenville ministry on the Wilkes issue; it modified the cider tax and banned the importation of French silks. But its most important measures were the repeal of the Stamp Act and the revision of the Revenue Act of 1764. All these things were done despite the opposition of the Grenvilles, the Bedfords, the followers of Lord Bute, some members of the ministry itself, and the uncertain support of the king. The Rockinghams succeeded only because they had behind them the solid backing of the merchants and manufacturers of England trading with America, and for once the support of the West Indians, who were as much opposed to the Stamp Act as the Americans on the mainland.[8]

By the middle of 1764 English newspapers and magazines were reporting the bad economic effects of the measures of the Grenville ministry and the growing colonial opposition to them. In July 1764 a story from Jamaica declared that the admiral in charge of the navy and the governor, between them, had already stopped importation from Spanish possessions to the amount of at least a million dollars, with which Spaniards would have purchased British manufactures. Jamaica would be depopulated if such a

---

[8] Lucy S. Sutherland, "Edmund Burke and the First Rockingham Ministry," EHR, XLVII (1932) is the best account of the ministry and its problems. See also Lecky, *England*, III, 93–96.

policy were continued![9] In October it was asserted that the mainland colonies would be ruined if the trade with foreign possessions was blocked; from the profits of that trade the colonies paid for British manufactures which in turn would decline.[10] Within a short time it was said that British artisans, hurt by unemployment, were leaving for America to start manufactures there, all because of the policies of the Grenville ministry.[11] In April 1765 the *Gentleman's Magazine* reported that all America was "in a violent agitation" and that the Bostonians were singing in the streets of the fall of Old and the rise of New England. It also summarized a pamphlet attacking the Revenue Act of 1764 and the foolishness of stationing unneeded troops in the colonies in peacetime—a measure which had raised the issue of the right of taxation.

No city in England was more concerned with colonial trade than Bristol, and its newspapers set forth at length the plight of both Bristol and America. In 1763 the merchants of Bristol had given George Grenville a banquet and the keys of the city; by mid-1764 they were damning him and his American policy for the economic depression. Early in 1765 they sent a petition to Parliament which was largely a summary of the economic protests of American merchants: lumber, iron, hemp, and flax, which had been placed on the enumerated articles list in the act of 1764, should be removed and colonial surpluses of these products sent to the foreign West Indies and sold for specie. The cockets for inland and coastwise shipping in America should be abolished and British naval vessels forbidden to stop British ships bound for America within two leagues of shore. The vice-admiralty court at Halifax should be moved, since it was unusable in winter. Additional bounties should be given for those American products that England paid cash for to foreign countries. American timber should be given a bounty when imported into Great Britain and be allowed free export to Ireland and to Europe south of Cape Finisterre.[12]

By August 1765 the news of the American revolt against the Stamp Act had reached Britain and stories of the growing vigor of that revolt followed week by week. The *Gentleman's Magazine* summarized the supposed Virginia resolution which denounced as enemies those who supported the right of any legislature except the House of Burgesses to tax Virginians.[13]

[9] *The Gentleman's Magazine*, July 1764, 337.   [10] Ibid. October, 493.
[11] Ibid. January 1765, 7.
[12] W. R. Savadge, The West Country and the American Mainland Colonies, 1763–1783, with special Reference to the Merchants of Bristol (B. Litt. Thesis, University of Oxford, 1952), passim; Walter E. Minchinton, "The Stamp Act Crisis: Bristol and Virginia," *The Virginia Magazine of History and Biography*, LXXIII (1965).
[13] August 1765, 389.

Like American newspapers, the magazine apparently did not know that the resolve had never been presented to the House of Burgesses. The accounts of riots throughout America were soon printed,[14] while English pamphleteers debated the rightness and wrongness of British policy and of colonial reactions thereto. Americans were charged with seeking independence, with being a republican race, a mixed rabble of Scotch, Irish, foreign vagabonds, and convicts. Others declared that Americans "are not, never were, nor ever will be our slaves." [15] One pamphleteer proclaimed that Americans are "our brethren," freeborn subjects equally entitled to the rights of Britons. The first right of a Briton is that he cannot be tried except by his peers, and the second is that he cannot be taxed except by the parliament in which he is represented.[16]

By the time Parliament met in December 1765, the pamphleteers had set forth most of the arguments that the politicians were to use in their debates, and doubtless the pamphleteers had worked in collaboration with, if not in the pay of, the political leaders. In October the Privy Council had before it the Virginia Stamp Act resolutions and the news of the calling of the Stamp Act Congress. It decided that such matters were of "too high a nature" and that they must be submitted to Parliament. A few days later when the Privy Council received Bernard's accounts of the August riots in Boston, it ordered letters sent to the colonial governors, the admiralty, and the secretary at war, telling them that the military should support the civil power, if necessary, to maintain order in the colonies.[17]

Meanwhile the merchants in England who had supported American protests and demanded "commercial reform" before news of American opposition to the Stamp Act reached Britain, continued to demand reform, and agreed with American contentions as to the unconstitutionality of the Stamp Act. They decried too the economic burden imposed by the Stamp Act, for the stamps had to be bought with scarce specie. By December 1765 the merchants of Bristol were receiving cancellations of orders as a result of the American non-importation agreements. Again they petitioned

---

[14] See *The Gentleman's Magazine*, October 1765, for accounts of the August riots in Boston, and the November issue for events in Philadelphia.
[15] Ibid. Dec., "The Right of Taxing the Americans Considered," 572–73; "The Claims of the Americans impartially represented," 573–74.
[16] Ibid. "The Importance of the Colonies of North America . . . ," 569–72. For a discussion of public opinion see Dora M. Clark, *British Opinion and the American Revolution* (New Haven, 1930), chapter II, and Fred J. Hinkhouse, *The Preliminaries of the American Revolution as Seen in the English Press, 1763–1775* (New York, 1926), chapter III.
[17] APC:CS, IV, 732–36.

Parliament, telling of the decline of trade with America and denouncing naval officers and customs officials in America. Other towns soon joined in. Liverpool, Lancaster, Halifax, and Leicester sent memorials to the treasury complaining of government interference with American trade.[18]

Such protests were capitalized upon by the Rockingham ministry, which realized that it might stay in power if it could organize the support of British merchants and manufacturers. It was not that the ministers had any ideas of what to do about an America in flames, for they had none. Their first worry was the meeting of Parliament in December. They knew that the king considered them as only a stopgap ministry until he could come to terms with Pitt; they knew too that Grenville and his followers were determined to unseat them; and they could not find out what William Pitt would do or say.

Rockingham and his secretary, Edmund Burke, began meeting with the "American" merchants in London, that is, merchants whose principal trade was with the colonies. These merchants organized a committee of twenty-eight to produce a "national commercial agitation." The chairman, Barlow Trecothick, had spent his early life in Boston, Massachusetts, and his old mother still lived there. The committee wrote all over England and Scotland for help, and similar committees were set up in Bristol, Manchester, Liverpool, and Glasgow. The result was a flood of petitions which poured in on the House of Commons during January 1766.[19] Nothing quite like it had ever happened before, and many of the landed gentry and nobility were shocked at Rockingham's turning to merchants and manufacturers for political support: however useful or rich such men might be, they were hardly of the "gentry."

Before the campaign could produce results, the ministry had to face Parliament on 17 December, and it had no policy. The shadow of William Pitt lay over every thought. Many members, like the two secretaries of state, Conway and Grafton, wanted Pitt in the cabinet. Other members despised him. Pitt himself was at Bath suffering from gout, fulminating against the Duke of Newcastle and writing to his followers that "the country is undone." [20] His followers in turn insisted that only he could save the country.[21] Pitt was in complete agreement with his admirers on this point but was determined to act as a savior only on his own imperious terms. He

---

[18] Savadge, West Country and American Colonies, 209–25.
[19] Sutherland, EHR, XLVII, 60–64; HCJ, XXX, 462–63.
[20] Pitt to Thomas Nuthall, 10 Dec. 1765, W. S. Taylor and J. H. Pringle, eds., *Correspondence of William Pitt, Earl of Chatham* (4 vols., London, 1838–40), II, 345.
[21] Nuthall to Pitt, 14 Dec., ibid. 349.

refused to give any hint of what he really thought; perhaps he did not know. To one admirer he wrote, "whenever my ideas, in their true and *exact* dimensions, reach the public, I shall lay them before the world myself." [22] On receiving an account of the opening of Parliament from Shelburne he declared that "the legislative and executive authority over America" must be upheld, but that "the ruinous side of the dilemma to which we are brought is, the making good by force there, preposterous and infatuated errors in policy here. . . ." [23]

No one, friend or enemy, knew where Pitt stood. But George Grenville's position was clear, and had been ever since his last audience with the king in July. He believed that his policies must be maintained; that the disturbances in America were serious; and that if the colonies were to be independent of the mother country, the sooner the issue was settled the better. He denounced ministerial propaganda that he had interfered with the trade to Spanish America, but said that if he were in office, smuggling would be stopped. He warned his followers to be in Parliament when it met in December in order to "prevent the surprise that is intended." He even knew the contents of the king's speech and the proposed reply before Parliament met.[24]

The hapless Rockinghams had written the understatement of the year for the king's speech: "matters of importance have lately occurred in some of my colonies in America," which Parliament should consider after the holidays. The Commons merely promised to attend "to those important occurrences in America. . . ." Grenville leaped to the attack. He proposed that the Commons should "express our just resentment and indignation at the outrageous tumults and insurrections which have been excited and carried on in North America, and at the resistance given by open and rebellious force" to the execution of the laws, and should promise to do everything necessary "for preserving and securing the legal dependence of the colonies upon this their mother country; for enforcing their due obedience to the laws; for maintaining the dignity of the Crown, and asserting the indubitable and fundamental rights of the legislature of Great Britain." [25]

[22] Pitt to George Cooke, 7 Dec., ibid. 343.
[23] To Shelburne, Dec. 1765, ibid. 359. For a sympathetic account of Pitt, see O. A. Sherrard, *Lord Chatham and America* (London, 1958). Sherrard makes a convincing case for the proposition that Pitt, whatever his defects, was a towering statesman compared to such figures as Grenville, Rockingham, and Burke.
[24] Grenville to Whately, 4 Aug., 13 Oct.; to Lord Botetourt, 3 Nov.; to Robert Nugent, 27 Nov., Grenville Letter Books, II, HEHL; Charles Jenkinson to Grenville, 15 Dec., GP, III, 111.
[25] *The Parliamentary History of England* . . . [PH], XVI, 83–90.

Grenville's hope of a knockout blow was foiled, and he withdrew the amendment; but the line he and his followers were to take was clear.

The ministry was still without any idea of what to do when Parliament adjourned on 20 December for the holidays. Debate had revealed that at least two members of it were for enforcing the Stamp Act. During the interval Rockingham failed to get agreement among the ministers. Charles Yorke, attorney general, demanded a declaratory act asserting the unlimited power of Parliament over the colonies. The Duke of Newcastle insisted that commerce was the important thing, a declaratory act useless, and that the Stamp Act should be repealed. Still others wrangled, fearful of Pitt and not knowing what he wanted. Rockingham, with no ideas of his own, was unable to make decisions about anything, while the two secretaries of state could think of nothing except to replace him with Pitt.[26]

When Parliament met again on 14 January the ministry was still policy-less and virtually leaderless. George III hoped that the ministry might last long enough to take care of American affairs, and that afterward he could stand on his own feet.[27] The issue of American policy was taken from the hands of the ministry at once when Pitt and Grenville met in dramatic combat. The occasion was the answer to the king's speech to the reassembled Parliament. One of Grenville's followers, Robert Nugent of Bristol, ignored the wishes of his constituents and began the debate by defending Grenville and his policies. He declared that "the honor and dignity of the kingdom obliged us to compel the execution of the Stamp Act, except the right was acknowledged, and the repeal solicited as a favor." The cost of the Stamp Act to the Americans was nothing compared with the British land tax used to pay the expenses of the British troops in America. He "expatiated on the extreme ingratitude of the colonies" and denounced the ministry for its campaign of petitions from merchants and manufacturing towns. So far as he was concerned, "a pepper-corn, in acknowledgment of the right, was of more value, than millions without."

William Pitt was at last ready to tell what he thought and he did so in one of the greatest speeches of his life, a speech that shines through the dull pages written by two men who heard it. He was not a party man, he said, and he turned on the ministry and denounced it for not earlier informing Parliament of the troubles in America. The characters of the ministers might be "fair" but he had no confidence in them, and he implied

---

[26] Ritcheson, *British Politics*, 50–52.
[27] To Lord Egmont, 11 Jan. 1766, Sir John Fortescue, ed., *The Correspondence of King George the Third* [Geo. III *Corres.*] (6 vols., London, 1927–28), I, 220.

that they were probably taking orders from Lord Bute, that long since worn-out whipping boy of politicians out of power. He also turned his vast scorn on his brother-in-law, George Grenville, and his ministry: "every capital measure they have taken, has been entirely wrong!" He then boasted of his own achievements as a minister of the Crown, of how he had been the first to look for merit in men he appointed to office.

At last he turned on the Stamp Act. When it was passed he had been ill, but if he could have endured to be carried, he would have been laid on the floor of the House of Commons to speak against it. He ridiculed Nugent's talk of honor: there was only one point to discuss and that was the "right" to levy the stamp tax, for if members of Parliament made it a point of honor, "they leave all measures of right and wrong, to follow a delusion that may lead to destruction."

No American had yet equaled the eloquent statement of colonial rights that followed:

> It is my opinion, that this kingdom has no right to lay a tax upon the colonies. At the same time, I assert the authority of this kingdom over the colonies, to be sovereign and supreme, in every circumstance of government and legislation whatsoever. They are the subjects of this kingdom, equally entitled with yourselves to all the natural rights of mankind and the peculiar privileges of Englishmen. Equally bound by its laws, and equally participating of the constitution of this free country. The Americans are the sons, not the bastards, of England!

He then made a distinction as difficult for posterity as for his hearers to understand: "Taxation is no part of the governing or legislative power. The taxes are a voluntary gift and grant of the Commons alone." "But in an American tax, what do we do? We, your Majesty's Commons of Great Britain, give and grant to your Majesty, what? Our own property? No. We give and grant to your Majesty, the property of your Majesty's commons of America. It is an absurdity in terms."

As for the notion that America was "virtually" represented in Parliament, "the idea . . . is the most contemptible idea that ever entered into the head of a man; it does not deserve a serious refutation." "The Commons of America, represented in their several assemblies, have ever been in possession of the exercise of this, their constitutional right, of giving and granting their own money. They would have been slaves if they had not enjoyed it. At the same time, this kingdom, as the supreme governing and legislative power, has always bound the colonies by her laws, by her regulations, and restrictions in trade, in navigation, in manufactures, in everything, except that of taking their money out of their pockets without their consent." Little wonder that "a considerable pause ensued after Mr. Pitt had done speaking," or that Americans ordered statues of him when they read his speech.

George Grenville, angry at Pitt, the ministry, and the Americans, rose to reply. If Pitt's doctrine were confirmed, he said, "a revolution will take place in America." He could not understand the difference between internal and external taxation. "They are the same in effect, and only differ in name. That this kingdom has the sovereign, the supreme legislative power over America, is granted. It cannot be denied; and taxation is a part of that sovereign power." No one denied the right to tax America when he proposed to do so. If America is not bound to yield obedience, "tell me when the Americans were emancipated"? When they want protection they ask for it, and Britain has run into an immense debt to give them that protection. But when they are asked to contribute a small share of the expense, "they renounce your authority, insult your officers, and break out, I might almost say, into open rebellion." The seditious spirit in America owes its birth to factions in the House of Commons itself, and in effect, Americans are told to disobey the law. "Ungrateful people of America!" They have been given bounties, the act of navigation has been relaxed for them. Grenville defended himself against newspaper charges that he was an enemy of the trade with America, and that he had tried to stop the trade with Spanish America that provided the Americans with cash to send remittances to England. All that he ever tried to do was to stop illegal trade. Otherwise he had offered to do everything possible to encourage American commerce.

William Pitt "seeming to rise, the House was so clamorous for Mr. Pitt! Mr. Pitt! that the speaker was obliged to call to order." Pitt declared that he proposed to "combat" Grenville's arguments on every point, whereupon a member cried point of order. Pitt and Grenville had wandered from the subject, which was the answer to the king's speech, and by the rules members could not speak twice on the same subject. But the House of Commons had not heard its greatest orator for a long time and clamored for more; the speaker ruled that Pitt could go on. He went further than before in defending America, and heaped contemptuous scorn on George Grenville. He rejoiced, he said, in American resistance. "Three millions of people, so dead to all the feelings of liberty, as voluntarily to submit to be slaves, would have been fit instruments to make slaves of the rest." He came not, he said, armed with law cases and acts of Parliament and "the

statute-book doubled down in dogs-ears, to defend the cause of liberty. . . ." He would not debate points of law with Grenville, that "diligent" researcher, "but, for the defense of liberty upon a general principle,
upon a constitutional principle, it is a ground on which I stand firm; on
which I dare meet any man." Not since William III had any minister until
George Grenville "thought, or ever dreamed, of robbing the colonies of
their constitutional rights." He boasts of bounties, but are not those for
the benefit of Britain? If Grenville cannot understand the difference between internal and external taxes, Pitt cannot help it. One is for raising a
revenue and the other is for regulating trade.

Grenville wants to know when the colonies were emancipated, "but I
desire to know, when they were made slaves?" As for money, the profit of
the trade with America is two millions a year and that profit carried Britain
through the last war. The great increase in the rents of landed estates in
Britain during the last thirty years is owing to America. "This is the price
that America pays you for her protection. And shall a miserable financier
come with a boast, that he can fetch a peppercorn into the exchequer, to
the loss of millions to the nation!" The regulations of American trade are
wrong. The islands have been favored over the mainland. The right things
are prohibited, the wrong things encouraged; "let not an English minister
become a custom-house officer for Spain, or for any foreign power."

At the end, Pitt at last laid down the program which the ministry had
been unable to formulate for itself. His real opinion, he said, was "that the
Stamp Act be repealed absolutely, totally, and immediately. That the reason for the repeal be assigned, because it was founded on an erroneous
principle. At the same time let the sovereign authority of this country over
the colonies be asserted in as strong terms as can be devised, and be made
to extend to every point of legislation whatsoever. That we may bind their
trade, confine their manufactures, and exercise every power whatsoever, except that of taking their money out of their pockets without their consent." [28] Thus Pitt demanded repeal of the Stamp Act while at the same
time insisting on a sweeping declaration of the absolute authority of Parliament over the colonies.

Secretary Conway made it clear that he agreed with Pitt and thus committed the Rockingham ministry to the repeal of the Stamp Act. But the
ministry did not know if it had the votes, for the followers of Grenville,
Bedford, and Bute were certain to oppose; some members of the ministry
itself were for enforcement; and it was uncertain what the king and his

[28] PH, XVI, 95–108.

"friends" would do. Week by week tempers rose. When one of Pitt's supporters tried to present the petition of the Stamp Act Congress, Pitt went further than ever before in demanding its acceptance. He proclaimed that the Stamp Act had broken the original compact between America and Britain and that the Americans had every right to resist it. Little wonder that he was called a "trumpeter of rebellion" and that some thought he should be put in the Tower of London.[29]

The Commons refused to accept the petition of the Stamp Act Congress, and on 3 February the ministry presented resolutions declaring that Parliament had the power to legislate for the colonies "in all cases whatsoever." Pitt and his followers at once demanded that the words "in all cases whatsoever" be left out because they implied the right of internal taxation. The ministry and the opponents of America united to beat down this proposal, leaving it clear that so far as the majority was concerned Parliament could tax the colonies at any time it chose to do so; and it was so interpreted by the English newspapers.[30]

Four days after the House of Commons agreed on the basis of the Declaratory Act, George Grenville suddenly proposed an address to the king calling for outright enforcement of the Stamp Act. The debate was heated and dramatic. Pitt spoke against the proposal and then enraged Grenville by walking out during his reply. Henry Cruger, Jr., of Bristol, who was lobbying against the Stamp Act, wrote to his father in New York that old General Howard got up and said that if the motion passed, and he were ordered to enforce the Stamp Act, "before he would embrue his hands in the blood of his countrymen who were contending for English liberty he would, if ordered, draw his sword, but would soon after sheathe it in his own body." Grenville had made a blunder: had he moved for an amendment to the Stamp Act it might well have passed and the ministry have fallen. As it was, the amazed ministry won a rousing victory it had neither planned for nor expected. Grenville's motion was rejected, 274–134.[31]

When George III heard the news he at once wrote Rockingham that the "great majority must be reckoned a very favorable appearance for the

---

[29] Conway to the King, 28 Jan., Geo. III *Corres.*, I, 246–47; Sherrard, *Chatham*, 198–99.
[30] W. T. LaPrade, "The Stamp Act in British Politics," AHR, XXXV (1929–30), 752; Conway to the King, 4 Feb., Geo. III *Corres.*, I, 254–55. For an account of the debates from 3 to 22 February, see Lawrence H. Gipson, "The Great Debate in the Committee of the Whole House of Commons on the Stamp Act, 1766, as Reported by Nathaniel Ryder," PMHB, LXXXVI (1962).
[31] Conway to the King, 7 Feb., Geo. III *Corres.*, I, 266–67; Henry Cruger, Jr., to Henry Cruger, Sr., 14 Feb., EHD, IX, 692–94; Sherrard, *Chatham*, 200–1.

repeal of the Stamp Act in that House." The king had made it clear that he preferred that the Stamp Act be amended, but the ministry was committed to repeal. Therefore he had to support repeal or the ministry would fall. George III had no respect for the Rockinghams but his negotiations with Pitt were bogged down and he preferred repeal of the Stamp Act to the awful possibility that George Grenville and the Bedfords might be forced upon him once more. He therefore told Rockingham that while he preferred amendment, he "thought repealing infinitely more eligible than enforcing, which could only tend to widen the breach between this country and America. . . ." [32] A few days later when the Duke of Bedford offered the assistance of his followers in amending the Stamp Act, George III coldly rejected the offer on the ground that he did not think it proper "for the Crown personally to interfere in measures which it has thought proper to refer to the advice of Parliament." [33] George III, however, could not bring himself to order his "friends" to vote for repeal.

Armed with the support of the king, the ministry now turned to the petitions from the merchants and manufacturers of Britain which had been pouring in on the House of Commons for weeks. The ministry had tried to avoid the constitutional issues and principles which Pitt and Grenville debated so hotly, and wanted to justify repeal entirely on economic grounds. Its approach was essentially that of Lord Dartmouth, who said in the House of Lords that "not less than fifty thousand men in this kingdom were ripe at this time for rebellion, for want of work, from the uneasy situation in the colonies. . . ." [34] The petitions before the House all emphasized the decline of trade with America and its consequences, and the ministry turned to them with relief, deciding to call on one representative from each town to explain its petition. There were those of course who thought it quite indecent to call upon "those wretched merchants," but such men were ignored. [35]

The first petition considered was that of the London merchants, and Barlow Trecothick, chairman of their committee, was questioned for three and a half hours. [36] The questions and answers revealed that the merchants knew far more about the realities of trade with America than their questioners, however eminent. Trecothick elaborated the statements in the

[32] The King to Rockingham, 7 Feb.; Memorandum by the King, 10, 11 Feb., Geo. III Corres., I, 268–70.
[33] The King to Duke of York, 18 Feb., ibid. 273.
[34] Will Crowle to [Earl of Huntingdon], 16 Jan., HA 1815, HEHL.
[35] Ritcheson, British Politics, 56.
[36] HCJ, XXX, 462; EHD, IX, 686–88. The London petition was widely printed in American newspapers. See PG, 17 April and VG(P), 25 April 1766.

London petition about the decline of exports to America and the importance of American trade with foreign colonies as a source of gold and silver, and tried to explain to an uncomprehending audience the complex mechanisms of American trade with Africa and the West Indies. He defended American slowness in paying debts and offered figures to show that Americans owed British merchants and manufacturers at least four and a half million sterling. He told the Commons bluntly that the only solution was to repeal the Stamp Act so that normal business could be resumed.

William Reeve of Bristol was clearly not impressed by his questioners, and his answers were short and pointed. He said that trade was totally stagnated because of the Stamp Act, and that he had received 500 letters from Americans declaring that they would not send orders unless the act were repealed. And he would not send any more goods to America until it was done. When someone asked Reeve if opposition to the Stamp Act was not the cause of the stagnation of trade, he replied, "I know the Stamp Act is the grievance." He declared that 300 men had been laid off in one day as a result of cancellation of one of his orders for nails. When asked if he would fill orders from America if he got them, he replied, "Not a single one." Asked whether he would ship goods if his correspondent in America would comply with the act, Reeve said, "No, one swallow does not make a summer." When asked if he would ship goods if Americans generally complied, he said, "No"; and when asked why, replied, "Because my affairs are in my own hands and if the Stamp Act is not repealed I will never ship or lance off goods for America. That is explicit."

The Commons then turned to John Glasford of Glasgow, a tobacco merchant trading to Virginia and Maryland, but his replies were as short as those of Reeve and showed that he too felt that his business was his own affair. When asked about the extent of his trade, all he would reply was "to a considerable extent," and he made the same answer when asked about the amount of money owing him in America. A series of questions about the method of collecting debts in Virginia revealed that the members knew nothing of colonial courts, and Glasford made no effort to enlighten them. He did finally admit that the total amount of debts owed by Virginia and Maryland was large but that the debts could not be collected as matters then stood. He admitted cautiously that the merchants of Glasgow would attempt to lessen the amount of debt if the Stamp Act were repealed.[37]

Grenville and his followers were furious. When Barlow Trecothick said that the Americans would not be content with anything except total re-

[37] The interrogations of Trecothick, Reeve, and Glasford are in EHD, IX, 686–91.

peal, Grenville's party was "inflamed" and called the Americans "insolent rebels." Grenville tried to prove that the debts owed the merchants were not as large as they claimed, and to force the merchants to admit that the Americans would eventually submit to the act.[38] But the merchants stood their ground: the Stamp Act must be repealed or the result would be outright ruin.

One of the last witnesses was Benjamin Franklin. The performance, carefully "stage managed" by agreement between him and the ministry, was a skillful one indeed, with none of the abruptness of the interrogation of the merchants. Furthermore, Franklin's testimony, unlike theirs, soon appeared in print, and every line bore the mark of his facile mind and pen. It was a remarkably able piece of pro-American propaganda which, incidentally, helped Franklin regain some of his popularity in Pennsylvania. Forcefully he defended Americans who, he said, paid heavy taxes, who had supported the last war to the best of their abilities, and who no longer needed British troops to protect them from the Indians. Americans once respected Parliament as the bulwark of their liberties but they had lost much of their respect because of the restrictions on their trade, the prohibition of paper money, and the Stamp Act. Americans would never submit to the Stamp Act unless compelled by an army, but even an army could not force a man to buy stamps if he did not want to. In fact, the use of an army would create a rebellion where none existed.

Franklin followed Pitt's arguments on taxation. Americans, he said, did not object to external taxes or duties levied by Parliament for the regulation of trade, but they would never consent to any internal taxes except those levied by their own representatives. As for the proposed declaratory act, it would not concern them unless Parliament tried to act upon it. The colonial legislatures would never rescind their resolutions against the Stamp Act, and there was no way to make them do so except by force of arms. And even arms would not achieve the result, for "No power, how great soever, can force men to change their opinions."

The questions and answers scattered through the long session skillfully played on Britain's ever lively fear of the growth of colonial manufactures. Franklin told the Commons that there was nothing the Americans could not do without or else make for themselves. They had made surprising progress in the manufacture of cloth, their wool was good, and within three years they would have enough for their needs. Of course it was cheaper to buy cloth in England, but if the Stamp Act were not repealed

[38] Henry Cruger, Jr., to Henry Cruger, Sr., 14 Feb., ibid. 692.

they would make their own. Repeal the Stamp Act and Americans will buy their cloth in England again. The very end of the "examination" was a subtle summation of the inquiry:

> Q. What used to be the pride of the Americans?
> A. To indulge in the fashions and manufactures of Great Britain.
> Q. What is now their pride?
> A. To wear their old clothes over again, till they can make new ones.[39]

Franklin gave his testimony on 13 February and was excused from further attendance.

Eight days later the ministry introduced resolutions calling for the repeal of the Stamp Act. The debate was long and heated, with William Pitt again taking the lead. His first speech lasted two hours and he talked again and again after that. He insisted that the Stamp Act must be repealed because it was illegal, and once more he abused George Grenville and found fault with the ministry. "Heavens, what a fellow is this Pitt!" wrote one who heard him. "I had his bust before; but nothing less than his statue shall content me now." [40] The vote was taken at two o'clock in the morning of 22 February. William Pitt, the fifty-odd merchant members, the twenty "West Indians," and such members as the ministry could control, rolled up a vote of 275 for repeal. The forces of Grenville, Bedford, Bute, some fifty of the king's "friends," and two members of the ministry itself, could muster only a total of 167 against repeal.

At four that morning Pitt wrote to his wife: "Happy, indeed, was the scene of this glorious morning (for at past one we divided), when the sun of liberty shone once more benignly upon a country, too long benighted." [41] An hour later Rockingham reported to George III that "the joy in the lobby of the House of Commons which was full of considerable merchants both of London and from different manufacturing parts of this country, was extreme." [42]

The vote of 22 February was the essential victory, although Grenville and the minority balked every step of the way, as did a minority in the House of Lords. On 24 February the House of Commons agreed on seven resolutions that were to be the basis of three laws and of a circular letter to the colonial governors. The laws were the Declaratory Act, the repeal of the

[39] Franklin, Writings(S), IV, 412–48. The most detailed and sympathetic account of Franklin and the Stamp Act, and of his growth as the most able pro-American propagandist in Britain, is Verner W. Crane, "Benjamin Franklin and the Stamp Act," CSMP, XXXII (1937).
[40] Pitt, Corres., II, 390n.   [41] Ibid. 393.   [42] Geo. III Corres., I, 275.

Stamp Act, and an indemnity act. Four resolutions declared that tumults and insurrections had been carried on in North America in manifest violation of the laws and legislative authority of Britain; that these had been "greatly countenanced and inflamed" by the votes and resolutions of the colonial assemblies, which had a tendency to "destroy the legal and constitutional dependency" of the colonies on the Crown and Parliament of Great Britain; that people in the colonies who had tried to execute acts of Parliament, and who had suffered damage, "ought to have full and ample compensation made to them" by the colonies; and that such people were entitled to and would have the protection of the House of Commons. These four resolutions were sent to the king with the request that the colonial governors be told to lay them before their legislatures.

The Declaratory Act and the repeal of the Stamp Act passed the House of Commons on 4 March, and after the House of Lords wrangled, it too passed them. On 18 March, George III signed both bills. On 6 June he approved the act indemnifying those who had disobeyed the Stamp Act because they were unable to get stamps, and validating all legal documents executed while the Stamp Act was law.[43]

The merchants of Britain felt that the victory was entirely theirs. Henry Cruger, writing to a merchant in Rhode Island, stated their feeling precisely. The repealing act will soon be law, he said. "You'll be informed that the Parliament have settled their *right* of taxing you. When that was done they proceeded to the expediency of repealing the act, which never would have come to pass had it not been for the merchants and manufacturers of England. Trade here was totally stagnated; not one American merchant gave out a single order for goods on purpose to compel all manufacturers to engage with us in petitioning Parliament for a repeal of the Stamp Act, by which thousands were out of employ and in a starving condition." Thus did he describe the methods that had been used, and said he, "I hug myself the Parliament will never trouble America again." [44]

The campaign of the British merchants and manufacturers for repeal of the Stamp Act was merely an interlude in their program of "commercial reform" which began before the Stamp Act became an issue in British politics and which continued after its repeal. The day the repeal resolutions

[43] HCJ, XXX, 602, 626–27, 839, 843–44. The Declaratory Act and the Repeal Act are in EHD, IX, 695–98. The Indemnity Act is in Pickering, XXVII, 273–74.
[44] To Aaron Lopez, 1 March, EHD, IX, 694–95.

were introduced, the House of Commons agreed to continue sitting as a committee on American trade. The Rockingham ministry knew little or nothing about commerce and it had no commercial policy, but its merchant and West Indian backers and the Americans had many complaints.

They all agreed on the need of encouraging the bullion trade with Spanish America, which had been hit hard by the new enforcement policies. For several years Spanish vessels had been coming to the British West Indies, particularly to Jamaica, with gold and silver to purchase slaves, British manufactures, and other goods. According to the Navigation Acts it was strictly illegal for foreign ships to trade in British colonies, and according to Spanish law it was equally illegal to export gold and silver to any place but Spain. But British governors and customs officers had cheerfully connived at so profitable a trade, and merchants on both sides of the Atlantic were convinced that Spanish bullion was an essential part of their commercial prosperity.

The Grenville measures of 1763 and 1764 empowering naval officers to seize foreign ships hovering off the shores of the British colonies threatened to put a stop to this trade. The West Indians and British merchants at once protested, and Grenville had secretly ordered customs officials in Jamaica to permit the entry of Spanish vessels if they did not carry goods. The purpose was to encourage illegal trade while avoiding all public mention of it. Protests continued to pour in and the Rockingham ministry, like the Grenville ministry, thought that orders to customs officers would be enough. But the West Indians said that legislation was needed and they were supported by Newcastle, who went so far as to suggest that the Navigation Acts be broken to the extent that Spanish ships be allowed to carry goods from American ports in order to prevent the decline of woolen exports to America.[45]

The merchants of the northern colonies were particularly concerned over the threepenny duty on molasses in the Revenue Act of 1764 and the new enforcement policies which so hampered their trade with the foreign West Indies, from which they too acquired gold and silver and bills of exchange with which to pay for manufactured goods bought in Britain. Here the Americans and the West Indians were at odds, for the West Indians felt that the traffic between North America and the foreign islands was a threat to their sugar monopoly within the empire. Hence they had secured the Molasses Act of 1733 and the duties on foreign sugar and molasses in the

[45] Frances Armytage, *The Free Port System in the British West Indies* (London, 1953), chapters I, II.

Revenue Act of 1764. The duties were unrealistic in terms of the economic needs of North America, and smuggling was the result, with enough British West Indians conniving to make it possible.

The "American" merchants in Britain supported the complaints of the mainland merchants and demanded repeal of the strict trade regulations of the Grenville ministry and of the duties on foreign molasses. British sugar refiners soon joined the chorus. By 1763 British West Indian sugar was hardly adequate to supply the market within the British Empire, and it was high priced. British sugar refiners, trying to compete with the French in European markets, wanted a cheaper supply of raw sugar and the way to get it, they argued, was to establish free ports in the West Indies. Beginning in 1763, they repeatedly suggested that the newly acquired island of Dominica be made a free port. To it would flow, they hoped, foreign raw sugar; and from it, they promised, foreigners would take away British manufactured goods. They could point to the example of St. Eustatius, where vessels of all nations could buy and sell freely, for the Dutch, where profit was concerned, were never inhibited by such ideas as those underlying the navigation acts.[46]

Such were some of the proposals facing the Rockingham ministry in the spring of 1766 as its supporters clamored for "commercial reform." Its hold on office was uncertain, for although Pitt had once more returned to Bath to nurse his gout, George III continued to dicker with him for the formation of a new ministry. And since the ministers had no real conception of commerce, the merchants and West Indians proceeded to formulate and offer a program.[47]

At first the "American" merchants and the West Indians were able to reach a compromise. At a meeting in March they agreed that the duty on foreign molasses entering the mainland colonies should be reduced to a penny a gallon, but that the prohibition of foreign rum should be continued. They agreed too that foreign sugar, coffee, and cocoa could be brought to the mainland freely if warehoused and re-exported to Britain, where they would also be free of duty if re-exported. But foreign sugar would have to pay a duty of five shillings a hundredweight when imported into the mainland colonies; and if re-exported to Great Britain it would be treated as foreign sugar and required to pay the usual duties.[48]

---

[46] Ibid. 36–38.   [47] Sutherland, EHR, XLVII, 65–69.
[48] Minutes of Meeting of West India and North American Merchants, 10 March 1766, Lillian M. Penson, *The Colonial Agents of the British West Indies* (London, 1924), 284–85. The minutes were printed in the *Boston Gazette*, 12 May, and the *Virginia Gazette*(P), 23 May 1766.

This compromise "treaty" was soon shattered, for other groups in England made further demands. Early in April the merchants and manufacturers of Manchester petitioned for the opening of a free port in the West Indies, where foreign ships could bring cotton and other products used in the manufactures of Britain in general, and of Manchester in particular. A few weeks later the London merchants backed the request with a petition of their own.[49] Then in a few days the sugar refiners of Bristol and London struck a low blow at the West Indian sugar monopoly: they demanded the reduction of the high duties on foreign sugars, declaring that British raw sugar was so high priced that they could not compete with French refiners in the continental sugar market.[50]

The West Indians were furious. They would accept a free port in Jamaica to encourage the Spanish bullion trade but they did not want one in Dominica: the mainland merchants would simply use such a free port to convert foreign sugar into British sugar. And they objected violently to lower duties on foreign sugar.

With their chief supporters at loggerheads, the ministers were in confusion. Some thought they should yield to the merchants; others were afraid of the political power of the West Indians. Inevitably they worried about which side Pitt would take, and well they might, for the great man flip-flopped. At first he sided with the West Indians, and a deputation of London merchants could not make him change his mind. But finding his popularity in London fading fast, he finally came out on the side of the merchants. The beleaguered West Indians at last agreed to another "treaty," in which they won some handsome concessions. The "treaty" was agreed to on 8 May [51] and the next day it was introduced in the House of Commons as a series of resolutions which formed the basis of the Revenue Act of 1766 and of the West India Free Port Act.[52]

The victors in the Revenue Act of 1766 were the British merchants and manufacturers and the West Indians; the forgotten men were the merchants of the mainland colonies. The old seventeenth-century duty on foreign sugar imported into the colonies was repealed. Such sugar was made free of duty if warehoused and re-exported to Britain within a year. If sold in either America or Britain, the sugar must pay the usual duties on foreign sugar. But what hurt the Americans most was that all sugar shipped from the mainland colonies to Britain, whether British or foreign, was labeled

[49] Manchester petition, 8 April; London petition, 21 April, HCJ, XXX, 708, 750.
[50] 24 April, ibid. 759.   [51] Sutherland, EHR, XLVII, 71–72.
[52] HCJ, XXX, 811, 812–13.

"French sugar." Furthermore, British importers of such sugar must pay a duty of threepence a hundredweight on it, even if it was re-exported. Such was not the case with truly foreign sugar if shipped directly from the West Indies to Britain. Not only did this provision attempt to block the Americans from carrying foreign sugar to Britain, it also attempted to prevent them from carrying British sugar as well. Many American merchants took British sugar in payment for supplies sold in the West Indies and some of it they shipped to Britain to pay bills there. They were understandably bitter when this form of remittance was made more expensive if not actually prohibited by the Act of 1766.

The mainland merchants had a small but growing trade with both the foreign and British West Indies in such tropical crops as coffee and pimento, some of which they shipped to Britain. The Revenue Act of 1764 placed coffee and pimento on the list of enumerated articles and levied an export duty on shipment from the colony where grown. Now the export duty was abolished and replaced with an import duty when brought into another British colony. Mainland consumers must pay the tax if they used the articles; the only way to escape the tax was to warehouse and re-export the articles to Britain. Foreign coffee and pimento were also freed of import duties in the colonies if warehoused and re-exported to Britain. Since the mainland merchants seldom carried such products directly from the West Indies to Britain but took them first to their home ports before reshipment, the requirement of warehousing and bonding threatened to eliminate the profits of this small but important trade and to place it entirely in the hands of British merchants.

British cloth manufacturers came off well at the expense of both British and American consumers. Foreign cotton and indigo were freed from all duties if brought to Britain either directly or indirectly. New duties were placed on foreign cloth brought into Britain, and special taxes were levied on it if sold within the country. The duties levied in the Act of 1764 on foreign cloth imported into America were replaced by export duties on shipment from Britain to America.

Finally, instead of freeing Americans from the many restrictions imposed in 1763 and 1764, and to which the British merchants at first loudly objected, the Act of 1766 actually increased them. As in 1764, customs officials in the colonies were again virtually guaranteed against damage suits in the common law courts. But what was new and more serious was the requirement that all ships loading non-enumerated goods in the colonies must now give bond that those goods would not be landed in Europe north of Cape Finisterre except in Britain and in the Spanish ports on the Bay of Biscay. Not only was this a threat to the development of any American trade with northern Europe, it was also an immediate blow at the shipment of flaxseed to Ireland, where the linen industry was largely dependent on seed supplies from America.

Only one of the many complaints of the northern mainland colonies was answered in the Revenue Act of 1766; the duty on molasses was reduced to a penny a gallon. But the act abandoned the pretense that the duty was a regulatory measure, for the tax applied to all molasses, British and foreign.[53] It was frankly a revenue measure, with the money collected set aside for the same purpose as that of the Stamp Act. And it proved to be very successful indeed. In time Americans discovered that their economic victory was won at the price of being taxed by Parliament for the purpose of raising revenue.

Although the Free Port Act that accompanied the Revenue Act of 1766 was designed to encourage the bullion trade, in which the Americans were interested, it had the further purpose of encouraging the importation of foreign sugar into Dominica for the use of British sugar refiners. It was hoped that a free port would increase the sale of British manufactures to the foreign colonies. The mainland merchants were interested in this too, for they peddled manufactured goods throughout the West Indies as well as cargoes of lumber and provisions. The act carefully protected the powerful sugar interests of Jamaica by forbidding entry into Jamaica of foreign sugar and other products competing with crops grown on that island. Foreign vessels could come into Jamaica and take away British products with the exception of enumerated articles, which by law must go to Britain or to other British colonies. As for Dominica, the purpose was to attract foreign sugar and other products, except tobacco, to that island. Once there, they must be shipped directly to Great Britain and nowhere else. The British West Indies were further protected because every product shipped from Dominica to Britain, except the rum and sugar produced on the island, was labeled foreign.[54]

The act never worked as intended. Great quantities of French sugar did not flow to Britain, and the Spanish government tried to stop its merchants from exporting bullion, now that Britain openly acknowledged the existence of the traffic. The mainland merchants continued to trade as be-

---

[53] The Revenue Act of 1766 is in Pickering, XXVII, 275–87 and in part in EHD, IX, 696–98. For the American criticism of these acts see Chapter VIII below.
[54] Pickering, XXVII, 262–70.

fore and the Dominicans and the Jamaicans smuggled when it was to their economic benefit.[55]

With the passage of these last two acts the Rockingham ministry was through with the colonies, for in July 1766 it was replaced by a new ministry headed by William Pitt. The Rockinghams' achievements during the spring of 1766 were interpreted variously on both sides of the Atlantic. Grenville and his followers opposed the Free Port Act as bitterly as they had fought the repeal of the Stamp Act, for Grenville predicted that the mainland colonies would use it for the purpose of furthering illegal trade.

It was not illegal trade, however, but the repeal of the Stamp Act that hardened British political attitudes toward America, and the reception of repeal in America merely convinced men such as Grenville that they had been right in insisting on maintaining in practice as well as in theory British sovereignty over the colonies. Grenville himself alternated between bitter sarcasm over the past and gloomy predictions for the future. He described repeal as a "shameful and pernicious measure" that "is intended to give up now and forever the fundamental rights of the Kingdom and legislature of Great Britain." [56] He had no doubt, he said, that "our brethren in America" would express great joy, despite the Declaratory Act, because they will understand that "they are thereby exempted forever from being taxed by Great Britain for the public support even of themselves which this kingdom is to pay for them. I think they will be very ungrateful to our American patriots and our American merchants." If, Grenville said, such people would do the same for Buckinghamshire "and double tax themselves to take off our taxes," he would guarantee as universal joy and even more gratitude than they would ever receive from America.[57]

The victorious merchants had little more liking for the Americans than did Grenville. They were particularly irritated by the violence of American opposition, and never after 1766 were they to present so united a front in opposition to the colonial policies of the government. Shortly after the passage of the repeal resolutions the London merchant committee wrote to merchants in America telling the news, and of the prospects for new trade regulations. They warned the Americans not to boast of repeal as a victory of America over the authority of Parliament. To do so would merely provide more ammunition for the opponents of America. In fact, the main obstacle to repeal had been the news of riotous proceedings in the colonies,

[55] Armytage, *Free Port System*, 42–45.
[56] To ————, 3 March 1766, Grenville Letter Books, II, HEHL.
[57] To Robert Nugent, 21 June, ibid.

which had awakened "the honor of Parliament, and thereby involved every friend of repeal in the imputation of betraying the dignity of Parliament." The Stamp Act would never have been repealed if the members had not been in some measure satisfied with the Declaratory Act. Therefore Americans should hasten to express their duty and gratitude to the parent country. But if they continued violent measures and talked of the point gained as a victory, and that Parliament had yielded the "right," "then indeed your enemies here will have a complete triumph—your tax masters probably restored; your friends must certainly lose all power to serve you; and such a train of ill consequences follow, as are easier for you to imagine than for us to describe." [58]

On 18 March, the day George III signed the repeal bill, the London merchants wrote again and told American merchants bluntly that had the Americans accepted the law and represented their hardships, "your relief *would* have been more speedy and we should have avoided many difficulties, as well as not a few *unanswerable* mortifying reproaches on your account." [59] As the program of "commercial reform" got under way, the bluntest letter of all came from Bristol. Americans should do three things: keep their rejoicings in bounds and burn no effigies; keep "indecent reflections" against Parliament out of their newspapers; and inform the government of any illegal trade. "This very thing has brought on all that has happened." [60]

The Americans paid little attention to the warnings of British merchants, nor were they particularly grateful to a Parliament which had, from their point of view, legislated wrongfully to begin with. Americans were grateful most of all to William Pitt, and to a lesser extent to George III. As for the British merchants, most Americans knew little of the part they played and thought instead that Americans had won the victory. No Virginia tobacco planter could conceive of a British merchant, especially if he were a Scot, acting from anything but selfish motives, and New England merchants felt the same way about British merchants in general and West Indians in particular. Furthermore, many issues remained to be settled. There were the new customs regulations about which there was talk but no action, and explosive questions such as the Quartering Act and the demand for compensation for the sufferers from the Stamp Act riots.

[58] NYM, "Special Bulletin," 26 April; PG, 1 May.
[59] VG(P), 30 Oct.; BEP, 1 Sept.; Massachusetts Historical Society *Proceedings* [MHSP], LV, 215–23.
[60] MdG, 5 June. See also letter from the London Merchant Committee to the Philadelphia Merchant Committee, 13 June, in VG(R), supplement, 5 Sept.

Many Americans did not remain quiet. They celebrated the repeal of the Stamp Act, and some legislatures passed resolutions expressing gratitude; but they continued their opposition to British officials and policies with as much vigor as ever.

Part 2: The Widening Rift

The men in America and Britain who hoped that repeal of the Stamp Act and the passage of the Revenue Act of 1766 would heal the breach between mother country and colonies, hoped in vain. The Americans displayed a minimum of gratitude for repeal and scorned the new commercial legislation. They continued to oppose the operation of the customs service and they defied the Quartering Act in a variety of ingenious ways. They made life miserable for political officials in America, whether British or American, who in any way had supported the attempt to enforce the colonial policies of Britain.

In Britain a group of leaders not only subscribed to the principles of the Declaratory Act but also insisted that they should be put into practice. American ingratitude for the repeal of the Stamp Act, the disintegration of the Chatham ministry after 1766, and the continuing clamor of British taxpayers, gave such men their opportunity.

During 1767–68 a series of new parliamentary acts and administrative measures in a real sense continued and even extended the Grenville program which had led to the Stamp Act crisis. Parliament once more tried to raise a revenue in America, this time for the purpose of paying British civil officials in the colonies. It sought to strengthen the customs service and attempted to enforce the Quartering Act by taking the unprecedented step of suspending the New York Assembly until it obeyed that act. In 1768 the ministry went the whole road when it ordered the military occupation of the town of Boston.

It was inevitable that Americans would fight back against a program that seemed to some even more ominous than that of the Grenville ministry. Once more they denied the right of Parliament to tax them, whatever the guise, and some moved on to the point where they began denying the right of Parliament to legislate for them in any case whatsoever, and asserted that Parliament was merely one of the many co-equal legislatures in the empire. Colonial legislatures insisted that they had the right to take united action in opposition to British policies, and when most of them were dissolved or prorogued on orders from Britain for doing so, the struggle was dramatized as it had not been before. On the everyday level, Americans continued to intimidate customs officers and to defy the British army. Above all they achieved an unprecedented union of action in the non-importation movement in an effort to apply economic pressure against Britain.

Widespread though it was, American opposition to the Townshend program was not achieved easily. There were bitter disputes as to the means and ends of opposition; there was none of the relative unity of purpose that characterized opposition to the Stamp Act. Many Americans had been frightened by mob violence and radical political ideas and behavior during the Stamp Act crisis and they did not want to see their revival. Many importing merchants, in particular, resented political interference with their business operations which the demand for non-importation involved, but they were forced into it anyway. Hence in 1770, when the new North ministry, wanting an end to controversy with the colonies for a variety of domestic reasons, repealed most of the revenue features of the Townshend Act of 1767, American resistance collapsed. It was followed by a welter of mutual recrimination within colonies and between colonies, and left a legacy of distrust. By the end of 1770 it seemed that opposition to any policies Britain might adopt in the future would be more difficult than ever, if not impossible, to achieve.

Despite the "conservative reaction" in America in 1770, the rift which had widened did not narrow, for there was no return to the state of affairs in 1763. Controversy was merely suspended and any new British measure infringing, or seeming to infringe, on American rights, was bound to meet opposition. The colonies had gained experience in united action and had established precedents and relationships that were not to be forgotten.

They had refined and advanced their interpretation of the constitution of the empire. And the events of the years since 1763 had provided the opportunity for the rise of a new generation of alert and vigorous political leaders. Whatever their setbacks in 1770 these men would not, in the future, remain quiet in the face of new or suspected attacks on American rights and liberties, as they defined them.

VII

The Aftermath of the Stamp Act in America

In September 1765, when the Americans learned of the fall of the Grenville ministry, they began predicting the repeal of the Stamp Act, and week by week through the winter, as they nullified the act themselves, endless rumors circulated. One moment Americans were sure of repeal, the next that the British army would enforce the law. In New York excitement reached such a pitch by the end of March 1766 that street gossips reported that Colonel Putnam and 10,000 Connecticut troops would come at a moment's notice to defend the city against the British. That night when a vessel arrived with the tale that the Stamp Act would not be repealed, the town crier and newsmongers ran through the streets crying "Bloody news for America. . . ." The next afternoon when an express arrived from the Sons of Liberty in Philadelphia, hundreds of boys ran about shouting "the Stamp Act's repealed." [1]

By April the New York Sons of Liberty were making further demands: if the Stamp Act were repealed, Americans should also insist on the removal of all restrictions on trade, the abolition of post offices and admiralty courts, and they should do so "while the colonies are unanimous." [2] Rumor followed rumor throughout April. One spread from Maryland. On 5 April a man rode into Baltimore with a letter from George Maxwell of Benedict who reported that a London merchant had congratulated him on the repeal. Within a quarter of an hour the Baltimore Sons of Liberty sent off an express to Philadelphia.[3] Two days later, gentlemen in Chestertown, Maryland started collecting money for a statue of William Pitt.[4] On

[1] Montresor, NYHSC(1881), 354-55.   [2] Ibid. 358, 360.   [3] PG, 10 April.
[4] MdG, 10 April.

10 April the *Maryland Gazette* and the *Pennsylvania Gazette* printed the story, and four days later the *Newport Mercury* ran a copy of Maxwell's letter, but by 18 April the *Virginia Gazette* was merely hoping the news was true.

When another rumor of repeal reached New York from Boston on 23 April, and along with it a copy of Pitt's speech, "one Swinney, an inflammatory news-carrier and monger, galloped on horseback through the street crying 'Pitt and no King,' 'til meeting with an English butcher, who silenced him." [5] Three days later bells began ringing at three in the morning when a packet boat arrived with mail. The captain reported that the Stamp Act had been repealed, and the Sons of Liberty put him in a chair and carried him to the post office "with great acclamations of joy, cheering him all the way." The captain's hour of glory, like that of George Maxwell in Maryland, was brief. The mail revealed that the House of Commons had not yet passed the act. The bells stopped ringing and "great discontent ensued owing to their having been so premature in their rejoicings." [6]

The uncertainty soon ended. On 2 May the *Virginia Gazette* printed copies of the repealing act and the Declaratory Act. Within two weeks all the colonies had the news, and the celebrations began. They were of a pattern from one of the colonies to the other: fireworks, bonfires, lighted windows, bell ringing, and the drinking of innumerable toasts to Liberty, George III, Pitt, and to a long list of British politicians.

There were some pleas for moderation. A Newporter congratulated his fellow citizens but urged that "public exhibitions of joy" be conducted "with decency and good order," for Americans should try to conciliate and secure the esteem of the parent state. More to the point, the Newport Sons of Liberty warned the inhabitants against giving away quantities of liquor during the evening.[7] The Newport celebration was elaborate. Bells began ringing at one in the morning. A signal gun was fired at sunrise and houses and ships in the harbor were decorated with flags. A four-part painting, eight feet high and fourteen feet wide, was hung before the courthouse. One section displayed the harbor of Newport, another the Goddess of Liberty surrounded by Conway, Rockingham, Cornwallis, Shelburne, Barré, and others. A third section was devoted to George III in his royal robes. At his right stood the "immortal Pitt" with "one hand on his breast, his thoughts distended with the patriot virtues, and with the other holding

---

[5] Montresor, NYHSC(1881), 361. Much of the speech appeared in American newspapers. See VG(P), 9 May; BEP, 12 May.
[6] Montresor, NYHSC(1881), 363.   [7] NM, 26 May.

forth Magna Charta. . . ." Lord Camden, "the British Aristides," stood at
the king's left hand. The fourth section was a "beautiful landscape,
charged with vegetable productions, representing the blessings which liberty bestows on agriculture and rural life."

At three o'clock in the afternoon a grand procession moved to the courthouse where twenty-eight toasts were drunk, beginning with the king and
ending with "success to the friends of liberty throughout America—may
they never want money, interest, or spirit to maintain their just rights." A
trumpet was sounded and five cannon were fired at each toast, and "joy
and gratitude sparkled on each face. . . ." That night lights were lit and
the tree of liberty was hung full of glass lanterns. Rockets were fired in
"continuous flights." The twenty-three-hour celebration ended at midnight. The local newspaper reported happily that the gentlemen and ladies
who spent the evening on the streets "met with no kind of indecent treatment from the populace; indeed the people seemed to be ambitious to
outvie each other in civility and politeness." [8]

Franklin warned his party in Pennsylvania to celebrate quietly in order
to make a good impression on the ministry, and to give the lie to those
who said that repeal would make the Americans more insolent than ever. A
Philadelphia newspaper appealed for quiet and apologized for past disturbances, which were to be "ascribed to the best of passions, a love of liberty." The "few instances of misguided zeal in what was deemed a good
cause" were not to be "ascribed to us as a people." [9] The Quaker party did
its best to keep things quiet but the city was illuminated by the proprietary party, and at a banquet at the State House, the diners promised to give
their lately purchased homespuns to the poor and to appear in fine English
broadcloth on the king's birthday.[10]

Charlestonians rang bells, built bonfires, illuminated the city, and on the
whole conducted themselves with joyful dignity. The joy of the New
Yorkers was less restrained. They too rang bells, drank toasts, and fired
guns. Some of the Sons of Liberty went to Trinity Church when the rector
informed them that he was adding "a congratulatory discourse" to a sermon on another subject. Then they adjourned to their usual tavern where
they "cheerfully drank" twenty-eight toasts to the music of a band.[11] According to an unfriendly onlooker, the night ended in "drunkenness,
throwing of squibs, crackers, firing of muskets and pistols, breaking some

[8] Ibid. 2 June.
[9] PG, 8 May; Franklin to Charles Thomson, 27 Feb., *Writings*(S), IV, 411.
[10] Thayer, *Pennsylvania*, 125.   [11] NYM, 26 May.

windows and forcing off the knockers off the doors." [12] In Hartford, Connecticut, a "tragical accident" turned "the intended rejoicings into lamentation and mourning." When twenty-two men met in a brick schoolhouse to prepare fireworks, they left three barrels of powder on the lower floor. The inevitable small boy set fire to some loose powder and blew up the schoolhouse, killing some of the men and wounding the rest.[13]

Bostonians awaited news of repeal with mixed emotions. Governor Bernard reported that the "thinking" people did not know which would be the more dangerous: repeal or enforcement. Repeal would mean the triumph of the mob; enforcement would make the people mad with desperation.[14] While Boston waited, James Otis talked. No matter what Parliament did, Americans would repeal the Stamp Act themselves. He told the town meeting that there was no distinction between internal and external taxes and that the merchants were great fools if they submitted to the laws of trade. The governor feared that "the ravings of this man" would be taken for the sentiments of all Americans.[15]

The popular leaders began to worry and decided to "quiet the minds of the people." [16] At town meetings in April the people were told that plans should be made to prepare for the news of repeal. The meeting agreed that the selectmen should take charge. They proposed the illumination of all the houses in Boston except those of the poor, the sick, and those with religious scruples. Such people were promised protection. People doing damage, such as breaking windows, would be prosecuted by the town.[17] The news of repeal reached Boston on 16 May, and three days later the town was illuminated. The whole affair demonstrated that the popular leaders could control their followers if they chose to do so.

ह‍

When the colonial legislatures met, their actions seldom reflected the gratitude the British expected, or if they did it was not always a heartfelt response. The South Carolina Commons House voted its thanks to George III, and a £1000 marble statue of William Pitt; a motion to substitute a statue of the king could not obtain a second.[18]

The New York assembly reluctantly adopted an address to the king be-

[12] Montresor, NYHSC(1881), 368.   [13] VG(PD), 20 June.
[14] To John Pownall, 13 April, BP, V, 103–5, HUL.
[15] To Richard Jackson, 17, 28 April, ibid. 106–11.
[16] Thomas Hutchinson to [Richard Jackson], 21 April, Hutchinson Letter Books, Massachusetts Archives [Mass. Ar.], XXVI, 227.
[17] BTR, XVI, 174–6.   [18] Wallace, South Carolina, II, 74.

cause of its "fears of the populace, for the swellings of the great multitude were not yet assuaged." John Cruger, the mayor of New York, "who was afraid of his constituents and urged by instructions from them," proposed that the assembly vote for a statue of Pitt. Most of the members were opposed but they agreed because they "durst not speak for fear of the people." Warned by the New York agent that any favoritism to Pitt might make the king jealous, the assembly then voted for a statue of George III, but it was "certain that if they had not voted a statue for Pitt, the King would have had none, for in truth they were disposed to give none. . . ." [19] The statues were of lead, and were later converted into shot to be fired at the soldiers of George III.

The Pennsylvania assembly, controlled by the Quaker party, expressed its gratitude to the king for his approval of its "dutiful behavior" as compared with the "too prevailing distractions which have agitated the other colonies. . . ." After thus patting itself on the back, the assembly adopted a resolution designed to place the blame for any future trouble upon the proprietors. It promised that whenever it was asked to grant money for the king's service "in a constitutional way," it would do so cheerfully unless the proprietors' instructions to their governors "shall continue to interfere." [20] The Rhode Island assembly quietly adopted an address which it voted to keep secret until the king had received it.[21]

No legislature adopted a more fulsome, or more hypocritical, address than the Massachusetts House of Representatives. The Boston leaders had at last won control of the house in the May election and they were engaged in an all-out attack on Governor Bernard and Thomas Hutchinson. James Otis, Samuel Adams, and Speaker Thomas Cushing were members of the committee to prepare an address. They defended their past conduct and, by implication, called the governor and the chief justice liars. Their gratitude to the king and Parliament was warm and deep, said the committee, but they hoped that the king would not believe reports that his American subjects had "manifested some kind of disaffection to their constitutional dependence on the parent country," or that they had taken advantage of the "lenity and tenderness" of king and Parliament "to abate of their respect and submission to the supreme legislative authority of Great Britain." Such reports had been made and they were true enough, but the address assured the king that the members of the house abhorred such ideas,

[19] W. H. W. Sabine, ed., Historical Memoirs from 16 March 1763 to 9 July 1776 of William Smith (New York, 1956), 32–33; NYAJ, 23 June.
[20] 6 June, Pa. Ar., 8 ser. VII, 5884–85.   [21] June 1766, RICR, VI, 496, 498–99.

for "they esteem their connection with their fellow subjects in Great Britain, and a constitutional subordination to your Parliament, their great privilege and security." At the same time the committee prepared an eloquent address to Pitt praising him for his "noble and generous efforts" and his "great abilities" and voted thanks to numerous members of Parliament.[22]

The New Jersey legislature assured the king that it was loyal and grateful and explained that the people had opposed the Stamp Act because "Americans have ever been free." [23] The North Carolina house and council joined to address the king in glowing terms.[24] But the Virginia House of Burgesses did nothing. When it met in November, Governor Fauquier congratulated it on the repeal of the Stamp Act; the house merely replied that it was grateful. The governor considered the reply "extraordinary" and thought that it showed weakness, want of judgment, and "much heat in the composers. . . ." He prepared an answer in which he used "more art than I ever practised with them before," but even so, the burgesses did not prepare a loyal address to the king. The house did consider a bill for a statue of him and an obelisk to various British leaders, but soon abandoned it. All the burgesses did in the end was to create Pittsylvania county, one parish of which they named Camden.[25] The burgesses had all their attention fastened on something of far greater interest.

Even while Americans were celebrating repeal, they turned upon one another with more fervor than ever. Old political divisions were sharpened and the foundations for new political alignments were laid. The Stamp Act crisis brought to the fore new and aggressive leaders as defenders of American rights; men who had no intention of surrendering the positions they had gained. The Stamp Act might be dead but it could be and was kept alive as a political weapon with which to attack political opponents, who were charged with indifference, or subservience, or even downright connivance in securing the hated law. Such was the case in Pennsylvania, Connecticut, and Massachusetts, and to a lesser extent in Virginia. Some colonies remained relatively quiet, notably Delaware, New Jersey, and New

[22] 19, 20 June, Bradford, *Speeches*, 91–93.
[23] 20 June, William A. Whitehead, *et al.*, eds., *Archives of the State of New Jersey, First Series* . . . [N.J. Ar.] (33 vols., Newark *et al.*, 1880–1928), IX, 560–61.
[24] 28 Nov., William L. Saunders, ed., *The Colonial Records of North Carolina* [NCCR] (10 vols., Raleigh, 1886–90), VII, 332–33.
[25] Fauquier to SS, 18 Nov. 1766, C.O. 5/1345; JHB (1766–69), ix, 12, 23–24, 44, 48, 75.

Hampshire. The Carolinas, for a time, were mainly concerned with the rising discontent of the backcountry.

The proprietary party in Pennsylvania did its best to regain control of the legislature by insisting that Franklin and the Quaker party were supporters of the Stamp Act. Franklin's role had been equivocal at best, but many leading Quakers had been strong opponents of the act. By 1766 all the newspapers in the colony were opposed to the Quaker party, even the *Pennsylvania Gazette*, which had been taken over by David Hall, Franklin's former partner. The newspapers made much of Franklin's supposed sell-out of American rights. They got copies of letters written to England by former stamp distributor John Hughes and printed these at large in Pennsylvania and other colonies.[26] On the other side, Franklin was busy supplying letters from prominent men in England testifying that he had played a vigorous role in opposition to the Stamp Act; but the best ammunition of the Quaker party was Franklin's "Examination" before the House of Commons, which Joseph Galloway published widely before the October elections in 1766.[27]

The result of the campaign of charge and countercharge was a landslide victory for the Quaker party. Franklin's daughter told him that "we have beat three partys, the Proprietary, the Presbyterians, and the Half and Halfs." [28] The Quaker party then elected Joseph Galloway, open defender of the Stamp Act and of the sovereignty of Parliament, as speaker of the assembly. The next spring the Quaker party struck at Chief Justice William Allen, leader of the proprietary party. Thinking him too old to ride horseback, the assembly established circuit courts throughout the colony, but the chief justice did not resign; he rode circuit.[29]

As for Franklin, he was now safe to continue to work for the abolition of the proprietary government, although increasingly he turned to the promotion of speculative land schemes for the benefit of himself and his friends on both sides of the Atlantic. And far from losing prestige as a result of the Stamp Act, the circulation of his "Examination" won him widespread popularity. In fact he became what amounted to an ambassador from America. Not only did he continue as deputy postmaster general for North America and agent for Pennsylvania, he also became agent for Georgia in 1768, New Jersey in 1769, and Massachusetts in 1770. Equipped with a more than adequate income, Franklin stayed on in Europe until the out-

[26] PJ, 4 Sept.; NM, 22 Sept.; BEP, 15 Sept.
[27] PG, 8, 16 May 1766 for examples. Publication of the "Examination" in Boston was announced in the *Boston Evening Post*, 29 Sept., 6 Oct.
[28] Thayer, *Pennsylvania*, 136.   [29] Ibid. 136–37.

break of the war for independence, the best-known American on either side of the Atlantic and an outstanding promoter of pro-American propaganda in British newspapers.[30]

The attempt to defeat the dominant party in Pennsylvania by smearing it as a supporter of the Stamp Act failed completely. The reverse was true in Massachusetts, where a political revolution took place in the spring of 1766. The popular party, centering in Boston, had fought the Hutchinson machine in vain for five years. Hutchinson maintained his control despite the barrage of propaganda against him; but by 1766 the popular leaders at last had an "issue" with which they thought they could win. They accused Hutchinson and Governor Bernard of being the promoters, if not actually the authors, of the Stamp Act. The rumor was started early in the summer of 1765 [31] and by 1766 newspapers were asserting that the names of the contrivers, promoters, and executioners of the Stamp Act were no longer a secret. The voters should "cut off and remove wicked men and evil councilors from places of trust and power." [32] The newspapers reiterated the argument about the iniquity of multiple office-holding and charged great corruption in the grants of public money to certain men, all of whom were supporters of Thomas Hutchinson.

As the elections neared, the Boston newspapers printed "model instructions," as examples for the country towns. These stated that holders of other public offices should not be elected to the council, that no man should hold more than one office at a time, that legislative sessions should be open to the public, and that the fees collected by public officials should be established by new and rigid legislation. Money taken from the treasury without the consent of the house should be returned. The liberty of the press should be preserved. Those who had suffered losses during the Stamp Act riots should not be compensated. Thus did the Boston leaders lay their program before the colony.[33]

They went even farther and proposed a "purge." The newspapers listed the names of thirty-two members of the former house as "friends" of the Stamp Act. In April the list was republished with the assertion that men who had approved the Stamp Act were enemies of their country and their names should be posted and exposed to the contempt of every town in the province. The voters should reject "the old leaven" and "look out for good

30 Carl Van Doren, *Benjamin Franklin* (New York, 1938), chapter XV, "Agent-General." On Franklin as a propagandist see Verner W. Crane, *Benjamin Franklin's Letters to the Press, 1758–1775* (Chapel Hill, 1950).
31 Hutchinson to Thomas Pownall, 31 Aug. 1765, Hosmer, *Hutchinson*, 101.
32 BEP, 3 Feb. 1766.   33 BG, 31 March 1766.

and honest and free men—men that are unshackled with posts and preferments; men who will not warp, nor be cajoled into any measures that will tend to impoverish and enslave their country." [34]

The continuous campaign against such "tools of power" as Bernard and Hutchinson, and charges of "treason" and "corruption" against Hutchinson's supporters, did not go unchallenged. The main target of Hutchinson's friends was the leader and hero of the popular party, James Otis. Otis had stopped wavering after his return from the Stamp Act Congress and was steadily and publicly violent against the Stamp Act, but his contradictory pamphlets were in print and the opposition quoted them gleefully.[35] Could such a man be a true patriot and an enemy of the Stamp Act? Not one of the thirty-two representatives whose "purge" was demanded could be accused of such slavish doctrines as those of James Otis. How could Otis's inconsistencies and prevarications be reconciled with honesty, patriotism, and common sense? Otis was a "double-faced Jacobite Whig," for ". . . one day he writes a book to prove his extreme love for his country, and his veneration to its glorious constitution; the next he prostitutes himself to the idol on the other side of the water, writes another book, and advances with a brazen front, principles that would cut the very throat of liberty." [36]

Otis's defenders were stricken, for the record was before the people. The best that his partisans could suggest was that he had been motivated by fear of being called a traitor, or that he had been in the depths of despair.[37] The day following this wobbly argument in the popular party newspaper, Otis once more defended himself before the town meeting. He did not admit authorship of the contradictory pamphlets. According to an unfriendly witness, he was a "mere buffoon" who told his audience that "he was under the unhappy influence of weak nerves, or as it is vulgarly called, cowardice," and that he cited Cicero and John Locke, who had similarly suffered, although otherwise "Great Men—like himself." In the end the great orator won his audience by offering to meet George Grenville in single combat on the floor of Faneuil Hall to decide the fate of the colonies.[38]

Once more James Otis was re-elected by the town of Boston, and by a safer margin than the year before, but he did run third behind Samuel Adams and Thomas Cushing.[39] And as returns came in from over the

[34] BEP, 28 April; BG, 31 March, 14 April, 5 May.   [35] BEP, 28 April.
[36] Ibid. 5 May.   [37] BG, 5 May.   [38] "Q" and "A Merchant," BEP, 19 May.
[39] BTR, XVI, 176–77.

colony, it was clear that the popular party had at last won a majority of the members of the House of Representatives. Nineteen of the thirty-two men listed for purging had been defeated. "Several gentlemen of respectable characters, considerable property, and heretofore of uninterrupted authority [in] their towns were flung out and ignorant and low men elected in their stead" was the way Governor Bernard saw it. At the same time he felt optimistic, for he heard from England that his letters on the economic state of the province had been influential in obtaining repeal of the Stamp Act; and this news won him the favor of the merchants, who now denounced Otis for the lies he had told.[40]

When the legislature met on 28 May, more than forty new men were present, but the popular party majority was narrow indeed. The house elected James Otis speaker by a margin of only seven votes out of 112 cast. Samuel Adams was elected clerk of the house by a majority of one. Governor Bernard promptly vetoed Otis so the house elected Otis's ally, Thomas Cushing, and the governor accepted him, for he had been relatively quiet—and vetoing a speaker was a rare thing. That afternoon the house turned to the election of councilors. Otis had announced before the election that fifteen councilors would not be re-elected, but now he attacked only the Crown officers, probably because of the small majority he commanded. Judge Lynde of the superior court resigned rather than face the humiliation. Judge Peter Oliver, Secretary Andrew Oliver, and Attorney General Trowbridge were easily defeated, but Thomas Hutchinson lost his seat by the narrowest of margins. These leading Crown officers were replaced by inconspicuous but loyal supporters of the popular party. The governor had served public notice that he would not have such men on the council, and he now vetoed them and, in addition, James Otis, Sr. and Nathaniel Sparhawk, members of the old council who had been re-elected. He had never used this veto power before but he said that he was applauded by "almost every liberal thinking man in the town and country."[41]

The next day Bernard formally opened the session with what John Adams called "a most nitrous, sulphurous speech."[42] He congratulated the house on the repeal of the Stamp Act and then turned angrily on the popular leaders. It was not unusual, he said, in times of public calamity, for private resentments to mix themselves with popular discontent "under the

[40] To John Pownall, 30 May, BP, V, 114–17, HUL; to BT, 7 July, C.O. 5/892.
[41] To John Pownall, 6 June, BP, V, 124, HUL; BG, 21 May.
[42] *Diary*, 29 May 1766.

borrowed mask of patriotic zeal." This was why unlimited abuse had been heaped on some of the most respectable men of the province, and why the fury of the people had been heaped on the man to whom they owed more than any other in the Stamp Act crisis. Bernard meant Thomas Hutchinson, and his hearers knew it. Tactlessly, the governor told the house that its refusal to elect Hutchinson and other officers to the council was an "ill-judged and ill-timed oppugnation" of the king's authority, which had deprived the government of the services of its best and most able men.[43]

Before the house could reply, Bernard received official news of repeal of the Stamp Act, and passage of the Declaratory Act, the resolutions of Parliament recommending compensation, and praise for the usefulness of his letters in obtaining repeal. He promptly made a second speech, telling the house that he had been ordered to recommend full and ample compensation to "the late sufferers by the madness of the people." This order, he said, was most unusual, for it was based on resolutions of the House of Commons. Furthermore, the "justice and humanity of this requisition is so forcible, that it cannot be controverted." Again he accused the house of ingratitude for refusing to re-elect the Crown officers to the council. He charged flatly that "the private interests, passions, or resentments of a few men" would ruin the country simply because they could not get enough offices to satisfy them. He would compromise, however. If the house would reconsider the election of councilors, he would not veto its other choices.[44]

Bernard's charges, whatever their merit, set him up as an ideal target for the special literary talents of the popular leaders. They replied to him, as he said with some justice, "by prevaricating and perverting my words from what they know I meant to what they know I did not mean, and then arguing upon such perversion." [45] James Otis and Samuel Adams, the new clerk of the house, apparently wrote the replies to the two speeches and did so with vast skill. They expressed surprise and astonishment that Bernard had revived partisan animosities by using words such as "private interests." The house was interested only in the public good and aimed only at the cultivation of harmony. As for injustice to Hutchinson, strangers would think the riots against him had been the action of the whole people instead of a few unknown villains. The house knew of no one trying to inflame the country; the governor must be misinformed by enemies of

[43] Bradford, *Speeches*, 74–76; BG, 9 June.
[44] Bradford, *Speeches*, 81–84; BG, 2, 9 June. As early as 2 March the *Boston Evening Post* contained extracts from various people in London praising Bernard's letters for help in repeal of the Stamp Act.
[45] To John Pownall, 6 June, BP, V, 122–26, HUL.

the people. And the house was unable to understand how the governor could treat the free election of councilors as he did. His statement that its action was an "oppugnation" of the king's authority was a direct impeachment of the two houses for high treason!

As for depriving the colony of the services of some of its most able men, "we have released those of the judges of the superior court . . . from the cares and perplexities of politics, and given them opportunity to make still farther advances in the knowledge of the law," and given other gentlemen more leisure to perform the duties of their important offices. "This surely is not to deprive the government of its best and ablest servants, nor can it be called an oppugnation of anything but a dangerous union of legislative and executive power in the same persons; a grievance long complained of by our constituents. . . ." [46]

Bernard clearly had lost the battle of words and he was left muttering that "what I am now endeavoring at is only to patch up a rotten constitution. . . ." [47]

The popular leaders, fresh from their triumph in the elections and in the verbal exchanges, proceeded to niggle and haggle until Bernard prorogued the legislature. When it met again in September it deferred compensation for the Stamp Act riots until the next session, although only by one vote. At first the house postponed the grant of the governor's salary for fear that he would dissolve it, but then voted the money, knowing that Bernard would welcome a refusal so he could ask for a salary from British customs revenues. Finally, the house voted to open its debates to the public and to build a gallery for visitors. This was more than a symbol, for it meant that the gallery could be and was packed with adherents of the popular party in Boston who could exert "moral" pressure in support of their leaders on the floor. [48] Bitterly, at the end of the year, the governor wrote that "the demagogues who have got the lead, are determined to bring all real power into the hands of the people. . . ." If he would submit and be content to be "reduced to the standard of a Rhode Island governor," he could live in peace. But this he would not do, for he could not surrender the prerogatives of the king. [49] Prejudiced though he was, Governor Bernard's analysis of the political revolution that had taken place in May 1766 was sound. For the next four years the leaders of the popular party in Boston were to rule the colony through control of the House of Representatives, although

[46] Bradford, *Speeches*, 76–81, 88–91; BG, 9 June.
[47] To John Pownall, 24 July, BP, V, 136–37, HUL.
[48] Thomas, Massachusetts, 321–22.
[49] Bernard to SS, 6, 24 Dec. 1766, C.O. 5/756.

they did not gain the support of the majority of the council until the stationing of British troops in Boston in 1768.

The passage of the Stamp Act resolves in Virginia in May 1765 had not been the work of a "party" but of a small group of younger men who found in Patrick Henry a spokesman bold enough to challenge the clique of great planters who had long governed the colony. Governor Fauquier and the council, knowing that the legislature was the only real source of radical political action in Virginia, decided at the end of 1765 not to call it into session until November 1766. It would be useless, said the governor, to expect men "to consider coolly of the circumstances of the times when they are so heated as to shut up all avenues to reason." [50] After the repeal of the Stamp Act, the governor stuck by his decision. Some men suggested a meeting but he was dubious, afraid the assembly might pass seditious or offensive resolutions. Such being the case, an early call would mean that "I should only give them a liberty effectually to cut their own throats, and lose every friend they now had. . . ." [51]

The problems of Virginia were described by a Virginia merchant who refused to rejoice with an English friend over the repeal. "This country," he wrote, "is immersed under a load of debts." Trade languished because restrictions prevented monied men from entering into trade and because "the pimping commanders of our men of war, add much to the distressing of our trade." The only "recipe" he said, was frugality and industry, "which is a potion scarcely to be swallowed by Virginians, brought up from their cradles in idleness, luxury, and extravagancy, depending on their myriads of slaves, that bane (if not curse) of this country. . . ." [52] Governor Fauquier reported that the people were "sour," partly because of their private distress and partly because they were "spirited up by the newspapers. Everything is become a matter of heat and party faction . . . a spirit of discontent and cavil runs through the colony. . . ." Nor did he look forward to the meeting of the legislature which he had put off as long as possible. He feared it would be "warm" because the members differed on so many things and because "the blood of the people is soured by their private distresses and party feuds will run high." [53]

The governor was right on both counts. Ever since July, Virginians had

[50] To SS, 11 Dec. 1765, C.O. 5/1345. [51] To SS, 27 June, 1766, C.O. 5/1345.
[52] Nathaniel Savage to John Norton, 22 July 1766, Brock Collection: Savage-Norton Papers, HEHL.
[53] To BT, 4 Sept., 8 Oct. 1766, C.O. 5/1331.

been diverted by a newspaper brawl between the Mercer family and Richard Henry Lee. Lee, second only to Patrick Henry as a popular patriotic leader, was in difficulties. The brilliant but erratic orator, born in 1732, was the seventh of the children of Thomas Lee of Westmoreland county. He was educated by private tutors and then sent to school in England. In 1758 he entered the House of Burgesses, an easy matter because the Lees had been members of it or the council for a century. Despite its aristocratic standing, the Lee family, like other families such as the Washingtons and the Masons in northern Virginia, was outside the inner circle of James River families that really ruled the colony. Furthermore, Lee's father, Thomas Lee, had long been a political rival of Speaker John Robinson.

Richard Henry Lee himself was relatively poor and the father of many children. He became an inveterate office-seeker and appealed for a seat on the governor's council as early as 1762, and was eager to become speaker of the House of Burgesses. In 1764 and 1765 his letters throbbed with opposition to British policies. He predicted independence if Britain continued on the course she had begun. He asserted that the Stamp Act was as bad as "Egyptian bondage," that the mother country was converted into "an arbitrary, cruel and oppressive step-dame," and he denounced Grenville and "his infernal crew of hireling miscreants. . . ." [54] He led the opposition to the Stamp Act in his county. When effigies of George Mercer, the Virginia stamp distributor, and of George Grenville were burned in Williamsburg in September 1765, Richard Henry Lee apparently wrote a "dying speech" for Mercer, which was published in Maryland but not in Virginia.[55] Yet in November 1764 Richard Henry Lee himself had asked for the post of stamp distributor!

The Mercers, who were anxious to defend their relative, heard rumors of Lee's application. When George Mercer went back to England after resigning as stamp distributor, Lee said that Mercer planned to bring back troops. He had gone back, in fact, to continue his work as agent of the Ohio Company of Virginia, but he also looked for evidence of Lee's application. He found it and informed his brother James Mercer, who let fly in the *Virginia Gazette*.[56] The next week an even more violent attack followed. Not only had Lee applied, he had not opposed the Stamp Act until he found that Mercer had been appointed, and then, "to hide his cloven foot, did, proteus like, change his dress, and take upon himself the

[54] James C. Ballagh, ed., *The Letters of Richard Henry Lee* (2 vols., New York, 1911–14), I, 1–12 for letters from 1762 to 1765.
[55] MdG, 17 Oct. 1765.   [56] VG(PD), "An Enemy to Hypocrisy," 18 July 1766.

outward apparel of a Son of Liberty," when in fact he was nothing but "a wolf in sheep's clothing, and not having the fear of God before his eyes, but being instigated and seduced by the very Devil (to wit, envy, and disappointment)," proceeded to burn an effigy before a group of Negroes.[57]

Lee admitted that he had applied, but insisted that only a few days after he sent off his letters he had decided that he had been wrong and had determined to do all he could to fight the Stamp Act. He had not felt it necessary to publish his application for he believed that his actions would be clear proof to his countrymen of his principles.[58] Despite the weakness of this statement, his defenders took to the newspapers and attacked both James and George Mercer. Outraged, Colonel John Mercer came to the defense of his sons. Do not Lee's anonymous defenders who step forth "with malice in their hearts, and the poison of asps under their lips, belch out and publish to the whole world their malicious and venomous lies and slanders, deserve to be treated as assassins and murderers?" The "gang-leader," Richard Henry Lee, should be called "Bob Booty," for he asks friends in England to help him get every job he hears of. Lee's own defense was proof of his hypocrisy. The charges circulated against his son, John Mercer told Lee, are "a crime that richly deserves the gallows, and cannot be expiated or executed by any of your hypocritical appeals, or proud and insolent boastings." [59]

The next week James Mercer followed his father with a signed article of his own. Lee was an arrant hypocrite, a forger, and a liar. He had not opposed the Stamp Act until he learned of George Mercer's appointment. It was notorious that Lee had been a "solicitor general" for every vacancy in the colony for more than seven years. He had not been in the House of Burgesses when the Stamp Act resolves were passed, although he had been in perfect health. Such absence was quite "contrary to his former custom, he usually giving close attendance for fear the speaker should die and he not be there to fill the chair." He approved the Stamp Act resolves only after he learned he had not been appointed distributor.[60]

ह२

Richard Henry Lee's political career might have ended in 1766 had not Virginia been rocked by the greatest scandal in the century and a half since

---

[57] Ibid. 25 July. [58] VG(R), 8 Aug. Reprinted in *Letters*, I, 16–18.
[59] VG(PD), 28 Sept.
[60] Ibid. 3 Oct. The fight continued. Arthur Lee returned from London and he and James Mercer agreed to a duel. Each insisted that he could not find the other at the appointed place and time and various affidavits were published in the newspapers "proving" that all concerned were liars. VG(PD), 28 May, and VG(R), 23 July 1767.

its founding. In May, John Robinson died. He was one of the wealthiest men in the colony and ever since 1738 he had been both speaker of the House of Burgesses and treasurer of the colony. He dominated Virginia politics, for as speaker he controlled the political futures of new members of the house, and as treasurer he wielded great economic power, which had its political advantage. It was his responsibility to collect and account for taxes, and, since the passage of the first paper money act of 1755, to burn the money as it was paid into the treasury. But he had not burned the money as the issuing laws required; he had loaned it to friends and political allies. And even before 1755, apparently, he had secretly used treasury funds to finance the land speculations and business ventures of himself and his friends. The fall of tobacco prices during the early 1760s threatened to bankrupt some of Virginia's most prominent citizens as well as lesser men, and the Currency Act of 1764 which forbade new issues of legal tender paper money and the extension of old issues was a blow to a colony already suffering from a staggering depression. As treasurer, Robinson had two choices: "He could burn the paper money and bankrupt his friends, or ignore the law and make the paper available to those in desperate need. He chose to save his friends."

But Robinson was constantly threatened by exposure. Richard Henry Lee had opposed Robinson from the day Lee entered the house in 1758, and as early as 1760 he had demanded an investigation of the treasury to see if the paper money had been burned according to law. Lee made a similar demand in 1763, but Robinson managed to circumvent him. Nevertheless, suspicion was growing and in May 1765 Robinson and his allies devised a scheme to enable them to escape from the consequences of a public revelation of what they had done. They proposed to create a loan office by borrowing £240,000 from British merchants. If such a loan office could be established, they could "borrow" from it and then pay the money they had acquired illegally back to the treasury. It is uncertain whether or not British merchants would have made such a loan, but the Robinson group never had a chance to find out. The House of Burgesses passed a bill to establish a loan office but the council rejected it. Then came the dissolution of the house for the adoption of Patrick Henry's Stamp Act resolves and a crisis was avoided, but only for a moment, for within a few months Robinson died.[61]

Fulsome eulogies followed Robinson's death on 11 May 1766, but within days alarm was spreading. When the King and Queen county court ap-

[61] Mays, *Pendleton*, I, chapter XI, "The Robinson Affair"; Ernst, WMQ, 3 ser. XXII, 53, 64–65; JHB (1766–69), xviii–xxi.

pointed Edmund Pendleton, Peter Randolph, and Peter Lyons administrators of the Robinson estate in June, the court fixed the bond at the astonishing figure of £250,000. The onlookers probably did not know that two of the three administrators, five of the six justices of the court, and two of the eight sureties for the bond owed the Robinson estate a total of £10,000, and that some of the guarantors of the bond were themselves insolvent. Edmund Pendleton, the principal administrator, soon found that about £130,000 was owing to the estate and that over £100,000 consisted of paper money which Robinson had loaned to his friends instead of burning it. The list of names was a roll call of the aristocracy: Byrds, Braxtons, Burwells, Carters, Carys, Grymeses, Pages, Randolphs, and many others. Some amounts were small, others were large. William Byrd III, a member of the council, owed nearly £15,000; the members of the house more than £37,000. Even Robinson's political opponents were debtors to his estate: Richard Henry Lee owed £12 and Patrick Henry, £11. While there were other small debtors such as shopkeepers and tavernkeepers most of the money had been lent to a relatively few men in the tidewater counties of southern Virginia.

It is easy to see why the Virginia aristocrats wanted their names kept hidden, even though the fact that they had gotten away with the money could not be. Governor Fauquier appointed Robert Carter Nicholas treasurer until the legislature could elect a new one. Nicholas at once announced that sheriffs were in arrears and that there was gossip about shortages in the treasury. At the end of June he published a letter running more than six columns in the *Virginia Gazette*. He praised Robinson but argued that the offices of speaker and treasurer be separated. He said that since people were gossiping about shortages, he might as well admit them, although he did not know how great they were. The shortages explained why credit was scarce, for "now it comes out that a great part of the money, squeezed from the people for their taxes, instead of being sunk at our Treasury, as it ought to have been, was thrown back into circulation." [62]

The best defense against public revelation was attack. Nicholas was accused of currying favor with the governor and council and seeking to "ingratiate himself the more in the public's favor" by preaching the separation of the offices. That is why he "very hastily published to the world the misconduct of his predecessor." [63] "An Honest Buckskin" objected to the "slur of embezzlement" cast upon the late treasurer, arguing that if time had been taken it might have been found out that there was no fraud and

[62] VG(PD), 27 June 1766.   [63] Ibid. 25 July.

that Robinson had acted "from that humane disposition, charity, so much recommended by Christianity. . . ." [64] Nicholas insisted that he had not charged Robinson with "peculation," but no one came to the new treasurer's defense until October, when a "Freeholder" flatly declared that something had been wrong in the treasury ever since 1753 and that "the Speaker would not have dared to embezzle the public money if he had not obtained an influence in the House by indirect methods. . . ." [65]

Little wonder that the people of Virginia were "sour" as the governor had reported, for most of them had not benefited from Robinson's "benevolence." When the counties instructed their delegates, they made this sourness clear. Accomac denounced the misapplication of public money and insisted that past misconduct in the treasury must be "searched out." James City voters told their delegate, Lewis Burwell, that it was self-evident that the possession of any office of high dignity gives weight and authority to its possessor, and that the combination of two such offices must convey a weight and power "which may lay a foundation for such undue influence as is inconsistent with the liberty of a free people." He must, they said, work for the separation of the offices of speaker and treasurer, promote measures for the effective collection of taxes, and for the prevention of future frauds. Burwell's constituents apparently did not know, nor did he tell them, that he owed more than £7000 to the estate of John Robinson.[66]

When the legislature met, the governor did not even mention the most exciting news in Virginia in his speech, nor did the house refer to it in its reply. But the next day it appointed a committee to investigate the treasury. On the committee were Patrick Henry and Richard Henry Lee, three others who owed large amounts—including Archibald Cary, whose debt was nearly £7500—and six members who were not debtors. They reported in December that a little over £100,000 was still due to the public from Robinson's estate. Furthermore, sheriffs, inspectors, and county clerks were greatly in arrears. Some had not rendered accounts for several years and others had turned in only partial ones.

The administrators of the Robinson estate then submitted a petition which agreed with the figures given by the committee. They listed Robinson's property and asked for three years to settle his affairs, promising to pay the colony one-third of what was due it each year. They said that the distress of the country was so great and money so scarce that if they were

[64] Ibid. 1 Aug.   [65] Ibid. 17 Oct.
[66] Ibid. 17, 30 Oct.; Mays, *Pendleton*, I, appendix II.

forced to settle at once they would ruin many families. In April 1767 the legislature agreed, but it took far longer than three years to settle the tangled affairs of John Robinson. As late as 1792 Edmund Pendleton still had not collected all that was due.[67]

Inevitably the Robinson affair had an impact on Virginia politics and gave younger men a political weapon. Governor Fauquier described the spring session of the legislature in 1767 as one of great heat. Legally, he reported, he was ignorant of what was said in debate by the "young, hotheaded, inexperienced members. The cool old members by their great steadiness and moderation, will, I am in great hopes, regain that lead in the house which they formerly had, but at present it is lost." [68]

The great families were successful in keeping their names hidden and in retaining their political power, but they were suspect as never before. Gossip as to names must have spread throughout the colony and added to the existing discontent. From time to time it broke into the newspapers. A cynical "Prophecy from the East" indicated one attitude.[69]

> And it shall come to pass, after the people of Virginia shall prevail against their Stamp Masters, that he who is over their treasury, even the Speaker of the great Assembly shall be gathered unto his fathers;
>
> 2. And he shall die an old Man, in a good old age, and full of days: and there shall be great confusion in the land.
>
> 3. Party shall menace party, and dunce shall enflame dunce; and the Gazette of Purdie and Rind shall contain wonders.
>
> 4. And it shall come to pass that the principles of judging shall be perverted; men's understanding shall be darkened; For this shall be the Era of Delusion.
>
> 5. And then men who cannot write for themselves, shall write for the public; the Great Men, even the Men of fortune, shall write controversies.
>
> 6. And they shall call themselves lovers of truth and lovers of justice; and much paper shall be wasted and words shall lose their meaning.
>
> 7. . . . but we will not write about the dead; for our friend is dead, and the dead ought not to be evil spoken of. . . .
>
> 9. And they shall say, come and let us write about benevolence. And they shall write about it, and they shall call peculation benevo-

[67] The preface to JHB (1766–69), x–xxvi, has an outline of events and includes many documents. See also Mays, *Pendleton*, I, chapters XI–XII and appendices I–VI. One result was the separation of the offices of speaker and treasurer. John Carter Nicholas, who had officially "exposed" the scandal, was elected treasurer, but Peyton Randolph was elected speaker. Both held their jobs until the war for independence. VG(PD), 27 Nov. 1766.

[68] To SS, 27 April, C.O. 5/1345.   [69] VG(R), supplement, 15 Aug. 1766.

lence, and they shall say that it is a very great virtue, and of infinite service to the public.

10. And they shall say, let us write about patriotism . . . and they shall say it is a very fine thing, and that it will make a man guilty of malversation, and ruin his country.

As the end of the three years given to settle the estate drew near, "Aristides" made it clear that bitterness was very much alive. He trusted, he said, that Virginians would no longer be "amused" with memorials asking for indulgence. The Robinson estate should be sold and its debtors made to pay at once or the debt would never be paid. The writer said he was not void of humanity "but he who is intrusted by his country, and wantonly betrays that trust, and prostitutes his honor for his own private emolument, had no right to expect that the virtues of humanity will be shown to himself while living, or to his estate, when dead." [70]

Men like Richard Henry Lee and Patrick Henry used the scandal to achieve a measure of power, despite the animosity they incurred. Many years later John Adams remembered that there were sharp divisions in the Virginia delegation at the Second Continental Congress and that George Wythe had told him that many influential families in Virginia had never forgiven Lee for his part in the exposure of Robinson's affairs, and that he "was still heartily hated by great numbers." [71]

While American politics seethed after the repeal of the Stamp Act, gratitude toward Britain cooled rapidly. As they took a second look at the Declaratory Act, the Revenue Act of 1766, and the request for compensation of the sufferers from the Stamp Act riots, many Americans came to feel that all too little had been done for them. Some at first thought that the Declaratory Act, since it did not mention taxes, meant that Parliament had given up the claim to a power which it had wrongly assumed. Pitt's speech making a distinction between the power of legislation and the power of taxation was widely known. But there were those who wondered. Colonial assemblies were told to lay the Declaratory Act on their tables as a mark of respect but otherwise to ignore it and to enter on their own journals the strongest declarations of their own rights.[72] Christopher Gadsden warned the Charleston Sons of Liberty that the preamble to the act declaring null and void all the resolutions of colonial legislatures was dangerous indeed.[73]

[70] Ibid. 19 Oct. 1769.   [71] Autobiography, III, 367–68.   [72] BG, 11 Aug. 1766.
[73] Edward McCrady, The History of South Carolina under the Royal Government, 1719–1776 (New York, 1899), 590.

Before they heard of the Revenue Act of 1766, many Americans had high hopes of commercial reform, and they were encouraged by letters from British merchants. They were joyful over the proposed reduction of the molasses duty. They expected freer trade with the Spanish colonies. They wanted limitations on the power of the vice-admiralty courts and the elimination of irksome regulations of the coastwise trade. They looked forward to a restoration of the power to issue paper money. In these and other matters, American newspapers clearly hoped for a wholesale reversal of the Grenville program.[74]

Americans were soon disillusioned. The generalities and promises in the letters of British merchants could not hide the fact that nothing had been done about paper money and about the restraints placed upon trade by the Revenue Act of 1764.[75] Even before the news of the "commercial reforms" reached America, some Americans were saying that the British merchants were acting for their own selfish interests. And they were more than a little irked when British merchants declared that American misbehavior was the principal obstacle in the way of concessions to the colonies.[76]

The South Carolinians reacted more mildly than most. Shortly after the legislature voted a statue of Pitt, a committee listed some of the grievances that still remained. It asked for the appointment of judges during good behavior, for the establishment of courts in the backcountry, for the end of multiple office-holding, for the abolition of restrictions on paper money, and for the right to export rice directly to northern Europe and to export lumber and provisions anywhere in the world.[77]

Resentment in Virginia was far more intense, and particularly against the patronizing tone of the letters from merchants and others in Britain. No one summed up that resentment better than George Mason, who sent a reply to the *Public Ledger* in London, which published it in September 1766. He began by saying that the words parent and child had long been applied to Britain and the colonies but that Americans rarely saw anything from Britain "free from the authoritative style of a master to a school boy."

"We have with infinite difficulty and fatigue got you excused this one

---

[74] BG, 16 Sept. 1765; MdG, 5 June 1766; VG(P), 13 June 1766; London Merchants to New York Merchants, 18 Feb. 1766, NYM, 26 April.
[75] London Merchants to Boston Merchants, 13 June 1766, BEP, 1 Sept. 1766.
[76] VG(P), 30 May 1766; London Merchants to the "Gentlemen of Virginia," 18 March 1766, VG(PD), 30 Oct. 1766.
[77] Wallace, *South Carolina*, II, 75.

time; pray be a good boy for the future, do what your papa and mama bid you, and hasten to return them your most grateful acknowledgments for condescending to let you keep what is your own. . . ." If you don't behave, your parents will whip you and your friends will be ashamed of you. "Is not this a little ridiculous," Mason asked, "when applied to three millions of as loyal and useful subjects as any in the British dominions, who have been only contending for their birth-right, and have now only gained, or rather kept, what could not, with common justice, or even policy, be denied them?" As for the Declaratory Act, Americans do not deny the supreme authority of Great Britain but that authority should be exercised with caution. The new procedures in trade and the admiralty courts are not instances calling for filial gratitude to the mother country. The people of Britain should remember that "we are descended from the same stock with themselves, nurtured in the same principles of freedom," and then they will know how the late regulations have been relished in America.

Mason told the merchants that they need not worry about Americans breaking into intemperate strains of triumph and exultation, for they had not as yet much reason for joy. "Some bungler in politics" will probably try to frame new restraints in addition to the existing ones. "There is a passion natural to the mind of man, especially a free man, which renders him impatient of restraint." Mason's warning was clear and prophetic: Americans would not long submit to oppression if it were tried again. "Such another experiment as the Stamp Act would produce a general revolt in America." [78]

Mason spoke for many Americans in 1766 as he did ten years later when he drafted the Virginia Bill of Rights. They realized the wide gap between promise and performance when they read the Revenue Act of 1766 and as they tried to carry on trade within the framework of the Revenue Act of 1764. The merchants of New York sent a forceful petition to the House of Commons in November 1766. Once more they explained the complex trade patterns of the northern colonies, as the Boston merchants had done in 1763 and the Rhode Island merchants in 1764. [79] Again they outlined the importance of the trade in lumber and provisions to the foreign West Indies and the relationship of the profits from that trade to the trade with Africa and the Mediterranean, and the ultimate use of the over-all profits to pay for British manufactures. They reiterated the obvious fact that the

[78] "To the Committee of Merchants in London," 6 June 1766, Kate M. Rowland, *The Life of George Mason, 1725–1792* (2 vols., New York, 1892), I, 381–89; GP, III, 315–16.
[79] See Chapter III above.

British West Indies could neither supply the demands of the British Empire for tropical produce nor consume the surpluses of the mainland colonies.

These were the usual arguments, but the New York merchants next attacked British legislation that gave unfair advantage to the British West Indies and to British merchants. Sugar was a "capital" article. The mainland merchants needed sugar from the foreign islands to make up adequate return cargoes, yet the five-shilling tax per hundredweight was too high and too difficult to pay in specie. And compelling American merchants to land foreign sugar in Britain and store it before exporting it to Europe was a "most expensive and dilatory restriction." Worse than that, labeling all sugar from the mainland colonies as "French" sugar was a hardship, especially since the British West Indians could export sugars for what they really were. The trade to the Danish West Indies was hampered by prohibiting the importation of foreign rum, for the Danish islands could not pay except with rum. The enumeration of logwood was killing the trade in foreign logwood between the mainland colonies and Europe and handing it over to foreigners. The restrictions on the shipment of lumber, potash, and flaxseed to Ireland not only hurt the Americans and the Irish but were ridiculous, since they forced the Irish to buy what they needed in the Baltic. The restrictions on the wine trade hurt the export of wheat, flour, and fish to the "Wine Islands" and produced no revenue for Britain. The opening of free ports in Dominica and Jamaica was of no benefit to the mainland colonies since all they could bring back in effect was molasses, and molasses could not begin to pay for the products sold in the foreign West Indies. In fact, the New Yorkers concluded, despite all the talk, the new legislation had added to the burdens on trade, not lessened them.[80]

The New York merchants asked the Boston merchants to join in and they did so. They had been listing and relisting their grievances ever since 1763. They soon had a petition covering the same ground as the New York petition but emphasizing the importance of the fisheries. The Boston merchants also deplored the many bonds and cockets required for most shipments, whereas the New York petition had mentioned only the inadequacy of the admiralty court at Halifax.[81]

The New York petition was tabled in high indignation by the House of Commons. The Massachusetts petition was not presented by the colonial

[80] BEP, 11 May 1767; HCJ, XXXI, 158–60.
[81] Andrews, CSMP, XIX, 174–75. A copy of the petition is in the Samuel Adams Papers, NYPL. It was also embodied in a letter of the House of Representatives to agent Dennys De Berdt. See Arthur Lee Papers, I, HUL.

agent, who thought it useless to do so. When such petitions with their honest, if somewhat exaggerated, statements were ignored, it is not surprising that many Americans were cynical about the motives of British merchants and the impartiality of Parliament in the commercial "reforms" of 1766. Furthermore, other issues soon showed that all was not well between the colonies and the mother country.

ॐ

Among the resolutions accompanying the repeal of the Stamp Act was one in which the House of Commons declared that those who had lost property during the Stamp Act riots "ought to have full and ample compensation made to them. . . ." [82] The secretary of state sent the resolutions to the colonial governors and told them to do their utmost for those who had suffered "from the madness of the people. . . ." [83] The governors followed orders but the legislatures concerned made political capital out of the demand, and delayed, obstructed, or gave in with ill grace.

The New Hampshire distributor, George Meserve, insisted that he had "suffered" but the legislature replied that he offered no proof, and in any case, the resolution did not apply to him.[84] Shortly after Rhode Island gave thanks for repeal, Governor Samuel Ward asked for the payment of over £2600, which he said was due Rhode Island for expenditures during the Seven Years War. The treasury in England refused because Rhode Island had not compensated the sufferers. Martin Howard and Dr. Thomas Moffat were in Britain at the time, telling their stories of the violence done them. When the Rhode Island assembly met in October 1766 it instructed the governor to write to all concerned that it knew nothing of the story that the Rhode Island mobs had been "encouraged and animated by . . . persons of consequence," and that it hoped its word was as good "as the suggestion of any evil minded persons on the other side of the water. . . ." Furthermore, no one had applied for compensation. If anyone did, he would be given consideration. Eventually Howard, Moffat, and Augustus Johnson did appeal to the assembly, but they appealed in vain.[85]

As might be expected, the fight in Massachusetts was conspicuous, and for once not devoid of humor. Shortly after the riots in August 1765 a committee of the Massachusetts council evaluated the damages. When the

[82] 24 Feb. 1766, HCJ, XXX, 602.
[83] Conway to the colonial governors, 31 March 1766, RICR, VI, 486–87; NYCD, VII, 823–24.
[84] BG, 21 July; VG(PD), 8 Aug. 1766.
[85] RICR, VI, 504–5, 508–14; BEP, 22 June, 14 Sept. 1767.

legislature met in September, Governor Bernard said that it should pay as an "act of justice," and do so before a "requisition" was made. The house replied that it deplored the riots but that payment might encourage further violence. And what did the governor mean by an "act of justice" and who had a right to "requisition" money from Massachusetts? If the house did anything at all it would be an act of generosity.

There the matter rested until June 1766, when Bernard sent the resolution of the House of Commons to the House of Representatives. He said flatly that since Parliament had asked for compensation, the representatives should stop disputing and pay. Once again the hapless governor had led with his chin. The house told him that a "recommendation" by Parliament meant something quite different from the word "requisition" he had used the previous September. The house then put off action until the next session, saying that since any grant would be an "act of generosity," and since it would be a gift of its constituents' money, it must first consult them. Bernard offered to co-operate in discovering the guilty rioters, and the house responded by appointing a committee of five obscure country members. Naturally the committee discovered nothing, although everybody in Boston from the governor on down knew who the leaders of the riots were.

When the legislature met in the fall of 1766, the house and the governor went round and round, for the Boston leaders had no intention of paying damages, particularly to their old enemy Thomas Hutchinson, who claimed more than £2000 sterling. In the midst of the haggling it began to dawn on some of the country members that the town of Boston ought to pay for the damages, not the government of the colony. The startled Boston leaders suddenly changed their tactics. They threw clouds of rhetoric at the governor, insisting that his request was a violation of the inherent right of the people to dispose of their money as they saw fit, and that it was just as important to pardon the rioters as to compensate the sufferers. Then, during a brief adjournment, the Boston leaders got a complete reversal of their instructions from the town meeting. They came back to the legislature with orders to compensate Hutchinson and the others, but at the same time, to secure a general pardon for the rioters. The instincts of country members were right, but they were simply no match for the political agility of the Bostonians. On 5 December 1766 the house passed a compensation bill, 54-35, which included a pardon. The power to pardon did not lie with the legislature, but the next day the governor and council approved the bill. The act was bitterly attacked by the anti-American members of Parliament, but not until the spring of 1770 did the Privy Council get around to vetoing it, and by then Hutchinson had his money.[86]

For once, however, it was the behavior of New York, not Massachusetts, which aroused anger in Britain and triggered a series of parliamentary acts which once more embroiled the colonies with the mother country. To begin with, the assembly refused to grant Cadwallader Colden the £195 he asked for his losses in the Stamp Act riots, and did so in the committee of the whole so there would be no record in the journals. Then by a vote of 11 to 10 it agreed to compensate the commander of the fort, Major James, as well as the owner of the mob-wrecked house in which James had lived. Apparently James's first bill was not approved, for in November the assembly agreed to pay him his "real loss" if he would take an oath to its correctness. The major appeared before the house, expressed his gratitude for £1745 and promised to tell the ministry of his feelings. The assembly then publicly refused to pay Colden because his loss "was occasioned by his own misconduct." The furious old man promptly wrote a pamphlet, which he sent to England. The next year when it was printed, both council and assembly, professing to be outraged, appointed a joint committee to discover the author, knowing perfectly well who it was, and instructed Governor Colden to prosecute him if he were ever found.[87]

&

The evasion or defiance of the Quartering Act of 1765 was far more serious than the bickering over compensation. Before the law was passed, South Carolina complained because it was supplying troops at frontier outposts while other colonies contributed nothing. Then in October 1765 the Commons House seized on the Stamp Act as an excuse for refusing further money: the Stamp Act would provide for troops so why should South Carolina? Secretary Conway in London was forced to admit that "she has some color for declining this expense. . . ."[88]

However, New York's evasion of the law was the most serious and conspicuous, for New York was the headquarters of General Thomas Gage. As he moved more troops into the colony during the Stamp Act crisis, he asked for supplies. Gage applied first to the Albany magistrates, who refused unless the legislature would compensate them. He then appealed to

[86] Thomas, Massachusetts, 326–37; APC:CS, V, 86–87.
[87] NYAJ, 19 June, 26, 29 Nov., 9 Dec.; Colden to SS, 24 June, 26 Dec. 1766, NYCD, VII, 832–34, 886–87; to BT, 23 Nov. 1767, Colden Letter Books, II, NYHSC(1877), 137–40.
[88] Gage, Corres., I, 69; II, 31, 284–85, 306.

the new governor, Sir Henry Moore, who sent the request and a copy of the Quartering Act to the assembly. The members examined the treasurer's accounts and found that he had £5000 granted for "refreshing" his Majesty's troops back in 1755, and another £4790 for the same purpose in 1762. They blandly resolved to give £400 to buy candles and firewood for the garrison at Fort George in the city. The house then adopted three resolutions: when the king's troops were in royal barracks they were supplied at no expense to the places in which they were stationed; there were adequate royal barracks in both New York and Albany; and if any money was needed for troops on the march the assembly would consider a grant after the money was spent.[89]

The irritated general once more approached the Albany magistrates and once more they refused unless the legislature acted first.[90] Meanwhile Gage continued to abandon or reduce frontier posts and move men toward the coast. By filling up what the assembly called royal barracks, he hoped to force it to obey the Quartering Act.[91] When the legislature met in May 1766 there was a large body of troops in the colony. The Sons of Liberty in the city were still rioting and were quarreling with the soldiers. The tenant-farmer rebellion seemed out of hand and the local militia could not be depended upon. The legislature, dominated by the great landlords, asked Gage for British regulars to suppress the tenants. He furnished the troops, but without enthusiasm. He said that "the rich and most powerful people of the province" were the most affected by the tenant uprising and "they certainly deserve any losses they may sustain, for it is the work of their own hands. They first sowed the seeds of sedition amongst the people and taught them to rise in opposition to the laws. . . ."[92]

Gage naturally enough expected supplies in return. Instead of complying, the legislature passed still more resolutions: supplies would be too expensive since no one knew how many troops might come in the future and the articles requested were "unprecedented"; if there was a "proper" requisition, the house would pay for barracks, bedding, kitchen utensils, firewood, and candles; and finally, if the house did not comply, the service would not suffer since the troops had done well enough in the past. In any case, the legislature declared, the treasurer had nearly £4000 on hand, sub-

[89] Gage to SS, 21 Dec. 1765, ibid. I, 76–77; NYAJ, 3, 5, 13 Dec. 1765.
[90] Gage to SS, 22 Feb. 1766, Gage, Corres., I, 84.
[91] To SS, 16 Jan., 28 March, 6 May, ibid. I, 81–91.
[92] Gage to SS, 24 June, ibid. I, 95. Gage reported that "every branch of the legislature" wanted his help but no request is recorded in the journals. When the governor asked the legislature to pay the extra expenses of the two regiments used, the assembly even rejected a proposal to pay the privates a few shillings each. NYAJ, 9, 12 Dec. 1766.

ject to the orders of the commander in chief. Once more the governor demanded supplies and the assembly was at last forced to act, although it could still evade the letter of the law. It granted £3200 from the old funds of 1762 to provide the New York and Albany barracks with beds, bedding, firewood, candles, and kitchen utensils for two battalions of not more than 500 men each for a period of one year. The salt, vinegar, cider, and beer or rum demanded by the Quartering Act were ignored, as was the very name of the act itself.[93]

The governor was outraged but Gage advised him to accept the bill as better than nothing at all, and because it might have a good effect on other colonies. When Moore had arrived in New York during the Stamp Act crisis, he had listened approvingly to tales about Cadwallader Colden, but now his letters began to sound like those of the old lieutenant governor. The assembly had treated his message as a mere "requisition," and had avoided the "least mention" of the act upon which it was based. He was convinced that every act of Parliament "not backed by a sufficient power to enforce it" would suffer the fate of the Quartering Act in New York.[94]

Nor was New York's action the good example Gage hoped for. Previously he had sent troops through New Jersey and Pennsylvania without encountering difficulty from their legislatures. Now the New Jersey council declared that the Quartering Act was as much of a tax as the Stamp Act and even more unfair, since it did not tax colonies where there were no troops. In December the New Jersey legislature, like New York's, granted some supplies but not others, and avoided all mention of the Quartering Act.[95]

New York's action brought an immediate response from the new secretary of state in the Pitt ministry, Lord Shelburne. New York must obey the Quartering Act to the letter and without quibbling.[96] Meanwhile, New York was concerned with another dispute, that over paper money, which was to be tied up with the fight over the Quartering Act until New York won a victory in both disputes. Almost to a man the New York leaders objected to the Currency Act of 1764, for their own currency had been conservatively managed, highly successful, and, they insisted, indispensable to their prosperity. The assembly proposed an issue in June 1766 and Governor Moore supported the demand, saying that New York's old issues of paper would end in 1767. The governor was wrong, replied the board of

[93] NYAJ, 13, 19, 20, 23 June, 3 July 1766.
[94] To SS, 20 June, NYCD, VII, 831–32.
[95] To SS, 24 June, Gage, Corres., I, 93–96; N.J. Ar., IX, 577.
[96] 9 Aug. 1766, NYCD, VII, 847–48.

trade—New York's issues did not run out until November 1768—but recommended that New York be allowed to issue new money under certain restrictions. Accordingly the Privy Council told Governor Moore that New York could issue £260,000 if an adequate sinking fund were provided, if the issue were called in within five years, and if the bill were submitted to Britain for approval before going into effect.[97]

When Governor Moore received this instruction, he called the assembly together in November 1766. Tactfully he held back Shelburne's letter and laid his new instruction before the assembly as an example of the king's "paternal regard and protection." The assembly was contemptuous: since no paper money bill could pass without a suspending clause, "we are prepared to bear our distresses as well as we are able" unless the governor would approve a money bill without such an "unusual clause." [98] The governor replied by delivering a copy of Shelburne's letter demanding compliance with the Quartering Act. The assembly delayed an answer for a month and then flatly refused. Both the house and its constituents were unanimous, said the governor. He could have dissolved the assembly and called a new election but had he done so the same members would have been re-elected and "a flame would have lighted up throughout the country, and not a single advantage derived from it. . . ." [99]

The complaints against the Revenue Act of 1766, the delay in compensating sufferers in the Stamp Act riots, and the refusal of New York to obey the Quartering Act reached a Parliament already indignant at American "ingratitude." Even the friends of America had no defense to offer. The emotions generated by the news of the aftermath of the Stamp Act in America lay behind much of the legislation of the Townshend program in the spring of 1767, a program which brought on a new crisis between Britain and the colonies. And among the laws passed, none was more striking or regarded by many Americans as more dangerous than the act suspending the New York assembly until it agreed to obey the letter of the Quartering Act of 1765.

[97] NYAJ, 17, 19 June; NYCD, VII, 827–28; APC:CS, IV, 754–55.
[98] NYAJ, 10, 13 Nov.
[99] Ibid. 18 Nov., 15 Dec.; Moore to SS, 19 Dec., NYCD, VII, 883–84.

VIII

The Aftermath of the Stamp Act in Britain:
The Townshend Program

The Rockingham ministry repealed the Stamp Act and enacted the commercial reforms demanded by English merchants and manufacturers, but its hold on power was tenuous for it was no secret that George III wanted to be rid of it. Meanwhile the king was acquiring a following in the House of Commons, men who looked to him as a leader and the source of office, rather than to the leaders of the old factions. George III had deplored "faction" ever since 1760 and he still did so, but the "king's friends," as their enemies called them, were now a "faction" and an ever more powerful one. Many of them voted against repeal of the Stamp Act, and they intrigued constantly for the downfall of the Rockinghams, as did Pitt's followers who were members of the ministry.

At the end of April 1766, Pitt's supporter, the Duke of Grafton, a secretary of state, struck the first blow. He declared that he could not "retain any degree of honor, if he remained part of a ministry that set Mr. Pitt at defiance," and urged the king to send for Pitt and "offer him his own terms." At the moment, however, George III was willing to retain the ministry in the hope that "the chapter of accidents may be favorable to me. . . ." [1] But a month later, when Rockingham proposed to delay a grant of money to the king's brothers, George III denounced the ministers as "weak boys" and said that "my prudence is now exhausted; I am inclined to take any step that will preserve my honor." [2]

Meanwhile, rumors of the American response to the repeal of the Stamp Act affected political speculation. American legislatures, on hearing of

[1] To the Lord Chancellor, 28 April, Geo. III *Corres.*, I, 295.
[2] To Lord Egmont, 28 May, ibid. I, 347.

215

Pitt's speech against the Stamp Act, had reportedly passed resolutions going far beyond anything Pitt had said. There were predictions that only Pitt could handle the situation, and rumors that the king would offer Pitt his own terms to form a ministry. Pitt had been playing a very tricky political game ever since the repeal. To frighten the ministry, he appeared on the point of reconciliation with George Grenville; then he voted against Grenville to make the king hope that he could be won over.

What Pitt wanted, wrote David Hume, was "to be minister with full power of modeling the administration as he pleases." And if the rumors from America were true, Pitt was "the only man who can either bring the Americans to submit peaceably by his authority; or subdue them by his vigor. It does not seem probable that the repeal of the Stamp Act will alone suffice." [3] Hume was only partly right. Pitt was waiting to form a ministry on his own terms, and there was trouble in America, but the American policies of his ministry added to the confusion, multiplied the problems, and widened the breach between Britain and America.

Early in July, George III told Rockingham that his ministry was too weak to continue. He then asked Pitt for his thoughts on the formation of an "able and dignified ministry." The king made it plain that he was in hearty accord with Pitt's ideas, for both despised "faction" and believed that "measures" not "men" should govern. Neither of them seemed to realize that the king himself was the leader of a "faction," that Pitt was dependent upon it, and that "men" made "measures."

Pitt's ministry contained an even more discordant group of personalities than its predecessor. Pitt wanted men who would take orders from him. In naming the ministers, he apparently paid no attention to their ideas or to their attitudes on American affairs, and hence he included both friends and enemies of the colonies. His brother-in-law, Lord Temple, refused to join. Temple was no man to take orders and he demanded a share of the patronage, but under Pitt he would have to do the former and do without the latter. He would not, he wrote his sister, Pitt's wife, be "stuck into a ministry as a great cipher at the head of the Treasury, surrounded with other ciphers, all named by Mr. Pitt. . . ." [4]

What Pitt did, said his other brother-in-law, George Grenville, was to bring in his "immediate dependents, who joined the rump of the last administration. . . ." [5] As for himself, Pitt became the Earl of Chatham and

[3] To Lord W——, 8 May 1766, HM 7203, HEHL.
[4] To Lady Chatham, 27 July, Pitt, *Corres.*, II, 468.
[5] George Grenville to Lord Trevor, 19 July, Grenville Letter Books, II, HEHL.

took the sinecure office of Lord Privy Seal. Grenville commented cynically that Pitt, who had formerly refused to be responsible unless he could guide, now insisted on guiding without being responsible: "the Great Commoner retreats from the scene of business into the House of Peers from whence he is to issue his mandates. . . ." Bitterly Grenville hoped that the "new made peer" would "taste the fruits of his own public spirited, comprehensive, temperate, and disinterested principles, but I sincerely lament for the King and his people the instability and weakness of government and the misfortunes which I fear must be the consequences of it. These are my sentiments as a public man. . . ." [6] George Grenville, who had a way of being wrong, was right for once, and the history of the Chatham ministry was one of disaster for Pitt personally, and of further chaos for Britain and for America.

Lord Barrington, an enemy of America, stayed on as secretary at war. Charles Townshend, who openly favored taxation of the colonies, and who resented giving up his lucrative job as paymaster of the forces, became chancellor of the exchequer. Lord Camden, who as chief justice in 1763 had released Wilkes, became lord chancellor. He was friendly toward America, as was General Henry Conway, who stayed on as a secretary of state. Lord Shelburne, who became secretary of state for the southern department and hence was in charge of colonial affairs, spent so much time collecting information that he had little time to formulate, or at least to further, policies. Isaac Barré (maker of the "Sons of Liberty" speech) was rewarded with an Irish post. The Duke of Grafton, who had resigned from the Rockingham ministry and thus helped topple it, became virtual head of the ministry as first lord of the treasury. Grafton, however, cared little for the business of government. No wonder then that George Grenville despaired, as did George III.

Pitt made the political mistake of his life in becoming the Earl of Chatham. His great power had been in part due to his ability to dominate the House of Commons. In addition, as the "Great Commoner," he had for years pictured himself as the defender of "the people" of Britain against the corrupt politicians. He had been the hero of the middle class, the merchants, and the mob of London, but now they were disillusioned with and furious at their former idol: to them he became "Lord Cheetem." The city of London refused to congratulate him, and the lamps set up for a great celebration of his return to power were torn down by mobs. Popular broadsides and pamphlets denounced him for his apostasy, and in high places

[6] To the Earl of Fife, 31 July; to Alexander Wedderburn, 5 Aug., ibid.

Lord Temple inspired vicious attacks. Chatham's followers replied in kind to that conceited, empty-headed nobleman.[7]

The new ministry was faced with a widespread domestic crisis. The grain harvest was bad in the summer of 1766 and the price of wheat, flour, and bread went up and up. Bread riots occurred all over England and mobs destroyed flour mills and seized food supplies and sold them at low prices. Soldiers were called out and men were killed. In September the ministry decreed that an old statute against forestallers, engrossers, and regraters was in effect; and then went even further and prohibited the export of all grain from England, despite a law of Parliament that exports could not be prohibited until grain reached a certain price. As soon as Parliament met in November the opposition attacked the use of such "arbitrary power." George Grenville proclaimed, in terms familiar on the other side of the Atlantic, that the suspension of an act of Parliament was founded on the "dangerous and exploded doctrine of a legislative power in the Privy Council in cases of necessity. . . ." The poor should be taken care of but an end should be put to the idea that the Privy Council might "suspend or supersede the laws and constitution, a plea which has more than once brought us to the brink of slavery and destruction." [8]

In the House of Commons a spokesman for the ministry argued that the king had the suspending power whenever the public welfare demanded it. Grenville pounced on him and forced him "further to explain himself" to the point where he confessed that only necessity could make it excusable, and only an act of Parliament could justify it. A few days later, when a bill was brought in to indemnify officials who had acted under the proclamation, Grenville insisted that the ministry itself be named in the bill. The ministry agreed and all Chatham's praise of the act could not hide the humiliation his ministry suffered, or the gloating of George Grenville, who wrote: "What a disgrace is this at the outset of an administration calling themselves friends of liberty. . . ." [9]

The ministry of the "strong man" was tottering even before what amounted to its first defeat. Lord Egmont resigned as head of the admiralty almost as soon as the ministry was formed because he was irked by Chatham's dictatorial ways. Attempts were made to bring in the Bedfords,

[7] Sherrard, *Chatham*, 211–20; John Brooke, *The Chatham Administration, 1766–1768* (London, 1956), chapter I. For a typical attack on Chatham see *The Gentleman's Magazine*, August 1766, 347–52, and for an answer, ibid. 370–76.
[8] To George Chalmers, 5 Oct., Grenville Letter Books, II, HEHL.
[9] PH, XVI, 245–314; Grenville to the Earl of Bucks, 22 Nov., Grenville Letter Books, II, HEHL.

but Chatham would not give them enough room at the public trough. Before the end of November Rockingham pulled out seven of his followers in an effort to bring the ministry down, but he failed; and his man, General Conway, refused to resign. It was not a matter either of principle or of policy; Chatham had removed a Rockingham follower from a minor post to make way for another man. A second attempt to bring in the Bedford faction failed because they had raised their price and in return for votes were now demanding more jobs and titles than ever. The ministry was kept in power only by calling in still more of the king's friends.[10]

Far more significant were the defeats Chatham suffered in the field of finance. He knew little of the subject and cared even less, but the plight of the government was real and the British taxpayers were very clamorous. The repeal of the Stamp Act meant that no more money could be raised in America. As William Beckford, one of Chatham's supporters, put it, "we must look to the East and not to the West." [11] The "East" meant the East India Company, whose reputedly fabulous profits were a temptation to any government desperate for funds. The company had made great territorial gains during the Seven Years War, and reports reached England that the new revenues from Bengal alone would add £2,000,000 a year to the company's profits. These stories set off a boom in East India Company stock and many of the stockowners demanded greater dividends. Meanwhile, Chatham proposed to raid the company and force it to disgorge for the benefit of the government. Thus he began a political struggle which was to last for years and which was to help shape the future of the American colonies in a way that no one could foresee in 1766.

Chatham proposed a parliamentary inquiry into the affairs of the company preliminary to divesting it of its territories in India and of most of its revenues. The proposal at once split the ministry. To General Conway, it looked like a raid on private property, while Charles Townshend thought the affair should be handled by private negotiations, not by Parliament. Politics was at once involved, for various members of Parliament and the ministry either were or became stockholders and supported one or another of the various warring groups fighting for control of the company, and the company in turn played politics with members of Parliament. Lord Shelburne, a stockholder, took one side; Charles Townshend acquired stock and took another.

10 Brooke, *Chatham*, chapter II.
11 Quoted, Ritcheson, *British Politics*, 80. For accounts of the supposedly lush profits of the East India Company and arguments for a government raid upon it, see *The Gentleman's Magazine*, Sept. and Oct. 1766, 395-97, 443-46.

Once the proceedings against the East India Company were started, they were left in the hands of Chatham's warring colleagues, for he retired to Bath in December 1766, and by the spring of 1767 was apparently demented. He either refused to see his colleagues or gave them advice so vague as to be meaningless. George III, desperate for a stable ministry, pled with Chatham for help, but he ignored the king as he did the ministers. The attack on the East India Company collapsed. Shelburne eventually took charge of negotiations and in May 1767 the ministry accepted an offer of £400,000 a year and left the company in control of its territories in India.[12]

The man who had gone into office to end "faction" and to bring the East India Company under government control, failed in both. Above all, he had promised to "settle" the affairs of America, but his illness meant that American policy as well was left to others. What Chatham had in mind, if anything, is unknown. His magnificent oratory contained no practical program nor did he offer any. It is unlikely, given the situation in America, that Chatham would have had any more success than had others who tried. When he organized his ministry in July 1766, he at first considered the creation of a third secretaryship of state in direct charge of American affairs, and for a brief time he thought of holding it himself.[13]

Reform was long overdue, for colonial affairs were directed or misdirected by a great many overlapping boards and officials: the board of trade, the secretary of state for the southern department, the admiralty, the war office, the treasury, and the Privy Council. As a result, even when a clear-cut policy was established, or a problem arose, decisions were often delayed or lost sight of in the confusion, as papers were shuffled from office to office and often mislaid or ignored. The advantage, of course, lay with the Americans, who sometimes managed for years to do in practice what in theory they were not supposed to do.

Reforms had been attempted. A secretary of state for the colonies had been proposed as early as 1751. The next year the board of trade was given more influence. Until then colonial governors had reported on political matters to the secretary of state for the southern department, and on economic matters to the board of trade. In 1752 the board was given the power to nominate all governors and lesser officials in the colonies, and the governors were told to send all correspondence to the board. Then in 1761

[12] Lucy S. Sutherland, *The East India Company in Eighteenth-Century Politics* (Oxford, 1952), chapter VI, "The First Parliamentary Intervention, 1766–7."
[13] Charles R. Ritcheson, "The Elder Pitt and an American Department," AHR, LVII (1951–52).

the right to nominate was taken away. Confusion increased as Parliament interfered increasingly in American affairs after 1763. However inefficient the various boards and agencies might be, they did know something of America. All too many members of Parliament knew nothing, and they showed no interest in learning—although perhaps no member was as ignorant as the man whom an American heard ask whether Philadelphia was in the East or West Indies, and say that "he had a notion it was upon the coast of Sumatra." [14]

In 1766, Chatham added to the confusion. He appointed Lord Hillsborough president of the board of trade and then stripped the board of what little influence it had. The correspondence with colonial governors and matters of commercial and financial policy were turned over to the ministers, with most of the authority going to the secretary of state for the southern department.[15] In this post was Chatham's devoted follower, the Earl of Shelburne, known as a friend of the colonies because he had fought for the repeal of the Stamp Act in the House of Lords.

Even before the Chatham ministry took over, rumors of American reactions to the repeal of the Stamp Act, some of them bordering on fantasy, reached London. Late in May the Americans were said to be arming, and that repeal of the Stamp Act would not satisfy them. In June the story spread that South Carolina had declared its independence of Britain. By September some facts were at hand which embarrassed friends of the colonies and convinced men such as Grenville that they had been right all along. New York had refused to obey the Quartering Act, and both that colony and Massachusetts were ignoring or evading Parliament's resolution asking for compensation of victims of the Stamp Act riots. On 4 September the London *Public Ledger* printed George Mason's letter to the London merchants which made it distinctly clear that at least some Americans were not going to abase themselves in gratitude for Parliament's repeal of the Stamp Act. Parliament had merely righted a wrong; and even then had not acknowledged the rights of the colonies but had acted only for the sake of commercial expediency.[16]

When Parliament met in November the domestic economic crisis prevented consideration of the colonies. By the time it met again in the mid-

[14] APC:CS, IV, 154–57; NYCD, VII, 848–49. For the quotation, see Michael G. Kammen, "The Colonial Agents, English Politics, and the American Revolution," WMQ, 3 ser. XXII (1965), 252.
[15] NYCD, VII, 848–49; Shelburne to BT, 26 Aug. 1766, CHOP, II, 70–71.
[16] Thomas Whately to George Grenville, 23 May, 25 June, 5 Sept., GP, III, 236–37, 253, 315–16.

dle of January 1767, the news from America was causing excitement everywhere. New York had again refused to obey the letter of the Quartering
Act and it still refused to compensate Cadwallader Colden. Massachusetts
had compensated the victims of the Stamp Act riots but had pardoned the
rioters. To make matters worse, the forthright petition of 240 New York
merchants demanding freer trade, and sharply criticizing the Revenue Acts
of 1764 and 1766, had reached London.

As the news came in, Shelburne reported it to Chatham at Bath. The
Americans' refusal to obey the Quartering Act was due "to their jealousy of
being some time or other taxed internally by the Parliament of Great Britain." The Declaratory Act had spread alarm throughout America. Such
stories were likely to be the talk of the town, said Shelburne, and doubtless
George Grenville would say in the House of Commons that the Americans
were in rebellion.[17] Chatham was shocked. The actions of the Americans,
he replied, would leave no room to say anything in their defense. The New
Yorkers were infatuated and "doing the work of their worst enemies themselves." He predicted that "the torrent of indignation in Parliament"
would become irresistible. He denounced the petition of the New York
merchants as "highly improper; in point of time, most absurd; in the extent of their pretensions, most excessive; and in the reasoning, most grossly
fallacious and offensive." A few days later he blamed everything on the
Stamp Act, which, he said, "has frightened those irritable and umbrageous
people quite out of their senses." The problem of the Quartering Act and
the New York merchants' petition must be laid before Parliament. If the
ministry did not, the opposition would make political capital. But Chatham had nothing else to offer except the rhetorical and meaningless statement that "in pursuing steadily one's duty, one cannot lose one's way." [18]

Shelburne knew that New York's behavior could not be ignored but neither the king nor the cabinet replied with anything except assertions that
the Quartering Act must be enforced. Politically, as he told Chatham, the
"government appears called upon . . . to support the authority of Parliament and the coercive power of this country." Shelburne then proposed to
Chatham a measure far more drastic than anything finally adopted: that a
military man be sent as governor of New York and that he be given power
to quarter troops in private homes. Yet Shelburne recognized the danger
of establishing such a precedent. And he predicted that if the Americans
resisted, France and Spain would not hesitate to break the peace, "the days

[17] Shelburne to Pitt, 1, 6 Feb. 1767, Pitt, *Corres.*, III, 184–85, 191–93.
[18] Pitt to Shelburne, 3, 7 Feb., ibid. 188–89, 193–94.

of which they already begin to count." Chatham, by now almost completely incompetent, repeated that the whole issue should be laid before Parliament.[19]

Shelburne seemed as incapable of independent action as Chatham, yet he understood, as few men did, the complexities of America. He realized that each of the colonies had different interests, and yet that they had much in common. He knew that the Currency Act of 1764 was unrealistic. He was aware of the problems created by the acquisition of western territory, of the Indian trade, and of political relations with the Indians. He knew too that political pressure in Britain demanded the establishment of some form of American revenue. He worked hard at gathering information, for he believed that long-range policies were the only possible solution, and that they must be based on facts.[20]

But it was no time for a scholarly approach in a Parliament dominated by emotions and stirred up by opposition politicians who seized on every issue that might topple the ministry. Furthermore, Shelburne's colleagues neither liked nor trusted him, and while he dallied, control of colonial policy was taken from him. By the spring of 1767 it was in the hands of Charles Townshend, chancellor of the exchequer, and to a degree, in those of George Grenville. Grenville insisted that America must be taxed, partly to save money, partly to demonstrate the sovereignty of Parliament, partly to justify the colonial policies of his own ministry, and not least, to bring about the downfall of the Chatham ministry. And, in effect, Townshend was Grenville's ally. The emotions generated by news from America aided both of them in a campaign which for sheer irresponsibility has seldom been matched in a legislative body.

Late in January 1767 when Parliament heard that the army in America would cost about £400,000, Grenville at once proposed to cut the amount in half and to require the Americans to pay the balance. Only Grenville's followers voted for the motion, but in the course of the debate Townshend delighted the opposition and astounded his colleagues, whom he had not consulted. He agreed that America should pay part of the cost of the army, approved of the principle of the Stamp Act, and ridiculed Pitt's distinction between external and internal taxes as "absurd, nonsensical, and ridiculous to the highest degree. . . ." Gaily he promised to find enough revenue in America to pay all the expenses there. How it could be done, no one knew,

---

[19] Ritcheson, *British Politics*, 88–89; Shelburne to Pitt, 16 Feb., Pitt, *Corres.*, III, 206–11, deletes Shelburne's drastic proposals concerning New York.
[20] For example, see Shelburne to Gage, 11 Dec. 1766, Gage, *Corres.*, II, 47–51.

least of all Townshend. Gleefully Grenville reported that "the Earl of Chatham is still at Bath and consequently the king's administration has got the gout and hobbles horribly. Mr. Charles Townshend indeed seems to wish to move a little more nimbly and to try to walk without crutches." [21]

In February, Grenville renewed the attack. He moved that the expenses in America be reduced and that the troops be moved from the frontiers to the older provinces. Again he was beaten, but the minority on his side was larger than ever before. Townshend harangued "inimitably on both sides of the question, and by turns was cheered by every party in the house." [22] Meanwhile the various opposition groups were planning a move ever popular with politicians: a cut in taxes. In January, Grenville had said it could be done if the Americans were made to pay a part of the expense of the army. The only fear among the opposition was that Grenville might get the credit if taxes were lowered. George III was furious. He said that Grenville was riding his "hobby horse, the reduction of expenses," and that his conduct was "as abundant in absurdities as in the affair of the Stamp Act; for there he first deprived the Americans by restraining their trade, from the means of acquiring wealth, and [then] taxed them. . . ." Now, said the indignant king, Grenville objects to the only means of restoring government finance which is to deprive the East India Company of its territorial revenues, and yet he proposes to cut the land tax. He bewailed the fact that no one seemed to realize that "the great acquisitions made by the successful war must necessarily give rise to an increase of expense in the peace establishment. . . ." [23] Whatever his limitations, George III was the only person in power thinking like a statesman.

On February 25, Townshend proposed that the land tax remain at four shillings in the pound. At once a Rockingham follower moved that it be reduced to three shillings; and the House of Commons voted for the motion 206-188. Grenville got the credit anyway, for as he wrote in his diary, "the joy in the House of Commons was very great, all the country gentlemen coming round Mr. Grenville, shaking him by the hand, and testifying the greatest satisfaction." [24] The ministry had been caught napping, and even some of Chatham's followers voted for the reduction—for once, more afraid of the voters than of their leader. Cynically George III commented that "those who have voted for it can have been guided only by the incite-

[21] To Earl of Bucks, 27 Jan., Grenville Letter Books, II, HEHL.
[22] Lord Charlemont to Henry Flood, 19 Feb., Pitt, Corres., III, 210n.
[23] To Conway, 18 Feb.; to Grafton, 24 Feb., Geo. III Corres., I, 450–52.
[24] GP, IV, 211–12.

ments that too frequently direct the conduct of politicians, the shadow of popularity. . . ." [25]

The House of Commons voted the budget out of balance at a time when the government was desperate for money, so much so that Chatham himself was asked to pay back the thousands of pounds he had held ever since he had been paymaster of the forces years before.[26] An agreement with the East India Company was still in the future. It was up to Townshend to make good the irresponsible promise he had made in January. Chatham, when he heard of the reduction of the land tax, and of the stalling of the attack on the East India Company, roused himself enough to make the trip to London, where he tried to replace Townshend with Lord North. But North refused, and shortly thereafter Chatham collapsed completely, leaving his confused colleagues virtually at the mercy of "Champagne Charlie" Townshend.

More self-assured than ever, Townshend delivered an ultimatum to the cabinet: either it must agree to his proposals or he would resign and bring down the ministry. American expenses must be cut by withdrawing the troops from the frontiers and stationing them near the great towns. The expense of Indian affairs must be charged to the colonies. Finally, the ministry must sanction import duties to be collected in American ports.[27] Spinelessly the ministers agreed, and Townshend went ahead with his plans, some of which had originated with George Grenville. Shelburne gave up all but one thing: he asked for time to propose a different plan for the American West and his request was granted. Other than that, American policy was determined by an irresponsible chancellor of the exchequer and by a majority of Parliament more determined than ever to demonstrate British sovereignty over the colonies.

Townshend spelled out his program in May. He offered three resolutions aimed at New York: that its assembly had refused to obey the Quartering Act; that the provision it had made was inadequate; and that the legislature should be forbidden to pass any legislation until it obeyed.[28] In addition, he proposed the establishment of an American board of customs. As

[25] To Conway, 27 Feb., Geo. III *Corres.*, I, 454.
[26] Grafton to Pitt, 29 March, Pitt, *Corres.*, III, 239. Several paymasters in the eighteenth century made fortunes. They collected commissions on foreign subsidies and pocketed interest on government money they loaned. Pitt opposed such practices but apparently did not turn over all the funds in his hands when he gave up his post.
[27] Grafton to Pitt and Shelburne to Pitt, 13 March, reporting on cabinet meeting of 12 March, ibid. 231–36.
[28] HCJ, XXXI, 364. Townshend seems to have originated the idea of suspending the New York Assembly. See Sir Lewis Namier and John Brooke, *Charles Townshend* (London, 1964), 176–77.

for revenue, he suggested that taxes in the form of import duties be collected in American ports. He admitted that the duties would not bring in more than £35,000 or £40,000 a year. On the whole, his tone was moderate, but he urged that by one act Parliament should demonstrate its sovereignty, although he was opposed to the use of military force which some demanded. His speech, "so consonant to the character of a man of business, and so unlike the wanton sallies of the man of parts and pleasure, was (however modified) but too well calculated to inflame the passions of a legislature whose authority was called in question, and who are naturally not prone to weigh the effusions of men entitled to as much freedom as themselves, while in an apparent situation of dependence."

The speech, Horace Walpole went on, "could but expand the narrow heart of Grenville with triumph." Nevertheless, Grenville damned the ministers for their faults and insisted that the authority of Parliament be enforced to the full.[29] He proposed that Parliament adopt an oath law which in effect would require every colonial governor, councilor, and elected assemblyman to subscribe to the Declaratory Act. The oath would read that "the colonies and plantations in America are, and of right ought to be, subordinate unto, and dependent upon, the imperial Crown and Parliament of Great Britain," and that the king and Parliament had the right, power, and authority to make laws "to bind the colonies and people of America . . . in all cases whatsoever." [30] The Commons rejected it, but nine years later Richard Henry Lee used some of its language when on 7 June 1776 he moved that the American colonies "are, and of right ought to be free and independent states."

The Commons then approved the suspension of the New York Assembly, the enactment of a new American revenue act, and the creation of an American board of customs commissioners.[31] The Townshend acts, as they have been known ever since, were passed by the end of June. Born of emotional heat and of a determination to bring the colonies to heel, they were as certain to arouse opposition as if they had been specifically designed for the purpose.

The Revenue Act of 1767 was one of the most futile and inept laws of

[29] Horace Walpole, *Memoirs of the Reign of King George the Third* (G. F. Russell Barker, ed., 4 vols., London, 1894), III, 24–25.

[30] HCJ, XXXI, 364–65. The *Boston Evening Post* printed the proposed oath and noted its rejection on 6 July.

[31] 12, 16 June, HCJ, XXXI, 403, 408. The three acts are reprinted in EDH, IX, 701–4. Namier and Brooke, *Townshend*, 178–79, point out that Townshend first proposed the payment of officials' salaries when he was a junior minister in 1754. This policy was therefore the only consistent one in his entire career.

the age. It had its origin in Townshend's promise that he could find revenues in America to make up for the reduction in the British land tax. But the law did nothing to make up the deficit; instead of placing the money at the disposal of Parliament, it was put in a separate fund for the use of the Crown, which meant in practice that it was at the disposition of the prime minister as first lord of the treasury. In addition, the act completely reversed the old policy of encouraging British exports. Instead, import duties collected in American ports on British glass, red and white lead, painter's colors, paper, and threepence a pound on tea, would within a few months hinder British exports. The attempt to collect such duties in America was an open challenge which Americans did not ignore.

Even careful planning could not have created a law more certain to arouse American opposition, for its purpose was to interfere in the internal politics of the colonies. The money collected was to be used to pay the salaries of royal governors, judges, and other officials, and thus, presumably, to free them from their dependence on colonial legislatures. Inevitably, therefore, it raised a "constitutional" issue, for colonial legislatures ever since the seventeenth century had had no more cherished claim than their "right" to vote the salaries of officials. Furthermore, the law raised the constitutional issue of the right of taxation, for it was as frankly a revenue measure as the Stamp Act, despite its guise as an "external tax."

Then too the duties were payable in sterling. This requirement, at a time when money was scarcer than ever in the colonies, when Parliament was ignoring the bad effects of the Currency Act of 1764, added fervor to American opposition. And finally, as if to guarantee that nothing that might give offense was omitted, colonial supreme courts were specifically authorized to issue writs of assistance to customs officers. These general writs allowed them to search anywhere for goods presumed to be smuggled or prohibited.

The act suspending the New York Assembly was a striking example of parliamentary encroachment on the powers of the Crown, for royal governors had always called, prorogued, and dissolved legislatures. It had also been the sole prerogative of the Crown to approve or veto acts of colonial legislatures. Parliament now forbade the governor of New York to approve legislation passed by the assembly after 1 October 1767, forbade the assembly to pass acts, and if it did, declared them "null and void" in advance. These multiple prohibitions were to remain in effect until the New York Assembly agreed to all the provisions of the Quartering Act of 1765. The one thing the assembly could do was elect a speaker. Every American, whatever his political complexion, was alarmed by this act; its implications for the very existence of independent colonial legislatures were obvious.

The establishment of an American board of customs had been talked of from time to time, and there was a clear need for one if the customs service in the colonies was to operate efficiently. Officials and merchants often had to submit problems to the commissioners of the customs in England, who knew little of colonial conditions, and the result had been endless delay and confusion. The law of 1767 created a board of five members in America with all the powers of administration and enforcement possessed by the customs board in England. The ministry then appointed five men, some of whom were already unpopular in America, and with a perversity amounting to genius, placed the board in the town of Boston.

Parliament passed only one more act concerning the regulation of American trade before the outbreak of the war for independence. The Revenue Act of 1764 had authorized the establishment of a vice-admiralty court over all America, and in 1765 one had been created at Halifax, Nova Scotia. The law gave customs officials a variety of choices: they might, as before, take seizures to a colonial vice-admiralty or a common law court, but now they could take a case directly to the new court if they chose. It was soon obvious that the court at Halifax was almost useless, not only because of the distance from the centers of commerce but also because the weather during a large part of the year made it difficult to get there. In the spring of 1768 parliament therefore authorized additional courts, and in July the admiralty established three new courts in addition to the one at Halifax: at Boston, Philadelphia, and Charleston. The courts served as courts of appeal from the colonial courts, but were given original jurisdiction in their districts as well.[32]

No area of British colonial policy was more beclouded or more subject to the vagaries of ministerial change than that relating to the vast acquisitions of 1763: Canada and the Mississippi Valley.[33] The new territories were never so much in the public eye as the old seacoast colonies, but they were close to the hearts of many people on both sides of the Atlantic: fur trad-

[32] Order in Council establishing the courts, 6 July 1768, EHD, IX, 707–8. For an illuminating study of the role of the vice-admiralty courts, see Carl W. Ubbelohde, *The Vice-Admiralty Courts and the American Revolution* (Chapel Hill, 1960).
[33] The account of western policy which follows is based in large measure on Alvord, *Mississippi Valley in British Politics*; hence only a few citations are given. However, reference should be made to the various works listed in the bibliographes in EHD, IX, 623, 630–31, which qualify some of the conclusions offered by Alvord.

ers, land speculators, and politicians. They were, furthermore, the source of keen intercolonial rivalries.

The Proclamation of 1763 outlined broad policies but did not specify methods for carrying them into effect. The West was reserved to the Indians by a boundary line; the power to purchase land within the area was reserved to the Crown; and the regulation of the fur trade and of political relations with the Indians was placed in the hands of royal officials. Beyond these generalities the proclamation did not go. The Grenville ministry was clearly for imperial control of the West, and it asked General Gage and the two Indian superintendents for advice on practical details. John Stuart and Sir William Johnson not only sent advice, but Johnson also sent his deputy, a tough Irish fur trader, George Croghan, to London to explain his ideas. Despite his rough life on the frontier, Croghan was soon able to analyze the political situation in England: "The people here spend their time in nothing but abusing one another and striving who shall be in power with a view to serve themselves and their friends, and neglect the public." [34]

A plan for imperial regulation of the frontier was ready by July 1764. It proposed to make the two Indian superintendents into virtual dictators, free from control of the colonial governors and the commanding general in America, and responsible only to the ministry in London. The Indians were to be grouped into districts and subdistricts. In each subdistrict, commissaries appointed by the Indian superintendents were to regulate the fur trade, fix prices, prevent the sale of rum and ammunition, and act as justices of the peace in disputes, with final appeal only to the Indian superintendents. In addition, a permanent boundary line was to be run between the whites and the Indians, for the Proclamation of 1763 had left whites west of the line and Indians to the east.

The plan was expensive: it would cost at least £20,000 a year, and the hard-pressed Grenville ministry never adopted it officially. The Indian superintendents were told to carry out the policies as best they could. John Stuart, south of the Ohio, went to work with considerable success, if with great expense, while Sir William Johnson, north of the Ohio, did little until 1766. Meanwhile the Rockingham ministry took over. The two men directly responsible for American affairs—Conway, secretary for the southern department, and Lord Dartmouth, president of the board of trade—had neither knowledge nor ideas about the American West, and apparently

---

[34] Quoted, Alvord, I, 220. See Nicholas B. Wainwright, *George Croghan: Wilderness Diplomat* (Chapel Hill, 1959), for an excellent account.

they did not read the files in their offices. The ministry was divided: some members thought the West should be maintained as an Indian reservation and that the fur trade should be developed; some that settlements should be encouraged; while still others believed that settlements in the Mississippi Valley would be so far from the old colonies that inevitably they would separate, not only from them but also from Britain.

In the fall of 1765 the ministry ordered the governors of Pennsylvania and Virginia to remove settlers from beyond the boundary line, and General Gage was to help them. But the task was futile, for Gage had too few troops. In the spring of 1766, shortly before the Rockingham ministry fell, the secretary at war came up with a simple solution: abandon the West and thus save the expense which Grenville had hoped would be paid for in part by the Stamp Act. Barrington thought that there was plenty of land east of the mountains to provide for settlers for ages to come; that the troops and the forts did not help the fur trade; and that the Indians should be made to come east if they wanted to barter furs. Hence, Britain should abandon virtually all of the posts and reduce the number of troops in the three or four remaining. If the colonies got into an Indian war, let them take the consequences and pay for it themselves. The troops should be moved to East Florida, Nova Scotia, and Canada, and from there they could be moved to the old colonies to maintain order whenever necessary. Thus Grenville's imperial scheme of 1764 would be abandoned.

Before any action could be taken, the Pitt ministry took office, with Shelburne as secretary of state for the southern department and with wide additional duties taken over from the board of trade. No policy had yet been adopted and Shelburne set about elaborate research. He wrote to governors and to generals; he talked to Franklin and other Americans. He wanted time and yet more time, but Charles Townshend threatened to take control of western policy out of his hands. During the spring of 1767, George Grenville, like Barrington the year before, proposed to scuttle his own imperial program by moving that the West be abandoned. Grenville was defeated and Shelburne continued to plan.

Shelburne realized that the boundary line of 1763 was no barrier and that Americans could not be stopped from moving westward, but he believed there ought to be some method of orderly settlement. He felt that the fur trade should be regulated, and in 1766 he ordered Johnson to do so. Yet the expense of regulation was great, as John Stuart was proving, and Shelburne was alarmed at this further burden on the English taxpayer. He hoped that quitrents might be used for the purpose of paying the cost, but a careful inspection of the quitrents showed how very little was collected, and that was coming from only five colonies. In the course of his planning he got no help from his colleagues.[35]

In addition, he was under constant pressure from two groups: the fur traders and the land speculators. After 1763, fur traders rushed to capture the riches they hoped to find all the way from Hudson Bay to the Gulf of Mexico, an area which had been controlled by the French for a century. Scottish merchants took over from the French in Canada and moved westward immediately, establishing stores at Detroit and Green Bay and at Michilimackinac. The Philadelphia fur-trading firm of Baynton, Wharton, and Morgan spent over £30,000 and hired 300 boatmen to capture the trade of the Ohio Valley. In the Southwest, traders from Carolina and Georgia fought with one another and with the French and the Spanish for control of the trade in deerskins. Virginians, who had had an eye on the fur trade of the Ohio Valley ever since the middle of the century, were still making plans.

None of the fur traders liked the idea of regulation. John Stuart in the Southwest tried hard but he had little authority and less money, and many small traders with licenses from the colonial governors pushed in to challenge the big companies. The Virginians ignored Stuart and appointed their own commissioners to regulate the trade. The Philadelphia merchants did not like price-fixing. Most effective of all were the Scots in Canada, whose influence extended back to London and into the House of Commons.

In fact, the plan for conducting a regulated fur trade at a few military posts was unrealistic, for it ignored the way the French had carried on the trade for more than a century. The French had gone to the Indians, lived with them, and brought the furs back to Montreal and Quebec. The Indians resisted change and the French traders, whom the Scottish merchants hired, continued to trade in the old way. They paid no attention to the demand for passes and for conducting trade at specified places, and they defied the agents appointed by Johnson.[36] Meanwhile the Scottish merchants protested against any regulation, and the governor of Canada, Guy Carleton, agreed that regulation was useless. Even worse, it was driv-

[35] R. A. Humphreys, "Lord Shelburne and British Colonial Policy, 1766–1768," EHR, L(1935).
[36] Marjorie G. Reid, "The Quebec Fur-Traders and Western Policy, 1763–1774," *The Canadian Historical Review* [CHR], VI (1925).

ing the Indians to sell their furs to the French traders at New Orleans and St. Louis. As a result of such pressures, imperial regulation of the fur trade was defeated by the end of 1767.[37]

Of far greater long-range importance was the rise of land speculation as a force in British and American politics. The speculators in the first half of the eighteenth century dreamed of thousands of acres, those in the last half dreamed of millions. If they could only stake out vast areas in the Ohio and Mississippi valleys, they could grow rich, as the inevitable flood of small farmers moved westward. Although the speculators' hopes of riches were destined to be frustrated, their faith in the future growth of the American West was a far more accurate guess of what was to come than the skepticism of those who thought it would take untold ages to settle the American continent. The speculators and planners of the last half of the century realized also that individuals alone could not achieve success; therefore they organized companies. The Ohio Company of Virginia pointed the way shortly before midcentury, when it got a royal grant of 200,000 acres in the region south of Pittsburgh. After 1763 there were multitudes of schemes for great land grants in the Ohio and Mississippi valleys, and most of the promoters appealed to Britain to give them what they wanted.

The central political fact in such schemes was that the colony of Virginia had a "legal" claim to the whole region to the north and west of the Appalachians. Her royal charter declared that Virginia extended to the Pacific Ocean. Britain might claim the right to buy and grant land west of the mountains, but she still had a great respect for charter rights, particularly where land was concerned. Virginians were content therefore to organize companies and ask for land in an area which most Virginians believed to be within the bounds of their colony.[38] But Pennsylvania and Maryland had definite western boundaries. If speculators within those colonies wanted to stake out claims in the West, they had to circumvent the fact that Virginia "owned" it, whatever they might think of her real rights. The answer of such speculators, therefore, was to appeal for the establishment of new colonies in the West. Only by appeal to a central government could Pennsylvania and other American speculators get around Virginia's claims. As early as 1754, Franklin and others proposed that the central government envisioned in the Albany Plan of Union should have the power to fix west-

[37] Alvord, *Mississippi Valley*, I, chapter XI, "Indian Management and Western Trade." For the work of John Stuart see Alden, *John Stuart*.
[38] Thomas P. Abernethy, *Western Lands and the American Revolution* (New York, 1937), contains a detailed account of Virginia speculation.

ern boundaries for the seacoast colonies and to grant lands within the areas thus set off. This idea was a continuous factor in British politics before 1776, and in American politics afterwards.

The Proclamation of 1763 was ignored by settlers who moved westward and settled where they pleased, but it was a legal obstacle to land speculators. It was obvious that any big projects for land grants or new colonies would have to be west of the line and that it must either be moved or evaded. John Stuart was making a serious effort to draw a permanent boundary line. By 1767 he had drawn a line from Georgia through South and North Carolina and had reached the southern boundary of Virginia. There he ran head-on into the Virginia speculators and politicians, who had no intention of being stopped by a boundary line, however far it might be beyond the area of actual settlement. Their visions of the future were every bit as large as those of Benjamin Franklin. The Virginians told Stuart that the plan of 1764 had never been officially adopted, and they were right; so for the moment he was blocked. North of the Ohio, Sir William Johnson had done little except to attempt to regulate the fur trade; and he was involved with certain of the land speculators.

Meanwhile plans were being laid to secure a new boundary line north of the Ohio River. In 1754 a large group of Indian traders lost their goods when young George Washington "took" their horses to carry his cannon and stores when he fled from the French back across the mountains. The French promptly seized the trading goods of George Croghan and William Trent, as well as those of lesser men. For years these men sought compensation. They appealed to Virginia and failed, they appealed to the Crown and failed, and they continued to make demands after 1763.

In that year a new and more important group of Indian traders suffered losses, and they too demanded redress. When Pontiac's Rebellion broke out in the spring of 1763 there were hundreds of fur traders scattered through the Ohio and Mississippi valleys as usual. Many were killed and their goods were seized. The important fact was not the killing of the fur traders but that the trading goods of many of them had been supplied by two great fur-trading companies of Philadelphia: Baynton, Wharton, and Morgan, and Simons, Trent, Franks and Company. The two companies joined forces to seek compensation and sent George Croghan to England to ask for a money grant. There was little chance of this, considering the state of English finances, and so the members of the two Philadelphia companies turned to the idea of creating a new colony in the West. They were sure of the support of Johnson, who did much of the financial business of his office through Baynton, Wharton, and Morgan. They organized a company that included Sir William Franklin, governor of New Jersey, and leaders of the Quaker party in Pennsylvania, such as Joseph Galloway. Benjamin Franklin, in England, became a member and was elected the company's representative. Franklin, who had gone to England in 1764 to promote a royal government for Pennsylvania, was authorized to give memberships to "such gentlemen of character and fortune" in England as would be likely to promote the company's schemes.

Franklin's appointment was strategic. It came at a time when the Pitt ministry took power, and Shelburne, now in charge of the colonies, was a friend and admirer of Franklin. Franklin went to work to secure Shelburne's support for a new colony in the Illinois country, and to persuade him to ignore all rival claimants for lands in the West. By August 1767 Franklin had converted both Shelburne and Secretary Conway to his scheme.[39]

Shelburne finished his long researches and at last came up with a plan in September, a plan which owed much to the advice of Franklin and the letters of Johnson. It was based on two assumptions: that it was unwise and impossible to limit American expansion; and that the regulation of the fur trade, whatever the evils involved, could be best managed by those familiar with conditions. He proposed to abolish the system of Indian superintendents and their deputies and hand over the regulation of the fur trade and political relations with the Indians to the colonial governments. In addition, he proposed at least two new colonies in the West: one in the Illinois country, and one around Detroit. He reasoned that they would be able to supply the British forts, which could be reduced in number, and that within a few years the quitrents collected in the new colonies would pay all their expenses. The board of trade balked at once. Shelburne, Franklin, and various London merchants lobbied for approval, and eventually a compromise was arranged. It was agreed that the Indian superintendents should be retained to handle political relations with the Indians.[40]

Meanwhile the wealthy merchants and politicians, who called themselves "Suffr'ing Traders," had another scheme. If Johnson could be ordered to draw a new boundary line north of the Ohio, and far enough to the west, they might secure a land grant east of it. The eager Americans realized how slowly the bureaucratic wheels in England turned and they

[39] Franklin to William Franklin, 28 Aug., *Writings*(S), V, 45–46; Alvord, *Mississippi Valley*, I, 321.
[40] Alvord, *Mississippi Valley*, I, 345–53.

planned to speed them up. Joseph Galloway, Thomas Wharton, and George Croghan in Pennsylvania organized a letter-writing campaign in which they asserted (quite falsely) that an Indian war was imminent and that the only way to head it off was to draw a new boundary line north of the Ohio River. When Franklin got the letters he sent them to Shelburne and urged him to order Johnson to run the line. Apparently the idea of a permanent boundary line had been forgotten, for officials were seemingly unaware of the work of Stuart south of the Ohio—except when they chided him for spending too much money.[41]

The letter-writers' campaign got results, for their tale of the dangers of Indian war was supported by reports from such people as Governor Fauquier of Virginia, and of course by Johnson, whose motives were unknown in Britain. Ever since 1763 Fauquier had been reporting Virginia's objections to the proclamation line, largely because Virginia speculators had great grants lying beyond it. But he had also been reporting the movement of small settlers into the forbidden area, men who were as indifferent to boundary lines as they were to speculators. The settlers hated Indians and killed them when they could. The governor issued proclamations offering rewards, but few guilty white men were captured, and when they were, their friends released them from jail, or county courts in the West refused to convict them. If they needed help, the Paxton Boys of Pennsylvania stood ready, meanwhile killing Indians in their own colony.[42]

General Gage and his subordinates also issued proclamations and removed settlers when they could find them; but the settlers always came back and were followed by an ever larger number of others. The migration could not be stopped, for as Fauquier reported, "the lands between the Allegheny hills and the Ohio are said to be so extremely fine that people will run all risks, whether from governments or Indians, to take possession and seat themselves without the least plea of right for so doing." [43]

Sir William Johnson in letter after letter to the board of trade and the secretary of state told of the movement of settlers, their hatred of the Indians, and of the unpunished murders. By the summer of 1766 his predictions of imminent Indian war were gloomy indeed; it would come because of encroachment on Indian lands and the murder of peaceful Indians. Settlers and speculators alike, he said, laughed at the Proclamation Line of

[41] Franklin to William Franklin, 25 Nov. 1767, *Writings*(S), V, 67–68; Alvord, *Mississippi Valley*, I, 354–55.

[42] Fauquier to SS, 31 Jan. 1764, C.O. 5/1345, and to BT, 13 Feb., 27 Dec. 1764; 26 May, 14 June, 1 Aug. 1765, C.O. 5/1331.

[43] Fauquier to Shelburne, 18 Dec. 1766, C.O. 5/1345.

1763. His solution was to run a new boundary line and to put into effect the plan of 1764 which gave the Indian superintendents full control of trade and political relations with the Indians.[44] The American speculators and their partner and chief lobbyist, Franklin, jarred Shelburne into action. The board of trade and the Privy Council were also aghast at the prospect of a costly new Indian war, and early in January 1768 Shelburne ordered Johnson to run a new boundary line north of the Ohio.[45] The American speculators had achieved their purpose, and the Indian war they and Johnson had predicted did not occur, although settlers continued to push westward and to murder Indians as they had in the past.

No sooner had the decision been made than Shelburne lost control of American policy. A secretaryship of state for America was at last established. Shelburne stayed on as secretary for the southern department, and the new position was given to Lord Hillsborough, who had been president of the board of trade. He ratified Shelburne's order to run the boundary line but objected to other parts of his plan. He opposed the formation of new colonies, for he was convinced that they would mean Indian war. He listened to the fur traders who wanted to keep the West as an Indian reservation, and to British speculators in lands east of the Alleghenies who feared that new western colonies would drain off prospective purchasers.

Once more the question of western policy went the rounds from office to office. Finally, in March 1768, a decision was reached to abandon control, although the Indian superintendents would be retained to manage land purchases from the Indians and to survey boundary lines. Regulation of the fur trade would be handed back to the colonies. The British forts in the West would be reduced in number. New colonies would not be established, for they would be contrary to old principles of British policy. In letters to General Gage and the colonial governors, Hillsborough's constant refrain was the necessity of saving money: "The present state of this kingdom, its future safety and welfare do in great measure depend on relieving it from every expense that is not of absolute necessity. . . ."

He told Gage that the fraudulent practices in the Indian trade were well known and that the British troops and the Indian agents had done much to stop them. Nevertheless, Britain would save money by abandoning most of the forts and returning regulation to the colonies. If the colonies wanted

---

[44] See Johnson to BT, 28 June, and to SS, 28 June, 16 Dec. 1766, NYCD, VII, 834–38, 880–83.
[45] NYCD, VII, 1004; VIII, 2. For the results of this decision in America, see chapter XV. See Sosin, *Whitehall*, chapter VI, "Shelburne and the Lobbyists," for a detailed account of the maneuverings of the land speculators.

to maintain peace with the Indians and profit from the fur trade, they would have to act. After the boundary lines were run, the colonies would have to pass laws to punish settlers beyond them. As for the troops, a few forts should be maintained but the bulk of the men should be concentrated in Quebec, Nova Scotia, East Florida, and the middle colonies, ready to serve in any emergency whatever.[46]

The policy, finally established after five years of muddling, lasted five years, and the results were chaotic from any point of view. Land speculators, disappointed at the rejection of new colonies, soon evolved even bigger schemes. The colonies did not regulate the fur trade or stop western expansion. General Gage did withdraw troops and presumably saved money, but the troops stationed in the town of Boston in 1768 cost more money and caused far more trouble than the scattered garrisons in the West ever had. Officials in Britain were informed of such matters but their attention was elsewhere, for in the fall of 1767 the Americans along the Atlantic seaboard started a campaign against the Townshend program that lasted until a portion of the Revenue Act of 1767 was repealed in the spring of 1770. As a result, when Britons, from George III to the lowliest member of the House of Commons, thought of America at all, they did not think of the American West. Not until the end of 1773 did Britain once more take up the question of what to do with it, and by then it was too late.

With the legislation for the colonies in 1767–68, Parliament was finished with America until 1773, except in the spring of 1770 when it repealed most of the revenue features of the Townshend Act of 1767. That act had been a fiasco from the start, and men soon talked of repeal. Yet when repeal came it was incomplete, for Parliament retained the tax on tea as a symbol (however futile) of the principle of the Declaratory Act of 1766.

The Chatham ministry which had started out with high hopes of settling the affairs of America had virtually disintegrated by the end of 1767. Then in January 1768 colonial policy was put in the hands of Lord Hillsborough, who issued orders, blustered, threatened, and finally used military power in an effort to force the colonies to acknowledge what he and other

---

[46] Circular Letter to colonial governors, 15 April 1768, C.O. 5/231. To Gage, 15 April, EHD, IX, 704–7. The report of the board of trade, 7 March 1768, on which the letters were based, is in NYCD, VIII, 19–31.

Britons insisted was their proper subordination to the will of Parliament. He suffered one defeat after another at the hands of the Americans, who fought him and the Townshend program with various and considerable weapons that ranged all the way from constitutional arguments to economic coercion.

IX

The Constitutional Protest Against the Townshend Program

The Americans reacted at once to the Townshend program. Regardless of internal political differences, most American leaders were alarmed by the political and constitutional issues raised by the Revenue Act of 1767. It meant taxation for revenue, whatever the guise, and it meant more political interference within the colonies than ever before. The granting of salaries to royal officials by colonial legislatures was more a symbol than an effective force in the maintenance of colonial self-government, but it was cherished nonetheless. The payment of the duties in specie was still another economic burden on a people for whom money of any kind was all too scarce. But worst of all in the eyes of some Americans was the suspension of the New York Assembly; to them the political and constitutional implications seemed far more drastic and dangerous than those of the Stamp Act.

American opposition appeared in many places: in legislatures, in town meetings, in merchant meetings, in extra-legal mass meetings called by popular leaders, and in pamphlets and newspapers. Equally various were the methods of opposition proposed and used. Colonial legislatures drafted the traditional petitions. Popular leaders, particularly in the northern colonies, soon urged the non-consumption of British goods as they had done at the time of the Stamp Act. Most merchants, torn between profits and patriotism, and with vivid memories of the Stamp Act riots, were reluctant to take any action at all. Meanwhile, Americans continued to oppose the customs service and to protest against British troops. But as opposition spread, Americans soon divided far more sharply than they had at the time of the Stamp Act. The memory of violence in 1765 caused a growing number of leaders to be as much, if not more, concerned with the threat of internal upheaval as with the threat of British interference.

Rumors of the new measures appeared in the colonial newspapers during the spring of 1767. At first there was doubt that Parliament would again attempt to tax the colonies [1] but that soon disappeared when Americans heard from England that the reduction in the English land tax would have to be made up by America.[2] One report prophesied that either North America must support its own civil and military establishment "or must be declared to be independent of us." [3] Americans heard also that Charles Townshend wanted to send more troops to be quartered in the large towns; and they read his declaration that the distinction between internal and external taxes was nonsense.[4] Americans learned too that they were not well liked. New York's refusal to obey the Quartering Act, Massachusetts's quibbling over compensation for the Stamp Act sufferers, and even the Americans' orders for British goods while complaining of hard times, were all counts against the colonists.[5]

By July 1767, newspapers predicted the punishment of New York, and before the end of the month the outlines of the Townshend program were clear. Newspapers printed accounts of the proposed acts suspending the New York Assembly, establishing an American board of customs commissioners, and levying duties on imports into the colonies. Newspaper readers also learned that governors and judges would be made independent by the payment of their salaries from the new duties.[6] Within a short time the suspension of the New York Assembly was known to be a fact,[7] and the other acts followed close on its heels.[8]

The Stamp Act Congress had summed up the American position on taxation when it declared that "no taxes ever have been, or can be constitutionally imposed on them, but by their respective legislatures." The proposal of James Otis and some others for American representation in Parliament was rejected by most Americans. George Grenville's argument that the Americans were "virtually" represented was jeered on both sides of the Atlantic, most notably by William Pitt, who called it the "most contemptible idea that ever entered into the head of a man; it does not deserve seri-

[1] MdG, 30 April 1767.   [2] VG(PD), 4 June; BG, 15 June.
[3] MdG, 11 June; BG, 15 June.   [4] VG(PD), 27 May.
[5] Ibid. 30 April, 18 June; BG, 20 April.
[6] BG, 6 July; MdG, 23 July; VG(PD), 30 July.   [7] BG, 27 July; VG(PD), 6 Aug.
[8] NYM, 5 Oct.; GG, 14 Oct.

ous refutation." All such arguments were swept aside by the Declaratory Act, which asserted the absolute sovereignty of Parliament over the empire in "all cases whatsoever."

But in 1767 Charles Townshend ignored Parliament's claim to ultimate authority. He attempted instead a superficial political trick, and he died before he could know how badly it had failed. The Americans had denied that Parliament had the right to levy "internal" taxes but they had admitted that Parliament could levy duties to regulate trade. The distinction was ridiculous in the eyes of everyone except the Americans, said Townshend, but since they had made it, let Parliament raise money in the colonies by placing taxes on trade. William Pitt had not thought the distinction ridiculous in his great debate with Grenville in 1766, nor did the Americans, to most of whom it meant what it did to Pitt.

The American position had been challenged in the Revenue Act of 1764 but only the New York legislature understood it. Parliament could regulate, said the New York Assembly, but "all impositions, whether they be internal taxes, or duties paid for what we consume equally diminish the estates upon which they are charged" and the "whole wealth of a country may be as effectually drawn off by the exaction of duties, as by any other tax upon their estates." James Otis made the same distinction between internal and external taxes in his *Vindication of the British Colonies* in 1765, but unlike the New Yorkers, he openly proclaimed Parliament's right to levy both kinds of taxes as implicit in "the idea of a supreme legislature, or sovereign power of a state." [9]

Otis's argument represented his own fears, not the feeling of most Americans. The New York legislature had provided the answer in 1764, and in 1767 it was elaborated by John Dickinson, a wealthy Philadelphia lawyer who had been trained at the Middle Temple. On 2 December the *Pennsylvania Chronicle* carried the first of his *Letters from a Farmer in Pennsylvania*—and the next day it appeared in the *Pennsylvania Gazette*. On 17 December the *Maryland Gazette* printed it, and a week later, Rind's *Virginia Gazette*. The New England newspapers began publishing the letters before the end of December, and in January 1768 the first letter appeared in the far-off *Georgia Gazette*. In fact, all but four colonial news-

[9] For a brief discussion of the political thinking of the period see Merrill Jensen, "Commentary," in R. G. Adams, *Political Ideas of the American Revolution.* For a far more detailed account, with a different interpretation, see Bernard Bailyn, "The Transforming Radicalism of the American Revolution," *Pamphlets*, I, 3–202. Edmund S. Morgan, "Colonial Ideas of Parliamentary Power, 1764–1766," WMQ, 3 ser. V (1948), argues that Americans were consistent and did not change their arguments about "internal" and "external" taxation, an interpretation with which I do not agree.

papers ran the series. By March 1768 the letters were in pamphlet form. At least seven American editions were printed, and one in Dublin, two in London; a French translation circulated on the Continent.

Dickinson's argument was simple enough. He admitted that Parliament had the right to regulate trade but denied that it had the right to raise revenue in the guise of duties on trade. In the Townshend revenue act "we may observe an authority *expressly* claimed and exerted to impose duties on these colonies; not for the regulation of trade; not for the preservation or promotion of a mutually beneficial intercourse between several constituent parts of the empire, heretofore the *sole objects* of parliamentary institutions; *but for the single purpose of levying money upon us.*"

"This I call an innovation; and a most dangerous innovation." He scoffed at those who said the Stamp Act was wrong because it was an "internal" tax, but said that Americans should submit to the Townshend revenue act because it was an "external" tax. "To this I answer, with a total denial of the power of Parliament to lay upon these colonies any 'tax' whatever." "To the word '*tax*,' I annex that meaning which the constitution and history of *England* require to be annexed to it; that is—that it is *an imposition on the subject, for the sole purpose of levying money.*" "It is true, that *impositions for raising a revenue*, may be hereafter called *regulations of trade*. But names will not change the nature of things." Americans should be watchful, declared Dickinson, for if they are not, "a new servitude may be slipped upon us, under the sanction of usual and respectable terms." [10]

Dickinson rescued Americans from a theoretical dilemma and he was applauded from one end of the colonies to the other. You have not, said a Marylander, "like most of our flimsy politicians, taken up the loose undigested principles of the day" and sought to please the ears of readers "with the labored harmony of a polished period." [11] The Boston town meeting hailed him as "the friend of Americans, and the common benefactor of mankind," but prefaced its praise with a long disquisition aimed at Massachusetts leaders willing to submit to the "Rod of Power" in exchange for place and patronage.[12] The freemen of Lebanon, Connecticut, praised him for the "clear knowledge and solid argument" with which he vindicated the rights of America and told him that he had erected a "monument which will last when those of marble and brass are moulded to

[10] The quotations are from Letters II, IV, VI, in P. L. Ford, ed., *The Writings of John Dickinson* (Memoirs of HSP, XIV, 1895).
[11] MdG, 7 Jan. 1768.   [12] 22 March, 1768, BTR, XVI, 243–44; BEP, 28 March.

dust. . . ." [13] The merchants of Norwich, Connecticut, rhapsodized that "Posterity, who must reap the fruits of your toil in the fields of freedom, will raise in every bosom an altar to your memory." [14] Providence, Rhode Island, declared its "ineffable gratitude." [15] Grand juries in Maryland and Pennsylvania heaped their praises, that of Cumberland county, Pennsylvania, declaring that "though we are little, very little, among the many who have become your tributaries, yet, believe it, sir, we love our country; we love our liberty" and hope that "your name may be transmitted to distant, very distant generations." [16] Amateur poets greeted him in verse that had fervor if not merit.[17]

No previous writing had had such wide popularity as the *Farmer* letters, a popularity not equaled until Thomas Paine's *Common Sense*. And one wonders with what grim irony John Dickinson must have remembered such acclaim in 1776, when, as a leading opponent of independence, he was one of the most maligned men in America.

As at the time of the Stamp Act, some Americans were convinced that constitutional arguments were inadequate to meet the threat they saw, and once more, as in 1765, the town of Boston led the colonies. The popular leaders were more powerful than ever. They had an organized mob to enforce their will, and they had won control of the house in the election of 1766, although Thomas Hutchinson remained in the council in his capacity as lieutenant governor.[18] The popular leaders again won control of the house in the spring elections of 1767 but the ensuing legislative session was deadlocked by a council which temporarily showed courage.[19]

Governor Bernard regained his easily recovered optimism. In July he doubted that there would be fresh troubles because the friends of government, "among which is almost every person of fortune and fashion throughout the province," were gaining ground.[20] Even the more realistic Thomas Hutchinson thought that the Sons of Liberty would find it difficult to make trouble, although he feared the consequences if a mob were raised.[21] Once more he and the governor were wrong. On 14 August 1767 the populace celebrated the anniversary of that day in 1765 when it had

[13] BEP, 25 April.   [14] Idem.   [15] PrG, 25 June.
[16] *Pennsylvania Chronicle* [PC], 5 Sept.; PrG, 25 June.
[17] CC, 30 May. For examples of Dickinson's modest replies see letter to Boston town meeting, BEP, 2 May, and to the merchants of Norwich, PrG, 16 July.
[18] Thomas, Massachusetts, 338–48.
[19] Ibid. 358–69.   [20] To SS, 27 July, C.O. 5/756.
[21] To ———, 18 July 1767, Mass. Ar., XXVI, 281.

hanged the effigy of stamp distributor Andrew Oliver and wrecked his house, and the Sons of Liberty adopted resolutions that were reprinted as far away as Virginia. The governor was now convinced that some of the Boston "desperadoes" wanted to break with Britain and intended another "insurrection." He identified the "desperadoes" as "Otis and his gang." [22]

The *Boston Gazette*, the popular newspaper, pointed the way, and its influence extended far beyond the borders of Massachusetts. Its stories were probably more widely reprinted by editors all the way from New Hampshire to Georgia than those of any other newspaper. The *Gazette* began the campaign on 10 August when it asserted that Thomas Hutchinson and Secretary Andrew Oliver would have been appointed to the new customs board except for the fact that their salaries would now be paid from the new customs revenues. Thus they and all other Crown officers would be "rendered independent of the people." The next week the *Gazette* reprinted the Petition of Right and urged editors throughout America to follow suit. In the same issue "Britannus Americanus" declaimed against the "tools of arbitrary power" who wanted to free governors and judges from their dependence on the legislatures. Those who want to set up tyranny say that duties will be imposed "by which the monster is to be fed. What a daring insolence is it to think we are to be intimidated by such impotent threats!" Have such people forgotten the "old new English spirit" aroused by the Stamp Act? Do they think it "evaporated and lost? Let them not deceive themselves: the colonies are still united . . . rather than submit to slavery, they would risk their all." [23]

Ever since the autumn of 1766 the *Gazette* had been telling its readers that Governor Bernard was promoting payment of officials' salaries by the Crown.[24] Early in May 1767 Speaker Thomas Cushing privately warned the Massachusetts agent in England that if duties on trade were used to pay such salaries, the people would declare them unconstitutional.[25] However the popular leaders got their information, and they got it in various ways, it was accurate. The governor had been urging reforms in colonial governments ever since 1761, and in particular, the payment of salaries, including his own, from revenues collected by Britain.[26] The proposal not

[22] Bernard to SS, 24 Aug., C.O. 5/756; VG(PD), 17 Sept.; Bernard to Richard Jackson, 30 Aug., BP, VI, 42–45, HUL.
[23] BG, 17 Aug.; MdG, 10 Sept.   [24] For example, 16 Nov., 21 Dec. 1766.
[25] To Dennys De Berdt, 9 May, MHSC, 4 ser. IV, 348–49.
[26] See Edward Channing and A. C. Coolidge, eds., *The Barrington-Bernard Correspondence* . . . (Cambridge, Mass., 1912), 42–45, 75–77, 84–86, and Bernard's petition to the king for an increase in salary, 259–63.

only offended an ancient principle of colonial legislatures, it also enraged the popular leaders, particularly James Otis, whose campaign against Hutchinson seemingly could not be won. Peter Livius in New Hampshire reported that if Hutchinson were paid by the Crown, James Otis's "rage and envy hereupon would be sufficient to kill him. He might perhaps burst like a toad with his own venom." [27]

Yet when the Boston leaders started their fight against the Townshend acts, they based it not on the salary question but upon the highest of constitutional issues, the suspension of the New York Assembly, and they did so while New York remained strangely quiet. Governor Bernard believed that there was an agreement between the "factions" in Boston and New York whereby the Boston leaders were to lead the protest movement, using their newspaper, the *Boston Gazette,* with the New York papers reprinting the materials from it.[28] This was in fact what happened. The popular newspaper in New York, Holt's *Journal,* faithfully copied propaganda from the *Boston Gazette* during the winter of 1767–68.

On 31 August two writers in the *Gazette* proposed the non-importation of British goods as a means of opposing British policy.[29] At the same time the Boston leaders insisted upon the necessity of once more making a constitutional protest. Early in October the four Boston representatives—James Otis, Samuel Adams, John Hancock, Thomas Cushing—and "a stray member whom they picked up in the streets," petitioned the governor to call a session of the legislature. All they wanted, said Bernard, was to "blow up a flame," and so he treated the petition with "silent contempt." [30] The leaders then turned to the town meeting where they met a startling setback, for it refused to adopt new instructions to its representatives and turned down the demand for non-importation. The most the town meeting would accept was a voluntary non-consumption agreement.[31]

This defeat of the popular leaders was due in part to the presence of the "better sort," who usually did not attend, and in part to the "extraordinary conduct" of James Otis. As moderator of the meeting he warned against

---

[27] To his brother in London, 18 Oct. 1768, Arthur Lee Papers, I, HUL.
[28] Bernard to SS, 14 Sept. 1767, C.O. 5/756.
[29] The *New York Journal* printed the second proposal 10 September 1767 and the *New York Mercury* printed both 14 September.
[30] Bernard to SS, 8 Oct., and copy of memorial, C.O. 5/756.
[31] BTR, XVI, 221–25; Bernard to SS, 30 Oct., C.O. 5/756. The records of the meeting and the governor's letter give two quite different versions of what happened. The records do not show a hint of opposition, whereas the governor declared there was an almost "universal" voice against the program of "the faction," including its demand for a special session of the assembly.

giving offense to Britain. And despite talk on the streets that the new customs commissioners would be forced to resign when they arrived, verbal assurances were given that there would be no violence.[32] And when the commissioners arrived on 5 November there was none.

Another town meeting was called for 20 November, the day the Townshend revenue act went into effect. Again there were rumors that the commissioners would be forced to resign, and that morning a handbill posted on the Liberty Tree exhorted the Sons of Liberty to rise and fight for their liberties. The alarmed governor called the council together only to be informed that the selectmen had torn down the handbill. Hutchinson persuaded his friends to attend the town meeting and they exerted themselves with such spirit that they "silenced the Sons of Liberty." [33] Not only that, but James Otis "made a long speech entirely on the side of government. He asserted the king's right to appoint officers of the customs, in what number and by what denominations he pleased," and furthermore he declared that it was imprudent for Boston to oppose the new duties when the other towns in the colony, and other colonies as well, seemed to be contented.[34] If Bernard's account was accurate, the speech must have been a bombshell. The *Boston Gazette*'s report was evasive. All it said was that Otis had made an "animated address" and that he had exhorted the people to be steadfast in the steps they had resolved upon. The town, said the *Gazette*, was for "good order," and the handbill on the "venerable elm" was a "dirty trick" of some enemy of Boston's civil rights.[35] The *Evening Post* applauded Otis's speech on behalf of order and declared that Edes and Gill of the *Gazette* did not dare give a full report since it would have been an "antidote to the poison" they had been spreading. The *Post* also printed a letter from Otis which did little to clarify matters, for he denied saying things which no one had accused him of saying and proclaimed that he was devoted only to the party of "truth and right reason" which he would embrace wherever he found it.[36]

The opposition saw a chance to drive a wedge between Otis and his allies. Otis was praised as having nothing but "profound contempt for this town's well-known incendiaries; for the characters and proceedings of that

[32] Bernard to SS, 30 Oct., C.O. 5/756.
[33] Hutchinson to Richard Jackson, 19 Nov., Mass. Ar., XXV, 226–27; BTR, XVI, 225–26.
[34] Bernard to SS, 21 Nov., C.O. 5/756. As far away as Virginia, Otis was reported as defending the customs commissioners. VG(PD), 24 Dec.
[35] 23 Nov.   [36] 23, 30 Nov.

junto herd of small statesmen, who rave and drivel out their political frenzy and idiotism." All America would soon see the disgrace of these "shallow, dirty Politicasters, this execrable set of scrawling miserables, together with their flimsy systems of ridiculous politics, and their despicable, quack expedients. . . ." [37]

The *Gazette* did its best to insist that Otis had been misrepresented,[38] but the offensive grew more furious. The peak was perhaps reached when the *Post* said of a *Gazette* writer:

> . . . the genius and puny efforts of this agonizing reptile are really contemptible, [and he is in every way a fit member of] that pretending, superficial, ridiculous club political! that factious, seditious combination! that unhallowed conclave! of mean slander-mongers and truth adulterers, miserable and dirty scribes, pharisees, hypocrites, dogs, sorcerers, publicans, and sinners! who under the Patriot mask, to the scandal of religion and morality, of decency and common sense, have, for these seven years, been indefatigably stabbing the most distinguished virtuous characters, poisoning the minds of the people, sapping and assaulting the whole structure of our government, and even bursting the bands of all civil society. The deluded rabble still following, huzzaing, and adoring the audacious maxims and violent proceedings of this scandalous, infamous, thrice execrable Juntocracy.[39]

Otis himself was only briefly exempt from the torrent of mud-slinging. Versifiers had at him in "The Jemmiwilliad," in which he and William Cooper, the town clerk, were labeled "Jemmy Split" and "Cooper Will," and which ended with the verse:

> And may kind Heaven joint exit bring,
> And their fond hopes, and ours fulfill;
> Nor quit this life without full swing!
>   May Jemmy Split and Cooper Will! [40]

This was followed shortly by "Jemmyicumjunto," an even more violent assault on Otis than "Jemmibulero" in the spring of 1766. It made much of his waverings and expressed the utmost contempt for the "Junto," as well as for Otis. Its last lines declared:

[37] BEP, 7 Dec.   [38] 7 Dec.   [39] 21 Dec.   [40] BEP, 30 Nov.

> Since Freedom, dear Freedom so much has been taught,
> And Freedom of Speech without action is naught,
> We'll speak our own thoughts and we'll do as we're wont to,
> And a f—— for the schemes and the dreams of the Junto! [41]

The best the Boston leaders had been able to achieve in the town meeting was an agreement for a voluntary consumer boycott of reluctant local merchants, but those leaders were men who never accepted defeat. Furthermore, because a vital constitutional principle was at stake, they had far wider support than the newspaper attacks on them would indicate. Speaker Thomas Cushing voiced the convictions of many moderate men throughout America, although because of his associates he usually did so privately. The colonists, he said, claim the rights and privileges of British subjects, and as such "they cannot be constitutionally taxed without their consent." They admit their subordination to Parliament and its right to regulate trade, and even to levy duties in the course of "proper regulation," but they are convinced that "there is an evident distinction between an act imposing a tax for the single purpose of a revenue and an act made for the regulation of trade." Cushing in a private letter thus anticipated John Dickinson by several weeks. Such objections, he said, "are not thrown out by warm and hot people but are the sentiments of all sober and moderate men among us who wish well to Great Britain and her colonies and are very solicitous to the welfare of both countries." [42] The wide acceptance of Dickinson's *Farmer* letters not only testified to the soundness of Cushing's analysis but helped to transform a local squabble in Massachusetts into an all-American fight for a constitutional principle. No one recognized this more clearly than the governor of Massachusetts, who warned that unless Dickinson were refuted his letters would become a "Bill of Rights" for Americans, and then Parliament might "enact declaratory acts, as many as they please, but they must not expect any real obedience." [43]

Dickinson's first letter appeared in the *Boston Gazette* the day before the town met on 22 December to instruct its representatives. As usual the instructions set forth the program of the town's leaders. They pictured the dismal economic plight of the colony resulting from the debts and taxes arising from the war, the growing private debts to British merchants, the importation of superfluous goods, and the heavy burden imposed on trade by British duties and restrictions. The representatives were told to encour-

---

[41] Ibid. 11 Jan. 1768.
[42] To Dennys De Berdt, 15 Oct. 1767, Arthur Lee Papers, I, HUL.
[43] To Richard Jackson, 20 Feb. 1768, BP, VI, 90–94, HUL.

age economy and American manufactures. The Townshend revenue act must be opposed because it was "the natural right of every man, and the constitutional right of every British subject" to dispose of his own property in person or through his elected representatives. Beyond this, the act would further depress an already depressed trade.[44]

The Boston leaders went to the legislature, where they secured the appointment of a committee on the state of the province dominated by themselves and their followers. There was strong opposition, but by the end of January 1768 the house had agreed to a series of letters to officials in England and a petition to the king. The latter, the work of Samuel Adams, summed up the constitutional argument of the popular leaders: Parliament was the supreme legislative authority of the whole empire in cases consistent with the rights of nature and of the constitution, but its authority did not extend to taxation. The colonies were not and could not be represented in Parliament and therefore the sole right to tax Americans lay with their several legislatures.[45]

All this was merely preliminary to the central goal of the Boston leaders: a union of all the colonies. This idea had not been mentioned in their instructions, but the Boston town meeting had proposed such a union as early as 1764, and the governor was well aware of it.[46] The committee proposed a circular letter to the other colonial legislatures and the news appeared in the Boston Gazette a few days later.[47] The house rejected it by a resounding two to one majority. Gaily the governor reported that "the faction has never had so great a defeat . . . it cuts off their hopes of once more inflaming the whole continent."[48] He was further delighted when he received a letter from Shelburne approving his veto of the six popular party councilors elected in the spring of 1766. Shelburne also approved Hutchinson's continuing to sit in the council as lieutenant governor. In general, he censured the popular party for its heated behavior. Bernard promptly sent what one of his supporters called the "heavenly letter" to be read to the house.[49]

The house ignored it for the moment while the Boston leaders turned defeat into victory by means which have never been clear and with conse-

[44] BTR, XVI, 227–30.
[45] 20 Jan. 1768, H. A. Cushing, ed., The Writings of Samuel Adams (4 vols., New York, 1904–8), I, 162–66, and BEP, 21 March. For letters to Shelburne, Conway, Rockingham, Camden, and Chatham see BG, 21, 28 March, 4 April, and BEP, 28 March, 4 April.
[46] Bernard to SS, 21 Jan. 1768, C.O. 5/893.   [47] 25 Jan.
[48] To Richard Jackson, 1 Feb. 1768, BP, VI, 77–81, HUL.
[49] Hutchinson to ———, 17 Feb. 1768, Mass. Ar., XXVI, 289.

quences which even they probably did not anticipate. They won approval for a circular letter, and then capped their triumph by erasing the record of their previous defeat from the journals of the house.[50]

The Circular Letter of 11 February 1768 was, in form, a report of the actions of the Massachusetts House of Representatives. It began by suggesting that the acts of Parliament levying taxes and duties were of common concern to all the colonies, and that every care should be taken that the colonial assemblies "upon so delicate a point should harmonize with each other." All the colonies should join in petitioning the king for a redress of grievances. And despite its guise as a "report," the letter reiterated the constitutional ideas of the Boston leaders. Parliament was the supreme legislature of the empire but "in all free states the constitution is fixed" and Parliament derives its authority from that constitution. Therefore, it "cannot overleap the bounds of it without destroying its own foundation. . . ." As for Americans, they enjoy all the "fundamental rules" of the British constitution and it is "an essential, unalterable right of nature, engrafted into the British constitution, as a fundamental law" that no man can be deprived of his property without his consent. Furthermore, Americans, beyond any charter rights, as freemen and subjects, may "assert this natural and constitutional right."

The duty acts are an infringement of those rights because Americans are not and cannot be represented in Parliament. Colonial legislatures were established long ago to enable Americans to enjoy "the unalienable right of representation. . . ." The letter also questioned the payment of the salaries of governors and other officials without "the consent of the people," attacked the hardships imposed by the Quartering Act, and asserted that the unlimited power of the new customs board to appoint officials might endanger the liberties of the people. The letter concluded by denouncing those "enemies" who pictured Americans as factious and disloyal and tending to independence, insisted that Massachusetts had no ambition either to lead or to dictate to other legislatures, and piously closed by expressing confidence in the king, "our common head and father." [51] Speaker Cushing sent the letter to the speakers of the other colonial assemblies, and not one of them could have kept it quiet for it was given an honored place on the first page of the *Boston Gazette*.[52]

---

[50] Thomas, Massachusetts, 30–32.   [51] EHD, IX, 714–16.
[52] BG, 14 March. The *Boston Evening Post* was more cautious. It first mentioned the letter on the same day but merely reported that it had been read to the Rhode Island assembly. The *Post* finally printed the letter on 27 June when the Massachusetts legislature was on the eve of dissolution for refusing to rescind it.

ఇ❧

The Circular Letter did produce a "union" of the colonies, not because of its merits but because it was answered by a circular letter from England presenting a challenge no colonial legislature could ignore. Meanwhile, all but one of the legislatures in session during the spring of 1768 answered the Massachusetts letter, beginning with the Virginia House of Burgesses. It had not met since April 1767 and hence Virginia had remained politically silent while opposition grew in the North.

Virginians were well informed by Purdie and Dixon's *Virginia Gazette*, however, which reprinted materials from northern newspapers, particularly from the *Boston Gazette*. Thus Virginians read of economic distress, of the need for American manufactures, of the economic and constitutional dangers of the Revenue Act of 1766, and of the threat to self-government explicit in the act suspending the New York Assembly. They read too of the "great ones" of Massachusetts who were greedy for salaries paid from customs revenues, and of a "certain furred Patagonian, who is NO JUDGE . . . ," a clear reference to Thomas Hutchinson.[53] In addition, Purdie and Dixon's *Gazette* and Rind's *Gazette* printed John Dickinson's *Farmer* letters during the first three months of 1768. And Rind also printed the fiery essays of "Monitor," which supported Dickinson. These were written by a brother of Richard Henry Lee, Dr. Arthur Lee, who had recently returned with an Edinburgh degree to practice medicine in Williamsburg.[54]

When the House of Burgesses met on 31 March, it therefore had plenty of ammunition at hand. Ever since the Stamp Act crisis, Governor Fauquier had met the assembly only when absolutely necessary. He died on 1 March and the aged John Blair, president of the council, assumed the office of governor and met the burgesses at the time appointed by Fauquier. He informed them of illegal settlements on the frontier and the resulting danger of Indian war. Most of all, he deplored the heavy taxes which the people "have long groaned under," and said that if they could be ended it "would be great consolation to me in the decline of life." He did not mention the Massachusetts letter.[55]

But the burgesses knew all about it.[56] Speaker Peyton Randolph had received it in March and had replied to Speaker Cushing in what the *Boston Gazette* hailed as a very "genteel letter," for Randolph had praised the people of Massachusetts as "very vigilant and steadfast guardians of Ameri-

<hr/>

[53] VG(PD), 10, 17 Dec. 1767, 10 March 1768.   [54] VG(R), 25 Feb., 28 April.
[55] VG(PD), 3, 31 March; JHB (1766–69), 141–42.   [56] VG(PD), 21 April.

can rights." Not to be outdone, the *Gazette* praised the Virginians for "their noble, timely, and spirited resolutions in the year 1765," and assured its readers that Virginia would support Massachusetts.[57]

The burgesses were prepared. Several counties were ready with petitions protesting against the suspension of the New York Assembly and against the revenue act and demanding a petition to the king.[58] Speedily, and with skill, for they had had much practice in stating their constitutional position, the burgesses adopted a petition to the king, a memorial to the House of Lords, and a remonstrance to the House of Commons. Calmly and plainly the burgesses told the Commons that they were equal legislatures, that the burgesses were "the sole constitutional representatives of his Majesty's most dutiful and loyal subjects, the people of Virginia. . . ." However, they denied any desire for independence and said they rejoiced in the "constitutional connection" between the colonies and the mother country. They admitted that Parliament could legislate to maintain that dependence but denied that it could tax them.[59]

In a more leisurely fashion the burgesses prepared a reply to Massachusetts, and then went on to draft a circular letter of their own.[60] The Virginia letter went much further, for where Massachusetts proposed only joint action in petitioning the king, Virginia told the colonial legislatures that they should go "hand in hand in their opposition to measures which they think have an immediate tendency to enslave them," and declared that Virginia was not "without hopes that by a hearty union of the colonies the constitution may be again established on its genuine principles. . . ."[61]

In May the New Jersey assembly approved the Massachusetts letter and instructed its agent in England to act jointly with other colonial agents.[62] The Pennsylvania assembly, safely in the hands of the Quaker party managed by Joseph Galloway, listened to the Massachusetts letter on 10 May but took no action.[63] Connecticut approved in June and expressed fears for the future.[64]

Before any other colonial assembly met, Lord Hillsborough, secretary of the new American department, took action which created a storm in Amer-

---

[57] BG, 2 May.   [58] JHB (1766–69), 145–46, 148.   [59] Ibid. 165–71.
[60] 3 May. BG, 27 June; CC, 11 July.   [61] Pa. Ar., 8 ser. VII, 6189–92.
[62] 9 May. BG, 27 June; CC, 11 July.
[63] Gov. John Penn to Thomas Penn, 15 June, Penn Mss., HSP.
[64] 11 June. BG, 27 June; CC, 11 July.

ica and a "union" of the colonies such as the Boston leaders perhaps imagined only in their rosiest dreams. London was in turmoil when the Massachusetts Circular Letter reached the ministry. Parliament had been dissolved on 11 March and new elections were under way. Rioting mobs seethed through the streets of London, and the ministry moved troops here and there in futile attempts to preserve order. The outlawed John Wilkes suddenly returned from his exile and was elected to the House of Commons from Middlesex at the end of March.[65]

Hillsborough was in no mood to take any nonsense from America. He told the proprietor of Pennsylvania that the action of Massachusetts was improper and illegal,[66] and the Massachusetts agent that the colonies' insistence on "right" simply could not be allowed.[67] The Massachusetts letter was laid before the cabinet on 15 April and a few days later Hillsborough sent orders to Governor Bernard. The Circular Letter, he declared, had been adopted by a "thin house" at the end of a session, and "procured by surprise." He denounced the "attempts made by a desperate faction to disturb the public tranquillity." At the next session Bernard must "require" the House of Representatives to rescind the Circular Letter and declare its "disapprobation of and dissent to that rash and hasty proceeding." If the house refused, Bernard should dissolve it immediately and send an account of the proceedings to be laid before Parliament if further steps were needed "to prevent for the future a conduct of so extraordinary and unconstitutional a nature." [68]

This letter was followed by a circular letter to all the American governors. Hillsborough described the Massachusetts letter as "of a most dangerous and factious tendency, calculated to inflame the minds of his [the king's] good subjects in the colonies, to promote an unwarrantable combination, and to excite and encourage an open opposition to and denial of the authority of Parliament, and to subvert the true principles of the constitution. . . ." The governors were to persuade their assemblies to treat the Massachusetts letter with the "contempt it deserves." If they did consider the "seditious paper," the governors were to prorogue or dissolve them immediately.[69]

The colonial assemblies treated Hillsborough's circular letter with the

---

[65] See Chapter XII below.
[66] Thomas Penn to Gov. John Penn, 20 April, Penn Mss., HSP.
[67] Dennys De Berdt to Thomas Cushing, 27 June, CSMP, XIII, 332.
[68] 22 April, C.O. 5/757. Printed, BEP, 4 July. Hillsborough's letter was based on Bernard's version of events.
[69] 21 April, C.O. 5/241, and EHD, IX, 716–17.

"contempt" they thought it deserved. Massachusetts and Maryland were the first to do so.

Ever since the dispatch of the Circular Letter, Boston had been in an uproar extraordinary even for that unruly town. The House of Representatives accused Bernard of lying to the secretary of state and demanded copies of his letters. He naturally refused and was excoriated in a letter which he said "outdoes even Otis' outdoings." The house then defended itself to Shelburne and asked for the governor's removal.[70] The interchange was followed by an attack on Bernard in the *Boston Gazette* as vicious as any colonial governor was ever subjected to. It was the work of a new recruit to the popular party, young Dr. Joseph Warren, whom the British later called the "rascally apothecary," and who died at Bunker Hill. The governor was malicious, diabolical, treacherous, a man-hater, and "totally abandoned to wickedness. . . ." "If such men are by God Appointed, the Devil may be the Lord's Anointed."

Bernard's name was not mentioned but he and his supporters were outraged, and the council denounced the article as "a false, scandalous, and impudent libel" and an insult to God. A committee of the house, including Hancock and Otis, blandly replied there was no reason for alarm. It then went on to defend the "freedom of the press" as the great bulwark of the people's liberties.[71] James Otis, said the governor, "behaved in the house like a madman" and even invaded the council chamber and threatened the political lives of its members in the next election. The frightened council then refused to indict Edes and Gill of the *Gazette* for libel.[72]

Up to this time Bernard had ignored suggestions from England that he ask for an indictment of the "popular printers" because members of the house were involved,[73] and he knew who they were: "two of the chief leaders of the faction in the House (Otis and Adams) are the principal managers of the *Boston Gazette*." [74] He was right. The next year John Adams noted in his diary: "Spent the remainder of the evening and supped with Mr. Otis, in company with Mr. Adams, Mr. William Davis, and Mr. Jno. Gill. The evening spent in preparing the next day's newspaper—a curious employment. Cooking up paragraphs, articles, occurrences, &c.—working the political engine!" [75]

[70] Bernard to Richard Jackson, 20 Feb. 1768, BP, VI, 90–94, HUL. The documents are in the *Boston Gazette*, 22 Feb., and the *Boston Evening Post*, 11 April.
[71] BG, 29 Feb., 7 March.   [72] To SS, 5 March, BP, VI, 272–77, HUL.
[73] To SS, 30 Jan. 1768, C.O. 5/757.   [74] To SS, 5 March, BP, VI, 272–77, HUL.
[75] 3 Sept. 1769.

Failing to get an indictment from the legislature, the governor turned to the superior court, which met only a few days after he in a fury prorogued the legislature. Chief Justice Thomas Hutchinson delivered an eloquent appeal to the grand jury for an indictment of Edes and Gill. At first it seemed willing, but the "managers of the paper were seen publicly to haunt the grand jurymen wherever they went. . . ." The next day the jury refused an indictment and Hutchinson's private hope that he could "eradicate the absurd notion of the liberty of the press" was thwarted.[76]

Freed from the threat, the *Gazette* outdid itself. It was necessary to expose the guilt of villains.[77] Only tyrants and their tools are afraid of a free press and these are the men who forged the Stamp Act and who have forged other "chains and manacles" for the people. It urged the people "to choose liberty and refuse chains" and to "strip the serpents of their stings" and consign to disgrace all "guileful betrayers of their country." [78] The writers in the *Gazette* were attacking Governor Bernard, Thomas Hutchinson, and their allies of the "government party," not George Grenville or George III.

The newspaper war was accompanied by rising tension on other levels. In February, Daniel Malcolm, a petty merchant, openly and successfully defied the customs officials. Early in March some reluctant merchants signed a tentative non-importation agreement. During the celebration of the repeal of the Stamp Act a howling mob terrified the customs officials, who appealed to the navy at Halifax and to Britain for protection.[79] In April, Samuel Adams, preparing for the spring elections, discovered an alarming degree of "popery" in certain towns which usually elected supporters of the government party to the legislature.[80] In May the *Romney* sailed into Boston harbor, and troubles over "impressment of seamen" began at once. In June came the seizure of Hancock's sloop *Liberty*, the most violent riots since 1765, and the flight of the customs commissioners to the *Romney*.[81]

Such was the atmosphere when the legislature received Hillsborough's order to rescind the Circular Letter. Bernard asked for compliance on 21 June. The house demanded a complete copy of Hillsborough's letter and copies of Bernard's own letters. Bernard sent Hillsborough's letter and threatened the house with dissolution. Furthermore, he said that he would not call a new election unless instructed to do so from England. The Bos-

---

[76] Hutchinson to [Richard Jackson?], 23 March, Mass. Ar., XXVI, 295–96; Bernard to SS, 12 March, BP, VI, 278–80, HUL.
[77] 7 March.   [78] 14 March.   [79] See Chapter X below.
[80] "A Puritan," BG, 4, 11 April.   [81] See Chapter X below.

ton leaders made the most of this political gift, and James Otis excelled himself. An anonymous spectator reported his attack on the nobility and Commons of England. Who are these nobility with titles which have raised them above those whom "they are pleased to style the vulgar" and whom "the unthinking multitude are taught to reverence . . . as little deities"? It is certainly not for their virtue, for "there are no set of people under the canopy of Heaven more venal, more corrupt and debauched in their principles." It is certainly not for their learning. They go to Oxford and Cambridge and all they learn is "whoring, smoking, and drinking." As a finishing stroke they are sent to France and all they see is "the outside of a monkey," and when they return home they are "complete monkeys themselves." As for the members of the House of Commons who affect to make laws for the colonies, they are nothing but "a parcel of button-makers, pin-makers, horse jockeys, gamesters, pensioners, pimps, and whore masters." [82]

After waiting a week while the house was regaled with such oratory, the governor once more demanded action. The house asked for a recess, and when refused, defeated a motion to rescind the Circular Letter by a rousing majority, 92 to 17. Bernard dissolved it the next day.[83] But the dissolution did not stop the house from denouncing the governor for his "lies." As the *Boston Gazette* summed it up, "some of the most virulent as well as perfidious enemies of the Province, are residents in it; and a man needs not his political spectacles, clearly to discern who they are." [84] The dissolved house went even further and petitioned the king for the removal of Bernard. The petition accused him of every political crime, and significantly, the first count against him was that he had attached himself to the wrong party when he came to the province.[85] The Boston leaders could never forget that their chief enemy was Thomas Hutchinson. And the council finally joined the popular party, it too petitioning the king to remove Bernard. As far away as Virginia it was reported that he "has been capable of a piece of chicanery below the character of the meanest member of the community." [86] "It is all over now," wrote the despairing governor. Britain has done nothing to check "the demagogues of America," and the vote against rescinding "gave the precise turn to the council. . . ." He pre-

[82] Sparks Mss., "Papers Relating to New England," II, 81, HUL.
[83] The relevant documents are in the *Boston Gazette*, 27 June, 4 July, and in the *Boston Evening Post* on the same dates.
[84] 18 July.
[85] BG, 8 Aug. The petition was also printed in the *Virginia Gazette* (PD) on 8 September and in other newspapers.
[86] VG(PD), 12 Jan. 1769.

dicted rightly that "popular leaders and popular measures will wholly prevail in that body. . . ." [87]

ॐ

The news of Massachusetts's refusal to rescind spread rapidly: within a month the *Virginia Gazette* and many other newspapers printed the relevant documents.[88] Americans began drinking toasts in numbers that must have staggered all but the most hardy. Toasts to the "Glorious 92" of Massachusetts were combined with toasts to "No. 45," for American newspapers reported the affairs of John Wilkes as fully as those of Massachusetts. The *Boston Evening Post* asserted that "the famous Ninety-two will live forever in the annals of America." On the same day the *Gazette* echoed the sentiment and sneered at a governor who, to double his salary, would be guilty of "the basest projects, by the basest misrepresentations, and even of attempts to overturn the Constitution." [89] Ninety-two freeholders at Marblehead praised the "Glorious 92" [90] and Providence toasted them too.[91] In Newport "45 Sons of Liberty," after raising a church tower, dined on forty-five dishes and drank to the "Ninety-two Anti-Rescinders." [92] A new song was addressed to the Sons of Liberty and "particularly to the Illustrious, Glorious, and never-to-be-forgotten Ninety-two of Boston." [93] A climax of the celebrations occurred in Boston. On 8 August the *Boston Gazette* described a new punchbowl fashioned by Paul Revere in honor of the "92" and John Wilkes. The bowl weighed forty-five ounces, held forty-five gills, and was engraved with the names of the "Glorious 92." It was initiated on 1 August when eighteen men, including Otis, Adams, Hancock, and Daniel Malcolm, met and drank forty-five toasts. On that same day, too, many reluctant Boston merchants were at last forced to agree to non-importation.

In Philadelphia, John Dickinson, with the help of a few lines from Arthur Lee of Virginia, wrote a "Liberty Song" to be sung to the tune of "Heart of Oak." It soon became the "official" anthem of the popular parties in the colonies.[94] Hillsborough and his letter were denounced in no uncertain terms, while at the same time Americans whose "private views and evil machinations" had produced his letter were warned that they must answer for the coming crisis.[95] Very few indeed cared or dared to

87 To Barrington, 30 July, *Barrington-Bernard Corres.*, 170. Cf. letter to Hillsborough, 26 Sept., C.O. 5/757.
88 VG(PD), 27 July.   89 4 July.   90 BG, 18 July; CC, 1 Aug.
91 PrG, 9 July.   92 *Essex Gazette* [EG], 2 Aug.   93 PJ, 4 Aug.; EG, 16 Aug.
94 Dickinson, *Writings*, 431–32.   95 BEP, 18 July.

defend the seventeen men who had voted to rescind, or to attack the majority, although one writer had the temerity to write, and a newspaper the courage to print his statement, that he had long known the "pretended champions of liberty" and that he did not know one who was "not in his heart and in his family a tyrant." [96]

During the next few months one legislature after another defied Hillsborough, and by the end of 1768 they had achieved the "union" he tried to prevent. The Maryland legislature read the Massachusetts letter and ordered a petition to the king before Governor Sharpe laid Hillsborough's order before it. The day after he did so, the legislature adopted the petition, read the Virginia letter, and ordered it answered. It then replied to the governor. Bluntly the house told him that what it proposed to do was its own business; that it would not ignore the Massachusetts letter or treat it with contempt for the letter was loyal to the king and "replete with just principles of liberty. . . ." The house then passed resolutions objecting to parliamentary taxation, and the governor prorogued the legislature at once.[97]

Rhode Islanders were so busy with political bargaining to end the old and corrupt political battle between Stephen Hopkins and Samuel Ward for the governorship[98] that they did not take up the question until fall. However, Rhode Island newspapers made it plain that Hillsborough had "missed of his aim" if he thought he could separate Rhode Island from the other colonies; his letter only confirmed "the necessity of a general union, when the oppression is common."[99] In September the legislature not only petitioned the king, it also told the governor to tell him that it supported Massachusetts.[100]

Delaware, like Rhode Island, was small but it had large ideas. The legislature received only the Virginia letter but it declared the Townshend

---

[96] NHG, 12 Aug. Another defense of the rescinders is in the *Boston Evening Post*, 17 Oct. The two Salem representatives who voted to rescind were denounced by a majority of the town but defended by thirty of the "principal inhabitants." BG, 11 July; BEP, 25 July.

[97] Speaker Robert Lloyd to Speaker Thomas Cushing, 24 June, VG(PD), 14 July; MdG, 28 July; William H. Browne, *et al.*, eds., *Archives of Maryland* [Md. Ar.] (70 vols., Baltimore, 1883–1964), LXI, 334, 360–61, 399, 406–9, 413–20.

[98] Ward of Newport and Hopkins of Providence had fought over the governorship for years. In 1768 both withdrew from the race after dividing up offices among their respective supporters, a political deal fully reported in the *Providence Gazette*, 5, 19 March, 2, 9 April.

[99] Ibid. 9 July; BEP, 18 July.   [100] RICR, VI, 559–63; BEP, 3 Oct.

revenue act unconstitutional and told the king that the right to vote taxes was "derived to them from God and nature. . . ." [101] The Massachusetts and Virginia letters were read to the North Carolina legislature in November but it avoided dissolution by giving verbal orders to its speaker to answer both of them. Then it petitioned the king, but Governor Tryon did nothing and lamely defended himself on the ground that the assembly had acted with "moderation." [102]

No such moderation was to be found in South Carolina. Speaker Peter Manigault received the Massachusetts and Virginia letters in July, answered them, and reported that the South Carolina agent had already been ordered to co-operate with those of other colonies.[103]

Meanwhile a new election was due in the fall and the gentry were faced with internal threats as well as the external one. After years of futile demands for circuit courts, the backcountry people threatened a march on Charleston. The alarmed legislature had passed a circuit court act in the spring session of 1768, but included a provision—tenure of judges during good behavior—that ensured a royal veto. During the summer, backcountrymen formed a "Plan of Regulation," denied the jurisdiction of the Charleston court, refused to pay taxes, and announced that they agreed with the legislature that there should be no taxation without representation. These people, said Governor Bull, "are not idle vagabonds, the Canaille, the mere dregs of mankind, they are mostly tenants of his Majesty, landholders, though poor; they are in general an industrious, hardy race of men. . . ."

They demonstrated that they were law-abiding when Bull called an election for early October. At their own expense they surveyed parish lines into the backcountry so that they could find their way to the legal polling places, at least 150 miles away. The governor estimated that the backcountry contained at least half of the legal voters of the colony and many of them made the journey to the seacoast polling places. There they behaved "with decency and propriety." The *Gazette* also reported: "They mentioned many intolerable grievances they had long labored under, and seem to have most immediately in view a more equal representation in the assembly," an act for fixing officers' fees, and one for establishing county

---

[101] House of Representatives, *Votes and Proceedings* . . . (Wilmington, 1769), 27 Oct. 1768.
[102] Speaker John Harvey to Speaker Cushing, 10 Nov., in CC, 3 April 1769; NCCR, VII, 928–29, 980–82; Tryon to Hillsborough, 15 Dec., ibid. 881.
[103] Speaker Peter Manigault to Speaker Cushing, 30 July 1768, SCG(T), 12 Sept. 1768; McCrady, *South Carolina Under Royal Government*, 603–4.

courts.[104] But they managed to elect only one or two of their own men and hence offered no legal threat to low-country rule.

The gentry were far more startled by events in Charleston, where a few days before the election, the "mechanics" held an unprecedented meeting to "nominate" candidates. They picked Christopher Gadsden, who had been courting them ever since the Stamp Act crisis, and pointedly rejected Henry Laurens and Charles Pinckney. Then they marched to Mazyck's pasture, where they "consecrated" an oak tree as the "Tree of Liberty" and sang John Dickinson's "Liberty Song." That night they decorated the tree with forty-five lights and fired off forty-five rockets in honor of John Wilkes. Afterward, carrying forty-five candles, they marched to Governor Bull's house and toasted the "Massachusetts Ninety-two." Festivities concluded at Dillon's Tavern, where a table held forty-five each of lights, bowls of wine, bowls of punch, and ninety-two glasses. The first of many toasts was "May the ensuing members of assembly be unanimous, and never rescind from the resolutions of the Massachusetts Ninety-two." The evening ended with "civil mirth and jollity, without the least irregularity happening." [105]

Gadsden won handily in the election that followed, but so did Laurens and Pinckney. Bull cannily delayed calling a session, leaving that for the return of Governor Montagu, who told the Commons House that he trusted it would treat with contempt any letter or paper with a tendency to seditious and unwarrantable combinations. He was hardly out the door before Speaker Manigault read the Massachusetts and Virginia letters and his reply to Speaker Cushing. The house told the governor that no letters tending to sedition had ever been laid before it, and if any were, they would be treated with contempt. The house then voted that the circular letters were loyal and founded upon undeniable constitutional privileges. The next day a committee called upon the governor who warned it of "disagreeable consequences." After the committee returned, the house, just as the governor's proclamation of dissolution reached its doors, ordered all the documents concerned published in the newspapers. A few days later the *South Carolina Gazette* demonstrated the futility of the governor's action when it published an "extraordinary" issue containing all the letters, messages, and speeches.[106] While the low-country leaders thus maintained

[104] Bull to SS, 10 Sept. 1768, C.O. 5/379; SCG(T), 10 Oct. 1768.
[105] SCG(T), 3 Oct.; BG, 7 Nov.
[106] SCG(T), 24 Nov. The same documents appeared in the *Virginia Gazette*(PD), 2 Feb. 1769, and Speaker Manigault's letter to Cushing, 21 Nov. 1768, is in the *Connecticut Courant*, 16 Jan. 1769.

great principles, the news of the royal veto of the circuit court bill reached Carolina, and the men of the backcountry were left more desperate than ever—and more cynical about the principles proclaimed in Charleston.

Party politics in Pennsylvania and New York delayed action on the Massachusetts letter. Joseph Galloway and the Quaker party were determined that Pennsylvania must avoid any action that might offend Britain and thus hinder Franklin's campaign for a royal government. Galloway was contemptuous of Dickinson and his *Farmer* letters, which he said might be fit "for the selectmen of Boston and the mob meetings of Rhode Island," but which should be despised in a colony where the people were "none of your damned republican breed. . . ." [107] But Galloway could not control all the people of Philadelphia or its newspapers. As one paper put it, if Americans lost their liberties, it would make no difference whether Pennsylvania had a royal or a proprietary government.[108]

The arrival of the Hillsborough circular sharpened public opinion. Governor Penn wrote his brother, the proprietor, that "even those persons who are the most moderate are now set in a flame and have joined in the general cry of Liberty." [109] A great mass meeting was held at the end of July to "instruct" the city's delegates in the assembly, one of whom was Galloway. The meeting was told that "the iron rod of power is stretched over us"; that restrictions on trade and the invasions of rights would deprive the colonies of "even the shadow of liberty, and reduce us to a state of abject slavery." British measures from the Stamp Act onward were converting colonial assemblies from "the representatives of a free people, to be the abject tools of ministerial power. . . ." The most recent and worst example was Hillsborough's circular letter. The instructions adopted praised the Massachusetts and Maryland legislatures for their courageous stand and demanded that Pennsylvania unite with the other colonies.[110]

Such pressure forced the assembly to act when it met in September. It resolved that it had the right to correspond with the other colonial legislatures and prepared petitions to king and Parliament spelling out conventional constitutional arguments. But it did not answer either the Massachusetts or Virginia letters, and in instructions to agents Franklin and

107 Dickinson, *Writings*, 281.   108 PC, 30 May.
109 John Penn to Thomas Penn, 31 July, Penn Mss., HSP.
110 The meeting was widely reported. See PG, 28 July; NYJ, 11 Aug., containing the address to the meeting; VG(PD), 1 Sept., containing a copy of the instructions. The Boston papers were of course intensely interested.

Jackson it emphasized the economic inexpediency of the Revenue Act of 1767.[111] Meanwhile the merchants of the city continued to resist popular demands that they join with Boston and New York in non-importation of British goods.[112]

The suspension of the New York Assembly had set off the campaign in Boston which led to the Massachusetts Circular Letter and the non-importation movement, yet New Yorkers themselves were seemingly indifferent. The New York newspapers, particularly the *Journal*, faithfully copied articles from the Boston papers, but New Yorkers themselves wrote little. As one of them said, "our poor printers would starve if it was not for the dirty trade of copying, which they are forced to submit to for want of originals. . . ." [113]

The New York Assembly, despite Parliament's act suspending it, had done business as usual in the fall of 1767 on the assumption that the grant to the British troops the past summer had in effect suspended the act of Parliament.[114] The assembly did not meet again until the fall of 1768 because New York had a septennial act which meant an election in the spring of that year. Hence during the crisis over the Massachusetts Circular Letter it was in no position to act.

Nor did it seem likely at first that it would. One reason was that the aristocracy feared a new mob might be raised. As Governor Moore put it, "the apprehensions which every person of property was under during our late commotions [the Stamp Act crisis] from the licentiousness of the populace are not yet forgotten. . . ." [115] Equally important was the fact that the Livingston party did not want to risk losing the control of the assembly it had won in 1761, and which it retained in the election of March 1768, but only after conspicuous defeats. Its rivals, the De Lanceys, assumed the role of "popular leaders" and, in a campaign aimed at lawyers, defeated John Morin Scott, a Livingston henchman, in New York City, and even more startling, defeated the head of the Livingston clan, Robert R. Livingston, in his home county of Dutchess.[116] Furthermore, many of the Sons of Liberty, angry at the assembly's support of British troops, were now backing the De Lanceys in the city.

Hence the constitutional issue raised by the Massachusetts Circular Letter and Hillsborough's order to ignore it was entirely subordinated to the

[111] Pa. Ar., 8 ser. VII, 6187–88, 6243–44, 6271–81.   [112] See Chapter X below.
[113] John Watts to General Monckton, 23 Jan. 1768, MHSC, 4 ser. X, 600.
[114] See Chapter XIV below.   [115] To SS, 7 July 1768, NYCD, VIII, 80.
[116] Becker, *New York*, 59–60.

struggle for power between the two rival factions. When the assembly met in October 1768, Philip Livingston's strategy, as speaker, was to adopt various popular constitutional resolutions and thus gain credit for his party, but to ignore the Massachusetts letter. If he could ignore it, the Livingstons might stay in power until the next regular election in 1775. The De Lancey strategy was the reverse: force the assembly to consider the Massachusetts letter and thus produce a dissolution and a new election which might mean a victory for the De Lanceys.

The Livingston majority voted to delay consideration of the Massachusetts and Virginia letters until all the business of the session was finished. It then adopted petitions to Britain declaring the Townshend revenue act unconstitutional and insisting that it was not essential to the dependence of America on Britain for Parliament, in which Americans were not and could not be represented, to have the power to tax the colonies.[117] Such petitions were safe enough and no one in the colony could quarrel with them.

The only hope of the De Lancey minority was to build up outside pressure. An early newspaper article had excoriated the "mean, selfish men" who would make New York "odious to all the British colonies." It was predicted that British troops would be used in New York as in Boston. Did or did not the assembly receive the Massachusetts letter? asked a "Westchester Farmer"; of what use is an assembly to the people if it yields to the "dictates of a minister"?[118] The De Lanceys also stirred up a mob to burn the effigies of that symbol of tyranny, Governor Bernard of Massachusetts, and his weak-kneed appointee, the sheriff of Suffolk county. The Livingstons denounced the affair as a fiasco, but persuaded the governor to issue a proclamation and the assembly to offer a reward for the arrest of the perpetrators who were labeled "a very few persons of the lowest class."[119]

The De Lanceys next adopted the strategy of the popular leaders in Philadelphia and called a vast mass meeting to "instruct" the city's representatives in the assembly. The instructions declared the suspension of the assembly by Parliament to be more dangerous than the Stamp Act and "a most flagrant infraction of your sacred rights and privileges," which should be countered by a full statement of the assembly's "natural and constitutional rights." As for Hillsborough's letter, it was the "most daring insult

117 NYAJ, 1768, passim.   118 NYJ, 14 April, 20 Oct., 17 Nov.
119 Ibid. 17 Nov.; BEP, 28 Nov.; VG(PD), 15 Dec.; NYAJ, 22 Nov. 1768.

that ever was offered to any free legislative body." The Massachusetts Circular Letter should not only be read, it should be answered in a "respectable manner." [120]

The pressure built up by the De Lanceys and their Sons of Liberty was too great to resist. Governor Moore's view was that the majority of the assembly were "plain well meaning men" who did not want to act, but who were afraid of being called enemies of their country. The result was that on 31 December, after all legislation was completed, including an act granting more money for British troops, the assembly adopted resolutions. These asserted the sole right of taxation, denied that the assembly could be constitutionally suspended except by the governor acting in the name of the king, and asserted its right to consult with other colonial legislatures. After beating down James De Lancey's move to make the resolutions even more pointed, the assembly appointed a committee of correspondence. And then, at last, Speaker Philip Livingston officially laid the Massachusetts Circular Letter before the house, which promptly ordered him to answer it.

Governor Moore got a copy of the proceedings on Sunday, New Year's Day 1769, and on Monday dissolved the assembly as he was required to do, although he was forced to act without the consent of his council, which divided four to four.[121] Shortly thereafter he called a new election, which fulfilled all the hopes of the De Lanceys: the Livingstons went down to an inglorious defeat.[122]

By the end of 1768 all of the colonies except New Hampshire had joined Massachusetts in making a constitutional protest against the Townshend acts, thanks in large measure to the arrogance of Lord Hillsborough, and despite internal political quarrels. At the same time this movement for constitutional protest was paralleled by a movement for economic pressure. The non-importation movement, like the constitutional protest, was hampered by internal politics and intercolonial jealousies. In the end common action was achieved, but as in the case of the Massachusetts Circular Letter, it was largely because Britain again raised a constitutional issue which only a few Americans dared leave unchallenged.

[120] NYJ, 1 Dec.
[121] NYAJ, 31 Dec. 1768; Moore to SS, 4 Jan. 1769, NYCD, VIII, 143–44.
[122] For the election and its consequences see Chapter XIII below.

X

Politicians, Merchants, Customs Officers, and Non-importation in the North, 1767–1769

Americans in the Revolutionary era, unlike some who have written about them since, never depended on constitutional arguments alone. Theory was a useful weapon but so was economic coercion, and many believed that the non-importation agreements at the time of the Stamp Act had more to do with its repeal than all the talk about colonial rights. Merchants in Philadelphia and New York had adopted the measure in 1765. Only the Boston merchants had been reluctant, and they had been forced into non-importation by popular pressure.

In 1767 it was the popular leaders in the northern colonies who were the first to propose non-importation, not the merchants. Merchants as a group did not like the Townshend acts but they feared the revival of popular activity and its seemingly inevitable corollary of mob action, which had so frightened "men of property" in 1765. Hence most merchants opposed non-importation in 1767.[1] There were merchants, of course, who were involved in popular politics, as were John Hancock in Boston and Christopher Gadsden in Charleston, but with some exceptions, they were not the mercantile leaders of their colonies.

[1] The two indispensable studies of non-importation are Charles M. Andrews, "Boston Merchants and the Non-Importation Movement," CSMP, XIX, and Arthur M. Schlesinger, Sr., *The Colonial Merchants and the American Revolution, 1763–1776* (New York, 1918). It is their view that the merchants began non-importation for purposes of "commercial reform" but that control of the movement was taken from them by popular leaders for political purposes of their own. It is my view that the evidence demonstrates that the non-importation movement was actually begun by the popular leaders who forced or persuaded merchants to take part in it by threats of non-consumption, and even of physical violence.

 є❧

The leadership in the non-importation movement, as in the statement of constitutional theories, was taken by the popular leaders of Boston. On 31 August 1767 a writer in the *Boston Gazette* proclaimed: "my blood is chilled, and creeps cold through my stiffened veins. To what alas! is America reduced. This land for which our fathers fought and bled, must now become the den of slavery. . . ." The civil and religious liberties for which they fled to a wilderness will be lost and a "degenerate posterity" will possess no spark of the heavenly fire which glowed in the venerable bosoms of the founding fathers. Is it necessary to sail to the coasts of liberty through seas of blood? Not at all. The remedy is to "put a stop to the importation of all English goods" and show Britain that Americans can "freely part with the gay trappings of a butterfly." [2]

That same day Governor Bernard hurriedly sent a copy of the *Gazette* to London. He said the scheme was "outrageous," and could not be put into effect without violence because more than half the Boston merchants were opposed to it. Even at the time of the Stamp Act, when Americans were far more "estranged," the "faction" had had to force the merchants to agree to non-importation and had done so with the "greatest threats, even to marking houses in the daytime for nightly ruin. . . ." [3]

The *Evening Post*, a moderate, pro-merchant newspaper, at once began a campaign against the popular leaders and non-importation that lasted for months and grew in violence and made it clear that name-calling was not a monopoly of the *Gazette*. The *Post* insisted that Boston owed its greatness largely to its merchants and asked why they should be condemned "to a state more to be dreaded than ten thousand deaths?" [4] It asked: Who are these people who "style themselves patriots" and who try to "poison the minds of the people" when they know they cannot oppose the strength of Great Britain? All sensible men "detest the ridiculous parade and poisonous performances" of those "Blow Coals" who "sour the minds of the unwary and ignorant at this side of the water." If trouble came, those "canker worms of the state . . . men of desperate fortunes" would "slip their necks out of the halter. . . ." [5]

Week by week the *Post* continued the attack. Non-importation would cause economic hardship for all classes, and property owners would be taxed for the "relief both of the innocent miserable, and the abandoned

---

[2] The proposal for non-importation was reprinted in the *New York Mercury*, 14 September. The *Boston Gazette* also proposed a partial non-importation agreement on 31 August.
[3] Bernard to SS, 31 Aug., C.O. 5/756.   [4] BEP, 7 Sept.   [5] Ibid. 21 Sept.

wicked and idle. In that all will be in common and free plunder." And as for the motives of the promoters of the scheme, everyone knows "the pretended one of their love to their country," but it is impossible to believe, despite "their reiterated exclamations and bombast, echoed through the mouths of bawling boys and hectoring bullies in newspapers" that they are in earnest. If one looks at the characters "of these entirely new and strange politicians, we may unveil their real designs; they consist chiefly of persons who have no property to lose, therefore subject to no danger on that account, and whose only hopes of living are founded in anarchy and confusion; who borrow all their importance in life from deceiving others; who know themselves to be despised by men of sense and honor, and therefore through the pretended medium of patriotism, endeavor to gain the esteem of the unguarded populace." [6]

The *Boston Gazette*, accustomed to handing out such brutal assaults not to receiving them, soon counterattacked. Anyone who opposed non-importation when faced with "the spectacle of a whole country in chains" was a "wolf in sheep's clothing. . . ." Non-importation had worked at the time of the Stamp Act and it would work again. Readers were warned against those who "with reptile wiles would cozen you out of your just rights" and "would pilfer away your liberty." One writer denounced those who wanted to bring in British troops to "dragoon us out of our liberties," who called the colonists "rebels, traitors, revolters, rioters, outlaws . . ." and who wanted to destroy the freedom of the press because it stood in the way of those who wanted to enslave America. As for those who say that men of "approved worth" and of "fortune" are opposed to non-importation, "it is no uncommon thing for a man of *high fortune* to be an oppressor, a tyrant in principle, and the basest scoundrel on earth," whereas those of "low fortune" are often "possessed of great virtues. Those obscure and contemptible persons have been the guardians of the liberties of their country. They have delivered a whole continent from being enslaved to your *men of high fortune*. . . ." [7] Thus in three articles in one week's issue the *Boston Gazette* answered its critics. The next week it circulated a rumor that troops were coming from Halifax and predicted that Americans would be ready to defend themselves. [8]

It was soon rumored in Boston that the members of the new board of customs commissioners would meet with violence when they arrived. [9] Over and over the *Gazette* insisted that the suspension of the New York legislature and the payment of officials' salaries from customs duties would

[6] Ibid. 12 Oct.   [7] BG, 14 Sept.   [8] Ibid. 21 Sept.
[9] Bernard to SS, 21 Sept., C.O. 5/756; BEP, 28 Sept.

mean slavery, and that the depressed state of trade called for non-importation and non-consumption of British goods.[10] The charge that only propertyless men were opposed to the Townshend acts was met by the countercharge that the men who favored them were "desirous of fattening themselves upon the spoils of a plundered people." [11] The reference to local officials was obvious and the imagination boggles at what the *Gazette* would have said if its publishers could have seen the private letters of Thomas Hutchinson and Andrew Oliver expressing their pleasure at the prospect of receiving their salaries from customs duties.[12]

The popular leaders sought support from the Boston town meeting, but on 28 October it rejected their proposals. It refused to consider a non-importation agreement. All the meeting would accept were the resolutions praising the prospect of domestic manufactures and a voluntary non-consumption agreement. Those who signed agreed to buy American manufactures and not to buy a list of goods normally imported from Britain. Oddly enough, this list did not include any of the dutied articles in the Townshend revenue act. The defeat of the popular program was due partly to the attendance of an unusual number of the "better sort," and partly to James Otis, the moderator, who warned against giving offense to Britain.[13]

Despite the town meeting's rejection of non-importation, the Boston leaders did their best to win support for non-consumption. The Boston agreement was sent throughout the colony and to the principal towns in other colonies. Rival newspapers in Boston soon gave two quite different versions. The *Boston Gazette* insisted that people were eager to sign, that country towns were calling meetings to adopt similar agreements, that merchants would ship the listed articles back to England, and that Boston's action was widely approved in other colonies. Even the *Boston Evening Post* carried accounts of its adoption in some small towns.[14] But the *Evening Post* presented another side of the story: the New Yorkers and Pennsylvanians were contented and could see no good purpose in the inflammatory pieces in the *Gazette*.[15]

The *Massachusetts Gazette*, the paper of the governor and council, said

---

[10] 28 Sept., 5, 19, 26 Oct.   [11] 19 Oct.

[12] Hutchinson to Richard Jackson, 19 Nov. 1767, Mass. Ar., XXV, 227; Andrew Oliver to Jasper Mauduit, 30 Oct. 1767, Andrew Oliver Letter Books, I, MHS.

[13] BTR, XVI, 220–25; Bernard to SS, 30 Oct., C.O. 5/756. See Chapter IX above for a more detailed account.

[14] BG, Nov.–Dec.; BEP, 7, 23 Nov.; 7, 14, 28 Dec.; CC, 23, 30 Nov., 7 Dec.

[15] 16 Nov.

that the people in general were delighted to be relieved of taxes to pay the salaries of British officials.[16] Ridicule was heaped on the non-consumption agreement. "Naked Truth" was shocked to find that mustard was "an enumerated enemy of liberty, nothwithstanding its famed reputation for wisdom"; but he looked forward happily to the day when the ladies of Boston would strip off their ornaments and "appear in their native beauty" for love of their country.[17] "A True Patriot" in the *Evening Post* ridiculed the Boston "junto" and its manufactures, which he said existed only in the newspapers. The so-called unanimous town meeting was no more than the result of "the very few and impotent junto" to whom no one paid any attention except a few ignorant dependents who voted as they were told. The non-consumption agreement was signed only by such people while "the most wealthy and respectable among us, have treated the thing in the ludicrous light it deserves." [18]

This last charge hurt. Draper, printer of the *Massachusetts Gazette*, had already been threatened with a boycott, if not worse, for saying that towns outside of Boston were contented.[19] The selectmen of Boston denounced the "True Patriot." They publicly called him a liar and insisted that non-consumption was not "merely a party business, and the proposal only of a Junto." The *Evening Post* printed the selectmen's statement and then ridiculed the "princely gentry" who talked of liberty of the press while trying to force the printer to reveal the name of "A True Patriot." And it heaped scorn on the "inimitable performance" and the "shining talents" of the selectmen.[20]

Clearly the non-consumption movement was not going well and even the *Boston Gazette* admitted it when "Liberty" called on the merchants to "ward off the blow, that every moment threatens me with certain and eternal death." [21] And in January 1768 the *Gazette* conceded that the town had adopted non-consumption because of large imports and "the difficulty of bringing about a speedy agreement among the trade. . . ." [22] The merchants continued to resist. In December 1767 the Reverend Andrew Eliot reported that "few of the trading part have subscribed"; [23] and two months later the customs commissioners said that the merchants were still refusing to sign.[24]

The Boston leaders carried their campaign into the legislature which adopted the Circular Letter. However, the legislature rejected any thought

[16] 12 Nov.; CC, 23 Nov.   [17] MG, 12 Nov.   [18] BEP, 23 Nov.
[19] MG, 26 Nov., 4 Dec.   [20] 30 Nov., 7 Dec.   [21] BG, 30 Nov.
[22] Ibid. 4 Jan. 1768.   [23] To Thomas Hollis, MHSC, 4 ser. IV, 418.
[24] To Treasury, 12 Feb. 1768, C.O. 5/757 and MHSP, LV, 263–67.

of economic coercion. Only toward the end of the session did the house finally agree to resolutions urging the suppression of extravagance, vice, and idleness; the promotion of industry, economy, and good morals; and the encouragement of domestic manufactures in order to prevent unnecessary exportation of money. The vote was 82 to 1. The lone dissenter was Timothy Ruggles, a friend of Hutchinson who as chairman of the Stamp Act Congress had refused to sign its petitions.[25] The *Boston Gazette* hailed the vote as proof that non-consumption was not the measure of an "expiring faction"; [26] but in terms of reality it was a defeat. The resolutions were merely good intentions; effective action depended upon the merchants.

Meanwhile non-consumption was making some progress elsewhere in Massachusetts and in the other New England colonies. By mid-January twenty-four Massachusetts towns had adopted agreements, and others followed shortly.[27] Some of the Boston merchants finally yielded to the pressure from the popular party and the merchants allied with it. A meeting was held on 1 March 1768, apparently at the instigation of Captain Daniel Malcolm, and a committee of nine was appointed to draft a non-importation agreement. Six of the nine members, including merchants John Hancock and John Rowe, were adherents of the popular party. On 4 March some of the Boston merchants agreed to the non-importation of European commodities for a year, except for salt, coal, lead, shot, and fishing supplies. But the agreement was conditional: it would not go into effect unless the merchants of "the neighboring colonies," meaning New York and Philadelphia, took similar action.[28]

Why had Boston adopted even this tentative agreement? Governor Bernard was sure that he knew. "The merchants," he wrote, "are at length dragged into the cause; their intercourse and connection with the politicians and the fear of opposing the stream of the people have at length brought it about against the sense of an undoubted majority both of numbers, property, and weight." Many signed because they were told "they would be obnoxious to the lower sort of people; others were threatened with the resentment of the higher. Some were afraid for their persons and houses, others for their trade and credit." But, he pointed out, some of the most substantial merchants had refused, many signers had no intention of keeping the agreement,[29] and more than half of those who signed did so from fear of the mob.[30]

[25] BG, 29 Feb.; BEP, 7 March.   [26] BG, 29 Feb.
[27] Schlesinger, *Colonial Merchants*, 110.   [28] Andrews, CSMP, XIX, 201–2.
[29] To SS, 21 March, C.O. 5/757.   [30] To SS, 19 May, C.O. 5/757.

Speaker Thomas Cushing naturally did not mention mobs but asserted that economic pressure had forced the merchants into the agreement. "The traders here in the English way," he wrote the Massachusetts agent, "begin to feel the effects of the measures entered into last fall by the people. . . . As the consumption of British goods lessens, their sale diminishes. . . . I believe the gentlemen in trade are one and all convinced that it will be to no good purpose for them to import English goods as usual. . . . They despair of ever selling them, and consequently of ever being able to pay for them." [31]

It would seem evident that the Boston merchants as a group, far from adopting non-importation as a means of "commercial reform," were forced into it by popular pressure. Temporarily, however, they were saved from enforced patriotism by the even more reluctant Philadelphians, and by a conditional agreement of the New Yorkers.

ß❧

The New York newspapers faithfully reported events in Boston during the winter of 1767–68 and the *Journal* in particular supported the non-consumption movement.[32] But New York as a whole, and notably the legislature, showed that it had no enthusiasm for Boston leadership by its reluctance to consider the Massachusetts Circular Letter. Nevertheless, appeals for economy and frugality were frequent. The *New York Mercury* opposed the opening of a theater because it would "strip the poor" and endanger the "morals of youth" and urged instead the promotion of economy and thrift.[33] Inhabitants' meetings were called to approve measures to "promote frugality and industry." Merchants were urged to start a bank to encourage industry and thus to benefit the poor.[34]

New York City was suffering from an economic crisis which many blamed on the rapid disappearance of paper money. Hence, the merchants were sympathetic to joint action with Boston. But there were sharp differences of opinion. A few wanted to demand repeal of the Quartering Act as well as the Townshend revenue act, while others wanted an immediate stoppage of trade. In mid-April, however, the majority adopted an agreement to stop importation in October, and virtually every merchant in the city signed it. But the agreement, like that of Boston, was conditional. It

[31] 4 March, MHSC, 4 ser. IV, 350–51.
[32] NYJ, 26 Nov. 1767. The *New York Journal* reprinted most of the significant articles from the *Boston Gazette* and even verbatim proceedings of the Boston town meeting.
[33] 7 Dec.   [34] NYM, 18 Jan., 8, 22 Feb. 1768.

would not go into effect unless Boston and Philadelphia adopted similar agreements by mid-June.[35]

There was early support for the Boston proposals in the Philadelphia newspapers, which echoed the complaints about stagnation of trade and scarcity of money and praised the idea of frugality and home manufactures.[36] Such appeals had no effect on those Philadelphia merchants who followed the lead of Joseph Galloway. They held a meeting on 26 March, after receiving Boston's invitation to join in non-importation. They listened to a stirring appeal but adjourned without taking action.[37] At another meeting, on 25 April, John Dickinson addressed them. In his *Farmer* letters he had done more than any other American to popularize the use of economic pressure to bring about recognition of American constitutional rights. He now told the merchants that the best method of opposition was non-importation. The Philadelphia merchants were as stolid and as unmoved as they had been the month before.[38]

The supporters of non-importation continued their campaign in the newspapers. Charles Thomson, who within a few years was to be known as the "Sam Adams of Philadelphia," declared that the selfish interest of merchants should not prevail over patriotism, and that if it did, the "curses of thousands" would be upon them.[39] Another writer warned that Philadelphia would be ruined by the "vices of slavery" unless it returned to the path of virtue and liberty.[40] The merchants had their defenders. One newspaper declared that Boston was jealous of Philadelphia's flourishing commerce as compared with its own "long-declining state": hence Boston proposed non-importation. And the idea of home manufactures was ridiculous. Would farmers produce cloth as they had at the time of the Stamp Act, only to have city people refuse to buy it, as after the repeal? [41] The most Philadelphia should do was stop the importation of duties goods but a general economic boycott should be avoided; and the decision should be left to the merchants who knew best, not to the "vox populi." [42]

The Philadelphia merchants continued adamant. Early in June when New York reminded them that the New York agreement would lapse unless Philadelphia agreed, they took no action.[43] The New Yorkers then abandoned their own agreement, and thus, almost a year after the first proposal in the *Boston Gazette*, non-importation was dead in the North, while

---

[35] Ibid. 18 April; Schlesinger, *Colonial Merchants*, 115–16.   [36] PC, 2 Dec. 1767.
[37] PG, 31 March; VG(PD), 21 April.
[38] Dickinson, *Writings*, 411–17; PJ, 28 April; BEP, 23 May.
[39] PG, 12 May; Dickinson, *Writings*, 435.   [40] PC, 30 May.   [41] PG, 16 June.
[42] PC, 25 July.   [43] Schlesinger, *Colonial Merchants*, 119.

the southern colonies remained indifferent. But once again, as it had been in the past and would be in the future, the conflict between Massachusetts and Britain brought the dead to life. Boston's continuing battle against the customs service led to British measures attacking Massachusetts, which united the colonies in the non-importation movement and in still another reiteration of constitutional principles.

Most Americans opposed the more rigid enforcement of customs regulations, but none more vigorously than the people of Boston. According to the *Boston Gazette*, the customs service was staffed by ever larger swarms of greedy vampires feeding on the vitals of America and sucking the life blood of its economy. Its officials were crooks and potential if not actual tyrants. Customs officers, on the other hand, presented themselves as honest hard-working men doing their duty at the daily risk of their lives from vicious mobs urged on by smuggling merchants and unscrupulous politicians.

The battle against the customs service was of long standing and was merely intensified by the Townshend program. It was a battle that did not rise and fall with events as did the constitutional debate, nor did it vary with shifts in local politics. It was the product of British laws, of the behavior of the men enforcing them, of American determination to carry on trade in ways that seemed profitable, and of the constant propaganda waged by popular leaders against all British interference in America.

The task of the customs service was enormous. The laws were complex and often contradictory, and the measures in 1767 did not lighten the burden, although the revenue act of that year continued to exempt officials from the danger of damage suits in American courts. The act, too, tried to help them by providing that colonial supreme courts "shall and may" issue writs of assistance, thus settling so far as mere law could the issue raised by James Otis in 1761. The establishment of the American board of customs in Boston in 1767, with the powers of the British board, was designed to make the service even more efficient and effective. The creation of vice-admiralty courts at Halifax, Boston, Philadelphia, and Charleston in 1768 capped the whole reorganization of the customs service. To these courts, officials could take cases directly or could appeal cases from local colonial vice-admiralty and common law courts.

With the adoption of the Townshend program the framework within which the customs service operated until 1775 was complete, but the result was not the efficiency which was the purpose of its creation. Its failure was due to the dubious methods of some of the customs officials, to squabbles among the officials themselves, and to persistent American opposition. Americans blasted away at the new measures as they had at the old. They denounced the admiralty courts as further evidence of British tyranny while producing glowing tributes to trials by jury. But this attack was partly fraudulent, for most American shipowners, merchants, captains, and sailors usually preferred to try their disputes in admiralty courts rather than in the slower and often more expensive common law courts with their jury trials. And despite the uproar, the admiralty courts tried relatively few cases involving customs laws as compared with the day-to-day disputes involving cargoes, contracts, wages, and other matters concerned with maritime commerce, disputes brought to them voluntarily by Americans.[44] As for writs of assistance, with only a couple of exceptions, colonial supreme courts flatly refused to use the new power given them by the act of 1767.[45]

A major cause of the failure of the customs service was the endless quarreling among British officials, which delighted and encouraged the Americans. Trouble began with the establishment of the British navy in American waters in 1763. The navy, usually moribund in peacetime, acted fast, and before the end of the year more than forty vessels, each commander having the power of a customs officer, were ranging American waters from Newfoundland to the West Indies. American alarm was immediate and vocal, but effective opposition first came from British officials.

Under the old rules, when a ship and/or cargo was seized, condemned, and sold for violation of trade regulations, one-third of the proceeds went to the customs officer who prosecuted, one-third to the governor of the colony where the seizure occurred, and one-third to the king, which in practice meant to the treasury of the colony. This rule remained unchanged if a customs officer made the seizure, but what caused anguish and bitterness from one end of America to the other was that now the navy could capture illegal traders before they came in reach of land-bound officials, and when that happened the navy would get the profits. The Privy Council decided that the proceeds from naval seizures and sales should be divided equally between the officers and crew of the seizing ship and the king's exchequer.

---

[44] Ubbelohde, *Vice-Admiralty Courts*, passim. For a typical example of an attack on the admiralty courts see instructions to the Boston representatives in the legislature, 8 May 1769, BTR, XVI, 287–88.

[45] For a detailed discussion of the writs of assistance, see O. M. Dickerson, "Writs of Assistance," in Morris, *Era of the American Revolution*, and Frese, NEQ, XXX.

The enthusiastic co-operation of the commander in chief of the navy at Halifax was assured by the fact that he was to have one-fourth of the king's half.[46]

Officials on land at once refused to co-operate. They charged, rightly enough, that naval officers were totally ignorant of complex customs and trial procedures. The navy was totally contemptuous of civilian officials.[47] Even more important was the clamor of colonial governors who saw their one-third share vanishing into naval pocketbooks, and they balked every step of the way. Cadwallader Colden of New York was an ardent imperialist but he had an equally ardent concern for his income. When Captain James Hawker of the *Sardoine* seized a vessel off Sandy Hook late in 1763, Colden at once demanded a one-third share if the ship were condemned, but he was willing to leave the decision to the judge of the New York vice-admiralty court. The captain was not willing, and he appealed to Admiral Colville at Halifax. The admiral at once wrote the judge so sizzling a letter that the judge evaded the issue. The money, he said, should go to the king and to such other persons as were entitled to it. Colden at once appealed to the board of trade and to friends in England to help him get the share he demanded.[48]

Governor Bernard of Massachusetts was equally alert. When a naval vessel seized a ship in Massachusetts waters early in 1764, Admiral Colville promptly demanded one-half of the proceeds for the crew, plus his one-fourth. Bernard was wildly indignant. He wanted his traditional third, he told the board of trade, although he was willing to settle for an annual cash payment in lieu of his share from seizures. Otherwise he would fight the navy to the end.[49] Governors all the way to the West Indies carried on a similar battle against the commanders of naval vessels in their waters, and they too appealed to England for help.[50]

The attorney general of England decided that the laws were unclear and, until amended, the old division into thirds should stand. The law-makers soon added to the confusion, for the Revenue Act of 1764 declared that governors were entitled to their thirds of seizures under that or any

46 1 June 1763, APC:CS, IV, 560–62.
47 John Temple to Treasury, 10 Sept. 1764, PRO: Treasury, 1/429; Bernard to BT, 28 April 1766, C.O. 5/892.
48 Colden to General Monckton, 21 Jan. 1764, MHSC, 4 ser. X, 512–13; and to BT, 19 Feb., C.O. 5/1071.
49 To BT, 10 April 1764, C.O. 5/891; Admiral Colville to Philip Stephens, 24 Nov. 1763, 22 Jan. 1764, PRO: Admiralty, 1/482.
50 For example see Governor Fauquier of Virginia to BT, 25 Jan. 1765, C.O. 5/1331.

other act, except for seizures at sea, which should be divided between the king and the prosecutors. But the law did not define "the sea" and British officials in America at once provided a definition of their own. As Admiral Colville put it, "American lawyers, judges and governors . . . would say that nothing was the sea but that part of the ocean which is without the coast." [51] And so they did, for eager governors and officials claimed shares of everything seized by the navy within the multitude of bays and rivers along the coast, where most seizures were naturally made. The navy demanded and finally got a legal statement that the navy could make seizures "anywhere at sea, or in or upon any river, and which [seizures] shall not be actually made on shore. . . ." [52]

But the fight continued, with naval officers, fearful of losing their shares, defying orders to consult with governors, and with governors and customs officials appealing to England to order the navy to bring its seizures within reach of officials on land. In the end the navy won out. At least in 1771 Governor William Tryon of New York was plaintively asking that colonial governors be given a share of naval seizures equal to that given the naval commander at Halifax. [53]

Americans were equally delighted with quarrels among officials on shore, and nowhere was there a more furious brawl than that between Governor Bernard of Massachusetts and John Temple, surveyor general of customs in the northern district. The origins of the fight are obscure but politics was apparently involved. Temple remained on good terms with Massachusetts merchants despite his position, and in 1767 he married a daughter of James Bowdoin, one of the popular leaders in Boston. [54] In 1764 he struck a conspicuous blow at Bernard's friend William Cockle, collector of the port of Salem.

Salem had long been notorious for exporting far more molasses and sugar than legally entered its customs house, and no one assumed that sugar cane was grown in the Bay Colony. Temple began an investigation but bided his time until a vessel entered Salem with a cargo of sugar purported to be from the British West Indies. Cockle and Governor Bernard decided the papers were forged but let the vessel go after levying a "fine." They then informed Temple, who fell into a rage and denounced them. Temple gathered depositions stating that Cockle had taken bribes, and then suspended him from office. So far as Temple was concerned, Cockle

[51] To Philip Stephens, 22 Sept. 1764, PRO: Admiralty, 1/482.
[52] 5 Geo. III, c. 45, Pickering, XXVI, 443.
[53] William Knox to Robinson, 31 Jan. 1772, CHOP, III, 425.
[54] BEP, 26 Jan. 1767.

was the governor's "milch cow." Both Bernard and Temple carried their fight to England, charging one another with what amounted to corruption, but since they had influential friends at home, each held on to his job.[55]

An even more diverting battle occurred in Rhode Island, for the admiralty court which had been established during the Seven Years War was presided over by John Andrews, who had been hand-picked by the local merchants. John Robinson, who became collector of the customs in 1764, had trouble from the start. One of the first vessels he seized for smuggling molasses was stripped and then grounded by a mob. The owner sued Robinson for damages and had him jailed. Temple got him out and a British naval vessel recaptured the sloop. It was finally taken to the Halifax court and sold, but only after strong opposition from Governor Bernard of Massachusetts. He insisted that the case should be tried in the Massachusetts court because the sloop had been seized in an overlapping customs district.[56]

But Judge Andrews was the big stumbling block. In March 1765, Robinson and his comptroller seized two vessels. The advocate general of the admiralty court refused to examine witnesses or to argue the case for the Crown, while Judge Andrews scheduled the case only three days after the seizure and before evidence could be collected. He finally granted a week's delay, but no witnesses could be found and he acquitted both vessels.

The Rhode Island customs officials told their tale to England, declaring that even when Judge Andrews did condemn a vessel he allowed it to be sold at far less than its value. They urged that if he were not replaced he should at least be given orders to hold court in Newport and not at his house in the woods or at other private places they could not locate. The treasury asked the governor of Rhode Island to investigate; he turned the request over to the legislature; it appointed a committee which ignored the matter. Meanwhile Judge Andrews wrote to England, denying everything and in turn accusing the customs officials of conniving with the merchants. The judge filed suit against Robinson for defamation of character and the grand jury returned an indictment stating that the customs officers, "not having God before their eyes, but moved by the instigation of the Devil," had written false statements to England. In the spring of 1767 Judge Andrews sued Robinson for £10,000 damages (Rhode Island currency) and won the case, but Robinson escaped when he was appointed to the new

---

[55] Bernard to SS, 16 Nov., 7, 29 Dec. 1764, C.O. 5/755 and letters of Bernard and Temple in PRO: Treasury, 1/429.
[56] Ubbelohde, *Vice-Admiralty Courts*, 67–69; Bernard to SS, 11 May 1765, C.O. 5/755.

American board of customs commissioners and transferred his residence to Massachusetts.[57]

With British officials at odds among themselves, it is little wonder that Americans were encouraged to obstruct the customs service. The Boston merchants had tried by means of court action in 1760–61, but they had been thwarted by the new chief justice of the superior court, Thomas Hutchinson.[58] The trial procedures established by the Revenue Act of 1764 made such legal tactics almost useless and Americans turned more and more to outright violence, especially after it proved so effective in defeating the Stamp Act. And they were encouraged to use violence by some of their leaders. According to Governor Bernard, James Otis told a town meeting shortly before the repeal of the Stamp Act that the merchants were fools to submit to any restrictions on their trade. One result of such advice, said the governor, was common talk in the streets of Boston that no more seizures would be permitted. Customs officers were frightened and told the governor they did not dare seize illegal goods, and that even if they did, mobs would recapture them. Nor could the government help, for "the popular leaders have labored so successfully that the very principles of the common people are changed. . . ." [59]

A conspicuous example of defiance occurred in Boston in the fall of 1766. An informer told customs officials that Captain Daniel Malcolm, a petty merchant and popular politician, had smuggled wine in his house. One morning in September two customs officers went to Malcolm's house and were admitted and allowed to look around until they found a locked door in the cellar. Malcolm said that the room belonged to a tenant and that he did not have a key; but when the officials proposed to break down the door, Malcolm armed himself with two pistols and a sword and threatened to shoot the first one who tried it. They beat a retreat and returned in the afternoon with a writ of assistance and the sheriff. By then a large crowd had gathered, including schoolboys, and someone told the sheriff that Malcolm and his friends would offer armed resistance. Torn between the law and discretion, the sheriff delayed action until sundown, after which a writ of assistance was invalid. He and the customs officer departed, and Malcolm treated the crowd to buckets of wine.[60]

57 Ubbelohde, *Vice-Admiralty Courts*, 95–97. For a survey of the troubles between 1763 and 1768 see Barrow, *Trade and Empire*, chapter IX.

58 See Chapter III, above.

59 To BT, 18 Aug. 1766, C.O. 5/892.

60 G. G. Wolkins, "Daniel Malcolm and Writs of Assistance," MHSP, LVIII (1924–25), is a detailed account with copies of many documents.

The governor and council collected depositions from the officials, copies of which the town meeting promptly asked for and got. It declared them a "partial" account, and then collected depositions of its own from "persons of credit" and sent them to the colonial agent in England, along with a letter signed by James Otis. The letter defended the town's behavior and attacked "a set of men in America who are continually transmitting to the mother country odious and false accounts of the colonies: which is a crime of the most dangerous tendency." Such accounts have probably excited "a groundless jealousy in the nation," which will, if not checked, "too soon prove fatal to both countrys." [61] By the "set of men" the Boston leaders of course meant Bernard, Hutchinson, and their allies, as well as the customs officials.

The customs officers appealed to England but the attorney general ruled that colonial courts did not have power to issue writs of assistance.[62] Malcolm thus escaped punishment, and Boston was prepared to defy the new American board of customs commissioners when it arrived.

ɞ๑

The stationing of the customs board in Boston was one of the major political blunders of the age; in any other American city it would have had less trouble. Most of its members landed on "Pope's Day," 5 November 1767. Henry Hulton, the first commissioner, reported that the "mob carried twenty devils, popes, and pretenders, through the streets, with labels on their breasts, Liberty, and property, and no commissioners." Hulton "laughed at em with the rest," laughter the Boston mob was to make him pay for twenty times over in the years ahead.[63]

Hulton had served as a clerk in the Plantation Office in London since 1763. William Burch was an Englishman about whom nothing is known. Two other members were regarded as public nuisances by many Americans. Charles Paxton had been collector of the port of Boston for years and was a bitter enemy of the popular leaders of the town. John Robinson, former collector in Rhode Island, was unpopular far beyond that colony. The fifth member, John Temple, was the former surveyor general of customs in the northern district. He regarded his appointment as a demotion, for not only was his income less but two former subordinates were now his equals. He was soon at odds with his colleagues and both sides began

61 BTR, XVI, 187–94; Otis to DeBerdt, 26 Oct., Arthur Lee Papers, HUL.
62 Frese, NEQ, XXX, 503–6. It was this incident which led to the provision in the Townshend Revenue Act of 1767 empowering colonial supreme courts to issue writs of assistance.
63 Ann Hulton, *Letters of a Loyalist Lady* (Cambridge, Mass., 1927), 8.

writing letters to England. Temple's charges sound remarkably like the propaganda of the popular leaders in Boston; his colleagues in turn accused him of favoring the popular party—and with some justice, since he was married to James Bowdoin's daughter and suffered from none of the troubles that beset the other four members of the board. The bickering went on until 1770, when Temple was replaced by Benjamin Hallowell, former comptroller of the port of Boston.[64]

The customs board began its career by investigating, and it soon reported that only six seizures had been made in all of New England during the preceding two and a half years, and that only one had been successfully prosecuted. Three vessels had been rescued by mobs and two had been acquitted in the Rhode Island admiralty court. The board complained bitterly to London of the weakness of the colonial governments, of the "licentious" publications in the newspapers, and of town meetings where the "lowest mechanics discuss upon the most important points of government. . . ." It predicted that the laws could not be enforced unless government was strengthened and proposed that the solution was the use of armed force.[65]

Shortly thereafter Captain Daniel Malcolm again defied the customs service. Late in February 1768, the customs board alleged, he asked officials for a kickback of the duties on a cargo of wine he was expecting. They refused, and the next day a vessel anchored several miles from town. That night a cargo of wine was brought into Boston on drays, each guarded by men armed with clubs. The next day the ship's captain entered the customs house and swore that he had come from Jamaica in ballast, but the new waterline of the vessel showed plainly that cargo had recently been removed. Desperate customs officers sought in vain for witnesses although everyone in town knew what had happened.[66]

Meanwhile, merchants, including one in the legislature, were saying that they would not allow customs officers on board their ships. The distraught governor reported that people in Boston were demanding total repeal of all trade laws imposing duties and declaring that they would suspend those laws as they had the Stamp Act.[67]

[64] Dora M. Clark, "The American Board of Customs, 1767–1783," AHR, XLV (1939–40), is a good brief account. See also Alfred S. Martin, "The King's Customs: Philadelphia, 1763–1774," WMQ, 3 ser. V (1948). Examples of the conflict in the board are in Temple to George Grenville, 7 Nov. 1768, GP, IV, 396–97, and Charles Paxton to Viscount Townshend, 6 Nov. 1769, MHSP, LVI, 349–50.

[65] To Treasury, 12 Feb. 1768, MHSP, LV, 263–67.

[66] Customs Board to Treasury, 28 March, MHSP, LV, 268–71; Bernard to SS, 21 March, C.O. 5/757.

[67] Bernard to Barrington, 4 March, *Barrington-Bernard Corres.*, 147–48.

Mobs too threatened the customs officials. Early in March when the first Boston non-importation agreement was adopted, men surrounded the houses of members of the customs board, blowing horns and beating drums. This was merely preliminary to the combined celebration of the repeal of the Stamp Act and of St. Patrick's day on 17 March. That morning effigies of Commissioner Paxton and Inspector General Williams were found hanging on the Liberty Tree. Governor Bernard and the customs board demanded satisfaction for the "atrociousness of this insult" but the governor's council refused to act. That night mobs appeared before the houses of the governor and of various customs officials, but they did no damage because many "gentlemen" united to keep things relatively quiet.

Why had not the governor asked for troops? Bernard told the secretary of state that the king's governors must have the consent of their councils before requesting troops and that it was useless to ask the Massachusetts council, "considering the influence they are under from being creatures of the people, and the personal danger they would be subject to. . . ." [68] But the governor wanted troops desperately, and so did the customs commissioners. They wrote harrowing accounts of the riots to officials in England and to General Gage in New York.[69] Earlier they had written to Commodore Samuel Hood at Halifax suggesting that a war vessel be stationed in Boston harbor.[70] They wrote him again and Hood responded at once. He dispatched the fifty-gun *Romney* and two armed schooners with orders to support the customs service.[71]

Meanwhile the outraged commissioners turned upon the moneybags of the popular party, John Hancock. Did they attempt to "frame" Hancock and make an example of him, or did Hancock deliberately offer an affront to the commissioners? There is evidence on both sides. Hancock had gone out of his way to insult them. As captain of the local militia he had refused to lead a parade in their honor when they arrived, and he had refused to go to dinners to which they were invited. He had trouble early in April when his ship, the *Lydia*, arrived from London and two tide-waiters were put on board to watch the unloading. Hancock and some followers threw them off the vessel after one of them tried to search it without proper papers. Hancock was on solid legal ground, and he resisted Captain Malcolm's advice to knock the tide-waiters in the head.

Then on 10 June the customs officers seized Hancock's vessel, the *Lib-*

[68] Bernard to SS, 19 March, EHD, IX, 736–39.
[69] Customs Board to Treasury, 28 March, MHSP, LV, 268–71 and Paxton to Townshend, 18 May, ibid. LVI, 349.
[70] 12 Feb., ibid. LV, 278.
[71] Hood's instructions to Captain John Corner of the *Romney*, ibid. 271–72.

erty, and had it towed out to the *Romney* in the harbor. When they returned to shore a mob attacked them with stones, clubs, and brickbats. Collector Harrison and his son and Comptroller Hallowell were badly injured. That night mobs broke the windows of the houses of many officials and then took a "pleasure boat" of Collector Harrison to Boston Common and burned it.

Four of the commissioners, afraid for their lives, fled to the *Romney*, and then to Castle William in the harbor, where they remained for months. John Temple, with his popular party connections, stayed safely behind in Boston. Ann Hulton, sister of Henry Hulton, who had just arrived in Boston was shocked to the roots. "We soon found," she wrote to her friend Mrs. Adam Lightbody back in Bristol, "that the mobs here are very different from those in Old England where a few lights put into windows will pacify, or the interposition of a magistrate restrain them, but here they act from principle and under countenance, no person daring or willing to suppress their outrages. . . ." After surrounding houses "with most hideous howlings as the Indians" and injuring officials, "these sons of violence . . . consulted what was to be done next, and it was agreed to retire for the night. All was ended with a speech from one of the leaders, concluding thus: 'We will defend our liberties and property, by the strength of our arm and with the help of our God, to your tents O Israel.' " [72]

More than the seizure of Hancock's ship lay behind the riot. As soon as Captain John Corner arrived with the *Romney* early in May, he began impressing seamen from inbound vessels and, as Hutchinson said, added "more fuel to the great stock among us before." [73] Corner continued on his arrogant way, indifferent to public opinion. He began firing on merchant vessels which refused to acknowledge his Majesty's ships when passing. And he followed this by publishing advertisements in the Boston newspapers ordering ship captains to obey his orders! [74]

In addition to rioting on Friday, 10 June, the Bostonians held a mass meeting of thousands of the Sons of Liberty which was transformed into a legal town meeting on the following Tuesday. The meeting petitioned the governor to order the *Romney* from the harbor. When he replied that he had no authority to do so, the town's leaders prepared a remarkable piece

[72] 30 June, *Letters*, 11–12. The *Boston Gazette*, 13 June, gave a very brief account with little hint of the extent of the riot, while the *Boston Evening Post*, 20 June, gave a full one. See also Bernard to SS, 11 June, C.O. 5/757. The seizure of the *Liberty* and the consequences are discussed more fully in Chapter XIII, below.
[73] To Richard Jackson, 16 June, MHSP, LV, 283.   [74] BEP, 15 Aug.

of propaganda in the guise of instructions to the town's representatives in the legislature, then on the eve of dissolution for refusing to rescind the Circular Letter of February 1768. The instructions deplored the collection of revenue for "the maintenance of swarms of officers and pensioners in idleness and luxury" and expressed fears of designs on American liberties from a "multitude of placemen and pensioners, and an enormous train of underlings and dependents, all novel in this country. . . ." The seizure of the *Liberty* was a scheme of the customs board to awe the people "into base compliances, and unlimited submission. . . ." There were rumors of new revenue acts and new officers and pensioners "to suck the life blood of the body politic, while it is streaming from the veins. . . ." Furthermore, new ships of war and a body of troops were to be expected "to dragoon us into passive obedience. . . ." A "parliamentary enquiry" should discover if the customs board had asked for troops.[75] The writers of these instructions were obviously informed of the contents of letters on the way. Then came the dissolution of the legislature at the end of June for its refusal to rescind the Circular Letter and the widespread applause for the "Glorious 92" who had defied Hillsborough's order.

In the midst of this turmoil the popular leaders determined to go ahead with non-importation, no matter what the Boston merchants might think or the other colonies might do. The agreement on 4 March had been conditional on the acceptance of New York and Philadelphia. Boston accepted the New York agreement on 2 May; but when Philadelphia refused, New York backed out, and the Boston agreement itself was dead. The "standing committee" appointed in May, with John Hancock as chairman, was dominated by the popular party. In July this committee prepared a new non-importation agreement and called a meeting at Faneuil Hall on 1 August to ratify it. The agreement called for the non-importation of all goods from Britain between 1 January 1769 and 1 January 1770, except salt, coals, fishhooks and lines, hemp, duck, bar lead and shot, wool cards and card-wire. As for tea, glass, paper, and painter's colors, none of these would be imported until the Townshend duty act was repealed. Furthermore, no British goods brought in by factors or from other colonies would be bought.[76]

The *Boston Gazette* praised the "unanimity" shown but in fact there were only sixty signers as compared with the ninety-eight who had signed

[75] BTR, XVI, 253–59; BEP, 20 June.
[76] Andrews, CSMP, XIX, 204–6; BG, 25 July, 1, 8, 15 Aug.

the March agreement. Furthermore, it is likely that many of those who did sign were shopkeepers rather than importing merchants. Further meetings were held to secure more signers.[77] The governor reported that forty merchants had refused although they said they would abide by the agreement, and that thirty-five importers, some of whom were the "principal importers of the town," refused either to sign or to stop importation. The latter, he predicted, "are to be brought [to] reason by mob law; otherwise thirty-five importers only will defeat the scheme." Furthermore, he said, the scheme would fail because many of the merchants had ordered such quantities of goods in advance that they would not need to order any more for a year.[78] Whether true or not, this charge was widely believed and it led to a vast amount of distrust among the commercial towns in the northern colonies during 1769.

New York merchants soon followed Boston, for they were more irked than ever with things British. Governor Moore reported in May that New York's paper money would be gone by November and that money was so scarce that "many of the poorer inhabitants have been ruined and all ranks greatly impoverished." "Numberless" suits against farmers had resulted in the sale of their lands for less than they had paid.[79] Then the customs commissioners in Boston hit the New York merchants where it hurt: they ordered the collector of the port to accept only silver in payment of duties. Previously he had taken promissory notes from merchants and allowed them to unload their cargoes. Governor Moore said that silver was non-existent and that he would have countermanded the order, had he dared, since it served no purpose except to furnish those "inclined to be riotous with some pretense for complaint, and lay the foundation for future disorders." [80]

New York merchants were not inclined to be riotous, but they were indeed angry, and on 27 August they adopted a new non-importation agreement. With some exceptions they agreed to order no more goods for the fall and to countermand all orders sent after 16 August unless the revenue act were repealed. And they went farther than the Boston agreement in more than one respect. The agreement, unlike Boston's, which was only for 1769, would remain in effect until the repeal of the Townshend revenue act. Moreover, it prohibited the importation of goods shipped from Britain after 1 November, and provided that any merchandise imported contrary to the agreement would be stored in public warehouses. Furthermore,

[77] Andrews, CSMP, XIX, 206. [78] To SS, 9 Aug., C.O. 5/757.
[79] To SS, 14 May, NYCD, VIII, 72. [80] To SS, 18 Aug., ibid. 96–97.

those who signed and then imported goods would be "deemed enemies to this country"—an idea the Boston leaders either had not thought of or had not dared to include in their agreement. To keep merchants in line, the "tradesmen" of New York, or the "mechanics and other inhabitants" as the *Boston Evening Post* called them, signed an agreement to boycott any merchant who imported British goods.[81]

The example of Boston and New York encouraged the popular leaders in Philadelphia. The bluntest attack on the Philadelphia merchants came from John Dickinson, this time disguised as a "gentleman from Virginia." During the Stamp Act crisis, he told the merchants, "your patriotism and private interests were so intimately connected that you could not prostitute the one without endangering the other." But now, since you can pass on the new duties to your customers, "you did not esteem it your duty, as merchants nor as American freemen, to oppose it; BECAUSE IT DID NOT DIRECTLY AFFECT YOUR PRIVATE INTERESTS." How unlike the merchants of the northern colonies, who despise such inglorious motives and would rather lose their trade than have their country enslaved! [82]

Dickinson's attack was widely published in other colonies and Philadelphia's reputation sank ever lower, nowhere more so than in New York. A writer in the *New York Journal*, after deploring the use of troops in Boston, turned on the Philadelphia merchants, whom he described as "contemptible to the last degree for their mercenary principles, and abject pusillanimity," and then finally exploded that they were "dastards!" He blamed Philadelphia's reluctance on a few dry-goods importers and appealed to the retailers to adopt non-consumption and treat the importers with "contempt and disgrace on all occasions, publish their names in all the newspapers, that the present may hand down with infamy to their last posterity the reproachful memory of those despicable wretches. . . ." He ended by declaring that "Vox Populi, Vox Dei, is the best political creed that was ever invented for a free people. . . ." [83]

By now the Philadelphia merchants were on the defensive and they attempted to answer such assaults by insisting that they were as aware as anyone of the bad effects of trade restrictions, and of the danger of Parliament's attempt to raise a revenue in America. They argued that violent action would result in still more violence and that Philadelphia should wait to see the result of the legislature's petition, and of the merchant petition

[81] Andrews, CSMP, XIX, 206–7; NYJ, 15 Sept.; BEP, 19 Sept.
[82] "A Copy of a Letter from a Gentleman in Virginia, to a Merchant in Philadelphia," Dickinson, *Writings*, 439–45; BEP, 15 Aug.
[83] NYJ, 6 Oct.; BG, 24 Oct.

which soon would follow. As for the voice of the people being the voice of God, what America had to fear was "arbitrary ministerial tyranny on the one hand, and republicanism on the other. . . ." The spirit, if not the hand that wrote that, was Joseph Galloway's.[84]

Despite their reluctance as a group, Philadelphia merchants as individuals were opposed to British policies. Chief Justice William Allen, who had little love for the Quakers, said that even they were "in their way as zealous in claiming the right [of self-taxation] as their neighbors." [85] Repeatedly, individual merchants wrote to English merchants telling them that they would be forced into non-importation unless Parliament repealed the Townshend duty act, and in November more than 200 merchants sent a petition saying the same thing. But British merchants could offer them no hope and in February 1769 the merchants of Philadelphia at last caved in.

There was a quality of desperation in their action, for they agreed not to order any goods until 10 March unless they heard that the duty act might be repealed, and to countermand all orders that could not be shipped from England before 1 April. The good news did not come and at last on 10 March, a little over a year after the first Boston agreement, the Philadelphia merchants adopted non-importation. They excepted from the list of goods they would not buy some twenty items, including materials used for ballast, for medicinal purposes, and for manufactures. To discourage smuggling they agreed that prohibited goods would not be imported directly from Europe except linens and provisions from Ireland. The agreement was to last until amended by the subscribers or until the Townshend duties were repealed.[86]

Now that they were at last committed, the Philadelphians did their best to recover their reputations. They declared publicly that they were united with all classes of people in the colonies in resistance to parliamentary taxation, and explained that their slowness was due to their desire to try every other means first. When the London merchants told them that appeals based on the economic inexpediency of British legislation would be more effective than constitutional objections, the Philadelphia merchants replied that they would never presume to petition Parliament on such grounds when the assemblies in America were basing their appeals on right. That

[84] PG, 20 Oct.   [85] To Thomas Penn, 12 Oct., Penn Mss., HSP.
[86] The best account is in Arthur L. Jensen, *The Maritime Commerce of Colonial Philadelphia* (Madison, 1963), chapter XII, "The Townshend Acts and Non-Importation, 1767–1770." The original agreement with signatures is in the Charles Thomson Papers, I, LC.

these were not mere catchwords is indicated by the merchants' private correspondence, in which they said the same thing: they would insist on their constitutional rights even if it made the attainment of their goal less certain.[87]

With the adherence of Philadelphia, the three major northern seaports were united, but lesser ports had taken no action. Portsmouth, New Hampshire, still under the control of the Wentworth family, took no action at all, but the slowness of Newport and Providence was surprising, since Rhode Islanders had never before shown any reluctance to act. However, it was expected that these ports would soon join the great ports. The crucial question was what the southern colonies would do. So far they had shown little interest in non-importation although they were fully informed by their newspapers of the events in the North. We hope, said one writer in October, that the "southern colonies will have more virtue and spirit than to be tame spectators of the ruin of their country." [88] They did have spirit, but it was not aroused until an indignant Parliament, stirred by events in Boston, made a proposal that excited alarm from one end of America to another.

It was Boston's response to the coming of the troops in September 1768, which the town's leaders either guessed at or knew about in June, that set off the chain of events on both sides of the Atlantic that made non-importation possible throughout America.

[87] Jensen, *Maritime Commerce*, 180–81.   [88] EG, 25 Oct.

XI

The British Army, Boston, Parliament, and Non-importation in the South

The decision to leave regiments of the British regular army in America after the Seven Years War was the source of much of the trouble between Britain and the colonies. Officially the soldiers were left to guard the frontiers, although most of them were always kept along the Atlantic seaboard. The conviction that Americans should pay a part of the cost led to the Stamp Act, and the obstructions Americans placed in the way of the marching and quartering of troops led to the Quartering Act of 1765. Both laws were extraordinary interventions in the internal affairs of the colonies, but what Americans feared most of all was that the army would be used to support British civil officials.

That possibility had been in the minds of some of the British who made the decision in 1762–63, and almost at once both military and naval authorities in America were ordered to support the customs service if called upon. The Stamp Act crisis brought the issue to the fore. General Gage moved troops to strategic places, but his instructions forbade him to use them unless called upon by civil authorities. At the same time the ministry told colonial governors to ask General Gage for help, but like him, the governors were limited by instructions: they could not ask for military aid without the consent of their councils, consent their councils were not willing to give.

Thus the Stamp Act crisis passed without the military intervention that many governors yearned for and many Americans feared. When intervention did come, it was the result of orders from Britain. Parliament acted first in 1767, when it suspended the New York Assembly until it obeyed the letter of the Quartering Act of 1765. Then in 1768 the ministry ordered

British troops stationed in Boston and created another storm within the very mother of political storms. And while many Americans deplored the behavior of Boston, the stationing of troops in that town aroused the deep distrust of military power in civil affairs which Americans had inherited from England, and presented them with the very real threat that in the future, force would be Britain's final answer to American opposition.

The *Boston Gazette* had been telling its readers ever since 1765 that troops were coming to "dragoon" the inhabitants into "supine submission." In 1768 the American board of customs commissioners demanded military and naval aid and got the latter from Commodore Samuel Hood in May. The arrival of the *Romney* and attendant vessels and the seizure of the *Liberty* on 10 June led to the most violent riot since the summer of 1765. The commissioners sent accounts to General Gage, to Commodore Hood, and, by special messenger, to the ministry in England.[1] General Gage replied that he could not send troops unless requested by the civil power, and that Governor Bernard had not asked for them. He offered troops to Bernard and authorized him to apply directly to officers in Nova Scotia.[2] Bernard explained that his council had repeatedly denied requests for troops ever since 1765, and had refused again after the *Liberty* riot, its members saying that they did not care to be knocked in the head. The governor sympathized, for one of the chiefs of the Sons of Liberty had publicly declared that anyone concerned in asking for troops would be killed. But, added Bernard, "my not applying is no argument that they are not wanted."[3]

His hopes rose high when he got sealed orders from Gage to transmit to Halifax: he thought Gage was taking responsibility. But the general had no intention of letting the governor off the hook; he merely told Colonel Dalrymple to send troops if Bernard asked for them. When Bernard heard this he told Gage that troops would never come if it depended upon him, but he did make another desperate appeal to his council.[4] This time the council replied in a political manifesto blaming all the trouble on the customs board and asserting that "the civil power does not need the support of troops." All is lost, cried the governor, the popular party now completely controls the council.[5] Bitter, he wrote that troops were needed, not to

1 Samuel Venner to Treasury, 20 June 1768, C.O. 5/757.
2 To Commissioners, 21 June, and to Bernard, 24, 25 June, C.O. 5/757.
3 2 July, C.O. 5/757.   4 To Gage, 3, 18 July, C.O. 5/757.
5 To SS, 30 July, C.O. 5/757.

quell riots but "to rescue the government out of the hands of a trained mob" and that troops should have been sent two and a half years ago. "Boston has been left under the uninterrupted dominion of a faction supported by a trained mob from August 14, 1765, to this present July 23, 1768." [6]

Meanwhile, Colonel Dalrymple and Commodore Hood gathered troops and vessels at Halifax, but they waited in vain for a call from Bernard. What came instead were orders from England. As we have seen, Lord Hillsborough tried vigorously to bring the colonies to heel, but without success. His orders to ignore the Massachusetts Circular Letter of February 1768 were defied everywhere, while the Massachusetts legislature resoundingly refused his order to rescind. The customs board's report of the "riots" in March produced the crucial decision. Parliament was not in session, and so the ministry acted alone. On 8 June 1768, Hillsborough ordered Gage to send one regiment to Boston, or whatever forces he thought necessary, and to quarter them in the town. He was fully aware of the significance of the order, for he told Gage it was "a service of a delicate nature, and possibly leading to consequences not easily foreseen. . . ." [7]

Late in July, Comptroller Benjamin Hallowell of Boston arrived in London with reports of the *Liberty* riot and of the flight of the customs board from the town. The news created a furor. Thomas Whatley told George Grenville that he found "the alarm about America very great. The stocks have fallen two and a half percent upon it. The ministers are in great confusion." But action was impossible until the Duke of Grafton could be persuaded to return to town for a full meeting of the cabinet. [8] When it did meet, it decided to send two regiments from Ireland in addition to those previously ordered. Again Gage was told to use them as he saw fit, when properly called upon by the civil magistrates. [9]

But this was not "policy," as Grenville pointed out. His informants were legion, both in America and in the ministry, many of them doubtless with an eye out to his possible return to power. [10] Grenville was not surprised at events, for the Americans had been "notoriously and avowedly encouraged in Great Britain. . . ." What had happened in Boston was a "natural"

[6] To Barrington, *Barrington-Bernard Corres.*, 167–68.
[7] Gage, *Corres.*, II, 68–69; to Bernard, 1 June, C.O. 5/757; to Lords of the Admiralty, 11 June, C.O. 5/757.
[8] 26 July, GP, IV, 321–22; William Knox to Grenville, 23 July, ibid. 319–20. On the fall in stocks see *Gentleman's Magazine*, Aug. 1768, 358.
[9] Hillsborough to Gage, 30 July, Gage, *Corres.*, II, 72–73.
[10] Commodore Hood, for instance, sent long informative letters to Grenville as well as such things as seeds and Canadian geese.

consequence of such encouragement and of the "torpor" of government. It needed no spirit of prophecy to foretell that the Americans, thus encouraged, would go to extremes of one kind which would probably be met by extremes of another. It was futile to send troops without some plan for settling the affairs of America upon a permanent and solid foundation of obedience to the legislature of Great Britain.[11]

The confused ministry had no plan. Hillsborough exhorted Bernard to bring the Boston magistrates to a sense of their duty or else remove them, to enquire into the causes of the riots, to search for evidence of treason so that the accused persons could be brought to England for trial under the treason statute of Henry VIII. He fulminated against the "erroneous doctrines and dangerous principles inculcated with so much art and diligence by wicked and designing and probably self-interested men," principles which tended only to "anarchy and confusion, to the subversion of our constitution, and to the destruction of the British empire, the defence and protection of whose liberties can be nowhere so safely placed as where the constitution has placed it, in the hands of the supreme legislature." [12] What Hillsborough, like Grenville, refused to admit was that some Americans had a quite different version of the "constitution," and believed that the sending of troops to Boston was itself "subversion."

ह≫

Americans had written thousands of words since 1765 to define their conception of the constitution of the empire. Most of them at first had ignored Parliament's assertion of absolute power over the colonies in the Declaratory Act of 1766, but by 1768 some of them faced it squarely. John Dickinson did not. In fact he consistently supported Parliament's power. In his second *Farmer* letter he wrote: "We are but parts of a whole; and therefore there must exist a power somewhere, to preside, to preserve the connection in due order. This power is lodged in Parliament. . . ." A fellow Philadelphian did challenge the Declaratory Act. Little is known of William Hicks except that he was a supporter of the proprietary party in the 1760s. His *The Nature and Extent of Parliamentary Power Considered* began as a series of newspaper essays which soon appeared in pamphlet form. The first essay appeared in the *Pennsylvania Journal* on 21 January 1768. Several newspapers reprinted his essays at the same time they were

[11] Grenville to William Knox, to Cadwallader Colden, to Michael Collinson, 28 July, to Lord Trevor, 8 Aug., and to Whately, 14 Aug., Grenville Letter Books, HEHL.
[12] 30 July, C.O. 5/757.

reprinting Dickinson's *Farmer* letters, and the *Boston Evening Post* even dropped Dickinson for a time to publish Hicks.

Hicks's argument, which he called "this doctrine of independence," was clear. The emigrants brought with them "the spirit of the English government" and their "duty" to their sovereign but they did not leave "their brethren, the freemen of England, vested with a sovereign, supreme power to restrain their natural liberty, or to dispose of their acquired property." Englishmen in America could no longer join in the national council, and so governments of their own were created under the Crown "as the very spirit of the English constitution required it. . . ." With such governments established, the people of America "totally disclaim all subordination to, and dependence upon, the two inferior estates of their mother country." The only laws they submit to are those made by themselves by agreement with the deputy of the Crown. Perhaps it is not an "irreconcilable paradox" to assert that the freemen of America may be "absolutely independent of their fellow subjects" and yet be loyal to their sovereign. "The colonies may . . . be considered as so many different counties of the same kingdom, the nature of whose situation prevents their joining in the general council. . . ." The restraining power of the Crown guarantees that no one distinct part of the kingdom may interfere "with the general welfare of the whole. . . ." True, as a commercial people, the interests of America may sometimes clash with those of the inhabitants of Britain but is this "sufficient authority for stripping us of all the most valuable privileges in society?" [13]

Such arguments were carried much farther in Boston as tension mounted during the spring and summer of 1768, a tension heightened by the *Liberty* riots, the dissolution of the assembly, and the constant rumor that troops were coming. Months later an innkeeper deposed that he heard Samuel Adams, Dr. Benjamin Church, and others talking wildly on the streets and in his tavern. The day after the *Liberty* riot, he said, Samuel Adams told seven men on a street in South Boston: "if you are men, behave like men. Let us take up arms immediately and be free and seize all the king's officers; we shall have thirty thousand men to join us from the country." Adams talked even more wildly in the tavern: our ancestors

---

[13] Hicks's pamphlet is reprinted in Jensen, *Tracts*, 164–84. For a shorter denial of subordination see the *Boston Evening Post*, 1 Aug. The "commonwealth" conception of "A Citizen" and other "advanced" political ideas of the times are to be found in the newspapers long before well-known pamphleteers like James Wilson and John Adams, who are usually given credit, either cared or dared to publish them.

were free and therefore "we are free and want no king." Shortly before the troops arrived Adams predicted that 30,000 men would come to Boston and that "we will destroy every soldier that dare put his foot on shore." [14] Such "evidence" is naturally suspect.

Then, on 9 July, the selectmen of Boston ordered the town's arms cleaned and put on display for several hours in the town hall, and no one could miss the implications.[15] Nor could they when the *Boston Gazette* declared that "however meanly some people may think about the populace or mob of a country, it is certain that the power or strength of every FREE country depends entirely upon the populace. . . ." [16] All was blamed on the "wicked faction" in America which had tried to enrich itself by taxes levied on America and which had sent "one of their prostitutes after another" to England. The faction secured the Stamp Act and was defeated. And then it secured the revenue act, and when the assemblies protested they had been dissolved. The government of Massachusetts has become a monarchy and "there is not in it a spice of democracy or democratical power." [17]

What shall a "wise people" do if troops come, asked "Sidney"? The next week "Clericus Americanus" offered a solution: a declaration of independence. Parliamentary taxation of the colonies, the dissolution of assemblies, and the attempt to bring troops to Boston all mean that the charter is abolished. The colonies have reverted to a state of nature and all bonds with Britain are severed. The people of the towns should choose representatives to an assembly to create a temporary government from which all Crown officers and pensioners are excluded.[18]

These were not the "casual ravings" of an "enthusiast," said Governor Bernard, a faithful if horrified reader of the *Boston Gazette*. On 9 September, in an effort to head off the violence he feared, he deliberately "leaked" the news he had received on 27 August: the troops were coming. That night the Sons of Liberty met and talked of calling in men from the backcountry to repel the landing. The next night another meeting proposed to capture Castle William and use it to prevent troopships from entering the harbor. A turpentine barrel was put on the beacon, supposedly to be fired to call men from the country. The council met on Sunday and

[14] Deposition of Richard Silvester before Chief Justice Hutchinson, 23 Feb. 1769, C.O. 5/753.
[15] Bernard to SS, 9 July, C.O. 5/757.   [16] 25 July.   [17] 15 Aug.
[18] 29 Aug., 5 Sept. The "Queries" of "Clericus Americanus" were reprinted in the *New York Journal*, 15 Sept.

ordered the selectmen to take it down. They ignored the order, but when the sheriff finally removed the barrel a few days later it was empty.[19]

Cooler heads took over and called a town meeting for Monday, 12 September. The meeting asked the governor for the source of his information about the troops and requested that he call the legislature to meet at once. Bernard lied twice in reply. He said his information about the troops was "private" not "public," and that he could not call an assembly without permission from England.[20] Meanwhile the meeting listened to a report on measures to be taken in "the present emergency." It was a long statement of American rights, "natural" and otherwise, and replete with citations to British laws and precedents. After the governor's reply the town meeting took the startling step of calling a convention of the province. The town's four delegates in the legislature—Otis, Cushing, Adams, Hancock—were elected a "committee in convention" to meet with similar "committees" on 22 September in Boston.

This open defiance of the royal prerogative was accompanied by an even more extraordinary recommendation. After citing an act of Parliament of William and Mary to the effect that all Protestant subjects should be armed to defend themselves, and praising it as founded in "nature, reason, and sound policy," the meeting declared that the inhabitants of Boston should observe a "good and wholesome law" of Massachusetts which provided that every soldier and householder should have arms. The reason offered was that "there is at this time a prevailing apprehension in the minds of many, of an approaching war with France." [21] It was not lost upon anyone that chests containing 400 muskets lay in the middle of the town hall during the meeting. And when it was suggested that they be distributed immediately, it was objected that they might fall into the hands of people who would not use them against the troops. James Otis reportedly told the meeting that the arms would be distributed at the proper time and that there was no need to be specific since they all understood one another well enough.[22] Little wonder that the government party feared violence

---

[19] Bernard to SS, 9, 16 Sept., C.O. 5/757.

[20] When Bernard dissolved the assembly in June, he said he could not call it again without permission. Hillsborough's order did not say this and Bernard asked him to "cover" him. To SS, 6 Aug., C.O. 5/757. Hillsborough did so, 12 Oct., C.O. 5/757. Hillsborough's official letter of 10 June saying troops were coming was hardly "private" information.

[21] BTR, XVI, 259–64; BEP, 19 Sept.

[22] Bernard to SS, 16 Sept., C.O. 5/757; to Gage, 16 Sept., BP, VII, 196–99, HUL; Minutes of Town Meeting, Sparks Mss. X, Papers Relating to New England, II, 81, HUL.

and felt that the convention was part of the plot. Hutchinson's friends even warned him that he might be killed before the troops arrived.[23]

A few days before the convention met, the *Boston Gazette* said that troops were coming merely because of some "children's hallooing" back on 18 March, while "Hyperion" pictured the ghastly future in store for the town in an obvious bid for drastic action. "Hyperion" asserted "that as soon as the troops shall be quartered upon us, some were to be pilloried, some whipped, some to lose their ears, and others their heads. . . ." There will be "dragoons and executioners to awe and terrify with fire and sword every man who should dare give his countrymen one timely caution." What wonder then that a nation should remain inactive "till their hands were fast-manacled, and the whole herd of great and little tyrants rush violently on, seeking whom they may devour? A people in this state, it is likely, would never be roused from their lethargy till the soldier was ravaging their fields, invading their most sacred property, and tearing the dearest pledges of nature from their bosoms, till the executioner was at the door, the scaffold erected, and the fire kindled." [24]

The convention which met on Thursday, 22 September, ignored this hysterical "call to arms." Before it was over, delegates from ninety-six towns and eight districts were present and there was little visible difference between it and the recent assembly, for Thomas Cushing was elected chairman and Samuel Adams, clerk. The convention at once petitioned the governor to call the legislature, but he refused to receive the petition and sent a note, in his own handwriting, declaring that the convention was an illegal body, and that while ignorance of law might now excuse its members from charges of criminal action, in the future it would not. A second petition defending the legality of the convention and its necessity to quiet the minds of the people was likewise rejected by the governor.

Thereafter the meeting went into a secret session which wrote a petition to the king and a "Result of the Convention." These consisted of a review of constitutional theories, a denial of criminal activity, an assertion of loyalty, and an appeal to God and posterity.[25] Considering the background of rumors and threats of violence, the convention was indeed "moderate," as the governor claimed, and he took the credit.[26] But the credit was not his alone, if at all. The majority of towns had not sent delegates; rural

[23] Hutchinson to Thomas Whately, 9 Oct., Mass. Ar., XXV, 281–82.
[24] BG, 19 Sept. and supplement.
[25] Ibid. 26 Sept., 3 Oct.; BEP, supplement, 26 Sept., 10 Oct.; VG(R), 27 Oct., 3 Nov.
[26] To SS, 3 Oct., C.O. 5/757.

Hatfield had issued a blistering denunciation of Boston which probably reflected the opinions of many.[27] The Boston leaders were themselves at odds. Thomas Cushing opposed violent resistance to the landing of troops; he was for "moderate" measures such as driving Bernard and Hutchinson from the colony and then having the council call the legislature into session![28] James Otis did not appear in convention until near the end, and then he was "perfectly tame." Samuel Adams's tirades were easily squelched.[29] The main fact was that the country delegates had no intention of following the Boston firebrands. If the purpose of the Boston leaders was violent opposition to the troops, the convention was a miserable failure. However, they had set an extraordinary precedent in calling what amounted to a meeting of the legislature in defiance of the "constitution." The convention disbanded and the delegates started for home with understandable speed as a British fleet and two regiments of troops arrived in Boston harbor on 28 September.[30]

The news of the Massachusetts convention had reached England by the time Parliament met on 8 November. The king's speech declared that Boston had taken "measures subversive of the constitution, and attended with circumstances that might manifest a disposition to throw off their dependence on Great Britain." In the debate that followed, George Grenville, who for months had been attacking a policyless ministry, united with Edmund Burke to blame the ministry for all the troubles in America. The majority, however, officially blamed the troubles on "the arts of wicked and designing men" in America who had rekindled the flame of sedition. Furthermore, the majority pledged itself to maintain "entire and inviolate the supreme authority of the legislature of Great Britain over every part of the British Empire," thanked the king for sending troops to Boston, and promised to support any future measures to establish the "constitutional dependence of the colonies on Great Britain. . . ."[31]

Resolutions did not constitute policy, but Hillsborough tried to provide one. In July he had ordered Governor Bernard to find evidence and to prosecute those guilty of rioting. He had also ordered him to look for evi-

---

[27] MG, 6 Oct.; VG(R), 3 Nov.
[28] Report of Nathaniel Coffin on conversation with Cushing, C.O. 5/758.
[29] Bernard to SS, 3 Oct., C.O. 5/757. Bernard wrote many letters then and later about the convention. He obviously had informants present.
[30] For events in Boston after the arrival of the troops see Chapter XIII below.
[31] PH, XVI, 467–69, 472–74.

dence which would justify bringing Americans to England for trial under the treason statute of 35 Henry VIII.[32] Bernard failed. Not a single witness would testify before the grand jury, of which Captain Daniel Malcolm, a mob leader, was a member. It was impossible to secure evidence, and Bernard, who had undercover agents among the Sons of Liberty, refused to reveal their names for fear that they would become known in Boston.[33]

Undiscouraged, Hillsborough sent Bernard's letters and other papers to Attorney General De Grey. What crimes have been committed, asked Hillsborough? Can the Massachusetts charter be forfeited? Rather coldly the attorney general replied there was not enough evidence to justify a charge of high treason. The principles expressed were bad, but overt acts were lacking. And as for the Massachusetts charter, there was not enough evidence to proceed judicially "upon a legal forfeiture. . . ."[34]

Hillsborough then turned to the House of Lords where he introduced eight resolutions denouncing Massachusetts and Boston, while the Duke of Bedford moved an address to the king recommending the gathering of evidence so that Americans could be brought to England for trial under the treason statute of Henry VIII. Hillsborough's resolutions charged that the Massachusetts House of Representatives, in January and February 1768, had denied the authority of Parliament "in all cases whatsoever," and that this was "illegal, unconstitutional, and derogatory of the rights of the Crown and Parliament of Great Britain"; that the Massachusetts Circular Letter was "of a most unwarrantable and dangerous nature, calculated to inflame the minds of his Majesty's subjects in the other colonies, tending to create unlawful combination, repugnant to the laws of Great Britain, and subversive of the constitution"; that Boston was in a state of disorder and that the customs officers were obstructed in doing their duty and their lives endangered; that neither the council nor civil magistrates had used their authority to suppress the riots; that military force was necessary to protect civil magistrates and customs officials; that the actions of the town meetings on 14 June and 12 September were "illegal and unconstitutional and calculated to excite sedition and insurrections"; that the issuing of writs by the selectmen in calling a convention was "subversive" and showed a design of people of Boston to "set up a new and unconstitutional

[32] 30 July, C.O. 5/757. The law referred to is 35 Henry VIII, c. 2. It provided that anyone committing treasonable offenses outside the realm of England could be tried within any shire of England by the Court of King's Bench or by commissioners in the same manner as if the offense had been committed within that shire. Pickering, V, 199.
[33] Bernard to SS, 9 Sept., C.O. 5/757.
[34] De Grey to Hillsborough, 25 Nov., C.O. 5/757.

authority, independent of the Crown of Great Britain"; and finally, that the election of delegates and the convention itself "were daring insults offered to his Majesty's authority, and audacious usurpations of the powers of government." The opposition was feeble; a few questioned the validity of Bernard's reports, and Lord Temple denounced the resolutions as a "paper war with the colonies" and stalked out.[35]

The real opposition centered in the House of Commons in January 1769. By then the defenders of the colonies had gathered materials from the colonial agents, and even from the Boston selectmen, and Barlow Trecothick was attempting to organize merchant opposition as he had at the time of the Stamp Act.[36] Alderman William Beckford began the fight by offering a petition from members of the Massachusetts council, which ignored the question of "right" and asked for repeal of the revenue acts because of economic hardships. The majority tabled the petition as it did one from William Bollan, agent of the Massachusetts council, protesting against the Lords' resolutions. The ministry's argument against it was feeble: it was too long, it contained legal arguments difficult for the members to judge, and it was presented at an unusual time. Length of a petition was no argument, said the opposition, and furthermore the right of a subject to petition is indisputable. But the ministry had the votes if not the better argument.[37]

The debate on the resolutions soon showed that Hillsborough was ignorant of some simple facts. Friends of the colonies such as Edmund Burke and Isaac Barré were joined by George Grenville, who was convinced that "force alone will not do; there must be system, firmness, and moderation, positive and intelligible instructions and certainty of support to those who obey them." [38] The ablest defender of the colonies was a former governor of Massachusetts, Thomas Pownall, who had recently published the fourth edition of his knowledgeable *Administration of the Colonies*. He flatly charged, and proved his case, that many of Hillsborough's resolutions were not based on fact. Pownall declared that the journals of the Massachusetts house contained no record that it had denied the supremacy of Parliament. Grenville then threw the ministry into utter confusion by demanding that

[35] PH, XVI, 476–79, and note.
[36] Thomas Whately to Grenville, 3 Jan. 1769, GP, IV, 408–09; Grenville to Whately, 8 Jan., Grenville Letter Books, HEHL; Thomas Pownall to the Boston Selectmen, 30 Jan., Samuel Adams Papers, NYPL.
[37] PH, XVI, 481–84.
[38] Grenville to Whately, 7 Aug. 1768, Grenville Letter Books, HEHL. It should be remembered that at this time Grenville was also opposed to the expulsion of John Wilkes.

it produce the journals and read them to settle the point. The ministry had no copies nor could it find any. The third and fourth resolutions were equally false, said Pownall, for the riot was sudden and over before the council or magistrates could interfere. As for charging that the Boston selectmen had issued writs for an election, the man who wrote that resolution simply did not know what a writ was, and Pownall produced a writ as defined by Massachusetts law. The selectmen had written letters, which was legal. The facts were on Pownall's side, and Lord North proposed an amendment to make the charge "writing letters" instead of "issuing writs." Inevitably, the question of Governor Bernard's veracity was raised, and he was defended by his cousin, Lord Barrington, secretary at war, with a "warmth and passion not usual."

With even more force, Pownall opposed the address to the king. The Crown itself had approved a Massachusetts law for treason trials in the colony back in the days of William and Mary; it was therefore illegal to bring Americans to England for trial under the old statute of Henry VIII. But far more dangerous in his eyes was the use of military power for political purposes, and particularly, the enforcement of revenue laws. The Americans were unalterably opposed to internal taxes except those imposed by their own legislatures, and therefore the "issue is well nigh brought to force." If this military power is not withdrawn "the union between Great Britain and North America 'is broken forever'. . . ." When a people is against a tax, no civil power can collect it nor can a military force. It may collect money but "that is not 'government,' it is 'war.'" If Britain uses military force, the Americans will come to hate Britain and then the people "whom it has governed . . . with a little paper and packthread, you will not for the future be able to govern it with a rod of iron. . . ."

Seven years later at Concord and Lexington the accuracy of Pownall's prophecy was borne out, but the majority of the House of Commons followed the leadership of men who, in their blind determination to force recognition of the sovereignty of Parliament "in all cases whatsoever," lost the American colonies forever. The answer to all arguments was the chanting of "Question, question" by the "chorus men," and at four in the morning "the whole House in confusion, laughing, etc." passed the resolutions and the address to the king, and thus another step in the dissolution of the empire was taken, in the midst of irresponsible gaiety.[39]

---

[39] PH, XVI, 485–90, 494–507; HCJ, XXXII, 185–86, 194. The resolutions and address of 9 February are reprinted in EHD, IX, 720–22. Pownall's speech was printed in the *Virginia Gazette*(R), 15 June 1769.

ℰ✥

While the ministry was sending troops to Boston, and Parliament was trying to resolve Massachusetts into submission, officials had been alarmed by the behavior of Virginia. "His Majesty's most ancient colony" had passed some remarkable resolutions, but its people had behaved decorously as compared with the rowdy Bostonians. Shortly after troops were ordered to Boston in June 1768, Hillsborough learned that in May the House of Burgesses had not only supported the Massachusetts Circular Letter, it had also adopted an even more radical circular of its own, and then prepared petitions which, among other things, blandly asserted the equality of the House of Burgesses with the House of Commons. The secretary was thoroughly rattled.[40] He sent the documents to George III saying that they were "still more alarming than those from Massachusetts," and he called for warships and marines to be ready "on very short notice." [41]

When the uproar subsided, it was decided to send a full governor of noble rank to Virginia in place of Lieutenant Governor Francis Fauquier, who had died in March. For decades the lucrative governorship had gone as a reward for services to someone who stayed in England while a lieutenant governor was the resident administrator. Jeffrey Amherst had been governor since 1759 but he had no intention of returning to a land he despised. Within weeks he was forced to resign and was replaced by Lord Botetourt, whose business practices had led him to the verge of bankruptcy, if not the gates of prison. The result of the appointment was a cloud of rumor and a political scandal relished equally by George Grenville and the Boston Gazette, the one and only time they were ever of one mind. Amherst was outraged, not because he lost the governorship but because his honor was not salved with a peerage, a future American peerage, an income equal to that from Virginia, and a grant of Cape Breton coal lands or other land in America.[42]

Botetourt was on his way by August, carrying with him speeches written by Hillsborough for delivery to the House of Burgesses. He was to denounce the petitions of May 1768 and lay the Declaratory Act before the house. If the burgesses did not behave he was to dissolve the house and remove any members of the council who agreed to anything derogating from the authority of Parliament. If there was a "sudden commotion of the populace" he was to call for military aid.[43] Time soon showed how

[40] Acting Governor Blair to SS, 18 May, and SS to Blair, 9 July, C.O. 5/1346.
[41] 22 July, Geo. III Corres., II, 36.   [42] Brooke, Chatham, 366–69.
[43] Additional Instructions to Botetourt, 21 Aug., and SS to Botetourt, 10 Dec., C.O. 5/1346.

futile such childish orders were when directed at the proud gentlemen of
Virginia in legislature assembled. Botetourt arrived in October on a man-of-
war which had orders to proceed to Boston to assist in the subjection of
that rebellious town. Whatever it thought of the ship, the *Boston
Gazette* had nothing but jeers for Virginia's new governor. While it
purported to give both sides of the story, it left the impression that Botetourt's appointment was merely a scheme of Hillsborough to save him
from the consequences of his crooked financial deals.[44]

The Virginia newspapers were discreet and Botetourt was greeted with
the usual fulsome addresses. But these were soon ridiculed as a "curious
species of lip-loyalty" unbecoming to men determined to be free. And the
prorogation of the assembly until May 1769 was scorned. "Is it to wait with
patience to see what steps our imperious lords and masters at home shall
be pleased, in their great wisdom to take? Lords and masters, by the by,
who are bought and sold like sheep in the markets." Virginians would not
give up their rights even if they did hear "awful sounds" about rescinding
and demands for due deference to acts of Parliament.[45] It was not surprising that the new governor soon found that the colonies would "never
willingly submit to the being taxed by the mother country; the reverse is
their creed. . . ." [46] His political education was under way.

ଛ

Most of the commerce of the southern colonies was such that problems
faced by northern merchants as a result of the Revenue Act of 1764 meant
little to them. Even the new enforcement politics had little impact before
1768, except for the activities of bumptious naval officers such as Captain
Jeremiah Morgan of the sloop *Hornet*. In 1764 Morgan had his arm
broken in the course of a fight with Maurice Moore, a prominent member
of the North Carolina legislature.[47] In April 1766 Morgan seized a ship in
Virginia. The captain of a Norfolk vessel, William Smith, was suspected of
being the informer and when he appeared in Norfolk he was seized by some
of the leading citizens, including the owner of his vessel, and tied behind a
cart. As Smith told the story to Morgan, "Maximilian Calvert, mayor of
the town, instead of suppressing the insult, encouraged and threw stones at
me himself." Smith was tarred, feathered, tied to a ducking stool, and
made the target for more stones and rotten eggs. He was then marched
through town by a mob which showed "all imaginable demonstrations of

[44] 17 Oct., 28 Nov.   [45] VG(R), 2 Feb. 1769.
[46] To SS, 17 Feb., C.O. 5/1347.
[47] Tryon to SS, 2 Feb. 1767, NCCR, VII, 435.

joy and all the principal gentlemen of the town being present." Proposals that he be thrown into the water tied to the stool were regarded as a bit extreme so he was thrown in without it. He was picked up by a boat and taken to Portsmouth, from whence he wrote Captain Morgan asserting his innocence, asking for protection, and claiming that he had almost lost the use of his limbs and his eyes.[48]

What happened to Smith thereafter is unknown, but Morgan departed for North Carolina, still seeking revenge for his broken arm. He challenged Maurice Moore to a duel, which Moore refused, whereupon Morgan publicly abused members of the legislature. The indignant legislators threatened his arrest and he fled downriver, much to the relief of Governor William Tryon, who said that although Morgan had done much to stop smuggling, "his conduct on the whole reflects no honor to his Majesty's service." [49]

Within a few months Morgan was back in Virginia. Late one night he raided a Norfolk tavern and impressed men for his crew. A mob gathered and when a magistrate arrived Morgan cursed him and threatened to run him through with a sword. When the mayor appeared, Morgan ordered his men to fire on the crowd but the sailors balked and Morgan fled to his ship, leaving some of his men behind to be jailed.[50]

Such activities as Morgan's did not stir Virginians to adopt nonimportation. What did rouse them was Parliament's proposal that Americans be brought to England for trial under the treason statute of Henry VIII. That news set going the events which led to the adoption of nonimportation agreements by Virginia, Maryland, and South Carolina before the end of the summer of 1769.

The Virginians learned of the proposal in March,[51] and somehow they heard of the order to Botetourt to lay the Declaratory Act before the House of Burgesses. They soon made clear what they thought. Fauquier county instructed its delegates that taxation by any other body except the Virginia legislature was "totally inconsistent with the principles of liberty, and the greatest insult that can be offered to free born subjects." And the delegates were to disapprove of the Declaratory Act as strongly as possible if it were laid before the burgesses.[52] An essay by "A British American" in the Virginia Gazette the next week predicted that Britain's ruin was im-

[48] Smith to Morgan, 3 April, and Morgan to Governor Fauquier, 5 April 1766, C.O. 5/1331.
[49] N. C. House Journal, 10 Nov. 1766, NCCR, VII, 358; Tryon to SS, 2 Feb. 1767, ibid. 435.
[50] VG (PD), 1 Oct. 1767.　　　[51] Ibid. 23 March 1769.　　　[52] VG(R), 27 April.

minent and warned that Americans should preserve their country, not only as an asylum for their own posterity but also for those inhabitants of Britain who could enjoy in America those rights they would lose at home when Britain was no longer an independent kingdom. As for the Declaratory Act, the burgesses should ignore both it and Parliament and resolve that Virginians could be taxed only by their own legislature.[53]

When the burgesses met four days later, Lord Botetourt disobeyed his orders from Hillsborough: he delivered a speech filled with innocuous generalities.[54] The gesture was futile, for on 16 May the House of Burgesses adopted four resolutions. Once more it asserted its sole right of taxation, the right to petition the king, and the right to join with other colonies in doing so. The members then challenged the proposal to take Americans to England for treason trials. Such trials should be held in the courts of the colonies concerned. To send Americans beyond the seas was "highly derogatory of the rights of British subjects, as thereby the inestimable privilege of being tried by a jury from the vicinage, as well as the liberty of summoning and producing witnesses on such trial, will be taken away from the party accused." The burgesses then decided to petition the king, and to make certain of widespread publicity, they ordered their proceedings sent to all assembly speakers in America and printed in the *Virginia Gazette*, where they appeared along with copies of the proceedings of the Boston town meeting, of the Massachusetts convention, and the resolutions of Parliament.[55]

Governor Botetourt was astonished and shocked and he abruptly dissolved the assembly. His only satisfaction was that none of the councilors apparently had "the smallest share in any part of this abominable measure." [56] A few days later he warned that "opinions of the independency of the legislature of the colonies are grown to such a height in this country, that it becomes Great Britain, if ever she intends it, immediately to assert her supremacy in a manner which may be felt, and to lose no more time in declarations which irritate but do not decide." [57]

He got proof of his warning the day after he dissolved the legislature, when the ex-members signed a non-importation agreement. The *Virginia Gazette* had been providing information ever since November 1767, when it printed the Boston non-consumption agreement of October and had followed it with such documents as the New York non-importation agree-

---

[53] VG(PD), 4 May.   [54] JHB (1766–69), 188–89.
[55] Ibid. 214–16; VG(PD), 18 May.   [56] To SS, 19 May, C.O. 5/1347.
[57] To SS, 23 May, C.O. 5/1347.

ment of August 1768.[58] The idea that Virginia should try economic coercion, however, made no headway until the spring of 1769. By April, plans were passing from hand to hand. George Washington sent one to his neighbor George Mason with his hearty approval, not knowing that Mason himself was the author. Petitions and addresses were inadequate to secure American liberty, declared the future father of his country. In the last resort men should not scruple to "use arms in defence of so valuable a blessing. . . ." Non-importation would be difficult but it should be tried. Mason agreed, but said they should wait for the legislature to meet, and meanwhile prepare the way with newspaper propaganda.[59]

It soon appeared. "Atticus" listed American grievances and urged non-importation as the remedy despite the difficulties involved. One was that most merchants in the tobacco colonies were agents for British houses and therefore could not join. Furthermore, since Virginia had no manufactures, it would have to import them from the northern colonies. But Virginians did not need to import food, drink, and finery, and they could stop the importation of slaves and turn from tobacco farming to manufactures.[60]

The planters did not consult the merchants, and if there was any opposition, it vanished as a result of the dissolution of the legislature on 17 May. That day the members met at a private house, elected Speaker Peyton Randolph moderator and agreed on a plan of non-importation, which the next day was signed by the "principal gentlemen" of the colony. It followed George Mason's earlier plan except that it omitted his proposal for the non-exportation of such items as hides, naval stores, and lumber. The agreement called for the non-importation, after 1 September 1769, of all articles taxed by the Townshend revenue act except paper costing no more than eight shillings a ream. The signers agreed also to the non-importation of a long list of luxuries, including liquors, foods, clothing, jewelry, and of tools, cloth, and leather goods. Most striking was the provision that they would neither purchase nor import slaves after 1 November. As a gesture in the direction of home manufactures, no lambs born after 1 May each year would be killed. The plan was to last until the revenue act was repealed or the subscribers agreed to abandon it.[61] The day after its adoption Richard Henry Lee, who had been railing against the Townshend rev-

[58] VG(PD), 19 Nov., 10 Dec. 1767; 21 Jan., 10 March, 29 Sept. 1768; 12 Jan. 1769.
[59] Washington cautiously spelled arms, "a--ms." 5 April, John C. Fitzpatrick, ed., *The Writings of George Washington* . . . (39 vols., Washington, 1931–44), II, 500–504.
[60] VG(PD), 4, 11 May.   [61] Ibid. 18, 25 May.

enue act, wrote his brother Arthur, who had returned to England, that "the flame of liberty burns bright and clear, nor can its light and luster be impaired by any ministerial art or delusion." [62] It was not; the flame was snuffed out by the Virginians themselves.

The agreement was essentially a non-consumption agreement among the planter-legislators, eighty-eight members signing at once and eleven more later. Once more they had supported a constitutional principle, and perhaps they hoped to relieve themselves of a part of their debts to British merchants. More importantly, they believed they had set an example for the other colonies, and in this they were not disappointed.

The resolution protesting against taking Americans to England for trial was soon adopted by New Jersey and Delaware.[63] The new governor of Maryland, Robert Eden, postponed the meeting of his legislature until November, but when it met, it did all the necessary business first and then adopted the Virginia resolves and sent a circular letter to all the colonies urging their support. The thwarted governor then ended the session.[64] Governor Tryon was ill when the North Carolina legislature met in the fall. It promptly adopted the Virginia resolutions and then prepared a petition to the king declaring the treason statute of 35 Henry VIII unconstitutional, illegal, and dangerous to the rights of the people. When the governor recovered and read the journals, he dissolved the assembly,[65] and in so doing ended the first legislature that had promised to do something about the grievances of the Regulators, thus helping to precipitate the crisis at Alamance Creek in 1771. The New York legislature, busy with internal quarrels, adopted the Virginia resolves without argument.[66]

In this way, as in the case of the Massachusetts Circular Letter the year before, British action brought about a "union" of the colonial legislatures, but this time in defiance of Parliament itself, not of a "mere ministerial order." Furthermore, British action helped to unite the southern and the northern colonies in the non-importation movement.

Maryland, like Virginia, had ignored the northern example although the *Maryland Gazette* kept the colony fully informed and the legislature supported the constitutional protests of Massachusetts and Virginia. Baltimore acted first when its merchants, upon request from Philadelphia,

---

[62] *Letters*, I, 34–35. [63] VG(R), 13 July. [64] Md. Ar., LXII, 110–11, 119.
[65] NCCR, VIII, 121–24, 140–41. [66] NYAJ, 22, 24, 29 Nov.

adopted a non-importation agreement on 20 March 1769, only ten days after the reluctant Philadelphians had finally yielded.[67] Annapolis took the lead when on 11 May four merchants called for an Anne Arundel county meeting, and for a meeting of delegates from all Maryland counties. On 23 May, Anne Arundel county adopted an agreement modeled on Virginia's of the week before, and in June a colony-wide convention did likewise. But there was one important exception: the Maryland plan said nothing about slaves. Unlike Virginia, Maryland did provide for a measure of enforcement. Signers agreed to refuse to rent or sell warehouses to nonsigners, and to boycott them to boot. Furthermore, they would be deemed "enemies to the liberties of America" and be treated "with the contempt they deserve." [68]

Although the Maryland agreement purported to be one of "merchants, traders, free-holders, mechanics," and other inhabitants, twenty-two of the forty-three signers were legislators and five more were destined to become such. It would seem that as in Virginia, non-importation was primarily the work of planter-legislators.[69]

৪১

Charleston was the last of the major seaports to adopt non-importation. Except during the Stamp Act crisis, South Carolinians were preoccupied with internal problems, particularly those of the discontented backcountry. They were willing, of course, to join other colonies in asserting constitutional rights as in November 1768, when the legislature defied British orders and was dissolved for approving the Massachusetts Circular Letter. And like other Americans, the Carolinians were increasingly irked with the implementors of British policy. In Carolina, as elsewhere, quarrels with customs officials, naval officers, and other British appointees did more to alienate opinion than the question of constitutional supremacy, for it was probably on the level of day-to-day life, rather than on the rarefied plateau of theoretical debate, that the opinions of most men were formed.

By 1768 Charlestonians were attacking the customs service with all the verbal violence of the Bostonians. They had had little quarrel with the laws of trade, and smuggling was almost nonexistent. They had shown little concern over the Revenue Act of 1764, which caused so much alarm in the North. The South Carolina merchants and planters, with profitable mar-

---

[67] Charles A. Barker, *The Background of the Revolution in Maryland* (New Haven, 1940), 320.
[68] MdG, 11 May, 29 June; VG(R), 13 July.   [69] Barker, *Maryland*, 322.

kets for rice and indigo, were a prosperous, proud, and arrogant little aristocracy, happy to stay within the British Empire as long as they were allowed to run South Carolina, in a manner, be it said, in no way at variance with the economic interests of either South Carolina or Britain.

But the Revenue Act of 1764 did provide a basis for trouble. The writers of the law, ignorant of both American geography and trade routes, assumed that only undecked vessels engaged in the coastwise trade. Hence the law required that decked vessels more than seven miles from shore must carry a multitude of papers. Aside from the fact that the busy coastwise trade of the Americans was not carried on in rowboats and open sailing craft, the law was particularly inept where South Carolina was concerned. Great cargoes of rice, indigo, and naval stores were shipped downriver in decked vessels too large to follow the coastal waterways. Hence, they put out to sea, often beyond the seven-mile limit, before turning into Charleston. Carolina law required such vessels to give bond but once a year since there were only three customs houses in the colony. The act of 1764 superseded the Carolina law, and busy naval captains at once took advantage of the technicality to seize rice and indigo boats in purely internal coastwise trade.[70]

Carolinians were furious and their fury increased when Daniel Moore arrived from London in the spring of 1767 as the new collector of the port. Moore and George Roupell, who had been searcher of the port for many years, soon united the colony against them.[71] Moore tactlessly announced to the law-abiding Carolinians that no breaches of the law would be permitted, and then began demanding higher fees. When Captain James Hawker of the *Sardoine*, who had tangled earlier with Governor Colden in New York, seized the sloop *Active* for sailing between two South Carolina ports without papers, Moore co-operated, but he could get no legal advice. To a man the Charleston lawyers ignored his appeals and offered their services to the owner of the *Active*. Egerton Leigh, the attorney general, refused his advice, for he was also judge of the vice-admiralty court. Leigh, like his father, was a prime example of what Americans meant when they talked of the evils of English "placemen." Peter Leigh had arrived from England in 1753 with a commission as chief justice. He alienated the

---

[70] Governor Bull carefully explained the problem to the board of trade but no action was taken. 8 Sept. 1765, C.O. 5/378.
[71] The following account is based in part on Dickerson, *Navigation Acts*; Leila Sellers, *Charleston Business on the Eve of the American Revolution* (Chapel Hill, 1934); Ubbelohde, *Vice-Admiralty Courts*; and Barrows, *Trade and Empire*, all of which vary in details.

powerful Pinckney family, for he displaced Charles Pinckney, the first South Carolinian ever appointed to the post. That same year he admitted his twenty-year-old son, Egerton Leigh, to the practice of law. Peter Leigh died in 1759 but his son accumulated one post after another. He was appointed surveyor general, justice of the peace, member of the governor's council, and, in 1762, judge of the vice-admiralty court. In 1765 he alienated the Rutledges when he displaced John Rutledge as attorney general. In the meantime he had married a niece of Henry Laurens and then had seduced her sister when she came to live in his home.

Somehow Egerton Leigh managed to survive the ill-will of the Carolinians. His decision in the *Active* case in June 1767 was popular to the extent that it freed vessels in the coastwise trade from carrying the papers required by the act of 1764, but he charged the owner £150 costs for the return of a vessel not worth £80 and he certified that Captain Hawker and Collector Moore had a "probable cause" for seizure and thus freed them from possible damage suits.[72]

Almost simultaneously Collector Moore made the mistake of picking on Henry Laurens, one of the richest merchants in America. Laurens was a shipowner, importer, exporter, banker, and plantation owner, with friends and partners in other American colonies and in Britain. Politically conservative, he had never had trouble with the customs service. Laurens had sent a vessel with supplies for his Georgia plantation, where it was laden with shingles for the return voyage. Since the nearest Georgia customs house was forty miles distant, Laurens followed the usual practice and secured a bond from a Georgia magistrate. Nevertheless, Moore seized the vessel in June 1767 for not having a proper lumber bond. He then offered to release it in return for a cash payment to himself, and when this was rejected, hinted that its "chastity" could be preserved by an escape at night. Laurens refused to connive, and the case was tried in Judge Leigh's court. Leigh condemned the vessel and cargo for not carrying proper papers but, since there was no evidence of fraud, he allowed Laurens to buy the vessel back for £175, far more than its value. And to make matters worse, he charged Laurens a fee of £277 for hearing the case.

At the same time still another Laurens vessel was seized on its return from Georgia. This time logs and chunks of wood had been thrown in as ballast. Moore seized it because it did not have a lumber bond and said he did so after giving Judge Leigh £50 for advice. Moore allowed his deputy

[72] SCG(C), 23 June 1767; BEP, 20 July. On the Leighs, see H. Hale Bellot, "The Leighs in South Carolina," *Transactions of the Royal Historical Society*, 5 ser. VI (1956).

Roupell to try the case, which was dismissed by Leigh as frivolous; he charged Roupell one-third and Laurens two-thirds of the costs. However, he declared that there was no "probable cause" for seizure. Laurens promptly sued Roupell for damages and won a verdict of £1400, which Roupell paid, not from his own pocket but from customs revenues.

The Charleston merchants now united to drive Moore from the colony. A grand jury indicted him for extortion,[73] and the hot-tempered Laurens, after promising not to lay hands upon him, did in anger "lay a finger upon his nose."

The next day Moore left after only a few months in the colony, but Roupell stayed on and soon showed that he had learned nothing. He wanted revenge on Henry Laurens and his opportunity came in the spring of 1768. The ship *Ann*, owned in partnership by Henry Laurens and merchants in Bristol and Philadelphia, arrived in Charleston. It unloaded and then began loading for the return voyage to Bristol. Laurens took out a permit to load and gave bond for the enumerated articles he knew would be shipped, and then left for Georgia. His captain and clerk completed loading with non-enumerated articles such as rum and cattle horns, but, as was the custom, did not ask for a permit or give bonds until they could know what the final cargo would be. When the *Ann* was ready to sail, they went to the customs house with manifests and asked for a permit and offered bonds. Roupell refused, and seized the ship, although the day before he had cleared a vessel under identical circumstances. Roupell offered to release the *Ann* if Laurens would drop the £1400 damage suit he had won earlier. Laurens refused and Judge Leigh dismissed the case but he charged Laurens a part of the costs and issued a certificate of "probable cause" for seizure so that he could not sue Roupell for damages.

This was the end so far as Laurens was concerned. He had already circulated accounts of the difficulties in Charleston to other colonies. In February 1769 he published *Extracts from the Proceedings of the Court of Vice-Admiralty*, which was little more than a collection of the legal documents. Leigh had resigned as judge, for he had received orders from England to give up that post or the attorney generalship, but he attacked Laurens in a pamphlet called *The Man Un-Masked*. The furious Laurens then prepared a new edition of his own pamphlet, which he advertised in the *South Carolina Gazette & Country Journal*. He described Leigh as "that POLE CAT" and later on called him a "greedy, coarse, and filthy wretch." News of the fray was widely reported in the colonial newspapers,

[73] SCG(C), 3 Nov. 1767.

and Laurens circulated his pamphlets everywhere in America and Britain. Leigh stayed on in the colony and in 1772 he was made a baronet, an act not calculated to win approval in America.

But the controversy had far wider implications. Henry Laurens was a man with an international reputation and his denunciation of the customs service, in language that Boston's popular leaders must have envied, did much to make opposition respectable. At the same time the conspicuous case in Massachusetts involving young John Hancock was equally well publicized. Furthermore, it was prosecuted, not by local officials as in South Carolina, but by members of the new American board of customs. Their motives were suspect, their evidence was dubious, and the result was a crashing defeat for them only a few short months after they had taken charge of the customs service in North America.

The normally conservative Carolinians were forced into violent opposition to the customs service, but they ignored the invitation of the Boston merchants to adopt non-importation in the fall of 1768.[74] The first demands for action came from the leader of the "mechanics," Christopher Gadsden, and from Peter Timothy, publisher of one of the three South Carolina gazettes. The mechanics had by no means the strength of their northern brethren but they willingly followed Gadsden's lead. Timothy was particularly intent and from February 1769 onward he urged non-importation and the use of American manufactures,[75] while Gadsden dramatized the issue by appearing at his wife's funeral clad in blue homespun instead of the usual black mourning imported from England.[76] Since a good deal of Charleston commerce was in the hands of "foreigners," who were either independent merchants or factors for British houses, they soon became the butt of propaganda. In June 1769, Timothy's *Gazette* attacked these "birds of passage" and asked whether they or the planters who lived in the colony suffered the most from the unconstitutional acts of Parliament. Carolinians should adopt non-consumption agreements and thus force the merchants into non-importation.[77]

Shortly thereafter Gadsden issued an address to the "planters, mechanics, and freeholders" urging them to stop buying to force merchants into line.[78] The *Gazette* then published a non-importation agreement suitable

---

[74] Sellers, *Charleston Business*, chapter X, "Non-Importation at Charleston," is the best account.
[75] SCG(T), 2, 16 Feb. 1769. Ever since December 1767 Timothy had reprinted detailed accounts of non-consumption and non-importation in the North, including copies of agreements.
[76] Ibid. 2 March.   [77] Ibid. 1 June.   [78] Ibid. 22 June.

for farmers and workers. It would allow for the importation of articles used on farms and in shops but exclude all others. It would last until the Townshend revenue act was repealed, and all who did not sign within a month were to be boycotted. The "mechanics" met on July third and fourth under the Liberty Tree and added two amendments: no Negroes would be imported after 1 January 1770 and no British goods would be bought from transient traders.[79]

The merchants were at last forced to act, and on 7 July they adopted an agreement of their own to last until 1 January 1771 unless the Townshend act were repealed. It called for the importation of far more goods than the mechanics' agreement, but added wine to the items excluded. As for slaves, the merchants would import none from the West Indies after 1 October and none from Africa after 1 January. But the merchants said nothing about dispensing with the use of imported mourning clothes: they had large supplies on hand. And as importers and sellers of manufactured goods they naturally said nothing about the promotion of domestic manufactures. The mechanics, also naturally, objected to these two omissions. The merchants complained bitterly that the mechanics' agreement gave special favors to mechanics and planters while burdening the merchants in a harsher manner than was ever "conceived by the most arbitrary minister of the most despotic king." [80]

The mechanics and planters once more threatened to boycott the merchants, who were thus forced to ask for joint action. The result was a new agreement which Gadsden read to a mass meeting under the Liberty Tree on 22 July. The agreement excluded all cloth except "Negro cloth" and canvas, and would permit the importation of drugs, tools, nails, firearms, bar steel, ammunition, wool cards and card wire, mill and grindstones, fishhooks, printed books and pamphlets, salt, and coal. Trade with transient vessels was forbidden after 1 November except for salt and coal. It included the merchants' proposal for the non-importation of slaves and of wine. Signers also agreed to maintain the usual prices and to promote American manufactures, to boycott all who did not sign within a month, and to treat all importers with the "utmost contempt." [81] The list of 268 signers was headed by the members of the legislature.

As assemblymen they took official action on another matter: the Virginia resolves of May protesting against the proposal for taking Americans to

---

[79] Ibid. 29 June, 6 July.   [80] Ibid. 13 July.
[81] Ibid. 27 July, reprinted EHD, IX, 725–26. See also Sellers, *Charleston Business*, chapter X.

Britain for trial. On 19 August the Commons House adopted the Virginia resolves and added one of its own declaring that the statute of 35 Henry VIII did not extend to the overseas dominions of the Crown, where there were sufficient provisions for impartial trials of persons accused of treason.[82] Governor Bull reported that it would have been useless to dissolve the house for its action: not only did it have considerable business to attend to, including the tax bill for 1768, but also because experience had shown that "a repetition of such marks of displeasure had not produced any good effects of changing men or measures in the present universal jealousies of the people, but had tended rather to furnish the more turbulent and factious with popular arguments to keep up their clamors and feed their discontent." [83] Few governors in America or officials in Britain were as wise as the lieutenant governor of South Carolina.

With the adherence of South Carolina all the major colonies were united, but some of the lesser ones had not yet acted. Georgia, controlled by a forceful and popular governor, held out and was denounced by the Carolinians, who said that it should be "amputated" from the rest of America "as a rotten part that might spread a dangerous infection." Charleston gradually shut off trade with Georgia and in September 1770, when non-importation was dead, Georgians adopted an agreement.[84] North Carolinians expressed sympathy and the legislature adopted an agreement, but North Carolina had little direct trade with Britain and no means of enforcement were provided. Rhode Island adopted the Boston non-consumption agreement of 1767, but both Newport and Providence ignored the non-importation movement. Other colonies charged that Rhode Islanders hoped to profit from the patriotism of their neighbors, and eventually boycotts by Philadelphia and New York, and even by Charleston, forced the two towns to adopt watered-down agreements by the end of 1769. Connecticut, with almost no direct trade with Britain, also ignored the movement until bitter attacks by the New York merchants' committee brought about some local agreements during the summer of 1769. Somewhat belatedly, Connecticut leaders saw an opportunity to free themselves from their economic dependence on New York and Boston, and the Connecticut merchants' adoption of a colony-wide agreement early in 1770 had as much to do with schemes for legislative aid for domestic shippers and manufacturers as it did with the Townshend program.[85] New Hampshire

[82] EHD, IX, 723–24.   [83] To SS, 28 Aug., C.O. 5/379.
[84] Sellers, *Charleston Business*, 216–17.
[85] New York Merchants Committee to the New Haven Merchants, 12, 27 July, Misc. Bound, XIII, MHS; Schlesinger, *Colonial Merchants*, 111–12, 150–55.

took no action, despite threats from Boston, until after the Boston Massacre, when Portsmouth and a few other towns agreed to non-importation.

It had been relatively easy for Americans to agree on constitutional principles in 1767 and 1768, for by then the reiteration of such principles was a familiar activity. But economic coercion on the scale achieved by 1769 was unprecedented, and two years of wrangling had taken place between the first proposal in August 1767 and the adoption of the Charleston agreement in August 1769. The very difficulty of achieving non-importation thus made it the principal symbol of American opposition to the Townshend program. But non-importation was a shaky method at best, for many American merchants objected to it from the start and had been forced into it by threats of non-consumption movements and open violence. Economic coercion of Britain was achieved, in part at least, either by the threat or the reality of coercion of Americans by Americans.

Another difficulty arose from the diversity of the non-importation agreements which produced intercolonial distrust and jealousy, and which led to charges of cheating on the part of prominent supporters of the movement. In addition, the methods of enforcement aroused alarm everywhere. Many men who in normal times could have had no influence on the flow of commerce, began interfering directly with the private business of merchants, and this aroused the fears of many conservative-minded Americans for the fate of private property, not only for the moment but for the future.

Hence there was constant opposition to non-importation, an opposition soon encouraged by the promise of a change in British policy. Even before the adoption of the Charleston agreement Americans had learned of the beginnings of the second British retreat. During the summer of 1769 their governors informed them that Hillsborough had promised repeal of the Townshend revenue act in the next session of Parliament, and the abandonment of any further attempts at parliamentary taxes on commerce.

More than one influential American therefore waited with ill-concealed impatience for the measure which would give them an opportunity to escape from what they felt was economic bondage to and political persecution by their fellow countrymen, whom they looked upon as belonging to the lower orders of society.

XII

The Second British Retreat, 1769–1770

For three years after the passage of the Townshend program in the spring of 1767, Parliament enacted no important laws affecting America. Administration of policy was left in the hands of an ever-changing ministry but there were no sharp overturns such as had occurred before 1766. Instead, there was a gradual transition from the ministry formed by William Pitt in the summer of 1766 to that headed by Lord North in the spring of 1770. Nevertheless there was no end to political bitterness, quarrels, and intrigue for position and power. The changing group of men who held office seemed incapable of developing or administering a coherent colonial policy except to insist that the colonists must acknowledge that which they would not: the subordination of their legislatures to the absolute sovereignty of Parliament. Aside from this futile insistence, they sent orders that were not obeyed, they blustered and were defied, and in the end they tried to use that last refuge of desperate and policyless politicians, military force. Having done all these things and having united all America as never before, they retreated when they committed Parliament to the repeal of the Townshend revenue act while still clinging futilely to the principle of the Declaratory Act.

It is one of the many ironies of the age that the renewed troubles were the result of laws sponsored by a ministry nominally friendly to the colonies on the issue of taxation, while the retreat was carried out by a ministry overtly committed to the absolute sovereignty of Parliament over the whole British Empire. The retreat was due to many things: to the constant struggle for power and the alterations in the ministry; to the rise of radicalism in England itself which seemed more dangerous than anything happening in America; to the threat of foreign war; and to the non-importation movement in the colonies. For such reasons the ministry and Parliament alike by the end of 1769 were anxious to end the dispute with America.

ह≈

In Britain, as in the colonies, the demands of domestic politics, and sometimes sheer chance, often shaped patterns of action. So it was with the ministry which bears the name of William Pitt, Earl of Chatham. It set out with high hopes in July 1766, but Chatham's illness left it leaderless within six months, and placed the concerns of a great empire in the hands of men who disliked and distrusted one another. A few of them, like Shelburne, were devoted to Chatham and wanted to follow his policies if only they could discover what, if any, policies he had. For the most part they had nothing in common except the desire for office and their fear that Chatham might recover and fall upon them for their misdeeds. The young Duke of Grafton, the acting head of the ministry, had little interest in leadership, and the ministry lost strength steadily during the spring of 1767 as Parliament passed one by one the measures that created a new storm of protest in America.

George III, desperate for stable government after years of administrative chaos, literally begged Chatham to provide the necessary leadership, but by the summer of 1767 Chatham, his mental balance uncertain at best, refused to see either the king or his colleagues. The only suggestion he made was to strengthen the ministry by an alliance with the noxious Bedford Whigs. Negotiations with the various factions came to naught, but the ministry staggered on until September 1767, when Charles Townshend died. Lord North took his post as chancellor of the exchequer and again Grafton tried to negotiate. Rockingham would have nothing to do with George Grenville, who continued to hammer away at the necessity of a forceful colonial policy. Meanwhile the Bedfords, who had no principle except lust for office, wondered if loyalty to Grenville was worth the price. In December 1767 they let it be known that they would join the ministry if Shelburne were removed. Since both Grafton and the king were anxious to be rid of Shelburne, this was no price at all. Shelburne had been alternately snubbed and ignored but he had refused to resign as secretary for the southern department and stayed on in the hope that Pitt would recover. Now the Bedfords, the king, and Grafton hit upon a scheme which they thought would force Shelburne out. They proposed to divide

his department and create a third secretary of state in charge of the colonies. The need was great and obvious, and had been for years, but the decision when it came was not the result of any concern for better administration. But Shelburne did not quit. He surrendered control of American
affairs and stayed on as secretary for the southern department. The Bedfords, despite the failure of the plot, took office anyway, and Lord Hillsborough, a king's friend, became the new secretary of state for America
and remained in that post until 1772.

During 1768 as the American protest mounted in intensity, it was countered by a growing demand in Britain for stringent measures. The attack
on Shelburne was renewed to force him to resign and Chatham roused
himself long enough to remove the mantle of his great name from a ministry that had no interest in the principles he had proclaimed.[1] From the
resignation of Chatham and Shelburne in October 1768 until the spring of
1770, affairs were managed or mismanaged by a ministry whose head, the
Duke of Grafton, did not want the office. Its American policy was one of
threat and retreat from threat, sometimes engaged in simultaneously, with
the result that there was no policy at all. If the Grafton ministry's vagaries
created contempt in the colonies, its domestic policy created a fear, both in
America and in Britain, that it was sapping the very foundations of English
liberties.

The steady drift in the direction of intolerance and coercion in British
politics after 1767 provided a legacy for Americans to ponder, and for the
popular leaders in the colonies to use for their own purposes. The American newspapers reported at length the events in what many Americans,
even those who had never been there, called "home." In addition, Americans carried on a great correspondence with merchants, agents, and Americans in Britain, and many of them went there to school or to travel. From
the newspapers, their correspondence, and from personal experience, more
and more Americans were convinced that "home" was rapidly becoming a
sink of corruption and the death-bed of liberty. American newspapers, for
instance, carried lengthy accounts in 1768 of Lord Baltimore's trial for
rape,[2] and in 1770 there appeared a premature account of his death, supposedly in Vienna: he "having been detected in an amour with the wife of
a German count, was run through the body by the injured husband and
expired on the spot. This unfortunate nobleman, whose inordinate passion

[1] Brooke, *Chatham*, chapters V, VII–VIII, X; Ritcheson, *British Politics*, chapter IV.
[2] VG(R), 4 Aug. See William L. Sachse, *The Colonial American in Britain* (Madison, 1956), chapter XI, for an account of Americans in Britain and their activities in the years before the war.

for the sex, obscured all his other good qualities," left "an only daughter and three illegitimate sons." [3] Nor were Americans unaware of the immorality of other members of the aristocracy who presumed to lecture Americans on the subject of their behavior. The buying and selling of seats in the parliamentary election in the spring of 1768 was told at length in American newspapers, and, among other places, in the letters of Benjamin Franklin.[4] American politics had its corruptions, but the Americans, being human, congratulated themselves on their own relative purity. The resignation of the Americans' hero, William Pitt, was evaluated as the triumph of lesser men and of the enemies of America. But above all, Americans gained a new English hero who received adulation such as Pitt had never had.

ॐ

The return of John Wilkes to England in 1768 and the Middlesex elections created a symbol of liberty for Americans, as for many Britons. The specter of a House of Commons uncontrolled by law frightened even George Grenville, and convinced more Americans than ever that their views of the rights of their own legislatures were not only constitutionally correct but practically necessary, if liberty were to survive anywhere in the world. Wilkes had been toasted occasionally in America during 1766, but by the end of 1768, "Wilkes and Liberty" was a toast from one end of the colonies to the other, and "45" was almost a sacred number. An unfrocked parson in Massachusetts wrote Wilkes that according to "rascally Tories" he was "an abominable blasphemer, and uncommonly wicked." The parson was sure that the last charge was false, but rather wistfully, said that he had never read the "Essay on Woman." If he were to see it, and found anything "which is called too luscious, I assure you I am well fortified by the revolution of sixty cold North American winters, which have hoared my head. . . ." [5]

Wilkes had lived on the Continent since 1764, fleeing from creditors and vainly seeking a pardon from the Rockingham and Chatham ministries— vainly because George III could neither forget nor forgive the scandalous publications of 1762 and 1763. Suddenly, in March 1768, Wilkes appeared in London. He petitioned the king for a pardon and announced that he was a candidate for election to the House of Commons from the City of

[3] BEP, 11 June 1770. The report was wrong, for Baltimore did not die until 1771. VG (PD), 16 Jan. 1772.
[4] Writings(S), V, passim.
[5] Benjamin Kent to Wilkes, 5 Oct. 1768, MHSP, XLVII, 194–96.

London. He avoided arrest during the election campaign by promising to surrender to the Court of King's Bench on the outstanding charges against him. Wilkes had powerful support but he did not win. He at once became a candidate for Middlesex with the powerful backing of such men as Lord Temple, who had long helped pay his bills. The London mob helped too. People who did not wear a blue cockade with "Wilkes" and "45" on it were kept from the polls. For two days London was at the mercy of the mob which broke windows of the houses and coaches of the aristocracy. The Austrian ambassador was dragged from his coach and had "45" chalked on the soles of his shoes.

Wilkes won the election at Brentford on 25 March. The ministry, which had hitherto ignored him, was completely taken aback. Those who were afraid of the mob thought he should be pardoned and allowed to take his seat, but George III insisted that he must be expelled from the house when it met.

Meanwhile Wilkes went to prison. The mob assumed that he would be released to take his seat in Parliament on 10 May. A large crowd surrounded the House of Commons shouting "Wilkes and Liberty," but a far larger number met in St. George's Fields at King's Bench Prison. The ministry ineptly, defiantly, or because it did not trust English soldiers, ordered Scottish troops to the scene, and Lord Weymouth, secretary of state, told the magistrate of the district to use them if necessary. On learning that Wilkes would not be released, the mob began threatening the prison and throwing rocks at the soldiers. The soldiers fired, killed five or six, and wounded several more, some of them women. In the course of the brawl soldiers chased into a private home and killed a young man, William Allen, who apparently had nothing to do with the rioting. A coroner's inquest found a Scottish soldier guilty of murder, but he was acquitted when tried. Only with difficulty was the mob prevented from tearing him to pieces. The "massacre" of St. George's Fields was to be followed less than two years later by a "massacre" in Boston, Massachusetts, and the example of the first massacre was not lost on the participants in the second.

Early in June, Wilkes appeared before Lord Mansfield who declared his outlawry illegal and thus restored his full rights as a British citizen. Wilkes then appeared to receive sentence for seditious libel and blasphemy of which he had been convicted in 1764. He had every reason to expect a mild sentence or perhaps no sentence at all, for in 1764 general search warrants, on which he had been arrested and his papers seized, had been declared illegal. But the court sentenced him to twenty-two months in prison and fined him £1000.

The London mob was outraged, and violence rose in London as the ministry puzzled what to do about Wilkes. George III was adamant, and one by one his ministers agreed to Wilkes's expulsion from the House of Commons. In December the other member from Middlesex died, and John Glynn, an ardent defender of Wilkes, set himself up as the popular candidate and won a violent election, in which one man was murdered. Two government supporters were convicted of the murder but were pardoned, and again the mob was infuriated. Wilkes, from prison, blasted away at the government. He accused Mansfield of irregularities in the trial in 1763, and accused a secretary of the treasury of bribing a printer to testify against him. Somehow he got hold of a copy of Weymouth's letter to the magistrate before the massacre in St. George's Fields. He sent it to a newspaper with a preface accusing the ministry of deliberately planning the massacre.

The ministry used this publication as the excuse for a new attack on Wilkes, and the House of Commons voted it a libel. Wilkes was brought before the house, but instead of repenting he declared that the country owed him its thanks for exposing "that bloody scroll" and that his only regret was that he had not used stronger terms. On 3 February 1769 Wilkes was expelled a second time for the publication of *North Briton* No. 45, for the "Essay on Woman," and for the preface to Weymouth's letter. Wilkes's leading defender was George Grenville, who had led the opposition to him in 1763. Narrow though Grenville might have been, he was a Whig of the Whigs, with an enormous respect for the constitution as he understood it, which understanding was far better than that of those who voted to expel Wilkes. Grenville knew the law and custom of Parliament, and that Parliament's action was contrary to it. Furthermore, the expulsion raised the issue of the right of electors to elect whom they pleased, and here high principle was at stake.

On 16 February, Middlesex re-elected Wilkes. The next day the House of Commons voted that he was incapable of sitting in Parliament because he had been expelled. On 16 March, Wilkes was unanimously elected a third time. The next day the house declared the election void. The ministry then persuaded young Colonel Luttrell to resign his seat and stand for Middlesex in still another election. Wilkes's supporters kept the election quiet, determined to prove that Wilkes was their choice. Wilkes won a fourth time, with 1143 votes to 296 for Luttrell. Thousands called to congratulate Wilkes, and that night all London was illuminated. But on 14 April the house declared Wilkes's election void, and two days later seated Luttrell. On 8 May it reconfirmed the decision after a bitter debate, and the next day when George III drove to Westminster to close the session he drove through a storm of shouted insults.

ह੶

The uproar surrounding John Wilkes brought to a focus and produced the organization of radical groups in England strikingly like those in America in terms of program and propaganda. During 1769 mass meetings were held to air radical opinions on the subject of government. The idea, long familiar and much used in the colonies, of instructing representatives in legislatures, was taken up throughout England in an effort to influence members of the House of Commons. The most important group was the Society of the Supporters of the Bill of Rights which was organized to help Wilkes but which soon demanded drastic political reforms. The guiding spirit at first was the Reverend John Horne Tooke, vicar of Brentford, who abandoned his clerical garb for the role of propagandist and agitator for which he was far better suited. The Society railed against "placemen" and "pensioners" with all the vigor of Samuel Adams in Boston, and proposed their exclusion from Parliament. It proposed full representation of the people in annual parliaments and the impeachment of ministers who had violated the rights of freeholders in the Middlesex elections, and of those responsible for the "massacre" in St. George's Fields. It supported Irish protests and the claim of the colonies to the right of taxing themselves.

Backing up this organized assault on the corruption of the government were the slashing, erratic attacks in the "Letters of Junius." The unknown author obviously knew the inside workings of government, and in letter after letter, without regard for truth, decency, or honor, he attacked men high and low, topping it all with a devastating letter to George III himself in December 1769. Master though he was of invective, Samuel Adams could seldom match "Junius," whose letters confirmed many Americans in the low views they held of the ministry "at home," and strengthened their belief in the rightness of opposition to "ministerial tools" in America.

The opposition groups in Parliament, distrustful though they were of one another, had an issue of principle on which they could at least partially unite; outside, the London mob rose to new heights of violence. Petitions to the king from counties, towns, and boroughs protested against the violation of the rights of electors and demanded a dissolution of the "corrupt"

Parliament and a new election. The ministry's attempts at a counter-campaign failed utterly. A London meeting to support the ministry was attended by only thirty persons and was broken up by a mob. Merchants carrying a petition to the king, offering their support, were attacked and routed. A London grand jury flatly refused to indict rioters seized by officers, and juries refused to convict them when indictments were presented. Colonel Luttrell did not dare appear on the streets for months. The Duke of Bedford was attacked within the very walls of Exeter Cathedral, and in another town he was stoned and bulldogs set upon him.

Radical language was soon heard in the House of Commons, where Colonel Barré declared that if the petitions to the king were ignored, it would teach the people to think of assassination. A London city alderman refused to pay the land tax on the ground that it was passed by an illegal parliament, and carried the case into court. London officials presented petitions to the king denouncing the conduct of the ministry as subversive of the constitution and drew certain deadly parallels with Charles I and James II. A violent speech, supposedly given by Oliver Cromwell when he drove out the members of the Long Parliament, was posted in the streets of London, and eventually it appeared in the American newspapers.[6]

In the fall of 1769 Chatham recovered his health, and early in 1770 he appeared in the House of Lords and pled with the members to "rescue" the constitution and limit the power of an unlimited legislature. But tension could not be maintained at such a high pitch, and in Britain, as in America during the early part of 1770, the conservatives, frightened by radicalism, united to suppress it.[7]

In London the release of Wilkes from prison in April 1770 helped to relieve the tension, for Wilkes free was not the symbol that he was in prison. He was of course the undisputed hero of the populace. Successively he was elected alderman, sheriff, and lord mayor of London, and he won suits for damages against various officials. Friends and admirers raised £20,000 to pay his debts and endow his future. Among others, the Commons House of Assembly in South Carolina voted £1500 sterling to the Society of the Supporters of the Bill of Rights.

The principles raised by the fight against the man were infinitely greater and more important than he. A Grenville, a Rockingham, and a Pitt could

6 VG(PD), 4 Feb. 1768, from the London *Public Advertiser*; NYJ, 9 Aug. 1770.
7 The account of the Wilkes affair is based on Bleackley, *Wilkes*, chapters XII–XIV, and Lecky, *England*, III, chapter XI. Ian R. Christie, *Wilkes, Wyvill and Reform* (London, 1962), and George Rudé, *Wilkes and Liberty* (Oxford, 1962), are more recent accounts which add much detail but do not alter the broad outlines presented here.

all agree on that. So too could the Americans whose battles Wilkes seemed to be fighting. Most of them knew not the man but they understood the principles, and from 1768 onward "Wilkes and Liberty" was as much their "war cry" as it was of the people of London.

ह~

It was in this setting of turmoil that Lord Hillsborough, the secretary of the new American department, tried to carry out the policies laid down by Parliament. He started out with vigor in January 1768 but everything he tried backfired. His first defeat came in connection with the Massachusetts Circular Letter of February 1768. His orders to Massachusetts to rescind it and to other legislatures to ignore it were greeted with contempt and defiance and the very kind of "union" he tried to prevent. His next step was to persuade the reluctant Duke of Grafton to sanction the stationing of troops in Boston. This was followed shortly by the decision to send a full governor to Virginia for the first time in decades, but even a governor of noble rank could not stop Virginians from lining up with their fellow Americans. The resolutions denouncing Massachusetts in February 1769 and the recommendation that Americans charged with treason be brought to England for trial caused the Virginians to take the lead, not only in denouncing the proposal but in the non-importation movement in the southern colonies.

Hillsborough's success in getting Parliament to adopt the resolutions attacking Boston and the colony of Massachusetts marked the end of his effectiveness as secretary after only a year in office. Such resolutions were empty gestures and perhaps he knew it, for he demanded more. A few days after they were adopted he sent a far more comprehensive program to George III, only to have it rejected. Hillsborough proposed an act of Parliament converting the elective Massachusetts council into a royally appointed body, and he wanted the same act to declare the Massachusetts charter automatically forfeit if the House of Representatives took any action denying the authority of Parliament "in all cases whatsoever." He also demanded the removal of the four members of the New York council who had refused to approve the dissolution of the legislature for supporting the Massachusetts Circular Letter. In addition, the governor of New York should call the assembly and demand that it "rescind" its action; if it did not the principal members involved should be disqualified from holding office. As for the assemblies of Georgia and South Carolina, their governors should deliver "proper exhortations in their speeches." In addition to such measures Hillsborough proposed to tighten the Quartering Act by allowing troops to be placed in private houses unless the colonies built barracks or hired quarters, and to provide punishment for civil officials who refused to obey the act. He would offer concessions in only one area: he would repeal the Townshend revenue act for colonies with permanent civil lists such as Virginia and some of the West Indies, and repeal it for other colonies if they made similar provisions.[8]

Hillsborough had learned nothing from a year in office. It was futile to order governors to lecture their legislatures, and the idea of ordering New York to rescind its support of Massachusetts was fatuous. His proposal to quarter troops in private houses, had it been adopted, would have lit a fire from one end of America to the other.

Once more George III demonstrated that he was more far-seeing than his ministers by vetoing most of Hillsborough's plans. He told Hillsborough that it might be necessary to alter the Massachusetts charter in the future, but that it should not be done at present because "altering charters is at all times an odious measure." He declared that the proposal for automatic forfeiture of the Massachusetts charter was of "so strong a nature that it rather seems calculated to increase the unhappy feuds that subsist than to assuage them." He did not object to making Governor Bernard a baronet, nor to giving him discretion as to the meeting place of the legislature, nor to allowing Gage to move troops as he saw fit. As for New York, it was all right to remove the councilors, and he did not find it "much objectionable" to ask the legislature to rescind its resolutions. He agreed also that governors should be firm with their legislatures, but he warned that they should be instructed to avoid "giving occasion to the assemblies again coming on the Apple of Discord." The king, however, was still indignant about Virginia's petitions of the previous May. Therefore he was unwilling to have a partial repeal of the Townshend revenue act during the current session, but he suggested that it could be hinted that if the colonies made proper provisions for their civil establishments, they might be exempted from all the Townshend duties except that on tea.[9]

George III, who had helped remove from the act of 1765 the provision for quartering troops in private homes, completely ignored Hillsborough's proposal to provide for it now. Nevertheless, the issue was brought into Commons in March 1769, which took time out briefly from the wrangle over John Wilkes to debate American affairs. The debate arose when Barlow Trecothick presented the petition adopted by the New York legislature

[8] Geo. III, *Corres.*, II, 82–84.   [9] "Memorandum by the King," ibid. 84–85.

in December 1768. The petition acknowledged the supremacy of Parliament but argued that the dependence of the colonies on Britain did not require that Parliament have the power to tax the colonies. Lord North opposed the petition because New York denied the right to tax and the debate went round and round. George Grenville made one of the few sensible speeches. He declared that the confusion could not be ended unless Parliament took a stand one way or the other. There was no middle way: "we must either resolve strictly to execute the revenue laws in America, or else with a good grace give up our right entirely, and repeal the declaratory laws and revenue laws directly." [10] Parliament ignored Grenville's statement of the fundamental problem and rejected the petition. Thus once more Parliament refused to face the issue, as it continued to do until war imposed the solution.

Any discussion of New York was bound to raise the question of its continuing refusal to comply with the Quartering Act, and of further punishment. But the day after the rejection of the New York petition, the opposition seized the initiative from the ministry and persuaded the house to retreat from the literal provisions of the act of 1765. It adopted two amendments offered by Thomas Pownall. They provided that the Quartering Act would not apply to those colonies which gave supplies to the troops, and that it would be legal for local officials and commanding officers to quarter troops in any way they could so long as it did not involve any expense for the Crown. In effect Parliament thus agreed to the refusal of the colonies, and above all of New York, to abide by the letter of the Quartering Act of 1765. When Lord Barrington offered Hillsborough's proposal to quarter troops in private houses if local officials refused to obey the law, it was beaten decisively.[11]

The second British retreat was now under way, and this became clear in April. Thomas Pownall seized upon Hillsborough's idea of repealing the Townshend revenue act for those colonies which had established civil lists: he proposed that the act be entirely repealed. The reply of the ministry was feeble: it was too late in the session and the ministry was unprepared, but it would take up the question in the following session.[12] The next month Hillsborough notified the American governors that, despite insinuations to the contrary, the ministry had no intention of asking Parliament to lay further taxes on America. Instead the ministry would propose

[10] PH, XVI, 603–5.
[11] Ibid. 605–7. The act (9 Geo. III, c. 19) is in Pickering, XXVIII, 167–68. See also Arthur Lee to his brother in Virginia, 23 March, Arthur Lee Papers, I, HUL.
[12] PH, XVI, 610–22.

the removal of duties on glass, paper, and colors. It had hit upon a face-saving formula: the duties would be removed because they had been levied "contrary to the true principles of commerce." [13]

As the months went by the promise of repeal was reinforced by troubles at home and abroad. The uproar over Wilkes mounted. War threatened with Spain over the Falkland Islands. There were rumors that France would try to regain her losses and that she was moving troops to the West Indies. Hillsborough therefore tried to convince himself and others that the colonies were "in a much more tractable disposition than they appear to be in from the common accounts." [14] When Parliament met in January 1770 the king's speech began by saying that "distemper among the horned cattle has lately broke out," and the only reference to America was a casual remark that people in some of the colonies were trying to destroy the commercial connection between them and the mother country. [15]

In the ensuing debates it was obvious that John Wilkes, not America, was the main issue. [16] Chatham in the Lords was "really divine," wrote William Lee to his brother Richard Henry in Virginia. [17] But Chatham was fighting a battle that was already lost. Opposition politicians might join him in excoriating the ministry on the Wilkes issue but they distrusted one another so much that a real union was impossible. Edmund Burke, for instance, hated Chatham. But the battle was lost primarily because George III now had a solid majority in Parliament. When the Duke of Grafton resigned in January, Lord North smoothly took his place as the head of the ministry. [18]

North, a skillful political organizer, witty and impervious to political attack, headed the ministry for twelve years, and through all those years he insisted that he was not the "prime minister" but only one among equals. Nevertheless he did lead from time to time and one of his first aims was to bring about peace with the colonies. On 5 March, the day of the Boston Massacre, North moved the repeal of the Townshend revenue act, except for the tax on tea. He professed astonishment that "so preposterous a law could originally obtain existence from a British legislature." It had "given umbrage" to North America, created dissatisfaction among British merchants, and given birth to "dangerous combinations." He knew that many

---

[13] NYCD, VIII, 164–65.
[14] William Knox to Grenville, 10 Nov. 1769, GP, IV, 480.
[15] PH, XVI, 642–44.
[16] Ibid. 647–66, for debate in House of Lords, and 668–727 for debates in the Commons.
[17] 6 Feb. 1770, Brock Collection: Lee Papers, HEHL.
[18] Ritcheson, *British Politics*, 133–35.

were "vehement" against America but said that they must not stand in the way of the prosperity of Britain. He had agreed with the other ministers during the last session on promising the Americans repeal on "commercial principles." In fact he would like to repeal the whole law to conciliate the Americans if there were any possibility of doing so without giving up the right to tax the colonies. But the colonies did not deserve the repeal of the tea tax. They would not be grateful and would merely suppose that Parliament had been terrified into submission and would make fresh demands and be even more turbulent. It had been evident ever since the repeal of the Stamp Act that lenient action had merely encouraged Americans "to insult our authority, to dispute our rights, and to aim at independent government." Nevertheless, while he was for the right of taxing America, he was for giving every relief possible. And canny politician that he was, he guessed that Americans were tired of non-importation.[19]

At once Thomas Pownall proposed that the tax on tea be repealed as well. He knew, he said, that anyone speaking in favor of America would be accused of doing so from partisan motives, from wishing to capitalize on the trouble in America. He disclaimed such motives. He was proposing complete repeal, not to redress a grievance, not as "an American measure," but simply because he wanted to remove restrictions on British trade.[20]

Pownall's professions of non-partisanship were probably sincere but others among the desperate opposition groups made no such pretense in their efforts to embarrass the ministry. Unable to gain power on purely British issues, there were men among them who encouraged Americans to keep up their opposition in the hope of a political overturn.[21] Thus they took the high road of principle in the debate on Pownall's motion. General Conway proclaimed that it was the right of every Englishman to have a voice in the laws by which he was taxed, and that Americans had as many rights as Englishmen. The Stamp Act was illegal; the Townshend revenue act is illegal and should be totally repealed. Sir William Meredith professed amazement at the perversity of a ministry persisting in error. The only reason for keeping the tea tax was to maintain the principle of "right." The tea duty would not pay the cost of collection and as a result Britain would plunder itself to maintain the preamble of the Declaratory Act. In language long familiar in Boston he declared that it would mean keeping up customs houses in America with "their long, their hydra-headed train of dependents, and yet cut off the very channels through

[19] PH, XVI, 852–55.   [20] Ibid. 855–70.
[21] Ritcheson, British Politics, 128–30.

which their voracious appetites are to be glutted." Colonel Barré demanded repeal of the tea tax because the Townshend duty was destroying the East India Company's market in America—and Parliament had pledged its faith to the company by removing the duty on exported tea in 1767. Furthermore, he raised the specter of foreign war: Americans should be conciliated before England's old enemies turned on her once again.[22]

During the debate George Grenville made his last speech on America. He spoke without offering any plan, without hope, and seemingly without bitterness. He said that whenever America was discussed, he felt called upon to speak because "the principal confusions of that country are supposed to originate with me." He had offered one system. The Stamp Act might have been wrong in method but the intention was for the common good. The Rockingham ministry had a totally different system and had restored matters to the state they were in before the Stamp Act, but at least it had maintained the dignity of the House of Commons with the Declaratory Act. Ever since then, ministries had acted without plan or system. One proposed a tax "repugnant to the principles of commerce" and of no consequence since the revenue was small, and threw America into a greater ferment than ever. The present ministry had no plan either. A partial repeal would not "reduce the colonies to temper," and a full repeal would not sufficiently provide for "the dignity of the nation. I shall not therefore give my voice upon the present question." [23] Argument did not matter, for the ministry had the necessary votes to beat down Pownall's motion for total repeal. By 12 April the repeal act was law, to take effect on 1 December 1770.[24] Before the end of the year George Grenville died and most of his followers soon became supporters of the North ministry.

A few weeks later the disorganized opposition made one last attempt to use American affairs to embarrass the ministry. The occasion was the news of the Boston Massacre. The use of military power in civil affairs was guaranteed to raise the hackles of most Englishmen although the opposition leaders had not previously made an issue of the use of troops in America. Thomas Pownall again took the lead by proposing an address to the king asking for clarification of the powers of the governors and of military officers in America, and for the elimination of the disputes among them. In the debate the opposition decried the use of military power. George Johnstone, who had had violent disputes with the military when he was gover-

[22] PH, XVI, 871–74.   [23] Ibid. 870–71.
[24] 10 Geo. III, c. 17, Pickering, XXVIII, 294–95. Pownall's amendment was beaten 204–142. North to King, 5 March, Geo. III, Corres., II, 132.

nor of West Florida, started his speech with Tacitus, talked about the troubles of Roman proconsuls in Africa, and ranged down through James II. The troops in America did no good; Englishmen could not be terrified into submission by soldiers; and the troops in Massachusetts had driven the people to madness. Lord Barrington, secretary at war, claimed that Johnstone did not know his history, but Barrington seemed completely befuddled by the legal questions involved. The use of troops in America is illegal, cried Chatham's supporter Alderman William Beckford of London; even the pensioners and the placemen of the ministry should support the address out of shame. Was it illegal? Calls for the law officers of the Crown revealed that they were not in the house.[25]

A mere address did not satisfy men like Edmund Burke. After the reading of such documents as Hillsborough's circular letter and excerpts from Lord Botetourt's speech to the Virginia House of Burgesses, Burke proposed resolutions censuring the ministry for its misconduct of American affairs and, in particular, Lord Hillsborough for his "ill-judged and inconsistent" instructions. Furthermore, the "dignity" of the House of Commons had been insulted and its privileges breached when the ministry promised to repeal taxes and attempted to define principles of taxation. And to inform the house of treasons in America when in fact there were none "is an audacious insult on the dignity of Parliament" and encourages treason in America. Burke's resolutions, like Pownall's address, were defeated with monotonous regularity by a ministry solidly entrenched after ten years of administrative chaos.[26]

Various factors contributed to the power of the North ministry. First of all, George III, who had worked for a decade to establish a stable ministry, stood solidly behind North. Furthermore, men who were concerned with the power and profits of office rather than with principles, saw little advantage in supporting the various warring factions in opposition. One by one they deserted their old leaders and began to support North and the king. Rising radicalism in England swung still others behind what promised to be a stable and conservative government. It was supported too by those who demanded that the colonies be firmly subjected to British control. Only a few leaders remained outside the new circle of power. Chatham remained a lonely, if powerful, voice in the political wilderness. Rockingham kept his followers together, and twelve years later first he and then

[25] 8 May, PH, XVI, 979–1001.
[26] Ibid. 1001–10; HCJ, XXXII, 970; North to King, 9 May, Geo. III, *Corres.*, II, 146.

Shelburne at last won office once more, only to preside over the dissolution of the first British Empire.

Despite its anti-American support, the policy of the North ministry was to avoid trouble with America so far as it could. It also avoided bringing American affairs before Parliament. As a result, Parliament passed no laws affecting America until the spring of 1773 and even then the legislation was only a minor part of a program to rescue the East India Company. Nevertheless the action taken set off an explosion in America that led directly to the war for independence.

Meanwhile, the immediate effect of the repeal of the Townshend revenue act in April 1770 was the collapse of American resistance. As Lord North had cannily surmised when proposing repeal, many Americans were tired of non-importation and of the political pressure of the "lower orders" on their "betters."

ह

The retreat in 1770 left unsettled all the fundamental issues that had arisen between the mother country and the colonies during seven years of controversy, yet no one in power stopped to evaluate the achievements of the past or to ponder the consequences for the future. Only a few men such as George Grenville and Chatham seemed to realize that nothing had really been settled; and Grenville died before the year was out while Chatham remained unheeded if not unheard. The assumption of most leaders in 1770 seemed to be that the issues that had been raised could be ignored as if the past did not exist, that disputes over such issues as the regulation of trade, the standing army, the right of taxation, and the nature of the constitution of the empire could be forgotten. Therefore no political leader tried to weigh the successes and failures of the policies that, in theory at least, still remained in force. Instead, British leaders turned to domestic concerns with relief as opposition in America collapsed in 1770, only to be shocked into a violent emotional reaction when the colonies once more dramatically defied an act of Parliament at the end of 1773.

ह

Had anyone in 1770 attempted or been able to analyze the results of British policies during the preceding decade, he would have found that those policies had either failed or produced results quite the opposite of their intentions. The reform of the customs service begun in 1763 had been completed by 1768. Superficially the reforms achieved a measure of success, but at the same time they had met with ever-mounting resistance. Underlying much of American opposition was the assumption of the reform measures that Americans were engaged in wide-spread illegal trade. It is true that the Molasses Act of 1733 had been widely ignored, but it also seems true that the great bulk of American trade flowed in the legal channels established by the Acts of Trade and Navigation.

Nevertheless, customs officials and naval officers in America seemed to spend more time using the technicalities of the laws to harass legal traders than in searching for smugglers. Thus they alienated an influential segment of American opinion and provided ample materials for attacks upon all British controls by the popular leaders of the colonies. And when the pleas of customs officials brought troops to Boston, more Americans than ever were ready to defy British law and officialdom. Simultaneously the navy did its share to alienate American opinion, and only partly because it helped to enforce the laws of trade. Arrogant naval officers treated Americans with contempt and were heartily despised in turn, not only by Americans but also by British civil officials. In short, it can be argued that because of legal technicalities totally unrelated to the nature of American commerce, and because of the stupidity of some and the cupidity of other British officials, the customs service was more effective in arousing American opposition to all things British than it was in catching law-breakers.

The presence of the British army in America was a source of even greater contention, and on various levels. The requirement that American legislatures pay a part of the expense of troops they did not want and insisted they did not need, led to endless disputes at a high level. At the same time, conflicts between the populace and the soldiers in such towns as New York and Boston led to "atrocities" such as the Boston Massacre. In enormously effective propaganda, Americans pictured the dangers of a standing army in peacetime, and argued that they, not the ministry in London, were the supporters of one of Britain's most deeply rooted traditions. The damage done by the British army to the connection between the colonies and the mother country was immeasurable.

Another fundamental source of conflict between Britain and America was Parliament's attempt to raise revenue in the colonies. The British government, desperate for funds and heavily dependent upon the land tax, was either unwilling or unable to tax the great commercial and industrial wealth of the nation. Instead, it turned to America, at first to make the customs service self-supporting, and then to collect money to pay a part of the cost of the British army, and finally, to secure funds with which to pay British civil officials in America. Inevitably this raised the constitutional issue, and the desire for money was lost sight of as the two sides took unalterably opposed stands. The Americans insisted that they could be taxed only by representatives of their own choosing; Parliament declared that it could legislate for America in all cases whatsoever, if it chose to do so.

The revenue acts of 1764 and 1767 and the Stamp Act all failed to raise the money hoped for. The only successful law was the Revenue Act of 1766, which lowered the duty on molasses imported by Americans to a penny a gallon and placed it on both foreign and British molasses. The money collected demonstrated the futility of the Molasses Act of 1733, and of the Revenue Act of 1764, and proved the Americans' contention that the British West Indies could not supply their needs. The low duty stopped most smuggling, and of the 4,000,000 gallons imported annually by the mainland colonies between 1768 and 1772, only 3 per cent came from the British islands. As a result the customs service collected revenue in America as never before—at least ten times as much as the annual average before 1763. After 1768 the molasses duty produced from 80 to 90 per cent of all the money collected: £24,390 of £36,706 in 1768, and £42,570 of £46,225 in 1772.

But despite the fact that the act of 1766 was as clearly a revenue measure as any other law of the times, almost no attention seems to have been paid to it on either side of the water. Perhaps this was because the Townshend program followed closely on its heels. Townshend estimated that the import duties of the Revenue Act of 1767 would bring in about £40,000 a year but only £13,000 was collected in 1768. Thereafter, colonial nonimportation was effective. The next year collections dropped to a little over £5000, and in 1770 when the law was repealed, to a little more than £2500. The tax on tea was retained, and in 1771 Americans paid a total of about £4600 in duties despite their insistence that they would not import taxed tea. They then turned more and more to smuggling, and by 1773 American officials were agreed that most of the tea consumed in the colonies came from the Dutch. At any rate, the tea duties collected that year dropped to about £2500, and there was no evidence that Americans had eliminated tea as one of the many beverages they drank in such remarkable quantities.

It has been estimated that Britain collected a total of about £367,000 in America between 1765 and 1774. The customs service and the navy provided very little of it by the seizure and sale of ships and/or cargoes of illegal traders. The customs service reported that its seizures and sales amounted to £6080 between 1768 and 1774, and the proceeds of the navy's operations came to £7639. The money collected in America gave no relief to the British taxpayer.[27]

The expense of the army in America, in any one year, was almost as much as the total collections for the whole period, and what the forty-odd naval vessels and their crews cost is unknown. Likewise the customs service cost far more, especially after the establishment of the American board of customs. The board and its staff at Boston required more than £30,000 in salaries between 1767 and 1774, and its well-padded "expense account" ran to at least £27,000 more. When one adds to this the unknown sums paid to the many customs officers in other colonies, the total levy against customs revenues must have taken a very large chunk indeed. In addition, various civil officials such as the chief justices of New Jersey, New York, and Massachusetts, and the governors of New York and Massachusetts were paid salaries totaling over £36,000 from customs revenues.[28]

Thus the attempt to raise money in America by act of Parliament aroused bitter American opposition, and it did nothing to relieve the payers of the British land tax whose constant clamors lay behind much of the legislation after 1763. During the debate on the repeal of the Stamp Act, William Pitt had pointed to the great wealth Britain derived from her trade with the colonies, but the speaker who demanded a peppercorn in acknowledgment of right was typical of those who dominated colonial policy. Britain collected its peppercorns in America after 1763 but ignored the far greater wealth accruing from commerce with America.

Furthermore British policy makers were seemingly unaware of the golden stream pouring directly into the treasury from the taxes paid in Britain on Virginia and Maryland tobacco. Not until midway in the war for American independence did some unknown member of Parliament call for a report on the tobacco trade before the war. The customs house then revealed that between 1761 and 1775 the net revenues to the treasury, after payment of drawbacks on re-exportation, amounted to an average of £224,000 a year in England alone.[29] The net revenues accruing in Scotland were far less because Scotland re-exported over 97 per cent of all tobacco imported, but even so the net averaged over £23,000 a year between 1761 and 1775. The politicians who insisted on the "right" of Parliament

[27] Dickerson, *Navigation Acts*, chapters VII and VIII.
[28] O. M. Dickerson, "Use Made of the Revenue from the Tax on Tea," NEQ, XXXI (1958), gives many of the details on the spending of the money collected.
[29] EHD, IX, 410.

to tax America, and who tried to collect thousands in so doing, thus ignored nearly a quarter of a million sterling a year derived from the pockets of the British consumers and the Maryland and Virginia planters.

But of all the many results of the various British laws and policies between 1763 and 1770 the most important was the creation of a powerful and vocal American opposition such as had not existed in 1763, and which might otherwise have lain dormant for decades, or even generations. On a high level Americans had refined their constitutional theories to the point where they were insisting upon a "commonwealth" conception of the empire; namely, that each American legislature was equal to Parliament within its own segment of the empire, and with the Crown as the only bond and the balance among them.

And even more important, in the realm of political action, was the fact that British policies provided the opportunity for the rise of a group of new political leaders in America. These "new men" were extraordinarily able and they became "popular leaders" because they challenged not only British policies but also the old order of political leaders—leaders whose political fortunes, so they thought, were dependent upon support of or acquiescence in British policies rather than upon their leadership of Americans in opposition to those policies.

XIII

The Climax of American Resistance, 1769–1770

Americans opposed the Townshend program with a reiteration and refinement of their constitutional principles, and, after much labor and mutual recrimination, with the non-importation agreements. During the same years they carried on opposition to the implementers of British policy in America: the British army and navy, the American board of customs and its "minions," and above all, British civil officials such as governors and holders of lesser posts, whether British-born or native American. Conflict centered in New York and Massachusetts, where it reached a peak in the spring of 1770. The New York Assembly won a victory over Parliament in both the Quartering Act and Currency Act disputes, a victory accompanied by ever more bitter disputes among New Yorkers themselves. The popular leaders in Massachusetts destroyed the last vestiges of Governor Bernard's power and hooted him from the colony in 1769. They frustrated the operations of the customs service and reached the climax of opposition to the British army in the Boston Massacre and the removal of the troops from the town in March 1770.

Parliament's suspension of the New York Assembly for refusing to abide by the specific terms of the Quartering Act had set off American opposition to the Townshend program. But as Americans well knew, the New York legislature had always granted some money for the British troops in the colony.[1] Furthermore, it continued to do so, and thus aroused the indignation of the New York populace and of other colonies, and gave a

[1] See Chapter VII above.

hollow ring to the cries of the defenders of New York's constitutional "liberties."

In June 1767 the assembly once more provided money, evading the Quartering Act this time by simply giving General Gage £3000 to do with as he pleased.[2] Astonishingly, Secretary Shelburne, who had earlier ordered New York to obey the law to the letter, now accepted New York's latest evasion. He informed the governor that the grant was adequate and that New York could ignore the suspending act. In the fall the assembly proceeded to do just that, still ignoring the Quartering Act but granting £1500 for the troops, and again the governor and the general accepted the money.[3] All concerned got away with this extraordinary behavior, for the Privy Council approved the acts of the legislature despite its defiance.[4] This victory over Parliament brought no lessening of tension. In August 1768 New York merchants adopted non-importation, while the populace, angry at grants to the troops, was ever more willing to riot. In the fall the De Lanceys built up such a popular demand that they forced the Livingston-controlled assembly to consider the Massachusetts Circular Letter, and the governor promptly dissolved the legislature and called a new election for January 1769.[5]

The campaign was vicious. The De Lanceys praised their own "patriotism" as contrasted with such Livingston candidates as John Morin Scott, who, they said, had declared the Virginia Stamp Act resolves treasonable. They asked: "what more could have been done by any of the minions of power, or by the detested George Grenville himself . . . ?"[6] The Livingstons, whose assembly majority had voted money for the troops and had tried to ignore the Massachusetts letter, ignored such charges. As in the past they tried to stir up the passions of the religious dissenters against the Anglican De Lanceys, and they cheerfully contemplated the use of force. One of them reported that "our people are in high spirits, and if there is not fair play shown there will be bloodshed, as we have by far the best part of the Bruisers on our side, who are determined to use force if they use any foul play." "Damn them all," roared one De Lancey supporter at the Presbyterian Livingstons; they are "a pack of hypocritical, cheating, lying, canting, ill-designing scoundrels."[7]

[2] NYAJ, 27 May, 1, 2, 3, 4 June 1767.
[3] SS to Moore, 18 July, NYCD, VII, 945; NYAJ, 18–20, 27 Nov., 2, 3, 21 Dec.
[4] Grenville to Whatley, 13 April, 1768, GP, IV, 266–67; APC:CS, V, 137–39.
[5] See Chapter IX above.   [6] NYJ, 12 Jan. 1769.
[7] Peter R. Livingston to Philip Schuyler, 16 Jan. 1769, Edwin B. Livingston, *The Livingstons of Livingston Manor* (New York, 1910), 181–82; John Wetherhead to William Johnson, 9 Jan. 1769, Smith, *Memoirs*, 50.

The leaders of the Sons of Liberty had been split ever since 1765. "King" Isaac Sears and John Lamb supported the "patriotic" De Lanceys while only Alexander McDougall and one or two others of the "old Sons" remained loyal to the Livingstons. Smear tactics were in order. Sears asserted that one Livingston supporter had called Philip Livingston a "snake in the grass." [8] The Livingstons charged that the philanthropic reputation of a De Lancey candidate, James Jauncey, was utterly false. His supporters produced affidavits to the effect that he was a great, if secret, giver to the poor. As for John Morin Scott, declared a De Lancey broadside, he "puts money into the box (true charity no doubt!) and dances with, and *kisses* (*filthy beast!*) those of his own sex." [9] All in all, the two aristocratic factions demonstrated that dirty politicking was not a monopoly of the Bostonians.

The De Lanceys' gamble paid off: they swept New York City and won enough seats in the counties to gain control of the new assembly.[10] When it met in April, the triumphant De Lanceys began a purge of the Livingstons. The former speaker, Philip Livingston, had been beaten in the city, but his nephew, Peter Livingston, who had represented Livingston Manor since 1761, resigned so that his uncle Philip could be elected from it. On 12 April a De Lancey henchman moved that Philip Livingston be denied a seat because he was not a resident of the manor. Livingston countered by proposing that the assembly readopt the resolutions of 31 December 1768. If this were done, the governor would dissolve the new assembly as he had the previous one. The De Lanceys had already voted for the publication of the "safe" petitions of the previous session, but would have nothing to do with the resolutions whose adoption they had forced but a few months before. Then on 12 May they threw Philip Livingston out of the assembly.[11] But Associate Justice Robert R. Livingston of the supreme court was a resident of the manor, which at once elected him in place of his ousted cousin. To meet this threat the De Lanceys now adopted the arguments the Boston leaders used against Thomas Hutchinson: it was improper for a judge to be a legislator as well. Judge Livingston was thrown out, and despite a royal veto of the action, and repeated re-elections of the judge by the manor, no Livingston sat in the New York Assembly between 1769 and

[8] NYJ, 12, 26 Jan.; NYG, 16 Jan. The *Gazette* and the *Mercury* combined on 1 February, 1768 as *The New York Gazette and the Weekly Mercury*.
[9] NYJ, 19 Jan.; A Contrast: Read My Fellow Citizens, and Judge for Yourselves [New York, 1769], Clifford K. Shipton, ed., *Early American Imprints, 1639–1800*, No. 11223.
[10] NYJ, 26 Jan., 2, 16 Feb.   [11] NYAJ, 7, 12 April, 12 May.

1774, at which time Peter Livingston resumed the seat he had given up in 1769.[12]

The Livingstons, out of power, at once assumed the role of "popular" leaders which the De Lanceys had played between 1765 and 1769. The reversal of roles was apparent at once. The De Lancey minority had always opposed grants to the troops, but as the majority it now began voting money, while the Livingston faction opposed. Such tactics might mislead the Sons of Liberty, but not cynical Cadwallader Colden, who saw them as merely a struggle for "popularity" and for control of the assembly.[13] Thus, when Governor Moore asked for funds in April 1769, Philip Livingston, as yet unpurged, at once proposed a bill to issue £120,000 in paper currency. This was popular, for New York's old money was gone. The assembly told the governor that land was selling for half its value and that trade was on the verge of ruin. He would have to agree to the money bill or the troops would get nothing.[14] The governor was in fact even more eloquent than the assembly in supporting paper money, but he forgot to send a copy of the bill to England for approval.[15]

Sir Henry Moore died in September and Lieutenant Governor Cadwallader Colden became governor once more. For half a century he had denounced the aristocratic factions and above all, the De Lanceys, with whom he now made a political alliance. The "bargain" involved compensation for his losses in the Stamp Act riots and the promise of no trouble over his salary. In return Colden promised to support paper money and to avoid a dissolution of the assembly, which the De Lanceys would control for the next seven years. Under New York's septennial act the next regular election would come in 1776.[16] Colden at once informed British officials that New York would probably not grant more money to the troops unless it were permitted to issue paper money.[17]

By November 1769 General Gage had spent the money granted in May, and Colden asked for more. The assembly replied by introducing a paper

---

[12] Robert R. Livingston to SS, 4 Dec. 1769, NYCD, VIII, 192; NYJ, 12 March 1772; Livingston, *Livingstons of Livingston Manor*, 185–92. See Roger J. Champagne, "Family Politics versus Constitutional Principles: The New York Assembly Elections of 1768 and 1769," WMQ, 3 ser. XX (1963), for an account of the elections and their consequences.
[13] To SS, 16 May 1770, NYCD, VIII, 214.   [14] NYAJ, 4, 5 April, 20 May.
[15] Moore to SS, 26, 29 May, NYCD, VIII, 168, 169–70; SS to Moore, 15 July, ibid. 177.
[16] Smith, *Memoirs*, 59–60, 67.
[17] To SS, 4 Oct. 1769, NYCD, VIII, 189–90.

money bill identical with that passed in the spring, and not until it was ready for final passage did it consider Colden's request. Meanwhile, not knowing what Parliament might do about paper money, the members were "careful not to lose their popularity." Without argument they adopted the Virginia resolves of May protesting against taking Americans to England for treason trials.[18]

When the issue of a grant for the British troops was finally taken up in mid-December, the two factions met head on. Apparently the Livingstons wanted to make a grant payable in paper money, if and when the paper money bill was approved in Britain. If so, the De Lanceys outmaneuvered them. One of their henchmen moved that the grant be paid in paper money, and then they voted it down. The De Lanceys then proposed a grant of £2000, half to be paid in funds from the treasury and half in paper money after the paper money bill was approved. Repeated attempts by the Livingstons to make the entire sum payable in paper money—and thus to delay the grant—were beaten decisively if narrowly.[19]

The Currency Act of 1764 did not contain a clause suspending its operation until approved by Britain, although colonial governors had strict orders to refuse to sign paper money bills without such a clause.[20] Colden signed it anyway and defended himself on the ground that the assembly would have refused to do business if he had not agreed, and somewhat feebly, he argued that since the law did not go into effect until June 1770, there was plenty of time for Britain to act upon it.[21] Hillsborough rebuked him but at the same time promised that Parliament would probably allow New Yorkers the money "they do appear to be so desirous of." [22]

British officials had realized ever since the passage of the Currency Act of 1764 that its flat prohibition of the issuance of currency was unrealistic but they had done nothing to change the law. Now New York forced the issue by making further grants to British troops dependent upon an issue of paper money. In the spring of 1770 Parliament amended the act of 1764 to allow New York to issue currency which could be loaned out on farm mortgages and which could be used to pay taxes and import duties, al-

[18] NYAJ, 22, 23, 29 Nov.; Colden to SS, 4, 16 Dec., NYCD, VIII, 191, 193–94.
[19] NYAJ, 15, 29, 30 Dec.
[20] Leonard W. Labaree, ed., Royal Instructions to British Colonial Governors, 1670–1776 (2 vols., New York, 1935), I, 218–19.
[21] To BT and to SS, 6 Jan. 1770, NYCD, VIII, 198–200.
[22] 17 Feb., ibid. 205–6. On British dawdling, see Hillsborough to Colden, 9 Dec. 1769, 18 Jan. 1770, and reports of the board of trade 28 Dec. and 8 Feb. 1770, NYCD, VIII, 193, 195–96, 201–2, 202–3. The currency bill of May 1769 was not vetoed until 9 February 1770. The bill of January 1770 was vetoed 14 February, APC: CS, V, 215–16.

though legally it could not be used to pay private debts.[23] Even Hillsborough was forced to admit, in a half-hearted apology to Colden, that there were times when a governor might find it necessary to ignore his instructions.[24]

The concession to New York in 1770 was followed by a similar act in 1773 allowing the other colonies south of New England to issue paper money. Most of those colonies had managed to evade the Currency Act of 1764 in one way or another, but it had been an irritant nonetheless, and the permission came too late to do any good.[25]

৶

Despite the New York Assembly's success in both the Quartering Act and Currency Act quarrels with Britain, it won no popularity with either the people of New York City or of the other colonies. After all, it did continue to supply the British troops while the legislatures of South Carolina and Massachusetts conspicuously and successfully refused to do so. Royal barracks in Charleston were put in order in 1768 and the *South Carolina Gazette* predicted that troops would be used to enforce the revenue acts.[26] Then in the spring of 1769 a regiment of troops and a company of artillery arrived with a request from General Gage for supplies until the soldiers could be moved to permanent quarters at St. Augustine.

They were transients, replied the Commons House, and let Gage use the proceeds from the Revenue Act of 1767 for supplies.[27] The house told the governor that Carolina had not asked for troops; however, if the unconstitutional revenue acts which took property without consent, and subverted liberty, were repealed, it would comply with such requisitions "as shall appear to us just and reasonable or necessary." [28] The loophole was large but even Hillsborough admitted that Carolina's reasons had a "face of plausibility," and in the end he had to concede that the Quartering Act could not be enforced.[29]

The New York legislature was in an awkward position. As early as 1767

---

[23] 10 Geo. III, c. 35, Pickering, XXVIII, 306.   [24] 12 June, NYCD, VIII, 215–16.
[25] 13 Geo. III, c. 57, Pickering, XXX, 113–14. The law of 1773 was broader than that of 1770, for it allowed colonial treasuries to pay public creditors in paper money. For an account of methods by which many colonies evaded the letter of the Currency Act of 1764, see Joseph A. Ernst, Currency in the Era of the American Revolution (Ph.D. Thesis, University of Wisconsin, 1962).
[26] SCG(T), 25 July, 1 Aug., 10 Oct. 1768.
[27] SCHJ, 30 June, 1, 4, 27, 29 July, 10, 16 Aug.   [28] 19 Aug., C.O. 5/379.
[29] To Gage, 9 Dec. 1769, Gage, Corres., II, 93. Later on in the year South Carolina did partially comply. See Gage to Barrington, 16 Dec. 1769, ibid. 533.

the *Boston Gazette* asked if it had retreated from "first principles" [30] and by 1769 the New York newspapers were giving detailed accounts of South Carolina's successful resistance to the Quartering Act.[31] Furthermore, New Yorkers could read the Boston propaganda about the "bestial" behavior of British soldiers to be found in John Holt's *New York Journal*. The populace of New York was thus encouraged to carry on a quarrel with British soldiers which had started when Gage moved troops into the city during the Stamp Act crisis. The attacks ranged from name-calling to threats of death for the soldiers.[32] The conflict centered around a "Liberty Pole" erected in the spring of 1766 and inscribed with the names of George III, Pitt, and Liberty. In August 1766 some soldiers cut it down.[33] A new pole was put up, and it was cut down also. And so it went year after year, with mounting enmity on both sides, an enmity not lessened because of competition from soldiers hired to do work in the town during their free hours.

The climax came in mid-January 1770. On the 16th the Sons of Liberty published a broadside attacking those who hired soldiers to work for them. That night the soldiers cut down the pole once more, and then delivered the supreme insult by sawing it into chunks and dumping them before the door of the tavern which was the headquarters of the Sons of Liberty. The next day a mass meeting of some 3000 participants erected a new pole, whereupon the soldiers distributed a handbill questioning the legitimacy of the Sons of Liberty and the virtue of their ancestors. "King" Isaac Sears and his supporters captured several soldiers and took them to the mayor, while other soldiers armed with cutlasses and bayonets came to the rescue. A mob armed with clubs appeared and the hapless mayor ordered the soldiers to their barracks, but the mob and the soldiers merely retreated to "Golden Hill" and there did battle. One man was killed and many were badly beaten. The next day they renewed the fight, both sides ignoring the mayor, who appeared and bleated that they should disperse. Some soldiers even attacked the crowd in front of the jail, where Alexander McDougall, the new-crowned "Wilkes of America," was holding court.[34]

Alexander McDougall, born in the Hebrides, had been brought by his parents to New York in 1738, where his father became a milkman. The

[30] BG, 12 Oct.; NYJ, 29 Oct.
[31] *New York Chronicle,* 5 October 1769, contains copies of interchanges between the governor and the Commons House.
[32] Montresor, NYHSC (1881), 382–83, 11–17 Aug. 1766.
[33] Leake, *Lamb,* 28, 32–33.   [34] Dawson, *Sons of Liberty,* 112–17.

boy went to sea and during the Seven Years War he commanded privateers with enough success to establish himself as a small merchant after 1763. But his chief interest was politics. He rapidly became one of the more radical leaders of the Sons of Liberty in 1765, and of them he alone continued to support the Livingston faction in the years that followed. In December 1769, when the De Lancey-controlled assembly voted £2000 for British troops, McDougall became the hero of the hour, and the old leaders of the Sons of Liberty were soon reunited.

The first vote was taken on 15 December. Two days later a broadside addressed "To the Betrayed Inhabitants of the City and Colony of New York," signed "A Son of Liberty," was on the streets. This merciless attack on the De Lanceys and their new ally, Cadwallader Colden, was a skillful combination of invective and political principle equal to the most striking achievements of the Boston leaders in their campaign against Bernard and Hutchinson. It began: "In a day when the minions of tyranny and despotism in the mother country and the colonies are indefatigable in laying every snare that their malevolent and corrupt hearts can suggest, to enslave a free people," when Americans are struggling to maintain their freedom, when the merchants have sacrificed their interests for the public good, "it might justly be expected that in this day of constitutional light, the representatives of this colony would not be so hardy, nor be so lost to all sense of duty to their constituents (especially after the laudable example of the colonies of Massachusetts Bay and South Carolina before them) as to betray the trust committed to them." This they have done in voting money for the British troops. Why have they done so? The sacrifice of the public interest is due "to some corrupt source. This is very manifest in the guilt and confusion that covered the faces of the perfidious abettors of this measure, when the house was in debate on the subject."

First of all there is Cadwallader Colden who, knowing that "from the nature of things" he will never be governor again "and therefore, that he may make hay while the sun shines, and get a full salary from the assembly, flatters the ignorant members of it" with the promise of success for the paper money bill. Colden is also interested in his posterity. Some of his children hold government jobs they would lose if he did not get money for the troops.

As for the De Lanceys, they hope to manage the new governor when he arrives and will do all they can to prevent a dissolution. The members of the assembly, "conscious to themselves of having trampled on the liberties of the people, and fearing their just resentments," are also anxious to save their seats and avoid a new dissolution, and thus will serve for seven years in the hope that the people will forget the injuries done them.

It was for such reasons that the De Lanceys, "like true politicians," formed a coalition with Colden although they had been at "mortal odds" with him and "represented him in all companies as an enemy to his country. . . ." Their purpose is "to secure to them the sovereign lordship of this colony," hence, "the abominable vote by which the liberties of the people are betrayed." In fact, "all the checks resulting from the form of our happy constitution are destroyed."

What shall the "betrayed inhabitants" do? They should meet in the fields next Monday and demand a rejection of the vote of money to the troops. If the assembly majority refuses, a statement of the case should be sent to the speakers of the colonial assemblies and to friends in England, and be published in the colonial newspapers.[35]

On Monday 1400 people met in the fields, and with John Lamb putting the questions, declared that no money should be voted the troops. The resolutions were presented to the four city representatives but, led by James De Lancey, they and the assembly ignored the demand.[36]

Colden and the De Lanceys were outraged by the broadside which contained more truth than they cared to admit, and Colden offered a reward for the author. James Parker, the printer, and holder of a royal job as deputy postmaster general, named Alexander McDougall, who was promptly jailed. There he stayed for eighty-one days, refusing bail, posing as the Wilkes of America, writing letters to the public, receiving crowds of visitors at special hours, entertaining guests at dinner, and receiving delicacies from the patriotic women of the town. Upon one occasion, a newspaper reported, forty-five virgins, each forty-five years old, appeared and sang a verse of the 45th Psalm.[37] A De Lancey writer insisted that the report was in error: only twenty-eight of the ladies could claim the status attributed to them.[38]

The rise of popular violence and the enormous popularity of the jailed McDougall alarmed the gentry as they had not been since 1766, and they gave Colden support such as he had not had in fifty years of battles with

[35] E. B. O'Callaghan, ed., *The Documentary History of New York* [NYDH] (4 vols., Albany, 1850), III, 317–21.
[36] NYJ, 28 Dec. 1769.
[37] NYDH, III, 321–24; Smith, *Memoirs*, 73–76.
[38] NYJ, 22, 29 March, 12 April, 3 May 1770. The New York and other colonial newspapers during these months are replete with accounts of McDougall in jail.

them. In their alarm, they tried to capture at least the name of "Sons of Liberty" for themselves. They hired Montaigne's Tavern, the headquarters of the Sons of Liberty, for a dinner to celebrate the anniversary of the repeal of the Stamp Act. The displaced Sons then bought a tavern near the Liberty Pole which they renamed Hampden Hall.[39] After the rival dinners on 19 March, the newspapers were filled with conflicting accounts.

It is clear enough that the more radical Sons met at Hampden Hall, for they drank forty-five toasts, including one to McDougall, and sent ten men to dine with him. Shortly before sunset the whole company marched to the jail "with music playing and colors flying" and gave him three cheers. He in turn "thanked them for this mark of their respect in a short address through the grates of the window of the middle story." McDougall was not toasted at the other dinner, but Colden was, perhaps the first time he had been so honored in more than half a century.[40]

The gentry, having failed to capture the name, did their best and worst to discredit the Sons of Liberty, and above all the now reunited Alexander McDougall, Isaac Sears, and John Morin Scott and their Livingston backers. A newspaper story that forty-five men visited McDougall on the forty-fifth day of his stay in jail also declared that forty-five members of the Chamber of Commerce, founded in 1768, had visited Colden to thank him for their charter of incorporation. There were outraged denials from the gentry: only thirty-eight had visited Colden, and why lug in the Chamber of Commerce "to give a sanction to their dirty politics?" As for McDougall, there were not more than fifteen of the seventy-three members of the Chamber who did not heartily despise him "as an empty, insignificant, self-conceited, impotent body, utterly incapable of writing the scandalous paper laid to his charge. . . ."[41] John Morin Scott defended the Livingstons, who were accused of writing "To the Betrayed Inhabitants," and he in turn was attacked as a liar, a false patriot, a man who refused to pay his debts, and as a denouncer of the Virginia Stamp Act resolves.[42]

"King" Isaac Sears, who had deserted the De Lanceys, was the object of their bitterest attacks. Sears, they declared, had said repeatedly that McDougall was not a true Son of Liberty and that he was a "rotten-hearted villain" who had been trusted but once and then had betrayed the cause. The De Lanceys asserted that they had "bought" Sears with an ap-

---

[39] NYJ, 22 Feb. 1770.
[40] Ibid. 29 March. All the New York newspapers were involved. The story can be followed in the New York Journal, 22, 29 March, 5, 12 April.
[41] Ibid. 29 March.   [42] Ibid. 5, 12 April, 3 May.

pointment as an inspector of pearl and pot ashes and that he had not deserted them and joined the Livingstons until they had refused to appoint one of Sears's friends as colonial agent.[43] Sears defended himself as best he could: he had thought the De Lanceys true patriots in 1765; he had called McDougall a "rotten-hearted fellow" but not a "villain"; and he had not been "bought" by the appointment as inspector.[44] The important thing. declared Sears and his defenders, was the liberties of the country; therefore they supported measures and not men.[45]

In the course of the campaign the Livingstons and the De Lanceys dug up political dirt as far back as the Zenger trial. The outcome was a victory for the De Lanceys. Although they failed to break up the reunited Sons of Liberty, they did manage to keep the Livingstons out of power until the war for independence. The De Lancey hold on the government was fortified by the support of most of the alarmed gentry who had had quite enough of popular activity. The mercantile element was well on the road to ending non-importation despite the clamors of the Sons of Liberty. Alexander McDougall was almost forgotten. He was indicted for libel late in April 1770 and released on bail. Eventually he escaped a trial when James Parker, the sole witness against him, died. Forgotten too were the British troops in New York, for by the spring of 1770 Boston was the center of conflict with the British army.

British troops were ordered to Boston as a result of the pleas of the new American board of customs which began insisting on the need for military aid shortly after it arrived in November 1767. Commodore Samuel Hood, then commanding the British navy in America, and uninhibited by the constitutional limitations on governors and army officers, sent the *Romney* to Boston Harbor in May 1768. Then, as a result of Gage's orders, Colonel William Dalrymple gathered two regiments at Halifax by early July and Hood had collected transports.[46] When the orders for the move arrived in September, Hood smugly informed the Admiralty that he had long been ready because he had been sure that soldiers would be sent to Boston sooner or later.[47]

On 1 October two regiments landed in Boston under the guns of British war vessels lined up in battle array. A stunned silence instead of ferocious

[43] Ibid. 3 May.   [44] Ibid. 10 May.   [45] Ibid. 10 May, 21, 28 June.
[46] Hood to George Grenville, 11 July, 8 Aug., GP, IV, 306–8, 332–35.
[47] Hood to the Admiralty, 15 Sept., C.O. 5/757.

opposition was Boston's answer. The Massachusetts convention was "planet stricken," reported Colonel Dalrymple. Governor Bernard announced that he had no power, and "providentially" retired to the country. The colonel took over. He encamped the 29th regiment on Boston Common and then "by tolerable management I got possession of Faneuil Hall, the school of Liberty, from the Sons thereof, without force, and thereby secured all their arms." And he was courted by some of the popular leaders. "I am much in fashion," he informed Hood, "visited by Otis, Hancock, Rowe, etc., who cry peccavi, offer exertions for the public good," thus hoping to discredit Bernard. Dalrymple quite naturally concluded that things were going well and that "prejudices are giving way fast—they now neither think us cannibals nor street robbers." [48]

The Bostonians soon recovered. Local officials refused to provide quarters for the troops. General Gage came up from New York but he got nowhere.[49] Eventually he persuaded a reluctant council to vote the use of the colony's empty "Manufactory House," but before morning it was packed with the poor of the town and thus no longer a "vacant" building as defined by the Quartering Act. Gage gave up and supplied royal funds to rent buildings. British cash was irresistible, even for some popular leaders. A story started in New York that John Hancock himself had offered to sell supplies for the troops, but Hancock issued vigorous denials.[50] However, William Molineux, later known as a "first leader of dirty matters," and a public opponent of the troops, did rent buildings for their use.[51]

The troops stopped personal intimidation. But they could not stop political intimidation.[52] The *Boston Gazette* stepped up its campaign against the customs board and the governor and started a new one against the troops. No one could miss the implications when the *Gazette* printed "The Heroic Deed of William Tell"; how William, after shooting the apple from his son's head, killed the cruel governor and started the fight for freedom which ended when "Switzerland became one of the most free and independent republics." [53]

No William Tells arose in Boston, but writers did their best with words. During September the Boston leaders began writing the "Journal of the

[48] To Hood, 4 Oct., C.O. 5/757 and in part in Hood to Grenville, 15 Oct., GP, IV, 374–76.
[49] Gage to Hood, 18 Oct., C.O. 5/757.   [50] BG, 7, 14 Nov.
[51] Alden, *Gage*, 164; John Rowe, 24 Oct. 1774, Anne Rowe Cunningham, ed., *Letters and Diary of John Rowe . . .* (Boston, 1903), 286–88. The *Gentleman's Magazine* reported this affair in December 1768.
[52] Bernard to John Pownall, 7 Nov., C.O. 5/757; to SS, 26 Dec., C.O. 5/758.
[53] 24 Oct.

Times." They sent it to New York, where it appeared in John Holt's *Journal*. It was then reprinted by the Boston papers, by newspapers throughout the colonies, and even in England. From October 1768 until November 1769, when the last issue of this occasional "journal" appeared, it presented the iniquities of the customs service and the army in the blackest detail.[54] The campaign had begun, of course, before the arrival of the troops. Samuel Adams early described the *Liberty* riot of 10 June as a "little, inconsiderable rising of the people" wherein a few panes of glass were broken. It was small wonder, he said, that people were aroused when private property was seized under "a pretence of law" and with the aid of that military power so dreaded by all "lovers of peace and good order." Little wonder too that the people were discontented when faced with arrogant and insolent swarms of placemen and hireling pensioners. The people would complain until their grievances were redressed or they became "poor, deluded, miserable, ductile dupes, fitted to be made the slaves of dirty tools of arbitrary power." [55]

The "Journal of the Times" rang changes on the themes of how honest traders were victimized, how the elaborate regulations hampered trade, and how minor officials were guilty of corruption, insolence, and arrogance. Charles Paxton and John Robinson of the customs board were the particular butts of propaganda. Paxton's supposed influence on Charles Townshend had brought the creation of the board itself, while Robinson was a fortune hunter, bribe taker, and the violator of at least one virgin at Newport.

There were political means too of attacking the customs board. In 1769 the Massachusetts legislature demanded rent for the four and a half months the board had spent at Castle William after the *Liberty* riot. In December 1769 the Suffolk county grand jury ordered the attorney general to indict Governor Bernard (who had returned to England), the customs board, and various minor officials for slandering the people of Boston. Customs officers were sued for charging higher fees than allowed by Massachusetts law. An "income tax" was levied on the salaries of the members of the customs board. They appealed to England, and the governor was ordered to

[54] The "Journal of the Times," sometimes called the "Journal of Occurrences," has been edited by O. M. Dickerson, as *Boston Under Military Rule, 1768–1769* (Boston, 1936). Dickerson tends to accept the charges made at face value. I think that although there was a factual basis for many of the stories they were highly distorted for propaganda purposes.
[55] BG, 8 Aug. The *Gazette*, 29 Aug., contains a "Specimen" of a conversation at Castle William which pictures the customs officials as profane thugs.

block the tax. Whether successes or failures, such harassments were useful for the propaganda mills of Boston and those in other colonies as well.[56]

The customs board itself was responsible for its most crushing defeat. John Hancock's vessel, the Liberty, arrived from Madeira, entered the customs house on 10 May 1768, and paid duties on twenty-five casks of wine, a rather light cargo for a vessel of her size. During the next four weeks she lay at Hancock's wharf while a cargo of whale oil and tar was put on board. Then Thomas Kirk, one of the two tidewaiters who had watched its unloading in May and had not reported any illegality at the time, swore under oath on 10 June that he had lied. He deposed that the night before the Liberty entered the customs house he had been forced below decks for several hours, and that while there, he had heard rumbles indicating that cargo was being unloaded. Kirk's fellow tidewaiter could remember none of this, but Kirk swore that the other had been drinking and had left before Hancock's men arrived. Kirk also swore that Hancock's men had been led by a Captain Marshall, who had died the next day. Such was the dubious evidence on which the customs board seized the Liberty on 10 June.

The seizure was followed by a riot and the flight of the customs commissioners to the Romney. At first they offered to return the Liberty and her cargo if Hancock would give bond and await the outcome of a trial in the admiralty court. Hancock argeed, but his political mentors, James Otis and Samuel Adams, persuaded him to make a political issue of the seizure, and he backed out. In August the admiralty court released the cargo of oil and tar to Hancock but condemned the sloop. Thereafter the Liberty had a brief career as a British revenue vessel [57]—brief because the irrepressible Rhode Islanders burned it the next year.[58]

The customs board then sued Hancock for smuggling wine on the Liberty. In October, Jonathan Sewall, the attorney general of Massachusetts, filed suit in the admiralty court against Hancock and five alleged accomplices, including the notorious Captain Daniel Malcolm. A judgment of £9000 was asked against each of the six, treble the value of the wine allegedly smuggled. The case dragged on all winter, the one against Hancock being all that mattered. John Adams, as Hancock's lawyer, fought every inch of the way. In desperation the customs board apparently got a witness to perjure himself; at least one man was indicted for perjury by the Suffolk county grand jury although he escaped punishment when the board gave

[56] Thomas, Massachusetts, 657–64.
[57] G. G. Wolkins, "The Seizure of John Hancock's Sloop 'Liberty,' " MHSP, LV (1921–22), gives a detailed account and reprints many of the documents.
[58] NM, 24, 31 July, 7 Aug.; RICR, VI, 593–96.

him a customs job. The trial ended on 26 March 1769 when Judge Robert Auchmuty opened court by reading his commission as judge of one of the four new courts of vice-admiralty. His tenure as judge of the Massachusetts court was at an end. Attorney General Jonathan Sewall, who had also received a commission as one of the new admiralty judges, moved that the case against Hancock be dropped, and so it was.[59]

The board had lost face everywhere as a result of the fiasco, but the tragic climax of the fight between Boston and the board came in the fall of 1769. In August a ship from London brought copies of letters written by the board between February and July 1768 telling of its troubles and accusing James Otis and others of causing them. The copies, as was so often the case, had been sent to the popular leaders. At once James Otis and Samuel Adams called on all the commissioners except John Temple and demanded their appearance at the British Coffee House. Henry Hulton and Charles Paxton refused but John Robinson and William Burch came. Burch refused to answer questions and went home, whereupon Otis sent a message after him calling him a "Poltroon and a Scoundrel," but Burch did not challenge Otis to a duel as the code demanded. Robinson's answers were unsatisfactory, and on 4 September the *Boston Gazette* printed extracts from the letters along with an advertisement by James Otis denouncing the four commissioners and minor officials for telling lies about the colonies and about him personally. As for Robinson, Otis announced, "I have a natural right, if I can get no other satisfaction, to break his head."

James Otis had asked for it and he got it. The next night he met Robinson at the British Coffee House, and when he demanded a "gentleman's satisfaction," Robinson contemptuously pulled Otis's nose. They fell upon one another with canes and fists, and soon British army and navy officers joined in the brawl. Otis and his friend John Gridley, badly beaten and bleeding, managed to escape through the back door.

The next day Dr. Thomas Young rushed the popular party's version of the fray off to John Wilkes in England, while William Palfrey informed Wilkes that it was an "infamous assassination." [60] The Boston newspapers took up the fight and the story soon spread throughout the colonies. The government party in Massachusetts thought Otis got what he deserved, while the *Boston Gazette* charged that there had been a plot to murder

[59] The best short account is in Ubbelohde, *Vice-Admiralty Courts*, 121–27. An elaborate discussion of the legal aspects of the case is in the *Legal Papers of John Adams*, II, 173–93.
[60] MHSP, XLVII, 209–10.

him and that he had been hit on the head by a sword, not a cane.[61] Otis sued Robinson for damages and won his case, but Otis was done for. He had long been erratic, but from September 1769 until he was killed by lightning in 1783, he was subject to violent fits of insanity. He was still the idol of the Boston populace but leadership of the popular party was at last in the hands of steadier and more determined men, and above all, in the hands of Samuel Adams.

ৡ

The fight with the customs service was paralleled by an endless campaign of propaganda and legal harassment against the British troops in Boston. Early in November 1768 the selectmen accused a British captain of advising slaves to beat their masters and cut their throats, and the justices of the peace ordered the captain to give bond for good behavior and to appear before the court of assize for trial.[62] The town meeting protested against the troops in "their very bowels." Church wardens objected to the playing of music on Sunday, and upon one occasion, to "a more gross affront and insult than they ever yet received." A church warden asked a young man to leave as the guard was being changed, but the captain urged him to stay and offered to protect him and then "immediately ordered the fifes to play (in derision as we supposed) what by them is commonly called the Yankee tune." [63] This was sabbath breaking, it was blasphemy, and it had a bad effect on the morals of "inconsiderate youth" and the lower class of people. And when the people gathered to watch horseracing and dice games on Boston Common, the world was clearly coming to an end.

Arrogant officers were bad but the common soldiers were worse. They stole goods from merchants and they brawled with the populace. The brutal whippings of soldiers nauseated the good people of Boston. But above all, the virtuous wives and maidens of Boston were unsafe. Soldiers used abusive language to women of "unblemished reputation" and engaged in endless seductions and rapes. Some even managed fake marriages and others turned honest husbands into cuckolds. Such was the burden of the "Journal of the Times."

[61] BG, 11, 18, 25 Sept.; MG, 7 Sept.; *Boston Chronicle* [BC], 11 Sept. The story spread fast. The *Virginia Gazette* (PD) printed the *Massachusetts Gazette*'s pro-Otis account and the *Boston Chronicle*'s anti-Otis account on 28 September.
[62] BG, 7 Nov.
[63] P. Halley [?], Jno. Joy, and H. Hill to Major General MacKay, 17 June 1769, Misc. Bound, XIII, MHS.

The British officers did what they could to defend their troops who were by no means innocent of all the accusations. The officers and General Gage reported endless attacks on the soldiers with sticks, stones, and brickbats, and, in season, snowballs enclosing rocks. The crowds constantly called them bloody-backs and lobsters, and often worse, and at the same time encouraged them to desert.[64]

In the midst of the campaign against the troops and the customs service, Governor Bernard departed America, never to return. He had had permission to leave in 1768 but stayed on after the troops arrived. The attacks grew ever more intense, with everyone from the Boston selectmen to members of the council denouncing him.[65] Then in the spring of 1769 he was made a baronet and ordered home to give a full report. He delayed his departure until August so that he might once more meet with the legislature.[66] The session was a fiasco. The "faction" was in such complete control of the House of Representatives that it still further "purged" the council, and Bernard vetoed eleven of the members elected.[67] His message that he was leaving for England but that he was still governor and that his salary should be shared with Lieutenant Governor Hutchinson was satirized: [68]

> Now Gentlemen, I think it proper
> To make you stare and tell a whopper,
> My noble master, Sirs, I'll tell you,
> Conceives me such a clever fellow
> As to command me to repair
> To court and bring my budget there,
> Where I, Sir Mungo Nettle 'em, Bart.
> By lying, pimping, fraud and art,
> Am now advanced to such great credit,
> "It must be true if Mungo said it."

But don't think that

> When Mungo's gone, that Mungo dies.
> For when I've taken my departure,

---

[64] Alden, *Gage*, chapter IX.
[65] Boston Selectmen to Bernard, 16 Feb., and to Agent Dennys De Berdt, 25 Feb. 1769, Arthur Lee Papers, I, HUL; James Bowdoin to Hillsborough and Massachusetts council to Hillsborough, 15 April 1769, C.O. 5/758.
[66] SS to Bernard, 24 March, C.O. 5/758 and Bernard to SS, 29 April, C.O. 5/893.
[67] Bernard to SS, 15 May, 17 July, C.O. 5/758; to SS, 1–17 June, 1–13 July, C.O. 5/893.
[68] BG, 3 July; VG(R), 27 July.

By Jupiter! you'll catch a Tartar;
Lord Paddy, faith, has taken care,
To place Tom Gripeall in the chair.
He'll spoil your fun, I won't bely him,
But he's a crooked dog, as I am.

He demands all his salary but "my brother Gripe" must have his part and
then "Good Lord! how stately Tom will ride." Nevertheless Bernard would
remain their "Great Bashaw" and must be paid.

Take heed then and observe our will
For I must have my money still,
So Sirs, conduct the matter fairly,
And make the grant as usual—early.

When Bernard sailed for England on 1 August 1769 the town of Boston
held a joyful celebration and speeded him on his way with a broadside, "On
the Departure of an infamous B-r---t." [69]

Go B——d, thou minion! to thy country go,
For Boston, loud proclaims you freedom's foe . . .
Go on, ye pilferer, with all the rage
That half-starved spaniels for a bone engage,
Be like your brothers here, a tyrant crew,
Do all that fell rapacious souls can do . . .
Must it not fill all men of sense with scorn,
To see a muckworm of the earth, low-born
The chance production of some amorous spark,
In ignorance supreme, profoundly dark? . . .
Fly cringing minion! from all converse fly,
Den with the wolves, and learn the wolverins cry,
Go join in concert with the croaking frogs,
Or howl in chorus with a pack of dogs;
With monkeys go and chatter on a stage,
Or turn a mastiff and each cur engage,
Better do worse! turn pander, pimp, or slave,
Turn highwayman, turn murderer, or knave;
All do, that thy fell soul can think as evil,
And be a tyrant, Verres, or a Devil.

Having composed this requiem for the departed, Boston continued its
fight against the troops. Tension mounted early in 1770 as more and more

[69] Ola E. Winslow, ed., *American Broadside Verse* (New Haven, 1930), 133.

merchants wanted to break the non-importation agreement, but were kept in line by the mob. In February, Ebenezer Richardson, a minor customs official and reputed informer, fired a shot at a mob which surrounded him and killed a twelve-year-old boy, Christopher Snider.[70] Richardson was beaten, arrested, and convicted of murder, and the town held a great patriotic funeral for the boy. At the same time the newspapers carried more and more tales of military brutality. There was increasing trouble too between soldiers and the populace, particularly near the rope-walk belonging to Samuel Gray. A whole series of fights took place there before the "fatal fifth of March."

Certain things that happened on the evening of that day are clear; a number of people and some soldiers came together at the customs house, there was an order to fire, the soldiers fired, three men were killed on the spot, several were wounded, and two died later. This was the "Boston Massacre." Beyond this, the clouds of evidence produced by both sides obscure the events of the evening beyond all hope of saying that this or that is "true." [71] What followed is also clear enough. A vast mob of people poured into the streets but Governor Hutchinson addressed the crowd and prevented further violence by ordering the arrest of Captain Thomas Preston and the soldiers involved, and by persuading the commander to order the rest of the troops to their barracks.

The next day the town meeting demanded the removal of the troops from the town. Hutchinson reluctantly ordered the 29th regiment to Castle William. This did not satisfy the town meeting. A new committee, headed by Samuel Adams, came to the governor and told him that if he had the power to remove one regiment he could remove the other. Said Adams to his old enemy: "it is at your peril if you refuse. The meeting is composed of 3000 people. They are become impatient. A thousand men are already arrived in the neighborhood, and the whole country is in motion. Night is approaching. An immediate answer is expected. Both regiments or none!" At least that is what one of Adams's descendants said he said, but whatever words were spoken, the governor and council agreed to avoid a "perfect convulsion." [72]

Within a few days all the troops were out of the town but the populace still thirsted for the blood of the "guilty" and demanded an immediate

---

[70] BG, 26 Feb. et seq.
[71] The accounts by the *Gazette*, 12 March, and by Captain Preston, 13 March, are first-rate examples of the conflicting stories. They are printed in EHD, IX, 745–53.
[72] Alden, *Gage*, 174–77; Shy, *Toward Lexington*, 303–20. William V. Wells, *The Life and Public Services of Samuel Adams* (3 vols., Boston, 1866), I, 323.

trial. Hutchinson was so beside himself that he wanted to resign as governor. However, the superior court displayed great courage and delayed the trials until fall.[73] By that time the power of the town's popular leaders had been shattered. The Boston merchants, who had been forced into nonimportation and kept there by the constant threat of mob violence, had followed the lead of merchants in other northern colonies and were ordering goods from Britain.

Everywhere in America by the end of 1770, resistance to British policies had collapsed and many American leaders hoped that it would never be revived. They had had enough of economic coercion and of political upheaval and they yearned for a return to the "good old days" before 1763. For a time it seemed that their hopes might be fulfilled.

[73] See Chapter XVI below.

XIV

The Collapse of American Resistance, 1770

American attacks upon British civil officials and British military power offered the most dramatic examples of resistance, but the non-importation agreements were the essential foundation of American opposition. Nevertheless, many Americans had opposed non-importation from the start, and the methods of enforcement aroused ever greater resentment. The opportunity to abandon non-importation came after 5 March 1770 (the day of the Boston Massacre) when Lord North moved repeal of the import duties, except those on tea, levied by the Townshend revenue act of 1767. When the news reached America, non-importation, which had taken years to achieve, collapsed in a few brief months. Merchants everywhere gladly joined to put an end to a measure which many of them thought dubious at best, and at worst, might overturn the established order.

The problems involved in enforcing non-importation varied from place to place although similar issues arose in most of the colonies where the agreements were at all effective. In the South the Charleston agreement was the only one with any real impact. The more than thirty merchants who refused to sign were denounced as men of no consequence,[1] but some of them were too conspicuous to be ignored. One was William Wragg, who had made the unseconded motion for a statue of George III in 1766, and another was the wealthy William Henry Drayton, nephew of Lieutenant Governor William Bull. Drayton openly denied the legality of the agreement and petitioned the legislature for redress, declaring it futile to appeal

[1] SCG(T), 14 Sept. 1769, 5 April 1770.

to the court, for the judges themselves were signers. Despite his courage and position, he was forced to sail to England in January 1770 with goods the enforcement committee refused to allow him to sell.[2]

The committee was made up of thirteen each of mechanics, planters, and merchants, but the presence on it of powerful and conservative men such as Henry Laurens and Miles Brewton meant that there was none of the public violence to be found in the North. However, the committee was kept on its toes by Christopher Gadsden and Thomas Lynch, whom Governor Bull called "tribunes of the people," and by publisher Peter Timothy, whom the governor described as one of the "numerous subalterns of this corps."[3] Enforcement was rigid and effective, and all cargoes from England were inspected and forbidden articles either stored or sent back.

As in other colonies, there were charges that committee members and wealthy merchants cheated or profiteered while lesser people were kept in line. Ann Mathewes, a widow who ran a small shop with the help of her son, was advertised as a violator.[4] She defended herself and attacked both John Rutledge, who had received two carriage horses, and a committee member who was allowed to sell goods ordered before adoption of the agreement. But she was a poor widow and they great men, and that made the difference, said she.[5] Her spirited defense was in vain, and her son was forced to sue for the committee's "pardon."[6] Shortly before the agreement ended, Governor Bull commented that the many had been forced to submit while "the rich leaders enjoy their trade in state,"[7] although earlier he had reported that the committee members "themselves are greatly hurt thereby."[8] Whatever the truth of the charges, and it is impossible to know, South Carolina's agreement was so effective that the value of imports from England dropped from £365,000 in 1769 to £202,000 in 1770.[9]

Non-importation in the two tobacco colonies was a farce. The Marylanders made a great deal of noise and in the spring of 1770 an Annapolis firm was forced to send a cargo back to England. The *Maryland Gazette* made much of Maryland's enthusiastic co-operation with the other colonies, but it is doubtful that reality matched the professions.[10]

After the first flush of enthusiasm, Virginians paid little attention. A few

[2] Ibid. 3 Aug., 21 Sept. 1769.   [3] Sellers, *Charleston Business*, 209–10.
[4] SCG(T), 31 May 1770.   [5] SCG(Wells), 8 June.   [6] SCG(T), 4 Oct.
[7] To SS, 20 Oct. 1770, quoted in Sellers, *Charleston Business*, 215.
[8] To SS, 6 March 1770, C.O. 5/379.
[9] EHD, IX, 393. These figures are approximate and include the negligible direct imports of North Carolina and Georgia.
[10] MdG, 8 Feb., 7, 21 June, 12 July 1770; Barker, *Maryland*, 323–25; EHD, IX, 393.

merchants signed the agreement but most did not.[11] When they held their annual meeting at Williamsburg in June 1769, they pointedly ignored non-importation.[12] Even the merchants who had signed continued to order goods from Britain as usual. The planters were as indifferent as the merchants. Less than two months after signing, George Washington sent an order for goods that ignored the spirit if not the letter of the agreement, and while he professed hearty support of the association, he left it up to the British merchant to exclude from his order the items contrary to it.[13]

In the spring of 1770 a writer in the *Virginia Gazette* lamented that the "glorious association" was so "soon forgotten, so basely deserted, and both the letter and spirit of it kicked out of doors. . . ." [14] The merchants were tempters and should be forced to agree, declared another.[15] Only after Virginians learned of the repeal of the Townshend act at the end of April [16] did they adopt an agreement with teeth in it. When the governor laid the repeal act before the burgesses, they "spurned at the pretended favor, and unanimously voted a petition to the king asserting their rights. . . . They did not expect this petition would produce any alteration in the conduct of the British ministry; but, they intended it as their protestation never to submit silently to the power of the Parliament to tax the colonies." [17]

On 22 June Virginians signed a new agreement. Merchants were forbidden to import restricted goods, planters to buy them, and county committees were given "authority" to inspect all imports and to publish the names of violators.[18] Governor Botetourt swore that this second agreement would never have been adopted had it not been for the advice from "the patriots of England" who had put pressure on the merchants and factors in Virginia "to promote distress to their mother country by all means." [19] The governor's fear of the new agreement was groundless. In 1769 Virginia and Maryland together imported goods worth £488,000 from England alone, and in 1770 when both colonies made much of enforcement, the value of their imports from England rose to £717,000! [20]

৪৯

11 VG(R), 25 May.   12 VG(PD), 29 June.
13 To Robert Cary & Co., 25 July 1769, *Writings*, II, 512–14.
14 VG(R), 8 March.   15 VG(PD), 22 March.   16 VG(R), 26 April.
17 "Letter from a Gentleman in Virginia," NYJ, 12 July 1770; JHB (1770–1772), 82–83, 85, 101–2.
18 VG(R), 31 May; Robert P. Thomson, The Merchant in Virginia, 1770–1775 (Ph.D. Thesis, University of Wisconsin, 1955), 324–29. My account owes much to Thomson's excellent discussion.
19 To SS, 30 June, C.O. 5/1348.   20 EHD, IX, 393.

Effective enforcement was possible only in the great commercial centers which contained substantial groups of artisans and political leaders to direct them as in Charleston, Philadelphia, New York, and Boston. The Philadelphia merchants had adopted non-importation in March 1769 only because of popular pressure, and the committee for enforcement was soon controlled by the popular leaders. Even goods which violated only the "spirit" and not the letter of the agreement were shipped back to England. In August 1769 a meeting decided that all goods shipped on consignment must be returned and that anyone who had ordered goods after 6 February would be deemed an enemy of American liberties "and the printers shall be justified in publishing his name." [21] Chief Justice William Allen, a hearty opponent of all British restrictions, although he became a loyalist in 1776, testified to the effectiveness of Philadelphia's enforcement. "Our people have left off going to the stores to buy what they usually took up, which they now make in their own families. The storekeepers universally complain that they do not vend one half of the goods they used to do. Even the lawyers allege their business is in a manner at an end, as there are very few contracts, of course few lawsuits." In fact he thought it would be well to maintain non-importation, for the colonies would soon be out of debt to Britain, and they might be cautious in the future about plunging into the "luxury too common among us within these fifteen years past." [22] Statistics backed up his assertions, for the value of imports from England dropped from £432,000 in 1768 to £200,000 in 1769, and to £135,000 in 1770. [23]

Such results were not achieved without injustice. The importers of dry goods from Britain were hit hard, while merchants specializing in the West Indian and southern European trade carried on as usual. Furthermore, the Baltimore agreement allowed for the importation of many kinds of cloth banned by Philadelphia, whose merchants feared the loss of markets in the backcountry and of the Indian trade to their rivals in the booming Maryland city. By the end of 1769 there were denials that the dry goods merchants would abandon the agreement, whether Parliament repealed the revenue act or not. It was said of them that they would never "sell their birthrights for a mess of pottage, even though they should be more distressed for food than Esau was. . . ." [24] But such denials plainly came from men like Charles Thomson, not from the merchants.

[21] PG, 3 Aug. 1769.
[22] To David & John Barclay, 7 Nov. 1769, Lewis B. Walker, ed., *The Burd Papers* (3 vols., [Pottsville, Pa.], 1897–99), I, 76–78.
[23] EHD, IX, 392.   [24] VG(PD), 22 Feb. 1770.

In fact, most dry goods merchants, refusing to have anything to do with enforcement, resigned during the winter of 1769–70, leaving Charles Thomson in control of the committee. In a letter to Franklin in November 1769, written to be published in England, Thomson said flatly that the nature of American grievances must be explained so that the "conduct of the merchants might not affect the general cause. . . ." He railed against the Townshend revenue act on constitutional grounds, against the admiralty courts, the customs board, and the attempts to break down the barriers erected by the forefathers against "arbitrary power." Plainly, he hinted that independence would be the outcome unless Britain mended her ways.[25] His language and his motives were like those of the popular leaders in other northern colonies. Because of such men as Thomson, the Philadelphia merchants could not escape until after New York abandoned non-importation in July 1770.

New York's agreement went into effect before that of any other colony, 1 November 1768, and it was enforced by a committee dominated by conservative merchants. One problem was to keep out goods from places like Philadelphia, which did not adopt its agreement until more than five months later. Such goods were sent back and one man who tried to cheat was boycotted. But the shopkeepers and artisans, who had adopted an agreement of their own in September 1768, took far more vigorous measures. A silversmith, merely proscribed by the merchants, was hauled up before a mass meeting and forced to admit his "crimes." A jeweler who received mild treatment from the merchants was taken to the Liberty Pole by a mob and put on a scaffold from which he quickly asked public forgiveness.[26]

Naturally the "people of property" were alarmed once more as in 1765 and 1766. And increasingly during the winter of 1769–70 they wondered if opposition was worth the price, especially during the uproar over Alexander McDougall and the riots against the troops. General Gage was convinced that the merchants were "tired" of non-importation as early as May 1769, and that while a few substantial ones had taken the precaution to have plenty of goods on hand, the majority would suffer. He reported too that while forbidden goods were stored in warehouses, they were soon delivered to the owners, and he predicted that the many small shopkeepers would be ruined.[27]

[25] 26 Nov. 1769, "The Thomson Papers," NYHSC (1878), 21–25.
[26] Schlesinger, Colonial Merchants, 186–90.
[27] To Barrington, 14 May 1769, Gage, Corres., II, 510.

There were charges and countercharges of profiteering and cheating,[28] but enforcement was effective as nowhere else in the colonies. The value of imports from England dropped from £482,000 in 1768 to £75,000 in 1769.[29] It is impossible to say how many merchants had anticipated a profitable scarcity and ordered in advance, but by the spring of 1770 most of them were ready to have done with non-importation.

ࡈꙴ

Compared with Boston, the other colonial cities were placid pools. The Boston agreement, achieved after a year of conflict, was only for the calendar year 1769, while those of the other colonies were to continue until the repeal of the Townshend revenue act. Originally enforcement was left in the hands of the standing committee of "merchants" but even that euphemism was abandoned in the spring of 1769 when control was openly taken over by "The Body," a mass meeting dominated by the popular leaders, whose decisions could be enforced by a well-drilled mob.

In April 1769 "The Body" appointed a committee to inspect manifests of cargoes. It was discovered that seven signers of the non-importation agreement, eight non-signers, and five ship captains had imported forbidden articles. Some of the "guilty" parties turned their goods over for storage and others refused, and the names of the latter were circulated around town with the suggestion that they be boycotted. Upon the arrival of Hillsborough's circular letter of 13 May 1769, promising repeal of the Townshend revenue act, the hopes of the non-signers and many reluctant signers rose, only to be quickly dashed. The Body adopted a new agreement demanding repeal of the revenue acts of 1764 and 1766 as well as that of 1767. It then appointed committees to inspect cargoes, to get signers, and to state commercial grievances.

In August The Body declared that the names of the "enemies" of the country should be published in the newspapers. The threat forced six non-signers into the agreement but the names of eight who still refused appeared in all the Boston newspapers and in the *Essex Gazette* at Salem. The "enemies" were John Bernard, son of the recently departed governor, Thomas and Elisha Hutchinson, sons of Thomas Hutchinson, James McMaster & Company, Richard Clark, Nathaniel Rogers, Theophilus Lillie, and John Mein.[30] In October the Boston town meeting voted to

---

[28] Colden to ———, 16 May 1770, NYHSC (1877), 220.   [29] EHD, IX, 392.
[30] Andrews, CSMP, XIX, 224–27. Actually names of importers appeared in newspapers even before this. See VG(R), 15 June 1769.

enter their names on its records so "that posterity may know who those persons were that preferred their little private advantage to the common interest of all the colonies . . . who not only deserted but opposed their country in a struggle for the rights of the constitution," and who, "with a design to enrich themselves, basely took advantage of the generous self-denial of the fellow citizens for the Common Good." [31]

One man on the black list was willing and able to fight back, for he was publishing a newspaper, and he fought so effectively that he created paroxysms of rage. John Mein, a Scot who had been a bookseller in Edinburgh, arrived in Boston in the fall of 1764. He soon started a bookstore and the first circulating library in Boston, and in 1766 in partnership with another Scot, John Fleeming, he began printing books.[32] On 21 December 1767 the two partners published the first issue of the *Boston Chronicle*, which was, until its demise in June 1770, the handsomest newspaper in America. It was also one of the most aggressive, and it met the *Boston Gazette* on its own ground and slugged it out. The *Chronicle* supported the "government party" and began by attacking William Pitt. The *Gazette* at once defended its hero and denounced its new rival.[33] The trigger-tempered Mein went to the *Gazette* office and demanded the name of the author of "Americus" from Benjamin Edes, who took the high ground that a publisher must protect his sources. Edes then refused to "take a walk" with Mein to settle the argument and the next day published a sarcastic account of the interview in the *Gazette*. The following day John Mein met Edes's partner, John Gill, on the street and clubbed him.[34]

Mein and the *Chronicle* were thus off to a fast start. Mein opposed non-importation, and when he was black-listed in August 1769 he fought back with devastating effect. The customs board gave him the manifests of all cargoes imported since the first of January. He published them in the *Chronicle* and reprinted them on thousands of sheets and in pamphlets which were broadcast from Nova Scotia to the Floridas by delighted customs officials and others. The lists demonstrated, according to the *Chronicle*, that some of the most ardent non-importers such as John Hancock were importing goods contrary to the agreement they had signed.[35]

[31] 4 Oct., BTR, XVI, 297–98. Richard Clark's name was not listed.
[32] See John E. Alden, "John Mein: Scourge of Patriots," CSMP, XXXIV (1943).
[33] "Americus," BG, 18 Jan. 1768.
[34] Ibid. 25 Jan., 1 Feb. With James Otis as his lawyer, Gill eventually collected £75 damages. Alden, CSMP, XXXIV, 584–86.
[35] See the issues from August 1769 to February 1770. It would be sheer guesswork to say whether Mein's charges were either true or false. Certainly they were widely believed, especially in other colonies.

The popular leaders were thunderstruck. The *Gazette* denied everything and defended Hancock, whose name "will shine in the records of fame when infamous Jacobites and Tories will sink in oblivion," [36] but on that level Mein was more than a match for the *Gazette*. In October he promised to publish some illustrated character sketches of the "Well Disposed," a name first used by the popular leaders to describe themselves, but which their enemies had turned into a gibe. He offered a taste of what was to come, however. John Hancock was

> Johnny Dupe, Esq.; alias the Milch Cow of the "Well Disposed"; a characteristic plate will be given with this history, representing a good natured young man with long ears—a silly grin on his countenance—a fool's cap on his head—a bandage tied over his eyes—richly dressed and surrounded with a crowd of people, some of whom are stroking his ears, other tickling his nose with straws, while the rest are employed in rifling his pockets; all of them with labels out of their mouths, bearing these words, "Our Common Friend."

James Otis was "Counsellor Muddlehead, alias Jemmy with the Maiden Nose"; Samuel Adams was "Samuel the Publican, alias the Psalm singer." There were many other nicknames which contemporaries doubtless recognized; fortunately for posterity, Mein left a "key" to them. The key indicates that Mein knew of many scandals or supposed scandals in Boston. "William the Horner," he explained, was William Dennie who "has kept Mr. Barnabas Clark's wife many years and employs her husband abroad while he is getting children for him at home." He said little of Dr. Joseph Warren, "The Lean Apothecary," in the *Chronicle*, although he promised revelations about his "married state." But in the key he wrote that Warren was "one of the greatest miscreants that walks on the face of the earth, who has cheated and back-bitten every person with whom he ever had the least connection—father, mother, and friend, and more than once poxed his wife." [37]

The tidbits in the *Chronicle* and the promise of more to come infuriated the popular leaders. The only solution was to drive Mein from the city, and two days after the article appeared, Mein, who had armed himself, was attacked by a mob. He escaped to the protection of a guardhouse and hid in the attic while a warrant was sworn out for his arrest on the ground that he had put "innocent people in bodily fear." Meanwhile the frustrated

[36] BG, 9, 23, 30 Oct. See also Andrews, CSMP, XIX, 228–29, n.2.
[37] BC, 26 Oct., and "Key to the Characters published in the *Boston Chronicle* of October 26, 1769," Sparks Mss., X: New England Papers, III(1768–70), HUL.

mob of between 1000 and 2000 tarred and feathered a man accused of being a customs informer. A constable, accompanied by Samuel Adams and William Molineux, could not find Mein, who escaped to a British warship disguised as a soldier. When Hutchinson refused to give him military protection, Mein left for England to meet the most ironic fate of all. He found that London booksellers to whom he owed money had given power of attorney to John Hancock to collect from his property in Boston, and shortly thereafter, on Hancock's suggestion, they had him jailed for debt.[38] Mein's end was inglorious but he had set Boston in an uproar and had confirmed the suspicion long held in other colonies that Bostonians were cheats and canting hypocrites.

Meanwhile, in the fall of 1769, when the rumor reached Boston that New York and Philadelphia merchants had sent orders to be filled upon the repeal of the Townshend revenue act, the Boston town meeting demanded the repeal of all revenue acts, abolition of the customs board, and removal of the troops before ending non-importation. The hapless Boston merchants were forced to agree and they asked New York and Philadelphia to join, but the merchants of those cities refused.[39] The Boston merchants then backed out. Some of them had already ordered goods; others had agreed to store goods; and Hutchinson's two sons had never signed. It seemed for a moment that they might be free to do business when the old non-importation agreement ended on the last day of December.[40]

Such hopes were futile, for, as Mrs. Henry Barnes of Marlborough, whose husband was on the Boston black list, informed a friend: "those daring Sons of Liberty are now at the tip top of their power and to transact anything contrary to their sentiments, or even to speak disrespectfully of the Well Disposed, is a crime equal to high treason." She could but hope that "people will not be much longer imposed upon with a cry of liberty when they see private property is only sought after." [41]

Early in December the threat of a break-through was met by the extension of the old non-importation agreement until the repeal of the Townshend act. The few remaining non-signers, including Hutchinson's sons, defiantly proposed to sell goods on hand. The answer was a great mass

[38] Alden, CSMP, XXXIV, 588–91. Mein apparently got compensation from the ministry and in 1774 wrote propaganda for it.
[39] Colden to SS, 4 Dec., NYCD, VIII, 191; Jensen, *Maritime Commerce*, 183.
[40] Hutchinson to SS, 20 Oct., C.O. 5/758 and 1 Dec., C.O. 5/759; Andrews, CSMP, XIX, 230–31.
[41] 20 Nov. 1769, to Mrs. Elizabeth Smith, Letters of Mrs. Henry Barnes of Marlborough, Mass., 1768–84, LC.

meeting on 17 January 1770. Hutchinson thought it illegal and wanted to stop it, but his council refused to co-operate. The threat of the mob was too great for Hutchinson's sons and they at last gave in.[42] In the months that followed, little shopkeepers as well as big merchants were intimidated by mobs, even of children, who went from door to door while magistrates refused to interfere.[43] One woman fought back. Mrs. Curtis, a small shop-keeper, was seen leaving the store of an importer and had her name published. She wrote to town clerk William Cooper, telling him that she had bought nothing and that the "worthy committee" had better inspect the Providence wagon and the big stores, which were always well supplied, instead of picking on a woman. "There is no accounting for so extraordinary conduct but that you would not dare to treat a man in so base a manner, but remember that no man but a coward will affront a woman." [44]

Thomas Hutchinson confessed that he was helpless and that the town was "under the government of the mob. This has given the lower part of the people such a sense of their importance that a gentleman does not meet with what used to be common civility, and we are sinking into perfect barbarism. . . ." [45] The aristocrat did not like the new day that had dawned, at least in Boston.

The Massacre on 5 March was but one part of the turmoil in the spring of 1770 as merchants continued to hope for an end of non-importation, and the mob, directed by the popular leaders, continued to enforce it as never before. The news of repeal of the act of 1767 reached Boston on 24 April, but within days The Body had met and agreed that non-importation would continue until the repeal of the tax on tea.[46] Nathaniel Coffin wrote to a customs official in Philadelphia that "our demagogues" have "unlimited uncontrolled power supported by 1500 or 2000 able-bodied men who are ready to receive any impression they may please to give them. . . . What resolutions they will take God knows. They have everything in their power." [47] So they had, and the Boston merchants had to wait until non-importation had been abandoned elsewhere before they

---

[42] Hutchinson to SS, 24 Jan. 1770, C.O. 5/759; Boston Merchants to Dennys De Berdt, 30 Jan., Misc. Bound, XIII, MHS. The eleven signing the letter were popular party stalwarts including such "merchants" as William Molineux. This event was widely and completely reported in other colonies. MdG, 8 Feb.; VG(PD), 8 March. The latter paper prints many documents.

[43] Hutchinson to SS, 28 Feb., C.O. 5/759.

[44] [30 Jan. 1770], Samuel Adams Papers, NYPL.

[45] To John Pownall, 26 March, Hosmer, Hutchinson, 189.

[46] Andrews, CSMP, XIX, 235.

[47] To John Swift, 14 May, Customs House Papers, Philadelphia, 1750–74, X, HSP.

could regain the freedom that had once been theirs. And despite all the charges of evasion made against them, their trade plummeted. New England's imports from England dropped from £420,000 in 1768 to about £208,000 in 1769.[48]

ૐ

The popular leaders in every colony wanted to continue non-importation despite the repeal of the duties levied by the Townshend revenue act. If Parliament retains one dutied article, said the *South Carolina Gazette,* "we shall not yet be restored to our former freedom" and our agreement must be maintained.[49] The repeal act kept the duty on tea and the Charleston committee at once broadcast a ringing appeal for unanimity. Americans would not be free until the customs board and admiralty courts with their uncontrolled power were abolished. The sister colonies should not take advantage of the repeal of "those trifling duties" and "sink into a slavish inactivity when a spirited and steady conduct can alone crown our hopes." [50]

Charleston remained "steady" but confusion reigned in the North where the final decision lay with the great commercial centers. Many Philadelphia merchants were as anxious to have done with non-importation as they had been to avoid it, and the unhappy dry goods merchants demanded a meeting of the signers.[51] Then came the news that Newport, Rhode Island, had abandoned its agreement. The tradesmen and mechanics of Philadelphia met at once and resolved to keep up non-importation, boycott all violators, and denounce what even one of the merchants called the "little dirty colony of Rhode Island." The lesson was clear and the merchants wrote to New York and Boston asking what they were going to do.[52] When the signers met on 5 June (apparently in company with many "mechanicks" brought in by Charles Thomson), they voted almost unanimously to continue non-importation.[53]

In New York the Sons of Liberty, abetted by the Livingston faction, were equally determined.[54] A popular mass meeting on 30 May denounced the apostasy of Newport, called for a boycott of that town and the maintenance of non-importation in New York, and proclaimed that any mer-

[48] EHD, IX, 392.   [49] SCG(T), 19 April 1770.
[50] John Neufville, chairman, General Committee of Charleston, to the Sons of Liberty in Boston, 25 April, Samuel Adams Papers, NYPL. The letter was printed in several newspapers. See VG(R), 31 May; MdG, 14 June.
[51] NYJ, 31 May.   [52] Ibid. 7 June.
[53] PG, 24 May, 7 June; Jensen, *Maritime Commerce,* chapter XII, which contains the best account of non-importation in Philadelphia.
[54] Colden to SS, 16 May, NYCD, VIII, 214–15.

chant who violated the agreement was an enemy of the liberties of America. The merchant committee resigned in a huff, only to stay on when asked to do so by another mass meeting.[55] But the merchants did not give up, and two days later they appealed to the merchants of the northern colonies to send deputies to a meeting at Norwalk, Connecticut, on 18 June, to adopt a common course of action.[56]

The proposal was roundly rejected in Connecticut and New Jersey, both of which imported most of their goods from New York, and by the popular leaders of Boston and Philadelphia, who spoke in the name of the merchants.[57] Meanwhile a number of merchants and mechanics asked the merchants' committee for a poll of the city. The poll was taken and the merchants claimed that the majority of the inhabitants wanted to end non-importation. Expresses were sent to ask the concurrence of Boston and Philadelphia. It was agreed that if they refused, New York would take another poll. The poll was denounced by a "Son of Liberty," who said the mechanics involved were the "tools of a party" and that the poll was dishonest. The two popular leaders on the merchant committee, Isaac Sears and Peter Van Devoort, dramatized the issue by publicly resigning.[58] Boston and Philadelphia flatly rejected the proposal, leaving the New Yorkers to act alone.[59]

The merchants gave up any further attempt at intercolonial action and decided to end non-importation, whatever the impact on their reputations, and they were backed by the De Lancey party and government officials.[60] They learned too that Parliament had at last allowed New York to issue paper money. Thus armed they called a meeting, but the opposition turned out and voted to retain non-importation. The merchants then held a private meeting and decided to poll the town again. Alexander McDougall and Isaac Sears called a meeting of their own, voted to retain non-importation, and that night paraded the streets hooting and hissing at the doors of would-be importers. This "mob" was met by another "mob" led by a future president of the chamber of commerce, and the two had at each other in Wall Street with clubs and canes.[61] The defeat of Sears's and McDougall's mob in the brawl was both real and symbolic, for when

[55] NYJ, 7 June.   [56] Ibid. 28 June.
[57] Ibid. 21, 28 June, 5, 26 July; BG, 11 June; MdG, 19 July.
[58] The *New York Journal*, 21 June, is filled with arguments pro and con.
[59] BEP, 2 July; Schlesinger, *Colonial Merchants*, 223.
[60] The *Boston Gazette*, 23 July, lists the names of the many men who worked to end non-importation.
[61] Schlesinger, *Colonial Merchants*, 225–26.

the poll of the town was completed on Monday evening, 9 July, the merchants claimed an overwhelming victory. Governor Colden had held up the sailing of the packet boat and within two days merchant orders for goods were on the way to England.[62] The popular leaders in New York were utterly defeated and all they could do was to bewail the loss of New York's reputation, "which has been meanly prostituted to serve the vile purposes of a party." [63] The merchants in turn made much of the cheating in Boston and Philadelphia as a justification for their own decision to import.[64]

New York's break-through brought bitter attacks from other colonies. The Philadelphia committee charged that "however you may color your proceeding, we think you have, in the day of trial, deserted the cause of liberty and your country"; [65] and some Philadelphians told New Yorkers to send their old liberty pole to them since New York would have no more use for it.[66] Princeton students tolled the bell on Nassau Hall, hired a common hangman to burn the New York letter, and hoped that the name of every promoter of the end of non-importation "may be blasted in the eyes of every lover of liberty, and their names handed down to posterity as betrayers of their country." [67] More practical New Jerseyites proposed a boycott of New York and the building up of their own ports.[68] In Connecticut, New Haven merchants told the Wethersfield merchants that the time "is now come for us to determine whether we will be FREEMEN or SLAVES." They should stop all business with the "degenerate importers" of New York. Connecticut people, for a little temporary wealth, should not "bequeath infamy, poverty, and slavery" to posterity by keeping up a connection with that city. Besides, they could probably get what they needed, and on better terms, "from our natural friends and neighbors of Boston, whose manly fortitude and persevering measures justly claim our preference." [69]

The "manly fortitude" of the Boston merchants was not of their own making or choice nor was that of the Philadelphia merchants. The popular leaders held a great mass meeting in Philadelphia on 14 July to denounce New York, to boycott her, and to publish the name of anyone having dealings with a New Yorker.[70] But the dry goods merchants began a propa-

---

[62] Colden to SS, 7, 10 July, NYCD, VIII, 217, 218; NYJ, 19 July; MdG, 26 July.
[63] NYJ, 26 July, 2 Aug.
[64] The *New York Gazette* published Mein's pamphlet, 27 Aug. For attacks on the "slander" against Boston and Philadelphia, see NYJ, 19, 26 July, 25 Oct.
[65] PG, 12 July.   [66] NYJ, 26 July.   [67] Ibid. 19 July.
[68] Ibid. 26 July, 2, 9 Aug.   [69] 26 July, Emmett Coll. no. 357, NYPL.
[70] PG, 19 July.

ganda campaign telling of their suffering and insisting that the non-importers were not merchants at all. They proposed to poll Philadelphia, following the example of the New Yorkers, but they did not want a public mass meeting, which they feared they could not control. Finally, on 20 September they held a carefully staged meeting with only subscribers present, and voted overwhelmingly to end non-importation. The enforcement committee, in control of supporters of the agreement, resigned, and then called a great mass meeting a few days later to censure the merchants. The meeting was futile, as were threats of a non-consumption agreement. The Philadelphia merchants, alarmed at New York's break-through and the competition from Baltimore, hurried off orders to England as fast as they could.[71]

ଓ

The news from Philadelphia was the final blow to the power of the popular leaders over the Boston merchants. As early as May, when they first heard that Philadelphia merchants wanted to end non-importation, about fifty Boston merchants met and decided to import. But the next day a mass meeting voted to retain non-importation until the repeal of the tea tax. Thomas Hutchinson countered by warning the governors of New York and Pennsylvania not to believe all the lies told of the unanimity in Boston, and the customs officials busily but secretly circulated accounts of cheating in Boston to other colonies.[72] Violence against importers increased, even in little towns like Marlborough,[73] and once more the customs commissioners fled to Castle William and their business came to a full stop.[74] James McMaster, who had held out against non-importation from the start, "lost his property and lost his senses." He was hauled about town in a cart and escaped tarring and feathering only by promising to leave.[75]

When New York ended non-importation, Hutchinson bewailed that Boston was not a corporation like New York; if it were, a poll of the town could be taken. As it was, the selectmen "were the creatures of the populace," for "the lowest class of people still have the rule in Boston," and were abetted by a few merchants.[76] Nine out of ten of the "best men" wanted to send orders, reported Samuel Prince, but were kept in constant

[71] Jensen, *Maritime Commerce*, 190–95.
[72] Hutchinson to SS, 27 May, C.O. 5/759; Thomas Irving to John Swift, 5 June, Philadelphia Customs House Papers, X, HSP.
[73] Mrs. Henry Barnes to Mrs. Elizabeth Smith, 6 July, Barnes Letters, LC.
[74] John Williams to John Swift, 16 July, Philadelphia Customs House Papers, X, HSP.
[75] Ann Hulton to Mrs. Adam Lightbody, 25 July, *Letters*, 26–27; NYG, 2 July.
[76] To SS, 26 July, C.O. 5/759.

dread by the noise and threats of a set of villains who would reduce everyone to "the same necessitous, desperate condition with themselves." John Fleeming, Mein's partner, had stopped publication of the *Boston Chronicle* and fled; "Edes and Gill reign triumphant"; and other printers were either seditious or dared not publish anything unpopular.[77]

The popular leaders not only had Boston under control, but they also began to inspect towns like Salem and Marblehead.[78] Then, with extraordinary presumption, they sent a committee, including William Molineux and the Boston town clerk, William Cooper, to investigate matters at Providence and Newport, which had re-adopted their agreements after an intercolonial boycott. The indignant Newporters threatened to tar and feather their visitors, who stayed only a few hours instead of the two or three days they had planned. One unfriendly Newport merchant broadcast to the world at large that Molineux had told that Boston merchants cheated by having two doors to a store: one for the goods to come in and another for them to go out. The committee had no better luck at Providence, and so it returned to Boston,[79] where Thomas Hutchinson asserted that "the frenzy was not higher when they banished my pious greatgrandmother, when they hanged the Quakers, when they afterwards hanged the poor innocent witches, when they were carried away with a land bank, nor when they all turned 'New Lights'. . . ." [80] He informed Bernard that "the infamous Molineux and Young, with Cooper, Adams, and two or three more, still influence the mob who threaten all who import," but that even the merchants who were at first zealous now wanted an end to non-importation.[81]

Such versions of life in Boston were denied in the newspapers and in private letters of the popular leaders to other colonies. Dr. Thomas Young blandly informed a New Yorker that the merchants had discovered the inconveniency of offending tradesmen and farmers and are "become very mild. . . . I thank God there never was so fine an appearance of a fair, firm, and rational harmony in this town since I . . . [have been] an inhabitant." [82] At the very moment he was writing, collapse of the Boston agreement was on the way. A mass meeting on 11 September proposed a general congress at Philadelphia to adopt a new agreement [83] but the Philadelphians abandoned their own agreement before the letter arrived. When the news of Philadelphia's action reached Boston the merchants

[77] To ———, 28 July, Misc. Bound, XIII, MHS.   [78] BG, 13 Aug.; VG(PD), 6 Sept.
[79] VG(PD), 4 Oct.   [80] To William Parker, 26 Aug., Hosmer, *Hutchinson*, 195.
[81] 28 Aug., ibid. 195–96.
[82] To Hugh Hughes, 15 Sept., Misc. Bound, XIII, MHS.   [83] BG, 17 Sept.

took courage, and in October they met and decided to import everything except the taxed tea.[84] The popular leaders sought to put the best face they could on their defeat by blaming it on the unpatriotic behavior of New York, New Hampshire, and Philadelphia.[85]

ဒ

The breakdown of non-importation in the southern colonies followed rapidly on the heels of breakdown in the North as the southerners combined denunciation of northern merchants with raucous charges of cheating against one another. Various county committees in Maryland met and resolved to boycott Rhode Island, and then New York. The Talbot county committee of inspection asserted that all commerce with New York should be ended so that New Yorkers "may be branded as the betrayers of their country, be despised of the people, and become an hissing among the Nations." [86] Marylanders soon attacked one another because the Baltimore merchants clearly wanted to end their agreement as soon as they could. When one Baltimore merchant was charged with profiteering on tea, he offered some rather precise details as to how his detractors—flaming patriots like Samuel Chase and other supporters of non-importation—had been profiteering and sneaking in cargoes.[87] After the defection of Philadelphia, the Baltimore merchants demanded a colony-wide meeting, but made it plain that whatever the decision, Baltimore itself was through with non-importation.[88] The meeting at Annapolis on 25 October voted to keep up non-importation and then resolved to boycott the merchants of Baltimore. A "Merchant" in turn called the meeting a "fortuitous collection . . . of councilors, representatives, lawyers, and others" who presumed to give law to the merchants.[89] Thus non-importation ended in Maryland in the midst of name-calling.

The second Virginia agreement of June 1770 was no better enforced than the one of the year before, although far more effort was made.[90] During the summer, county committees of inspection sent some cargoes back; yet at the end of August, Peyton Randolph announced that several counties had done nothing.[91] Enthusiasm died rapidly as the northern merchants abandoned their agreements. Virginia merchants regretted ever

---

[84] MG, 11 Oct.; VG(R), 1 Nov.
[85] See the ingenuous letter of William Palfrey to John Wilkes, 23–30 Oct., CSMP, XXXIV, 421–22, 426.
[86] MdG, 7, 21 June, 12 July, 23 Aug.   [87] Ibid. 26 July, 2, 9, 16 Aug.
[88] Ibid. 11 Oct.   [89] Ibid. 1 Nov., 6, 13 Dec.; PC, 17 Dec.
[90] VG(R), 19 July, 2, 23, 30 Aug., 6 Sept. for examples.   [91] Ibid. 23 Aug.

signing, while conservative planters worried about the extra-legal local committees and the danger to the sanctity of private property. "Mercator" gave tongue to such fears when he argued that the association had a tendency to defeat the "original end and design of all society" which was to protect private property from the assaults of individuals.[92]

Shortly thereafter Peyton Randolph called a meeting of the associators at Williamsburg for 14 December, a place difficult to reach in winter. Popular leaders like Richard Henry Lee were convinced that this was a "plot" to end non-importation, and the *Gazette* attacked the merchants, who, "accustomed, like post boys, to ride through thick and thin, in all weathers, for the sake of a little pelf," would be sure to attend the meeting.[93] The planters should come to the rescue. Among others, Richard Henry Lee responded to the call and rode off to Williamsburg. There, he declared, they defeated a "North British scheme"; but in fact not enough men were present to take action so the meeting was postponed until June 1771.[94] Non-importation was already a "sham affair" said one merchant, and many of its most ardent supporters had sent off such large orders that "dry goods were never a greater drug. . . ."[95]

Non-importation was in fact dead and always had been, for the planters wanted the goods and the merchants imported them. The farce ended on 18 July 1771, when George Washington and George Mason of the Fairfax county committee recommended that non-importation be abandoned except for such goods as were still taxed by Parliament.[96]

Non-importation was no farce in South Carolina, and during the summer it was kept going in full force. Charleston got the marble statue of Pitt which had been ordered in 1766 and dedicated it with enthusiasm in July.[97] In August a mass meeting reaffirmed the non-importation agreement while excoriating New York, Rhode Island, and Georgia.[98] "We are too apt to cast our eyes to the North Star of Boston in our political navigation," said Governor Bull,[99] but by December Charlestonians knew that even the "North Star" had failed them. On 13 December a mass meeting,

[92] VG(PD), 4 Oct.   [93] VG(R), 13 Dec.
[94] To William Lee, 8 Jan. 1771, *Letters*, I, 53; William Nelson to SS, 19 Dec. 1770, C.O. 5/1349.
[95] Nathaniel Savage to John Norton, 9 Jan., Brock Coll.: Savage-Norton Papers, I, HEHL.
[96] VG(R), 18 July. The best account of non-importation in Virginia is in Thomson, The Merchant in Virginia, 320–38.
[97] SCG(T), 31 May, 5 July.   [98] Ibid. 23 Aug.
[99] To SS, 10 July, C.O. 5/379.

with Henry Laurens as chairman, abandoned non-importation except for tea and appointed a committee to draft a protest against the northern colonies, whose conduct had forced Charleston to alter its agreement.[100] All the efforts of men like Gadsden could not sway the crowd; nor even those of Thomas Lynch, who rode in fifty miles from the country and "exerted all his eloquence and even the trope of rhetorical tears for the expiring liberties of his dear country, which the merchants would sell like any other merchandise." [101]

The breakdown of non-importation was accompanied by shrill protests that liberty itself had been abandoned, and by bitter charges that one colony or another had betrayed them all. During the summer of 1770, as the Bostonians maintained their agreement, they blasted the New Yorkers for their "immortal shame and infamy," and if any other colonies followed New York's example, "let them, like the parricides at New York, be despised, hated, detested, and handed down to all future ages as the betrayers of their country. . . ." [102] When the letter of the New York merchants announcing the end of non-importation reached Boston a mass meeting ordered it torn to pieces and cast to the winds.[103]

But Boston was vulnerable and New York counterattacked with plenty of ammunition. Boston had refused New York's invitation to the Norwalk conference of merchants because it wished to continue importing despite "pompous, ostentatious resolves against it," and therefore it was Boston's fault that New York ended non-importation.[104] The New York newspapers published lists of Boston's imports contrary to its agreement, and if correct, the lists were damning evidence of Boston cheating.[105] New York, said one writer, should be judged by honest men, not by Bostonians whose "vile and scandalous behavior" ruined non-importation. Despite its pretences and glorious resolves, Boston has been "the common sewer of America into which every beast that brought with it the unclean thing has disburthened itself!" [106] "Ichabod Snuffle" offered satirical resolutions addressed to the "wonderful Folk" of Boston, in which he suggested the erection of a "Janus-faced statue" to their "mightinesses near the Faction Pole of this sinful city." [107] The New Yorkers defended the integrity of their

[100] SCG(T), 13 Dec.   [101] Bull to SS, 13 Dec., C.O. 5/380.
[102] BG, 23 July.   [103] NYG, 6 Aug.   [104] NYJ, 30 Aug.
[105] NYG, 27 Aug.   [106] "Coriolanus," ibid.   [107] Ibid. 3 Sept.

own merchants while charging that "those of Boston are only for practising less and professing more than all the rest of the continent." [108] Or as one writer put it, the merchants of Boston were "a set of the most designing, hypocritical, perfidious beings that ever existed in any country. . . ." [109]

The widespread conviction that the Bostonians were cheaters—added to the dislike of many Americans for the everlasting tumults in Boston—destroyed, temporarily, the leadership of the colonies which that town had held ever since 1765. Two years later when Dr. Thomas Young tried to stir up the lethargic New Yorkers, he found that the suspicion created in 1770 was not dead, and his defense of his adopted city was lame at best.[110]

What has been called a "conservative reaction" followed the breakup of non-importation. Merchants, planters, and the well-to-do generally had had enough of popular agitation, enough of riots and of popular propaganda, and were as anxious as the North ministry to have an end to the disputes between the mother country and the colonies. Cadwallader Colden put it succinctly when he said that "all men of property are so sensible of their danger, from riots and tumults, that they will not rashly be induced to enter into combinations, which may promote disorder for the future, but will endeavor to promote due subordination to legal authority." [111] At any rate, the tax on tea was not worth fighting about, and if Britain was ready to call it quits, so were many leading Americans.

The popular leaders who had risen to fame and power after 1763 as the champions of American liberty were left without any real issue. They tried to keep up the fight over the tea tax but they got no effective support. The depression which had dogged many parts of America since 1763 was apparently at an end and trade boomed feverishly after 1770. The popular leaders continued, of course, to fight against local political leaders as they did in Massachusetts, but most of them returned, at least partially, to the obscurity from which they had emerged, to the great glee and relief of their American opponents.

[108] "Veritas," NYJ, 6 Sept.   [109] Ibid. 8 Nov.
[110] To Hugh Hughes, 20 Dec. 1772, Misc. Bound, XIV, MHS.
[111] To SS, 7 July 1770, NYCD, VIII, 217.

Part Three: The Final Break

The hope of a return to the "good old days" before 1763, so longed for by many Americans in 1770, was doomed to frustration by the events after 1763. For one thing, although British policy-makers wanted an end to trouble with the colonies, it was almost inevitable that those policy-makers would take actions in the future to which at least some Americans would object. And most Britons had learned very little about the colonies. They could not understand that many Americans meant what they said when they rejected the supremacy of Parliament "in all cases whatsoever."

Even more fatal for the future of the empire was that many Britons looked upon Americans as an inferior breed of men. Few of them recognized that some American leaders were the intellectual equals, and quite likely the superiors, of many members of Parliament, and that they led a vigorous people far more economically independent and politically literate than the comparatively poverty-stricken and politically powerless rural and urban masses of England. Given such attitudes on the part of the ruling class in Britain, it was certain that if the colonies offered violent resistance to British policies in the future, Britain would strike back with a grim determination to force Americans to yield.

A second fact that made a "return" impossible was that the older ways of American politics were gone beyond recovery. One consequence of the opposition to Britain after 1763 was the tradition-breaking use of extra-legal political methods and the participation of the people at large in extra-legal actions. Another consequence was the popularization of radical ideas of American rights and of the relationship that should exist between the colonies and the mother country.

Equally important was the rise of a group of new men in America: the "popular leaders," and their followers, the "popular parties." Eighteenth-century America took for granted the existence of political parties or "factions." "Government," "prerogative," and "court" parties were terms commonly used to describe the politically entrenched groups in the colonies. Increasingly after 1763 they were called "Tories" by their opponents. The opposition groups often called themselves the "country party," and increasingly after 1763 looked upon themselves as "Whigs." Such terminology, of course, followed the practice in England, but after 1763 a new name appeared in America, and most notably in Massachusetts, where "popular leaders" and "popular party" were first used by the "government party" to describe the outspoken opponents of British policies.

It is pointless to attempt to apply latter-day notions of what political parties ought to be to the eighteenth century. Parties then had neither the organizations nor the supposed principles of twentieth-century parties. They were usually the personal following of a leader, or a small group of leaders, and neither leaders nor followers saw anything incongruous in switching from one side to another if such a switch might gain political advantage. But British policies after 1763 presented issues both of principle and of economic importance to Americans, and forced them to line up as never before on the question of what could be or should be done.

Most of the well-established political leaders in 1763 had spent years climbing the political ladder, and they saw to it that younger men served an equally long apprenticeship. Ambitious beginners were carefully watched, and young men who had wealth and powerful family connections, or were able to win the sponsorship of the politically entrenched, usually began with a minor office. Given a capacity for an adequate amount of conformity on the part of the younger men and the removal of enough older men by death—which alone seemed to provide political openings—they might eventually reach the top.

The generation of men who were the councilors, judges, sheriffs, and justices of the peace in 1763 thus usually owed their positions to long apprenticeships, and to their wealth, social position, and family and political connections. They owed them also, in the royal and proprietary colonies, to their at least seeming co-operation with Britain, and particularly with the governors who made the appointments to practically all of the offices by which the colonies were governed. Colonial officials of high rank were therefore seldom in a position to lead vigorous opposition to British policies after 1763 although many of them, like Thomas Hutchinson, thought those policies mistaken. They might have resigned office, or acted as opposition leaders until removed, but few if any did. Most clung to the offices they had and constantly intrigued to acquire more.

The way was thus open for men out of power and for new leaders, most of them young, to win places for themselves in American politics. These "new men" as they were often called, would naturally have sought political preferment in any period: British policies after 1763 were for them an unearned political increment which made possible their sudden rise to actual if not always legal power. Some of these men were only "outs" who wanted "in" as their opponents charged, but others were far more than that. Seldom has any nation at one moment in its history produced so many men with such striking personalities and such talent for political leadership. Their mastery of political ideas and their ability to put them in enduring prose has not been equaled by Americans since then. Their capacity for political organization approached genius and their talent for propaganda has seldom been paralleled.

Such men were given an unusual opportunity after 1763, for, in effect, many of the established leaders abdicated their leadership of the colonies (but not their positions of political power) by refusing to take an open and aggressive stand against British policies. The new men therefore filled a political vacuum. Although most of them were not extremists at heart, they expounded extreme ideas and supported extreme measures, and from time to time they had the support of many normally conservative planters and merchants who were irritated or injured by British policies.

They were called "popular leaders" because they appealed to the people at large and proclaimed their rights. The mass meeting, held without regard to law or the political rights of those who attended, became a common means of asserting principles and exerting political pressure. When the statement of constitutional principles failed to achieve results, mobs, both informal and organized, were sometimes used effectively.

In the course of this activity the traditional patterns of political behavior were profoundly altered, for resolutions in mass meetings, and pamphlets, broadsides, and newspapers, denounced established colonial leaders as well as British policies. While there was no alteration in the constitutional framework of American society, a revolution was wrought in the minds and hearts of the people, not only in their attitude toward Britain, as John Adams said, but also in their conception of their own role in politics. Many people became accustomed to political action as never before, even if it was no more than shouting approval of half-understood resolutions presented to them, and they were publicly taught to suspect the gentlemen who held high office. This attack upon established leaders who considered themselves gentlemen, and the constant appeal to the people and their "rights," along with the doctrine of equality embodied in the Declaration of Independence, had a far-reaching impact on the political life of the new nation. The time was not far distant when a "gentleman" who wanted a political career, had either to hide his pretensions or deny his origins.

The methods of the popular leaders were those of political artists in any age, always deplored but always used, and concern for truth was not always uppermost in their minds. Yet at the same time these men preached ideals of the highest order and political theories profoundly appealing to the ordinary men of every land and every age. Despite their success after 1763, most of the popular leaders disappeared from the public eye in 1770, deserted by their followers and distrusted by the older leaders.

Nevertheless, there were issues and problems in America, some domestic and some arising from British actions, that make the years 1770–73 far more significant than is usually supposed. The popular leaders, although lacking overt issues, kept a watchful eye on Britain. They seized on every possible occasion to reiterate their ideas of American liberties, and increasingly they worked in the direction of an intercolonial organization of like-minded men. They were certain—and perhaps some hoped—that Britain would again adopt measures infringing on American rights. Before the end of 1773 Britain did act in a way that gave the popular leaders an opportunity to regain their leadership. Then within a few months Britain adopted measures that amply justified the warnings the popular leaders had dinned into seemingly deaf ears ever since 1770. When angry and determined British leaders turned from laws and resolutions to the use of armed force to impose Britain's will on America, an equally determined and ever-larger number of Americans united to meet force with force. British leaders refused to compromise or to accept any solution except absolute submission. The popular leaders in America and their followers refused to submit. The final break, the declaration of American independence, was inescapable.

XV

The Various Roads to Crisis: America South and West of New England

Many Americans welcomed the collapse of non-importation and what they hoped would be an end of agitation and extra-legal action which, equally with British policies, had seemed to many to threaten the very foundations of colonial society. Hence there was a "conservative reaction" after 1770. But it was such only by comparison with the preceding years. Extra-legal methods were not abandoned and some of the new leaders who had arisen did their best to keep issues alive, or to create them where none existed. As in the past, there was a real difference in the quality of the leadership, the issues, and the events in New England and in the colonies to the southward. In Massachusetts agitation never died down and in Rhode Island violence against the British navy continued, whereas there was little such overt drama elsewhere. Nevertheless many of the colonies faced problems that helped prepare the way, politically and emotionally, for the crisis with Britain in 1774.

Outside of New England only South Carolina engaged in a constitutional dispute with Britain in the early 1700s. In the course of it the aristocratic Commons House reiterated the constitutional ideas of the preceding years, defied British orders, and fought the governor and council to a standstill. The cause was John Wilkes. He had been much toasted in Charleston, as elsewhere, and Carolinians had founded a "Club No. 45." An appeal for financial aid from the Society of the Supporters of the Bill of Rights in England was answered by the Commons House in December 1769. It voted money to defend British and American liberties and directed the treasurer to give the money to a committee of the house which in turn sent £1500 sterling to England. The house did not consult the governor and council.[1]

Support for Wilkes, especially from a colony, was something the ministry would not tolerate. Britain's attorney general and the governor of South Carolina were ordered to investigate the constitutional history of the colony. The former promptly reported that the appropriation of money by one branch of the legislature was illegal. But Governor Bull pored over the journals for the past thirty years and explained that only from the "journals, not the bare representations of governors," could the truth be discovered. He found that as a result of a dispute between the two houses that began in the 1730s, the council had had no power over money bills since the 1750s.[2]

The Privy Council did not wait for Bull's report. It declared the practice illegal and unconstitutional and ordered the attorney general of the colony to sue the treasurer for the money, and the governor and council to disapprove any bill reimbursing the treasurer, or any other money bill, until the Commons House accepted London's interpretation of its powers.[3] In August 1770, Governor Bull delivered these orders to the Commons House, which at once adopted resolutions defending its "ancient right" to raise and dispose of money as it saw fit, and asserting that a "minister's dictating how a money bill shall be framed is an infringement of the privileges of this house. . . ."[4] It then passed a bill reimbursing the treasurer for the money. The council, as ordered, rejected it, and government came to a stop. A prorogation until January 1771 produced no change in temper. When Lord Montagu, the governor, returned from England, he dissolved the legislature. After an election in August 1772, he petulantly called the legislature to meet at Beaufort.[5] He thus threw away the little influence he had left, and shortly thereafter he resigned from the position which he had seldom honored by his presence in the colony. The Commons House refused to yield to British orders and the result was a deadlock which prevented the passage of tax bills between 1769 and the war for independence, and of all legislation after 1771.

The council, made up mostly of royal office-holders, finally lost all power in the summer of 1773. When Governor Bull made the usual request for a tax bill to pay the colony's debts, the house replied that it would never in-

---

[1] SCHJ, 8 Dec.; Bull to SS, 12 Dec., C.O. 5/379.
[2] Bull to SS, 8 Sept. 1770, C.O. 5/379.   [3] APC:CS, V, 229-35.
[4] SCHJ, 16, 30 Aug.; Commons House to Bull, 30 Aug., C.O. 5/379.
[5] SCHJ, 6, 7, 8, 17 Sept., 5 Nov. 1771; 8, 10 Oct. 1772.

sert the clause ordered by the royal instruction of 1770 and that it hoped no future assembly would be "so totally regardless of the most essential rights of the people as to do so. . . ." The council then took the offensive, asserting that the treasury was nearly empty and demanding an investigation. It charged that the merchants owed the treasury nearly £127,000 and asked that they be sued at once. Using some odd logic, a house committee headed by Christopher Gadsden replied that the £127,000 should be counted as being in the treasury, and then attacked the council for misrepresentation. If it would pass tax bills "agreeable to the constitution of the province," the public debts could be paid.[6]

The council had taken the unusual step of publishing its charges in the newspapers, but when the *South Carolina Gazette* published a protest by John and William Henry Drayton against a delay in passing an anti-counterfeiting bill, the council jailed the printer, Thomas Powell. The Commons House promptly recommended a writ of habeas corpus, and Speaker Rawlins Lowndes and another member, as justices of the peace, issued the writ freeing Powell from jail. When the council protested that the writ was not good against its actions, the justices replied that such an argument was a usurpation of the rights of Englishmen. Gleefully, Powell's paper reported:[7]

> Thus was defeated the most violent attempt that ever had been made in this province upon the liberty of the subject—probably intended to control the liberty of the press, one of the most valuable blessings that can be enjoyed by Britons, it being the best alarum to rouse us against the attacks of arbitrary power.

The attack on the liberty of the press and the integrity of the merchants completed the suicide of the council. As Governor Bull put it, "the merchants were alarmed at the unprovoked wound . . . at their credit here and abroad." In his explanation the governor ingenuously revealed how ingeniously the South Carolinians had managed to evade the provisions of the Currency Act of 1764, and their own laws issuing paper money as well. They simply did not pay currency into the treasury for import duties and taxes; if they had done so the money would have been burned as the issues expired. Instead, merchants had given the treasury their personal notes and bonds in payment of duties. Every fall when supplies of gold and silver

[6] SCG(T), 16, 23, and postscript, 25 Aug.
[7] Ibid. 30 Aug., 2, 13 Sept., and postscript, 15 Sept. Drayton, appointed to the council after his fight against non-importation, had now switched sides.

were brought in to pay for rice and indigo, the merchants paid in specie and the treasury then cancelled the accumulated notes.[8]

In this instance, as in others, the rulers of South Carolina defied British policies, governors, and councilors. They kept very much alive the popular ideas of the supremacy of elected legislatures and of the "rights of the people," ideas that were to prove highly embarrassing to those leaders once the war for independence had begun.

In North Carolina there was trouble of a different sort. The demand of the backcountry farmers for internal economic and political reforms was crushed by brute force at Alamance Creek in May 1771. Sir William Tryon, who had personally led an army of easterners against the farmers, left within a few weeks to become governor of New York. Josiah Martin, his successor, investigated and reported that the people did indeed have justifiable grievances.[9] The sympathy received from the new governor and from officials in England contrasted blatantly with the violence used against the backcountry by some of the anti-British leaders in eastern North Carolina. As a result, when the war came, some backcountry men remained loyal to Britain, while others went into the politics of the new state in an attempt to achieve the goals which had been suppressed by armed force only a few short years before.

Maryland's position in colonial America was unique because the charter of 1632 made the proprietor almost completely independent of English control and gave him the powers of a medieval monarch within the colony.[10] The government and the people of Maryland therefore had almost no direct political relations with England, nor were they much interested in neighboring colonies. One central political fact was that several strong proprietors had insisted on exercising their kingly prerogatives (such as George III did not dream of) and had built up in Maryland a "court party" of councilors and officials which was so effective that the personal income of the proprietors far exceeded that of the Crown in any royal colony, even so great a one as Virginia.

From the beginning, opposition to proprietary power centered in the elective branch of the legislature. By the eighteenth century it was controlled by a "country party" made up of leading families of wealthy land-

[8] Bull to SS, 26 Aug., C.O. 5/380.
[9] For the Regulator movement see above, Chapter I, and EHD, IX, 591–609.
[10] The Maryland Charter, EHD, IX, 84–93. The following account of Maryland is based on Barker's thorough study, *Background of the Revolution in Maryland.*

owners whose power was based on their firm control of the county governments. Long before 1763 these county leaders, in their struggle with the
proprietor, had used arguments that were to become common in the fight
against British colonial policies after 1763. In 1725, for instance, they proclaimed themselves the "people's representatives for whom all laws are
made and human government established." They appealed endlessly to the
constitutional history of seventeenth-century England and claimed the
"rights of Englishmen" as legislators and as men, and upon occasion asserted the "equality" of all men. On a practical level they opposed the seat-
ing of appointive officials in the legislature long before James Otis and
Samuel Adams began their attack on the Hutchinson oligarchy in Massachusetts. They began appealing directly to the voters in the 1720s by publishing the laws and the legislative journals. While irate governors might
charge that such men were poor, illiterate, and ignorant, they were in fact
aristocrats by instinct and position, however "popular" their political appeals and tactics.

Events after 1763 jarred Marylanders loose from concern with their internal affairs. They co-operated with other colonies by re-stating the constitutional theories they had long used against the proprietors, but now turning them against British policies. They organized extra-legal associations
and used mob violence to defeat the Stamp Act and to attack the Townshend program.

Maryland politics were never the same thereafter. The end of non-
importation in 1770 did not bring peace but instead a new and more vigorous assault on proprietary power. One proprietary supporter's view was that
"the patriots must distinguish their zeal for popular regulations, to recommend themselves to the suffrage of the people." The occasion was the ex-
piration in October 1770 of the Tobacco Inspection Act, first passed in
1747. There was common agreement about the need of inspection, but the
original law had also limited the incomes of the Anglican clergy and had
set maximum fees to be collected by proprietary officials. These last two
issues split the colony for the next three years and brought government almost to a stop.

The proprietor made all the clerical appointments, usually without regard to the wishes of vestries and parishioners. Some Anglican clerics were
low characters; there were drunkards among them and one was even accused
of murdering his wife. The issue was brought to the fore in the 1760s when
Lord Baltimore insisted that his friend and fellow rake (and fellow of
Wadham College, Oxford), Bennett Allen, be given two livings. The pop-

ular story was that one living was no more than enough to pay Allen's liquor bill. Marylanders, even members of the "court party," were outraged by such appointments and determined to reduce clerical incomes. Meanwhile the house had investigated the fees of proprietary officials and discovered that some of them were collecting sums as great as those received by many a colonial governor. The house decided that such incomes must be limited, and denied that the proprietor had the right to establish fees by proclamation, as a governor had done in a similar fight back in the 1730s.

As a result of the conflict between the house and the court party in the council the inspection law lapsed, and the house soon arrested an official for collecting fees illegally, declaring that he had overstepped the bounds of the British constitution. Governor Eden released the man from jail by proroguing the legislature briefly; when the deadlock continued, he dissolved the legislature. The house had taken the high road of popular principle. If the governor and council wanted the government to operate they had to take the highly unpopular step of establishing fees by proclamation. Governor Robert Eden did so immediately after he dissolved the legislature. His purpose, he said, was to protect the people from exorbitant fees; the delegates replied that his act was a denial of the right of Englishmen to be taxed only by representatives of their own choosing. Then, when the delegates returned to their counties, they took a step which would have been unthinkable before the furor of the 1760s: they organized popular associations to enforce tobacco inspection. Once more the ordinary citizens of Maryland were given a chance to take part in political action, and what amounted to economic coercion outside the bounds of law.

A new election and a new meeting of the legislature in October 1771 only tightened the deadlock. Governor Eden was accused of acting the part of a "tyrannical king" in issuing the fee proclamation, and the house asserted that there was no precedent in all English history for such arbitrary procedure. Once more Eden prorogued the legislature, and it did not meet again until 1773 because of the adjustments following the death of the sixth and last Lord Baltimore, and the accession to the proprietorship of his bastard infant son, Henry Harford.

Meanwhile the *Maryland Gazette* became the forum for public debate as never before in its history. Early in 1773, Daniel Dulany, a proprietary leader, defended the fee proclamation. He was answered by Charles Carroll of Carrollton. In the course of a long newspaper debate, Carroll achieved a position in Maryland politics that he was to maintain for decades. A wealthy aristocrat, educated on the Continent and at the Inns of

Court, he returned to Maryland during the Stamp Act crisis, but as a Catholic he could not hold political office. A dedicated philosophical liberal, but a conservative in politics, he was early convinced that independence was inevitable. In the six-month newspaper debate between him and Dulany, which involved everything from historical precedents to personal invective, the two men popularized the fee issue as no legislative resolutions could do.

In the election of 1773, the last in Maryland as a colony, there were public demonstrations throughout the province. The fee proclamation was buried at public "funerals" as the Stamp Act had been a few years before, and the result was a new assembly even more anti-proprietary than the old one. The three legislative sessions that followed were accompanied by the usual resolutions and by a running battle in the *Maryland Gazette*. The outcome was a political compromise. A new tobacco inspection law omitted the limitation of officials' fees—a victory for the proprietary party. That party in turn agreed to sacrifice the Anglican clergymen. Many clerics had done everything possible to render themselves even more unpopular. When the inspection law lapsed in 1770 they demanded forty pounds of tobacco from each parishioner instead of the thirty pounds set by the old law. In addition, some of the reformers among the clergy supported the request of Anglicans in other colonies for the establishment of an American bishop, and this aroused the wrath of every Marylander, from the proprietary officials on down.

As a consequence, from 1770 on, such lawyers as Samuel Chase and William Paca insisted that the act establishing the church in 1702 was illegal, and encouraged the people to refuse to pay tobacco taxes to the clergy. At the same time the *Maryland Gazette* kept up an attack against all clergymen. And in November 1773, both houses of the legislature agreed to limit clerical incomes to thirty pounds of tobacco per poll and gave the taxpayer the option of paying four shillings instead. The effect was to cut clerical incomes by 20 to 50 per cent, and although the clergy complained bitterly to England, the law was never repealed. One of the first acts of the new state in 1776 was to abolish the Anglican church as the state church.

The decade since 1763 had cracked, although it had not shattered, the century-old mould of Maryland politics. Maryland's union with other colonies, the unprecedented use of extra-legal associations and mob violence, and the ever greater appeals to the populace made it inevitable that government in Maryland would never again be the exclusive business of the gentry. New and more vigorous leaders appeared who combined Maryland's old attack on proprietary power with opposition to British policies. But these "popular leaders"—men like Thomas Johnson, Samuel Chase, William Paca, and Charles Carroll of Carrollton—were aristocrats by position or inclination. They led the colony into the war for independence, but with the utmost reluctance, and they struggled to maintain the rule of the landed aristocracy over the new state.

ᛆᐁ

As the "most ancient" royal colony, Virginia, unlike Maryland, had a long and intimate connection with England dating back to 1624, but in the course of its history it had achieved a remarkable degree of self-government in fact. The colony was controlled by a landed gentry numbering a very few hundred, made up of a far smaller number of interrelated families. The leaders might quarrel with one another but they usually presented a united front against any threat to their control of the colony. Governors and lieutenant governors appointed by the Crown were allowed to participate in government, but any governor who tried to rule Virginia did not last long. Nor was there any serious internal threat to concern the leaders. Virginia had a great population of independent farmers but their sole political right was to vote for two members of the House of Burgesses from each county, and they usually ratified the choice of the planter leaders. Occasionally, challenges were offered by a Patrick Henry or a Richard Henry Lee, but these merely irritated rather than displaced the tightly knit group in power.

Virginia was like Maryland in one respect: it had no economic independence. No matter how the people increased the production of other crops, tobacco was still the heart of the economy, and the return from it was dependent upon the fortunes of the international market. Furthermore, most of the tobacco shipped from American wharves to British, and through Britain to French and other consumers, was controlled by merchants in Britain, their agents in the colonies, or onetime agents who had established themselves as independent merchants in Virginia. Such men exported tobacco and imported manufactures, and in the course of doing so, great planters and small farmers alike acquired debts they never seemed able to pay, and which sometimes passed down from father to son. From the Virginian's point of view, most merchants were "foreigners" who kept the natives in economic bondage, and none were more disliked than the Scots, who took an ever larger share of the trade and who spread small stores throughout the colony to further their operations.

Given this ill will, it was natural for Virginians to blame the merchants for the failure of their two non-importation agreements, although the planters themselves were directly responsible.[11] They attacked the merchants as never before; a "Planter" probably voiced the feelings of most of them when he declared "we all know that we are slaves to the power of the merchants, for who can truly say he is free when there is a fixed price set upon his tobacco and the goods he purchases, at rates he does not like?" Do not the merchants meet twice a year at Williamsburg "and plan schemes to enslave us. . . . What a blind infatuated multitude must we be to suffer those, who ought to be dependent on us, to become our masters?" [12] His proposal that planters refuse to sell tobacco, except at prices set by themselves, was as futile as that for a co-operative "Patriotic Store," controlled by planters, for importing and selling goods at cost.[13] Most Virginians were simply not businessmen and, spread out as they were over a sprawling colony, they could not work together economically.

One economic crisis followed another after 1770. In the spring of 1771 the greatest flood in the colony's history swept down over the tidewater, wiping out plantations and stores, and destroying most of the previous year's tobacco crop. This made it impossible to pay debts or to secure new credit, while merchants in Britain continued to insist that their agents in Virginia collect, no matter what. What added to the bitterness of Virginians was that the colony had to pay for the tobacco in government warehouses, most of which belonged to the merchants, whereas the individual planters could get nothing for their losses. And bitterness was compounded when a special session of the legislature paid for the lost tobacco by issuing £30,000 in currency, an act applauded by merchants who had earlier opposed paper money and secured the passage of the Currency Act of 1764.[14]

Recovery from this crisis had only begun when in the summer of 1772 Virginians began hearing of financial turmoil in Britain. A rapid development of uncontrolled speculative banking, followed by a collapse of first one and then another of the get-rich-quick schemes, and in turn by a financial panic, drove many British mercantile firms into bankruptcy and threatened others. British merchants with great debts owing to them from Virginia and Maryland demanded payment at once to save themselves. The creditors of the bankrupt firms did likewise; and their agents went into the Virginia courts to collect, refusing delays or part payment. Tobacco buyers

11 Thomson, Merchant in Virginia, 338–40.   12 VG(R), 31 Oct. 1771.
13 Ibid. 31 Jan., 7 Feb. 1771.
14 Thomas Nelson to SS, 14 June, 15, 26 July 1771, C.O. 5/1349; Thomson, Merchant in Virginia, 310n, 340–42.

did not dare draw bills of exchange on British houses in payment. Merchants in Virginia could not get credit to buy goods in Britain and British merchants feared to send cargoes that might not be paid for. The sudden panic which hit Britain in 1772 and 1773 thus had a direct impact on American tobacco planters; in Virginia it led to even more bitter attacks on the local merchants, who were accused of collusion to force down tobacco prices, and above all on the "mercenary Scotch factors" who bore the brunt of the antagonism.

Fortunately for Virginians, recovery was quick. In 1773 and 1774 they raised and exported more tobacco than ever before in their history, and at higher prices than during the preceding few years. In addition, crop failures in Europe meant profitable markets for their rapidly expanding wheat and corn crops. Thus in 1773 and 1774 many planters and merchants saved themselves from the bankruptcy with which the international financial crisis had threatened them.[15]

Virginia's economic plight was an old story but a new danger haunted the dreams of its leading men in the early 1770s: the threat that Virginia would be cut off at the Appalachians.[16] Virginians had been expansionists from the beginning, impelled ever onward by the twin motives of need for new tobacco land and, increasingly, the hope of riches from acquiring land in advance of actual settlement. By mid-eighteenth century such hopes were fastened on the vast reaches beyond the mountains. Before 1750 the governor and council granted 100,000 acres to James Patton and others, and 800,000 acres to a group calling itself the Loyal Company. The Washingtons, Lees, Masons, and others in northern Virginia organized the Ohio Company, and in 1749 received a royal grant of 200,000 acres south of the forks of the Ohio River, with a promise of 300,000 more if they fulfilled the terms of the grant. Meanwhile the legislature encouraged ordinary settlers to move beyond the mountains by promising them land free of taxes and quitrents for a period of years.[17]

---

[15] Ibid. 342–47; Richard B. Sheridan, "The British Credit Crisis of 1772 and the American Colonies," *The Journal of Economic History*, XX (1960); and the Virginia newspapers for 1772–73. To make matters worse, the ubiquitous counterfeiters who plagued every colony began counterfeiting Virginia money so successfully that business was brought to a stop and the legislature had to meet in special session in an effort to solve the problem.

[16] See EHD, IX, 623, 630 for a list of works on the West between 1763 and 1776, and Chapters II and VIII of this book for British western policy to 1768.

[17] Fauquier to BT, 13 Feb. 1764, C.O. 5/1330 gives a good summary of Virginia's prewar ventures beyond the mountains. Botetourt to BT, 24 June, 31 July 1770, C.O.

The Seven Years War put a stop to such ventures, and at its end the Proclamation of 1763 forbade all settlement west of the mountains and placed all land purchases from the Indians in the hands of imperial officials—the Indian superintendents north and south of the Ohio River.[18] There were settlers beyond the boundary line and more and more joined them, defying troops, speculators, and governors' proclamations to stop them. But the Virginia speculators with pre-war claims, and with new ones they hoped to establish, were interested in tens of thousands of acres, not mere clearings in the wilderness. Such men could not believe the boundary line would be permanent, protested against it, and made plans to go beyond it.[19] George Washington, for instance, proposed surveys beyond the line so as to be ready to secure title the moment it was abandoned. He instructed his agent to search out good land, but above all to keep his plans a "profound secret" because he did not want to be censured for open opposition to the Proclamation, or to have his speculating rivals adopt his methods.[20]

The line of 1763 was temporary, but in 1768 Britain ordered the running of a new and permanent boundary. John Stuart had begun surveying such a line south of the Ohio in 1763, and by 1767 he had reached Virginia. There he was stopped. The Virginians, from the governor on down, wanted no limitation on Virginia expansion, and ignored Stuart's demands.[21] They could not ignore the orders from England in 1768, however, and at Hard Labor in October 1768 Stuart agreed with the Cherokee Indians that the line through Virginia should run from Chiswell's Mine directly to where the Great Kanahwa River emptied into the Ohio.[22]

One possible escape from such a limitation was to discredit the Cherokee claim to the land, and opportunity offered at Fort Stanwix in New York, where, simultaneously with the negotiations at Hard Labor, Sir William Johnson was agreeing with the Iroquois on a line north of the Ohio. And there, oddly enough, the Iroquois did claim the land south of the Ohio as far as the Tennessee River, denied the Cherokee right to it, and then ceded it to the Crown. The claim was dubious and the cession of it

5/1333, includes a list of land grants. Abernethy's *Western Lands and the American Revolution* is the most detailed account of Virginia speculation.
18 See above, Chapter II.
19 See the protest of the House of Burgesses, JHB (1766–69), 69. The board of trade reported on 10 June 1768 that no settlements should be made beyond the line, or whatever new line was drawn. C.O. 5/1346.
20 To William Crawford, 21 Sept. 1767, *Writings*, II, 467–71.
21 Stuart to Botetourt, 19 Jan. 1769, C.O. 5/1347.
22 Alvord, *Mississippi Valley*, II, 62–64.

was not for the benefit of Virginians, but they at once demanded a new line farther west and the board of trade agreed.[23] Of course the Virginians wanted no boundary at all as they made clear in an ingenuous memorial of the House of Burgesses in December 1769. They proposed that the line run due west from the North Carolina boundary to the Ohio River! John Stuart, who knew some geography and had a dim view of Virginians, acidly replied that such a line would intersect the Mississippi, not the Ohio River.[24]

The House of Burgesses backed down and in June 1770 agreed to accept a line running from the intersection of the Holston River with the North Carolina boundary to the mouth of the Great Kanawha. This line was agreed upon at the Treaty of Lochaber in October 1770, but when the surveyor ran the line the next spring he moved it westward to the Kentucky (then Louisa) River,[25] to the great delight of the Virginians. Lord Dunmore, the new governor, praised the line as a "natural boundary" and asserted that it represented only a small gain,[26] whereas in fact it opened up more than half of Kentucky to Virginia speculators.[27] Yet in this moment of triumph, the way west for Virginians was blocked by a new threat, for it seemed inevitable that the entire region between the Alleghenies and the Kentucky River would be established as a new colony. And what was even more galling, it would be the property of a group of Pennsylvania speculators and their British partners.

The British order in 1768 to run a permanent boundary line was in large part the result of the intrigues of Pennsylvania merchants and Indian traders who had lost property during Pontiac's Rebellion in 1763. At first they called themselves the "Suffering Traders of '63." Then in 1765 they organized the Indiana Company and sought political support by giving shares to such non-suffering non-traders as Sir William Johnson, Joseph Galloway, Sir William Franklin, governor of New Jersey, and his father, Benjamin Franklin, who had gone to England in 1764. Franklin used their letters predicting the danger of a new Indian war, at a time when there was no danger, to frighten British officials into ordering the running of permanent boundary lines.[28]

The Pennsylvanians expected that the new boundary would be west of the Proclamation Line of 1763 and they planned to get a land grant within the new area. They had reason for their optimism because their secret part-

[23] JHB (1766–69), 226–27.
[24] Ibid. 13 Dec., 335–36; Stuart to Botetourt, 13 Jan. 1770, C.O. 5/1348.
[25] Sosin, Whitehall, 192.   [26] To SS, March 1772, C.O. 5/1350.
[27] Alvord, Mississippi Valley, II, 85–89.   [28] See above, Chapter VIII.

ner, Sir William Johnson, superintendent of Indian affairs north of the Ohio River, had persuaded the Iroquois and Delaware Indians to promise such a grant as early as 1765. When the news of the order to run the boundary line reached America in the spring of 1768, Samuel Wharton and William Trent of the Indiana Company went to New York. George Croghan, Indian trader, land speculator, and Johnson's deputy was already there, and shortly thereafter they were joined by Sir William Franklin and other interested parties.

Like the Virginians, the Pennsylvanians and their allies wanted the Iroquois to cede their claims to lands south of the Ohio, but for a quite different reason. Virginia's charter claim extended to the Pacific Ocean from the northern boundary of North Carolina and the still unsurveyed western boundary of Pennsylvania. Vast though the area was, it was entirely unlikely that the governor and council of Virginia would grant land within it to anyone except influential Virginians. The only way eager speculators from other colonies could hope to get land within the area was to appeal to some higher power, or to devise some "legal" stratagem to by-pass Virginia's charter. The "promised land" at the moment lay south of the Ohio and it was to secure a grant at Virginia's very back door that the "Suffering Traders of '63" went to New York in the summer of 1768.

They were successful, for prior to agreeing to the new boundary line in the Treaty of Fort Stanwix, the Iroquois not only insisted on ceding their claims south of the Ohio but also insisted on giving a tract within it to George Croghan, and a huge grant south of the forks of the Ohio to the Suffering Traders. This area, soon to be known as "Indiana," contained within it the land granted by the Crown to the Ohio Company of Virginia in 1749, a fact that embittered American politics down to the nineteenth century. Although the cession and grants had nothing to do with the purpose of the boundary line treaty they were included in it, and it was signed by, among others, Dr. Thomas Walker, official commissioner from Virginia. Perhaps he, a leading Virginia speculator and agent for the Loyal Company, was not unwilling to see this blow at his rivals in the Ohio Company.[29]

The grant from the Indians was only a first step: it would need confirmation by British officials. Samuel Wharton, and later William Trent, went to England to secure approval. Wharton soon found that as far as Lord Hillsborough, secretary of the American Department, was concerned, there would be no approval. Wharton therefore set about securing political

[29] Alvord, *Mississippi Valley*, II, 61–72; Abernethy, *Western Lands*, 33–38.

support. The Quaker merchant from Philadelphia proved to be a genius at intrigue and he was helped by the fact that prominent men in and out of government were as anxious as any American to get rich by speculating in American lands. In the course of time he acquired such influential partners as Lord Camden, Sir George Colebrooke of the East India Company, Thomas Walpole the banker, Earl Temple, George Grenville, and Lord Hertford, who as court chamberlain had direct access to the king. In addition to members of Parliament, the Privy Council, and leading financiers, Wharton cannily won the support of such useful bureaucrats as present and future under-secretaries of the treasury, the most notable being John Robinson.

Wharton and his supporters enlarged their project by organizing the Grand Ohio or Walpole Company. Then they offered to buy 2,500,000 acres of land south of the Ohio by paying the Crown what it had spent for Indian presents at the Treaty of Fort Stanwix. When they presented their offer to the board of trade in December 1769, Hillsborough astonished them by suggesting that they buy enough more land to create a new colony. Apparently Hillsborough hoped that the price would be so high they could not raise the money. If so, he was thwarted when treasury officials (some of whom had already swallowed Wharton's bait) agreed to sell the Grand Ohio Company an estimated 20,000,000 acres south of the Ohio River for £10,460, the amount the Crown had spent at Fort Stanwix.

Nevertheless, years of delay followed. The Virginians protested mightily although some of them, such as George Washington, secretly tried to buy into the Grand Ohio Company. As American secretary and president of the board of trade, Hillsborough used all his considerable powers of obstruction. Wharton did not give up. He distributed further shares among influential Englishmen and he promised that all prior Virginia claims would be honored. He offered George Mercer, agent of the Ohio Company of Virginia, two shares for that company's claims, and Mercer accepted without consulting his company. The board of trade was at last forced to make a report on the proposed colony in the summer of 1772, and when it did, it reported against its establishment. The Privy Council, which contained at least three members of the Grand Ohio Company, rejected the report, and Hillsborough resigned as he had threatened to do. His place was taken by the pious Lord Dartmouth, step-brother of Lord North and a speculator in Florida lands. Even then, the board of trade did not report in favor of the new colony until May 1773. It suggested that the colony be named Vandalia in honor of the queen, who, so it was said, was a descendant of the Vandals!

The report, achieved after four years of intrigue and political maneuvering, was only a temporary victory. When Attorney General Edward Thurlow and Solicitor General Alexander Wedderburn were ordered to prepare the necessary legal papers, they objected and delayed, and they continued to do so even after a second order from the Privy Council to get on with the business. At one point, Wharton and his partners concluded that the law officers' opposition was due to their dislike of Benjamin Franklin. In January 1774, Franklin therefore publicly withdrew from the Grand Ohio Company, although he secretly retained his shares. Two weeks later, Wedderburn denounced him publicly for his part in the affair of the Hutchinson letters. Meanwhile, news of the Boston Tea Party reached London in the same month and British officialdom turned all of its attention to Massachusetts.[30] As a result, the charter for the colony of Vandalia was never issued, but its promoters did not give up: they turned to the new government of the United States and they bedeviled it in the years after 1776 as they had British officialdom in the years before.

క్వ

Meanwhile, the decision to create a new colony, so far as Virginians were concerned, seemed to doom their efforts of a decade,[31] during which they had pushed back boundaries and established land claims, often by methods as dubious as those of their rivals. In 1773 they were as busy as ever establishing new claims on new foundations. One was the Dinwiddie proclamation of 1754. The governor, blending public interest with the private ambitions of the Ohio Company to which he belonged, promised 200,000 acres of public land to officers and soldiers who would build a fort at the forks of the Ohio and defend it against the advancing French. In 1769 Washington and others who had bought up soldiers' claims under the proclamation, received permission to make a survey. Washington's own agent, William Crawford, was appointed, and in 1773 Washington published the results. Over 127,000 acres had been surveyed, and Washington's share was more than 20,000.[32]

Another basis for speculation was the Proclamation of 1763 itself. It empowered governors to grant land to British soldiers and sailors who stayed on in America after 1763. Virginians easily convinced themselves that this meant colonial soldiers as well, and William Byrd III asked for a grant as early as 1764.[33] By 1770 Washington had seen the possibilities, for he in-

---

[30] The foregoing account is based on Alvord, *Mississippi Valley*, II, passim, and on Sosin, *Whitehall*, chapter VIII.
[31] See VG(PD), 18 March, 5 Aug., and VG(R), 2 Dec. 1773.
[32] VG(R), 14 Jan. 1773.   [33] Fauquier to BT, 13 Feb. 1764, C.O. 5/1330.

structed his brother to buy up the "claims" of Virginia soldiers but to play up their uncertainty, to buy cheaply, and above all, to keep Washington's interest secret.[34]

By 1773 the Virginians had a governor after their own heart, willing to grant land on almost any pretext. John Murray, Lord Dunmore, arrived in Virginia in September 1771, but he came filled with bitterness. He had been appointed governor of New York in January 1770 and assumed that office in October, only three days after the death of Lord Botetourt, governor of Virginia. Dunmore was then appointed to Virginia and was replaced in New York by Sir William Tryon, governor of North Carolina. Dunmore was incredulous and he was outraged. He had come to America to make his fortune and he had soon acquired 50,000 acres in New York. His only setback came when he tangled with a fellow Scot, Cadwallader Colden, who refused to surrender half the proceeds of the governor's office between Dunmore's appointment and his arrival in New York. Councilor William Smith, Jr., a Livingston henchman, always eager to make trouble for the ruling De Lanceys and "Old Caddy," urged Dunmore, after the supreme court sided with Colden, to rule in his own behalf as chancellor. This was too much, even for Dunmore, and he submitted the dispute to England where, as was so often the case, the attack on Colden died.[35]

Nevertheless, Dunmore was happy with New York. He pled to stay there. He tried to trade jobs with Tryon, but Tryon had had enough of the southern colonies. The night after Tryon took office Dunmore gave a party, at which he got drunk and went berserk. He called Tryon a coward, struck councilors, and then ran into the streets crying, "Damn Virginia, did I ever seek it? Why is it forced upon me? I asked for New York, New York I took, and they have robbed me of it without my consent."[36]

The Virginians were at first uncertain that he would come to their colony. Furthermore, they had a very low opinion of him. One legislator returned from New York and told the House of Burgesses a tale of how Dunmore and his drunken companions had "sallied about midnight from his palace" and destroyed the coach and cut the tails from the horses of Chief Justice Daniel Horsemanden of the supreme court. When Dunmore finally arrived in Virginia he did little at first to improve his reputation, for he began appealing to England for a bigger income, for more power over political appointments, and for 100,000 acres of land for himself and

[34] To Charles Washington, 31 Jan. 1770, Writings, III, 1–4.
[35] Smith, Memoirs, 83–87; Dunmore to SS, 25 May 1773, C.O. 5/1351.
[36] Smith, Memoirs, 99, 106–7; Dunmore to SS, 4 June, 2 July 1771, CHOP, III, 261, 272.

20,000 for his private secretary.[37] But he soon became popular, at least with land speculators, for he confirmed pre-1754 grants, issued patents for land under the Dinwiddie proclamation of 1754, and began granting lands to Virginians under the Proclamation of 1763.[38] He was doing so in 1773, to the fury of the Vandalia promoters, who demanded that he be ordered to stop. Secretary Dartmouth did so, and told him that colonials were not entitled to land under the Proclamation of 1763. Dunmore bluntly replied that it was impossible for him to pay any attention to Vandalia, "if any was due, to what I was entirely ignorant of but by common report," and that not even "common report" had informed him of the limits of the proposed colony.[39] Dunmore was as anxious as any Virginian to extend Virginia westward as far and as fast as possible.

Meanwhile the Virginians were determined to establish control over the key to migration westward, Fort Pitt. The western boundary of Pennsylvania had not been run and the Virginians had long believed that the forks of the Ohio belonged to them, no matter what Pennsylvanians might claim. Dunmore visited the region in 1773, put speculator Dr. John Connolly in charge of the militia, and appointed magistrates. The purpose, said one Virginian, was to "give a check to the aspiring and encroaching spirit of the princely proprietor" of Pennsylvania, who had extended his power a hundred miles beyond his true limits "far into the government of Virginia." Dunmore had protected the people from the "intolerable inconvenience" of being dragged off to the Pennsylvania courts. Connolly acted with a high hand. He repaired Fort Pitt, which had been abandoned by the British in 1771, and appropriately renamed it Fort Dunmore. He jailed people who claimed allegiance to Pennsylvania, confiscated their lands, and shot their livestock. Then, just as Connolly was about to call the militia together, "the haughty Pennsylvanians realized their threats, and conducted him to prison." [40]

The "war" with Pennsylvania was accompanied by growing Indian trouble, vicious murders by both sides, and with the Pennsylvania Indian traders encouraging the Indians to attack the Virginians. "An Indian war is inevitable" reported the *Virginia Gazette* in May 1774, "but whether the Indians or the white people are most to blame we cannot determine, the

---

[37] Richard Bland to Thomas Adams, 1 Aug. 1771, WMQ, 1 ser. V, 156; APC:CS, V, 595; Dunmore to SS, 24 Dec. 1774, C.O. 5/1353.
[38] List of lands patented by Dunmore, in Dunmore to SS, 24 Dec. 1774, C.O. 5/1353.
[39] SS to Dunmore, 6 April, and Dunmore to SS, 9 June 1774, C.O. 5/1352.
[40] VG(PD), 3 March 1774. Dunmore's version with attached documents is in his letter to SS, 18 March, C.O. 5/1352.

accounts being so extremely complicated." [41] Most Indians were for peace except the Shawnee, who were alarmed at Virginia penetration into the Ohio country and angry at Connolly, who had ordered his militia to fire on any Indians appearing in the company of Pennsylvania Indian traders.

Despite Dunmore's dissolution of the House of Burgesses for its protest against the Boston Port Act in May 1774, the legislators supported him heartily when shortly thereafter he set off to the frontier again, this time with an army. He reached Fort Dunmore in September, and on 9 October one wing of the army under Colonel Andrew Lewis defeated the Shawnee at Point Pleasant.[42] Dunmore's War in the fall of 1774 may not have been a speculators' war to establish a Virginia foothold northwest of the Ohio, but some Virginians, most Pennsylvanians, and British officials thought it was.[43]

If so, like all other Virginia plans for expansion, it was brought crashing to the ground in 1774. Vandalia south of the Ohio seemed inevitable, Britain took control of land granting in the West, and then in the Quebec Act, attached the region northwest of the Ohio to the government of Quebec. After 1768 Britain had reduced or abandoned military garrisons, returned regulation of the Indian trade to the colonies, and reduced the authority of the Indian superintendents, all in the name of economy. The results were chaotic. Indian traders lobbied to prevent regulation of the Indian trade by individual colonies.[44] An intercolonial congress in New York in the summer of 1770 to agree on regulation was a fiasco. Virginia sent commissioners, but Pennsylvania, which had urged the congress, did not; and Governor Guy Carleton of Quebec who approved officially, in fact helped block the congress by declaring that Canadians could not go to New York in the summer. Secretary Hillsborough in England was so alarmed at any evidence of colonial "union" that he denounced the congress and secured a royal veto of Virginia's law appointing commissioners.[45]

Meanwhile there was growing anarchy in the Indian trade, and the relentless push of settlers into Indian territory embittered the Indians more and more. The boundary lines were meaningless. The Indian attitude, sel-

---

[41] VG(R), 26 May.

[42] See R. G. Thwaites and Louise P. Kellogg, eds., *Documentary History of Dunmore's War, 1774* (Madison, 1905).

[43] See Alvord, *Mississippi Valley*, II, 191–94, and Randolph C. Downes, "Dunmore's War: An Interpretation," *The Mississippi Valley Historical Review* [MVHR], XXI (1934–35).

[44] Alvord, *Mississippi Valley*, II, chapter VII.

[45] SS to Colden, 14 April and Colden to SS, 7 July 1770, NYCD, VIII, 210–11, 216–17; Botetourt to SS, 31 July, C.O. 5/1348; Dunmore to SS, 3 Oct. 1771, C.O. 5/1349.

dom heard and even less often heeded, was well put by the Cherokee chiefs:

> Father: the white people pay no regard to all our talks that we have had. . . . They are in bodies in the middle of our hunting grounds . . . the whole land is full of white hunters and the guns rattling every way, and horse paths on the river both up and down. . . . You have often told us for to talk to our young fellows that they should not steal anything belonging to the white people, but the Virginia people will not listen to anybody, but do as they please for they steal our deer and our land. . . .[46]

Hillsborough's only solution was to exhort governors and legislatures to stop settlers from encroaching on Indian lands and to prevent traders from using rum. William Nelson, acting governor of Virginia after Botetourt's death, pointedly replied to Hillsborough that as for rum, "when I consider how bewitching the passion for strong drink is among the lower and unthinking part of mankind; insomuch that it is one of the greatest evils, I am told, in England, which cannot be suppressed by all the wisdom of the wisest legislature in the world," colonial assemblies could not be expected to stop such abuses perhaps a hundred miles from any magistrate.[47]

Eventually even British officials discovered that exhortation was futile, and once more they made plans to resume control. In April 1773 the Privy Council forbade colonial governors to make further land grants,[48] perhaps in part to protect Vandalia. Then in February 1774 new rules were prescribed, a policy in some ways anticipating the first land policy of the United States for the national domain. Governors were ordered to survey all ungranted lands into lots of from 100 to 1000 acres which were to be sold to the highest bidder at public auctions and be subject to a quitrent.[49] This was still another blow to Virginia speculators, long accustomed to acquiring huge tracts of land almost free. A few months later, plans for Virginia expansion northwest of the Ohio were blocked by Parliament, which passed the Quebec Act just as Lord Dunmore was setting off for his "war" to open the region northwest of the Ohio to Virginia settlement.

The problem of Quebec had bothered the British ever since the Proclamation of 1763. With a curious bifurcation of conscience they showed far more concern for the French Catholics and the problem of law and gov-

[46] Abstract of talk from the headmen and great ruling chiefs of the Cherokee Nation to John Stuart, 29 July 1769, C.O. 5/1348.
[47] 5 Feb. 1771, C.O. 5/1349.   [48] NYCD, VIII, 357-58.
[49] 5 Feb., C.O. 5/241; NYCD, VIII, 409-13.

ernment in Canada than for the abysmal plight of the Catholics in nearby Ireland. In 1764 Lord Mansfield, for instance, professed himself startled when he heard that the French had been subjected to British law. It is a fundamental maxim, he told George Grenville, that a conquered country keeps its own laws until the conqueror gives new ones. Even colonists, he said, anticipating Samuel Adams, are bound by only those laws of England which are adapted to or proper for their situation.[50]

Quebec had been ruled by British appointees since 1760, first by the military and then by a governor and council after 1764. Religious freedom had been guaranteed to the French Catholics in the surrender of 1760 and the Treaty of Paris in 1763, but the role of the church hierarchy was left unclear. So too were questions of law, of taxation, and of land tenure. Whenever British officials thought of Quebec, their solution was the creation of an elective legislature, an idea heartily supported by the few hundred British and American merchants and fur traders who moved to Quebec after 1760. Since Catholics could neither vote nor hold office, this tiny minority would have been able to govern the vast majority of French inhabitants.

There were several investigations concerning Quebec and innumerable reports, but the details of the Quebec Act were not settled upon until the end of 1773. However, action was delayed until after Parliament had adopted the Intolerable Acts to punish Massachusetts for the Boston Tea Party, and the Quebec Act was not adopted until June 1774. So far as government was concerned, most of the provisions of the Quebec Act were the result of the persuasiveness of a governor whose ideal was the maintenance of a feudal society. Guy Carleton, who became governor in 1766, was a member of the landed gentry and a military man who soon became enamored of "the decayed remnants of a feudal hierarchy." In repeated reports he urged the establishment of permanent government based upon the power of the French seigneurs and the Roman Catholic hierarchy in Canada. He vigorously opposed British officials who thought an elected legislature was the answer, and the Anglo-American merchants in Canada who demanded one. He went to England in 1770 and was so successful that by 1771 the idea of an elected legislature was dropped and it was agreed that future land grants should be made upon the feudal basis used before the conquest. Under the Quebec Act, government continued to be by a governor and an enlarged council, which included French Roman Catholic landlords. It meant that in the future as in the past the mer-

[50] 24 Dec., GP, II, 476–78.

chants and the common Frenchmen would be ruled by a military man at the head of a "foreign" aristocracy.[51]

The merchants, most of whom were interested in the fur trade, did gain one economic advantage: the guarantee that the great interior would once more be under the government of Quebec as it had been in the days of French rule before 1760. The fur traders had combined with American land speculators to end imperial control of the West in 1768, but they were soon alarmed by the threat of anarchy which followed, and the longer range threat that the fur-trading areas northwest of the Ohio River would be ruined by agricultural settlements. They appealed to the governor and council of Quebec. A committee investigated and reported in April 1769 that there was only one solution: the annexation of the region northwest of the Ohio River to Quebec. In terms of past history, geography, and economics, the contention was sound.[52]

Pressure from the fur traders was but one source of the action taken. By 1773, British leaders realized that the abandonment of regulation in 1768 was a mistake. The iniquitous practices of fur traders and the constant push of settlers toward Indian lands raised the specter of new and expensive Indian wars. Most of the pioneer settlers were simply men who wanted farms of their own, but the image of them in Britain, as along the American seaboard, was one of murderers and bandits, not of noble pioneers in the wilderness. The conviction that such people should be stopped, and the realization that they could not be stopped by the "permanent" boundary line of 1768, contributed to the decision to attach the Old Northwest to Quebec.

The "permanent" boundary line was a failure in another respect, for it was opposed by powerful land speculators in Britain and America. Official support of Vandalia in Britain rendered the line south of the Ohio meaningless, and by the end of 1773 the line north of the river seemed on the point of becoming so. The threat there came not from ordinary settlers but from a group of Pennsylvania speculators and their London friends and relatives, some of whom were involved in the Indiana-Vandalia scheme. They were impatient with the delays of British bureaucracy and looked for a "legal" device to by-pass the need for British approval. They found it in the so-called Camden-Yorke opinion. Back in 1757, Lord Camden, when

---

[51] See Donald Creighton, *The Empire of the St. Lawrence* (Toronto, 1956), part I, from which I have quoted.

[52] For the best account of the background of the Quebec Act see A. L. Burt, *The Old Province of Quebec* (Minneapolis, 1933). See also Marjorie G. Reid, "The Quebec Fur-Traders and Western Policy, 1763–1774," CHR, VI (1925).

he was Charles Pratt, the attorney general, and Charles Yorke, the solicitor general, had advised the Privy Council that grants of land to the East India Company by the "Mogul or any of the Indian Princes or Governments" did not need confirmation by the Crown. By the 1770s Lord Camden was an eager participant in the Vandalia project but whether or not he told the speculators of his opinion in 1757 is unknown. What is known is that William Murray, Indian trader and agent for a group of Philadelphia speculators, was back in America by the spring of 1773 with what purported to be a true copy. It was in fact a carefully edited version which left out the word "Mogul" and any reference to the East India Company. It declared that in any land acquired by treaty or grant from "Indian Princes or Governments," the king's letters patent were unnecessary, "the property of the soil vesting in the Grantees by the Indian Grants. . . ." [53]

Armed with this bit of forgery, which promoted American Indian chiefs to princes, the speculators went to work. In 1773, William Murray, as agent for the newly formed Illinois Company, purchased from the Indians a tract of land lying north of the Ohio and between it and the Mississippi. The new company sent a copy of the Camden-Yorke opinion and its deed to Lord Dunmore, and petitioned for his support on the ground that the land lay within the bounds of Virginia. Two years later the same group organized the Wabash Company, with Dunmore as a member, and bought two additional tracts lying on both sides of the Wabash River. Meanwhile, Dunmore was delighted with the new device for acquiring claims to land. He sent the petition of the Illinois Company to London with his hearty approval. He argued that even if the title were defective the lands would be settled anyway, for "experience shows nothing (so fond as the Americans are of migration) can stop the concourse of people" toward those lands. He insisted that it was wise to encourage "men of credit and ability" to take up land in the "back countries" to prevent "their becoming the asylum, as they now are, of all the disorderly and unruly people of the colonies, people who fly from debts and from punishments due to their crimes, and who, carrying with them an abhorrence of all authority and control, establish themselves in defiance of both and become the continual plague and embarrassment of every government in America, and may in the end prove dangerous to their very existence." [54] Despite his presentation of the accepted picture of frontiersmen, Dunmore was roundly denounced for his

[53] Sosin, *Whitehall*, 229–31, 259–67.
[54] Illinois Company petition to Dunmore, 19 April and Dunmore to SS, 16 May 1774, C.O. 5/1352.

support of the Illinois Company and was ordered to announce publicly that its purchase had been disallowed by the Crown.[55] The growing chaos in the West after the abandonment of imperial control in 1768, the futility of boundary lines to stop either settlers or speculators such as the Illinois Company and the Virginians, and the demands of the Canadian fur traders, all contributed to the decision to attach the Old Northwest to the Province of Quebec in the Quebec Act of June 1774.

The Quebec Act had an immediate impact on the colonies to the southward. To the New Englanders it was but another "Intolerable Act" aimed at them. The guarantee of the Catholic religion to the French in Quebec aroused the probably simulated but politically useful alarm of the popular leaders and the real fears of their less sophisticated but devoutly Protestant followers. The act's impact on the emotions of Virginia expansionists—already alarmed by Vandalia and the new land policy of February 1774—must be partially imagined, but it can be partially documented. Thomas Jefferson, who was not a land speculator, denied 150 years of history in his *Summary View of the Rights of British America* when he asserted that the idea of the king's ownership of American lands was a legal fiction and that the king should be told that he had no right to grant them. And two years later in the Declaration of Independence, Jefferson listed among the many "repeated injuries and usurpations" of George III his "raising the conditions of new appropriations of lands." [56]

ॐ

Pennsylvania and New York had few of the problems that concerned colonies to the north and the south of them. Political calm seemed to prevail, although in Pennsylvania there was evidence that the recent past could not be buried. The cracks opened in the Quaker party during the

[55] 8 Sept., C.O. 5/1352. For a good brief account of the Illinois Company and the other speculative land companies between 1749 and 1776, see Gipson, *British Empire*, XI, chapter XIII.

[56] That Virginia was driven into the Revolution by British western policy is affirmed by C. W. Alvord, "Virginia and the West: An Interpretation," MVHR, III (1916–17), and denied by such Virginia historians as H. J. Eckenrode, *The Revolution in Virginia* (New York, 1916) and Abernethy, *Western Lands*. The argument over British restrictions on western expansion as a "cause" of the Revolution is a sterile one. To assert that the restrictions were a main cause is to oversimplify a complex development. On the other hand, to argue that British restrictions had no impact on Virginia opinion is to ignore the evidence.

The debate over planter debts is equally futile. Some have argued that the debts were the principal reason for the Virginia planters' willingness to revolt, while others assert that they had no direct effect.

Seven Years War had not narrowed. Franklin, its mainstay, had been in England since 1764 and seemed likely to spend the rest of his years there, well paid by his deputy-postmastership for North America and his numerous colonial agencies. He reveled in the social and intellectual life so remote from his Boston beginnings, and even from his Philadelphia years. By 1770 he had largely abandoned his mission to convert Pennsylvania into a royal colony and was working to become one of the proprietors of a colony himself, that of Vandalia. His charm and political skill, which had kept the mechanics of Philadelphia within the ranks of the Quaker party, gradually lost its potency, separated as he was from his admirers. Furthermore, the other leader of the Quaker party, Joseph Galloway, had none of Franklin's political appeal, and his defense in 1765 of the right of Parliament to tax, and his opposition to non-importation, alienated the mechanics who had tasted power during those years. Then, shortly before the election in the fall of 1770, Galloway's former partner, William Goddard, attacked him in a pamphlet, *The Partnership*. Goddard told how in January 1767 Galloway and Thomas Wharton had secretly financed the founding of his paper, the *Pennsylvania Chronicle*, for the purpose of fighting the proprietors and of rebuilding Franklin's battered reputation after the Stamp Act crisis. Goddard's picture of Galloway as an enemy of American liberties had its impact. Many of the mechanics, already disillusioned, deserted the Quaker party. The proprietary leader, John Dickinson, whom Galloway had kept out of the legislature for five years, was elected from Philadelphia. Galloway himself was forced to seek election from Bucks county and he never regained his influence in Philadelphia, although he remained speaker of the assembly.[57] Franklin so little understood what had happened that he decried the "abuse and ingratitude" shown his friend.[58]

There were hints too of the revolution that was to take place in 1776. The Philadelphia artisans had long voted for the gentry presented for their approval, but shortly before the election in 1770 one of them proclaimed: "we glory in the despicable name of mechanic, let us . . . convince the great ones that truly wise and honest men, worthy to represent a free people, can be found amongst us." [59] None were found in 1770, but in 1775 and 1776 when the gentlemen leaders of both the proprietary and Quaker parties balked at independence, new leaders from the "lower orders" did

[57] Schlesinger, *Prelude to Independence*, 118–22; Thayer, *Pennsylvania*, 149–51.
[58] Franklin to Abel James, 2 Dec. 1772, *Writings*(S), V, 461.
[59] "A Brother Chip," PG, 27 Sept.

appear. As a result, the new state of Pennsylvania, unlike most others, was to be created by men almost unheard of before 1776, and they embedded their distrust of the aristocracy in the constitution they wrote.

New York was even calmer than Pennsylvania. The merchants who had defeated non-importation had had enough of interference in their affairs by the populace and its leaders. "Coriolanus" probably expressed the feelings of most merchants when he lashed out at "the aspiring demagogue whose unprincipled actions originate from a thirst for preeminence and popular applause, who, if he could thereby gratify the mob, would root up order and distinction, unhinge the portals of government, trample on the laws, and restore all things to their pristine level. . . ." [60] Certainly New York maintained "order and distinction" until the end of 1773. The Sons of Liberty were defeated in the city elections in the fall of 1770 and thereafter seemed to vanish utterly, and the onetime hero of the populace, Alexander McDougall, vanished with them. The supreme court never tried him for libel, and when the assembly jailed him for contempt the supreme court released him on a writ of habeas corpus. Finally, in the spring of 1771, without a ripple of excitement, the court dismissed the case.[61]

The assembly, firmly controlled by the De Lanceys, had no trouble with the new governor, Sir William Tryon, who was determined to avoid political rows after the tumultuous climax of his career as governor of North Carolina at Alamance Creek. The assembly had won its battle with Parliament over the Quartering Act and continued to give money to the troops on its own terms. It had won too the old dispute over paper money, and early in 1771 issued £120,000.[62]

The New Yorkers were in fact extraordinarily quiet, and when the indefatigable Boston agitator, Dr. Thomas Young, chided the New Yorkers for their lethargy, for their failure to agitate, or at the very least, to reprint articles from the Boston newspapers, schoolmaster Hugh Hughes replied that the common people were ignorant. The doctor retorted: "You complain of the ignorance of the common people. You may as well complain of the roughness of the desert! Our people would have known as little as yours had we taken as little pains to instruct them." As one of Boston's popular leaders, Young had no illusions about "mass" movements by the people at large, and he went on to give some advice about the methods of

[60] NYG, 27 Aug. 1770.
[61] Dorothy R. Dillon, *The New York Triumvirate* . . . *William Livingston, John Morin Scott, William Smith, Jr.* (New York, 1949), 118–21.
[62] Becker, *New York,* 95–96.

political agitation.[63] Such methods were being used in Boston, where by the end of 1772 the popular leaders were recovering from the setback they had suffered in 1770 and 1771 and were well on the way to their triumph at Boston Harbor in December 1773.

[63] 20 Dec. 1772, Misc. Bound, XIV, MHS.

XVI

The Revival of Popular Power in New England

New England, and above all Massachusetts, had been the storm center of opposition to British policies ever since 1760. The popular leaders of Boston got control of the Massachusetts legislature in 1766 and held it until 1770. They won popular support and achieved power because of their aggressive opposition to British policies, and because they charged that their domestic political enemies, who controlled the legislature until 1766, were supporters of British policies. When Britain retreated in 1770, the control of the popular leaders collapsed despite desperate efforts to maintain it. Whereas most popular leaders in the colonies remained quiet after 1770, some of those in Massachusetts did not, and one above all others. The war for independence had many "fathers," but among the fathers one is entitled to a very high place. His name was Samuel Adams.

෫෪

Samuel Adams has been the object of passionate defenses and equally passionate attacks from his day to this. He has been called the last of the Puritans, a demagogue, a democrat, a reactionary, a propagandist, and even a mercantilist, and he has been described as suffering from an inferiority complex. Since he destroyed most of his papers, one must depend on the slight written record he left to posterity and that points in only one direction—that of a defender of the liberty of his beloved Massachusetts against all outside interference, whether from the British government before 1776 or that of the United States afterwards.

The opinions of his contemporaries were as divergent as those of subsequent biographers. Loyalist Peter Oliver, the last chief justice of colonial Massachusetts, reported a celebrated artist as saying that if he wanted to draw a picture of the devil he would ask Samuel Adams to sit for him. Oliver agreed that anyone who saw his face could see the "malignity of his heart. He was a person of understanding . . . he understood human nature, in low life, so well that he could turn the minds of the great vulgar as well as the small into any course that he might choose . . . and he never failed of employing his abilities to the vilest purposes. . . . He was so thorough a Machiavellian that he divested himself of every worthy principle, and would stick at no crime to accomplish his ends." Oliver asserted that Adams was an embezzler and escaped punishment only because he ingratiated himself with John Hancock "in the same manner that the Devil is represented seducing Eve, by a constant whispering at his ear," and thus was "set at large to commit his ravages on government until he undermined the foundations of it, and not one stone had been left upon another." He soon outrivaled James Otis in popularity. "His was all serpentine cunning, Mr. Otis was rash, unguarded, foulmouthed, and openly spiteful," which disgusted the sanctimonious; Adams "had always a religious mask ready for his occasions; he could transform his self into an angel of light with the weak religionist, and with the abandoned he would disrobe his self and appear with his cloven foot and in his native blackness of darkness. He had a good voice and was a master in vocal music. This genius he improved by instituting singing societies of mechanics where he presided, and embraced such opportunities to the inculcating sedition till it had ripened into rebellion. His power over weak minds was truly surprising." [1]

John Adams, who was not weak-minded, gives an utterly different picture of the man in 1765: "Adams I believe has the most thorough understanding of liberty, and her resources, in the temper and character of the people, though not in the law and constitution, as well as the most habitual, radical love of it, of any of them—as well as the most correct, genteel, and artful pen. He is a man of refined policy, steadfast integrity, exquisite humanity, genteel erudition, obliging, engaging manners, real as well as professed piety, and a universal good character, unless it should be admitted that he is too attentive to the public and not enough so, to himself and his family." [2]

---

[1] Douglass Adair and John A. Schutz, eds., *Peter Oliver's Origin and Progress of the American Rebellion: A Tory View* (San Marino, Calif., 1961), 39–41. For an unfriendly twentieth-century view of Adams see Clifford K. Shipton, "Samuel Adams," *Sibley's Harvard Graduates*, X (Boston, 1958). The best biography, because it is relatively accurate and because it shows an understanding of Massachusetts politics, is Ralph V. Harlow, *Samuel Adams, Promoter of the American Revolution: A Study in Psychology and Politics* (New York, 1923).
[2] *Diary*, 23 Dec. 1765.

Perhaps the most penetrating tribute of all came from one whose plans he helped defeat at the First Continental Congress, Joseph Galloway. Giving Adams all the credit, Galloway described him as "a man, who though by no means remarkable for brilliant abilities, yet is equal to most men in popular intrigue, and the management of a faction. He eats little, drinks little, sleeps little, thinks much, and is most decisive and indefatigable in the pursuit of his objects."[3] Long after Samuel Adams was dead, John Adams provided the most lucid and perhaps the most valid estimate of his distant cousin's place in history: "Mr. Adams was born and tempered a wedge of steel to split the knot of *lignum vitae*, which tied North America to Great Britain."[4]

Born in Boston in 1722, he was one of the large family of a sea-captain who was also a prosperous brewer and a leader in the popular politics of the town. Adams was graduated from Harvard in 1740 and, after dabbling in law and business, went to work for his father. He inherited a third of his father's estate in 1748 but it soon wasted away, partly because he had neither interest in nor talent for business, and partly because the estate was subject to suits following the collapse of the land bank of 1740 in which his father had been a prominent stockholder. The bank had been declared illegal by act of Parliament at the urging of Boston merchants, and thereafter its stockholders were the legal prey of the bank's creditors. Samuel Adams was among the victims.

Adams's interest was in politics and his talent for it in time approached genius. He was first elected to office in 1753 as an assessor, and then in 1756 as one of Boston's tax collectors. After nine years in office he was in debt, living in a run-down house, and dependent upon his second wife and the neighbors for food and clothing for himself and his children. Furthermore, he and the other four collectors owed the town £18,000 in uncollected taxes, his share being £8000. Hutchinson and his followers charged that Adams was an embezzler, but plainly he was not. Whether from a kind heart or from political guile, he simply had not collected all the taxes levied, and the Boston voters joyfully re-elected him and the other delinquent collectors. Adams refused re-election in 1765, and in 1772 the voters finally excused him from collecting the amount still due.[5]

By 1763 Adams was a member of the inner ring, the "Caucus Club," which managed the popular politics of Boston from a "smoke-filled room." Wistfully, John Adams, still an outsider, reported that he had just learned that the club met in the garret of Tom Dawes, adjutant of the Boston regi-

[3] EHD, IX, 801   [4] To William Tudor, 5 June 1817, Works, X, 263.
[5] BTR, XVI, 150; XVIII, 69.

ment. "There they smoke tobacco till you cannot see from one end of the garret to the other. There they drink flip, I suppose, and there they choose a moderator, who puts questions to the vote regularly, and selectmen, assessors, collectors, wardens, fire-wards, and representatives are regularly chosen before they are chosen in the town." [6]

In the spring of 1764 Adams wrote the town's instructions to its representatives in the legislature, the instructions which were the first important blast at the new British policies, and at the same time an attack on the Hutchinson oligarchy. In the fall of 1765 after the death of Oxenbridge Thacher, a special town meeting elected Adams to the legislature. The next spring, after the political revolution which gave the popular party control of the House of Representatives, he was elected clerk of the house, a vastly important strategic post which he held until the final dissolution of the colonial legislature in 1774, just as it elected delegates to the First Continental Congress. As clerk he handled all the important documents, kept the journals, served on committees, and either drafted or helped to draft some of the most important of the stream of messages, resolutions, and petitions that kept the Massachusetts legislature at the very front of opposition to British policies. With James Otis's increasing insanity after 1769, Adams became the principal leader of the popular party in the legislature, and the undisputed leader of the Boston town meeting.

Constantly watching for younger men who could be brought into the popular party, he recruited a brilliant galaxy that included Dr. Joseph Warren, Dr. Benjamin Church, and Josiah Quincy, Jr. [7] One of the most remarkable was his country cousin, John Adams. In 1765 when Boston demanded that the governor and council open the courts despite the Stamp Act, it appointed James Otis, Jeremiah Gridley, and the almost unknown John Adams to argue its case. Puzzled, John Adams asked his cousin why he had been picked. The reply was candor itself: John Adams would be friendly to Boston out of gratitude, it would help his practice as a lawyer, and perhaps Braintree, finding the eyes of Boston upon him, would elect him to office the next March. [8] And that is what Braintree did, in a political revolution that shook the little town. [9]

In the spring of 1766 the newly rich John Hancock was elected one of Boston's representatives. As Samuel and John Adams walked past Hancock's mansion after the election, Samuel pointed to it and said: "this

[6] Feb. 1763, *Diary*, I, 238.
[7] John Adams to William Tudor, 8 Feb. 1819, *Works*, X, 364.
[8] *Diary*, 25 Dec. 1765.
[9] See John Adams's diary and the Braintree town records reprinted in EHD, IX, 303-9.

town has done a wise thing today. . . . They have made that young man's fortune their own." [10] From 1766 until 1775 Hancock was the money bags of the popular party and a tool in the hands of Samuel Adams. He was occasionally restive but Hutchinson understood his weakness: he was a vain man whose "ruling passion was a fondness for popular applause." [11] Peter Oliver was characteristically more bitter when he wrote that Hancock's "understanding was of the dwarf size, but his ambition, upon the accession to so great an estate, was upon the gigantic. . . . His mind was a mere *tabula rasa*" for Adams to write upon. Although Hancock sometimes tried to escape, "Adams, like the cuttlefish, would discharge his muddy liquid and darken the water to such an hue, that the other was lost to his way, and by his tergiversations in the cloudy vortex, would again be seized and at last secured." Hancock was, said Oliver, "as closely attached to the hindermost part of Mr. Adams as the rattles are affixed to the tail of the rattlesnake." [12]

Little did Samuel Adams realize in 1766 that the young man he handled so deftly would in time learn a few simple political lessons and that from 1780 until his death in 1793 Hancock would be the political boss of Massachusetts.[13]

In addition to all his other activities, Adams worked constantly to build up a political following and seized upon every occasion for a popular political meeting. "Pope's Day," 5 November, became an annual rally after 1765. In 1767, St. Patrick's Day and 18 March, the anniversary of the repeal of the Stamp Act, were combined in a political celebration. Even the date of Andrew Oliver's first resignation as stamp distributor became an occasion for annual rejoicing. John Adams attended such a meeting at Dorchester on 14 August 1769, when he dined with 350 Sons of Liberty. Later he noted in his diary: "Otis and Adams are politic in promoting these festivals, for they tinge the minds of the people; they impregnate them with the sentiments of liberty; they render the people fond of their leaders in the cause, and adverse and bitter against all opposers." [14]

The peak of popular agitation was reached with the Boston Massacre, and the peak of popular power with the removal of the troops from Boston

[10] John Adams to William Tudor, 1 June 1817, *Works*, X, 260.
[11] Thomas Hutchinson, *The History of the Colony and Province of Massachusetts-Bay* (L. S. Mayo, ed., 3 vols., Cambridge, Mass., 1936), III, 214.
[12] Oliver, *American Rebellion*, 40.   [13] Harlow, *Adams*, 304–6, 345–54.
[14] 14 Aug.

and the second flight of the customs board to Castle William in Boston Harbor. Thereafter that power declined. It began with the failure to secure an immediate trial of Captain Thomas Preston and the eight soldiers accused of murder. The popular leaders did not realize it nor did Thomas Hutchinson, who was so badly shaken he swore that he had not the "strength of constitution" to withstand the whole force of the other branches of government, and asked that a "person of superior powers of body and mind" be made governor in his place.[15] For months his courage failed him, and General Gage did not help by asking him to delay the trials of the soldiers, and then passing on a rumor that Boston had ordered enough "accoutrements and caps" in England to outfit 4000 men.[16]

Within a few days after the massacre the town printed its version, replete with ninety-six depositions attacking the soldiers, but omitting more than twenty in their defense.[17] The Boston selectmen hired Robert Treat Paine of Taunton to represent the families of the slain men, offered to arrange the evidence "properly," and sent him a copy of the town's printed narrative, "by the reading of which you will enter into the spirit of the thing." The "common enemy" had engaged most of Boston's lawyers, said the selectmen. This last was a lie, for very few Boston lawyers had the courage to defend Captain Preston. The agreement of two of them to do so, however, represented what appeared to be a startling break in the popular party ranks, and a forecast of what was to come. The day after the massacre one of Preston's friends asked John Adams to undertake the defense. Adams agreed to gather evidence and he was soon joined by Josiah Quincy, Jr.[18] But despite the popular uproar for blood, and threats of violence, the superior court courageously delayed the trials again and again.

Meanwhile, the news created a flurry in England. The ministry defeated the demand of the opposition for an investigation of the use of the military in America.[19] Governor Thomas Hutchinson was told that if the soldiers were condemned he was to order a stay of execution until the king could

[15] To SS, 27 March, C.O. 5/759.   [16] 30 April, Misc. Bound, XIII, MHS.
[17] Frederic Kidder, ed., *History of the Boston Massacre* . . . (Albany, 1870), 25–113, reprints *A Short Narrative of the Horrid Massacre in Boston*. It is also reprinted in Jensen, *Tracts*, 207–32.
[18] William Molineux to Paine, 9 March, Robert Treat Paine Papers, MHS. Something of a mystery surrounds Josiah Quincy, Jr.'s service as defense attorney. When his father expressed shock and swore he would not believe it, the son replied that he had at first refused and continued to refuse "until advised and urged to undertake it by an Adams, a Hancock, a Molineux, a Cushing, a Henshaw, a Pemberton, a Warren, a Cooper, and a Phillips." Josiah Quincy, *Memoir of the Life of Josiah Quincy* . . . (Boston, 3rd ed., 1875), 26–28.
[19] See Chapter XII above.

be heard from.[20] General Gage, as usual, was told to support the civil authority when called upon, and to occupy and improve Castle William as quarters for one regiment and as an "asylum in the last extremity for the officers of the Crown. . . ." [21] Finally, the headquarters of the British navy in North America were moved from Halifax to Boston, where it was supposed to check further violence, prevent illicit trade, and support the customs officials.[22]

Such measures had no immediate effect in Boston, where Thomas Hutchinson continued to worry about popular violence,[23] and he and British officers remained convinced that a fair trial would be impossible.[24] But when Captain Preston was tried between 24 and 30 October, the result was an acquittal. The popular leaders were furious. The jury was rigged, William Palfrey told John Wilkes: the sheriff packed it with Preston's friends after Preston had challenged so many properly chosen members of the panel that the sheriff was able to pick whom he pleased. "By this kind of management the last blow has been given to the expiring liberties of America." [25] But Hutchinson declared it a "fair trial" and Preston informed General Gage: "I take the liberty of wishing you joy of the complete victory obtained over the knaves and foolish villains of Boston." The verdict was to the "entire satisfaction of every honest mind, and great mortification of every bloodthirsty and malicious Bostonian." [26] In December six of the eight soldiers were acquitted and two were found guilty of manslaughter, but they pled benefit of clergy and were discharged after being burned on the hands.[27] Attempts to appeal Preston's acquittal and to sue him for damages failed and he sailed to England to be rewarded with a pension of £200 a year.

The abandonment of non-importation in October was a body blow to the popular leaders; the acquittal of the soldiers left them staggering, but the final trial of the series rendered them ludicrous and more suspect than

---

20 SS to Hutchinson, 14, 26 April, C.O. 5/759.
21 SS to Gage, 26 April, 12 June, Gage, Corres., II, 102–4.
22 4–6 July, APC:CS, V, 263–64; SS to Admiralty, C.O. 5/759.
23 To SS, 11 Sept., C.O. 5/759.
24 Randolph G. Adams, "New Light on the Boston Massacre," Proceedings of the American Antiquarian Society [AASP], n.s. XLVII (1937), reprints the correspondence among British officials in America between March and the end of the trials.
25 23–30 Oct., CSMP, XXXIV, 423–26.
26 Hutchinson to SS, 30 Oct., C.O. 5/759; Preston to Gage, 31 Oct., AASP, n.s. XLVII, 338–40.
27 Kidder, Boston Massacre, 123–285, reprints a "shorthand" record of the trial. Much valuable new material has been published in the Legal Papers of John Adams. The entire third volume consists of materials relating to the trials.

ever. Edward Mainwaring, a customs officer, and some others were accused of firing on the crowd from the windows of the customs house on 5 March. The only evidence against them was the testimony of Mainwaring's French servant boy. At the trial in December it was proved that the boy was on the other side of town on the night of 5 March; the jury acquitted Mainwaring without leaving their seats.[28] In the end, except for the two soldiers who were branded, the only one punished as a result of the Boston Massacre was Mainwaring's servant, who did not understand English. He was convicted of perjury, put into the pillory, and whipped twenty-five stripes, while the men who induced him to perjury were never legally identified.[29]

But Samuel Adams kept up the battle. As "Vindex" in the Boston Gazette he excoriated the "miscarriage" of justice that had allowed the escape of the "murderers." [30] As for John Adams, in March 1773, after he had heard the third of the orations commemorating the massacre, he wrote of his defense: "It was . . . one of the most gallant, generous, manly, and disinterested actions of my whole life, and one of the best pieces of service I ever rendered my country. Judgment of death against those soldiers would have been as foul a stain upon this country as the executions of the Quakers or witches, anciently. As the evidence was, the verdict of the jury was exactly right." [31]

The split between the cousins was symbolic of what happened to the popular party after 1770. For instance, on Hillsborough's orders the legislature had been meeting at Cambridge since 1769 and the house had refused to do anything except essential business until it was moved back to Boston. In October 1770, despite Samuel Adams's pleas, the legislature abandoned its "strike." [32] In the spring election of 1771 the popular leaders barely managed to keep control of the House of Representatives and Hutchinson was delighted to find himself well treated. "We have not been so quiet these five years," he reported. "The people about the country have certainly altered their conduct, and in this town, if it were not for two or three Adamses, we should do well enough." Hutchinson could not account for John Adams, but as for Samuel Adams, "I doubt whether there is a greater incendiary in the King's dominion or a man of greater malignity of heart, who less scruples any measure ever so criminal to accomplish his purposes. . . ." [33] Only in the Boston town meeting did the popular lead-

[28] Hutchinson to SS, 12 Dec., C.O. 5/760.   [29] VG(PD), 11 April 1771.
[30] Reprinted in Writings, II, 77ff.   [31] Diary, 5 March.
[32] Harlow, Adams, 159–68, contains the best account of the break-up of the popular party.
[33] To SS, 2 April 1771, C.O. 5/760; Hosmer, Hutchinson, 192, 215–16.

ers retain any real power, which, Hutchinson said, the persons of "best characters and best estates" did not attend because they were sure to be outvoted "by men of the lowest order, all being admitted and it being very rare that any scrutiny is made into the qualifications of voters." [34]

By the end of 1771 John Hancock was promising that he would never again follow the lead of Samuel Adams, and Hutchinson's friends undertook to "blow the coals." And to Hutchinson's joy, James Otis, who had recovered temporarily and was elected to the legislature in the spring of 1771, was in December "carried off . . . in a post-chaise, bound hand and foot. He has been as good as his word—set the Province in a flame, and perished in the attempt." [35] The very nadir of popular party fortunes was reached in the spring of 1772 when John Hancock and his new if temporary friends tried to prevent Samuel Adams's election from Boston. Of the votes cast for representatives, Thomas Cushing got 699, Hancock 690, William Phillips 668, and Adams but 505.[36]

By 1772 the Hutchinson-Oliver oligarchy seemed in an impregnable position. Hutchinson was governor, his brother-in-law, Andrew Oliver, the ex-stamp distributor, was lieutenant governor, and Andrew's brother, Peter Oliver, had succeeded Hutchinson as chief justice of the superior court. The family combine thus occupied the most powerful appointive posts in the colony. Furthermore, as in the days before 1766, the legislature supported Hutchinson, not the Boston leaders. Hutchinson, who had been appointed governor in October 1770, was a far abler man than his predecessor and he carried the fight to his political enemies by encouraging newspapers to fight the popular press with its own weapons.[37] But Hutchinson's satisfaction with the disasters of his enemies was short-lived. By the end of 1772 Samuel Adams had regained some of his support and was shortly to have more power than ever, both in Boston and in the colony. And by then he had a political organization such as the Boston leaders had not had before: the Boston committee of correspondence.

Samuel Adams never despaired and, unlike others, he never gave up. He still had some loyal allies such as Edes and Gill of the *Boston Gazette*, and a new recruit in young Isaiah Thomas, who began his remarkable career in American journalism when he founded the *Massachusetts Spy* in the

[34] To SS, 19 April, C.O. 5/760.
[35] Hutchinson to Gage, 1 Dec., and to Bernard, 3 Dec., Hosmer, *Hutchinson*, 222–24.
[36] Ibid. 226; BTR, XVIII, 78.
[37] Schlesinger, *Prelude to Independence*, 132–34, 143–44.

summer of 1770, a newspaper even more radical in language and views than the *Gazette*.[38] Perhaps the most extraordinary of Adams's co-workers was Dr. Thomas Young, who, unlike the devout Adams, was a religious radical. Young was born in New York and became a remarkably successful doctor. He moved to Albany, but finding it a dull place during the Stamp Act crisis, took his family to Boston, where he found full scope for his eloquent tongue and pen. He worked untiringly until the overthrow of the royal government in 1774. After a brief stay in Rhode Island, he moved to Philadelphia in 1775, where he soon became one of that small group which overthrew the Quaker assembly and wrote the constitution of the new state. The career of this able but little-known revolutionary was cut short in 1777 when, as a senior army surgeon in Philadelphia, he died of a fever.[39]

The Boston leaders had no great issues as before 1770, but they worked with what they had and they were geniuses at propaganda on every level. On the highest, they reiterated their political and constitutional ideas lucidly, brilliantly, and persuasively. On quite another level they appealed to religious prejudice, always easily aroused in New England. They began an attack on the Anglican church in the 1760s, which they continued during the 1770s. The occasion was the renewed demand on the part of certain English bishops and of American Anglican clergymen for the establishment of a bishop in America. The proposal aroused the ire of the multitude of dissenting sects and of many Anglican laymen as well. There was little likelihood that the ministry in London would agree to such a step, as Benjamin Franklin reported in 1768,[40] but the popular leaders ignored such reports, for men like Samuel Adams were well aware of the political uses to which the issue could be put. Canny politicians and ministers alike stirred up the bigotry of ordinary people, and most effectively when they blurred the distinction between the Anglican church and the "Whore of Babylon" at Rome, thus preparing the way for the violent if brief reaction to the Quebec Act in the northern colonies.[41]

[38] Ibid. 131–32.
[39] Henry H. Edes, "Memoir of Dr. Thomas Young, 1731–1777," CSMP, XI (1906–7).
[40] Franklin to John Ross, 14 May, *Writings*(S), V, 133–34. The same report reached Boston during 1768 in a letter from Thomas Hollis to the Rev. Andrew Eliot, an intimate of the popular leaders. See Eliot to Hollis, 17 Oct., MHSC, 4 ser. IV, 429. While the question of an Anglican bishop was a factor in the formation of American opinion, it was only one, and should not be overemphasized.
[41] Arthur L. Cross, *The Anglican Episcopate and the American Colonies* (New York, 1902), chapters VI–XI, is a detailed account of the newspaper and pamphlet warfare after 1763. For a summary of anti-Catholic propaganda in New England before 1774,

The Boston Massacre was likewise an ideal source for popular agitation. Beginning on 5 March 1771, orations to commemorate the event were given annually until after the war for independence. The orations followed a similar pattern, beginning with the devastation wrought by standing armies in all of history, and building up in the end to a climactic description of "the Massacre." On 5 March 1772 Joseph Warren declared that [42]

> . . . the fatal fifth of March, 1770, can never be forgotten. The horrors of that dreadful night are but too deeply impressed on our hearts. Language is too feeble to paint the emotions of our souls, when our streets were stained with the blood of our brethren; when our ears were wounded by the groans of the dying, and our eyes were tormented with the sight of the mangled bodies of the dead.
>
> When our alarmed imagination presented to our view our houses wrapped in flames, our children subjected to the barbarous caprice of the raging soldiery; our beauteous virgins exposed to all the insolence of unbridled passion; our virtuous wives, endeared to us by every tender tie, falling a sacrifice to worse than brutal violence, and perhaps, like the famed Lucretia, distracted with anguish and despair, ending their wretched lives by their own fair hands.

Warren was again asked to give the oration in 1775, only a few months before he died on Bunker Hill, and he outdid his earlier efforts.[43]

> Approach we then the melancholy walk of death. Hither let me call the gay companion; here let him drop a farewell tear . . . hither let me lead the tender mother to weep over her beloved son: come widowed mourner, here satiate thy grief; behold thy murdered husband gasping on the ground, and to complete the pompous show of wretchedness, bring in each hand thy infant children to bewail their father's fate: take heed ye orphan babes, lest, whilst your streaming eyes are fixed upon the ghastly corpse, your feet slide on the stones bespattered with your father's brains.

By 1775 his listeners had perhaps forgotten that the "massacre" was little more than the culmination of a series of street brawls, and that the five killed were all bachelors. Nevertheless, the orations did keep alive the ancient Anglo-American distrust of a standing army and the belief in the ne-

see Charles H. Metzger, S.J., *The Quebec Act: A Primary Cause of the American Revolution* (New York, 1936), chapter II.
[42] *Orations . . . To Commemorate the Evening of the Fifth of March, 1770 . . .* (2nd ed., Boston, 1807), 20.
[43] Ibid. 63.

cessity of the subordination of military to civil power, which was to find expression in so many of the new state constitutions.

Adams and his cohorts did have one political principle with which to carry on the battle against Thomas Hutchinson. After 1768 his salary as chief justice was paid from customs revenues, and in 1770, when he and Andrew Oliver were appointed governor and lieutenant governor, their salaries were ordered paid from the duty on tea.[44] The *Boston Gazette* learned of this fact as soon as the two men did of their promotions. The campaign against British salaries for colonial officials had gone on ever since the Townshend revenue act, and it was now redoubled. Samuel Adams reported in the fall of 1771 that Hutchinson had received his salary from funds which the customs board had collected from Americans without their consent, and that in time the money might be used "for the support of standing armies and ships of war; episcopates and their numerous ecclesiastical retinue; pensioners, placemen, and other jobbers, for an abandoned and shameless ministry; hirelings, pimps, parasites, panders, prostitutes, and whores." [45]

Even such fervent appeals aroused little interest in the doldrums after 1770. No success was achieved until the summer of 1772, when the ministry ordered the salaries of the five superior court justices paid from customs revenues.[46] The Boston leaders soon heard of the order and Dr. Thomas Young reported: "we are brewing some things which will make some people's heads reel at a very moderate age." And, he added, "ripeness for great enterprises advances slowly; but perhaps that is the best fruit which requires time to attain its perfection." [47] As "Valerius Poplicola," Adams helped prepare the "brew." He began by denouncing Hutchinson as an eager and assiduous tool of the ministry, independent of the people, and a "pensioned" dependent of the Crown, paid from revenues raised illegally and "extorted from the people in a manner most odious, insulting, and oppressive." He then asked: "Are we still threatened with more? Is life, property, and everything dear and sacred, to be now submitted to the decisions of PENSIONED JUDGES . . . ! To what a state of infamy, wretchedness, and misery shall we be reduced if our judges shall be prevailed upon to be thus degraded to *hirelings*, and the *body of the people* shall suffer their

[44] SS to Treasury, 7 Dec. 1770, C.O. 5/759. Hutchinson soon pointed out that the salary fund would be much larger if the illicit importation of tea from Holland were stopped. To SS, 25 Aug. 1771, CHOP, III, 290.
[45] BG, 11 March, 7 Oct. 1771; *Writings*, II, 247.
[46] SS to Treasury, 27 July 1772, CHOP, III, 527.
[47] To Hugh Hughes, 31 Aug., Misc. Bound, XIV, MHS.

free constitution to be overturned and ruined. Merciful God! Inspire thy people with wisdom and fortitude. . . . O save our country from impending ruin—let not the iron hand of tyranny ravish our laws and seize the badge of freedom, nor avowed corruption and the murderous rage of lawless power be ever seen on the sacred seat of justice!" What can be done? It should be talked of at every social club, every town should assemble and "let associations and combinations be everywhere set up to consult and recover our just rights." [48]

The last lines of this brilliant call to action revealed Adams's plan: it was nothing less than the creation of a colony-wide organization. Adams had the sympathy and advice of such men as Elbridge Gerry of Marblehead and James Warren of Plymouth, the husband of James Otis's sister Mercy, but in general the Boston leaders were suspect in other towns as in other colonies. Adams felt that Boston must act alone because "so much caution prevails." [49] And on 27 October, the day before the Boston town meeting, Adams revealed much when he wrote: "I wish we could arouse the continent." [50]

The town petitioned Hutchinson for information about the judges' salaries and adjourned for two days. Hutchinson, completely recovered from the insecurity of the months after the Boston Massacre, replied bluntly that the affairs of the colonial government were none of the town's business. The town then asked that the legislature be allowed to meet at the time appointed so that the "constitutional body" could examine into a matter "so important and alarming." This time Hutchinson replied sharply that the calling of the legislature was his prerogative, not the town's, and that he had put off the session to a later date. Samuel Adams then made his crucial move: he proposed the establishment of a committee of correspondence of twenty-one men to state the rights of the colonists "as men, as Christians, and as subjects," and to publish them to the towns of the colony and to the world at large.[51] The town agreed.

In establishing the Boston committee of correspondence the Boston leaders in effect proposed to create a popular party organization throughout the colony, something they had not needed when they controlled the legislature between 1766 and 1770. The "government party" had such an

---

[48] BG, 2 Oct.; *Writings*, II, 332–37.
[49] Gerry to Adams, 2 Nov., Adams Papers, NYPL; Adams to Gerry, 5 Nov., *Writings*, II, 346–47.
[50] To Gerry, *Writings*, II, 340.
[51] 28 Oct.–2 Nov., BTR, XVIII, 88–93; Harlow, *Adams*, 193; Adams to Arthur Lee, 3 Nov., *Writings*, II, 344–45.

organization, made up of appointed officials—of justices of the peace, county court justices, sheriffs, militia officers, and the family and personal ties of the Hutchinson-Oliver clan—and it was now headed by Hutchinson as governor. If successful, the Boston leaders would have a "grass roots" organization with official standing and would be able to spread their ideas and plans for action and put pressure on members of the legislature.

The plans were carefully laid with the writing of a "political platform." When, for instance, Gerry suggested that the support of the clergy could be gained by a "hint" at church innovations and the "establishment of those tyrants in religion, bishops," Adams replied that this was precisely what he intended, for some of the clergy were "adulators of our oppressors," and that even the best of them were afraid to recommend the rights of the country to heaven in public for fear "lest they should give offense to the little Gods on Earth. . . ." [52]

The committee of correspondence worked hard and on 20 November the town meeting adopted "The State of the Rights of the Colonists," a most able summary of popular political ideas and a reiteration of the many grievances against Britain. It began with an appeal to and a definition of the law of nature by asserting that among the natural rights of the colonists as men were those to life, liberty, and property, but pointing out that these were but "branches" of the "duty of self-preservation, commonly called the first law of nature." Men may remain in a state of nature as long as they please, but when they enter society it is by their voluntary consent, and they have a right to insist on the performance of all the conditions of the original compact. They retain every natural right not given up or ceded because of the nature of the social compact. All laws must conform as far as possible "to the law of natural reason and equity," and all men are entitled to liberty "by the eternal and immutable laws of God and nature, as well as by the law of nations. . . ." In case of intolerable oppression, whether civil or religious, men may leave one society and join another.

Here was the idea of the right of revolution which Jefferson summarized so lucidly four years later in the Declaration of Independence. It was followed by a long catalogue of grievances ranging from the Iron Act of 1750 through the judges' salaries to the threat of an Anglican bishop, which was denounced as a "design both against our civil and religious rights." The document was sent throughout the colony and to other colonies. It was accompanied by an eloquent letter asking the other Massachusetts towns to join with Boston in urging the legislature to oppose the "plan of despo-

[52] Gerry to Adams, 10 Nov., Adams Papers, NYPL; Adams to Gerry, 14 Nov., *Writings*, II, 348–50.

tism," and pleading with them not to "doze, or set supinely indifferent on the brink of destruction while the iron hand of oppression is daily tearing the choicest fruit from the fair Tree of Liberty. . . ." [53]

There was strong opposition in many towns, but one by one they were persuaded to adopt the Boston resolutions, or others of their own, and to appoint committees of correspondence. Meanwhile the Boston committee worked hard, writing letters and seeing to the publication of favorable replies in the newspapers. Before the legislature met in January 1773, perhaps a hundred towns had followed Boston's leadership. However, it was not all dry work, for on 2 February 1773 each member of the committee contributed a dollar to buy Rhode Island beer. [54]

Two years later loyalist Daniel Leonard labeled the Boston committee "the foulest, subtlest, and most venomous serpent that ever issued from the eggs of sedition," [55] but at first Thomas Hutchinson was not alarmed: the "faction" had not been able to revive "the old spirit of nobbing," and in desperation they had even hinted at the "lawfulness of assassination, poisoning &c," but the new scheme would only make them look foolish. [56] He changed his mind in a hurry as town after town joined Boston, and he placed the blame on Samuel Adams, "the grand incendiary," who, after trying "every measure besides to bring the province into an open declaration of independency," was now trying to unite Massachusetts, and the other colonies as well, by means of still another circular letter. [57]

The trouble, of course, had deeper roots, as Hutchinson knew. He declared that "the source . . . of all this irregularity, is a false opinion broached at the time of the Stamp Act, and ever since cultivated until it is become general, that the people of the colonies are subject to no authority but their own legislatures, and that the acts of the Parliament of Great Britain, which is every day in print termed a foreign state, are not obligatory." [58] Though reluctant, he felt he must challenge the "extravagant principles of government" set forth in the newspapers and town meetings, and that the legislature itself must take a stand. [59]

Hutchinson opened the session 6 January 1773 with a speech squarely

[53] Jensen, *Tracts*, 233–55.
[54] Boston Committee of Correspondence [BCC] Minutebooks, 184. The minutebooks and papers of the BCC in the Bancroft Collection in the New York Public Library are a remarkable source for the study of the internal political organization. Most of the references which follow are to the minutebooks, in which were copied the most important outgoing and incoming letters.
[55] "Massachusettensis," 2 Jan. 1775, reprinted in *Novanglus and Massachusettensis . . .* (Boston, 1819), 165–66.
[56] To John Pownall, 10 Nov., CHOP, III, 572–73.
[57] To Gambier, 14 Feb. 1773, Hosmer, *Hutchinson*, 249–50.
[58] To SS, 23 Oct. 1772, C.O. 5/761.   [59] To SS, 22 Dec., C.O. 5/895.

asserting that the supremacy of Parliament was founded in law and the charter and that their ancestors had understood this to be so. That supremacy had never been denied until a few years before, and this denial was the cause of all the disorder in government. The recent resolutions of the town meetings were "repugnant to the principles of the constitution," and the committees of correspondence were founded to maintain such false ideas. There is no line, he said, that "can be drawn between the supreme authority of Parliament and the total independence of the colonies: it is impossible there should be two independent legislatures in one and the same state. . . ." And independence would be full of horrors, with the colonies the prey of one or another of the European powers.[60]

Hutchinson spoke his honest convictions, but he had committed a fatal political error which helped destroy the leadership he had regained in the preceding two years. Only a few of his most loyal followers would openly support the supremacy of Parliament. Furthermore, he had set himself up as an ideal target for the unique talents of Samuel Adams. In the guise of an official reply, Adams won sanction for the ideas of the Boston committee of correspondence. The reply agreed that the government was in disorder, but not because the people of Massachusetts had adopted unconstitutional principles but because Parliament itself was acting unconstitutionally. Adams too examined the colonial charters but found that the colonies owed obedience only to the Crown; that they had never been annexed to the realm; and that Parliament had authority only within it.

With what must have been enormous glee, Adams used Hutchinson's own history of Massachusetts and the documents he had published to prove that he had misinterpreted the past. "Thus we see, from your Excellency's history and publications, the sense our ancestors had of the jurisdiction of Parliament under the first charter. Very different from that, which your Excellency in your speech, apprehends it to have been."

Deftly, Adams then turned to the issue of independence and piously deplored the fact that Hutchinson had raised it. But as for the terrors of independence, "there is more reason to dread the consequences of absolute uncontrolled power, whether of a nation or a monarch, than those of a total independence." However, the Massachusetts house would never think of drawing a line between the supreme authority of Parliament and independence. It would be an arduous undertaking and of great importance to all the colonies. The house would therefore "be unwilling to propose it, without their consent in Congress." Adams declared that the house

[60] Bradford, *Speeches*, 336–42.

was grief-stricken that the policy of a late administration had driven Americans even to consider such an idea, and that the house was much concerned that the governor's speech had reduced it to the "unhappy alternative, either of appearing by our silence to acquiesce in your Excellency's sentiments, or of thus freely discussing this point." After all, Americans were loyal subjects of the Crown, and if the people were left free to exercise the liberties and immunities granted to them by their charter, "there would be no danger of an independence on the Crown." [61]

Shortly thereafter the house sent a long address to Lord Dartmouth which embodied most of the grievances previously listed by the Boston committee of correspondence.[62] The new secretary of state for America had earlier lamented the behavior of Massachusetts but could think of nothing except to wait for the legislature to act upon the resolutions of the town meetings.[63] When it approved them, Dartmouth laid a report before the ministry, but all it could think of was to insist that the supremacy of Parliament must be maintained.[64] Obviously the ministry wanted things kept quiet in America, and Hutchinson got no credit for reviving a dispute it preferred to let lie.[65] At any rate, the ministry did not submit the problem to Parliament, for it was near the end of the session and many members had gone home. The remainder were occupied with the affairs of the East India Company, and with taking the action that within a few months set off the explosion that led to American independence.

ॐ

Meanwhile the Boston leaders were preparing still another attempt to destroy Hutchinson's influence. For years these leaders, like those in other colonies, had obtained copies of official letters from colonial agents and friends who had bribed clerks in government offices in London. Governors and other officials in the colonies complained constantly, but very seldom was anything effective done to stop the flow.[66] Benjamin Franklin, who was appointed Massachusetts agent in 1770, was equally obliging. In De-

---

[61] 26 Jan. 1773, Adams, *Writings*, II, 401–26.
[62] 6 March 1773, Arthur Lee Papers, I, HUL.
[63] To Hutchinson, 9 Dec. 1772, C.O. 5/761, and 3 Feb. 1773, C.O. 5/762.
[64] To Hutchinson, 2 June, C.O. 5/762.
[65] Arthur Lee to Samuel Adams, 11 June, Adams Papers, NYPL.
[66] For a typical appeal see Hutchinson to SS, 28 Sept. 1770, C.O. 5/759. Occasionally there was difficulty in getting copies, as Stephen Sayre explained to Samuel Adams after a conversation with a clerk who explained that of late Lord Hillsborough and his confidential secretary were the only people allowed to see Hutchinson's letters. London, 18 Sept. 1770, Samuel Adams Papers, NYPL.

cember 1772 he sent Speaker Thomas Cushing a packet of letters which he said had fallen into his hands.[67] Months later he insisted they must not be copied but could be shown or read to the proper people. He then explained that his "opportunity" arose because of the death of George Grenville, who had had the letters and loaned them to another but had died before their return. Franklin added that "more may possibly be obtained if these do not make too much noise." [68]

But "noise" is precisely what the letters made on both sides of the Atlantic. Among them were several from Hutchinson and Andrew Oliver, and a few from men in other colonies, all written to Thomas Whately, who had died in 1772. They were private letters but they contained the same ideas about colonial government and politics that the writers had expressed publicly and in official letters to the ministry. The Boston leaders kept the letters some months before they saw fit to use them, and they prepared the way by a great deal of mystifying talk. Then early in June 1773 Samuel Adams told the legislature that he had some letters written "with an intention to subvert the constitution." He read them in a secret session after saying that no copies could be made, and swearing the members to secrecy. Within a few days the letters, suitably edited to make Hutchinson and Oliver look as bad as possible, began to appear in the newspapers and were soon published in pamphlet form. Both houses of the legislature denounced the governor and lieutenant governor and petitioned the king for their removal.[69]

The Boston committee of correspondence broadcast the pamphlet, accompanied by a suitable letter pointing out the horrors intended for America. At the same time it smeared as "Tories" those few legislators who had dared oppose the petition for the removal of Hutchinson and Oliver.[70] The letters were a sensation. The *Virginia Gazette* reported the events in Massachusetts in detail and the *South Carolina Gazette and Country Journal* reprinted the letters in installments.[71] A New London, Connecticut, committee asked for copies of any letters written by people in Connecticut and

[67] 2 Dec. 1772, C.O. 5/118. The letters to Cushing in this small volume in the Public Record Office were taken from Cushing's house by the British and General Gage took them with him when he returned to England. See Gage to SS, 15 Oct. 1775, Gage, *Corres.*, I, 422–23.

[68] Ibid. 7 July 1773.

[69] To Bernard, 29 June, Hosmer, *Hutchinson*, 268–70; MHJ, 2, 16 June; BG, 28 June.

[70] BCC Circular Letter, 23 June, Minutebook, 223–24. For a defense of himself for objecting to the petition for removal, see John Pickering to Samuel Adams, 5 July, Adams Papers, NYPL.

[71] VG(PD), 1, 8, 22, 29 July, 5 Aug.; SCG(T), 9–30 Aug. 1773.

promised to follow Massachusetts in any action taken against "such traitors." [72] Within a short time Hutchinson reported that the flame raised "with so much art" was dying down as sensible people actually read the letters and that what prejudice remained was "principally in the minds of the lower class of the people. . . ." [73] Nevertheless, the Boston leaders were now reunited, and again in control of the legislature. They were able to demand that the superior court judges publicly renounce any intention of accepting salaries from customs revenues. The four associate judges abjectly agreed, but Chief Justice Peter Oliver scornfully refused. Impeachment proceedings were started against him which were terminated only by the end of the colonial legislature itself in 1774.[74]

The most conspicuous casualty of the affair was Benjamin Franklin. After he learned that the letters had been published he told Cushing that his role must be kept secret or his usefulness would be at an end, although he was canny enough to realize that secrecy would be impossible.[75] The news of the letters created an uproar in London. William Whately, a banker, and executor of the estate of his brother Thomas, remembered that John Temple, ousted from the American board of customs in 1770, had asked to read his own letters to Thomas Whately. He then charged Temple with the theft; Temple denied it, and they insulted one another in the newspapers. There followed a duel in Hyde Park with pistols and swords in which Whately was wounded; both men proposed to renew the fray as soon as Whately recovered. Franklin, whose name had not been mentioned so far, published a statement that he and he alone was responsible for securing and sending the letters to Boston. He then resigned as Massachusetts agent but in January he was called before the Privy Council to attend the hearing on the petition of the Massachusetts legislature for the removal of Hutchinson and Oliver. The hearing was held in the midst of the furor created by the news of the Boston Tea Party and emotions were at a high pitch. Bishops and members of the nobility listened to a diatribe by Solicitor General Alexander Wedderburn, who charged the silent Franklin with every crime from theft to the plotting of a revolution to set up an American republic. The next day Franklin was fired from his post

---

[72] Erastus Wolcott et al. to Mass. Comm. of Corres., 16 June, Emmett Collection no. 641, NYPL.
[73] To SS, 7 Aug., C.O. 5/895.
[74] Hutchinson to SS, 14–24 Feb., 9 March 1774, C.O. 5/763, and letters of the various judges to Speaker Thomas Cushing on 3, 5, 7, 8 Feb. 1774, in Misc. Bound, XIV, MHS; and Justice Trowbridge to Cushing, 26 Jan., Samuel Adams Papers, NYPL.
[75] 25 July 1773, C.O. 5/118.

as deputy postmaster general for North America,[76] and William Whately promptly brought suit against him.[77] Franklin now began planning to go back to America. Little did he or the men who watched his humiliation in the Cockpit know that the peak of the career of this sixty-eight-year-old man lay in the future.

Although few if any men knew what the future held, some Americans had been preparing for what they believed would be new attacks upon American liberties. They were convinced that when those attacks came, Americans must present a more unified and effective front than they had in the past. They therefore set about creating an inter-colonial organization and had achieved one by the end of 1773.

ૄ✍

The idea of an inter-colonial union dated back to the seventeenth century, but the various plans for uniting the separate colonies under a central government, ranging from William Penn's in 1697 to the Albany Plan of Union in 1754, had been either ignored or rejected in both America and Britain. After 1763 the popular leaders were convinced that united action among the colonies was the only way to achieve effective opposition to British policies. Thus in 1764 the Boston town meeting instructed its representatives to work for joint action by the colonial assemblies and they secured the appointment of a legislative committee of correspondence. The assemblies of Rhode Island and New York also appointed such committees, and various other legislatures in the North responded in one way or another.

In 1765 the Boston leaders forced the "government party" to agree to call the Stamp Act Congress. After this achievement, the idea of inter-colonial union of some sort was constantly in the minds of the popular leaders, and as constantly dreaded by British officials. For some time there was no very clear idea of what form that union should take. In 1766 the Reverend Jonathan Mayhew in Boston pointed to the "good foundation" laid by the Stamp Act Congress and urged the importance of friendship among the colonies.[78] That same year Samuel Adams introduced himself to Christopher Gadsden and asserted that the Stamp Act had been a blessing because of the union that had been formed. He too emphasized the importance of friendship and predicted correctly that Parliament would again

[76] Van Doren, Franklin, 458–76.
[77] William Whately to Andrew Oliver, 19 March 1774, MHSP, LVIII, 91.
[78] To Thomas Hollis, 8 June, Alden Bradford, ed., Memoir of the Life and Writings of Rev. Jonathan Mayhew . . . (Boston, 1838), 428–30.

try to raise revenue, this time in the guise of regulating trade. But his hopes were placed on the merchants, for he expressed the wish that "there was a union and correspondence kept up among the merchants throughout the continent."[79]

The merchants, as a group, were a poor foundation for united political action, as they proved in 1770. Their "union" was weak indeed as compared to that achieved by the legislatures as a result of the Massachusetts Circular Letter of 1768. In that year Richard Henry Lee introduced himself to John Dickinson and argued that each colony should appoint "select committees" and that "the lovers of liberty in every province" should correspond with one another.[80] However, as late as 1771 Samuel Adams apparently still pinned his hopes on an organization outside the legislatures. He proposed the formation of "societies" of "the most respectable inhabitants" in each colony which would correspond with one another and with a similar society in England and hold annual meetings of delegates. His model was the Society of the Supporters of the Bill of Rights in England.[81]

On the other hand, Thomas Cushing, who hoped for a revival of colonial union, was convinced that no dependence could be placed on "the virtue of the people. . . ." Only the legislatures could keep a watchful eye on Britain. Inevitaby Britain would get into a war and ask for help, and when it did the colonies should agree on a common program.[82] What he meant was spelled out bluntly by the Boston Gazette, which asserted that in case of war the colonies should refuse all help to Britain and then they could secure any bill of rights they demanded.[83] Meanwhile the Boston leaders set about creating an official political organization within Massachusetts —the committees of correspondence—but they made no attempt on the inter-colonial level. But when Hutchinson countered by declaring that the only alternative to complete submission to Parliament was independence, the assembly brought the idea of an American congress out in the open. The house asserted that independence could be decided upon only by such a congress, as indeed it was three years later. When the report reached London, Arthur Lee warned Samuel Adams against holding a congress. Earlier he had been worried that the northern colonies were moving too fast and felt that the "mutual faithlessness" demonstrated in the non-

[79] 11 Dec., Adams Papers, NYPL.   [80] 25 July, Letters, I, 29–30.
[81] To Arthur Lee, 27 Sept., Writings, II, 234.
[82] To Roger Sherman, 21 Jan. 1772, MHSC, 4 ser. IV, 358–59.
[83] 11 May 1772 and VG(PD), 11 June. The suggestion is printed as an "Extract" from a letter from London.

importation struggle made united action highly unlikely. Now he warned Adams that a congress would arouse Britain and might "incense her to some hostile measure." Wait, he said, until Britain gets into a war which would make it impossible for her to "hazard any military operation against us." [84]

It was Lee's own colony of Virginia, not Massachusetts, that took the crucial step in March 1773 when it called for the establishment of official legislative committees to correspond with one another. That this meant a congress eventually, all agreed. On hearing the news, Benjamin Franklin wrote Thomas Cushing that "it is natural to suppose, as you do, that if the oppressions continue, a congress may grow out of that correspondence." He predicted that "nothing would more alarm our ministers; but if the colonies agree to hold a congress, I do not see how it can be prevented." [85]

Virginia's move was the result of a series of events which began in Rhode Island where the citizenry carried on a relentless battle against the customs service. There was no letup of such opposition anywhere in America after 1770. A customs collector in New Jersey was beaten up by the citizenry and accused of smuggling and of probable insanity by no less a person than Governor Sir William Franklin.[86] The populace in Falmouth, Maine, repeatedly mauled the collector of the port.[87] In far away Newfoundland, officials complained that merchants refused to pay fees,[88] and Admiral Rodney down in the West Indies seemed unable to do anything to stop the vast illegal trade which, he said, went on with the French islands.[89] On the mainland most of the supreme courts refused to issue writs of assistance despite the provision in the Revenue Act of 1767 requiring them to do so. Customs officials complained that no justice was to be had, even from officers of the Crown. "No one will be our bail," wailed Captain Talbot of the *Lively*, "not a lawyer in the province that has a sal-

[84] To R. H. Lee[?], 14 Feb., Arthur Lee Papers, II, HUL; to Samuel Adams, 11 June, Adams Papers, NYPL. In less than two weeks Lee changed his mind about a congress. To Adams, 23 June, ibid. NYPL.

[85] 7 July 1773, C.O. 5/118. Hutchinson to SS, 1 Sept. 1773, C.O. 5/762, reported that the Boston leaders had been aiming at a congress in the last two sessions of the legislature and that he had "secret intelligence" that the speakers of the other assemblies had been asked to join Massachusetts.

[86] Franklin to Customs Board, 12 April 1771, C.O.: Treasury, 1/491. For the victim's version see ibid.

[87] Hutchinson to SS, 28 Nov. 1771, 15 July 1772, C.O. 5/761.

[88] John Robinson to John Pownall, 20 Dec. 1771, CHOP, III, 349.

[89] See documents in CHOP, IV, 52, 64, 83.

ary from the Crown, and any we may employ will seem to act for us, but strictly against us." [90]

The Rhode Islanders carried on after 1770 as they had before, certain of the support of their own government. They had fought the British navy ever since 1763. In 1764 two members of the council had ordered a naval vessel fired upon. In 1769 Rhode Islanders burned Hancock's *Liberty*, which the customs board in Boston had converted to its purposes after the seizure and sale in 1768.[91] In 1772 one vessel in particular aroused the ire of Rhode Island. In March the *Gaspee* returned to Rhode Island waters, this time under the command of an eager lieutenant, William Dudingston. The newspapers soon labeled him a pirate, a hog-stealer, and a chicken thief.[92] He quarreled with Governor Wanton and brought his commander, Admiral John Montagu in Boston, into the fray. The admiral and the governor wrote virulent letters to one another and the admiral reported back to England that the governor himself was a smuggler.[93]

Dudingston was doomed. On the afternoon of 9 June he set out in fast pursuit of the *Hannah*, which had left Newport for Providence. Captain Lindsey knew the waters of Narragansett Bay and it is not surprising that the *Gaspee* ran aground in the course of the pursuit while Lindsey sailed on to Providence. That night some of the leading citizens and others set out from Providence in longboats and soon came upon the *Gaspee*. As a contemporary broadside put it: [94]

> That night about half after ten,
> Some Narragansett Indianmen,
>
> Being sixty-four, if I remember,
> Which made this stout coxcomb surrender;
> And what was best of all their tricks,
> They in his britch a ball did fix,
>
> Then set the men upon the land,
> And burnt her up, we understand;
> Which thing provokes the King so high,
> He said those men shall surely die.

[90] John Robinson to John Pownall, 26 Oct. 1772, 25 Aug. 1773, CHOP, III, 565; IV, 79. See also Dickerson, "Writs of Assistance," in Morris, *Era of the American Revolution*, 49–73.
[91] Lovejoy, *Rhode Island*, 36–38, 157.   [92] PrG, 9 Jan.; VG(PD), 18 Feb. 1773.
[93] Admiralty to SS, 28 May 1772, CHOP, III, 503. For examples of the sulphurous correspondence between the admiral and the governor, see EHD, IX, 759–61.
[94] Winslow, *Broadside Verse*, 137. See also PrG, 13 June, VG(PD), 9 July, for various accounts as to location of the lieutenant's wounds. For Dudingston's own account see EHD, IX, 761–62.

Two days later Dudingston, suffering from his wound and the humiliation of its location, was charged with the illegal seizure of casks of sugar and rum and arrested by the high sheriff. He was tried, found guilty, and fined £365 by a Rhode Island court. The fine was paid by the customs board in Boston and eventually Admiral Montagu shipped him off to England to stand trial for the loss of the *Gaspee*.

Meanwhile Governor Wanton piously offered a £100 sterling reward to anyone who would "discover the perpetrators of the said villainy." No one stepped forward. In July Captain Linzee of the *Beaver* got hold of a Negro boy, Aaron Briggs. Aaron deposed that he had been rowing home from Providence when he was caught and forced to go along to the *Gaspee*. He swore that among the leading citizens who had attacked the vessel were John and Joseph Brown of Providence and Simeon Potter of Bristol.

Admiral Montagu demanded summary punishment but Governor Wanton now secured depositions to prove that Aaron was a liar. Two fellow indentured servants who lived on Prudence Island swore before the governor that they had slept in the same bed with Aaron for years and that on the night the *Gaspee* was burned he had been in bed with them as usual. The governor next procured a warrant for Aaron's arrest but Captain Linzee refused to surrender the boy to the sheriff. The governor then wrote a furious letter to the admiral denouncing the gross interference of military with civil authority, and in some confusion he first denounced Aaron as a liar and then declared that his admission of guilt was enough to convict him.[95] Meanwhile Aaron's owner had Captain Linzee arrested for stealing Aaron, whereupon Admiral Montagu bailed out his captain and took charge of Aaron himself. The admiral denounced the "lawless and piratical people" of Rhode Island, "this nest of smugglers," in reports to England, but confessed that it was impossible to bring the guilty to justice, opposed as he was by the whole government of the colony. It was up to Britain.[96]

The news reached London in mid-July. Secretary Hillsborough asked the attorney general and the solicitor general if the people concerned could be tried under the "Dockyards Act"[97] passed in the last session of Parliament. That act provided the death penalty, without benefit of clergy, for anyone setting fire to or otherwise destroying his majesty's ships, but the law officers decided that the law applied only when a ship was actually in a

[95] RICR, VII, 60–192, prints many of the documents.
[96] Montagu to SS, 12 June, 11 July, 12 Sept., C.O. 5/761.
[97] 12 Geo. III, c. 24, Pickering, XXIX, 62–63.

dockyard. However, they ruled that the attack on the *Gaspee* was high treason, that is, levying war against the king, and that the offenders could be indicted and tried in either England or Rhode Island.[98]

The result of this report was the appointment of a royal commission consisting of the chief justices of New York, New Jersey, and Massachusetts, the judge of the vice-admiralty court in Boston, and Governor Wanton of Rhode Island. They were told to call witnesses, take depositions, and if they found sufficient evidence, to turn it over to the civil authorities to make the arrests. These in turn were to hand the accused and all the witnesses over to Admiral Montagu for shipment to England. Furthermore, in light of the "outrages" committed in Rhode Island, the commission was authorized to call for military aid if it were insulted.[99]

The commission met at Newport on 5 January 1773 and at once refused to proceed without the presence of the admiral. He had been ordered to attend but he at first refused because the weather made it too "hazardous" to sail his ships around from Boston. When the commission still refused to act, the admiral finally went overland. Once on board the *Lizard* in Newport harbor he hoisted his flag, only to be infuriated when the fort refused to salute him. This he said was a "designed insult" and he appealed to England to instruct Governor Wanton as to the proper treatment of an admiral; he predicted that nothing would come of the inquiry.[100]

Nothing did, for while the commission was diligent, it met but a few days in January and then adjourned until the end of May. In its final report the commission concluded that there was no advance intention of destroying the *Gaspee*, and that Rhode Island officials had behaved properly. As civilians, the commissioners took a dim view of the navy. They reported that Captain Linzee had "treated the civil authority in a most contemptuous and unjustifiable manner" and that there was reason to believe that Lieutenant Dudingston had "from an intemperate, if not a reprehensible zeal to aid the revenue service, exceeded the bounds of his duty." As for Aaron's testimony, no credit was due it, and Captain Linzee had tried too hard to "extort from a weak or wicked mind, declarations not strictly true. . . ." The commission submitted its findings to the Rhode Island supreme court, which reported that the evidence was dubious, and the commission agreed.[101]

[98] 7, 10 Aug., CHOP, III, 531.
[99] Instructions to Commissioners, RICR, VII, 110–12; SS to Admiralty, 5 Sept., CHOP, III, 541.
[100] Admiralty to SS, 1 March 1773, CHOP, IV, 23.   [101] RICR, VII, 178–82.

Privately, of course, the attitude of the commissioners, except Governor Wanton, was probably that of Chief Justice Peter Oliver of Massachusetts, who wished that they had been able to discover the perpetrators of "that most abandoned piece of villainy." [102] What they thought of the admiral they did not say, but perhaps they agreed with John Adams, who reported that the admiral's wife was a snob and that "a coachman, a jack tar before the mast, would be ashamed—nay a porter, a shoe black, or a chimney sweeper would be ashamed of the coarse, low, vulgar dialect of this sea officer" whose "continual language is cursing and damning and God damning, 'my wifes d——d A——se is so broad that she and I can't sit in a chariot together'—this is the nature of the beast and the common language of the man." Adams declared that "an American freeholder, living in a log house twenty feet square, without a chimney in it, is a well bred man, a polite accomplished person, a fine gentleman, in comparison to this beast of prey." Adams noted: "This is not the language of prejudice, for I have none against him, but of truth. His brutal, hoggish manners are a disgrace to the Royal Navy and to the king's service." [103]

ço

The *Gaspee* commission ended in failure, but before it did the organization of official inter-colonial legislative committees of correspondence was under way. The news of the *Gaspee* incident spread fast—within three weeks it was reported by the *South Carolina Gazette*.[104] At first it was reported that Britain would do nothing because Governor Wanton's "true" reports had counteracted the "misrepresentations" of the affair.[105] By December the story of the appointment of the commission of inquiry was in the newspapers and the reaction was immediate. In 1769 the colonial legislatures had united in protesting against the parliamentary proposal to bring Americans to England for treason trials, and now they were faced with what seemed the reality. This, declared the *Providence Gazette*, "is shocking to humanity, repugnant to every dictate of reason, liberty, and justice, and in which Americans and Freemen ought never to acquiesce." A week later "Americanus" described the commission as a "court of inquisition more horrid than that of Spain or Portugal," a sentiment soon echoed in the *South Carolina Gazette*. "Americanus" concluded his long tirade by proclaiming that "ten thousand deaths by the halter, or the axe, are infinitely preferable to a miserable life of slavery in chains, under a pack of

---

[102] To SS, 20 July 1773, C.O. 5/762.   [103] *Diary*, 28 Dec. 1772.
[104] SCG(T), 2 July.   [105] PrG, 26 Sept.

worse than Egyptian tyrants, whose avarice nothing less than your whole substance and income, will satisfy; and who, if they can't extort that, will glory in making a sacrifice of you and your posterity, to gratify their master the devil, who is a tyrant, and the father of tyrants and liars." [106]

The *Boston Gazette* leaped to the attack and predicted that if the commission called for troops there would be as awful a slaughter of the inhabitants of Rhode Island as there had been of the innocent people of Boston in 1770. "How long!" cried the *Gazette*, "O LORD! How long!" [107] The Boston leaders, who were getting their committees of correspondence under way, promptly informed the Massachusetts towns, some of which responded with denunciations of the "court of inquisition" and of attacks on the "constitution." [108] Elbridge Gerry told Samuel Adams that the indignity offered Rhode Island and the other colonies was unequaled, that a "continent with many hundred thousand of warlike men" had been rendered scandalous, and that Rhode Island should not submit to this "star chamber" procedure or be bested by the "tools of tyrants." The paltry flyboats, the handful of troops, and "all the troops Great Britain can furnish can never enslave this continent if we behave like men." [109]

Samuel Adams was more cautious, and by now his stature was such that Stephen Hopkins, the chief justice, Darius Sessions, the lieutenant governor, and others wrote from Providence asking him what they should do.[110] Adams replied that the appointment of the commission "should awaken the American colonies, which have been too long dozing upon the brink of ruin." He bewailed the loss of "that union which once happily subsisted. . . ." He predicted that if the commission called in troops the result might be "a most violent political earthquake through the whole British Empire, if not its total destruction," and said that he had long feared that the unhappy contest would end in "rivers of blood."

His rhetoric was eloquent but his advice ambivalent. He believed, or at least tried to convince the Rhode Islanders, that behind it all was a plot to vacate their charter. He suggested that the assembly should protest and that the governor should refuse to call the commission together. In any case, Rhode Island should try to delay or evade taking action. The only concrete suggestion he offered was a circular letter to the other colonies asking them to order their agents in England to join in a protest. After he heard that the commission had held its first meeting at Newport, he hoped

[106] Ibid. 19, 26 Dec.; SCG(T), 1 March 1773.
[107] 14 Dec.; VG(PD), 21 Jan. 1773.
[108] PrG, 23 Jan.   [109] 16 Dec., Samuel Adams Papers, NYPL.
[110] 25 Dec., ibid.

that the governor would not take part in it and that the assembly would enter protests on its journals as Massachusetts had done for years.[111]

The Rhode Islanders did not follow Adams's advice nor did they need to, as we have seen. Once more, as in 1769, the British proposal to take Americans to England for treason trials was seized upon by Virginia to unite the colonies, and this time far more effectively. The *Virginia Gazette* carried full reports of events in Rhode Island, along with rumors that the Rhode Island charter would be vacated, and even one of a clash between British regulars and the citizenry in which men on both sides were killed.[112] But Richard Henry Lee, dubious about the "uncertain medium of newspapers," wrote to Samuel Adams for the first time and asked for a true state of the matter.[113] A week later he promised another correspondent in Massachusetts that when the House of Burgesses met it would assert the rights of America.[114]

And so it did. Most colonial legislatures had long had standing committees to correspond with the agents in England when the legislatures were not in session. As Jefferson remembered it much later, he, Patrick Henry, Richard Henry Lee, and a few others, "not thinking our old and leading members up to the point of forwardness and zeal which the times required," met in a private room at the Raleigh Tavern and made plans.[115] They picked Jefferson's brother-in-law, Dabney Carr, to offer the resolutions. On 12 March the burgesses agreed unanimously to appoint a standing committee of eleven to keep a watch on the acts of Parliament and of the ministry, and to correspond with the other colonies.[116] As Lee put it, "they have now adopted a measure which from the beginning of the present dispute they should have fixed on, as leading to that union and perfect understanding of each other, on which the political salvation of America so eminently depends." He explained, however, that the language of the resolutions was contrived so the Americans' enemies could not accuse them of treason as they had done in the past over "every honest attempt to defend ourselves from their tyrannous designs for destroying our constitutional liberty." [117] The caution, if such there was, was probably due to the "old and leading" members who, while they agreed to the proposal, included enough of their own group on the committee to control such members as Lee, Jefferson, and Henry.

---

[111] 28 Dec., 2 Jan., ___ Feb. 1773, *Writings*, II, 389–92, 395–401, 427–28.
[112] VG(PD), 7, 21, 28 Jan. 1773.   [113] 4 Feb., *Letters*, I, 82–83.
[114] To Thomas Cushing [?], 13 Feb., Misc. Bound, XIV, MHS.
[115] "Autobiography," P. L. Ford, ed., *The Works of Thomas Jefferson* (12 vols., New York, 1904–5), I, 9.
[116] JHB (1773–76), 28.   [117] To John Dickinson, 4 April, *Letters*, I, 83–84.

The resolutions were sent to the assembly speakers throughout America. When they reached Boston the committee of correspondence held a special session [118] and ordered 300 copies printed and sent to all the towns in the colony, along with a letter extolling them.[119] Meanwhile Boston told its representatives that the ministry had tried to render the "assemblies of Commons throughout the colonies mere ciphers in the Constitution" and instructed them to consider the Virginia resolves most seriously.[120]

The Rhode Island legislature appointed a committee on 7 May and before the end of the month the other New England assemblies had followed suit. By the end of the year only three legislatures had not done so, but by early February 1774 New York and New Jersey had established committees. Only Pennsylvania refused, once more as a result of the influence of Speaker Joseph Galloway.[121] When Pennsylvania did establish a committee, it was appointed by a Philadelphia mass meeting called to consider the Boston Port Bill.

The legislative committees of correspondence never had a chance to play a role in the events that led to independence, for within months power was seized by revolutionary committees, congresses, conventions, and mobs, and the legal legislatures soon disappeared forever. The legislative committees were important only as a symbol and the newspapers spelled out what that symbol meant. They greeted the Virginia proposal for colonial union as a bulwark of liberty and praised the "noble Virginians." A Rhode Islander described a union of the colonies as "a wall of brass against all the invaders of American rights." Americans should embrace it and "lay a sure foundation for the triumph of freedom in America, to the end of time." [122]

The newspapers, more bold than the legislatures, went beyond such generalities and by the end of 1773 were openly talking of independence. Only five days after Hutchinson raised the issue in January 1773, the *Boston Gazette* denied the right of Britain to make laws for America and then asserted that if "Britons continue their endeavors much longer to subject us to their government and taxation, we shall become a separate state," and that within a short time "Americans will be too strong for any nation in the world." [123] In June the *Providence Gazette* predicted that the time was not far distant when freedom would triumph over its enemies and that "more bright prospects for human happiness and glory are now opening

---

[118] Samuel Adams to R. H. Lee, 10 April, *Writings*, III, 25–28.
[119] 9 April, BCC Minutebook, 214–16.   [120] 5 May, BTR, XVIII, 132–34.
[121] The actions of the legislatures and the letters from their committees are printed in JHB (1773–76), 47–64.
[122] PrG, 22 May. See also issues of 10, 17, 24 April; BG, 14 June.
[123] BG, 11 Jan.

before the Americans, than ever gilded the dawn of any kingdom; and the imperial commonwealth of America will undoubtedly surpass all the political societies that have ever yet been formed by the sons of man." [124] Another writer put it that "America will soon be the glory of the world," and then went on to say that even the most exalted ideas would probably fall far short "of what will one day be seen in America." [125] An even greater destiny lay before the colonies, for as one man saw it: "the united Americans will be able not only to defend their own rights, but to be the guardians of the rights of mankind through the world." [126]

In Virginia "Hampden" declared that the House of Burgesses should be called a parliament and that no obedience was due the Parliament in England. The rights of the Virginia parliament were derived from a contract as binding as Magna Carta, and if the king invaded those rights, he ceased to be "king of the Dominion of Virginia." [127] Another Virginian called for the establishment of a permanent American congress, the publication of a bill of rights to the world, and the sending of an ambassador to reside at the court of Great Britain. He pointed out that the economic potential of America, linked to political liberty, was greater than that of any other country in history, and that Britain's existence as a nation might depend on America's growth. Britain should take note of this and act accordingly. "No people that ever trod the stage of the world have had so glorious a prospect as now rises before the Americans. There is nothing good or great but their wisdom may acquire, and to what heights they will arrive in progress of time no one can conceive." [128]

As usual it remained for the *Boston Gazette* to spell things out so that no one could mistake the intent of such writing. No redress can be expected from a corrupt Parliament, and the question of how the colonies can force their oppressors to terms "has been often answered already by our politicians, viz., 'Form an Independent State—An AMERICAN COMMONWEALTH.'" [129] Inevitably the balladeers seized upon a popular subject and one concluded "A Song on Liberty, made by a Bostonian," with the stanza: [130]

> Some fitter day shall crown us masters of the Main,
> In giving laws and freedom to subject France and Spain;
> And all the isles o'er ocean spread shall tremble and obey,
> The Lords, the Lords, the Lords, the Lords of North America.

[124] PrG, 5 June.   [125] Ibid. 12 June.   [126] Ibid. 19 June.
[127] VG(PD), 11 Nov.   [128] Idem.   [129] BG, 11 Oct.
[130] VG(PD), 6 Jan. 1774.

Thus by the end of 1773 the ideas of union, of an American congress, of independence, and of the future glory of America were widespread from one end of the colonies to the other.

Many Americans had moved far in their political thinking during a decade and by 1773 some of their leaders were asserting in unmistakable terms that they would oppose British interference of any kind in the future. Once more, and inadvertently, Parliament provided them with the opportunity. In the spring of 1773 it passed the "Tea Act" which allowed the East India Company to ship tea directly to America for sale by American merchants whom it appointed as agents. The popular leaders everywhere in the colonies seized upon the arrival of the tea to challenge Britain, and nowhere was that challenge more dramatic than in Boston where on 16 December 1773 a mob of "Indians" boarded the tea ships and dumped the tea into Boston Harbor.

XVII

From India to Boston Harbor: Tea, Tea Parties, and the Intolerable Acts

After the repeal of the Townshend duties, except on tea, and the collapse of American resistance in 1770, Britain turned its attention more and more to the empire on the other side of the world—to India, and to the tangled affairs of one of Britain's greatest corporations, the East India Company. By 1772 the king and the ministry were convinced that the company and its territorial holdings in India must be brought under government control, but they moved cautiously, for there was powerful opposition in and out of government. The Chatham ministry had made the first attempt at government intervention in 1767, but the ministry itself was divided and all it achieved was a requirement that the company must pay £400,000 a year to the government whenever its annual dividend was more than 6 per cent.[1] At the same time, however, Parliament did make an effort to help the company compete with its great rival, the Dutch East India Company.

The English company was required to ship all its tea to Britain, pay heavy import duties, and then sell its tea to merchants and others at public auction. In addition, heavy inland duties had to be paid on all tea sold in Britain. As a result, English tea was higher priced than Dutch tea, a fact that provided an opportunity for smugglers whose intense interest in illegal profits was matched by their skill in acquiring them. By the 1760s an estimated 7,000,000 pounds of Dutch tea was being smuggled into Britain each year. The Irish and the Americans smuggled tea too, but as in other forms of smuggling they could not match the achievements of their British counterparts. The success of the smugglers hit the East India Company

[1] See Chapter VIII above.

434

and hit it hard, since by mid-century tea sales had been the source of 90 per cent of its commercial profit.

The obvious thing to do was to lower the price of English tea, and in the "Tea Act" of 1767, Parliament reduced the inland duties on tea sold in Britain and provided for the repayment of all import duties on tea re-shipped to Ireland and America.[2] The immediate effect was the doubling of sales in Britain and of shipments to America, but at the same time, the Townshend Revenue Act of 1767 imposed a threepence a pound duty on all tea imported by Americans. Naturally, when the Americans adopted their non-importation agreements in 1768 and 1769, they agreed to stop importing English tea, and smuggled more Dutch tea than ever, and some of them continued to smuggle great quantities of it after non-importation was abandoned in 1770. In Britain, when the inland duties were raised again in 1772, smugglers stepped up an activity they had not suspended even during the five years of cheap English tea. Meanwhile, the East India Company had continued to import more tea than it could ever hope to sell, even if there had been neither taxes nor smugglers.

By the end of 1772 the company was on the verge of bankruptcy. It had nearly 18,000,000 pounds of unsold tea in its warehouses. The price of its stock had plummeted after wild speculation on the Amsterdam and London markets. Rival groups of stockholders fought for control of the company while its "servants" in India defrauded their employer and looted the Indians to build up private fortunes. The directors declared large dividends even when there was no money to pay them. The collapse of speculative banking schemes in 1772 and the ensuing credit crisis, which hurt American tobacco planters, staggered the East India Company. It owed the Bank of England £300,000 and in October 1772 the bank refused to renew a loan already long overdue. In addition, the company owed the government and other creditors another £1,000,000. The desperate directors were forced to conclude that the only way to escape bankruptcy was to ask for a government loan, whatever the dangers involved might be.

In the meantime a propaganda campaign pictured the horrors of company misrule in India, and the "nabobs" who returned from India with fortunes aroused the envy of many. Politicians fished about for political advantage and to vent personal spites. A parliamentary committee appointed to investigate the company was headed by John Burgoyne, who was soon to have a brief and inglorious career as a general in the American wilderness. Among those his committee investigated was Lord Robert Clive, who had

2 7 Geo. III, c. 56, Pickering, XXVII, 600–5.

won great military victories and a great private fortune in India. Soon thereafter Clive committed suicide.

The East India Company's request for a government loan of £1,500,000 early in March 1773 gave the ministry the opening it needed. In return for the loan the ministry insisted that the company must accept a "regulating act" which would give the government a measure of control over the company and over the government of India. The company and its supporters fought back with arguments that sounded much like those of the Americans. The company declared that such an act would deprive it of its property without its consent. The council of the city of London charged that the proposed regulating act was a "direct and dangerous attack on the liberties of the people." Edmund Burke and other members of the Rockingham faction denounced the act as an assault on sacred charter rights and an example of despotism unparalleled even in despotic France. The opposition had the rhetoric but Lord North had the votes, and although he tended to waver, his spine was stiffened by George III, who insisted that the company must "come on its knees" and accept the act.[3]

The Regulating Act became law on 21 June 1773 but, in the midst of the debate about it, Parliament had passed another act on 10 May that was to have far greater immediate consequences. It was the third law of its kind since 1767 in which Parliament had tried to increase the sale of tea in America.[4] As in previous laws, import duties collected in Britain would be repaid to the East India Company for all tea shipped to America. But the law contained a new idea. When the company petitioned for a government loan in March, it also requested that tea sent to America be exempt from the requirement that it be sold at public auction. The company proposed to sell such tea directly through its own agents in America. By eliminating middlemen it might thus sell cheaply enough to compete with smuggled Dutch tea.

Lord North approved and presented the request to Parliament late in April. At once, the Rockinghams, as they had in the debate over the repeal of the Townshend duties in 1770, argued that the tea duty should be repealed. One of them prophesied: "I tell the Noble Lord now that if he don't take off the duty they won't take the tea." Events soon proved him

---

[3] Benjamin W. Labaree, *The Boston Tea Party* (New York, 1964), chapter IV, from which I have quoted; Sutherland, *East India Company*, chapters VII–IX; Beckles Willson, *Ledger and Sword* . . . (2 vols., New York, 1903), II, 227–37. The Regulating Act, 13 Geo. III, c. 63, is in Pickering, XXX, 124–43.
[4] 13 Geo. III, c. 44, Pickering, XXX, 74–77.

right, but Lord North was not impressed at the moment. He knew that the Americans, despite their assertions, had imported more than 600,000 pounds of dutied tea in 1771 and 1772. Admitting that the duties collected were small, he argued that they were needed to support civil government in America. He finally admitted, when pushed to it, that he was opposed to repeal of the the tea duty for "political reasons." North clearly wanted to avoid still another debate over the principle of the Declaratory Act and all the emotions it would arouse. The tea duty was a symbol of parliamentary sovereignty over the colonies, and had its repeal been proposed by the ministry, it would have started a fight it might well have lost—and George III would have led the opposition.

Taking place as it did in the midst of the heated controversy over the proposed regulating act, the discussion of what the Americans were soon to call the Tea Act was desultory and almost unnoticed by those who took notes on the debates. The newspapers likewise paid almost no attention to it. Thus when the bill went to the House of Lords, one paper reported that "yesterday the upper assembly in a committee went through the East India tea bill. Also a bill to prevent the murdering or destroying bastard children, with amendments."

Americans in England and English merchants with American mercantile connections eagerly sought appointments as tea agents for themselves and their friends and clients. They no more suspected what would happen than the men who sought appointments as stamp distributors in 1765. By the end of July the East India Company had selected its agents who were to receive the tea in America and sell it for a 6 per cent commission. Among those picked were several merchants who were political enemies of the popular leaders in America. Thomas and Isaac Wharton were two of the agents in Philadelphia and two sons and a son-in-law of Thomas Hutchinson were among the agents in Boston.

By September, 600,000 pounds of tea worth over £60,000 were ready for shipment in more than 2000 chests to the four great ports in America: Boston, New York, Philadelphia, and Charleston.[5] Other colonies protested,

[5] East India Company to Dartmouth, 20 Dec. 1773, C.O. 5/133; Labaree, *Tea Party*, 73–77. The tea agents were Thomas and Elisha Hutchinson, Benjamin Faneuil, Jr., Joshua Winslow, and Richard Clarke & Sons in Boston; Henry White, Abraham Lott, Frederick Pigou, and Benjamin Booth in New York; Thomas and Isaac Wharton, Abel James, Henry Drinker, Jonathan Browne, and Gilbert Barkly in Philadelphia; Peter Leger, William Greenwood, and Roger Smith in Charleston. Some of the agents were partners, as were the Clarkes. Many important documents are printed in Francis S. Drake, *Tea Leaves . . .* (Boston, 1884).

but the people of the four seaports defeated the purpose of the Tea Act, and the action of Boston alone led Britain to take a long stride in the direction of war with America.

ह~

From time to time after 1770 American newspapers predicted the repeal of the tea duty.[6] By 1773 they were sure of it,[7] and Americans in England reported that the plight of the East India Company would bring it about. Benjamin Franklin was convinced that Parliament would eventually abandon the attempt to tax America and would repeal the tea duty when it could do so with dignity.[8] Early in 1773 he reported that he took the "opportunity of remarking in all companies" that because of the tea duty, Americans annually smuggled £500,000 worth of tea and other India goods from the Dutch, French, Swedes, and Danes.[9] Presumably he thought such tales would further repeal, but how he expected to win friends for the colonies is unclear. Even Arthur Lee, who would never admit to an illegal act by an American, seemed sure that the troubles of the East India Company would mean repeal of the tea duty.[10]

Both Franklin and Lee were highly indignant when Parliament proved them wrong in the spring of 1773. The English, declared Franklin, "have no idea that any people can act from any other principle but that of interest" and believe that cheap tea will "overcome all the patriotism of an American." [11] Lee, who always smelled plots, saw the new act as a "ministerial trick" of Lord North who was "treachery itself" and who probably wanted to create violence in America to justify coercion.[12]

Actually, violence in America was the last thing the ministry wanted or expected, and it opposed repeal of the tea duty because it wanted to avoid raising the issue of Parliament's power over the colonies. Thus when Secretary Dartmouth learned of Governor Thomas Hutchinson's speech to the Massachusetts legislature in January 1773 defending the sovereignty of Parliament, he told Hutchinson flatly to "avoid any further discussion whatsoever upon these questions." Dartmouth was shocked by the legislature's reply to Hutchinson, which was "replete with doctrines of the most dan-

[6] VG(R), 21 Nov. 1771; VG(PD), 11 June 1772; *South Carolina Gazette* (Powell), 7 May 1772.
[7] NYJ, 22 April; VG(PD), 1 July.
[8] To Thomas Cushing, 5 Feb. 1771, *Writings*(S), V, 292–93.
[9] To Thomas Cushing, 5 Jan. 1773, ibid. VI, 3.
[10] To [R. H. Lee?], 14 Feb. 1773, Arthur Lee Papers, II, HUL.
[11] To Thomas Cushing, 4 June 1773, *Writings*(S), VI, 57.
[12] To Samuel Adams, 22 Dec. 1773, Adams Papers, NYPL.

gerous nature," and he said the papers ought to be laid before Parliament. But he did not do so, and Franklin, who was close to Dartmouth, reported that the ministry wanted to keep Parliament out of American affairs. He said that Dartmouth did not lay the papers before Parliament because he feared that it would not let the declaration of the Massachusetts legislature, "asserting its independency," pass unnoticed and would thus widen the breach.[13] And when Shelburne expressed concern because American affairs had not been discussed in the House of Lords, Dartmouth blandly replied that he was a friend of the colonies and would redress their grievances.[14] As Franklin put it, the ministry's intention was to avoid all public debate about the colonies, let all contention subside, and "by degrees suffer matters to return to the old channel." [15] The intention was sensible but it had little to do with political reality in either America or Britain.

When Americans abandoned non-importation in 1770 many of them swore that they would not import taxed tea, but they did not stop drinking tea, whether taxed or not. The merchants of New York and Philadelphia continued to smuggle Dutch tea as they had in the past and thus combined profit with the maintenance of principle. New York's imports of English tea dropped from 320,000 pounds in 1768 to 530 pounds in 1772, while Philadelphia's dropped from 175,000 to a mere 128. However, other Americans drank taxed tea with no apparent effect on their principles. Virginia and Maryland imported more English tea in 1772 than they ever had before. Even more striking was that Boston, whence came so much noise about principles, imported nearly 265,000 pounds of taxed tea in 1771, about as much as the town imported in 1768 before the Townshend duty went into effect. Nor could the imports be blamed entirely on the mercantile allies of Thomas Hutchinson, for John Hancock collected freight charges on 45,000 pounds of duticd tea brought in by his ships in 1771 and 1772.[16]

In 1773 many Americans charged that the Tea Act was but another devious plot to seduce them into admitting that Parliament had the right to

[13] SS to Hutchinson, 10 April and 2 June, quoted in Bernard Donoughue, *British Politics and the American Revolution: The Path to War, 1773–75* (London, 1964), 18–19; Franklin to Thomas Cushing, 6 May, *Writings*(S), VI, 49–50.
[14] Arthur Lee to Samuel Adams, 23 June 1773, Adams Papers, NYPL.
[15] To Thomas Cushing, 6 May, *Writings*(S), VI, 48.
[16] Labaree, *Tea Party*, 51, 331.

tax them.[17] Others asserted that the act would make possible the entry of a vast monopoly into America, and that the East India Company, which had enslaved India, would enslave America.[18] Still other newspaper writers began attacking the use of tea itself. One declared that tea was an evil and dangerous as well as an "unconstitutional" drink. Another warned that a flea-like insect was to be found in old tea and that the company would ship no other kind.[19] Dr. Thomas Young of Boston assured his readers that newspaper charges that tea was a "pernicious drug" were wrong; "the sober truth is that tea is really a slow poison," and he offered "medical evidence" to prove it. A Virginia writer swore that the health of western Europe had so worsened since the introduction of tea "that our race is dwindled and become puny, weak, and disordered to such a degree, that were it to prevail a century more we should be reduced to mere pigmies." He offered such noxious substitutes as the hairy moss on the trees of the Virginia and Maryland lowlands which, he said, could be made into a brew good for bilious fevers, coughs, and catarrhs.[20]

Propaganda of all kinds prefaced the uprising against the Tea Act. What lay behind it: concern with constitutional principles, the fear of monopoly, the plots of tea smugglers? Such explanations were offered at the time and have been since, but one needs to distinguish between propaganda and the springs of political action. The idea that Americans could be taxed only by their own representatives was deeply embedded in their thinking by 1773. But the tea tax was not a new issue: it had been law since 1767; and in 1773 Americans virtually ignored the parliamentary taxes on molasses, sugar, and wine, which were producing the largest revenue ever collected in America. The ancient distrust of monopoly was a part of the colonists' English heritage, and warnings about monopoly doubtless helped to stir up public antagonism. However, it is likely that propaganda about monopoly had more impact on artisans than on the more sophisticated merchants. As for the tea smugglers, their opponents charged that they were the loudest defenders of constitutional rights.

Once one goes behind the propaganda in search of the instigators of the specific actions which in effect nullified a law of Parliament once more, it

[17] Virtually every American newspaper carried such articles week after week. For an example see Dr. Benjamin Rush's "Hamden" article, "On Patriotism," which first appeared in the *Pennsylvania Journal* on 20 October and was widely reprinted. It is reprinted in L. H. Butterfield, ed., *Letters of Benjamin Rush* (2 vols., Princeton, 1951), I, 83–84.
[18] "The Alarm" which appeared in New York during October is a good example of the anti-monopoly and other arguments. Shipton, *American Imprints*, Nos. 12799–12803.
[19] VG(R), 16 Dec. 1773.   [20] BEP, 25 Oct.; VG(PD), 13 Jan. 1774.

seems evident that, as in the days of non-importation, the popular leaders, supported by their artisan and shopkeeper followers, led the movement.[21] They had supporters, of course, among the merchants and professional men, but the leaders were those whose interests were essentially political, whatever their means of making a living.

Surprisingly enough the Philadelphians, who had always lagged behind, took the first concrete steps. In the doldrums after 1770 there were signs of change. The Philadelphia artisans organized a "Patriot Society" and began demanding representation in the legislature for themselves. The aristocracy was contemptuous at first. Before the election of 1772, one Quaker merchant sneered that the "patriots . . . would appear almost as weak and contemptible as they really are," and he was shocked when the anti-Galloway faction won seven of the ten seats from Philadelphia city and county.[22] The next year, Thomas Wharton, whom the mechanics had labeled "The Buckram Marquis of New Barrataria" because of his role in the Vandalia scheme, made plain his contempt for artisans in politics. One newspaper writer replied that mechanics, tradesmen, and farmers should not vote for those who would sell their liberties like merchandise, while another announced that the "lower orders" would meet to discuss candidates even if the "House of Wharton" disapproved.[23]

The Whartons were among the Philadelphia tea agents, and the election campaign in the fall of 1773 was paralleled by the campaign against the Tea Act. Thomas Mifflin, as "Scaevola," compared the tea agents to stamp agents and said they too must resign.[24] The result of the agitation was a great mass meeting on 16 October which agreed to resolutions that were to be a model for other colonies and were adopted by the Boston town meeting a few weeks later. The resolutions declared the tea tax to be taxation without consent and that the use of the proceeds for civil purposes had "a direct tendency to render assemblies useless and to introduce arbitrary government and slavery." They attacked the East India Company's part in the "plot" and declared that any American who aided it would be an enemy of his country. Finally, the resolutions called for a committee to demand the resignation of the tea agents.[25] Most of the agents promptly re-

[21] This interpretation differs from that of Schlesinger in his *Colonial Merchants and the American Revolution*, 270, where he asserts that "the fear of monopoly was the mainspring of American opposition. . . ." Arthur Jensen, who made a thorough study of the private correspondence of the Philadelphia merchants, says that in all the letters he read not a single merchant mentioned fear of monopoly as a reason for opposing the Tea Act. *Maritime Commerce*, 205.
[22] Ibid. 196–97; Thayer, *Pennsylvania*, 150–51.   [23] PG, 22 Sept.; PC, 27 Sept.
[24] Jensen, *Maritime Commerce*, 200.   [25] EHD, IX, 773–74.

signed, Thomas Wharton heading the list. His enemy, William Goddard of the *Pennsylvania Chronicle*, commented that Wharton was now "despised something less than he used to be." [26]

Philadelphia still faced the problem of what to do when the tea arrived. There were rumors that the company would pay the duty in England, but "William Bradford and others who are styled the Sons of Liberty" told two of the agents that the tea would be opposed, even if Parliament repealed the duty.[27] Clearly the popular leaders had taken over, and perhaps had been in control from the start. Many years later Charles Thomson remembered that the merchants had initiated the movement, but he also recalled that those who believed the Tea Act was but another maneuver of the ministry to stir up trouble "immediately adopted measures to bring the whole body of the people into the dispute and thereby put it out of the power of the merchants, as they had done before, to drop the opposition when interest dictated the measure." [28]

The popular leaders continued to agitate as they waited for the tea ship and they got out handbills threatening its captain and the Delaware River pilots with tar and feathers if they dared bring the ship to the city.[29] By the end of November, Abel James and Henry Drinker, two of the agents, were convinced that the popular temper was such that the tea could not be landed. As they saw it, some Philadelphians were opposed to violence, but most of them were also opposed to the revenue act, and therefore the agents were "unwilling to engage openly in opposition to the multitude. . . ." [30]

The popular leaders set up an unofficial committee of correspondence, and on hearing of the Boston Tea Party, approved Boston's action. However, they said that Philadelphia's plan of sending the tea back was best.[31] That night the tea ship *Polly* arrived at Chester with another tea agent, Gilbert Barkly, on board. He landed and promptly resigned when he heard the news from Philadelphia. The next morning Captain Ayres sailed up the river to the city where a large mass meeting resolved that he should return to England. He promptly agreed, took on stores, and started back. The *Pennsylvania Gazette* hailed the event and concluded that the attempt

[26] PC, 25 Oct.
[27] Jensen, *Maritime Commerce*, 204; Benjamin Rush to William Gordon, 10 Oct. 1773, *Letters*, I, 82.
[28] To William Drayton, n.d., NYHSC (1878), 279.   [29] EHD, IX, 774–76.
[30] Jensen, *Maritime Commerce*, 202.
[31] To BCC, 25 Dec., BCC Minutebook, 487–88.

to tax Americans without their consent had been broken and "the foundations of American liberty more deeply laid than ever." [32]

Although for once Philadelphia had taken the lead, it had, as usual,
acted mildly when compared to Boston. But behind the façade, Charles
Thomson, at least, was thinking of war. In response to a suggestion that
Samuel Adams and John Hancock would like to hear from him he wrote to
them at length on the need of union with Britain and of a constitutional
definition of that union. But with blunt realism he then went on and made
some specific suggestions: "the politicians and principal men" of the colonies should correspond with one another to unite the internal force of the
colonies; the military spirit of the people should be kept up by giving them
arms; and young men of fortune should visit foreign courts and establish
friendships and connections. Unless this were done, it would be madness
to hazard a break.[33]

Whatever the obscurity of the roots of opposition in Philadelphia, three
distinct groups were involved in the defeat of the Tea Act in Charleston—the mechanics, the planters, and the merchants. In mid-November
Peter Timothy's *Gazette* began reprinting attacks on the act from northern
newspapers. It also hinted that the people would not help land the tea and
that the merchants should "voluntarily" agree not to import it.[34] On 29
November the *Gazette* rumored that the inhabitants would meet. The tea
ship arrived on 2 December, and the next day a meeting, apparently mostly
of mechanics, voted that the agents of the East India Company should return the cargo.[35] The tea agents promptly resigned, but the merchants, as
a group, clearly had no intention of submitting, for they organized a
"Chamber of Commerce" a few days later.[36] The planters, who had remained aloof, now joined the mechanics in a meeting which was followed
the next day by a meeting of the merchants' committee. Finally, on Friday,
17 December, all three groups met together. A long-winded debate revealed so great a diversity of opinion that a formal organization was delayed,
although the meeting agreed that the tea ought not to be landed or sold.[37]

The inconclusive result gave Governor Bull a chance to act. Captain
Curling's tea ship was at the dock and the twenty days allowed before pay-

[32] PG, 29 Dec.; Jensen, *Maritime Commerce*, 203.
[33] 19 Dec., BCC Papers: General Correspondence.   [34] SCG(T), 15, 22 Nov.
[35] Ibid. 6 Dec.   [36] Ibid. 13 Dec.   [37] Ibid. 20 Dec.

ment of duties on a cargo were over on 22 December. Bull ordered the collector of the port to seize the tea for non-payment of duties, and the sheriff
to help him if need be. The collector landed and stored the tea without
opposition.[38]

When the news reached Boston, Samuel Adams sent back a startlingly
sharp reprimand. In view of Carolina's past, he wrote, "your sister colonies" had hoped for united opposition. "How great then was our chagrin
to hear that through some internal division the grand cause was neglected.
. . . Must then the liberties of the present and future ages be sacrificed
to some unhappy feuds in Carolina . . . ?" The lack of support by a
colony of far less importance would be bad enough, but if Carolina's divisions were not ended, it would be "a dreadful support of that truth 'that
by uniting we stand and by dividing we fall'. . . ." [39] Whether chastened
or not, the Carolinians finally had a "tea party" late in 1774, but it came
too late to affect the course of events anywhere.

The New Yorkers debated the issue far more bitterly than the Carolinians, but the non-arrival of a tea ship in 1773 freed them from the need to
act. Even so, the events in New York reveal much of the nature and complexity of American opposition. The *New York Mercury* printed the Tea
Act on 6 September and the newspapers were soon filled with the usual
charges that it was an attack on the constitutional liberties of America and
the grant of a dangerous monopoly. But some important people were not
impressed. Councilor William Smith noted that New Yorkers had been
smuggling all their tea from Holland since 1768 and that "now the Sons of
Liberty and the Dutch smugglers set up the cry of liberty." [40] Some found
it difficult to understand the Tea Act and interpreted it to mean that the
threepence a pound duty, first levied in 1767, had been repealed. Governor William Tryon reported that even if this were true, the smugglers, in
their efforts to mislead the people, would then use the "futile argument"
that the act was "a monopoly of a dangerous tendency . . . to American
liberties." [41] That smugglers were much interested, and that some were in
high places is clear. Hugh Wallace, merchant and member of the gover-

[38] Differing accounts of events in Charleston are in Sellers, *Charleston Business*, 220–26;
Schlesinger, *Colonial Merchants*, 295–98; and Richard Walsh, *Charleston's Sons of
Liberty* . . . (Columbia, S.C., 1959), 58–61.
[39] 20 Jan. 1774, BCC Minutebook, 719–20.   [40] Smith, *Memoirs*, 156.
[41] To SS, 3 Nov., NYCD, VIII, 400–401.

nor's council, virtually admitted at a council meeting that he was a smuggler.[42]

Of equal importance was the fact that the Tea Act presented Isaac Sears, Alexander McDougall, and John Lamb with an opportunity to regain a place in the political sun. Unheard of for three years, they now became extremely active at the familiar business of mass meetings and the adoption of resolutions, and they had the backing of the Livingston party, which still sought an issue with which to regain control of the legislature. They called a public meeting in October which thanked ship captains who had supposedly refused to take on tea cargoes in London.[43] Such activities led "Poplicola" to charge that the danger to New York's political liberties came not from Parliament but from a "cabal" in New York itself, to which John Holt's Journal replied that the miserable author had actually had to pay to get his article published.[44]

The propaganda campaign continued until 24 November when the "inhabitants" met again. A committee was sent to visit the tea agents, who agreed the next day not to sell duties tea.[45] Two days later some "Mohawks" threatened violence to anyone who helped land or store tea.[46]

The stage was now set for the formal reorganization of the Sons of Liberty by its old leaders, Sears, Lamb, and McDougall. On 29 November a mass meeting adopted "The Association of the Sons of Liberty." It began with the usual statement about the right of taxation and dangers of "slavery and its terrible concomitants," and concluded with some specific agreements. Anyone who helped bring in taxed tea would be deemed an enemy of the liberties of America, as would anyone who helped land, cart, or store it, or who bought it. Such a person "we will not deal with, or employ, or have any connection with him." Above all, it would make no difference whether the duty were paid in Britain or in America: "our liberties are equally affected." [47]

At the same time the tea agents got their commissions. They at once told the governor that they would not accept the tea, and Tryon and his council decided to land and store it in the military barracks when it arrived.[48] The decision seems to have been accepted by the populace, but a week later an express arrived with news that Boston would send its tea

42 Smith, Memoirs, 161.   43 NYJ, 21 Oct.
44 Rivington's New York Gazetteer [RNYG], 18 Nov.; NYJ, 25 Nov.
45 NYJ, 2 Dec.   46 RNYG, 2 Dec.
47 EHD, IX, 776–78. The correct date is 29 November when the agreement was made, not 15 December when it was published.
48 Smith, Memoirs, 157. The decision was made 1 December.

back in the ship in which it came. The "Liberty Boys now changed their tone" and decided that New York must do likewise. But they were anxious to know what the governor would do. Alexander McDougall explained to the Boston committee of correspondence that they had waited "for an accession of more respectable members" to the "Association," but that even so, the tea might be landed and stored. Two days later, the governor told his council that he would not use force to land the tea, and dramatically offered to throw himself "into the arms of the citizens" when the time came.[49] Upon hearing this news Sears and McDougall promptly called a mass meeting for the afternoon of 17 December.[50]

The alarmed governor and council finally agreed to send the mayor to the meeting with a message from Tryon urging that the tea be landed and stored in the fort while they awaited a decision from England. That afternoon a thousand or more met, with John Lamb in the chair as usual. He read letters from Boston and Philadelphia reporting their decision to return the tea. Then a committee was appointed to correspond with "our sister colonies," and the "Association" was read and approved "nem. con." The mayor was finally allowed to present the governor's message, but the crowd shouted down his proposal and voted that the tea should not be landed. The meeting did not dissolve—it merely adjourned to await the arrival of the tea ship.[51]

The conservative element had been out-maneuvered and out-shouted by the Sons of Liberty, and had been let down by the De Lancey representatives. One of them, a militia colonel, announced that he would do nothing to prevent the scuttling of the tea ship when it arrived.[52] The De Lanceys no more wanted violence than did the other conservatives, but they, like the Livingstons, had their eye on the next election, and they knew that the leaders of the Sons of Liberty and the bloc of voters they commanded were behind the Livingstons.

No one at the meeting knew that on that very Friday Paul Revere started from Boston with the news of its "Tea Party" of the day before. He got to New York on Tuesday night, 21 December,[53] and at once the conservatives abandoned hope of landing and storing the tea. Afraid of possible violence, they now agreed that the tea should be sent back, and Henry White, tea agent and member of the governor's council, made a secret agreement with the Sons of Liberty to that effect. Governor Tryon was just

---

[49] Ibid. 157, 159; McDougall to BCC, 13 Dec., BCC Minutebook, 472–73.
[50] NYJ, 23 Dec.   [51] Idem.; Smith, *Memoirs*, 160–61.
[52] Smith, *Memoirs*, 162.   [53] NYJ, 23 Dec.

as easily persuaded to give up his demand. William Smith commented that the governor wanted to be "popular" and that he was still worried about the reputation he had acquired when, as governor of North Carolina, he had suppressed the Regulator movement.[54] As the governor explained it to Secretary Dartmouth, the tea could have been landed "only under the protection of the point of the bayonet, and muzzle of the cannon. . . ."[55]

But the tea ship did not arrive until the next spring so the victory of the popular leaders in New York in 1773 was only one of principle and of organization. It was the news Paul Revere had brought from Boston that precipitated an explosion when it reached London.

The popular party in Massachusetts was not a monolithic group with a unified policy, as Thomas Hutchinson realized. "The conductors of the people are divided in sentiment," he reported in October 1773, just as the tea crisis was breaking. Men such as Speaker Thomas Cushing and other mercantile adherents of the party wanted to return to conditions prior to the Stamp Act, and were even willing to acknowledge the supremacy of Parliament. But the other wing of the party "declare they will be altogether independent. . . ." Each group needed the other's support, but both groups were dominated by one man: Samuel Adams. During the past seven years, said Hutchinson, "he has obtained such an ascendancy as to direct the town of Boston and the House of Representatives, and consequently the Council, just as he pleases." [56]

It was this extremist wing of the party, not the merchants, which directed the opposition to the Tea Act in Boston, but at first Adams and his followers seemed unaware of the political opportunity offered them. Ever since the publication of the Hutchinson-Oliver letters in June and the legislature's petition for the removal of the two men as governor and lieutenant governor, the *Boston Gazette* had carried on a campaign against Hutchinson unequaled in the previous decade, during which he had been the main butt of popular party propaganda. It was perhaps this concentration on his old enemy, plus the continuing attack on the payment of royal salaries to the superior court judges, that led Adams to ignore the Tea Act at first, although the *Boston Evening Post* contained a precise summary of it as early as 23 August, and a copy was printed in New York as early as 6 September.

54 Smith, *Memoirs*, 163, 173.　　55 3 Jan. 1774, NYCD, VIII, 407–8.
56 To SS, 9 Oct., Hosmer, *Hutchinson*, 289–92.

In fact, as late as 21 September, when the Adams-dominated Boston committee of correspondence sent out a circular letter bewailing the failure of the recent session of Parliament to redress American grievances, it still ignored the Tea Act. The letter warned of the danger of British oppression, but amidst all the rhetoric it cited but one specific example of what to expect—Parliament had "arbitrarily" deprived the East India Company of its "sacred charter rights"! [57]

Not until 11 October did the *Boston Gazette* begin the assault. It then asserted that the Tea Act was a scheme of Lord North to establish a precedent for parliamentary taxation and urged the Americans to show him that they were not ready for the "yoke of slavery" by sending the tea back. The next week the *Gazette* printed the names of the tea agents and suggested that the "mercantile spirit" which so distinguished the governor "bids fair to eternize" the names of his sons. As for the tea, if the people of Boston sent it back and did not destroy it as the people of New York and Philadelphia had resolved to do (said the *Gazette*, ignoring fact), Lord North would be forced to repeal the act. The only objection to returning the tea would be that "our excellent governor and superior judges" would have to "fall back into a dependence on the POPULACE for their support." [58]

The tea agents in Boston refused to submit as did agents in other colonies. They were supported by Governor Hutchinson, who believed that he could win in a showdown with the popular leaders, and by such men as Timothy Paine of Worcester. Paine wrote to one of the agents and told him that he hoped they would succeed in their "noble struggle against a set of cussed, venal, worthless rascals—for such I take Dr. Young and Molineux to be," and that they would convince "those lawless rascals that you even dare to withstand their devils, that call themselves Sons of Liberty. But from such liberty, good God deliver us!" [59]

The tea agents counterattacked vigorously and pointedly. They charged that the newspaper writers who harped on the danger of monopoly and of taxation without consent were either ignorant or trying to delude the people. Monopoly was not involved because tea could still be bought at auction in England and would be sold at auction in America. And it was hypocritical to charge that the Tea Act was a trick to raise money in America: "what consistency is there in making a clamor about this small branch of the revenue, whilst we silently pass over the articles of sugar, molasses, and rum," which are taxed by Parliament and which produce three-fourths

[57] 7, 10, 21 Sept., BCC Minutebook, 226–29, 234–35.   [58] 18 Oct.
[59] Timothy Paine to Isaac Clarke, 3 Nov., Misc. Bound Mss., MHS.

of all the revenue collected in America? Furthermore, the customs officials, as they had during non-importation in 1768–70, provided evidence showing that what Bostonians said did not square with what at least some Bostonians did. On 11 November the *Boston News-Letter* published customs house figures showing that Boston had imported more than 3000 chests of taxed English tea since the Townshend revenue act went into effect in 1768, an account that was soon reprinted in other American newspapers.[60]

The facts supported the tea agents and the customs officials, and since the popular leaders could not deny them, they ignored them. But they were well aware that Boston had a bad reputation in other colonies which dated back at least as far as the break-up of non-importation in 1770. Furthermore, as the weeks went by, letters from other colonies made it plain that men there expected Boston to do as it had in the past: proclaim high principles and then ignore them in practice.

The Boston committee of correspondence remained silent for a time but its leading members also belonged to an effective unofficial organization, the North End Caucus. On 23 October the Caucus met and decided that when the tea arrived it should not be sold. A few days later, handbills ordered the tea agents to appear at the Liberty Tree at noon on 3 November and resign their commissions. The Caucus met again on 2 November and "invited" the committee of correspondence to attend although many of its leading members were already present. It decided that the tea must be shipped back to England and Doctors Joseph Warren, Thomas Young, and Benjamin Church drafted a resolution to be read to the tea agents at the Liberty Tree the next day. It declared that they had "intolerably insulted" the Caucus and threatened that if they did not appear, the Caucus would esteem them enemies of their country and make them "feel the weight of their just resentment." [61]

The tea agents refused to appear; they met instead at Clarke's warehouse, where they were visited by a committee of nine from the Caucus Club, headed by William Molineux and backed up by a mob. The agents refused to resign and the committee departed, leaving the mob behind. The agents and their friends successfully opposed the mobsters.[62] The *Boston Gazette* and the *Evening Post* reported the affair in identical words: some of the people "being irritated with the haughty manner with

---

[60] "Z" in BEP, 25 Oct.; Drake, *Tea Leaves*, 281n.; Labaree, *Tea Party*, 112. Labaree's chapters VI and VII contain a marvelously detailed account of the events in Boston.
[61] Proceedings of the North End Caucus, E. H. Goss, *The Life of Colonel Paul Revere* (2 vols., Boston, 1891), II, 641–42.
[62] Clarke & Sons to Abraham Dupuis, Nov. 1773, Drake, *Tea Leaves*, 284–86.

which the answer was said to be given, turned back and showed some marks of their resentment and then dispersed." [63]

The Caucus Club and the mob had failed, and the town meeting took up the attack. It met on 5 November with John Hancock as moderator, adopted the Philadelphia resolutions of 16 October, and appointed a committee to demand the resignation of the tea agents. The agents in town refused, saying that they wanted to consult the Hutchinson brothers who were at Milton. They informed a second delegation headed by Samuel Adams that they had received no official word of their appointment and therefore could do nothing. The town meeting adjourned to the next day after appointing a committee headed by Hancock and Adams to visit the Hutchinsons at Milton. The next morning the delegation went to Milton, only to find that Elisha Hutchinson was in Boston, and when it got back to Boston, heard that he had returned to Milton. However, the committee did find Thomas Hutchinson, Jr., who said he could not possibly resign until he had definite information that he had been appointed.

The frustrated committee reported back to the town meeting, which voted that various letters of the agents were "daringly affrontive to the town." The comedy ended when both Hancock and Adams objected to a motion to thank Hancock for his services as moderator on the ground that a vote of thanks should be "only given upon very special and signal services performed for the public." [64]

The popular leaders had failed once more, but a few days later word arrived that the tea was on the way. The town met again on 18 November and demanded a direct answer from the agents. They replied that they had had no word from the East India Company and again refused to resign. The town meeting voted their answer unsatisfactory and then dissolved, not to meet again until 5 March 1774.[65]

The popular leaders gave up any pretense of legal action through the town meeting; subsequent opposition was guided by the committee of correspondence, that is, by Samuel Adams. Furthermore, within days he brought in committees from nearby towns to work with Boston in determining policy. On 22 November the committees of Boston, Dorchester, Roxbury, Brookline, and Cambridge agreed to prevent the landing of the tea. They also dispatched a circular letter requesting the support of other Massachusetts towns.[66]

The first tea ship, the *Dartmouth*, arrived on 27 November, and the next

---

[63] 8 Nov.   [64] BTR, XVIII, 141–46.   [65] Ibid. 146–48.
[66] 22–23 Nov., BCC Minutebook, 452–57.

day the Boston committee appealed to nearby towns for as many "friends" as possible to help Boston save "this oppressed country." [67] The five tea consignees and four of the customs commissioners fled to the protection of the British troops at Castle William in the harbor, and on 29 and 30 November more than 5000 people from Boston and the surrounding country met in Boston to pass resolutions.[68]

Once more, as during non-importation in 1769–70, this mass meeting, directed by the popular leaders, was known as "The Body." Now it was more powerful than ever, reinforced as it was by "voters" from surrounding towns. The merchant, John Rowe, long an associate of the popular party, reported that he had attended the meeting of "The Body" and had been chosen a committee man "much against my will but I dare not say a word." [69]

The Boston committee was the governing power in Boston. It took charge of the tea ships as they came in and placed guards upon them. It interrogated the captains and put pressure on them and the ship owners to ask for clearance papers so the ships could return to England. Meeting after meeting was held with committees from nearby towns, while still other towns in eastern Massachusetts adopted resolutions promising support for Boston. Day by day tension grew as the time approached when the *Dartmouth*, which had entered the customs house, would have to pay the duties on its cargo of tea or have it seized and landed by the customs service.[70]

But Governor Thomas Hutchinson was adamant. He refused to issue clearance papers and he ordered warships in the harbor to prevent the ship from sailing without them.[71] The twenty-day waiting period was up on 16 December, and that morning hundreds of people began pouring into Boston to attend still another great mass meeting. Further negotiations with the governor merely proved that he would not change his mind, and at last Samuel Adams arose and said: "This meeting can do no more to save the country."

Even before this "a number of brave and resolute men, dressed in the Indian manner, approached near the door of the assembly, gave the war whoop, which rang through the house and was answered by some in the galleries," but they were told to be silent. After the dissolution, "the Indians, as they were then called, repaired to the wharf where the ships lay

[67] 28 Nov. ibid. 458–59.
[68] 30 Nov. ibid. 459–60. Circular letter to Massachusetts towns, 1 Dec.
[69] 30 Nov., *Diary*, 256. [70] 3–14 Dec., BCC Minutebook, 460–64.
[71] Hosmer, *Hutchinson*, 302–3.

that had the tea on board, and were followed by hundreds of people to see the event of the transactions of those who made so grotesque an appearance." Three tea vessels lay at the wharf and the Indians "applied themselves so dextrously to the destruction of this commodity that in the space of three hours they broke up 342 chests . . . and discharged their contents into the dock. When the tide rose it floated the broken chests and the tea insomuch that the surface of the water was filled therewith a considerable way from the south part of the town to Dorchester Neck, and lodged on the shores. There was the greatest care taken to prevent the tea from being purloined by the populace." It was also "worthy of remark" that although there were other goods on board the vessels, they were not harmed. "Such attention to private property was observed that a small padlock belonging to the captain of one of the ships being broke, another was procured and sent to him."

Why was the tea destroyed? The first historian of the Revolution, the Reverend William Gordon, arrived in Massachusetts from England in 1770 and he soon became an intimate of the popular leaders and a supporter of their policies. When he wrote his history of the events in which he had taken part, he placed the blame on Thomas Hutchinson and the tea agents, but he went on to explain that there were other reasons for the event. He wrote that the Sons of Liberty realized that if the tea were landed it would eventually be offered for sale and that the people would buy it. The Sons of Liberty knew that "the virtue of the people . . . was too precarious a ground on which to risk the salvation of their country." Furthermore, they were obliged "to venture upon a desperate remedy" for "had the tea been landed, the union of the colonies in opposing the ministerial schemes would have been dissolved and it would have been extremely difficult ever after to have restored it. The fulfillment of their solemn declaration, that the tea should not be landed . . . secured them the good opinion and confidence of their co-patriots in other parts." [72]

If Gordon was right, and there is no reason to suppose that he was wrong, the Boston Tea Party was, in part at least, a desperate gamble by Boston's popular leaders to restore the town's reputation and to regain the confidence of the popular leaders in other colonies, a confidence they had lost. If such was the case, the gamble paid off handsomely within a few months.

The day after the Tea Party, Paul Revere mounted his horse and set off

[72] MG, 23 Dec. Reprinted, EHD, IX, 779; Gordon, History, I, 341–42.

on the first of his many rides as a confidential courier to other colonies. He went "express," carrying a letter from Samuel Adams to the popular leaders in New York and Philadelphia. "Yesterday," wrote Adams, "we had a greater meeting of the Body than ever, the country coming in from twenty miles round, and every step taken that was practicable for returning the teas. The moment it was known out of doors that Mr. Rotch could not obtain a pass for his ship by the Castle, a number of people huzzaed in the street, and in a very little time every ounce of the teas on board of the captains Hall, Bruce, and Coffin was immersed in the bay, without the least injury to private property." [73]

The newspapers and Adams alike ignored the fact that the tea was the private property of the East India Company, worth nearly £10,000. But John Adams did not. The next night he wrote in his diary: "This destruction of the tea is so bold, so daring, so firm, intrepid and inflexible, and it must have so important consequences, and so lasting, that I can't but consider it as an epocha in history.

"This however is but an attack on property. Another similar exertion of popular power, may produce the destruction of lives." And then, with remarkable foresight he predicted, in a series of rhetorical questions, several of the measures that Britain would adopt in response. "What measures will the ministry take, in consequence of this? Will they resent it? Will they dare to resent it? Will they punish us? How? By quartering troops upon us? By annulling our charter? By laying on more duties? By restricting our trade? By sacrifice of individuals, or how?" [74]

The first news of the Boston Tea Party reached London on 19 January. It was brought, fittingly enough, on John Hancock's ship the *Hayley*, captained by James Scott. Three days later an account derived from Boston newspapers brought by Scott was printed in a London newspaper, but the ministry had to wait several more days before it received Hutchinson's official account. Week by week as more news arrived, political England boiled

---

[73] 17 Dec., BCC Papers, Other Colonies, NYPL.
[74] 17 Dec. There are various estimates of the value of the tea destroyed. Donouzhue, *British Politics*, 25, n. 2, gives a value of £7521. Labaree, *Tea Party*, 141, says "about £9000." The tea on the four ships sent to Boston was invoiced at £10,994.5.6. East India Company to Dartmouth, 20 Dec. 1773, C.O. 5/133. The company informed Dartmouth on 14 February 1774 that the tea destroyed at Boston was valued at £9659.6.4. The discrepancy is due to the fact that the brig *William* was wrecked on Cape Cod.

with indignation. Be prepared, Arthur Lee warned Samuel Adams, "to meet some particular stroke of revenge." [75] Some weeks later Franklin reported that "I suppose we never had since we were a people, so few friends in Britain. The violent destruction of the tea seems to have united all parties here against us." [76]

At first, the ministry tried to devise a means of punishing Boston without turning to Parliament. On 29 January, the day Benjamin Franklin was denounced before the Privy Council for his part in the affair of the purloined letters, and accused of plotting revolution, the cabinet resolved that something must be done to secure the dependence of the colonies on the mother country. A few days later it followed up this vague statement with a decision to remove the government and the customs officials from Boston, and it was informed by the law officers that the Crown had the power to do so.[77]

Dartmouth also sent a detailed account of events in Boston prior to and during the Tea Party to the law officers. He asked if the acts amounted to high treason, and if so, who could be charged and how could they be punished? [78] Attorney General Edward Thurlow and Solicitor General Alexander Wedderburn had no love for America or Americans. Wedderburn in particular, had made this clear in his brutal assault on Franklin before the Privy Council on 29 January. Nevertheless, the law officers had respect for law and evidence. They delayed a reply until prodded by Dartmouth, and then they reported that the acts in Boston were indeed high treason and that Samuel Adams, John Hancock, Dr. Thomas Young, and others were chargeable. But, they said, the evidence brought by Captain James Scott, "the only person now in England who can give evidence," was inadequate for a prosecution.

Doubtless, John Hancock's captain was relieved, but Lord Dartmouth was irked. He gathered a dozen additional witnesses who had arrived from Boston in the meantime, interviewed them, and then took them before the Privy Council, where they were examined under oath on 19 February. At the end of the session the Privy Council was ready to sign warrants for the arrest of the Boston leaders and their removal to England for trial. The additional evidence was submitted to the law officers and once more they delayed. Then on the last day of February they declared flatly the charge of high treason could not be maintained on the basis of the new evi-

[75] 8 Feb., Adams Papers, NYPL.
[76] To Thomas Cushing, 22 March, Writings(S), VI, 223.
[77] Donoughue, British Politics, chapter III, "Deciding Measures."
[78] 5 Feb., CHOP, IV, 178–79; Donoughue, British Politics, 50–52.

dence. Entirely apart from the legal niceties involved, the law officers probably recognized, as Franklin commented, that if the "lower actors" were
disguised, it was highly unlikely that the leading inhabitants appeared
openly.[79]

After a month of frustration the ministry finally turned to Parliament,
which was ever more insistent that the issue be laid before it. Action by
Parliament meant, inevitably, far more than the punishment of Boston; it
meant a confrontation between a Parliament determined to assert its sovereignty over America and a group of Americans equally determined to
deny that sovereignty. Lord Dartmouth, despite his insistence for the need
of punishing Boston, apparently still hoped for moderation. As late as
14 March, the day the Boston Port bill was moved in the House of Commons, he assured Shelburne of his "determination to cover America from
the present storm," and even Lord North's language was reported to be of
a "moderate cast." [80] But it was too late for moderation.

On 7 March Lord North laid a message from the king and 109 documents describing resistance to the Tea Act before the House of Commons.
When he asked leave to bring in a bill closing the port of Boston, he said
that commerce was unsafe in Boston and that the customs house should be
moved and the port closed until the tea was paid for and the maintenance
of law and order could be guaranteed. But the real issue, he declared, was
that at "Boston we are considered as two independent states" and it was
therefore no longer a dispute about legislation and taxation. Parliament
must now consider "only whether or not we have any authority. . . ." [81]

The opponents of the bill raised questions and made charges. One declared that Britain had no right to tax America, but the house made so
much noise that he could not be heard. Another asked why Boston alone
should be punished, and above all, why shouldn't the town be heard in its
own defense? Captain Phipps denounced the Declaratory Act as one of
the most absurd and unconstitutional acts ever passed. Lord Cavendish
urged the Commons to forget idle ideas of superiority and warned that the
"country which is kept by power, is in danger of being lost every day."
Others predicted that the bill would "create that association of the Americans which you have so much wished to annihilate," and that a "sort of
rebellion will take place" when news of the bill reaches America. When
the bill passed, Edmund Burke solemnly declared: "this is the day, then,

[79] To Thomas Cushing, 22 March, Writings(S), VI, 224; Donoughue, British Politics,
58–61.
[80] Shelburne to Chatham, 15 March, Pitt Corres., IV, 335.
[81] PH, XVII, 1159–67.

that you wish to go to war with all America, in order to conciliate that country to this. . . ." [82]

Some of the questions were relevant, and events were to prove the dire predictions right, but both were brushed aside by a determined majority. To those who charged that Boston would refuse to obey the Port bill, Lord North replied that if a rebellion resulted, "those consequences belong to them, and not to us. . . ." It is useless to reason with Americans, said one speaker, because they "always choose to decide the matter by tarring and feathering"; while another hoped that the bill would "bring these tarring and feathering casuists to a little better reason," and said that it would not take military force to do it. No one outdid a Mr. Van who proclaimed that "the town of Boston ought to be knocked about their ears, and destroyed. Delenda est Carthago . . . you will never meet with that proper obedience to the laws of this country until you have destroyed that nest of locusts." [83]

On a wave of such emotion the Port bill passed the Commons on 25 March, went through the Lords without dissent, and was signed by the king on 31 March. The act abolished Boston as a port and forbade all shipping in and out except for food and firewood brought in coastwise. But even such vessels must carry cockets and passes, be searched by customs officers of the Salem district, and be accompanied to Boston by a customs officer and an armed force. Boston was not to be re-established as a port until it paid for the tea, and until the governor certified that it had compensated the customs officers who had suffered damage during the riots.[84]

Any hope Dartmouth had of stopping punishment with the Port bill was now gone. Three days later Lord North proposed a bill to alter the Massachusetts charter. There was no precedent for such parliamentary revision of a royal charter to a colony, although at the beginning of the century Parliament had tried and failed to abolish all colonial charters. The Massachusetts Government Act embodied many of the changes long urged by Francis Bernard and Thomas Hutchinson. It substituted a royally appointed council for the annually elected one, and gave the governor unchecked powers such as were possessed by no other executive in the thirteen colonies. The governor could appoint and remove all judicial and other officers without the advice and consent of his council, and no town meetings, except the annual spring election meetings, could be held without his con-

[82] Ibid. 1167–70, 1184–85.   [83] Ibid. 1170–73, 1178.
[84] EHD, IX, 780–81. Donoughue, *British Politics*, chapter IV, "The Massachusetts Legislation," is a detailed account of the passage of the Intolerable Acts.

sent. The election of juries, or their summoning by local constables, was abolished. The power of summoning juries was placed in the hands of the county sheriffs, who were the governor's appointees.[85]

The king signed the bill on 20 May, and on the same day approved the Administration of Justice Act. It provided that if magistrates or customs officials, or others acting under their direction, were indicted for murder as a result of their efforts to suppress riots or enforce the revenue laws, the governor, if convinced that a fair trial was impossible in Massachusetts, could order the trial held in another colony or in Great Britain.[86]

The fourth and last of what the colonies labeled the "Intolerable Acts" became law on 2 June. In effect it was an amendment to the Quartering Act. It empowered the commander of military forces in America to quarter troops wherever needed, even if outside regular barracks, and even in private houses.[87]

The debates on these bills were lengthy, as they had been on the Port bill, and opposition grew. But the pressure for such measures was overwhelming. Mr. Van, who had demanded that Boston be treated like Carthage, was an extremist, but he did represent the emotional state of the majority. During the debate on the Administration of Justice bill, he swore that if the Americans opposed any of the measures, "I would do as was done of old, in the time of ancient Britons, I would burn and set fire to all their woods, and leave their country open to prevent that protection they now have; and if we are likely to lose that country, I think it better lost by our own soldiers than wrested from us by our rebellious children." [88]

One striking fact that emerged from these debates was that the members of Parliament took it for granted that Britain and America were two different countries. The majority clearly looked upon Americans as an inferior, irresponsible breed of men, a rabble, a people who were and who should be treated like children with no will of their own and with no right to be heard in their defense. The majority assumed, despite all past experience, that the Americans would acquiesce in such punitive legislation, and that if they did not, a slight military force could soon whip them into submission.

The members of the disunited opposition saw that this was a fatal attitude, but some of them went along with the punitive measures. Colonel Isaac Barré, who had described Americans as "Sons of Liberty" in 1765, agreed to the Boston Port Act which he described as "harsh" but "moder-

85 EHD, IX, 781–83.   86 Ibid. 784–85.   87 Ibid. 785.
88 PH, XVII, 1210.

ate," although he balked at later measures. Thomas Pownall plaintively lectured the Commons about the real needs of the colonies, but no heed was paid to "experts." Such men were better at predicting consequences than in providing solutions. When Chatham heard of the Port bill he cried eloquently that if the ministry tried to "crush the spirit of liberty among the Americans . . . England has seen her best days"; and when he heard of the Government Act, he feared that "the cause [would] become general on that vast continent. If this happen, England is no more, how big words soever the sovereign in his Parliament of Great Britain may utter." [89]

But Chatham had nothing specific to offer in 1774, nor did the other opponents of the Intolerable Acts, except of course to do nothing, a politically impossible solution. In fact, the debates showed that both the majority and the minority were more concerned with attacking and defending the conduct of the various ministries since 1763 than they were with rational solutions for the current crisis. The Stamp Act was as much the hero or the villain as the town of Boston, as the debaters tried to place the blame for all the troubles with America on this or that or the other ministry in the past.

Thus when Rose Fuller proposed the repeal of the tea duty as the only way to render the Boston Port Act effective, the debate soon centered around the Stamp Act. Its repeal had been the great mistake and matters had gotten worse ever since. In other words, the Rockingham ministry was to blame for all the troubles in America, for it had abandoned a right which should have been, and should still be, maintained. This refrain had run through the debates ever since 7 March when Lord North first laid the issue before the Commons, and it now stirred Edmund Burke to make his speech on American taxation, a speech often cited but apparently seldom read.

It contained many quotable phrases and judicious statements about the nature of America and the rights of its people, but its main concern was to defend the policies of the Rockingham ministry and to attack all other ministries. Burke gave his version of "history," even going back as far as the first Navigation Act, but he concentrated his fire on the leaders since 1763. Grenville was a great and honest man but his training made him illiberal and unimaginative and incapable of dealing with great issues (Burke lacked only the word "bureaucrat" in its unpleasant connotations). Chat-

---

[89] To Shelburne, 20 March, 6 April, Pitt. Corres., IV, 337, 342.

ham was a great man too, but as a minister he was too much governed by "general maxims" which led him to adopt measures mischievous to himself and "perhaps fatal to his country." He put together a ministry which was a "tessellated pavement" all "pigging together, heads and points, in the same truckle bed." The result was chaos and it allowed Charles Townshend, a man of great wit and charm but so anxious to please that he had no principles, to carry out his mischievous policies. As for the partial repeal of the Townshend revenue act, it was carried out in a way to insult the dignity of Parliament; and Lord North, in the light of his past inconsistencies, was obviously irresponsible. Only one ministry in all these years of turmoil stood out—that of Rockingham—and its leader was pictured as a man of infinite wisdom and infallible judgment. Obviously, in Burke's eyes, Rockingham was the only possible savior of Britain, whose plight in 1774 was entirely due to the abandonment of his colonial policies.

But in the end Burke wound up on the side of the majority, for he too was devoted to the principle of the Declaratory Act passed by the Rockingham ministry when it repealed the Stamp Act. And although Burke would repeal the tax on tea, he would not give up the right of taxation which might be necessary, especially in time of war.[90]

Both the majority and minority in Parliament were blind to the fundamental position of a significant group of American leaders; and even the opposition leaders, despite their dire predictions, had little comprehension of the impact the Intolerable Acts would have on Massachusetts, much less on the rest of America. A final testimonial to British ignorance of American opinion was the appointment of General Thomas Gage, commanding general of the British army in North America, as governor of Massachusetts in place of Thomas Hutchinson who had permission to come to England.[91]

Whether most Britons knew it or not, they had abandoned any pretense of concern with constitutionality and right in the dispute with America. As Dartmouth put it baldly: "The supreme legislature of the whole British Empire has laid a duty (no matter for the present whether it has or has not the right so to do, it is sufficient that we conceive it has). . . ." The people of America, and particularly of Boston, have behaved treasonably, and laws have been passed to punish them. "The question then is whether

[90] PH, XVII, 1210–69.
[91] The decision was made between 9 March and 9 April and Hutchinson was assured that Gage's appointment would be temporary. To Hutchinson, 9 April, C.O. 5/763. See also Dartmouth to Gage, 9 April, Gage, *Corres.*, II, 159–62.

these laws are to be submitted to? If the people of America say no, they say in effect that they will no longer be a part of the British empire. . . ." [92]

To the enormous surprise of many Britons, some Americans did say "no," and then proceeded to make the answer effective.

[92] To Joseph Reed, 11 July, W. B. Reed, *Life and Correspondence of Joseph Reed* (2 vols., Philadelphia, 1847), I, 73–74.

XVIII

The Beginnings of American Union: The Creation of the First Continental Congress

The concept of an American union was an old one by 1774, but the various plans for such a union had always assumed that the colonies would remain an integral part of the British Empire and subordinate to its authority. By the end of 1773, however, anonymous newspaper writers had developed a new concept of American union. They argued that there should be an "American Congress" to speak for all Americans, and they made it plain that such a congress should have equal status with British authority as represented by king and Parliament. Furthermore, the relationship between an American congress and a declaration of American independence had been stated bluntly by the Massachusetts House of Representatives in its reply to Governor Hutchinson's speech asserting the sovereignty of Parliament in January 1773.

The arrival of copies of the act closing the port of Boston in May 1774, after weeks of rumors that it was on the way, was followed at once by almost simultaneous proposals in various colonies that a congress should meet and decide upon common policies of resistance. The intricate political maneuverings of American leaders as they brought about an agreement to meet in a congress, and elected delegates to it, resembled in many ways the politics involved in every congressional election from that day to this, although those American leaders in 1774 did not realize that they were establishing an institution, the Congress of the United States, whose history stretches in an unbroken line from their day to ours.

The Boston Tea Party was the climax of the campaign against the Tea Act. Some nearby Massachusetts towns approved, but men of "sense and property," such as George Washington in Virginia, did not approve. Their emotions, if not their words, were those of the New Yorker who in 1770 described Boston as the "common sewer of America into which every beast that brought with it the unclean thing has disburthened itself." [1] Yet so far as American newspapers reflected public opinion early in 1774, few Americans seemed to realize that Britain would retaliate so drastically that Boston would become, in popular opinion at least, a citadel of liberty, not a "sewer."

Many of the popular leaders who had emerged into political daylight once more as opponents of the Tea Act, found it difficult to keep agitation going during the first months of 1774. The Sons of Liberty in Charleston secured the appointment of a committee to prevent the importation of tea, but most Carolinians ignored their efforts. Philadelphia resumed its usual quiet. In New York, Sears, Lamb, and McDougall secured an agreement to return the tea after the arrival of the news of the Boston Tea Party, but no tea ships arrived in New York in 1773. They were frustrated and at the end of February 1774 they informed the Boston committee of correspondence that they had waited long and impatiently for the arrival of the tea ships. They urged the Boston newspapers to promote the idea of an absolute boycott of English tea. They said they could not mention it in New York "least it might divide us." [2] They agitated against using public funds to rebuild the governor's house after it burned, but all they achieved was a denunciation of themselves as "Generals Vox Populi, Vox Mobili, and Vox Diaboli." [3] A tea ship finally arrived in New York in April and was sent back. When the captain of another ship tried to smuggle tea ashore, "Mohawks" dumped it in the harbor, and the captain was lucky to escape with his life. But this event only further consolidated conservative opinion against the Sons of Liberty who were denounced as "cobblers and tailors" who wanted to take "upon their everlasting and unmeasurable shoulders the power of directing the loyal and sensible inhabitants of the city. . . ." [4]

The popular leaders reigned unchecked only in Boston. During the Tea Party crisis the customs commissioners had fled to Castle William once more and were joined there by the tea agents. John Malcolm, brother of the smuggler, Captain Daniel Malcolm, was a minor British customs official. One night in January he was beaten and tarred and feathered by a Boston mob. "They say his flesh comes off his back in stakes," reported

---

[1] NYG, 27 Aug. 1770.   [2] To BCC, 28 Feb., BCC Minutebook, 742–46.
[3] NYJ, 6 Jan.; RNYG, 13 Jan.
[4] RNYG, 28 April; Becker, *New York*, 108–10.

Ann Hulton. And the merchant, John Rowe, increasingly dubious about his association with the popular party, declared that the event was "looked upon by me and every sober man as an act of outrageous violence. . . ." [5] The committee of correspondence directed a campaign to catch and punish users of tea in and around Boston. On 7 March, when Captain Gorham arrived with twenty-eight chests of tea, a private shipment by a London merchant to a Boston merchant, the committee went through the motions of consulting with other towns, but on 8 March the "Indians . . . with great regularity and dispatch emptied the whole of them into the Sea." [6]

The committee congratulated other committees in the colony on how "political knowledge is catch'd and communicated from town to town," and on the adoption of legislative committees of correspondence at the invitation of Virginia. There was hope, declared the Bostonians, that a joint plan would be agreed upon which "will fix the liberties of America upon a basis not to be shaken by the rude hand of power." The spread of "intelligence" had defeated Britain's schemes, and had prevented her from taking money out of American pockets "to feed the State Caterpillars in Britain and America." [7]

But the "rude hand of power" still had force and the "State Caterpillars" were not mere worms, as Americans found out during the last two weeks of May 1774. By the end of the month the act closing the port of Boston had been printed in every leading American newspaper. At once there was a demand that the other colonies come to the aid of Boston, but distrust of that town was widespread in America. It was fortunate for Boston, wrote David Ramsay, that the other Intolerable Acts followed closely on the heels of the Port Act for they seemed to form a "complete system of tyranny" and a precedent dangerous to the liberty of all the colonies. The "patriots" in all the colonies therefore tried to "bring over the bulk of the people" but "much prudence as well as patriotism was necessary," for the other colonies were only remotely affected by the fate of Massachusetts and had no reason to oppose Britain.

"To convince the bulk of the people, that they had an interest in foregoing a present good, and submitting to a present evil, in order to obtain a future greater good, and to avoid a future greater evil, was the task assigned to the colonial patriots. But it called for the exertion of their utmost abilities. They effected it in a great measure, by means of the press. Pamphlets, essays, addresses and newspaper dissertations were daily presented to the

[5] 31 Jan., Hulton, *Letters*, 70–72; Rowe, *Diary*, 261.
[6] 7–9 March, BCC Minutebook, 726–29; Labaree, *Tea Party*, 164–66.
[7] To Sandwich CC, 9 March, BCC Minutebook, 730.

public, proving that Massachusetts was suffering in the common cause, and that interest and policy, as well as good neighborhood, required the united exertions of all the colonies, in support of that much injured province." However, Ramsay said, "the few who were at the helm, disclaimed anything more decisive than convening the inhabitants, and taking their sense on what was proper to be done. In the meantime great pains were taken to prepare them for the adoption of vigorous measures." [8]

Ramsay himself was one of the "patriots" whose activities he described in his history. One of the greatest achievements of these "patriots," or popular leaders, was the convening of the First Continental Congress, a meeting brought about despite the opposition of many powerful American leaders and widespread public indifference. And strangely enough, there was at first resistance from the popular leaders of Boston, and particularly, from Samuel Adams.

ॐ

Samuel Adams, John Hancock, Thomas Cushing, and William Phillips were "almost unanimously" re-elected Boston's representatives in the legislature on 10 May 1774. That same day the *Harmony* arrived from London with "the severest act ever penned against the town of Boston." John Rowe, a merchant, was shocked, but at least one of the popular leaders was delighted. That indefatigable agitator, Dr. Thomas Young, reported to John Lamb in New York that "at length the perfect crisis of American politics seems arrived and a very few months must decide whether we and our posterity shall be slaves or freemen." A few weeks later Ann Hulton summed up the "artifices and arguments" by which "the people are inflamed to the highest degree." They were told, she reported, that the Port Act was the best thing that could happen to America because it would unite the colonies, distress British manufacturers, and raise their friends in Britain. They could expect a rebellion in Britain "which will answer our purpose, and we shall become entirely free and independent. But if we now submit, our lands will be taxed, Popery introduced, and we shall be slaves forever." [9]

The popular leaders did not limit themselves to "artifices and arguments." Two days after the Port Act arrived, the Boston committee of correspondence met at noon and voted to request a town meeting the

[8] Ramsay, *American Revolution*, I, 108, 112–14.
[9] Rowe, *Diary*, 269; Young to Lamb, 13 May, quoted in Labaree, *Tea Party*, 220; Ann Hulton to Mrs. Adam Lightbody, 8 July, Hulton, *Letters*, 75.

next morning. By three o'clock on the same afternoon, committees from eight nearby towns had arrived in Boston. With Samuel Adams as chairman, they prepared letters to committees of correspondence in the northern colonies asking them to support Boston by stopping their trade with Britain, a "great but necessary sacrifice to the Cause of Liberty. . . ."[10] The next day, Adams, as moderator of the town meeting, secured ratification of the previous day's decisions. A committee headed by Adams brought in two specific proposals: (1) that all imports from Britain and the West Indies be stopped; (2) that all exports to Britain and the West Indies be stopped. The town meeting approved "nem. con." and directed Adams to send copies of the votes and his letters to all "our sister colonies."[11]

Ever since 1765 economic coercion of Britain had been limited to the non-importation of British goods, and only a partial non-importation at that. Now the town of Boston, whose port was closed to such trade, was asking the other colonies to sacrifice their trade with the British Empire, and to do so at once. Paul Revere carried the request to Hartford, New York, and Philadelphia. Letters to places nearer by were simply put in the mail.[12]

The town meeting on 13 May was but one important event. During the same day, General Thomas Gage, commanding general of the British army in America, arrived in Boston from London with a commission as governor of Massachusetts.[13] He was taking the place of Thomas Hutchinson, who was to sail to England on 1 June for a visit. Hutchinson never returned to his native land and Gage did not know that for all practical purposes he would be governor for only a month. On 17 June he dissolved the Massachusetts legislature for electing delegates to the First Continental Congress, and it never met again. A year later, to the day, his troops were slaughtered at Bunker Hill, and shortly thereafter he lost his post as commanding general.

Towns throughout New England responded at once to Boston's plea by adopting resolutions. None were more resounding than those of Farmington in Connecticut, which denounced the British cabinet as "instigated by the devil, and led on by their wicked and corrupt hearts," and "those pimps and parasites" who advised their master to adopt such measures. Farmington concluded by resolving "That we scorn the chains of slavery; we despise every attempt to rivet them upon us; we are the sons of free-

---

[10] BCC Minutebook, 755–56, 810–11.   [11] BTR, XVIII, 172–74.
[12] BCC Minutebook, 757–58.   [13] Rowe, *Diary*, 269.

dom, and resolved, that, till time shall be no more, that god-like virtue shall blazon our hemisphere." [14]

The Bostonians could provide their own rhetorical flourishes. They wanted concrete help, but their proposal that trade be stopped created bitter disputes in other colonies. The popular leaders in them demanded immediate action to support Boston. The more conservative leaders and many powerful merchants were opposed to any support at all, although some of them thought the Port Act too severe, and a dangerous precedent. Most merchants had had enough of economic coercion and popular agitation back in 1768–70, and the belief that Boston merchants had cheated during those years was still very much alive. Above all they could not condone Boston's destruction of property, whatever the principles at stake. For such reasons many merchants in New York, Philadelphia, and Charleston opposed the adoption of Boston's proposals. Yet they had to take some action if they were to retain any influence on events, for popular opinion was soon stirred up as it had not been since the Stamp Act.

The solution that the leaders turned to was a continental congress, which had been widely publicized by the newspapers and which for some time had been a goal of most of the popular leaders. Conservative-minded men in New York and Philadelphia also agreed to the idea of a congress to delay or to avoid the stoppage of trade, or hoped that if one did meet, they could dictate its measures. In any case there was general agreement that if any economic measures were to be adopted, they must be uniform for all the colonies. The chaos of the non-importation movement against the Townshend program would have to be avoided.

Four days after the Boston town meeting sent out its appeal for the stoppage of trade, Providence, Rhode Island, voted that it would support Boston if the other colonies would co-operate. Providence also voted that a congress of all the colonies was needed to adopt specific measures and instructed its delegates in the legislature to propose one.[15] The Boston committee of correspondence was taken aback. It replied to Providence that "*a congress of the merchants* . . . would effectually do the business." However, it approved of "your plan of a *Congress of American States*," and said the Massachusetts legislature would take it up, but insisted that "there must be both a *political* and a *commercial* congress." [16] The Rhode

[14] EHD, IX, 792.   [15] BG, 30 May.   [16] 21 May, BCC Minutebook, 796–98.

Island legislature ignored the advice and on 15 June elected delegates to a continental congress.[17]

The Bostonians met an even sharper rebuff from Connecticut. On 3 June, Silas Deane replied for the legislature that a continental congress was needed, that the resolves of merchants would be partial, and that the united measures of the colonies as a whole would carry more weight and influence with the people. The next day the legislature adjourned after instructing its committee of correspondence to write to other colonies suggesting a congress and authorizing it to pick Connecticut's delegates.[18]

Resistance soon developed in Boston itself. On 20 May the committee of correspondence prepared a "merchants agreement" to stop importation. Some merchants signed it and then backed out when merchants in other colonies took no action.[19]

Meanwhile, it was obvious that if the destroyed tea were paid for, the port could be re-opened. Therefore, a number of Boston merchants and their allies prepared an address and presented it to Thomas Hutchinson on 28 May, four days before he was to sail for England. The address lamented that Hutchinson was no longer governor, deplored the destruction of the tea, and promised to find money to pay for it. Two days later the committee of correspondence wrote the New Yorkers that the address was "set on foot by some worthless wretches capable of being instigated to any degree of prostitution to prop the character of their tottering hero. . . ." Shortly thereafter the committee wrote Philadelphia that the signers of the address were a "wretched group of subscribers consisting of placemen, pensioners, and needy expectants. . . ." The facts were quite otherwise. Among the signers were some of the wealthiest merchants in Boston and members of several of the most distinguished families in the history of the colony. Sixty-three merchants, factors, and tradesmen, twenty artisans and mechanics, twelve royal officials, and a scattering of others thus publicly declared themselves enemies of the popular leaders—and consigned themselves, ultimately, to oblivion.[20]

---

[17] Lovejoy, *Rhode Island*, 167–68.
[18] Peter Force, ed., *American Archives* . . . [Force] (4th series, 6 vols., Washington, 1837–46), I, 304–5.
[19] BCC Minutebook, 759; Schlesinger, *Colonial Merchants*, 315–18.
[20] Force, 4 ser. I, 361–62; BCC to New York committee, 30 May, and to Philadelphia committee, n.d., BCC Minutebook, 807–08, 817; Schlesinger, *Colonial Merchants*, 317 n.2. On 8 June the signers of the address to Hutchinson presented an address to Governor Gage and again promised to make an effort to pay for the tea. Force, 4 ser. I, 398–99.

The popular leaders had learned about the preparation of the address to Hutchinson as early as 22 May. On 27 May the committee of correspondence appointed a committee to prepare a "counter address." However, when it was published in the *Boston Gazette* it was dated 24 May and presented as the "unanimous" opinion of the merchants and tradesmen of Boston.[21] The assertion was as false as the date, and not a single name was attached. The popular leaders then aimed a body blow at the Boston merchants who opposed them. On 30 May the town meeting voted for the preparation of a non-consumption agreement to be taken to each family in town for signing, and directed the committee of correspondence to circulate the agreement throughout the colony. The committee at once prepared a "Solemn League and Covenant," which harked back, in name at least, to the Cromwellian compact aimed at Charles I. Buried in the pseudo-religious prose was a simple agreement to stop buying British goods and to end all dealings with the importers, and with those who refused to sign.[22]

Despite the order of the town meeting, the Solemn League was not circulated in Boston, where there was a growing demand that the tea be paid for, and where even the tradesmen refused to support the committee.[23] The committee therefore sent the document throughout the colony, implying that Boston had approved, and within a short time, unblushingly tried to pass it off as the creation of the farmers and mechanics of the country towns. The Reverend Charles Chauncy had pointed the way when he denounced the merchants as so mercenary that they were willing to become slaves and then proclaimed that "our dependence, under God, is upon the landed interest, upon our freeholders and yeomanry."

Within two weeks the *Boston Gazette* assured its readers that the country people were adopting non-consumption because they were impatient at the delay in adopting non-importation, and the committee of correspondence blandly informed the New Yorkers that the Solemn League and Covenant had originated with the "two venerable orders of men, styled mechanics and husbandmen, the strength of every community."[24] Whatever Samuel Adams and his colleagues were, they were neither mechanics nor farmers, and their discovery of the virtues of farmers was as belated as it was temporary. All their propaganda could not hide the fact that the Sol-

[21] BCC to Marblehead, 22 May, BCC Minutebook, 814–15, 761–62; BG, 30 May; Force, 4 ser. I, 362–63.
[22] BTR, XVIII, 176; BCC Minutebook, 763–64; Force, 4 ser. I, 397–98.
[23] Joseph Warren to Adams, 14 June, Samuel Adams Papers, NYPL; Rowe, *Diary*, 275.
[24] Schlesinger, *Colonial Merchants*, 318–20; BG, 13 June; BCC Minutebook, 819–20.

emn League and Covenant was a failure. At first only a few Massachusetts towns adopted it and one town accused Boston of trying to cheat country people by getting rid of its old goods.[25]

Meanwhile, the harbor emptied of shipping and the merchants and tradesmen held meeting after meeting without coming to any agreement as to what to do. One merchant declared that unless the tea were paid for and the port opened, Boston would face the worst of all evils, civil war. The "trading part" he said was willing to pay for the tea, but "those who have governed the town for years past and were in great measure the authors of all our evils, by their injudicious conduct, are grown more obstinate than ever. . . ."[26] Some merchants had offered to provide money from their own pockets; but naturally they thought the town itself should pay for the tea. The popular leaders were opposed to any payment whatever. Joseph Warren was so afraid that the merchants would capture a town meeting on 17 June that he told Samuel Adams, who was at the legislature in Salem, that he must return: "The party who are for paying for the tea . . . are too formidable," he explained.[27]

Adams did not return. He had finally given up his opposition to a continental congress and on 17 June he locked the door of the room where the legislature was meeting. One of the members, realizing what was happening, pleaded a "call of nature" and then ran to tell Governor Gage. While the governor's secretary stood outside the locked door reading a proclamation which ended the colonial legislature of Massachusetts, the men inside elected five delegates, including John and Samuel Adams, to the First Continental Congress, and set the date for 1 September at Philadelphia.[28]

At the Boston town meeting on the same day, Joseph Warren's fears proved unjustified, although there were hints of difficulty. James Bowdoin was elected moderator but he could not be found. Then John Rowe was elected but he professed to be too busy. Finally, John Adams was named moderator and all went smoothly. The meeting voted warm thanks to the committee of correspondence and then adjourned until 27 June.[29] Merchants who wanted the town to pay for the tea had not been ready on 17 June, but they were ready on the 27th and they made a desperate attempt to capture the town meeting. It was so large that it had to move to Old South Meeting House, where it was voted that the letters of the committee of correspondence and the Solemn League and Covenant

25 BCC to Westborough, 24 June, BCC Minutebook, 822–24.
26 John Andrews to William Barrell, 12 June, MHSP, VIII, 329–30.
27 14 June, Adams Papers, NYPL.   28 Force, 4 ser. I, 421–23.
29 BTR, XVIII, 176–77.

should be read. The merchants were furious at what the committee had written about them and they moved that the committee be censured and annihilated. Samuel Adams retired from the chair as moderator and he, Dr. Thomas Young, Dr. Joseph Warren, and other popular leaders defended the committee, which they controlled. Harrison Gray, treasurer of the colony, and several merchants led the attack. The debate continued into the second day, when the motion to censure and annihilate the committee of correspondence was negatived "by a great majority" and a motion to approve the committee and its "honest zeal" and to express the town's wish that the committee continue "steadfast in the way of well doing" was passed "by a Vast Majority." [30]

"The better sort of people," reported Governor Gage, "were outvoted by a great majority of the lower class. . . ." [31] Ann Hulton was more perceptive. She said that even those who supported "Government" did so more from interest than from principle, for very few of them would acknowledge the authority of Parliament. But whatever their motives, they were "overpowered by numbers, and the arts and machinations of the leader, who governs absolutely the minds and the passions of the people. . . ." [32] All the defeated merchants could do was to publish a protest signed by 129 people. The protest denounced the Solemn League and Covenant, attacked the committee of correspondence for the troubles of the times and for "falsely, maliciously, and scandalously" abusing the characters of "many of us, only for dissenting from them in opinion; a right which we shall claim so long as we hold any claim to freedom or liberty." [33]

The protest was the despairing cry of a lost cause. Samuel Adams and the popular leaders had triumphed at home. Further success depended on aid from the other colonies, and the Massachusetts leaders looked first of all to New York. As Joseph Warren put it, "I fear New York will not assist us with a very good grace but she may perhaps be ashamed to desert us—at least if her merchants offer to sell us, her mechanics will forbid the auction. . . ." [34]

೪ॐ

The struggle between the popular leaders and the merchants and their political allies in New York was under way before Paul Revere reached the

[30] Ibid. 177–78; Rowe, *Diary*, 276–77; John Andrews to William Barrell, 22 July, MHSP, VIII, 331–32.
[31] To Dartmouth, 5 July, Gage *Corres.*, I, 358–59.
[32] To Mrs. Adam Lightbody, 8 July, *Letters*, 74.   [33] Force, 4 ser. I, 490–91.
[34] To Samuel Adams, 14 June, Samuel Adams Papers, NYPL.

city on 17 May.[35] News of the passage of the Boston Port Act got to New York on 11 May and a copy of it the next day. Government officials at once insisted that the act did not concern New York and that Boston should pay for the tea. But the news was an opportunity for Isaac Sears, Alexander McDougall, and John Lamb. On 14 May, unaware of Boston's vote the day before, Sears called for a merchants' meeting on 16 May to discuss a non-importation agreement and the appointment of a committee of correspondence to bring about an inter-colonial congress.

The next day Sears and McDougall sent a secret letter to the Boston committee of correspondence. They asserted that "great numbers" of New Yorkers wanted to close their port in sympathy with Boston, and reported that they had "stimulated the merchants" to hold a meeting. Its purpose would be to agree upon non-importation and non-exportation under regulations to be established by a "general congress" which would be held in New York.[36] Sears and McDougall, like their opposite numbers in Boston, never balked at lying when a lie would serve their purpose. The fact was that "great numbers" of New Yorkers were opposed to their ideas, and that the leading men in New York objected to a stoppage of trade and to a continental congress. The New York merchants were indeed "stimulated," but their purpose was to block the schemes of Sears, Lamb, and McDougall.

To begin with, New York's response to the Boston Port Act was but another incident in the old struggle between the Livingston and De Lancey factions. The De Lanceys had won control of the legislature in 1769 and they had every intention of winning the next election in 1776. The Livingstons had all the advantage of a party out of power. Therefore they encouraged the Sons of Liberty to take extreme measures, although in fact they had no more sympathy for Boston, no more concern with principle, and no more liking for extremism than the De Lanceys. Both factions turned out for the "merchants" meeting on the night of 16 May. The De Lanceys appeared with their merchant and political allies and hosts of merchants' clerks to provide both noise and votes. They insisted that Boston should pay for the tea and that it was useless to talk of non-importation without consulting the other colonies. But they had to make a gesture if they were to retain control. Therefore they agreed to a committee of correspondence. Then, despite the demand of the Sons of Liberty for a small committee,

---

[35] The following account of events in New York is based largely on Roger Champagne, "New York and the Intolerable Acts, 1774," NYHSQ, XLV (1961).
[36] BCC Papers, "Other Colonies," NYPL.

the De Lancey-controlled meeting nominated a fifty-man committee, a majority of whom were De Lancey supporters.

The Sons of Liberty had been out-generaled and out-voted. But after Paul Revere arrived the next day, McDougall and his allies called a meeting of "mechanics" and nominated a twenty-five man committee to be submitted to still another mass meeting. Again the conservatives turned out in force and the meeting broke up in confusion after Isaac Sears was shouted down when he attempted to read the letters Revere had brought from Boston. Finally, on 20 May, Sears and McDougall gave up and accepted the committee (now of 51) controlled by the De Lanceys. If they had not, they would have been utterly defeated. On that day, Gouverneur Morris called them and their followers "sheep" who had been "gulled" again and again by the aristocracy, but he predicted that such "reptiles" could not always be misled, and that if the disputes with Britain were not settled, the aristocracy would be overturned by a "riotous mob." [37]

On 23 May the committee of 51 replied to Boston's appeal. The prose was elaborate but the meaning was clear. "The cause is general, and concerns a whole continent" and New York could do nothing for Boston unless all the colonies acted together. Therefore a congress of deputies from all the colonies should meet and form a "unanimous resolution." But the committee did not suggest a time or a place for such a meeting. McDougall, who was a member, was convinced that the De Lanceys did not want a congress. He told Paul Revere, who had returned from Philadelphia and was waiting for New York's reply, that New York would not call a congress, and that Massachusetts should do so. [38]

The Boston reply deliberately cut the ground from beneath New York's popular leaders. As in the letter to Providence, the Boston committee agreed that a "general congress" was necessary, but argued that it would take too long for one to assemble. The solution was the suspension of trade, "so wisely defined by you." But not all trade, as the Boston town meeting had voted on 13 May. Without consulting the town, the committee of correspondence casually reversed its vote. Each town in America could decide for itself what goods to stop importing, and a general congress was not necessary for the purpose. [39] Then, when Sears and McDougall's

[37] To John Penn, 20 May, EHD, IX, 861–63.
[38] New York committee to BCC, ibid. IX, 790–91; Roger Champagne, The Sons of Liberty and Aristocracy in New York Politics, 1765–1790 (Ph.D. Thesis, University of Wisconsin, 1960), 326.
[39] 30 May, BCC Minutebook, 807–8.

secret letter of 15 May was edited for publication in the *Boston Gazette* on 23 May, their proposal for a congress was deleted.

When a copy of the *Gazette* reached New York, Sears and McDougall denied that they had written the letter, as well they might considering what had been done to it. The New York committee told the Bostonians that the idea of suspending trade had not originated in New York and that only a congress could decide such matters. Sears and McDougall were further discredited when Boston replied that the idea of suspending trade came from a letter written by "your former committee of correspondence," ignoring the fact that the letter was written two days after Boston had voted for a complete stoppage of trade. However, the Boston committee at last promised that the Massachusetts legislature would call a meeting of a congress as New York had suggested.[40]

Opposition to a congress was as strong in Philadelphia as in New York. On 14 May the *Pennsylvania Journal* printed the Boston Port Act, but there was no public reaction until Paul Revere rode into the city on 19 May with letters from Boston.[41] Charles Thomson and other popular leaders at once called a mass meeting for the next evening but they were afraid that it would fail. They knew that the Philadelphia merchants deplored Boston's behavior. Nor did they have powerful backing such as the Livingstons gave the Sons of Liberty in New York. If they were to have any success they needed at least one distinguished supporter, and they turned to John Dickinson. He was conservative and he deplored Boston's destruction of the tea, but as the author of the *Farmer* letters of 1767–68, he had enormous prestige.

Charles Thomson, Thomas Mifflin, and Joseph Reed went to Dickinson's home and persuaded him to attend the mass meeting. But they had to agree to his terms as to precisely how the meeting was to be managed, and it went as planned. Joseph Reed gave the first speech, which was very moderate. All he proposed was that the governor should be requested to call the assembly so that it could prepare a petition for a redress of grievances. Mifflin and Thomson then followed with fire-breathing orations. Thomson fainted dramatically in the midst of his while demanding immediate and unlimited support for Boston. Dickinson then made the conclud-

[40] New York to BCC, 7 June, Force, 4 ser. I, 307; BCC to New York, 16 June, BCC Minutebook, 817; Champagne, Sons of Liberty, 327–28.
[41] The account of events in Philadelphia is based on Jensen, *Maritime Commerce*, 207–11 and Schlesinger, *Colonial Merchants*, 341–44.

ing speech supporting Reed's proposal. The pre-planned and beautifully stage-managed affair was effective.

Not more than 200 or 300 attended but among them were a good many merchants and political conservatives who did not normally attend mass meetings. Like the New Yorkers, they had received a painful education during the past decade and had turned out to protect their interests. Their votes made certain the adoption of the Reed motion. The meeting then agreed to Thomson's motion for the appointment of a committee to answer the Boston letter, but saw to it that the committee of 19 elected was controlled by the conservatives.

The committee answered Boston's letter the next day. It deplored the destruction of property, told Boston that it should pay for the tea, and declared that a stoppage of trade should be a last resort. However, the letter suggested that the people of Pennsylvania would be agreeable to having a congress meet to prepare a petition to the king. In Philadelphia, as in New York, the conservatives had made a gesture, but that was all. Governor John Penn commented that the backers of the meeting knew that he would not call the assembly, and that their only motive was to gain time while they waited to see what other colonies would do.[42] At the end of May, if the meeting of a congress had depended on Boston, New York, and Philadelphia, it would never have met, but those cities did not exist in political isolation, and their popular leaders continued to agitate.

Charles Thomson, who had sent Adams's letters on to the southern colonies, told Adams that Pennsylvania was "rather slow in determining" and that "our people think they should pursue the line of the Constitution as far as they can. . . ." But he expected more from the southern colonies. He reported that Maryland was "all in motion" and that he hoped that Virginia would "take a decisive part in the common cause." [43]

෫෫

Back in 1768–70 the southern colonies had been far from "decisive," and Virginia least of all except for the glowing rhetoric of its resolutions. But now the southern colonies acted quickly, and Virginia, alone among the colonies, supported Boston's appeal by adopting a wide-sweeping non-importation, non-exportation agreement, to take effect whether a congress met or not.

The Virginians had paid little attention to the Tea Act or the Tea Party

[42] Schlesinger, *Colonial Merchants*, 341–42.
[43] To Samuel Adams, 3 June, Samuel Adams Papers, NYPL.

for they were more concerned with the threat to Virginia's westward expansion and with preparations for war against the Indians northwest of the Ohio River. Then on 12 May the *Virginia Gazette* printed dire reports from London, and a week later it contained a summary of the Boston Port Act, along with a tale that Samuel Adams, John Hancock, John Rowe, and Ebenezer Mackintosh would be taken to England in irons.[44]

The House of Burgesses was in session when the news arrived but the cooler leaders insisted upon completing the regular business of the session before considering the Port Act. They were soon outmaneuvered by the younger men who presumably shared the attitude of Richard Henry Lee. He had anticipated drastic measures to punish Boston, and after the House of Burgesses had been dissolved, he proclaimed that it was a time of "immense danger to America, when the dirty ministerial stomach is daily ejecting its foul contents upon us. . . ." [45] At any rate a group of younger men persuaded the respectable Robert Carter Nicholas, chairman of the committee on religion, to introduce a resolution calling for a day of fasting, humiliation, and prayer. On 24 May it was adopted without dissent. Two days later, unanimously supported by the council, Governor Dunmore dissolved the legislature for usurping his prerogative of proclaiming fast days.

The next day, eighty-nine of the 103 former legislators met at the Raleigh Tavern, elected ex-speaker Peyton Randolph moderator, and adopted an association. It condemned Britain's tax policies and the Boston Port Act, agreed to stop the use of tea and other East Indian products, and directed the committee of correspondence to write to the other colonies about calling a general congress. The association concluded, perhaps ironically, that only a "tender regard" for English merchants prevented Virginians from recommending a total stoppage of trade with Britain. That night the ex-burgesses attended a ball in honor of Lady Dunmore at the Governor's Palace.[46]

By Sunday afternoon, when Samuel Adams's letters and the vote of the Boston town meeting reached Williamsburg, most of the burgesses had left for home. However, Peyton Randolph managed to round up about twenty-five of them for a meeting on Monday morning. They agreed that non-importation was needed, but disagreed about non-exportation. Finally they decided that they could not speak for the whole colony. Therefore, they issued a call for the members of the recent house to meet at Williamsburg on 1 August.[47] Governor Dunmore wavered. First he refused to

[44] VG(PD), 19 May.   [45] R. H. Lee to Arthur Lee, 26 June, *Letters*, I, 114–15.
[46] VG(PD), 26 May.   [47] Ibid. 2 June.

call an election, then issued writs for one, but in the end he put off a meeting of the burgesses until November.[48] Then, on 10 July, he set off for the frontier to fight Indians and did not return to Williamsburg until 4 December. By that time a "revolution" had taken place in Virginia and in America as a whole.

During June and July the people of Virginia had an unprecedented opportunity to meet and discuss their grievances and the policies to be adopted. Their grievances were many and varied, as George Washington explained early in June. The cause of Boston is "the cause of America," he declared, although Virginians did not "approve their conduct in destroying the tea. . . ." Never had the minds of the people been so disturbed. The invasion of their rights and properties by the mother country, the attacks on their lives and properties by the Indians, and a "cruel frost" succeeded by a drought which would mean only half a crop, were all sources of distress. The dissolution of the legislature had prevented the passage of a fee bill, and hence the courts of justice had stopped. Meanwhile there was very little "circulating cash" among them, and the merchants were to blame.[49]

At least half of the counties held mass meetings and the *Virginia Gazette* printed their resolutions week by week, as well as news from other colonies. Most of Virginia's leaders agreed to denounce British policy toward Boston and denied Britain's right to tax the colonies, but disagreed about particular measures. Patrick Henry, Richard Henry Lee, and other popular leaders argued for a complete stoppage of trade, the closure of courts, and the non-payment of debts owed British merchants. The more conservative leaders such as Edmund Pendleton, Peyton Randolph, and Carter Braxton opposed non-exportation and the non-payment of debts. The attorney general, John Randolph, was one of the very few who insisted upon submission to Britain, and he attacked the policy of allowing the "ignorant vulgar" to debate matters that should be left in the hands of their betters.[50]

The resolutions and instructions of the county mass meetings proposed all sorts of measures, but in general they agreed upon a congress and some form of economic coercion. When delegates from sixty of Virginia's sixty-one counties met at Williamsburg on 1 August they soon compromised their differences and adopted an association. It provided for complete non-importation after 1 November, including slaves; and if grievances were not

[48] Dunmore to Dartmouth, 29 May, 6, 20 June, C.O. 5/1373.
[49] To G. W. Fairfax, 10 June, *Writings*, III, 224–25.
[50] See Terrance Mahan, Virginia Reaction to British Policy, 1763–1776 (Ph.D. Thesis, University of Wisconsin, 1960), 265–82.

redressed before 10 August 1775, Virginians would stop all shipments to England, including tobacco. Counties were told that they should appoint committees to enforce the association and to prevent merchants from raising prices. Furthermore they were to get merchants to sign the association and to boycott all who refused. But there was one step the convention would not take, at least openly: it refused the plea of the popular leaders for a stoppage of debt collections by the courts. Unofficially, however, it was understood that the courts would not accept such cases because the act regulating fees had lapsed in April and the governor's dissolution had prevented the passage of a new one.

The convention concluded its work by electing delegates to a continental congress and committing itself to policies to be adopted by it, if the Virginia delegates agreed to them. Virginia's two oratorical firebrands, Patrick Henry and Richard Henry Lee, were delegates, but they were surrounded by more conservative and stable men: Peyton Randolph, George Washington, Richard Bland, Benjamin Harrison, and Edmund Pendleton.[51] Little did such men realize that Lee and Henry would team up with John and Samuel Adams and, by a combination of oratory, guile, and sheer persistence, so dominate American politics that they and their followers would soon be known as the "Lee-Adams Junto."

By the time Virginia had adopted its sweeping stand at the convention of 1–6 August, two other southern colonies had also decided, and one was about to do so. Only Georgia failed to join in the protest. A small group of Georgians tried to gain support for distant Boston but most Georgians were more concerned with the threat from the Creek Indians than with the less tangible threat to their constitutional rights. British troops defended their frontiers, the British treasury paid the expenses of their government, and Governor Wright was both tough and competent. Not until blood was shed in the spring of 1775 did Georgia unite with the rest of America.[52]

In Maryland, Governor Eden prorogued the assembly in April, left the colony, and did not return until November. The leaders of the antiproprietary party were equal to the occasion. Samuel Chase, William Paca, and others called a meeting at Annapolis on 25 May. The meeting resolved that the cause of Boston was the cause of America, that the complete stoppage of trade was the best way to secure repeal of the Port Act, and that

[51] The Virginia Association is reprinted in EHD, IX, 794–97. The proceedings of the Virginia convention are printed in Force, 4 ser. I, 686–90.

[52] On Georgia during these years see Coleman, *Revolution in Georgia*, and W. W. Abbot, *The Royal Governors of Georgia, 1754–1775* (Chapel Hill, 1959).

Annapolis would join with other counties and other colonies in stopping all trade. Such resolutions were safe enough, but another resolution aroused powerful objections as it had in Virginia. It proposed that lawyers should not bring suits to recover debts owed by Marylanders to Britons. A second meeting on 27 May reaffirmed the vote, 47 to 31. Thereupon, 161 citizens of Annapolis, including proprietary officials and merchants, published a protest denouncing the resolution as "founded in treachery and rashness." [53]

The Annapolis meeting elected Chase, Paca, and others to a committee of correspondence to arrange for a convention. Within weeks the counties held meetings and elected delegates. On 22 June ninety-two delegates from all the Maryland counties met at Annapolis for a four-day session. The convention agreed to join with the principal colonies in the stoppage of trade at a time to be fixed by a general congress. However, Maryland would not stop exporting tobacco unless Virginia and North Carolina did likewise. The convention ended by electing delegates to a congress.[54]

The Marylanders could ignore merchants but the South Carolinians could not. Welles's *South Carolina Gazette* printed the substance of the Port Act on 31 May; on that same day the Boston letters, via Charles Thomson in Philadelphia, also reached Charleston. Peter Timothy's *Gazette* at once began a campaign for the adoption of the Boston proposals and Christopher Gadsden assured Samuel Adams that he would sacrifice his fortune on behalf of American liberties.[55] But most Charleston merchants were deeply opposed to stopping trade, and they reminded their fellow citizens how Boston four years earlier had abandoned non-importation without telling Charleston. The merchants got the support of the rice planters who objected to non-exportation, at least until after their crops were shipped in the fall. The two groups demanded delay, and the way to achieve it was to propose a general congress to decide upon policy.

The Charleston committee therefore called a convention of the "inhabitants" to meet in Charleston on 6 July. On that day, 104 men, including forty-five from Charleston, attended. There was an easy agreement on principles but agreement on instructions to delegates to the proposed congress was another matter. The chamber of commerce was opposed to both non-importation and non-exportation, and the day before the convention met, had picked a slate of delegates pledged to oppose both measures. Gadsden and his followers insisted that the delegates should have unrestricted powers. Compromise was necessary and the convention finally

[53] Force, 4 ser. I, 352–54. [54] Schlesinger, *Colonial Merchants*, 360–62.
[55] Ibid. 373 n.3; SCG(T) 13 June.

agreed that the South Carolina delegates must agree to measures of a congress before they could be binding on the colony.

The make-up of the delegation was therefore crucial. The chamber of commerce slate was opposed by the popular leaders who insisted on Gadsden, Thomas Lynch, and on Gadsden's son-in-law, Edward Rutledge. The convention voted that every free white in the province could vote. This sudden and temporary abandonment of property qualifications was a merchant maneuver to take advantage of the fact that the delegates would be elected by Charleston and the nearby areas. The merchants gathered up their clerks and went to the polls in a body but this was a game at which Gadsden and Timothy were far more expert. They gathered up people from all over the city. Gadsden, Lynch, and Edward Rutledge were elected by a majority of nearly 400, as were Henry Middleton and John Rutledge, the merchants' nominees, who were acceptable to the popular leaders.

The convention concluded by naming a general committee for the colony to replace the Charleston committee, and gave it unlimited power to correspond with other colonies and "to do all matters and things necessary." The committee of 99 consisted of fifteen merchants and fifteen mechanics from Charleston and sixty-nine planters from the colony at large. When the legislature met on 2 August, all but five of its members had been members of the convention. Early in the morning, before the governor was awake, the assembly ratified the election of delegates and appropriated the handsome sum of £1500 sterling to pay their expenses.[56]

North Carolina, with no urban center, moved more slowly. A convention of six counties finally met on 21 July with William Hooper, a former Bostonian and law student of James Otis, as chairman. It called for a convention and one met at New Bern on 25 August with thirty-two of the thirty-eight counties represented. It adopted the association the Virginians had agreed to earlier in the month, promised to boycott anyone in the colony who did not abide by it, and elected delegates to the Continental Congress which was to meet within a few days in Philadelphia. Governor Martin's futile proclamation against illegal meetings had no result except to further alienate his subjects.[57]

The hopes of many conservative Philadelphians and New Yorkers that a congress could be delayed or avoided were crushed by events. In the middle of June, William Smith in New York recorded that as a result of news

[56] Schlesinger, *Colonial Merchants*, 373–79; Force, 4 ser. I, 671–72.
[57] Schlesinger, *Colonial Merchants*, 370–73.

from other colonies "the Liberty Boys here in the committee of 51 drive those who came in, to repress their zeal, before them. . . ." [58] In both New York and Philadelphia the tactics were the same. The popular leaders either called or threatened to call mass meetings of "mechanics" and thus forced the conservative-controlled committees of correspondence to yield inch by inch in order to retain control of events.

After the Philadelphia mass meeting of 20 May, more than 900 men petitioned the governor to call the assembly into session. Governor John Penn refused and the committee of 19 appointed at the mass meeting took no action. The popular leaders then issued a call for 1200 mechanics to meet on 9 June. The committee of correspondence headed off that meeting by agreeing to call a mass meeting of the whole city. The committee made careful preparations. On the night of 10 June "a number of gentlemen of different classes, societies, and parties" met and prepared the proceedings of the general meeting to the last detail. They decided upon the contents of speeches and resolutions, and the personnel of a new and larger committee. Furthermore, they decided to call a colonial convention. Many of the men present disliked such measures intensely but were afraid of "the People's resentment. . . ." [59]

The city-wide meeting on 18 June ratified the plans of this "caucus." John Dickinson, as chairman of the new committee of 43, then wrote to the counties which within a few weeks created committees of correspondence and approved a continental congress. The committee also called a colonial convention to meet on 15 July. Joseph Galloway was now convinced that the legislature had better act to head off something worse, and Governor John Penn suddenly discovered that there were "Indian troubles" and called the assembly to meet on 18 July. There was a tacit understanding that the convention would write instructions for the delegates to Congress and that the assembly would elect the delegates.

When the convention met it voted that the Congress should petition the king before suspending trade but agreed that Pennsylvania would support the Congress if it did suspend trade. The convention then prepared instructions. The assembly ignored them, and in effect denounced the convention as "THE BEGINNING OF REPUBLICANISM" and deplored the fact that it had given each county one vote, thus making the frontier counties equal to "this opulent and populous city and county." [60] The assembly

[58] 15 June, Memoirs, 188.
[59] Charles Thomson, Notes of a Meeting of a Number of Gentlemen Convened on the 10 June 1774, Memorandum Book, Charles Thomson Papers, HSP.
[60] Force, 4 ser. I, 607–8.

elected seven delegates with Galloway at the head, and he wrote instructions which left him free to oppose any stoppage of trade and to work for some form of constitutional union with the mother country. Governor Penn was pleased: the assembly had thwarted the committee of 43 and the convention.[61]

In New York the committee of 51 took no action to call a congress after writing to Boston on 23 May that only a congress could adopt measures for all the colonies. The populace burned effigies of Thomas Hutchinson, Lord North, and Alexander Wedderburn, but to no effect. Once more, as in the past, Alexander McDougall and Isaac Sears told Samuel Adams that Massachusetts must provide leadership.[62] The Philadelphia mass meeting of 20 June provided them with the boost they needed. McDougall almost chortled when he reported to Adams that "since the advice received from Philadelphia . . . stocks have risen in favor of Liberty." [63] On 29 June McDougall told the committee of 51 that a convention should be called to elect delegates to a congress. The conservatives replied that the assembly should elect them, knowing perfectly well that Cadwallader Colden, now eighty-four and acting governor once more, would never call the assembly for such a purpose. And their argument that a meeting of a congress was uncertain was jeered at the next day by the New York Journal.

Sears and McDougall kept up constant pressure on their fellow committee members. McDougall moved that the committee nominate five delegates for the city and that the slate be approved by the mechanics before submitting it to the voters. Sears nominated five men: Isaac Low and James Duane of the De Lancey faction and Philip Livingston, John Morin Scott, and McDougall of the Livingston faction. The committee majority was outraged by the last two names and substituted John Alsop and John Jay, thus committing itself to the idea of electing delegates. But the majority still refused to write a statement of principles.

The popular leaders then went outside the committee, picked a slate of five delegates, and wrote a ringing statement of popular principles. These were ratified by a mass meeting the next day, 6 July, and the conservatives realized that they had to yield once more. The next day they agreed that each faction should present a slate of delegates (to be voted on as a whole) and that all taxpayers, whether voters or not, could vote. That night the committee of 51 denounced the mass meeting, whereupon Sears and McDougall and nine followers resigned, hoping to break up the committee.

[61] Penn to SS, 30 July, ibid. 661.   [62] 20 June, McDougall Papers, NYHS.
[63] 26 June, Samuel Adams Papers, NYPL.

The committee did not dissolve. It revised its statement of principles and presented them and its own slate to still another mass meeting. The popular leaders turned out in force and shouted down the principles, appointed a committee to write "proper" ones, and added McDougall and Leonard Lispenard to the slate of five delegates proposed by the conservatives. A further mass meeting to approve the "proper" principles did nothing and that night the conservative members of the committee of 51 decided to poll the city on 28 July. The popular leadership gave in. The next day they agreed to support the five candidates nominated by the committee of 51 if they would agree to non-importation. Four of them did so, although somewhat equivocally, and the election on 28 July was a mere formality. Apparently the popular leaders gave in for fear that they would lose what they had gained.[64]

The popular leaders in New York and Philadelphia had failed to elect any of their own men to the First Continental Congress, but in a broader sense they had won a great victory. They had managed to push the reluctant merchants and conservative leaders in both cities into agreeing to a congress, and then into electing delegates to it. And when the Congress met, the popular leaders from other colonies with whom they had worked closely, if not always happily, achieved the goals of all of them. Before the First Continental Congress was over, they had ridden roughshod over the conservative delegations from New York and Pennsylvania, and a scattering of like-minded men in the delegations from the other colonies.

[64] Champagne, Sons of Liberty, 330–41.

XIX

The First Continental Congress

The direct intervention of Parliament in American affairs for the first time since 1767 set in motion the events that led to the meeting of the First Continental Congress. The news of the passage of the Boston Port Act was followed within days, from one end of America to the other, by proposals for the meeting of an American congress to decide upon common policies. At the same time most of the popular leaders proposed that the means of opposition should be more drastic than anything tried in the past: a complete stoppage of trade with Great Britain. The opponents of the popular leaders believed that Britain had gone too far in punishing Boston, for they realized that such a precedent, if established, might well be dangerous. Nevertheless, they opposed drastic measures of opposition and were dubious about, if not opposed to, a congress. In the end they yielded, partly because of popular pressure, and partly because they hoped they could control the decisions of a congress. Thus, despite a diversity of motives, most American leaders did agree, for the first time in their history, to submit policy-making to a single body of men who represented, in name at least, all Americans.

The delegates who met in Philadelphia had been elected in various ways: by legislatures, by colony-wide conventions, by New York City, and by certain New York counties. However elected, the members of the first Congress, like members of Congress since then, represented their "states" first of all. When John Adams described Massachusetts as "our country" and the Massachusetts delegation as "our embassy" he simply put in words

483

what most delegates felt.[1] After debating for a month, the Connecticut delegates informed their governor that "an assembly like this . . . coming from remote colonies, each of which has some modes of transacting public business peculiar to itself, some particular provincial rights and interests to guard and secure, must take some time to become so acquainted with each one's situations and connections as to be able to give an united assent to the ways and means proposed for effecting what all are ardently desirous of." Therefore every delegate had to be listened to on matters of no importance. "And indeed it often happens, that what is of little or no consequence to one colony, is of the last to another." [2]

Most of the delegates were determined to present a united front to the world, no matter how sharply they divided in their secret session. And they did divide despite their common heritage of language, ideas, and political institutions. As the Connecticut delegates pointed out, each colony had its own rights and interests to protect. Furthermore, the individual colonies often looked upon one another as "foreign" countries, split as they were by trade rivalries, by boundary disputes which had led to petty wars, and by political and religious differences which seemed very real to Americans in 1774.

At the same time, Americans recognized that certain groups of colonies had characteristics which set them apart from one another. Thus the New England, the middle, and the southern or "Plantation" colonies had differing political, religious, and economic interests and attitudes that transcended purely local boundaries. Upon occasion, therefore, the members of Congress voted as representatives of their sections as well as of their native colonies.

But there were other bases for voting that could not be explained by either local or sectional interests. The colonies with large populations were pitted against small ones when it came to the number of votes they should have in Congress, and the colonies with claims to western lands running to the "South Seas" fought with those colonies that had definite western boundaries. On these issues neither local nor sectional loyalties mattered at all.

Such diverse loyalties, ideas, and interests were to play a part in the decisions of the first and succeeding congresses, and the meeting of the first

[1] To Abigail Adams, 18 Sept. In this and the following notes, where only dates are given (except for John Adams's *Diary*), the references are to the first volume of E. C. Burnett, ed., *Letters of the Members of the Continental Congress* [LMCC] (8 vols., Washington, 1921–36).
[2] 10 Oct.

Congress had been brought about in spite of them. Americans had been forced to meet together, some willingly and some reluctantly, by what many viewed as a greater threat from Britain than ever before. As members of Congress, therefore, they were forced to act as Americans, to define American rights, and to devise means for defending them.

Americans had been debating their rights and the means of maintaining them among themselves ever since 1763, and by 1774 two major and opposed bodies of opinion had emerged. Most of the popular leaders had taken the position that each colonial legislature was all-powerful within its own territory, and that the British Parliament had no power to legislate for the colonies, either collectively or individually. They insisted that the Crown was the sole bond of the empire and the umpire among the equal legislatures within it. This view was summed up best of all by Thomas Jefferson in his *Summary View of the Rights of British America* which he wrote for the delegates to the Virginia Convention in August 1774. And Jefferson went even further and cast doubts on the power of the Crown itself, doubts he spelled out two years later in the Declaration of Independence.

The other group of leaders agreed that Americans had rights with which Britain should not interfere, but they insisted that in every political society there must be a supreme legislature with the power to establish common policies, particularly in economic matters such as the regulation of trade and finance. Parliament might have defects but of necessity it had to be the supreme legislature of the whole British Empire. Thomas Hutchinson had argued thus in defending the sovereignty of Parliament before the Massachusetts legislature in January 1773. James Duane and Joseph Galloway reasserted the idea in the debates in the First Continental Congress, and pamphleteers, including Galloway, elaborated the theme during the winter of 1774–75 after Congress revealed its decisions to the world.

The debate over concrete measures of opposition had likewise been intense, and while most of the colonies had adopted some form of economic coercion against the Stamp Act and the Townshend program, the agreements had varied in kind and effectiveness and had led to distrust and antagonism within and between colonies. As in the debate over American rights and the power of Parliament, the debate over means and methods of opposition had produced opposing bodies of opinion by 1774. At the one extreme were the men who insisted that all economic relations with Britain must be severed and that debt payments to British creditors should be suspended. At the other extreme were those who held that all the colonies should do was to petition for a redress of grievances, or at most, adopt a limited non-importation of British goods as in the past.

In agreeing to meet in a continental congress, Americans, whether they knew it or not, consented to a major political revolution, for they transferred the debate over theories and policies from the local to what was in effect the "national" level. Such a debate was inescapable because the delegates represented the wide spectrum of political thought and feeling in America. At one extreme was Joseph Galloway, a member of the old order that had long ruled the colonies, and a man who had defended the sovereignty of Parliament ever since the Stamp Act crisis. At the other extreme was Samuel Adams, the most conspicuous example of the new group of popular leaders, who had risen to eminence since 1763 and who denied the authority of Parliament over America in "all cases whatsoever." Most of the delegations contained men whose views ranged from one extreme to the other and thus individual delegations were divided among themselves. It was natural, therefore, for men who thought alike, to form alliances or "parties" which cut across colonial and regional boundaries, alliances based on common convictions and feelings, not on local or regional loyalties.

Six years later, Joseph Galloway, an embittered exile in Britain, declared that the Congress divided at once into two almost equal parties. One of them, he said, wanted to define American rights explicitly, to petition dutifully for a redress of grievances, to form a constitutional union between the two countries, and to avoid every measure tending to sedition or violent acts of opposition. The other party consisted of men who, ever since the Stamp Act, had wanted to throw off all subordination to Britain. They were men "who meant by every fiction, falsehood, and fraud to delude the people from their due allegiance, to throw the subsisting governments into anarchy, to incite the ignorant and vulgar to arms, and with those arms to establish American independence. The one were men of loyal principles and possessed the greatest fortunes in America; the other were Congregational and Presbyterian republicans, or men of bankrupt fortunes, overwhelmed in debt to the British merchants." [3] Galloway's description of the two "parties" was distorted by prejudice, but his assertion that the Congress divided into parties was sound.

Many years later, John Adams agreed that the Congress had divided although he described it differently. "America," he wrote, "is in total ignorance, or under infinite deception concerning that assembly. To draw the characters of them would require a volume, and would be considered as a

[3] EHD, IX, 801. '

caricature print; one third tories, another whigs, and the rest mongrels." [4]

Whatever the differences of opinion, and they were wide and deep, the first Congress contained some of the ablest men in America. A few of them, when forced to choose, remained loyal to Britain, as did Joseph Galloway. Most of them became leaders of the new nation whose birth they proclaimed less than two years later. Among them were future presidents of Congress, the first two presidents of the United States after 1789, the first chief justice of the United States Supreme Court, and many a state governor and state and national legislator.

Other galaxies of talent were to gather in the years to come, as at the Philadelphia Convention of 1787, but not even in 1787 did American leaders deal with matters more crucial than those at Philadelphia in 1774. After more than a century and a half as members of the British Empire, they took the first steps that led to the break-up of that empire and to the creation of what some newspaper writers were already hailing as the "American Empire."

Most of the delegates to the first Congress had never met before, but the reputations of some of them were widely known. Thus the New Englanders heard before they reached Philadelphia that Richard Henry Lee and Patrick Henry were known to their fellow Virginians as the Cicero and Demosthenes of the age.[5] It was natural enough for these men to display their talents on a greater stage than they had ever occupied before. Entirely aside from their deep differences of opinion, they orated and quibbled at length. At one point, an irritated John Adams exclaimed: "The business of the Congress is tedious beyond expression. This assembly is like no other that ever existed. Every man in it is a great man, an orator, a critic, a statesman; and therefore every man upon every question must show his oratory, his criticism, and his political abilities. The consequence of this is that business is drawn and spun out to an immeasurable length. I believe if it was moved and seconded that we should come to a resolution that three and two make five, we should be entertained with logic and rhetoric, law, history, politics, and mathematics, and then—we should pass the resolution unanimously, in the affirmative." [6]

[4] To Jefferson, 12 Nov. 1813, *Works*, X, 78–79.
[5] John Adams, *Diary*, 28 August. All citations to John Adams's diary, as in previous chapters, and to his Notes of Debates are to the Butterfield edition and are cited by date only.
[6] To Abigail Adams, 9 Oct.

One of the most serious obstacles to common action was the conviction that New Englanders, and especially the Bostonians, were "republicans," religious bigots, cheaters during non-importation in 1768–70, and bent upon independence. When John and Samuel Adams arrived in New York on the road to Philadelphia, Alexander McDougall warned them to be careful to "avoid every expression here, which looked like an allusion to the last appeal." He explained that New York was divided into several "parties" dominated by fear of civil war, by fear that the "levelling spirit" of New England would spread to New York, by Episcopalian prejudice against New England, by opposition to the stoppage of trade, and by those who looked up to government for favors.[7] The two Adamses received similar warning from the popular leaders in Philadelphia, where the Quakers had not forgotten that Quakers had once been hanged in Massachusetts. And the reputation for religious bigotry was enhanced during the first Congress when a delegation of New England Baptists, led by the Reverend Isaac Backus, appeared and charged at a public meeting that the popular leaders of Massachusetts were denying religious freedom to their fellow citizens while talking about the glories of freedom in general. Samuel and John Adams defended their colony, but it was a sorry defense indeed, at least so far as a delighted audience of Philadelphia Quakers and members of Congress was concerned.[8]

The Adamses were realists and set about improving their reputation and that of their colony. John Adams explained how they did it. "We have had numberless prejudices to remove here. We have been obliged to act with great delicacy and caution. We have been obliged to keep ourselves out of sight, and to feel pulses, and to sound the depths; to insinuate our sentiments, designs, and desires by means of other persons, sometimes of one province, and sometimes of another." [9] Fortunately for the Bostonians, the flamboyant oratory of some of the southern delegates made them look like moderates. Christopher Gadsden proclaimed that he was for taking up his firelock and marching to Boston, and that if his wife and all his children were in that city and due to perish by the sword, "it would not alter his sentiment or proceeding for American liberty. . . ." He "leaves all New England Sons of Liberty far behind" Silas Deane of Connecticut reported admiringly.[10] It is little wonder that some delegates concluded, as did one from Delaware, that "the Bostonians who (we know) have been con-

[7] John Adams, *Diary*, 22 Aug.
[8] Alvah Hovey, *A Memoir of the Life and Times of the Rev. Isaac Backus* (Boston, 1859), 204–12.
[9] To William Tudor, 29 Sept.   [10] To Mrs. Deane, 7 Sept.

demned by many for their violence are moderate men when compared to Virginia, South Carolina, and Rhode Island." [11]

The Bostonians could further their cause openly when opportunity offered and they did so brilliantly on the second day of the Congress. Thomas Cushing of Boston proposed that they open the next morning with prayer. John Jay and John Rutledge opposed because so many different religions were represented that they could not possibly worship together. At that point, Samuel Adams, who for years had been identifying the Church of England with the "Whore of Babylon," arose and announced that "he was no bigot, and could hear a prayer from a gentleman of piety and virtue," and that although he was a stranger in Philadelphia, he had heard that the Reverend Jacob Duché was such a man.[12] He later explained to Joseph Warren that since "many of our warmest friends are members of the Church of England, I thought it prudent, as well on that as some other accounts, to move that the service be performed by a clergyman of that denomination." [13] Duché later became a loyalist but he served the Adamses well that morning. Two days later a Pennsylvanian told them that they "never were guilty of a more masterly stroke of policy . . . it has had a very good effect, etc." [14] As a result of such "masterly" strokes, Samuel Adams was able to inform his co-workers in Massachusetts that "heretofore we have been accounted by many, intemperate and rash; but now we are universally applauded as cool and judicious, as well as spirited and brave." But he was worried about a "certain degree of jealousy in the minds of some, that we aim at a total independency, not only of the mother country, but of the colonies too" and that "we shall in time overrun them all. However groundless this jealousy may be, it ought to be attended to. . . ." [15]

One opportunity to "attend" to the "jealousy" came when a solemn and worried Virginia delegate spent an evening with the Adamses, Richard Henry Lee, and Dr. Edward Shippen of Philadelphia. George Washington had been warned by a friend, a British army captain in Boston, that the New Englanders wanted independence. What was said that evening is unknown, but Washington replied to Captain MacKenzie in words that sounded much like those of Samuel Adams. He told him that he had been led astray by "venal men" whereas Washington had talked to the real lead-

---

[11] Caesar Rodney to Thomas Rodney, 9 Sept.
[12] John Adams to Abigail Adams, 16 Sept.   [13] 9 Sept.
[14] John Adams, *Diary*, 10 Sept.
[15] To Joseph Warren, 25 Sept., *Writings*, III, 158.

ers of the people and could "announce it as a fact" that neither in Massachusetts nor elsewhere was there any desire for independence. "I am as well satisfied as I can be of my existence that no such thing is desired by any thinking man in all North America. . . ." [16] It was not the last time the future father of his country was to be misled by men subtler than he.

As the Congress ended, people in Massachusetts heard that it had gone as well to Samuel Adams's liking as if he had been the "sole director," [17] and six years later Joseph Galloway asserted that he had been just that. While the political talent of Samuel Adams should not be underestimated, he did not work alone. He needed and got the help of such men as Richard Henry Lee and Christopher Gadsden to overcome the formidable opposition to the measures proposed in and adopted by the First Continental Congress.

ॐ

The delegates met at a tavern on Monday morning 5 September and their first decisions were a victory for the popular leaders. Joseph Galloway, as speaker of the Pennsylvania legislature, offered the State House as a meeting place. The carpenters of Philadelphia offered their hall. The delegates went first to Carpenters Hall whereupon Thomas Lynch of South Carolina proposed that Congress meet there. James Duane of New York objected that they should at least look at the State House out of courtesy to Galloway, but there was a "general cry" that this was a good room and a "great majority" voted to stay where they were.[18] Lynch then proposed Peyton Randolph, speaker of the Virginia House of Burgesses, for presiding officer. The delegates agreed and decided to call him "President." "Our president," reported Silas Deane, in words applicable to certain future presidents of the United States, "seems designed by nature for the business. Of an affable, open, and majestic deportment, large in size, though not out of proportion, he commands respect and esteem by his very aspect, independent of the high character he sustains." [19] The delegates then appointed a secretary who was not a member of Congress. Again Thomas Lynch made the motion: he nominated and Congress elected Charles Thomson who held the post until 1789.

[16] Captain Robert MacKenzie to Washington, 13 Sept., and Washington to MacKenzie, 9 Oct., Washington, *Writings*, III, 244–47 and note; John Adams, *Diary*, 28 Sept.
[17] James Lovell to Josiah Quincy, Jr., 28 Oct., Force, 4 ser. I, 949.
[18] John Adams, *Diary*, 5 Sept.; James Duane, Notes of Proceedings, 5 Sept. The notes on debates taken by John Adams and James Duane and John Adams's *Diary* are the principal sources for the history of the disputes in the Congress.
[19] To Mrs. Deane, 5–6 Sept.

The decision to meet at Carpenters Hall and the appointment of Charles Thomson were "highly agreeable to the mechanics and citizens in general, but mortifying to the last degree to Mr. Galloway and his party, Thomson being his sworn opposite. . . ."[20] Both decisions had been made before Congress met, for the methods of the Caucus Club worked quite as well in Philadelphia as in Boston. John Adams discovered as soon as he arrived that "this Charles Thomson is the Sam Adams of Philadelphia" but he was too canny to propose him directly.[21] Joseph Galloway, who had been busy politicking to find out who was "cool" and who was "warm," noted that the Bostonians had been busy among the Virginians and South Carolinians and thus made the arrangements without appearing openly.[22]

With organizational details out of the way, the Congress at once turned to an issue which in one way or another has pervaded American politics from that day to this: how should Congress vote? Should it be by the majority of members present, should it be by population, should it be by area—that is by colonies—or by "interest," or by some combination of these. Virginia, which contained 20 per cent of the American population, insisted in 1774, as in 1776 and 1787, that voting should be by population. The small colonies insisted that each colony should have one vote. The South Carolinians, as in 1787, argued that wealth should also be counted. Speaking for the large colonies, Patrick Henry declared that all government was dissolved, that the colonies were in a "state of nature," and that "the distinctions between Virginians, Pennsylvanians, New Yorkers, and New Englanders are no more. I am not a Virginian, but an American."

Some latter-day commentators have seen in Henry's rhetoric the rising spirit of American "nationalism." His hearers knew better: he was merely arguing for more votes for Virginia. Benjamin Harrison made the point clear: if Virginians did not have more votes than a small colony it was unlikely that they would ever come to another convention. And Henry himself concluded his grandiloquent statement by saying he would not demand consideration of slaves, but would be satisfied "if the freemen can be represented according to their numbers. . . ."

The small colonies, like the small states in 1787, insisted that they should have equal weight. John Sullivan of New Hampshire declared that "a little colony had its all at stake as well as a great one." Samuel Ward of Rhode Island added that the delegates had come to make a sacrifice, if necessary, and that the "weakest colony by such a sacrifice would suffer as

20 Idem.   21 Diary, 30 Aug.   22 To Governor William Franklin, 3, 5 Sept.

much as the greatest," and he replied tartly to Patrick Henry, who orated about the evils of unequal representation, that there was no such equality in Virginia itself.[23]

There were eight small colonies opposed to the three large colonies (Massachusetts, Pennsylvania, Virginia) in Congress and they would not yield. Furthermore, Congress did not have adequate information to assess the respective weight of the colonies, and the delegates did not trust one another to make honest reports. As John Adams put it, "it will not do in such a case, to take each other's words. It ought to be ascertained by authentic evidence, from records." [24] Congress finally agreed that each colony would have one vote. In practice this meant that the majority of each delegation decided the vote, and where a delegation was divided evenly, the colony's vote did not count.

The decision was made Tuesday afternoon. Then Samuel Adams had proposed that an Anglican clergyman open the next morning's session with prayer. At that point a rumor arrived that British soldiers had killed six Americans while seizing powder near Boston and that the British fleet had bombarded Boston for a whole night. "All is in confusion," wrote one delegate, "the bells toll muffled, and the people run as in a case of extremity, they know not where nor why." [25] The Reverend Mr. Duché thus prayed in a highly charged emotional atmosphere on the morning of 8 September. Later on in the day Congress learned that the tale was false.[26] Nevertheless, the fear that armed conflict might begin shadowed the mind of many a delegate as the Congress set about its work.

ह∙

The members of Congress summed up their main task when they resolved unanimously on 6 September to appoint a committee "to state the rights of the colonies in general, the several instances in which these rights are violated or infringed, and the means most proper to be pursued for obtaining a restoration of them," and elected two men from each colony to the committee.[27] Unanimity ended with the adoption of the resolution. The committee began a debate which went on and on while Congress adjourned from day to day to await the outcome.

[23] John Adams, *Diary*, 5 Sept.; Notes of Debates, 6 Sept.; James Duane, Notes of Proceedings, 5, 6 Sept.

[24] *Diary*, 5 Sept.   [25] Silas Deane to Mrs. Deane, 7 Sept.

[26] For an account of the event, see Chapter XXI below.

[27] W. C. Ford *et al.*, eds., *Journals of the Continental Congress 1774–1789* [JCC] (34 vols., Washington, 1904–37), I, 26–29. At the same time Congress appointed a committee of one from each colony to report on British laws affecting the trade and manufactures of the colonies.

The committee split at once over the theoretical foundation of American rights. Richard Henry Lee led off for the popular leaders. He declared that American rights were "built on a fourfold foundation—on nature, on the British constitution, on charters, and on immemorial usage." He could not see, he said, why "we should not lay our rights upon the broadest bottom, the ground of nature." John Jay, for the moment at least, agreed that it was necessary to "recur to the law of nature and the British constitution," and went on to assert that "emigrants have a right to erect what government they please." What this meant in practical terms was put bluntly by Roger Sherman of Connecticut, who declared that the colonies were bound to the Crown only by their consent and that "there is no other legislative over the colonies but their respective assemblies."

Such ideas were shocking to the more conservative members of the committee. The "law of nature" was undefined and undefinable and could be used to justify the wildest kind of political upheaval. Therefore it had to be opposed. John Rutledge of South Carolina asserted flatly that emigrants did not have a right "to set up what constitution they please," that a subject could not alienate his allegiance, and that American rights were "well founded on the British constitution, and not on the law of nature." James Duane agreed. He said that American rights must be based on "some solid and constitutional principle" and that those rights could be based on two sources: upon the charters and upon the common law and the statutes in existence at the time of colonization. He did not want to recur to the law of nature which would be a feeble support. Joseph Galloway joined in the attack. He had looked for American rights in the law of nature but had not found them there. He had found them instead in the "constitution of the English government" and "we may draw them from this source securely." [28] Despite such opposition the committee voted to base American rights "upon the laws of nature, the principles of the English Constitution, and charters and compacts," but the decision was not a final one and the debate dragged on. [29]

The question of the power of Parliament was debated just as heatedly and inconclusively. Roger Sherman stated the extreme position of the popular leaders when he denied that Parliament had any authority whatsoever over the colonies. The conservatives, led by Duane and Galloway, at first made a partial, and fatal, concession, and Galloway recognized it. He said that he thought all American rights could be reduced to one: "an exemp-

---

[28] John Adams, Notes of Debates, 8 Sept.; James Duane, Address before the Committee to State the Rights of the Colonies, 8 Sept.
[29] Samuel Ward, Diary, 9 Sept.

tion from all laws made by [the] British Parliament since the emigration of our ancestors." He admitted that such a concession tended to "an independency of the colonies" and was contrary to the maxim that "there must be some absolute power to draw together all the wills and strength of the Empire." [30]

Galloway and the others soon retreated when the specific issue of such concern to most American merchants was raised: the power of Parliament to regulate trade. Gadsden, although a merchant himself, took the extreme popular view. He was "violent against allowing to Parliament any power of regulating trade, or allowing that they have anything to do with us." If the Congress acknowledged that Parliament had the power to regulate trade, it would be as bad as agreeing that it had supreme legislative power in all cases whatsoever. The right of regulating trade was the right of legislation, and a right of legislation in one case, was a right in all: "This I deny." [31]

James Duane, a lawyer, spoke for most American merchants who found it difficult to conceive of carrying on trade without uniform regulations, or for that matter, outside the British Empire. He presented a series of propositions to the committee in which he said that while the Acts of Trade and Navigation were burdensome in some respects, they had, on the whole, established salutary regulations upon which the wealth, strength, and safety of the whole British Empire depended. Those acts had been submitted to and recognized in all the colonies for more than a century. They should therefore be considered as a compact between Britain and the colonies. Because of the spirit of the compact, "the necessity of a supreme controlling power," and the protection the colonies had received, Americans should "cheerfully acknowledge that it belongs only to Parliament to direct and superintend the trade of all his Majesty's dominions. . . ." And such authority should not even be questioned. However, Duane would exclude "every idea of taxation internal and external for raising a revenue on the subjects of America without their consent." [32]

Thus the committee divided during the first few days of debate and it remained deadlocked while Congress marked time and the Massachusetts "embassy" fumed at the delay in doing something for their "country." High level discussions were all right but they wanted action and wanted it at once. Galloway later gave credit for breaking the deadlock to Samuel Adams, "a man, who though by no means remarkable for brilliant abilities,

[30] John Adams, Notes of Debates, 8 Sept.; James Duane, Address before the Committee to State the Rights of the Colonies, 8 Sept.
[31] John Adams, Diary, 14 Sept.
[32] Propositions before the Committee on Rights, 7–22 Sept., LMCC, I, 38–44.

yet is equal to most men in popular intrigue, and the management of a faction." Adams "managed at once the faction in Congress at Philadelphia, and the factions in New England." He employed "expresses" between Boston and Philadelphia, and one of those expresses arrived with the "inflammatory resolves of the county of Suffolk, which contained a complete declaration of war against Great Britain." [33]

On 14 September, Adams wrote to the Boston committee of correspondence that he was waiting with "great impatience" for a letter from it. Two days later Paul Revere arrived with the Suffolk Resolves which had been drafted by Adams's lieutenant, Dr. Joseph Warren, and adopted by Suffolk county on 9 September. They were indeed "inflammatory resolves" and were prefaced by a preamble which was one of the more magnificent pieces of rhetoric of the age. The resolves began by declaring that Massachusetts's rights were based on nature, the British constitution, and the charter, declared that George III was sovereign only by virtue of a "compact," and that the Intolerable Acts were a gross infraction of American rights and need not be obeyed. All trade with Great Britain, Ireland, and the West Indies should be stopped. Furthermore, the resolves urged the people to ignore the courts, the tax collectors to retain public money in their hands, and the people to elect their own militia officers and learn the art of war as soon as possible. However, Suffolk county would act only on the defensive.[34]

The more conservative members of Congress were aghast at resolves which, in effect, declared independence and pointed in the direction of open warfare, however "defensive." But they were caught in a dilemma. To reject the resolves would imply approval of British policies, and most members of Congress did not approve. Yet if they agreed to the resolves they would vote for everything they objected to, from the law of nature to the denial of the power of Parliament to regulate trade, and to the stoppage of trade itself. The popular leaders were enthusiastic, and Congress not only approved the resolves but also ordered them printed in the newspapers.[35]

John Adams declared that it was one of the happiest days of his life and that he was now convinced that "America will support the Massachusetts or perish with her." The next day he said that when the resolves were presented to Congress he had seen tears gush into the eyes of the "old grave pacific Quakers of Pennsylvania." [36] Such tears might well have gushed if

[33] EHD, IX, 801.   [34] JCC, I, 31–37. 39n.   [35] Ibid. 39–40.
[36] Diary, 17 Sept.; to Abigail Adams, 18 Sept.

what Galloway wrote later is true. He said that the debates were warm, that the "republican faction" had a mob ready to execute its secret orders, and that the practice of tarring and feathering had long since been introduced. "This lessened the firmness of some of the loyalists; the vote was put and carried." [37]

ε➣

The vote for the Suffolk Resolves was an enormous strategic victory for the popular leaders for it committed Congress to their entire program. Four days later Congress adopted a resolution which it ordered printed in newspapers and handbills. Merchants were requested to stop ordering goods from Britain and to cancel previous orders until Congress decided upon the "means" of opposition and made them public.[38] Congress then began to debate the "means," a debate that at once brought inter-colonial rivalry and suspicion into the open. John Adams discovered to his dismay that the distrust of Boston merchants was still a very lively ghost. One night John Dickinson and other Philadelphians questioned Adams about the importation of dutied tea by Boston merchants since 1770, and about the freight that popular hero John Hancock had collected on dutied tea brought in by his ships. John Adams was defensive, even in his diary. "I think the Bostonian merchants are not wholly justifiable—yet their conduct has been exaggerated. Their fault and guilt has been magnified. Mr. Hancock I believe is justifiable, but I am not certain, whether he is strictly so." [39]

The debate began in earnest on 26 September when Richard Henry Lee moved that non-importation from Britain and Ireland begin on 1 November. The Massachusetts delegation at once protested. Thomas Cushing declared that non-importation, non-exportation, and non-consumption should start at once. Samuel Chase said that they should stop lumber exports to the West Indies at once. This would soon bring Britain to its knees, for the West Indians could not ship sugar without barrels. But talk of immediate non-exportation ran head-on into the instructions of the Virginia delegation which forbade it to agree to non-exportation before 10 August 1775. The reason was simple: Virginia insisted on marketing its 1774 tobacco crop which would not be shipped until the spring of 1775. Gadsden proposed that Congress should go ahead anyway but the Marylanders and North Carolinians at once declared that under no circum-

[37] EHD, IX, 802.   [38] 22 Sept., JCC, I, 41.   [39] Diary, 20 Sept.

stances would they agree to start non-exportation without Virginia. If they did, their tobacco would be shipped through that colony and they would lose their trade.

Richard Henry Lee's defense of his colony was feeble. He argued that "all considerations of interest, and equality of sacrifice should be laid aside." Virginia tobacco was an exception. All the other colonies shipped their goods during the same year in which they were produced. Not at all, replied John Sullivan of New Hampshire: his colony's lumber was produced in the winter and shipped during January and February. Edward Rutledge of South Carolina tartly reminded the "gentleman" on the other side of the room who had talked of generosity, that "true equality is the only public generosity." If Virginia would raise wheat instead of tobacco it would not suffer. He was for immediate non-importation and non-exportation.[40]

The South Carolinians had their own interests to protect, and, except for Gadsden and Edward Rutledge, were really opposed to non-exportation. The bulk of South Carolina's commerce consisted of trade to and from Britain because rice and indigo were enumerated commodities which had to be shipped to Britain, although rice for southern Europe could be sent there directly. In any case, they would not agree to non-exportation if Virginia were exempt.[41]

The two-day debate revealed much about colonial rivalries and suspicions but the motion before Congress related only to non-importation. Some delegates supported 1 November while others wanted non-importation put off as long as possible, and perhaps forever. The delegates agreed that merchants would try to cheat, no matter what the date. Patrick Henry finally declared that "we don't mean to hurt even our rascals, if we have any" and moved that non-importation begin in December. Congress then agreed to stop the importation of all goods from Britain and Ireland on 1 December, and to stop the use and purchase of any goods brought in thereafter.[42]

The next day, before the much hotter issue of non-exportation could be taken up, Joseph Galloway, James Duane, and other conservatives made a

[40] John Adams, Notes of Debates, 26–27 Sept.
[41] Report of the South Carolina Delegates to the South Carolina Provincial Congress, LMCC, I, 85–87.
[42] John Adams, Notes of Debates, 26–27 Sept.; JCC, I, 43.

desperate effort to change the direction of the Congress. Galloway explained later that the "loyal party" had little hope of "stemming the torrent" after the adoption of the Suffolk Resolves but that it did try to base American rights on "just and constitutional principles" and to provide a "plan for uniting the two countries on those principles. . . ." The other purpose, he said, was "to probe the ultimate design of the republicans" to find out if they would be satisfied with anything except absolute independence.[43]

Therefore on 28 September Galloway offered a written constitution calling for a "grand council," a colonial parliament, with members elected by the colonial legislatures. The presiding officer would be a "president general" appointed by the king and holding office at his pleasure. The individual colonies would retain control of their internal affairs (then known as "internal police"), but all matters involving more than one colony, or of mutual concern to Britain and the colonies, would be handled by the American parliament. Galloway's solution for settling disputes between Britain and the colonies was simple, and might have been workable. Galloway proposed that either the British or the American parliament could originate legislation affecting both the colonies and Britain, but that such legislation must be adopted by both parliaments before taking effect.[44]

Galloway opened the debate by declaring that the non-importation they had agreed to the day before would not provide relief for Boston, and that non-exportation was an "undigested proposition" which would wreck America. The colonies had been and were disunited. Galloway declared: "I know of no American constitution; a Virginia constitution, a Pennsylvania constitution we have; we are totally independent of each other."

Galloway's basic assumption was that "in every government, patriarchal, monarchial, aristocratical, or democratical, there must be a supreme legislature." Above all it was necessary that the trade of the empire be regulated by some power or other. The colonial legislatures could not do it. "Where then shall it be placed? There is a necessity that an American legislature should be set up, or else that we should give the power to Parliament or king." James Duane seconded Galloway. New York had come to the Congress in part to aid Massachusetts, but in part to "lay a plan for a lasting accommodation with Great Britain." Congress had departed from that plan. Above all there was the problem of trade. Justice required that "we should expressly cede to Parliament the right of regulating trade." Edward

[43] EHD, IX, 802–3.   [44] Ibid. 811–12; JCC, I, 48–51.

Rutledge of South Carolina, unlike his older brother John, had tended to be on the side of the popular leaders. He now declared that he had come to the Congress with the idea of "getting a bill of rights, and a plan of permanent relief. I think the plan may be freed from almost every objection. I think it almost a perfect plan."

The popular leaders were clearly taken aback. They professed to want an end to disputes with Britain and the establishment of American rights on a constitutional basis. Galloway offered a solution but they wanted none of it and they offered no alternative. Richard Henry Lee asserted that the plan "would make such changes in the legislatures of the colonies that I could not agree to it without consulting my constituents," the typical reply of any eighteenth-century politician who wanted to avoid taking a stand or to delay consideration of an issue. John Jay replied that he supported Galloway's plan and asked Lee to explain wherein it gave up any one liberty or interfered with any one right. Lee made no attempt to answer the question. Patrick Henry charged that while the plan would liberate Americans from a corrupt House of Commons, it would throw them into the hands of an American legislature which might be bribed by "that nation which avows in the face of the world, that bribery is a part of her system of government." However, the basis of the popular leaders' opposition to the Galloway plan was that they were either unwilling to compromise with Britain, or believed that compromise was impossible, an attitude revealed in Patrick Henry's concluding remark: "I am inclined to think that the present measures lead to war." [45]

After a day-long debate, Galloway's plan was deferred for later consideration by a vote of six colonies to five, but the popular leaders had no intention of considering it if they could avoid doing so. It is unknown how individual delegates voted then or on 22 October when Congress "met, dismissed the plan for a union, etc.," but it is significant that even the Rhode Island delegates split, with Samuel Ward opposing and Stephen Hopkins favoring the plan.[46] However narrow the victory, the opponents of the plan went ahead and provided a striking example of what a later generation was to call "managed news." When the journals of Congress were published in November, all mention of the plan and the votes upon it were

[45] John Adams, Notes of Debates, 28 Sept. In his *Historical and Political Reflections on the Rise and Progress of the American Rebellion* in 1780, Galloway gave a version of his speech which coincides with John Adams's brief notes of what Galloway said. It is reprinted, JCC, I, 44–48.
[46] Samuel Ward, Diary, 22 Oct.

omitted. It was left for an outraged Joseph Galloway to present his plan of union to the American people in a pamphlet he published shortly thereafter.[47]

With the Galloway plan defeated, if only by a narrow margin, Congress turned once more to the means of opposition: this time the issue of non-exportation. After further debate it voted on 30 September that the "exportation of all merchandise and every commodity whatsoever" to Great Britain, Ireland, and the West Indies should be stopped on 10 September 1775, and appointed a committee to prepare a plan for putting non-importation, non-consumption, and non-exportation into effect.[48]

During the debate one of the delegates, probably from Massachusetts, proposed that non-exportation begin immediately if there were any further "hostilities" in Massachusetts, or if an American were arrested to be taken to England for trial. Such an arrest, declared the resolution, should be considered as "a declaration of war . . . against all the colonies. . . ." Congress shunted the resolution aside so firmly that it was not given a place in the journals. The delegates were not about to accept "hostilities" or a "declaration of war," especially as defined by a New Englander, as a basis for action.[49]

Meanwhile, when Congress had voted for non-importation on 27 September there had been a striking omission: nothing had been said about the imports from the West Indies, which loomed so large in the trade of the northern colonies. Thomas Mifflin had proposed that no articles subject to duties should be imported, and presumably this included West Indian products, but the southerners were suspicious of the motives of their northern colleagues. How does one know, asked Edmund Pendleton of Virginia, whether molasses, coffee, or sugar has paid a duty? With no tact whatsoever, Thomas Lynch of South Carolina charged bluntly that several members of Congress knew how to smuggle goods without paying duties. Isaac Low, a wealthy New York merchant, declared himself outraged by such insults to a group of men "who deserve it the least of any men in the community." Low wanted no part of the proceedings and he charged flatly that certain delegates aimed at independence. He urged Congress to adjourn for six months and argued that the people could not live without

---

[47] A Candid Examination of the Mutual Claims of Great Britain and the Colonies (New York, 1775), reprinted in Jensen, Tracts, 350–99.
[48] JCC, I, 51–53.   [49] Ibid. 52, n.1.

West Indian products. However, if they were going to have non-importation, they had better exclude Dutch tea as well as English.[50] To avoid further charges of bad faith, Congress voted to stop the importation of molasses, coffee, and pimento from the British West Indies and Dominica, wines from Madeira and the "Western Islands," and foreign indigo.[51] Brown sugar and Dutch tea were added later by the committee appointed to draft the plan for putting the votes of Congress into effect.

In the midst of the embarrassing debate over smuggling and the West Indies trade, Massachusetts again presented the conservative members of Congress with a painful dilemma. The Massachusetts delegates were more and more irked at the delay in doing something concrete for their colony. John Adams soon got over his enthusiasm for the vote on the Suffolk Resolves. Congress applauds you, he wrote to a friend, but if you ask what should be done, the answer is "stand still, bear, with patience, if you come to a rupture with the troops, all is lost. Resuming the first charter, absolute independency, etc., are ideas which startle people here." [52] A few days later he warned another friend not to expect too much from Congress, and he snorted at the "figurative panegyrics upon our wisdom, fortitude, and temperance" while doing nothing at all.[53]

Then, on 6 October, Paul Revere arrived with a letter from the Boston committee of correspondence declaring that the fortifications being erected in Boston could be explained only by the supposition that "the town and the country are to be treated by the soldiery as declared enemies," and that the inhabitants were to be held "as hostages for the submission of the country. . . ." What advice will Congress give? Shall the people of Boston abandon the town, or shall they stay? The Bostonians will do whatever Congress says, no matter what the hardships and dangers involved. And what about government? The recent acts of Parliament have forced the suspension of all law and the governor has prevented the legislature from meeting. "They therefore request the advice of Congress." [54]

The last thing the more conservative members of Congress wanted was to take a stand that might lead to a clash with British troops. They could remember vividly how thousands of men had sprung to arms only a month before with the spread of the false rumor that British soldiers had killed Americans and that the British fleet had bombarded Boston. The day after the letter arrived John Adams wrote: ". . . if it is the secret hope of many,

[50] John Adams, Notes of Debates, 6 Oct.   [51] 6 Oct., JCC, I, 57.
[52] To Joseph Palmer, 26 Sept.   [53] To William Tudor, 29 Sept.
[54] JCC, I, 55–56.

as I suspect it is, that the Congress will advise to offensive measures, they will be mistaken." He said that the majority of the delegates would not vote "to raise men or money, or arms or ammunition. Their opinions are fixed against hostilities and rupture, except they should become absolutely necessary; and this necessity they do not yet see. They dread the thoughts of an action, because it would make a wound which would never be healed; it would fix and establish a rancor which would descend to the latest generations; it would render all hopes of a reconciliation with Great Britain desperate; it would light up the flames of war, perhaps through the whole continent, which might rage for twenty years, and end in the subduction of America as likely as in her liberation." [55]

The delegates wiggled and squirmed and maneuvered from Friday the 7th until Tuesday the 11th of October as they adopted and rejected resolutions and prepared a letter to General Gage. Some of the popular leaders proposed drastic measures. Richard Henry Lee wanted Congress to advise the evacuation of Boston while Christopher Gadsden, apparently, moved that Gage be attacked and beaten before he could receive reinforcements.[56] Congress rejected all such motions and George Ross and Joseph Galloway counterattacked by moving that Massachusetts be abandoned to do as it pleased with respect to government, justice, and defense. That motion too was rejected.[57]

What most of the members did not know, as we shall see, was that the ambivalent resolutions they adopted served the purposes of the Boston leaders, who were resisting demands for evacuation of the town and trying to prevent an outbreak of hostilities. The resolutions declared that if an attempt was made to execute the late acts of Parliament by force, "all America ought to support them in their opposition." However, the evacuation of Boston would have such important consequences it should not be done unless the Massachusetts provincial congress decided upon it. Nevertheless, the people of Massachusetts should submit to the suspension of the administration of justice if it could not be obtained legally under the present charter. The only clear-cut resolution was a safe one: it denounced those who had taken office under the Massachusetts Government Act as people who "ought to be held in detestation and abhorrence by all good men, and considered as the wicked tools of that despotism, which is preparing to destroy those rights which God, nature, and compact have given to America."

[55] To William Tudor, 7 Oct.   [56] JCC, I, 59n.; LMCC, I, 65n.
[57] To Edward Biddle, 12 Dec.

The words bore the brand of Samuel Adams, but Congress rejected the fiery letter he wrote to General Gage. The letter sent urged Gage to stop fortifying Boston and to stop irritating the people while Congress was peaceably trying to restore American liberties and harmony with the "parent state." Congress had been assured that the people of Boston would be peaceable if they could be certain of their safety.[58]

With Massachusetts shoved aside once more, Congress finally turned to the declaration of rights and grievances which had been completed on 22 September. Since then Congress had taken no action except to vote to include only those grievances which had occurred since 1763.[59] The opponents of the "law of nature" had given up; in fact, approval of the Suffolk Resolves had committed Congress to using it. Many years later John Adams declared that he had been "very strenuous for retaining and insisting on it, as a resource to which we might be driven by Parliament much sooner than we were aware." [60] Adams had no more use than Joseph Galloway for the law of nature as a guiding principle, but like many of his contemporaries, he realized that theories could be used as practical tools in an argument, and like them, he was adept at using them as such.

The crucial issue in the debate over the declaration of rights was the power of Parliament to regulate trade. On one side Christopher Gadsden denied that Parliament had any such power and insisted that Congress must not concede it. At the other extreme was James Duane, who declared that "the right of regulating trade" was the "great point." To those who proposed that Congress "consent" to allow Parliament to regulate trade, Duane replied that the power must be grounded on "compact, acquiescence, necessity, protection, not merely on our consent." After two days of debate Congress deadlocked. Five colonies voted to concede the power to Parliament, five voted against it. The Rhode Island delegation split as it had before, but surprisingly, so did the Massachusetts delegation.[61]

John Adams finally provided a formula which satisfied no one but which Congress accepted because "upon this depended the union of the colonies." [62] His statement became the fourth (and longest) resolution in the bill of rights. It began by declaring that since the colonies were not and could not be represented in Parliament, they were entitled to the exclusive right of legislation in all cases of taxation and internal polity, subject only

[58] JCC, I, 57–62; LMCC, I, 68–69. For the controversy in Massachusetts, see Chapter XXI below.
[59] 24 Sept., JCC, I, 42.   [60] Autobiography, III, 309.
[61] James Duane, Notes of Debates, 13 Oct.; John Adams, Diary, 13 Oct.
[62] Autobiography, III, 309–10.

to the veto of the Crown. "But, from the necessity of the case . . . we cheerfully consent to the operation of such acts of the British Parliament, as are bona fide, restrained to the regulation of our external commerce, for the purpose of securing the commercial advantages of the whole empire to the mother country, and the commercial benefits of its respective members; excluding every idea of taxation, internal or external, for raising a revenue on the subjects in America, without their consent." [63]

This fourth section of the bill of rights was a victory for the popular leaders, for while they had been forced to agree that Parliament should regulate trade, they had not conceded that Parliament had a "right" to do so. Instead, they based the power on "necessity" and on the "consent" of the colonies. In December, after John Adams had returned to Massachusetts, he reported to a Pennsylvanian that the "resolution" was "extremely popular" and that the provincial congress considered it "a great point gained." How, he asked, was it "relished and digested among the choice spirits along the continent?" [64]

The bill of rights finally agreed to on 14 October, began with a long preamble explaining why Congress had been forced to meet. It cited the Declaratory Act, taxation without consent, the board of customs commissioners, the extension of the power of the admiralty courts, the threat to take Americans to England for treason trials, the dissolution of assemblies when they tried to petition for a redress of grievances, the acts aimed at Massachusetts, and the Quebec Act. Americans, proclaimed the bill of rights, "by the immutable laws of nature, the principles of the English constitution, and the several charters or compacts, have the following rights." Eight of the ten resolutions summed up most of the principles Americans had been reiterating for years. They were entitled to their life, liberty, and property and had never ceded to any sovereign power whatever the right to dispose of them without their consent; their ancestors had been entitled to all the rights and liberties of the free and natural-born subjects of the realm of England; they had not forfeited those rights by emigration and their descendants were now entitled to them; they were entitled to the common law of England, and in particular, to the privilege of being tried by juries of their peers of the vicinity; they were entitled to all the privileges and immunities granted by royal charters, or secured by the several codes of laws of the colonies; they had the right to assemble peaceably and petition the king; and the keeping of a standing army in the colo-

[63] EHD, IX, 806–7.   [64] To Edward Biddle, 12 Dec.

nies in peacetime without the consent of the colonial legislatures was illegal.

The fourth resolution asserting absolute freedom from parliamentary control, except by consent of the colonies, was in effect a reply to the Declaratory Act of 1766. The tenth resolution was a striking attack on a fundamental part of the constitution of the royal colonies, and on royal power itself. The royal councils were as old an institution as the elected assemblies but Congress resolved that the "exercise of legislative power" by a council appointed by the Crown was "unconstitutional, dangerous, and destructive to the freedom of American legislation." Who proposed this radical assertion and whether or not it was debated is unknown. Whatever its origins, it did point the way to an attempt to reduce the power of the upper houses of legislatures when Americans began writing their first state constitutions less than two years later.

The bill of rights concluded with a list of the acts and measures "which demonstrate a system formed to enslave America." Included was virtually every act of Parliament relating to America between 1763 and 1774.[65] James Duane made an effort to delete mention of the Quebec Act as irrelevant to the purposes of the bill of rights but such men as Richard Henry Lee saw to it that it was retained.[66]

ॐ

During the final debate on the bill of rights, the most important measure Congress was to adopt, the Association, was laid before it. Four members of the committee that prepared the Association—Thomas Cushing, Thomas Mifflin, Thomas Johnson, and Richard Henry Lee—were supporters of drastic measures. The fifth member, Isaac Low of New York, obviously had little influence. Congress began debating the Association on 15 October and it was ready for signing on the 20th. At that point four South Carolina delegates threatened to break up the Congress: they refused to sign and walked out. Christopher Gadsden remained and offered to sign but his was a meaningless gesture. The South Carolinians had insisted that rice and indigo be exempted from non-exportation but Congress had refused to agree. Eventually John and Edward Rutledge, Thomas Lynch, and Henry Middleton returned. They offered to stop the exportation of indigo if South Carolina could continue to export rice to southern Europe.

[65] EHD, IX, 805–8.   [66] James Duane, Notes of Debates, 17 Oct.

The South Carolinians, like most of the delegates, assumed that, aside from Britain and the British possessions, trade would continue as usual, for they did not expect war to wreck all the patterns of American trade within a few months. What they demanded, therefore, were the same privileges that most of the northern colonies would have under the Association. The wheat, flour, fish, lumber, and other products of the northern colonies would go as usual to southern Europe and the foreign West Indies. Those colonies would thus sacrifice a far smaller portion of their trade than South Carolina, even if it continued to ship rice to southern Europe, and doubtless their delegates knew it. Congress therefore gave in to South Carolina's demand.[67]

The Association contained many ideas derived from the non-importation agreements in 1768–69 and copied several parts of the Virginia association of August 1774. It exhorted Americans to be frugal and to develop manufactures and agriculture. Extravagance and dissipation were to be discouraged, particularly horse-racing, cock-fighting, plays, and shows. Those who attempted to profiteer would be boycotted, and American manufactures were to be sold at reasonable prices. Sheep would not be exported, the breed should be improved, and surplus stock should be sold to neighbors, "especially to the poorer sort, on moderate terms."

On 1 December 1774, the colonies would stop the importation of all goods from Britain and Ireland, East India tea from any part of the world, molasses, syrup, brown sugar, coffee, and pimento from the British West Indies and Dominica, foreign indigo, and wines from Madeira and the "Western" islands. The importation of slaves would likewise stop on 1 December and all commerce with those who continued in the slave trade would be cut off. Those who did import goods between 1 December 1774 and 1 February 1775 could have the choice of reshipping them or turning them over to a local committee for storage during non-importation, or for sale with the profit remaining, after reimbursing the owners, to be given for the relief of Boston. Goods imported after 1 February would be shipped back at once.

Non-consumption, "an effectual security for the observation of the non-importation," would start on 1 March 1775. Non-exportation would begin on 10 September 1775 unless the various acts of Parliament listed at the end of the Association had been repealed by that date.

The most significant part of the Association called for the establishment of committees in "every county, city, and town" in America to enforce the

[67] Report of the South Carolina Delegation, Nov. 1774, LMCC, I, 85–87.

Association.[68] In effect, if not in intent, this was a call for the creation of revolutionary committees throughout America, all charged with a common task. Such committees sprang into being everywhere and they did not limit themselves to publishing the names of violators of the Association in the newspapers. They took control of the economic life of the colonies and became centers of political power as well.

With the Association agreed upon, Congress hastened to a dissolution, for the delegates were anxious to return home, and some went early, leaving colleagues behind to sign their names to such documents as the Association. The principal remaining business was agreement on the final form of various documents that committees had prepared. These were a petition to the king, and addresses to the people of Great Britain, the people of North America, and the inhabitants of Quebec. Congress quibbled about the drafts, as about earlier documents, but finished them within days.[69] On Wednesday 26 October, "The Congress then dissolved itself." But the delegates looked forward to a second congress for on 22 October they had resolved, "as the opinion of this Congress, that it will be necessary that another Congress should be held on the tenth day of May next, unless the redress of grievances, which we have desired, be obtained before that time."

[68] JCC, I, 75–80.   [69] Ibid. 82–90, 90–101, 105–13, 115–21.

XX

The Road to Concord Bridge: The Way of Politics

The popular leaders of America won a victory at the First Continental Congress far greater than they could have expected or even planned for. They secured the inclusion of "the law of nature" as one of the bases of American rights and thus provided themselves with an infinitely flexible foundation for future arguments with Britain. They denied all power of Parliament over the colonies except for the regulation of trade, and even that power was based on necessity and the consent of the colonies, not on legal right. And by implication they questioned the power of the Crown itself by attacking the role of royal councils in the governments of the colonies. They defeated the Galloway plan of union and thus rejected any possible constitutional solution of the dispute with Britain except upon their own terms: the independence of each colony within the empire. In the Association they achieved the most drastic form of economic coercion ever attempted in America, and it was coercion aimed at the opponents of the popular leaders in America as well as at Britain.

Congress refused to sanction the use of force against the British troops in Boston, but the ambiguous advice to Massachusetts to act only on the defensive was a recognition that an armed clash might come. Whether or not it would come depended upon the response of each of the colonies and of the ministry and Parliament in London to the proceedings of the First Continental Congress.

"The proceedings of the Continental Congress astonish and terrify all considerate men," reported General Thomas Gage, whose governorship of

Massachusetts had become meaningless and whose optimism had long since vanished. The resolves of the Congress might not be observed, but they would be generally accepted because there "does not appear to be resolution and strength enough among the most sensible and moderate people in any of the provinces openly to reject them." [1]

"Sensible and moderate" men recognized that the Congress had taken such a stand that, if Britain did not back down, war might be the outcome. Thus the day after Congress adjourned, John Dickinson predicted that "the colonists have now taken such grounds that Great Britain must relax, or inevitably involve herself in a civil war. . . . The first act of violence on the part of administration in America, or the attempt to reinforce General Gage this winter or next year, will put the whole continent in arms, from Nova Scotia to Georgia." [2]

Above all such men feared that Massachusetts might bring about an open break. Toward the end of 1774, when the rumor spread that Massachusetts might defy Britain by resuming its old charter, John Dickinson wrote to Thomas Cushing: "I implore you, my dear sir, in the name of Almighty God to discourage by all the means in your power, this, not only useless, but pernicious scheme. Our province cannot *yet* bear the thought of arming for fear of dissensions." [3] On the same day a Baltimore merchant wrote Cushing that such a "wild measure" would ruin Massachusetts and all America and confirm the enemies of Massachusetts in the belief that "you were not only aiming at an independency on the mother country, but likewise a superiority dangerous to the other colonies." [4]

The threat of independence, so feared by moderate men, was real enough, as an anonymous newspaper writer in Philadelphia made clear two weeks after Congress adjourned. Anticipating *Common Sense* in both idea and language, "Political Observations without Order: addressed to the People of America" asserted that the history of kings was the history of the depravity of human nature. The power of the American Congress was derived from the people and opposition to its laws would be treason against the present generation, against generations yet unborn, and against God. Americans should constantly look forward to the time when the present connection between them and Britain shall be dissolved. The essay was

[1] To SS, 15 Nov., Force, 4 ser. I, 981.
[2] To Arthur Lee, 27 Oct., LMCC, I, 83.
[3] 20 Jan. 1775, C.O. 5/118. Some of Thomas Cushing's private correspondence was taken to England by General Gage which accounts for its presence in the Public Record Office. Gage to SS, 15 Oct. 1775, Gage, *Corres.*, I, 422–23.
[4] Samuel Purviance to Cushing, 20 Jan. 1775, C.O. 5/118.

welcomed by an opposition writer as proof that "the Republicans of North America, particularly those of New England, have long been aiming at independency. . . ." But at least the writer of "Political Observations" was not a hypocrite, as were the leaders of the "republican party of the Congress" who refused to admit that they had tried to throw off all subordination to Britain.[5]

The two anonymous newspaper articles illustrate the fundamental shift in the nature of the American debate that took place after the adjournment of the Congress. Prior to 1774, although Americans had attacked one another, most of their attention was centered on Britain and British policies. After the Congress, Americans turned upon one another as never before. Men who believed that the policies of the Congress would lead to armed conflict and prevent reconciliation with Britain attacked those policies and their supporters. They insisted that, bad though British measures might be, one basic cause of trouble was the ambition of American demagogues whose power was based on mob support. They argued (as some had ever since 1765) that were it not for such men the colonies and Britain could work out their differences peacefully.

One of the first to launch a full-scale assault on the Congress was Samuel Seabury, an Anglican rector in Westchester county, New York. He came from an old Connecticut family and was a physician as well as a parson. As the "Westchester Farmer" he wrote four pamphlets urging the merchants and farmers and the legislature of New York to reject the policies of the Congress. If they did not, he predicted open war for "the authority of Great Britain over the colonies must cease, or the force of arms must finally decide the dispute." If the Americans succeeded they would start a civil war and would probably shed the blood of a greater part of the inhabitants "to determine what kind of government we should have—whether a monarchy or a republic."

Seabury begged the New York legislature to reject the "laws" and "decrees" adopted by the "enthusiastic republicans of New England and Virginia," and denounced the "enthusiastic delegates and brain-sick committeemen" who were enforcing the policies of Congress in New York. That colony, he said, echoing the feeling of many another New Yorker, was in the power of a "faction using a mob to carry out its purposes." Seabury, who had no use for such, said that if he must be enslaved, "let it be by a king at least, and not by a parcel of upstart lawless committeemen. If I

[5] "Political Observations" from the *Pennsylvania Packet* and "M" 's reply from *Rivington's New York Gazetteer* are reprinted in EHD, IX, 816–20.

must be devoured, let me be devoured by the jaws of a lion, and not gnawed to death by rats and vermin." [6]

Massachusetts, like New York, had long been divided into parties, and in no colony had the inhabitants attacked one another more virulently. The results of the first Congress provided a unique opportunity for a review of the political history of the colony in an attempt to fix blame for what had happened. Daniel Leonard, a wealthy lawyer, presented one version of that history. His family came to Massachusetts early in the seventeenth century, and for a hundred years had been so powerful in Bristol county that John Adams once called it the "land of the Leonards." Leonard, who had been a member of the Massachusetts House of Representatives in 1774, was appointed one of the royal councilors under the Massachusetts Government Act, and because he accepted the post, his neighbors forced him to flee to Boston and the protection of the British army.

As "Massachusettensis" Leonard published the first of seventeen essays in the *Massachusetts Gazette* on 12 December 1774. He charged flatly that the "present calamity is in a great measure to be attributed to the bad policy of a popular party in this province" whose measures "have been diametrically opposite to their profession—the public good. . . ." "Party," he said, "is inseparable from a free state" and Massachusetts had long been divided between whigs and tories. While there were good men in both parties, some of the whigs depended on "popularity" and would have sunk into oblivion without it. Hence, they had created turmoil and engrossed all power in their hands. Massachusetts had been called a "democracy or a republic," but it was in fact "a despotism cruelly carried into execution by mobs and riots, and more incompatible with the rights of mankind than the enormous monarchies of the East." He had seen "the small seed of sedition when it was implanted; it was as a grain of mustard. I have watched the plant until it has become a great tree; the vilest reptiles that crawl upon the earth are concealed at the root; the foulest birds of the air rest upon its branches."

Such were the men who went to the First Continental Congress. "Fishing in troubled waters had long been their business and delight. . . . They were old in intrigue. . . . The subtility, hypocrisy, cunning, and chicanery habitual to such men, were practiced with as much success in this, as they had been before in other popular assemblies." Men of "first-rate abilities and characters" were outwitted and circumvented with the result that the

[6] C. H. Vance, ed., *Letters of a Westchester Farmer, 1774–1775* (Westchester County Historical Society *Publications*, White Plains, N.Y., 1930), VIII, 61, 98–99.

Congress did everything possible to make reconciliation impossible. For proof, said Leonard, look at a pamphlet by one of the delegates.[7]

That pamphlet was Joseph Galloway's *A Candid Examination of the Mutual Claims of Great Britain, and the Colonies*, perhaps the most important and thoughtful of the writings of those who opposed the first Congress. Like Seabury and Leonard, Galloway denounced "American demagogues" who had deluded "the unhappy people, whom they had doomed to be the dupes of their ambition." He asserted that nothing had been the result of the Congress except the "ill-shapen, diminutive brat, INDEPENDENCY," and that the "unthinking, ignorant multitude, in the east and west, are arming against the mother state, and the authority of government is silenced by the din of war." He pointed to the possible danger of foreign intervention and domination and the almost certain danger of civil war between the colonies over such matters as rival land claims if they became independent.

But Galloway's basic purpose was positive: on the one hand he sought to prove that Parliament did have legal sovereignty over America, and on the other that Americans had certain rights which they did not enjoy but must have. Britain, if she expected to retain the colonies, should "restore to her American subjects the enjoyment of the right of assenting to, and dissenting from, such bills as shall be proposed to regulate their conduct." To achieve this end, Galloway had presented his plan of union in the Congress, but it had been rejected and then omitted from the published journals as if it had never been presented and debated.

Aside from his basic conviction that there must be a "union between two great countries whose interest and welfare are inseparable," the core of Galloway's thought was based on the proposition that "there is no position more firmly established, in the conduct of mankind, than that there must be in every state a supreme legislative authority, universal in its extent, over every member." [8]

Galloway thus set forth one of the central issues in American political and constitutional thought during the revolutionary era—and ever since. He was concerned with the same problem and used many of the same arguments that James Madison, Alexander Hamilton, and John Jay used twelve years later, and in a very real sense his pamphlet is an introduction

---

[7] *Novanglus, and Massachusettensis*, 146, 149, 158, 159, 219–20. The essays of 19 and 26 December and 13 March are reprinted in Jensen, *Tracts*, 278–96, 341–49.
[8] The pamphlet is reprinted in Jensen, *Tracts*, 351–98.

to *The Federalist Papers* of 1787–88. He became a loyalist, but other Americans who fought for independence shared his social and political beliefs and his conviction about the need for a supreme central government within America. The Declaration of Independence merely altered the context, not the fundamental nature of the debate.

Some of the opponents of the Congress had long been as important, and every bit as "American," as the men who replaced them and became founding fathers of the new nation. Some of them remained loyal to Britain, as did Samuel Seabury, Daniel Leonard, and Joseph Galloway. Seabury became chaplain of a British regiment, received a doctor of divinity degree from Oxford University, but returned to America after the war as the first bishop of the American Episcopal Church and thus had a final revenge on his fellow New Englanders who had so long pictured bishops as dangerous ogres. Leonard became chief justice of Bermuda and, later on, one of the most prominent and successful lawyers in early nineteenth-century England. Galloway, after serving as civil administrator of Philadelphia during the British occupation in 1777–78, left for England, and despite his pleas to return to his native land, was never allowed to.

The tens of thousands of Americans who left their native land rather than accept independence demonstrated that such men represented a large and important segment of American thought and feeling. And no one knows how many tens of thousands of other Americans remained loyal to Britain at heart, or at least opposed independence, but could not or did not choose to leave.[9]

The supporters of the Congress had the advantage in the debate, for they had a single positive program to offer and they controlled or influenced most of the printing presses.[10] They insisted that Americans were not divided but were virtually unanimous in support of the Congress, except for a few "Tories" and British tools willing to sell the liberties of their country for power and cash. Most of them denied vociferously that they wanted independence and insisted that they wanted reconciliation with the mother country.

Samuel Seabury was answered by an undergraduate at King's College in New York who had recently arrived from the West Indies. Alexander Hamilton knew very little as yet about the mainland colonies but he defended the Congress and its policies and denied the supremacy of Parlia-

---

[9] For a brief discussion of loyalism see Chapter XXIV below.
[10] Gordon, *History*, I, 379.

ment with skillful invective and such rhetorical flourishes as the proclamation that the sacred rights of mankind "are written, as with a sunbeam, in the whole volume of human nature, by the hand of divinity itself; and can never be erased or obscured by mortal power." [11]

Where Hamilton dealt in generalities John Adams dealt in specifics for he had an intimate knowledge of Massachusetts politics. When he returned home from the first Congress he found "Massachusettensis" shining like a moon among lesser stars and making the tories happy and the whigs gloomy. As "Novanglus," Adams presented the popular party's version of recent Massachusetts history in the columns of the *Boston Gazette*. His purpose, he said, was to pursue "the tories, through all their dark intrigues, and wicked machinations; and to show the rise and progress of their schemes for enslaving this country." The villains were such men as former governors William Shirley and Francis Bernard, and Thomas Hutchinson and his allies. Among the "schemes of this junto, one was to have a revenue in America by authority of Parliament." They had no intention of sending the money to relieve Britain. "They chose to have the fingering of the money themselves" to provide handsome salaries for such avaricious characters as Bernard and Hutchinson. Furthermore, they proposed to "new model the whole continent of North America" by abolishing the charters and creating a nobility in each colony, "not hereditary indeed, at first, but for life." Unluckily for them, the "British financier," George Grenville, took the revenue for the British exchequer "because he had hungry cormorants enough about him in England whose *cooings* were more troublesome to his ears, than the croaking of the ravens in America." It was this junto then, and not the popular party, that was the cause of America's calamities.

As for the charge that the "whigs flattered the people with the idea of independence," Adams declared, "nothing can be more wicked or a greater slander on the whigs, because . . . there is not a man in the province, among the whigs, nor ever was, who harbors a wish of that sort." [12]

The truth of such charges and counter-charges is not as important as the fact that the debaters asserted that they were true, or at least tried to convince the American public that they were. Meanwhile, men in both Amer-

[11] Hamilton's two pamphlets replying to Seabury are reprinted in Harold C. Syrett and Jacob E. Cooke, eds., *The Papers of Alexander Hamilton* (New York, 1961), I, 45–78, 81–165.

[12] Adams's twelve essays were published in the *Boston Gazette* between 23 January and 17 April 1775. The essays for 23 and 30 January and 13 and 20 February are reprinted in Jensen, *Tracts*, 296–341. John Adams did not learn until a few years before his death in 1826 that Leonard was the author of the "Massachusettensis" essays.

ica and Britain were taking actions that would transform the spilling of ink on paper into the shedding of blood on the grass of Lexington Common.

The pamphleteers and newspaper writers spent months debating the implications of the first Congress, but the Association was a reality that had to be faced as soon as Congress adjourned. Whatever its impact on Britain, it would have a staggering effect on the American economy. Furthermore, many Americans were convinced that eventually they would reach a fork in the road ahead. One fork might lead to reconciliation with Britain; the other would probably lead to independence, and the Association pointed toward that fork.

The Association provided a "national" policy, but its effectiveness would depend upon action taken in each of the colonies. And as in the past, Americans responded in terms of the interests and the politics of what they looked upon as their "countries," not in terms of the interests of a nation as yet unborn. Whether from dislike of its economic restraints, or from a fear that it would lead to independence, a majority of Americans probably opposed the Association. William Gordon said that in the spring of 1774 the "great body" of the patriots in all the colonies wanted no more than a removal of the innovations adopted since 1763. This was true even in Massachusetts, although there were a few, led by Samuel Adams, "who hanker after independency" and would do all they could to achieve it.[13] The people, said Gordon, were "divided into two great classes": one wanted to rush headlong into extremities, and the other to avoid all violent measures except as a last resort. There was a "third party" which did not totally disapprove of British measures, but its voice was low and seldom heard.[14]

Several months after the Congress adjourned, reported Gordon, there was "to appearance, an amazing agreement through the continent" and it might be imagined that the people of twelve colonies had "but one heart, and but one understanding. Assemblies, conventions, congresses, towns, cities, private clubs and circles" all seemed to support the Congress. But appearances were misleading for "there are great numbers in every colony who disapprove of these measures—a few, comparatively, from principle and a persuasion that the same are wrong, and that they ought to submit to the mother country—some through attachment to the late governmental authority exercised among them—many from self-interest—but the

[13] Gordon, *History*, I, 347.   [14] Ibid. 378–79.

bulk for fear of the mischievous consequences likely to follow." Yet those who opposed "popular measures" had not been supported by Britain and had stayed away from town and other meetings. "The popular cry being against them, they have sought personal peace and safety in remaining quiet." [15]

The opponents of the Association thus contributed to their own defeat, but their freedom of choice was also limited by forces beyond their control. It was limited by British policy-makers, whose utter lack of comprehension of conditions in America led them to make decisions which justified the arguments of those Americans who insisted that compromise with Britain was impossible.

Freedom of choice was also limited by a political reality in America which the popular leaders had helped bring about. For a decade those leaders had appealed to "the people" and had won their support in opposing British policies. In 1774–75 "the people" greeted the Association enthusiastically and became members of or backed up the hundreds of local committees that sprang up to enforce the Association. What happened varied from colony to colony and even from community to community. Some local leaders were able to persuade their committees to act moderately; in other communities, committees ran roughshod over all opposition and acted in ways that ranged from the comic to the brutal. Each committee could establish its own standards for there was almost no centralized control. Colonial governments disintegrated during the winter of 1774–75 and the congresses and conventions that met made no attempt to regulate enforcement, except in South Carolina. It was not until after the outbreak of the war that any serious effort was made to supervise local committees and by then the Association was no longer the central issue.

The southern colonies—South Carolina, Maryland, and Virginia—put the Association into effect with dispatch and fervor and with none of the hesitation they had shown toward non-importation in 1768–69. Georgia was the scene of agitation but no action. North Carolina formally approved the Association, but it was divided and indecisive.

Charleston, which dominated the commerce of South Carolina, was the key to enforcement in that colony. The provincial meeting in July 1774, which elected delegates to the first Congress, had also elected a provincial committee consisting of fifteen merchants and fifteen mechanics from Charleston and sixty-nine planters from the colony at large. During the

[15] Ibid. 426–27.

summer and fall of 1774 the Charleston members had stopped merchants from exporting arms, warned them against raising prices, and campaigned against the use of tea. They even sent school boys from house to house to collect tea which was then burned publicly on Guy Fawkes' Day, or "Pope's Day" as the Bostonians called it.

But when the South Carolina delegates returned from Philadelphia, they were greeted by howls of outrage from the indigo planters because the rice planters could continue to ship their rice. The Charleston mechanics, following the lead of their hero, Christopher Gadsden, joined the chorus. So too did some of the backcountry people who professed to see but another example of hypocrisy on the part of the low-country leaders.

The Charleston committee called a congress to meet on 11 January 1775. Meanwhile, John Rutledge and his fellow delegates to Congress, except for Gadsden, tried to persuade the people that the exportation of rice was not contrary to principle, and promised that the indigo planters would be compensated for their losses. When the congress met it approved the proceedings of the Continental Congress, thanked the delegates, and then began a bitter debate over the Association. Gadsden moved that the freedom to export rice be cancelled. John Rutledge counter-attacked by appealing to the lively prejudice of the Carolinians against northerners, and went so far as to charge that the Association was, in large measure, a plot on their part to steal Carolina's markets. The debate went on and on until the rice planters and their supporters, somewhat to their surprise, retained the privilege of exporting rice. In turn, they promised to deliver one-third of the rice crop to compensate the indigo planters, but would in turn be compensated by the sales of other crops grown in the province. It is not entirely clear who would pay for the plan in the end, but war made it unnecessary for the Carolinians to find out.

South Carolina was the only colony where a central organization controlled enforcement of the Association from the start. The provincial congress appointed the local committees and prescribed rules for enforcement. It forbade suits for the recovery of debts, with certain exceptions. The congress also recommended that the people learn the use of arms, elected delegates to the Second Continental Congress, and agreed to meet again whenever called together by the Charleston committee. A few days later the legislature met briefly and approved the proceedings of the Continental Congress and of the provincial congress.[16]

16 W. E. Hemphill and W. A. Wates, eds., *Extracts from the Journals of the Provincial Congresses of South Carolina, 1775–1776* (Columbia, S.C., 1960), 3–30; Schlesinger, *Colonial Merchants*, 464–69.

The Association was enforced strictly and the mechanics remained alert for any wavering on the part of the gentry. When a native Carolinian returned from England with his furniture and two horses, a majority of the enforcement committee allowed him to land his property. Within days the populace denounced the landing of the horses. The committee then reconvened, with a great crowd to watch it. Gadsden moved that the two horses be banished, and among other things argued that the committee members were the servants of the people and must yield to their wishes. The Rutledges and others replied that allowing the horses to remain would not be contrary to the spirit of the Association, and besides, the committee would lose prestige if it reversed its vote. William Henry Drayton, who had publicly denounced the interference of the people in the affairs of their betters during non-importation in 1769–70, and had been appointed to the governor's council, had now changed sides as a result of the Intolerable Acts. He supported Gadsden's motion, which passed 35-34. What happened to the horses is not recorded, but later Drayton commented that the event was "the first instance of a point of importance and controversy being carried against those by whose opinion the people had been long governed." [17]

In Georgia the New England settlers in St. John's parish agitated to join the other colonies and so did a few men in Savannah. But less than half the twelve parishes sent delegates to a convention in January, and the legislature was prorogued before it could take any significant action. The St. John's people offered to secede and join South Carolina but were ignored. Samuel Adams's brother-in-law in Savannah told him that he blushed for the want of spirit among the "greatest part" of the province, "who, after their mock resolutions, lukewarm associations, and faint conventions, have thrown off the mark and remain a self-interested, penurious set not worthy of the freedom of Americans or the notice of its meanest subjects." [18]

North Carolina was a divided colony politically and its commerce, unlike South Carolina's, was divided among many small ports. Several of the tidewater counties adopted the Association and tried to enforce it but they were opposed by the merchants, many of whom were Scots who had come to the colony during the preceding decade. When a second provincial convention met on 3 April 1775, nine counties, mostly in the backcountry, did not send delegates, and some of the delegates from other counties were

---

[17] Schlesinger, *Colonial Merchants*, 526–27.
[18] Andrew E. Wells to Samuel Adams, 18 March 1775, Adams Papers, NYPL. For a detailed account see Coleman, *Revolution in Georgia*, chapter III.

elected by a very few men. The legislature met the next day and since all of its members except one were delegates to the convention, the two bodies sat in the same room and switched roles as each approved the Association and elected delegates to the Second Continental Congress. The angry and somewhat dizzy governor, Josiah Martin, denounced the convention and ordered it to disperse. He told the same men, as legislators, that he viewed events with "extremest horror" and ordered them to oppose the convention. As members of the convention, the legislators declared the governor's proclamation illegal, and as legislators they upheld the right of the people to assemble and petition for a redress of grievances. The governor then dissolved the legislature which never met again and he got support from the backcountry, where hundreds of citizens in four former Regulator counties sent him addresses swearing their loyalty to the Crown and denouncing lawlessness and the recent convention.[19]

The two "tobacco colonies" had responded more vigorously than any others to Boston's plea for help—more vigorously in fact than Massachusetts itself. The Virginians had adopted an association in June and a non-importation, non-exportation agreement in August, and the Marylanders made it clear that they would agree to an association adopted by a continental congress if Virginia and North Carolina tobacco planters were not given special concessions.

In Maryland, Governor Robert Eden had prorogued the legislature in March 1774 before he left for England, and when he returned in November, he neither dissolved it nor tried to call another session. Thus the popular leaders who had dominated the assembly were able to take over control of the colony without official opposition from higher authority. They called the first revolutionary convention held in any of the colonies and they controlled it and those that followed. For years they had proclaimed the "rights of the people," but they had no intention of allowing "the people" to decide policy in Maryland. They were therefore appalled when confronted with a practical demonstration of popular power.

On Friday 14 October the *Peggy Stewart* arrived at Annapolis with a cargo that included over 2000 pounds of tea. The vessel was owned by Anthony Stewart and his father-in-law, James Dick. Stewart entered the ship at the customs house and paid the duty on the tea, which was con-

[19] Journals of the Convention and the Assembly, NCCR, IX, 1178–1205; Schlesinger, *Colonial Merchants*, 462–64, 519–25; Force, 4 ser. II, 115–17.

signed to another firm. That afternoon four members of the Anne Arundel county committee of observation called a mass meeting which was attended by a throng of "inhabitants" and "gentlemen" from other counties who were in Annapolis for a session of the provincial supreme court. The meeting voted unanimously that the tea should not be landed, appointed a committee of twelve to oversee the landing of the other goods on the vessel, and adjourned until Wednesday the 19th.

"A great number of respectable gentlemen" from the surrounding counties appeared on Wednesday, but so did others. Stewart and the consignees appeared before the meeting and offered to burn the tea. The Anne Arundel county committee agreed that burning, and a public apology, would be adequate punishment. Thereupon, extremists insisted that the ship be burned but they were overwhelmingly defeated in a vote. A clamorous minority refused to agree and so did the shipowners. Fearful that his house might be burned, or that even worse might befall him and his wife, who was on the point of giving birth to a child, Anthony Stewart set fire to the vessel himself. Stewart and James and Joseph Williams, the tea consignees, signed an abject apology declaring that "we have committed a most daring insult, an act of the most pernicious tendency to the liberties of America. . . ." Then they "went on board said vessel, with her sails and colors flying, and voluntarily set fire to the tea; and in a few hours, the whole, together with the vessel, were consumed, in the presence of a great number of spectators." [20]

Marylanders, unlike people in Boston and New York, were not accustomed to such expressions of popular power. Their shock was expressed by a "gentleman at Bladensburg" who said that "since the burning of the ship at Annapolis, the common sort seem to think they may now commit any outrage they please; some of them told the merchants yesterday that if they would not sell them goods, they would soon find a way to help themselves." He also told of another merchant in a nearby town who hoped to sell imported goods at a higher price than usual but his prices were going to be fixed by a committee. He asked: "what think you of this land of liberty, when a man's property is at the mercy of anyone that will lead the mob!" [21]

The second Maryland convention met on 21 November and soon adjourned until 8 December when it approved the proceedings of the first

[20] VG(PD), 27 Oct. The story was dated Annapolis, 20 October. For a more detailed account, see Schlesinger, *Colonial Merchants*, 389–92.
[21] To his brother in Glasgow, 1 Nov., Force, 4 ser. I, 953.

Congress unanimously, set the percentage of profit a merchant could have, and recommended that lawyers boycott violators of the Association. Then, with the burning of the *Peggy Stewart* very much in mind, the convention "earnestly recommended" that decisions of the county committees be accepted and that "no persons except members of the committees, undertake to meddle with or determine any question respecting the construction of the Association. . . ." The delegates also resolved that "we do most earnestly recommend that all former differences about religion or politics, and all private animosities and quarrels of every kind, from henceforth cease and be forever buried in oblivion. . . ." [22]

Such resolutions were more expressive of hope than of reality as county committees searched out real and alleged wrongdoers and treated them harshly. Merchants who imported forbidden goods after 1 December 1774, if caught, had their goods stored, or sold, with the profits going to the relief of the poor of Boston. Merchants were boycotted, one so effectively that he complained that he could not get enough to eat. Others were humiliated and forced to make abject public apologies, and further punished when the populace sometimes broke their windows. Occasionally enforcement achieved the ludicrous, as when one county committee solemnly declared that for the sake of liberty an imported tombstone must be broken into pieces. [23]

જ

The second Virginia convention did not meet until March 1775, but Virginia's leaders did not wait. Virginia had adopted two associations before the first Congress met and the Virginia counties began organizing committees to enforce them during the summer of 1774. After the appearance of the Association, the Virginia counties continued to organize with the result that all of them probably had committees by the summer of 1775. Virginia's leaders had differed on policies, such as the payment of debts, and they continued to differ, but they took part in the work of the committees, with the most prominent acting as chairmen.

In the course of electing the committees, Virginia underwent a minor "revolution." Scores of men who had never held office before—nor would have in normal times—became members of the county committees. Many Virginians acquired a unique, if brief, opportunity to govern themselves.

---

[22] Proceedings of the Maryland Convention, 21–25 Nov., 8–12 Dec., Force, 4 ser. I, 991, 1031–33.
[23] Schlesinger, *Colonial Merchants,* 504–9.

They had been governed by appointed county officials over whom they had no control, and the only time they ever voted was at the occasional elections for delegates to the House of Burgesses. Now a whole new dimension was added, for at the mass meetings called to approve the Association and to elect members of the county committees, Virginians voted for the men who would govern them, since the county committees did in fact become the local governments. Furthermore, little or no attention was paid to voting qualifications, for "inhabitants" as well as "freeholders," that is, landowners, took part in many of the meetings.

In the summer of 1775 the Virginia convention partially recognized this "revolution" in an ordinance calling for the annual election of twenty-one freeholders in each county to enforce the Association and the measures of Congress and the convention. But the "inhabitants" were barred from voting: the suffrage was limited to those freeholders entitled to vote for members of the House of Burgesses.[24]

The leaders of the county committees might be fighting for freedom, but they made it clear at once that there would be no freedom of speech, at least for those who opposed them. Suppression began before the first Congress adjourned. When an undersheriff asked John Gray at Fredericksburg for a contribution to pay the expenses of the Virginia delegates in Congress, he asked: "Can't the poor dogs pay their own expenses?" They could, but Gray had to publish an apology and "cheerfully" agree to the Association. Andrew Shepherd, who had accused the delegates of "partiality," was likewise forced to print an apology.[25] Andrew Leckie of Caroline county was far more indiscreet. When he had been asked for a contribution for the Virginia delegates he had replied "damn them all." After Edmund Pendleton spoke to the people of Caroline county and the Association had been read to them, Leckie confessed that he had turned to a Negro boy and said: "Piss Jack, turn about my boy and sign." In a multiple apology, including one to the merchant whom he had charged with profiteering during the previous association, Leckie confessed to a "natural and unhappy peevishness of temper." [26]

County committees soon went far beyond requiring public apologies: they insisted that people either sign the Association or be boycotted. Thus four days after it was elected on 13 December 1774, the Northampton committee divided the county into seven districts and directed three or more of its members to present the Association to the people in each dis-

24 VG(P), 22 Sept. 1775; Force, 4 ser. III, 390, 420–24.
25 VG(PD), 13 Oct. 1774.   26 Ibid. 3 Nov.

trict. Asking people to sign the Association, said Madison, is "the method used among us to distinguish friends from foes and to oblige the common people to a more strict observance of it." [27]

Anglican rectors were no more exempt from attack than other inhabitants. The Nansemond county committee published a denunciation of the Reverend John Agnew for his obnoxious sermons. The Orange county committee conducted a public book-burning. It discovered the Reverend John Wingate had "several pamphlets containing very obnoxious reflections on the Continental Congress" and demanded that he surrender them. He refused at first but dared not resist for long. The committee considered the five pamphlets, four of them by Samuel Seabury, over the weekend, and on Monday, 27 March, held a meeting which resolved that because they were a collection of "audacious insults" against the Congress and the colonies, of "the most slavish doctrines of provincial government, the most impudent falsehoods and malicious artifices to excite divisions among the friends of America," they ought to be publicly burned. The sentence was "speedily executed in the presence of the Independent Company, and other respectable inhabitants of the said county, all of whom joined in expressing a noble indignation against such execrable publications, and their ardent wishes for an opportunity of inflicting on the authors, publishers, and their abettors, the punishment due to their insufferable arrogance, and atrocious crimes." [28]

The principal concern of the county committees was with the merchants, some of whom were natives of Great Britain, as were many agents of British mercantile houses. Virginians had carried on a campaign against merchants for years, particularly the Scots, and some Virginians looked upon the times as an opportunity to get rid of them. One of them declared that the Scots had signed the Association under compulsion, and if there were a rupture with Britain, "will they not be ready to come at our backs, and cut our throats? Let us then, my friends, whilst the disorder is curable, purge this our sickly colony of such filth." [29]

However, the merchants as a group professed a willingness to co-operate. They were holding their regular fall meeting at Williamsburg when the Virginia delegates returned from Congress. The whole body, "supposed to be between 4 and 500," went to the Capitol and expressed their gratitude

[27] Virginia Gazette (Dixon and Hunter) [VG(DH)], 4 Feb. 1775; to William Bradford, 20 Jan., in W. T. Hutchinson and W. M. E. Rachal, eds., The Papers of James Madison (Chicago, 1962), I, 135.
[28] VG(DH), 8, 15 April.
[29] Virginia Gazette (Pinkney) [VG(Py)], 19 Jan. 1775.

for what Peyton Randolph and his colleagues had done at Philadelphia, presented Randolph with a copy of the Association "voluntarily and generally signed," and promised to adhere strictly to it.[30]

Most planters remained suspicious and their suspicions were confirmed at the end of 1775 when intercepted letters proved that certain Scottish merchants had ordered goods, including Andrew Sprowle, leader of the group that thanked the Virginia delegates to Congress in November 1774.[31]

But the committees did not wait for such proof and they found enough to satisfy them as they went along. Merchants were caught bringing in tea and it was either burned or dumped overboard. The Northampton committee ordered all tea in the county surrendered to an officer and held at the risk of the owners until the Association was dissolved. But some "gentlemen" brought their tea to the courthouse and asked that it be burned, "in which reasonable request they were instantly gratified." [32] The Caroline county committee inspected merchants' books to see if they had raised prices. Some merchants refused to open their books, whereupon the committee published their names and announced that "a suspicion arises" that they had been selling goods at higher prices than usual, and advised the people to have no dealings with them. Those named soon changed their minds and were exonerated. In Gloucester county, Charles Marshall, who had declared that "every man had a right to sell his goods for as much as he could get," was soon brought to heel. He signed the Association and published a confession in which he said that "these are offenses I am (as have been some other North Britons) taught to know, at this time, deserve severe punishment. . . ." [33]

Examples could be multiplied although the pursuit of wrongdoing merchants did not keep the committees busy, for they also tried to stop gambling in a colony in which gambling was almost a way of life. In fact, the only Virginians who seemed to escape without being forced to mend their ways were the faculty members of the College of William and Mary, a majority of whom opposed the Association.[34]

ह‌

The bulk of the commerce of Pennsylvania and New York, like that of South Carolina, flowed through a single city in each colony. In addition, western Connecticut was an economic province of New York City and

[30] VG(PD), 10 Nov. 1774.   [31] VG(P), 22, 29 Dec. 1775.
[32] VG(DH), 4 Feb. 1775.   [33] Ibid. 14 Jan., 4 Feb. 1775; VG(Py), 19 Jan. 1775.
[34] VG(Py), 22 Dec. 1774, 26 Jan. 1775. For a fuller account of enforcement in Virginia see Schlesinger, *Colonial Merchants*, 509–19.

Delaware of Philadelphia, while the two cities divided most of the commerce of New Jersey between them. The two cities were also the political centers of their colonies and each contained popular leaders and their followers among the mechanics and tradesmen, although they had little of the power of the popular leaders in Boston. Nevertheless, backed by upper-class leaders out of power, they had pushed reluctant merchants and their political allies into agreeing to a continental congress.

The calling of a colony-wide convention in Pennsylvania had forced the legislature to elect delegates to the Congress but the convention achieved more than that. The Philadelphia leaders won the support of the back-country, long discontented with the lack of adequate representation in the legislature, by agreeing that each county should have one vote in the convention. Thus was laid the foundation for the alliance that would eventually bring Pennsylvania to agree to independence and would lead to the writing of the most revolutionary state constitution of the revolutionary era. But that future, if foreseen at all, was seen dimly. The Philadelphia leaders had quite another purpose in the summer of 1774. They had lost their faith in merchants during non-importation in 1769–70 and they were determined that the merchants must be forced to agree to a stoppage of trade if Congress recommended it. The weapon they readied was one the popular leaders had used or threatened to use ever since 1765: a buyer's strike against merchants who imported British goods. The Philadelphia leaders therefore undertook to build up support among "the body of farmers who compose the great strength of these provinces and to lay the foundations early of a non-consumption agreement which, if general, will give great effect to a non-importation agreement. . . ." The plan described by Joseph Reed in July was apparently successful, for two months later he reported that "should the merchants hesitate to comply with any suspension of trade the Congress direct, the people of the country will compel them, and I know no power capable to protect them." [35]

Then came the annual election for members of the assembly in October and the result was a blow for Joseph Galloway and his allies. His old enemy John Dickinson, and Charles Thomson, whom he despised even more, were elected, and the new assembly unanimously chose Edward Biddle of Berks county as speaker in place of Galloway who had been speaker for years. The next day, also unanimously, it added Dickinson to the Pennsylvania delegation in Congress.[36]

When the assembly reconvened in December it unanimously approved

---

[35] To Lord Dartmouth, 25 July, 25 Sept., Reed, *Life*, I, 70–71, 78.
[36] 14–15 Oct., Force, 4 ser. I, 869–70.

the proceedings of the Congress, asked the people to observe its recommendations, and elected the delegates who attended the first Congress to
go to the second Congress in the spring. A few weeks later, after the New
York legislature refused to consider the proceedings of the Congress, the
wealthy Quaker merchant, Thomas Wharton, commented bitterly that
"had our contemptible house done the same, we might have expected some
good, but Dickinson's politics turned the scale and caused the vote to pass
as it did. . . ." [37] Dickinson was entitled to credit but he was helped by
the fact that Galloway had gone off to New York to console himself and
did not return until three days after the action, which he deplored.[38]

Meanwhile, enforcement of the Association was in the hands of the
joint county-city committee of 43 that had been created in June with John
Dickinson as chairman, and with such conservatives as Thomas Wharton
as members, despite their distaste for some of their colleagues. As Wharton explained it, he had avoided taking part in public affairs for years, but
he agreed to serve because many had asked him to, and because he wished
"to keep the transactions of our city within the limits of moderation and
not indecent or offensive to our parent state." [39]

The popular leaders knew perfectly well that such men as Wharton intended to hold them in check, and writers professing to be "artisans" and
"mechanics" began a newspaper campaign for a new committee. The call
by Congress for election of local committees provided the necessary lever.
The committee of 43 set a date for the election of a new joint committee
for the city and county, whereupon a mass meeting demanded that the city
have a committee of its own, and that it be elected by ballot in each ward.
The old committee yielded and the new committee of 66 was at least a
partial victory for the popular leaders. Only seventeen members from the
old committee were elected to the new one, but among them were Dickinson, Charles Thomson, Joseph Reed, and Thomas Mifflin. Thomas Wharton and others like him were dropped and replaced by activists such as
William Bradford, publisher of the *Pennsylvania Journal*, and by several
mechanics and tradesmen who presumably had never before held a public
position of any kind.[40]

The membership of the committee, as well as its enforcement of the Association, inevitably aroused opposition. An embittered former "high

[37] To Samuel Wharton, 31 Jan. 1775, PMHB, XXXIV, 43.
[38] 10, 15 Dec., Force, 4 ser. I, 1023–24.
[39] To Samuel Wharton, 5 July 1774, PMHB, XXXII, 436.
[40] Schlesinger, *Colonial Merchants*, 456–59. All the counties except the two farthest
west had chosen committees by February.

Whig" swore in a coffee house that among the members of the committee were an "avowed republican," a man who had made a fortune in illicit trade during the last war, and an "illiterate merchant." Such people "aimed at a general revolution," and were trying to overthrow "our excellent constitution." They were "drunk with the power they had usurped, and elated with their own importance" and were determined to increase the discord and confusion by which they had risen to power. They realized that if the troubles were ended they would again "sink into their native obscurity" and that nothing would worry them more than "a speedy accommodation and reconciliation between the parent state and the colonies; they have nothing to lose in a general havoc, but all to gain from a scramble." [41]

Such ranting illustrated the strong feelings of important people, but it distorted reality. Members of the committee, such as the wealthy John Dickinson, privately dreaded the outcome of the policies of the Congress and were opposed to both independence and to political revolution, while at the same time they opposed British policies. Their plight was that of men who tried to steer a middle course between extremists on both sides of the Atlantic. Joseph Reed put it neatly in December 1774 when he said that he feared a "prudent person will find it difficult to act. A spirit of domination in the mother country has produced a spirit of libertinism rather than of liberty here, and . . . both sides will have something to concede before a settlement is made." A few weeks later he said that he could not support any British measure unless the system of colonial administration was changed, and then with considerable foresight said he doubted that the support of any individual, however important, would have any effect "in a country where people more generally read, discuss, and judge for themselves, than perhaps any other in the world." [42]

While such members of the committee as Dickinson and Reed were expressing their private doubts, the opponents of the Association grew more bold. In mid-January Galloway reported that many were uneasy because the assembly had approved the proceedings of Congress, that "the men of property begin to think and speak their sentiments. . . ." However, they would not act until they learned what Parliament would do "and they can hope to be protected in their upright conduct." [43]

The Quakers, as a group, did not wait for "protection." As early as June

[41] To Mr. Rivington, 16 Feb., Force, 4 ser. I, 1232.
[42] To Dennis De Berdt, 24 Dec. 1774, 13 Feb. 1775, Reed, *Life*, I, 88–89, 97.
[43] To [Samuel Verplanck], 14 Jan. [1775], PMHB, XXI, 478.

1774 they opposed the stoppage of trade and in December they reprimanded the Quaker members of the assembly who had voted to approve the proceedings of Congress. In January 1775 they denounced "all combinations, insurrections, conspiracies, and illegal assemblages" as contrary to their religious principles.[44] The Quakers were fearful as they peered into the future and Thomas Wharton gave voice to their fears in a letter to his brother in London. They believed, he said, that Britain was wrong but that she would redress American grievances if properly stated. However, "a particular sect" was making every effort to involve the whole continent with Boston, confident that they could oppose Britain successfully. "But," he said, "the thoughtful among us cannot help asking, what is the next step if England should be overcome? The question sinks deep in our minds . . . but what redress is to be expected, what civil or religious liberty enjoyed, should others gain the ascendancy?" [45] By "others" Wharton meant the Presbyterians who had long been enemies of the Quakers in Pennsylvania. Eventually, the "others," including many who were not Presbyterians, did "gain the ascendancy," and most Quakers stuck to their principles, and to a degree suffered the fate that Wharton anticipated.

The committee of 66 admitted that opposition was growing. As one member put it, the proceedings of the Congress "had been pitched on too high a key for some of these middle provinces," and that despite "general public approbation," men were speaking out instead of murmuring and that publications were more free than in former disputes. However, he warned, if Britain tried to enforce its measures, many who found fault with the Congress would change their minds.[46]

It was probably the growing opposition, and the possibility that the next session of the assembly might reverse its approval of the Congress, that led the Philadelphia committee to call a second convention to meet on 23 January. This convention "heartily" approved the proceedings of Congress and resolved that if any county committee met opposition in enforcing the Association, the other county committees should go to its aid. The convention also authorized the Philadelphia committee to act as a standing committee for the colony, and to call another convention whenever necessary.[47]

[44] Schlesinger, *Colonial Merchants*, 496–97.
[45] To Samuel Wharton, 31 Jan. 1775, PMHB, XXXIV, 41–43.
[46] Joseph Reed to Dennis De Berdt, 13 Feb., Reed, *Life*, I, 96.
[47] Proceedings of the Convention of the Province of Pennsylvania . . . , 23–28 Jan., Force, 4 ser. I, 1169–72. For the resolutions concerning defense, see Chapter XXI below.

The Philadelphia committee, whose most prominent members were also members of the legislature, did not use the authority until May 1776. Thus the legal assembly, unlike all other colonies except Delaware, remained the focal point in the struggle over policy until the very eve of independence, and remained opposed to independence until within days of its declaration.

It was to the assembly that Joseph Galloway turned in February 1775 in a last desperate effort to stop the drift toward independence. He was convinced that the people were changing their minds with "amazing rapidity" and said that the attempts of the "violent party" to get the people to prepare for war had been baffled. When the assembly convened, Governor John Penn suggested that it prepare a petition to the king "as the only proper and constitutional mode of obtaining redress. . . ." The New York and New Jersey assemblies had already agreed to do so and their example probably influenced the governor, although his father-in-law, ex-Chief Justice William Allen, declared that the message "meant no more than to save appearances."

Galloway began a fight for the petition, charging that the policies of the Congress were inciting the people to sedition and would end in independence. He was opposed by Allen, Dickinson, Thomson, and others, but in the course of the two-day debate, somewhat to his surprise, he won fourteen converts among the thirty-eight members. Then, to give himself more time, he moved that the debate be put off ten days, and won by a 19-18 vote. Before the debate resumed, he said, the "independent party" proposed to open the doors to the public and have "the mob let in upon me." He called some friends to be on hand, but the proposal to open the doors was beaten.

Although Galloway had won every vote so far, he still did not have a majority for a petition to the king, so he switched tactics by proposing the substance of an answer to the governor's message, including a motion to adjourn until some time before the Second Continental Congress met on 10 May. He hoped that the rapidly changing sentiments of the people and news of firm measures by Parliament would make possible "more rational and salutary measures" at a later date. Again the "independents" opposed but again Galloway won.

The speaker appointed a committee to prepare an address to the governor based on the principles proposed by Galloway and adopted by the house. Dickinson told Galloway that he should draft the message but while he was away doing so, the rest of the committee met and engaged in what

Galloway called "one of the most dirty and scandalous measures which ever was transacted in public life." The committee ignored the principles adopted by the house and drafted a quite different message. When Galloway returned and discovered what had been done, he denounced the committee for playing a "dishonorable, disingenuous, dirty, and fraudulent part" but despite the justice of his charge, the house adopted the committee's version by a vote of 22-15.

Earlier in the session a box containing a halter and a threatening letter had been left late at night at Galloway's lodgings. Such threats only fixed his determination "to oppose those lawless measures," but the days of his power were gone.[48] The assembly adjourned to meet again on 1 May, but his hope that something might be gained by the delay was shattered by the news of war in Massachusetts. On 12 May, after repeated requests from him, the assembly excused him from attending the Second Continental Congress, and before the end of the year he fled to the protection of the British army.

The ultimate irony is that some of the men who fought Galloway so bitterly soon began fighting for the ideas he had supported so openly and courageously. William Allen became a loyalist like Galloway, and within months after Galloway's departure, John Dickinson became the recognized leader of the men, from one end of America to the other, who opposed a declaration of independence. In fact, most of the leaders of the two Pennsylvania factions who had fought one another so long, joined forces to block independence. In this, Pennsylvania was unlike New York, where the leaders of the De Lancey faction controlled the legal government until it disintegrated, and then most of them became loyalists. On the other hand, the Livingstons, out of power, supported opposition to Britain and wound up, to the dismay of some of them, as American patriots.

New York's response to the Boston Port Act was confined almost entirely to the city of New York. The committee of 51 established in May was controlled by the De Lanceys who hoped to prevent the stoppage of trade proposed by Boston and demanded by New York's popular leaders and their Livingston backers. The committee evaded taking action by proposing a continental congress which the De Lanceys did not want, and

[48] Galloway to Governor William Franklin of New Jersey, 28 Feb., 26 March, N.J. Ar., 1 ser. X, 572–75, 579–86; 21, 23–25 Feb., 4, 8–9 March, Force, 4 ser. I, 1277–82. The journals reveal little of what happened.

then, when it became clear that a congress would meet, put off electing delegates as long as possible. When forced to elect delegates or lose control of the city, the De Lanceys named four of their faction to the delegation. Those men—Isaac Low, John Alsop, James Duane, and John Jay—fought manfully at Philadelphia but in the end they signed the Association and thus handed a resounding victory to the popular leaders of the city and to the Livingstons.

Despite the defeat, the committee of 51 tried to retain control of enforcement.[49] It proposed that each ward in the city elect ward committees by ballot, and these committees, presumably, would enforce the Association under the direction of the committee. The Livingstons and the popular leaders struck back through the "committee of mechanics" which threatened to call a mass meeting, and the result was an agreement to elect a new committee at a city-wide meeting. The new committee of 60 contained members of the Livingston faction and six members of the mechanics committee, while many De Lancey supporters were dropped. While the committee of 60 was more committed to drastic measures than the committee of 51, it still contained men who tried to prevent them.

Cadwallader Colden, at eighty-four, was acting as governor again, for Tryon had returned to England. He had no power but he retained all his old skill at cynical commentary about New York politics. He was surprised at first that "several gentlemen of property" were members of the new committee, but soon discovered that their purpose was "to protect the city from the ravage of the mob." They would support the measures of Congress for the time being, for if they did not "the most dangerous men among us would take the lead, and under pretense of executing the dictates of the Congress, would immediately throw the city into the most perilous situation." [50] Nevertheless, the Association was enforced rigidly and the populace saw to it that the committee did not waver. Even before the committee was elected, a mob of 200 prevented a ship captain from taking eighteen sheep to the West Indies.[51]

But most of the colony ignored the Association. Only three of thirteen counties responded favorably to the Association, efforts in three others to adopt it were suppressed, and most devastating of all, seven counties ig-

---

[49] The account which follows is based largely on Becker, New York, chapters VII–VIII. Bernard Mason, The Road to Independence: The Revolutionary Movement in New York, 1773–1777 (Lexington, Ky., 1966), offers a somewhat different interpretation and some new details.
[50] To SS, 5 Oct., 2 Nov., 7 Dec., NYCD, VIII, 493, 510–13.
[51] VG(PD), 24 Nov.

nored it entirely. If New York was to join with the other colonies, much would depend on the legislature when it met in January 1775. Early in the session ten members of the Livingston faction, "the whole strength of that party" according to Colden,[52] moved to consider the proceedings of the first Congress. Not all of the De Lancey faction had yet appeared but those present fought back. They denounced the members of the Congress as rebels and traitors. James Jauncey was reported "very high about the matter, but trembled like an aspen leaf all the time he was speaking." An opponent told an outsider that "he never knew the meaning of 'a d——d canting son of a b—ch' before he heard that speech." [53]

The De Lanceys defeated the motion by a narrow margin—the vote was 11-10—and then rallied their absent members. Thereafter, they overwhelmed the Livingstons. A motion to thank the New York delegates to the Congress was beaten 15-9, one to thank the merchants and inhabitants of the city for their "patriotic conduct" by 15-10, and most important of all, a motion to elect delegates to the Second Continental Congress was overwhelmed, 17-9.[54]

Far from joining the other colonies, the De Lancey-controlled New York assembly broke with them and appealed directly to Britain. The De Lanceys adopted a petition to the king, and petitions to the Lords and Commons as well. Colden hoped that the assembly's "loyalty and firmness" would appear in "a very striking light" as compared with other colonies, but neither house of Parliament bothered to discriminate. Both rejected the New York petitions without a hearing, as they did those of the first Congress. Meanwhile the assembly adjourned to meet in May; but it never met again because of events in Massachusetts.[55]

New York City's popular leaders insisted that New York must send delegates to the second Congress but the question was: how should they be elected? John Adams once described New York politics as "the devil's own incomprehensibles" and the devious machinations during the first two weeks in March illustrated his description.

The committee of 60 called a meeting for 6 March and both sides tried to pack it and an outright brawl was only narrowly averted. Then by shouting matches rather than orderly voting the popular leaders got the meeting to send delegates to a provincial convention and authorized the committee

[52] To SS, 1 Feb., NYCD, VIII, 531–32.
[53] Ebenezer Hazard to Silas Deane, 1 Feb., CHSC, II, 193.
[54] NYAJ, 26 Jan., 17, 21, 23 Feb.; Force, 4 ser. I, 1286–90.
[55] NYAJ, 31 Jan., 3, 8, 24, 25 March, 3 April; Force, 4 ser. I, 1287–1324; Colden to SS, 1 Feb., NYCD, VII, 532.

of 60 to nominate eleven delegates to it. The committee picked the five delegates to the first Congress—Isaac Low, John Alsop, James Duane, John Jay, and Philip Livingston—and six men from the popular faction headed by no less a person than the onetime "Wilkes of America," Alexander McDougall. The slate was presented to the voters on 15 March on a take-it-or-leave-it basis. Those who tried to vote only for the delegates to the first Congress were told to vote for all or none. The nominees were elected 825-163.

The next day the committee of 60 announced that a convention would meet in New York on 20 May. Eight counties responded despite opposition in some of them and the convention met as called and unanimously elected a delegation of eleven to the second Congress. Included were all the delegates to the first Congress plus six stalwart Livingstonians.

Isaac Low who had been chairman of the committee of 60 and a delegate to the first Congress refused to attend either the convention or the second Congress.[56] He had tried to temper the popular movement but gave up and became a loyalist. James Duane and John Jay were gradually shifting from the De Lancey to the Livingston factions (both had married into the Livingston family), a shift that was shocking to Jay's friends. One of them said that Jay must have thrown aside his principles "to please the populace" and suggested that all that could be done was to tell Jay his friends were glad that he was continuing "to counteract the views of our ambitious, republican demagogues" and hope that he would see his error.[57] Whatever his motives, Jay reluctantly accepted independence, but he did staunchly defend the old order against demands for change as the colonies made the transition to independent statehood.

ટ✎

The New York convention adjourned on 22 April. The next afternoon two vessels from Rhode Island and an express rider from Connecticut brought news of the fighting at Lexington and Concord.

The outbreak of hostilities marked a fundamental turning point for it changed the basis of American opposition from economic to military warfare. As an economic measure the Association was an astounding success for the value of imports from Britain was nearly 97 per cent less in 1775

---

[56] *Journals of the Provincial Congress* (Albany, 1842), I, 1–5. John Haring, who had been a delegate from Orange county to the first Congress, also declined election to the second.
[57] William Laight to John Vardill, 27 March 1775, quoted in Frank Monaghan, *John Jay* (New York. 1035), 65–66.

than it had been in 1774.[58] But Britain did not retreat, as many Americans had hoped she would. Instead she finally turned to the use of armed force to maintain a constitutional principle.

Politically, the Association had been a success in America, for it helped to prepare the way for the direct confrontation with Britain that some Americans believed inevitable. It provided more Americans than ever before with an opportunity to unite in a common program of action aimed at Britain, and at those Americans they commonly called "tories." And, in some colonies, Americans were preparing for war at the same time that they were enforcing the Association so effectively. Whatever they lacked in physical equipment, they were well prepared emotionally for the 19th of April 1775.

[58] Schlesinger, *Colonial Merchants*, 535–36. Schlesinger's chapters XI–XIII are indispensable for an account of enforcement of the Association in all the colonies, including those not discussed in this chapter.

XXI

The Road to Concord Bridge: The Way of Force

The news of the battle on 19 April 1775 shocked men from one end of America to the other. Yet the idea that Americans might fight British regulars was not new in 1775, nor had it been for a decade. In 1765 the New York Sons of Liberty made a formal written treaty of alliance with the Sons of Liberty in Connecticut to come to the aid of New York City if British troops were used to enforce the Stamp Act. Two years later, as Boston awaited the arrival of British troops, the popular newspaper predicted bloody days ahead and the town's leaders displayed the public arms and boasted in taverns and on the streets that thousands of people would come in from the country to stop the landing. The talk was empty bluster and the troops landed without opposition.

Nevertheless, the populace of Boston, like that of New York, was not cowed by the soldiers and engaged them in endless brawls that led to such events as the "massacre of Golden Hill" in New York, and the Boston Massacre a few months later. Tension died down after 1770, although the Boston Massacre orations each year told of the danger of unwarranted attacks upon a harmless and helpless civilian population.

But the threat of an attack, when it came, was from New England farmers upon the British troops, not the other way round. During the summer of 1774 tension mounted to greater heights than ever before with the arrival of the Intolerable Acts and of more and more soldiers and naval forces to support the new governor of Massachusetts, Thomas Gage, commanding general of the British army in America. Massachusetts farmers began collecting arms and ammunition and thousands of them demonstrated that they were ready and willing to fight the regulars when, early on the morning of 1 September, Gage's troops seized some powder stored near Cambridge.

By eight that morning between three and four thousand men had gathered at Cambridge. General William Brattle, who had advised Gage to seize the powder, fled to Boston. The crowd then demanded the resignations of the new councilors whom Gage had appointed after the arrival of the Massachusetts Government Act early in August. Lieutenant Governor Thomas Oliver, after resigning as councilor, hastened to Boston to urge Gage to keep his troops in town. If he had not, reported Joseph Warren, all of them would have been killed. Meanwhile the committees of correspondence from nearby towns called upon Joseph Warren and the Boston committee to help head off violence. They succeeded, and by the end of the day the crowd had disbanded and all seemed peaceful.[1]

But a "rumor propagated with uncommon dispatch"[2] that men had been killed in Boston and that the British fleet had shelled the town during the night reached Marlborough in time for two companies from that village to join the crowd at Cambridge by eight in the morning.[3] The rumor reached Worcester that afternoon and perhaps 6000 men from Worcester county started east before the story was contradicted.[4] By the next morning the "people from the river" in Hampshire county were on the march and the report was that 20,000 of them reached Worcester before they too learned that the tale was false.[5] Israel Putnam in Connecticut rushed the tale to Philadelphia while Connecticut men set out for Boston. When the rumor got to New York on 6 September one commentator remarked that "nothing so fully discovered the spirit of the lower classes as their countenances and speeches" on its arrival. "It is astonishing to observe to what a pass the populace are arrived. Instead of that respect they formerly had for the king, you now hear the very lowest orders call him a knave or a fool, and reproaching him for the diversity of his and his grandfather's conduct."[6]

In Philadelphia the story was contradicted within a day, but if it had not been, reported Joseph Reed, the fury was so great that "thousands would have gone at their own expense, to have joined in the revenge. It was difficult to make them doubt the intelligence, or delay setting out." If the news

[1] Joseph Warren to Samuel Adams [4 Sept.], Richard Frothingham, *Life and Times of Joseph Warren* (Boston, 1865), 355–56.
[2] Gage to SS, 25 Sept., Gage, *Corres.*, I, 376–77.
[3] John Andrews to William Barrell, 3 Sept., MHSP, VIII, 353.
[4] William Lincoln, *History of Worcester* (Worcester, 1837), 95–96.
[5] Thomas Young to Samuel Adams, 4 Sept., Adams Papers, NYPL.
[6] William Smith, *Memoirs*, 192.

had been true, he said, an army of 40,000 men well-armed with everything except cannon, would have marched to Boston, and he prophesied that "if blood be once spilled, we shall be involved in all the horrors of a civil war." [7]

Dr. Thomas Young, who had greeted the Boston Port Act as the "perfect crisis," said that he "was pleased with this little rising on many accounts. One great advantage will be this: every man will be led to advert to any deficiencies he may have, either in point of discipline or preparation." Young told Samuel Adams: "you will perceive the temper of your countrymen in the condition your every wish, your every sigh for years past panted to find it." [8]

John Adams was not inclined to pant but he noted complacently, on the road home from Congress, that he had seen men drilling in Connecticut, and in a little town in western Massachusetts he was shown a gun that "marched eight miles towards Boston on the late alarm. Almost the whole parish marched off, and the people seemed really disappointed when the news was contradicted." [9]

ह‍≈

Ordinary people scattered throughout America thus made clear their willingness to fight months before Lexington and Concord, and at least eight legislatures and conventions made preparations of various kinds for meeting force with force. However, many of them lagged behind the people, who did not wait for the guidance of either legislatures or conventions, or for advice from the First Continental Congress.

During the summer and fall of 1774 farmers and townsmen throughout New England prepared for war. In Connecticut there were "tory hunts," and the "enemies" of American liberties were forced to recant or go into exile. By early September, General Gage reported that the people in Connecticut were "as furious" as those of Massachusetts, and that they were "exercising in Arms." [10] During the first week in September delegates from two eastern counties met at Norwich and declared that both the towns and the government of the colony should take immediate steps to prepare for a military emergency because they might "be under the disagreeable necessity of defending our sacred and invaluable rights, sword in hand." [11]

[7] To Dartmouth, 25 Sept., Reed, *Life*, I, 78.   [8] 4 Sept., Adams Papers, NYPL.
[9] *Diary*, 5, 6 Nov.   [10] To SS, 2, 12 Sept., Gage, *Corres.*, I, 370, 374.
[11] Quoted in Oscar Zeichner, *Connecticut's Years of Controversy, 1750–1776* (Chapel Hill, 1949), 179.

The assembly convened on 13 October, and the first law it adopted ordered the militia to train at least twelve half-days between then and the next May, and ordered the officers to see to it that all weapons were ready for immediate use. Other laws doubled the amount of ammunition to be stored in each town and ordered that the cannon in New London be made ready and supplied with adequate powder and shot.[12]

Rhode Islanders displayed equal gusto. When the assembly met in October, it approved petitions from towns asking to establish independent military companies such as the "Newport Light Infantry." In December it approved the Association, revised the militia laws, authorized the creation of more military companies, ordered arms distributed to the county regiments, appointed Simeon Potter of Bristol major general of Rhode Island forces, and provided that Rhode Island troops could be marched to help the neighboring colonies if any of them were attacked.[13]

New Hampshire had lagged far behind the other colonies, and it continued to lag. However, the hold of the Wentworth family on the colony was finally broken at the end of the year. As the governor told the story, "one Paul Revere arrived express" at Portsmouth on 13 December and the next day about 400 men seized "his Majesty's castle," William and Mary, at the entrance to the harbor, and carried away about 100 barrels of powder and the next night took away sixteen cannon. Only the arrival of a British warship prevented the capture of the rest of the cannon and the destruction of the fort. Nothing is safe, said the governor, including the customs house and the treasury, "if it should come into the mind of the popular leaders to seize upon them." "The springs of government are relaxed," he concluded.[14]

They were indeed relaxed as towns elected delegates to a new provincial congress, which met for one day on 25 January, approved the Association unanimously, chose a committee to call another congress whenever it judged necessary, and urged the men and officers of the militia to practice diligently. It declared that the militia of the continent, if properly disciplined, would be of great service, "should it ever be invaded by his Majesty's enemies. . . ."[15] The resolution was pallid compared with the

---

[12] J. H. Trumbull and C. J. Hoadley, eds., *The Public Records of the Colony of Connecticut* (15 vols., Hartford, 1850–90), XIV, 325–28, 343, 346.

[13] RICR, VII, 260–71; Lovejoy, *Rhode Island,* 173.

[14] Wentworth to Admiral Graves, 14, 20 Dec., enclosed in Admiralty to Dartmouth, 21 Feb., 1775, CHOP, IV, 323–24; Wentworth to Gage, 14, 16 Dec., Force, 4 ser. I, 1041–42.

[15] Force, 4 ser. I, 1180–82.

forthright actions of Connecticut and Rhode Island, but for New Hampshire it was a significant turning point.

To the south, legislatures, conventions, and local committees in Maryland, Pennsylvania, South Carolina, and Virginia adopted a variety of defensive measures. In November, a Marylander reported that people there were imitating the Virginia counties which were raising companies of soldiers.[16] In December the Maryland convention approved the proceedings of the first Congress and resolved that if force were used to impose the acts of Parliament upon Massachusetts, or used in any colony to execute "the assumed power of Parliament to tax the colonies," Maryland would support opposition with all its power. Then, far more bluntly, the convention recommended that all inhabitants between sixteen and fifty years of age should form themselves into militia companies, choose officers, and drill. Furthermore, they should be provided with arms and ammunition and "be in readiness to act on any emergency." The county committees chosen to enforce the Association were advised to raise £10,000 "by subscription, or in such other voluntary manner as they may think proper" and buy arms and ammunition.

The response was erratic. Companies were organized in Annapolis in December and two more in Baltimore in January. According to one report, the Annapolis companies were "composed of all ranks of men in this city; gentlemen of the first fortunes are common soldiers." [17] But there was opposition. When "a turbulent man, of no consideration, unless with the needy and desperate like himself," called the people of Anne Arundel county together and sought approval of the Association "and the other wild, impracticable views of the Congress . . . ," he was blocked.

The indignant "Annapolis merchant" who described the event, said that the "busy demagogue" had "fascinated a multitude" but that his plan for levying money to buy arms and ammunition to "join the treasonable purpose projected by Adams and the eastern Republicans, to carry on a formal rebellion in the colonies" had been defeated. There was too much wisdom and loyalty among the "principal people of Maryland to suffer this firebrand's projects to throw the province into a state of further distraction. . . ." The merchant welcomed Samuel Seabury's *What Think You of Congress Now*, which would convince many who had been "misled by the loud unlettered orators of the Republican tribe," and then spluttered

---

[16] Gentleman from Bladensburg to his brother in Glasgow, 1 Nov. 1774, ibid. 953.
[17] Proceedings of the Maryland Convention, 8–12 Dec., ibid. 1031–33; J. T. Scharf, *History of Maryland* . . . (3 vols., Baltimore, 1879), II, 169n., 172–73.

that "Adams, with his crew, and the haughty Sultans of the South, juggled the whole conclave of delegates." [18] Within months it was evident that many Maryland leaders shared the views of the "Annapolis merchant" rather than those of the "turbulent man" who had tried to arm the people.

The Pennsylvania leaders were equally reluctant to use force despite Joseph Galloway's predictions that the convention in January 1775 would ask the townships to appoint military officers and raise troops to be used against the British.[19] The convention did nothing of the kind, for its members realized that the Quakers and other pacifist sects were unalterably opposed.[20]

Yet the convention had to face the issue of what to do if Britain used force. It finally resolved that "we hold it our indispensable duty to resist such force. . . ." And then, quite as ingenuously as New Hampshire, the convention recommended that the owners of powder mills manufacture powder "as largely as possible" because it might be needed in the future, "especially in the Indian trade. . . ." [21]

The South Carolina leaders were more forthright. Their convention in January 1775 recommended that all the inhabitants learn the use of arms and that their officers train and exercise them at least once a fortnight. Thereafter, preparations were left in the hands of the assembly until after Lexington and Concord.

The assembly, which had not passed a tax bill since 1769, and no legislation at all since 1771,[22] adopted resolutions designed to improve the military resources of the colony. But when someone moved to provide money to buy "a large quantity of stands of arms to be distributed among the poor people throughout this colony," the assembly put off consideration and thereafter ignored so bold an idea. However, some of the people armed themselves. Governor Bull told the legislature in April that "persons unknown" had taken large quantities of arms and powder from the armory, and powder from other magazines in the colony. The assembly investigated and concluded that "there is reason to suppose that some of the inhabitants of this colony may have been induced to take so extraordinary and

[18] 28 Jan., Force, 4 ser. I, 1194.
[19] To [Samuel Verplanck], 14 Jan. [1775], PMHB, XXI, 478.
[20] John Dickinson to Thomas Cushing, 26 Jan., C.O. 5/118.
[21] Convention Proceedings, 23–28 Jan., Force, 4 ser. I, 1169–72.
[22] See Chapter XV above and Jack P. Greene, "Bridge to Revolution: The Wilkes Fund Controversy in South Carolina, 1769–1775," The Journal of Southern History, XXIX (1963).

uncommon a step in consequence of the late alarming accounts from Great Britain." [23]

More was done in Virginia to prepare for war than in the other colonies, with the exception of Connecticut and Rhode Island. Virginia counties began forming "independent" or "volunteer" companies during the summer and fall of 1774 [24] and by the end of the year George Washington had been offered the command of one company and had been asked to buy supplies in Philadelphia for two others.[25]

An independent company was organized in Fairfax county sometime in 1774, and in January 1775 Washington and George Mason undertook to organize the whole county. The county committee voted a "tax" of three shillings on each tithable to provide money for military supplies, with the names of those refusing to pay to be reported to it. Meanwhile Mason and Washington used their own money to buy supplies in advance of the collection of the tax. Mason prepared a plan for a militia composed of "gentlemen freeholders and other freemen" and for a regiment. Those with rifles were to form a company to be garbed in "painted hunting shirts." In a striking departure from the past, the militiamen were to elect their own officers.[26] Other counties also were active. The Northampton committee offered a bounty of £40 sterling to the first person to settle in Virginia and produce 5000 pounds of gunpowder within eighteen months, and urged other counties to provide additional money.[27]

Enthusiasm spread to the frontier. In January the freeholders of Fincastle county declared their undying loyalty to the king, but concluded that if Britain did not adopt pacific measures they would never surrender their privileges, "but at the expense of our lives." [28]

Richard Henry Lee was delighted. He sent a copy of the newspaper containing the resolution to his brother in England, telling him that Fincastle county could furnish "1000 rifle men that for their number make [the] most formidable light infantry in the world," and that the six frontier

23 SCHJ, 26 Jan., 16, 22 Feb., 1, 3 March, 25, 27 April.
24 James Madison to William Bradford, 26 Nov., Madison, *Papers*, I, 129.
25 S. M. Hamilton, ed., *Letters to Washington* . . . (5 vols., Boston, 1898–1902), V, 56–57, 68–69, 78–79.
26 D. S. Freeman, *George Washington: A Biography* (7 vols., New York, 1948–57), III, 398–400; Hamilton, *Letters to Washington*, V, 94–95n. Mason found it difficult to collect and Washington accused Mason of trying to cheat him. Ibid. V, 107–12.
27 VG(DH), 4 Feb. 1775.   28 VG(P), 10 Feb.

counties could provide 6000 such men who were, above all, dextrous in the use of the "rifle gun." He boasted that "there is not one of these men who wish a distance less than 200 yards or a larger object than an orange. Every shot is fatal." [29]

A little later James Madison agreed that the "strength of this colony will lie chiefly in the riflemen of the upland counties" and that they were superb marksmen, although the targets he mentioned were the size of a man's face, not of an orange. Even Madison, who but two years earlier was reading "romances" and disclaiming any interest in politics, practiced with a rifle, and while admitting that he was not of the best, said that he could do rather well at 100 yards. Boasting about marksmanship was not confined to Virginians. A Bostonian told of a "countryman" who watched an entire regiment of British soldiers miss a target, and when invited to try, hit the target three times running. The British were astonished, whereupon the man said, "I'll tell you *naow*. I have got a boy at home that will toss up an apple and shoot out all the seeds as it's coming down." [30]

In Virginia the leaders marked time. Peyton Randolph had been authorized to call another convention, but he preferred legal assemblies to revolutionary bodies and soon showed that he deplored ideas that might disturb the status quo. And such ideas were spreading, even to the slaves. James Madison reported in November that he had heard of slaves in one county who "chose a leader who was to conduct them when the English troops should arrive—which they foolishly thought would be very soon, and that by revolting to them they should be rewarded with their freedom." They were discovered, said Madison, who added that "it is prudent such attempts should be concealed as well as suppressed." [31]

In any event, Randolph waited for the meeting of the House of Burgesses which had been prorogued until February 1775 because of the governor's expedition across the Ohio River. When Dunmore returned early in December he made no public statements but he wrote alarming accounts to officials in England. Publicly he basked in the popularity his victory over the Indians won for him, and named his infant daughter Virginia. A merchant commented acidly that "he is as popular as a Scotsman can be amongst weak prejudiced people." [32] Then, in January, Dunmore, on orders from Dartmouth, put off the meeting of the burgesses until May.

[29] 24 Feb. 1775, Lee, *Letters*, I, 130–31.
[30] To William Bradford, 19 June 1775, 25 Sept. 1773, 24 Jan. 1774, *Papers*, I, 153, 97, 105–6; John Andrews to William Barrell, 1 Oct. 1774, MHSP, VIII, 371–72.
[31] To William Bradford, 26 Nov. 1774, *Papers*, I, 129–30.
[32] James Parker to Charles Steuart, 27 Jan. 1775, *Magazine of History*, III (1906), 157.

Richard Henry Lee compared the delay with the "conduct of the tyrant Stuart race, whose wicked and ruinous policy made them fear to meet their people. . . . The event of their despotism is well known," he told Samuel Adams.[33]

Randolph was at last forced to act: he called for the election of delegates to meet in convention at Richmond on 20 March.[34] Dunmore predicted that the convention would regulate and confirm the power of the county committees, and probably provide for arming and supporting military forces, and that it would "certainly . . . erect their own body into the head which is to direct the new government, which supersedes that of his Majesty in this colony and entirely subverts the constitution." Nevertheless, he pointed out, there were some men "of the first property," in fact a greater number than dared appear, who foresaw ruin, and who placed their hopes "of being rescued from the tyranny of licentiousness" on the perseverance of king and Parliament.[35] There were indeed such men in Virginia and as they converged on Richmond they had no intention of creating a new government. They clung to royal government, and to Dunmore as its symbol.

During the first three days of the convention all was harmony as the delegates considered and approved the proceedings of the first Congress. The only unusual incident was a vote to admit two delegates from Virginia's farthest frontier—"that part of Augusta county which lies to the westward of the Allegheny Mountain." On the fourth day the convention thanked the Jamaica assembly for its petition to the king and resolved that "it is the most ardent wish of this colony (and we are persuaded of the whole continent of North America) to see a speedy return of those halcyon days when we lived a free and happy people." [36]

At that point Patrick Henry, as he had in 1765 when he presented the Stamp Act resolutions, rudely jolted those who looked longingly backward and forced them to look forward to an anything but halcyon future. After describing the dangerous insecurity of the colony, he offered a resolution proposing "that this colony be immediately put into a state of defense," and that a committee be appointed "to prepare a plan for embodying, arming, and disciplining such a number of men as may be sufficient for that purpose."

The idea of preparing for war shocked men such as Edmund Pendleton,

[33] To Samuel Adams, 4 Feb., Lee, *Letters*, I, 128.
[34] VG(DH), 21 Jan. 1775. Both Dunmore's proclamation and Randolph's call appear in this issue.
[35] To SS, 14 March, C.O. 5/1353.   [36] Force, 4 ser. II, 165–67.

Richard Bland, Robert Carter Nicholas, and Benjamin Harrison, and might well have contributed to Peyton Randolph's apoplectic condition from which he died before the end of the year. They argued that economic coercion would work, that reconciliation was still possible, and that in any case it was ridiculous to assume that Virginia could fight the greatest military and naval power on earth. Henry replied in a speech, which like his speech against the Stamp Act, was in large measure the creation of his first biographer, but a superb creation nonetheless. It concluded with the words:

> Gentlemen may cry peace, peace—but there is no peace. The war is actually begun! The next gale that sweeps from the North will bring to our ears the clash of resounding arms! Our brethren are already in the field! Why stand we here idle? What is it that gentlemen wish? What would they have? Is life so dear or peace so sweet as to be purchased at the price of chains and slavery? Forbid it, Almighty God—I know not what course others may take; but as for me, give me liberty or give me death! [37]

The only known contemporary account is quite different: "You never heard anything more infamously insolent than P. Henry's speech: He called the K—a Tyrant, a fool, a puppet and a tool to the ministry. Said there was no Englishmen, no Scots, no Britons, but a set of wretches sunk in luxury; they had lost their native courage and [were] unable to look the brave Americans in the face. . . ." Whatever Henry said, he was supported by Jefferson, Washington, and Richard Henry Lee, and his resolution squeaked through by a vote of 65 to 60.[38]

A committee was appointed to prepare a plan, and according to James Parker, "something very extraordinary was intended, but a disagreement amongst the patriots put a stop to it." The plan was to raise eighty-six men in each county and equip them with arms and ammunition, but the committee could not agree on how to support them. "What flattened them all down was a hint of a plea to be presented by P. Henry, no less than the taking of government into their hands, appointing magistrates and levying money." But Nicholas, Harrison, Bland, and others "saw into this and formed an opposition to this which overset the scheme. . . ."[39]

The tale might well be true for the convention did not raise troops or

[37] William Wirt, *Sketches of the Life and Character of Patrick Henry* [1817] (Hartford, 1854), 134–42. Wirt, who had never met Henry, based his work on the "oral history" given him by men who had known Henry and on letters from them.
[38] James Parker to Charles Steuart, 6 April 1775, *Magazine of History* (1906), III, 158. This letter is the only known source for the vote.
[39] Idem.

provide for their support, much less take over the government of the colony. Instead, it merely recommended that the counties do what some of them had been doing for months: raise troops and provide for their support. It did suggest, however, that the tidewater and adjacent piedmont counties raise troops of horse and that "all the counties above these" pay attention to raising infantry. One might venture a guess that the delegates assumed it more fitting that the gentry should ride while the backcountry farmers should walk. As for funds, the convention suggested that the county committees collect them from their constituents in any way they saw fit. The convention also ratified what the counties had been doing by recommending that the county courts not proceed with any suits "except attachments" (i.e. collection of debts), not give any judgments except for sheriffs and other collectors of money.

The convention showed no ambivalence whatever in a matter close to the hearts and pocketbooks of many of the delegates. It resolved that "the most cordial thanks are justly due to our worthy governor, Lord Dunmore, for his truly noble, wise and spirited conduct on the late expedition against our Indian enemy; a conduct which at once evinces his Excellency's attention to the true interests of this colony, and a zeal in the executive department which no dangers can divert or difficulties hinder from achieving the most important services to the people who have the happiness to live under his administration." The officers and soldiers were thanked with equal fulsomeness.

Meanwhile, on the second day of the convention, the governor had issued a proclamation. The king had ordered, said Dunmore, that the lands within the new western boundaries that were run at the request of the assembly, and all other vacant lands in Virginia, be surveyed in lots of from 100 to 1000 acres and then sold to the highest bidder at public auction. The purchasers must pay a halfpenny sterling per acre annual quitrent and surrender all gold and silver and precious stones found on their land.[40]

The delegates, some of whom were accustomed to receiving grants of thousands of acres from the governor and council at little or no cost, declared the terms an innovation and appointed a committee "to inquire whether his Majesty may, of right, advance the terms of granting lands in this colony. . . ."[41] One member of the committee, Thomas Jefferson,

[40] 21 March, Force, 4 ser. II, 174.
[41] The proceedings of the convention were printed in the Virginia Gazette (DH), 1 April 1775, only five days after the convention adjourned. They are reprinted in Force, 4 ser. II, 165–72, which I have used here. The proceedings give no hint of the controversies in the convention. The accounts in Freeman, Washington, III, 401–7, and Mays, Pendleton, II, 3–12, differ in detail.

had raised precisely that question in his *Summary View* the year before.

But the delegates did not blame Dunmore for he had served Virginia speculators well, even though their hopes of expansion northwest of the Ohio River had been thwarted by the Quebec Act. That Dunmore's War was a speculators' war was widely believed in other colonies. A few days after he got to the Second Continental Congress, Richard Henry Lee warned his brother: "For heaven's sake avoid compliments (except to the soldiery) on the Indian expedition last summer. Nothing has given more concern and disgust to these northern colonies than our unhappy vote of that sort in last convention." One of the "first men on the continent" told Lee that he had been much grieved for the honor and good sense of Virginia when he saw the vote. He also said that a few "scatter loping" Indians would never be lacking to "commit irregularities for the encouragement of these land-exploring schemes," and that land hunters ought to accomplish their purposes "upon terms less destructive than £100,000 charge to the public annually." [42]

There was no danger of another expedition, for Dunmore soon destroyed his popularity and brought Virginia to the brink of armed conflict. Within days after the convention adjourned on 27 March one of Virginia's most ardent speculators heard a rumor that all land patents issued under the Dinwiddie Proclamation of 1754 would be cancelled because the surveyor had not qualified under the law. George Washington had bought up soldiers' claims under that proclamation and received a patent to 23,000 acres of land from the governor and council in December 1773. The surveyor in question was Washington's hand-picked agent, William Crawford. Washington wrote Dunmore that he found the threat "altogether incredible" and "it appears in so uncommon light to me, that I hardly know yet how to persuade myself into a belief of the reality of it. . . ." Dunmore replied bluntly that the patents would be cancelled if the surveyor had not qualified.[43]

Within days after he had alienated some of the most powerful men in Virginia, Dunmore outraged the populace and provided Patrick Henry with an opportunity to acquire more popularity than ever before. Early on Thursday morning, 21 April, a British naval captain and his men took several barrels of powder from the magazine in Williamsburg, loaded them on the governor's wagon, and put them aboard a British naval vessel in the

[42] To F. L. Lee, 21 May, Lee, *Letters*, I, 136–37.
[43] Washington to Dunmore, 3 April, *Writings*, III, 280–83; Dunmore to Washington, 18 April, Hamilton, *Letters to Washington*, V, 158.

river. When the town awoke and found what had been done, a crowd of people, some of them armed, met and planned a march on the governor's palace.

Peyton Randolph and others of the alarmed gentry persuaded the crowd that the governor should be approached "in a decent and respectful manner." Randolph then presented a statement to the governor declaring that the colony had built the magazine and bought the powder, that it was needed in case of invasion or insurrection, and there was reason to believe that "some wicked and designing persons have instilled the most diabolical notions into the minds of our slaves." Therefore, attention to internal security was all the more necessary. What motives did the governor have for taking the powder and for what purpose, and would he order it returned to the magazine at once? Dunmore's excuse was that he had heard of an insurrection in a neighboring county and that the magazine was insecure. However, he promised that in case of insurrection, he would return the powder in half an hour.[44]

The gentry persuaded the dissatisfied crowd to disperse but grumbling continued and a week later "Civis" warned: "there is still a leaven of discontent among a few of us" which might spread and break out in serious disorder.[45] If the populace had heard the governor's threats there might well have been an outbreak. He told a doctor who came to the palace that "by the living God" if anyone threatened him or harmed the naval captains "he would declare freedom to the slaves and reduce the city of Williamsburg to ashes." He had once fought for the Virginians but "by God he would let them see that he could fight against them," and in a short time "he could depopulate the whole country." Dunmore told the doctor to tell Peyton Randolph and other gentlemen what he had said and the doctor lost no time in doing so. The governor then sent his wife and children on board the *Fowey* at Yorktown and readied himself with 200 loaded muskets, servants, and slaves to meet all comers at the palace.[46]

Meanwhile, expresses from Williamsburg carried the story throughout the colony and within days independent companies in the northern counties were gathering. On 26 April Hugh Mercer wrote Washington that mounted men were meeting at Fredericksburg and would start for Williamsburg on Saturday the 29th, but they would wait for Washington's approval and instructions.[47] Meanwhile, Mercer had sent Mann Page, Jr.,

[44] VG(DH), 22 April; Force, 4 ser. II, 371–72.   [45] Ibid. Supplement, 29 April.
[46] Testimony of Dr. William Pasteur before a committee of the House of Burgesses, 14 June 1775, JHB (1773–76), 231.
[47] Hamilton, *Letters to Washington*, V, 162–63.

to Williamsburg for information. He got there at one o'clock on Thursday afternoon the 27th after a twenty-four-hour ride. That night he started back with a letter from Peyton Randolph [48] reporting that the governor had given private assurances that the powder would be returned. Speaking for himself and the officials of Williamsburg, Randolph urged the troops to go home because there was no danger, "whereas we are apprehensive, and this we think upon good grounds, that violence may produce effects which God only knows the effects of." [49] Randolph's plea was supported by three of Virginia's delegates who were on the way to Congress: Washington, Richard Henry Lee, and Edmund Pendleton. [50]

On Saturday the fourteen companies of "light horse" at Fredericksburg elected a council of 102 to consider the plea that they disband. The council prepared a declaration condemning the governor but asserting that it abhorred civil war and preferred peaceful measures as long as any hope of reconciliation remained. The companies would return home but the men should pledge themselves "to be in readiness, at a moment's warning, to reassemble, and by force of arms, to defend the law, the liberty, and rights of this or any sister colony, from unjust and wicked invasion." The declaration, as printed, concluded: "GOD SAVE THE LIBERTIES OF AMERICA." [51]

James Madison commented scornfully of the tidewater gentry: "the gentlemen below whose property will be exposed in case of a civil war in this colony were extremely alarmed lest government should be provoked to make reprisals. Indeed some of them discovered a pusillanimity little comporting with their professions or the name of Virginian." [52] But there was one Virginia delegate to Congress who did not agree with his colleagues nor travel to Philadelphia with them. The news of Lexington and Concord reached Williamsburg on Friday night, 28 April, and was printed in Dixon and Hunter's *Gazette* the next day. Patrick Henry called the county committee and the volunteer company of Hanover county to meet at Newcastle on 2 May. There he denounced the British attack in Massachusetts and Dunmore's seizure of the powder, and demanded that the powder be paid for. The captain of the volunteer company then resigned in the orator's favor, and Captain Patrick Henry set out for Williamsburg with a body of armed men.

The next day they reached Doncastle's Ordinary, a tavern a few miles

[48] VG(P), Supplement, 28 April.   [49] Freeman, *Washington*, III, 414.
[50] Madison to Bradford, 9 May, Madison, *Papers*, I, 144–45; Resolutions of Loudon County Committee, 26 May, Force, 4 ser. II, 710–11.
[51] Force, 4 ser. II, 443; VG(DH), 13 May.
[52] To Bradford, 9 May, *Papers*, I, 144–45.

from Williamsburg, where they received word the powder would be paid for. On 4 May Captain Henry signed a receipt for £330 and promised to send the money to the Virginia delegates in Congress to buy powder. He also offered to remove the treasury from Williamsburg, but Robert Carter Nicholas said there was no need.[53] The "thick headed treasurer, who finds it more difficult to extinguish a flame than to kindle it, is in a terrible panic," commented one onlooker.[54]

Patrick Henry returned to Hanover county in triumph and prepared to go to Philadelphia. Back in Williamsburg the governor was in ever-deeper trouble, mostly of his own making. On 29 April the newspaper that printed the first news of the clash in Massachusetts, printed extracts from a letter Dunmore had written to Dartmouth in December. It was a highly unflattering picture of Virginia and Virginians, charging, among other things, that some of the leading men wanted to keep the courts closed to evade paying their debts.[55] Within weeks the letter was being denounced by county committees everywhere.[56] Then on 3 May, when he ordered the money paid for the powder, Dunmore issued a proclamation charging that "disaffected men" wanted to overturn the government.[57] Before dawn the next morning Captain George Montague of the *Fowey* told Thomas Nelson, president of the council, that the governor's palace would be attacked at daybreak. He was sending men to defend the governor, and if they were interfered with, he would shell Yorktown. Before the day was out the York committee met and declared that the captain's threat "has testified a spirit of cruelty unprecedented in the annals of civilized times" and that he "has discovered the most hellish principles that can actuate a human mind." [58] Other county committees soon echoed similar feelings.

Two days later the rattled governor issued a proclamation declaring that "a certain Patrick Henry . . . and a number of deluded followers" had "put themselves in a posture of war" and sent letters "exciting the people to join in these outrageous and rebellious practices, to the great terror of all his Majesty's faithful subjects," and had committed other "acts of violence," including the extortion of £330 for the powder. The people were charged not to aid or abet "the said Patrick Henry" or the country would be involved in the direst calamity.[59]

Virginia county committees started adopting resolutions thanking Henry

[53] VG(DH), 13 May; Wirt, *Henry*, 155–56, 158.
[54] James Parker to Charles Steuart, 6 May, *Magazine of History* (1906), III, 158–59.
[55] VG(DH), 29 April.
[56] For example, Resolutions of Caroline County, 19 May, ibid. 10 June.
[57] Ibid. 6 May.   [58] Ibid. 6 May.   [59] Ibid. 13 May.

and his men before the governor issued his proclamation. Within a few days after Henry's march, Madison reported that it "has gained him great honor in the most spirited parts of the county. . . ." [60] If anything, Dunmore's proclamation increased Henry's popularity and the citizens saw to his safety. When he set out for Philadelphia on 11 May, he was guarded by "respectable young gentlemen" volunteers from Hanover, Caroline, and King William counties who went with him as far as the Potomac River. At Mrs. Hooe's ferry they saluted him with "repeated huzzas" and a guard deposited him safely on the Maryland side, "committing him to the gracious and wise Disposer of all human events, to guide and protect him whilst contending for a restitution of our dearest rights and liberties. . . ." [61]

ॐ

No one in Massachusetts offered a dramatic performance like Patrick Henry's, but a far more dramatic struggle went on there. As a result the four sessions of the two provincial congresses between 7 October 1774 and 15 April 1775 were marked by deadlock after deadlock. The congress could not agree to establish an army until Gage forced the decision at Lexington. Another supremely ironic consequence of the continuing struggle was that Massachusetts, which had started opposition to Britain in 1760, never instructed its delegates in the Second Continental Congress to vote for independence despite their pleas for such orders.

A revolution began in the western counties and was well under way by the time Samuel Adams and his fellow delegates (all easterners) left for Philadelphia on 10 August 1774. For the first time the popular leaders in the east were challenged by men who demanded more violent measures against Britain than many of them were willing to take. Even more startling, the westerners began demanding revolutionary changes in government and started putting them into effect. The easterners were taken aback and began resisting change with all the intensity of a Thomas Hutchinson, and Boston was transformed, almost overnight, from a center of radical action into a citadel of opposition to violence.

Before Samuel Adams left for Philadelphia he told his followers to call a Suffolk county convention, but the Boston committee of correspondence bungled matters so that it was not until 9 September that Suffolk county

[60] To Bradford, 9 May, *Papers*, I, 144–45. For examples of addresses to Henry see Force, 4 ser. II, 529, 539–40.
[61] Force, 4 ser. II, 541n.

adopted the resolves so crucial in the affairs of the Continental Congress.[62]

Worcester county took the lead when on 9 August delegates from twenty towns denied parliamentary authority over America, called a county-wide convention for 30 August, and asked the Boston committee of correspondence to call a meeting of several counties to plan joint action. As a result, delegates from Worcester, Middlesex, Essex, and Suffolk counties met in Boston on 26 August.[63] They voted that the Massachusetts Government Act had rendered all judicial offices "unconstitutional" and that there should be a provincial congress. Meanwhile courts of every kind should be "properly opposed," if any attempt were made to hold them, and the people should begin to practice the "military art." [64] Such advice merely ratified what the westerners had begun doing. Early in August, Governor Gage heard that courts in Berkshire and Hampshire counties would be stopped, and a few days later a mob of 1500, including 300 from Connecticut, prevented the court from sitting at Great Barrington in Berkshire.[65]

The westerners had at last turned on the proud "river gods" who had ruled them for so long. Israel Williams of Hampshire, called "the monarch of the county" as early as 1762, was appointed a "mandamus councilor" under the Massachusetts Government Act. He had not accepted but did not deign to tell the people, and a huge mob in August forced him to declare publicly that he would not take the position. He remained arrogantly intransigent and in February 1775 he and his son were smoked all night in a smokehouse before they would sign a statement condemning the Intolerable Acts.[66]

Colonel John Worthington, who had ruled Springfield with "a rod of iron," was one of the justices of the Hampshire county court, which was surrounded by a great mob at Springfield on 30 August. "All opposition was in vain" and the justices "submitted to our Sovereign Lord the Mob." When Worthington was brought before the people, "the sight of him flashed lightning from their eyes. Their spirits were already raised and the

[62] BCC Minutebook, 776–78; Benjamin Kent to Samuel Adams, 20 Aug., Adams Papers, NYPL.
[63] William Lincoln, ed., *The Journals of Each Provincial Congress of Massachusetts in 1774 and 1775 . . .* [JPCM] (Boston, 1838), 627–31; Thomas Young to Samuel Adams, 19 Aug., Adams Papers, NYPL.
[64] BCC Minutebook, 778–85.
[65] 10 Aug., Albert Matthews, ed., "Documents Relating to the Last Meetings of the Massachusetts Royal Council, 1774–1776," CSMP, XXXII (1933–37), 473; Force, 4 ser. I, 724.
[66] Taylor, *Western Massachusetts*, 64, 66.

sight of this object gave them additional force." The proud Worthington argued, but "the people were not to be dallied with." He signed a statement that he would not serve as a councilor, and with the other justices, that he would accept no office under the Government Act.[67]

The attack on the county courts and the new royal councilors spread throughout the colony. The lives of the councilors were threatened, they were mobbed, and they were shot at. Only twenty-four of thirty-six accepted appointments but several soon resigned or fled to the protection of the British troops in Boston. The attack was so effective that early in September Governor Gage reported that "civil government is near its end, the courts of justice expiring one after another. . . ."[68]

The superior court made an attempt to hold a session in Boston, but the grand and petit jurors refused to take the oath. Finally, after broadsides were posted at the courthouse and about town "threatening certain death" to any lawyers who dared attend, the court adjourned on 3 September. "Thus ended the Superior Court and is the last common day court that will be allowed to sit in this or any other county of the province. . . ."[69]

The disintegration of the old colonial government at every level was accompanied by preparations for war in the backcountry, a movement beginning in Worcester county in July,[70] and all the towns sent delegates to the county convention on 30 August. It voted to prevent the county court from meeting on 6 September and invited all the inhabitants of the county to appear that day. A motion to ask the people to come "properly armed, in order to repel any hostile force," because it was "generally expected" that the governor would send one or more regiments, was withdrawn and a similar one adopted which left out any reference to the governor. Then, with pious resolves about keeping the peace, the convention adjourned to 6 September.[71]

By then many people in Worcester county had made it abundantly clear that they were ready for action. On 26 August 2000 men, many of them in militia companies, came to Worcester and forced Timothy Paine to resign as a royal councilor.[72] And, as we have seen, thousands of armed men from the county had started for Boston on hearing the false rumor that hostilities had begun there.

[67] Joseph Clarke to ————, 30 Sept., and diary of Jonathan Judd, quoted in James R. Trumbull, *History of Northampton* . . . (2 vols., Northampton, 1902), II, 346–47. Contemporary estimates of the size of the mob vary from 1000 to 4000.
[68] To SS, 2 Sept., Gage, *Corres.*, I, 370–71; Taylor, *Western Massachusetts*, 64.
[69] William Tudor to John Adams, 3 Sept., Adams Papers, MHS.
[70] Lincoln, *Worcester*, 96–97.   [71] JPCM, 631–35.
[72] Timothy Paine to Gage, 27 Aug., CSMP, XXXII, 476–78.

On 6 September 6000 men, many in military formation, arrived in Worcester to stop the county court. While waiting for the judges to appear, the convention voted a revolution in the militia system of the county. All militia officers were told to resign their commissions, and the field officers (who held royal commissions) were directed to publish their resignations in the Boston newspapers. The people of the towns were advised to elect their own militia officers, and each town to provide itself with one or more field pieces and ammunition.

Then the great men of the county were subjected to complete humiliation. The justices of the county court and forty-three men who had signed a protest against the "patriotic resolutions" of the Worcester town meeting in June were forced to walk "through the ranges of the body of the people," stopping from time to time to read their recantations.[73]

When the convention met again on 20 September it organized the militia into seven regiments and recommended that the officers in each town enlist one-third of the men between sixteen and sixty to be ready "to act at a minute's warning," and that the towns appoint committees to supply and support the troops "that shall move on any emergency." The officers of "the minute men" were told to meet and elect as many field officers as they thought necessary. The convention concluded by informing Governor Gage that there was no justification for his fortifications in Boston and that he should dismantle them. He had been "greatly misinformed of the character of this People" if he supposed that his acts would lead to submission or to reconciliation.[74]

Six other counties held conventions in late August and during September, and four of them made a gesture toward military defense, but most counties preferred to wait for the meeting of the provincial congress and for the recommendations of the Continental Congress.[75]

Nevertheless, people throughout the colony began arming and drilling.[76] William Tudor informed John Adams in Philadelphia that "the countrymen almost everywhere turn out and exercise three times a week," that 5000 small arms had been sold from Boston within a month, and that fifty cannon, ready for use, were supposed to be in upper Middlesex county.[77] One bystander thought it worth noting that "the parson as well as the squire stands in the ranks with a firelock."[78]

[73] JPCM, 635–39, 635–36n.   [74] Ibid. 640–46.
[75] The resolutions of the conventions may be found in the appendix of JPCM.
[76] To SS, 12 Sept., Gage, *Corres.*, I, 374.
[77] William Tudor to John Adams, 17 Sept., Adams Papers, MHS.
[78] John Andrews to William Barrell, 1 Oct., MHSP, VIII, 372.

The threat of an armed clash mounted after Gage began fortifying Boston Neck early in September, but the threat did not come from Boston. The committee of correspondence and the selectmen protested but did no more, although a committee of mechanics asked the New York mechanics to stop Gage from getting either supplies or workers in their city. Even so, Gage found no difficulty in hiring 200 laborers to construct barracks. Joseph Warren explained that "the employment was profitable to the tradesmen, and drew cash from the king to circulate in this impoverished town. . . ." [79]

People outside Boston saw it differently. "The country people," said Gage, "threaten to attack the troops in Boston, and are very angry at a work throwing up at the entrance of the town. . . ." [80] Their anger mounted when barracks were started and they notified the suppliers of building materials that "they would incur the resentment of the whole country" if they did not stop sending supplies into Boston. The "country people" then told the Bostonians bluntly that if the workmen did not stop building barracks it "would essentially affect the union now subsisting between town and country. . . ." [81]

Shortly before this, when a Worcester delegation proposed the creation of an alarm system, the Boston committee of correspondence had been indifferent, but the threat from the country stirred the committee and the selectmen to action. They voted that if the workmen continued building barracks, "our friends in the neighboring towns and the country in general," who had expressed "uneasiness," might stop contributing to the relief of Boston and deem Bostonians "enemies to the rights and liberties of America. . . ." The "contractors of workmen" were told of the vote but assured that "no offence is taken at what is past." [82]

General Gage protested to the selectmen and swore mighty oaths. They replied that "it was not in their power to influence the country," but so far as they were concerned, they would rather have the troops in barracks than scattered around town. [83] A few days later, in an effort to improve the town's reputation with the country people, the committee of correspondence called an "emergency" meeting of committees from near-by towns. The meeting denounced the governor and the admiral for starving Boston and for "harassing, insulting and vilifying the inhabitants," and then voted

[79] Force, 4 ser. I, 803–4; Warren to Samuel Adams, 29 Sept., Adams Papers, NYPL.
[80] To SS, 12 Sept., Gage, Corres., I, 374.
[81] John Andrews to William Barrell, 25 Sept., MHSP, VIII, 367–68.
[82] 19, 24 Sept., BCC Minutebook, 791, 793–94.
[83] To William Barrell, 25 Sept., MHSP, VIII, 367–68.

to ask the country people to do what they had demanded to begin with—stop sending building materials into Boston![84]

Gage seemed not to mind such rhetoric, for he was reported as saying that he could "do very well with the Boston selectmen, but the damned country committees plague his soul out as they are very obstinate and hard to be satisfied."[85] Gage and the town officials soon worked out plans for handling the soldiers and by mid-November his conduct was said to be "so unexceptionable of late that the most flaming Sons amongst us can't but speak well of him. . . ."[86] He was aided no doubt by the flight of Dr. Thomas Young to Rhode Island in September[87] and the death of William Molineaux in October, of whom John Rowe noted, " 'tis believed he was the first leader of dirty matters."[88]

Nevertheless, the town's leaders were ever more fearful of an outbreak of hostilities before the Continental Congress could agree upon policies. Shortly after Samuel Adams left for Philadelphia, Joseph Warren began sending advice, although he admitted that this was like lecturing on the art of war "to the illustrious general Hannibal." He reported that the mildest measures talked of were non-importation and non-exportation and that "nothing less will prevent bloodshed two months longer."[89] Two weeks later Warren declared "the utmost caution and prudence is necessary to gain the consent of the province to wait a few months longer. . . ."[90] William Tudor, in telling John Adams of the military preparations by the country people, predicted that if Gage committed one hostile act, a "civil war would inevitably be the consequence."[91] Gage realized it too.[92]

Those who wanted to avoid trouble were heartened when Paul Revere got back to Boston on 24 September with the response of the Continental Congress to the Suffolk Resolves: a resolution urging the people to continue their temperate conduct and to wait for the united actions of America to produce a change in British policies.[93] Then four days later trouble threatened again when Gage issued a proclamation dissolving the legislature which he had called to meet at Salem on 5 October.[94] By the time he

---

[84] BCC Minutebook, 795; Force, 4 ser. I, 807–8.
[85] John Andrews to William Barrell, 5 Oct., MHSP, VIII, 373.
[86] John Andrews to William Barrell, 17, 19 Nov., ibid. 385–86.
[87] John Andrews to William Barrell, 13 Sept., ibid. 360.
[88] Rowe, Diary, 286–87.   [89] 15, 21 Aug., Frothingham, Warren, 339–40, 343–44.
[90] 4 Sept., ibid. 357.
[91] William Tudor to John Adams, 17 Sept., Adams Papers, MHS.
[92] To SS, 25 Sept., Gage, Corres., I, 376.
[93] BCC Minutebook, 792. For the action of Congress on the Suffolk Resolves, see Chapter XIX above.
[94] 28 Sept., Force, 4 ser. I, 809–10.

did so it was well known that a provincial congress would meet, and many towns had elected delegates to it as well as to the legislature. Despite this, the day after Gage's dissolution, the Boston committee wrote a letter to Congress ignoring the forthcoming provincial congress and implying that Massachusetts was in a state of total anarchy. The committee said it was feared that the inhabitants of Boston would be "held as hostages for the submission of the country. . . ." If Congress advised them to, they would evacuate the town, but if Congress thought the people could serve the public cause better by staying, they would not shrink from the hardship and danger. Furthermore, the late acts of Parliament had made the administration of justice impossible, the laws had been suspended, and the governor had prevented the meeting of the legislature. "They therefore request the advice of the Congress." [95]

What the Boston leaders really wanted was the help of Congress in resisting mounting pressure from the country people, and they made that perfectly clear in private letters to Samuel Adams. Joseph Warren and Benjamin Church agreed that everything depended on Congress. Warren said if Congress had not cautioned "against any engagement" (in response to the Suffolk Resolves) he feared that "bloodshed would have ensued before this." While Warren was concerned at the time about brawling between the soldiers and the populace of Boston, Church was explicit about the danger from the country: "The country is very uneasy; long they cannot be restrained. They urge us and threaten to compel us to desert the town, they swear the troops shall not continue unmolested." [96]

The Boston committee's letter caused much anguish for most of the members of Congress, who looked upon it as a maneuver to secure approval for an outbreak in Massachusetts. Samuel Adams knew better, but whether he told any of the delegates, or even John Adams, is unknown. Certainly the two Adamses sent back somewhat different reports. Samuel Adams had told Warren earlier that he had been assured privately that if the people of Massachusetts were forced to defend their lives and liberties, the people of the other colonies would support them with every means in their power.[97] But John Adams did not hint at such private assurances. He declared that the delegates in Congress would not agree to military preparations, that they were utterly opposed to hostilities except in case of absolute necessity, and they did not see that necessity.[98] In the end, the dele-

---

[95] JCC, I, 55–56.   [96] 29 Sept., Adams Papers, NYPL.
[97] 25 Sept., Adams, Writings, III, 157–59.
[98] To William Tudor, 7 Oct., LMCC, I, 65.

gates, most of whom did not realize it, gave the Boston leaders the "advice" they wanted when they voted that Boston should not be evacuated and that the people should remain on the defensive.[99]

The further advice to submit to the suspension of justice, when it could not be obtained peaceably and legally under the charter of 1691, went to the heart of a debate which was under way in Massachusetts. By September the western counties were demanding the resumption of the charter of 1629, and while some easterners supported the idea, others opposed it, or suggested that an entirely new constitution be submitted to the king. The issue was clear. To resume the old charter would be to declare independence in fact if not in name. The issue was equally clear to members of Congress. "Resuming the first charter, absolute independency, etc., are ideas which startle people here," said John Adams.[100] The advice to cling to the charter of 1691, which Samuel Adams supported at the moment,[101] was born of fear of what Massachusetts might do, but it served the purposes of those eastern leaders in the colony who opposed western demands for the assumption of the charter of 1629.

The issue of government was before the first provincial congress before the advice from Philadelphia reached Massachusetts. Some eastern towns had followed Boston's lead in telling their delegates to "adhere firmly" to the charter of 1691, and Topsfield had ordered its delegate to secure the recognition of George III "as our rightful sovereign." But western towns like Worcester and Leicester made it perfectly plain that they considered themselves in a state of nature and were ready for a revolution. However, the struggle over government did not become the central issue until after Lexington and Concord. The immediate concern in 1774 was military policy. Boston ignored such matters but the western towns did not. Worcester told its delegate to secure the appointment of a "captain general" over the militia of the province, while Leicester voted that every town should be provided with field pieces and ammunition and that the militia should be properly disciplined "and taught the art of war, with all expedition, as we know not how soon we may be called to action." [102]

The first provincial congress met at Cambridge on 17 October after

---

[99] For the action of Congress see Chapter XIX above.
[100] To Joseph Palmer, 26 Sept., LMCC, I, 48.
[101] To Joseph Warren, [?] Sept., Writings, III, 156–57.
[102] 26 Sept., BTR, XVIII, 191–92; G. F. Dow, ed., Town Records of Topsfield, Massachusetts (2 vols., Topsfield, 1917–20), II, 335–36; F. P. Rice, ed., Worcester Town Records from 1753 to 1783 (Worcester Society of Antiquity Collections, IV, Worcester, 1882), 244; Emory Washburn, Historical Sketches of the Town of Leicester . . . (Boston, 1860), 451–54.

some of the delegates, as legislators, met at Salem where they declared themselves a congress.[103] The intense concern aroused was evident when more than 300 delegates appeared at the congress as contrasted with the 150 who had met in the legislature in May. And the westerners came in unprecedented numbers. Worcester county which had sent twenty men to the legislature sent fifty-six to the congress, and Hampshire which had sent eleven in May sent thirty-nine in October, whereas Suffolk county only doubled its representation from seventeen to thirty-four.[104]

The delegates did little at first for they waited to hear from the Congress in Philadelphia.[105] They appointed a committee on the state of the province which accused the governor of subverting the "constitution," to which he replied that the congress was guilty of subversion. The committee also prepared safe resolutions denouncing royal councilors and East India tea, and drafted others calling for non-consumption and a day of thanksgiving. The only decisive action was a vote requesting tax collectors to stop paying money to the treasurer of the colony, and to pay it to a receiver general elected by the congress.

Paul Revere got back from Philadelphia sometime between 16 and 18 October and the "advice" he brought was welcomed by John Andrews who hoped that it would check the "impetuous zeal" of the congress.[106] What impact it had is unknown, because the congress ordered the galleries cleared during debates and within a few days imposed absolute secrecy. The congress then agreed to a committee on defense consisting of one member from each county, except Suffolk with two, but the members were elected by the county delegations, not by the congress. An apparently intense debate began at once. In the midst of it a special committee was ordered to sit "forthwith" to consider the proper time to buy arms and ammunition. It reported forthwith that *now* was the proper time" and the next day the delegates were informed that the province should buy more than £20,000 worth of field pieces, mortars, bombs, powder, lead, and muskets and no less than 75,000 flints.

The congress then approved the much debated and amended report of

[103] JPCM, 3–48, 4n. The congress met briefly at Concord before adjourning to Cambridge. The only page references to the journals are for sessions as a whole. The journals contain very little evidence concerning the most hotly debated issues.
[104] See Stephen Patterson, A History of Political Parties in Revolutionary Massachusetts, 1770–1780 (Ph.D. Thesis, University of Wisconsin, 1968) for the above analysis. Patterson's work is the best study of the internal politics of Massachusetts during these years.
[105] Elbridge Gerry to Samuel Adams, 15 Oct., Adams Papers, NYPL.
[106] To William Barrell, 19 Oct., MHSP, VIII, 238.

the committee on defense. The key was to be a committee of safety, any five of whose members, provided that not more than one was from Boston, could call out the militia when needed, march them where needed, and provide them with supplies. The congress elected "three members of the town of Boston," then "six gentlemen of the country," and just before adjournment, added two more country members. Five commissaries, none of whom were from Boston, or even from Suffolk county, were chosen to buy military supplies, and eastern Massachusetts was shut out completely in the appointment of three generals. One was from frontier Maine and the other two from Worcester and Hampshire counties.

The journals of the congress do not mention a standing army, but there was gossip about it. Before secrecy was imposed Elbridge Gerry informed Samuel Adams that "standing armies" were not approved by those with whom he had talked, but that "a well regulated militia and under proper command will be closely attended to here." [107] However, a report reached Boston that some delegates had proposed a "standing army" of 15,000 men.[108]

As for the evacuation of Boston, Gage heard that some delegates had proposed to attack the troops in Boston immediately, and that others had proposed to value the estates in the town and then to set the town on fire. Still others proposed to invite the inhabitants to evacuate, "which has been talked of for some time." [109] The congress considered the idea and squelched a report concerning evacuation of Boston, as well as a motion to consider the removal of the Suffolk county records from Boston.

The Bostonians apparently led the opposition and were described as "by far the most moderate men" in the congress. James Lovell declared that "it is become a downright task for the warmest patriots of our town and county to confine the spirit of the other counties. . . ." He was afraid that the provincial congress, "with all their efforts to confine the inland spirits solely to the defensive, will surely fail" if the ministry continued hostile. Nothing but a speedy change of measures in England could "prevent a capital winter stroke. They press us to leave the town in the strongest manner." [110]

A little later Joseph Warren echoed the same feeling when he said that it would require "a very masterly policy to keep the province, for any considerable time longer, in its present state," and he agreed that Boston was

[107] 15 Oct., Adams Papers, NYPL.
[108] John Andrews to William Barrell, MHSP, VIII, 380–81.
[109] To SS, 17 Oct., Gage, Corres., I, 379.
[110] To Josiah Quincy, Jr., 28 Oct., Quincy, Memoir, 186–87.

"by far the most moderate part of the province. . . ." [111] John Andrews probably expressed the sentiments of many when he said he wished the congress had dissolved rather than adjourned on 29 October, for "it was principally composed of spirited, obstinate countrymen who have *very* little patience to boast of." [112]

The behavior of the Bostonians between the sessions did little to allay the suspicions of the country people. Gage did not try to prevent town meetings and he talked with the selectmen and various committees "more freely" about public matters than Hutchinson ever did. Joseph Warren had many meetings and private conversations with Gage and thought well of him, although he remained suspicious. And while the people quarrelled with common soldiers and refused to build barracks, some of them helped refit old houses and stores as winter quarters for the troops. [113]

When the provincial congress reassembled on 23 November the proceedings of the First Continental Congress were laid before it, [114] but Massachusetts, unlike other colonies, did not approve the Association at once. Then on 5 December, the congress adopted "further regulations" which were a thundering vote of no confidence in the integrity of the Massachusetts merchants. The regulations asserted flatly that the foes of America intended to import goods prohibited by the Association with the "assistance of such merchants and traders as . . . shall basely prostitute themselves." Furthermore, since it would be extremely difficult to distinguish between goods brought in before 1 December 1774 and those brought in afterward and "secretly dispersed throughout the colony," the sale of all goods prohibited by the Association should be stopped after 10 October 1775, no matter when imported. The local committees enforcing the Association were directed to take an inventory of all merchants' and traders' goods after 10 October 1775 and order them to stop selling those prohibited. The goods of those who refused to stop sales were to be seized and stored at the owners' risk and their names published so that "they may meet with the merits of enemies to their country."

The charge of cheating by the Boston merchants during non-importation in 1768–70, their refusal to agree to non-importation in May 1774, and Boston's failure to adopt the Solemn League and Covenant, which by December had been adopted by many country towns, especially in the

---

[111] To Josiah Quincy, Jr., 21 Nov., ibid. 206.
[112] To William Barrell, 29 Oct., MHSP, VIII, 380.
[113] Nathaniel Appleton to Josiah Quincy, Jr., 15 Nov., and Joseph Warren to same, 21 Nov., Quincy, *Memoir*, 202–3, 204–9.
[114] The journal for this session is in JPCM, 48–74.

backcountry, and the co-operation between the Boston leaders and General Gage, all lay behind the addition to the Association. James Lovell explained to a friend that he would not be able to understand it, "if you go only upon cool political principles; you must here for the first time admit the motives of anger and resentment, upon the too just evidence of mercantile chicanery in our former non-importation. . . ." He then said that "Boston seems to be put out of the question in most of the proceedings of our provincial congress, and all the seaports seem to have been in the case above mentioned. The country knows what it can do in inland places, and seems determined to let England know that in the present struggle, commerce has lost all the temptations of a bait to catch the American farmer. . . ." [115]

The amendment of the Association was the only success of the more aggressive delegates. The congress refused to consider a report on "assuming civil government." Nor was anything more done about military preparations except the election of two more generals. A special committee, which had been appointed during the first session to prepare a plan for organizing and disciplining the militia, did not report.

Such lack of action apparently did not satisfy the militant spirits. On 10 December the congress suddenly dissolved itself and called for the election of delegates to a new congress. Dissolution was justified because many states had learned from "fatal experience that powers delegated by the people for long periods have been abused"; therefore the people should elect delegates to a new congress. During the first session, a committee had been appointed to bring in a report "relative to the equal representation of the province," perhaps a move to curb the large rural delegations, but no such report was presented. Instead the towns were told to elect "as many members as to them shall seem necessary and expedient," and the only limitation suggested was that delegates be elected by those entitled to vote for representatives in the legislature.

Outsiders explained the dissolution quite differently. Two days later, John Adams, who had been present, wrote to a friend in Philadelphia that he would send a pamphlet so that he could see what the congress had been doing: "that is, you will see in part, not all." He added that he had sometimes wished since his return that the Continental Congress had agreed to the motion made by George Ross and seconded by Joseph Galloway that Massachusetts be left to its own discretion with respect to government, jus-

[115] To Joseph Trumbull, 26 Dec., Joseph Trumbull Papers, Connecticut Historical Society.

tice, and defense. "Our provincial congress had in contemplation some sublime conceptions, which would in that case have been carried rapidly into execution." [116]

Adams was cautious because his letter might miscarry, but another man wrote the same day that the congress had dissolved because a motion to take up arms at once against the king's troops had been opposed by a delegate who insisted that the other colonies would not oppose the British army.[117] Philadelphians heard that it was Samuel Adams who moved to raise 20,000 men to attack the king's soldiers at once, and Thomas Cushing who objected that the other colonies would not approve. Adams then insisted he knew the other colonies would help, whereupon Cushing called him a liar: "that is a lie Mr. Adams, and I know it and you know that I know it." [118] When Adams heard the story he denied that he and Cushing had had a "fracas," but also remarked, somewhat ambiguously, that "any difference between Mr. Cushing and me is of very little consequence to the public cause." [119]

There was no ambiguity about Gage's reports. He did not doubt that the "aim of the hot leaders" was to have a body of troops under their direction. They failed, and then they tried to "usurp the government entirely" as the surest means of getting both money and troops, but they had not been able to "bring the majority into their schemes." At the next congress "the chiefs will probably try to get members more inclined to serve their ends," but "their violence terrified many of their own party" who have helped to preserve the peace.[120]

The second provincial congress met on 1 February 1775, but how many of the 229 men elected actually attended is unknown. The three western counties again showed their concern by electing eighty-two men, whereas the three far more populous eastern counties elected but ninety-eight.[121] There was opposition to the "hot leaders," but they at least forced the congress to face the possibility of creating an army in the future. The congress appointed a committee to prepare rules and regulations for "the constitutional army which may be raised" and authorized the committee of safety to appoint a commissary to take charge of military stores "until the constitutional army shall take the field. . . ."

[116] To [Edward Biddle], 12 Dec., Works, IX, 348–50.
[117] Gentleman in Boston to his friend in New York, 12 Dec., Force, 4 ser. I, 1039.
[118] Stephen Collins to Robert Treat Paine, 14 Jan. 1775, Paine Papers, MHS.
[119] To Stephen Collins, 31 Jan., Writings, III, 173.
[120] To SS, 15 Dec., Gage, Corres., I, 387–88.
[121] The names of the men elected are in JPCM, 77–83. Pages 83–109 contain the journals for the 1–16 February session.

The congress, complained James Warren, did very little. It appeared to him to be "dwindling into a school for debate and criticism rather than . . . a great assembly to resolve and act." [122] The reason, said General Gage, was that many of the delegates "were purposely sent by their towns to oppose the violent party." [123] An anonymous letter from Boston declared the "principal object" of the session had been to "cajole the men of property," but that no impression could be made upon them for the "monied men are convinced that acts of rebellion will be punished with confiscation of their estates. . . ." The "republican leaders" would try again in the next session to raise money to put an army in the field, but he was hopeful, for "their dupes drop from them very fast, and it's expected the few demagogues will be soon left alone." [124]

He would not have been so optimistic if he had known of the actions of the committee of safety and the committee of supplies which had been meeting jointly since November. The congress made a tentative gesture toward the creation of an army, but there was nothing tentative about a vote of the two committees a few days after the congress adjourned. Nor is there any evidence that the three Boston members of the committee of safety—John Hancock, Dr. Joseph Warren, and Dr. Benjamin Church —dragged their heels. On 21 February the committees voted to buy enough military supplies to put an army of 15,000 men in the field, and the two doctors were told to prepare a list of the materials needed "in the way of their profession, for the above army to take the field." The next day the committees agreed that if Gage received more reinforcements, the congress should meet at once, and although congress had not delegated the authority to the committees, they drafted a letter to be sent to the delegates. The following day the committees decided to prepare a letter ordering the commanders of militia and minutemen companies to assemble one-fourth of their men. In meetings thereafter the committees continued to order supplies, organized artillery companies, established military depots, and moved stores from place to place. [125]

There were men who feared that the committee of safety might start a war. One of them was Joseph Hawley of Northampton, the only "river god" who had worked with the popular leaders ever since the Stamp Act

[122] To John Adams, 20 Feb., *Warren-Adams Letters* (2 vols., MHSC, LXXII(1917), LXXIII(1925)), I, 41.
[123] To SS, 17 Feb., Gage, *Corres.*, I, 392.
[124] To Gentleman of New York, 19 Feb., Force, 4 ser. I, 1248.
[125] The journals of the two committees from 2 Nov. 1774 through 18 April 1775 are in JPCM, 505–18.

crisis. As soon as he returned home he wrote Thomas Cushing that the time had come to drop "chimerical plans" and be practical. He was afraid that if the committee of safety called out the militia, the soldiers would fight and not stop to consider if it was the right time to fight. Hawley had no faith whatever in the resolution of the First Continental Congress declaring "all America ought to support" Massachusetts if Britain used force. This was not a guarantee of support and the members of Congress were not authorized to give one. It would be only a little "short of madness and infatuation" to begin hostilities before there was an explicit guarantee of help. If the committee of safety started a fight, the other colonies might well say "that we have unnecessarily and madly plunged into war, and therefore, must get out of the scrape as we can. . . ." Hawley begged Cushing to prevent the committee of safety from ordering out the militia "until we have the express categorical decision of the continent, that the time is absolutely come that hostilities ought to begin, and that they will support us in continuing them." [126]

Thomas Cushing was increasingly opposed to a break with Britain despite his long association—or perhaps because of it—with the popular leaders. He agreed completely that the committee of safety had too much power and hostilities should be avoided until the other colonies made an "express categoric decision" that the time had come to fight, and that they would support Massachusetts.[127]

When the congress reassembled on 22 March, there was the usual gossip about what it might do but General Gage no longer had to depend upon gossip: he had a spy in the midst of the congress, a man uniquely qualified. He was one of the inner core of Boston's popular leaders, a member of the Boston committee of correspondence, of the committee of safety, and of the congress. The man was Dr. Benjamin Church.[128]

The congress prepared the usual address to the people urging them not to relax, and the usual denunciation of the mandamus councilors who had not resigned. Unusual was a grant of money to buy a blanket and a yard of ribbon for each of the Indians at Stockbridge who had enlisted as "minute men."

The creation of a provincial army was the overriding issue. The committee appointed on 10 February to prepare rules for "the constitutional army which may be raised" presented its report on 27 March. Meanwhile, there

[126] 22 Feb., ibid. 748–51.   [127] 27 Feb., Hawley Papers, NYPL.
[128] Allen French, *General Gage's Informers* (Ann Arbor, 1932), *passim*. It is possible that Gage had more than one spy. The journals for the session, 22 March–15 April, are in JPCM, 109–47.

were "grand debates" as to what movements by British troops would justify calling out the militia.[129] General Gage had marched troops out of Boston from time to time and on the morning of 30 March they marched out again. There was an immediate alarm for fear that they might be going to Concord, and armed men in great numbers got ready to oppose them. But they only marched a few miles, "manfully laid siege to a certain swamp," and then marched back again.[130] If they had gone eight or ten miles and tried to destroy any magazine or abuse the people, "not a man of them would have returned to Boston." [131] Before the day was over, the alarmed congress, to prevent "any unnecessary effusion of blood," voted that the militia should not be mustered unless the troops marched out with baggage and artillery.[132] Immediately thereafter an attempt was made to adjourn without doing anything further, but the attempt failed. Two days later a majority made it clear that it still clung to the shreds of the old government. The congress voted that if Gage issued writs for an election as required by the charter, the towns should elect representatives. However, if he did not, they should elect delegates to a third congress to meet the last Wednesday in May.

Then another attempt was made to adjourn on 1 April. The delegates were about equally divided, but the argument finally prevailed that they should wait over the weekend in case news arrived from England.[133] And news did arrive on Sunday night. The next day the *Boston Gazette* published an account of proceedings in Parliament from a London paper of 11 February. Lord North had proposed a bill blocking New England's access to the Newfoundland fisheries and confining its trade to Britain, Ireland, and the British West Indies. Four regiments were to be sent from Ireland, and Parliament had adopted an address to the king declaring Massachusetts in a state of rebellion, urging him to uphold the power of "the supreme legislature," and pledging support for any measures he might take. For what little comfort it offered, the *Gazette* also published an eloquent speech by John Wilkes, now Lord Mayor of London and again a member of Parliament. He had defended Americans and declared that they would fight and declare their independence.[134]

Bostonians were shocked by the news. "The women are terrified by the

---

[129] Spy to Gage, 30 March, 3 April, French, *Informers*, 16–17.
[130] "Fidelis" [Samuel Swift] to John Adams, 31 March, Adams Papers, MHS; extract from letter from Boston to Gentleman in Philadelphia, 1 April, Force, 4 ser. II, 253.
[131] Joseph Warren to Arthur Lee, 3 April, Force, 4 ser. II, 256.
[132] Idem.; Spy to Gage, 3 April, French, *Informers*, 17–18.
[133] James Warren to Mercy Warren, 6 April, *Warren-Adams Letters*, I, 44.
[134] BG, 3 April.

fear of blood and carnage," reported William Tudor. As for the merchants, they were alarmed at the threat to their trade. "What cowards does interest make men! Thank God our salvation is not dependent on the virtue of merchants, if it was our perdition would be unavoidable." [135] As for the members of the congress, they were in "great consternation" and sent expresses to recall absentees, for attendance had been dwindling fast. On 30 March, 168 had been present, but by 8 April only 103 attended.[136]

There was one positive result of the news: the congress was forced to take a step toward the creation of an army. On 5 April the delegates adopted fifty-three rules and regulations "for the army that may be raised." But the next day the congress told Boston and eleven other towns they should continue to act on the defensive and advised them against any measures "that our enemies might plausibly interpret as a commencement of hostilities. . . ." Nor would the congress advise the evacuation of Boston; it only recommended that if poor people wanted to leave the town, help should be given them and employment ought to be found for them.

But the pressure for the creation of an army continued. Gage's spy summed it up neatly when he reported: "the people without doors are clamorous for an immediate commencement of hostilities but the moderate-thinking people within wish to ward off that period till hostilities shall commence on the part of government which would prevent their being censured for their rashness by the other colonies and that made a pretence for deserting them." And there were other motives. Delegates from the seaport towns were afraid their towns would be burned if hostilities began. On the other side "several members" were "positively required by their constituents to urge the immediate raising of an army. . . ."

The opponents of an army argued that Massachusetts could not act alone but must have the help of the other New England colonies. On 7 April Stephen Hopkins and Darius Sessions from Rhode Island and John Sullivan and John Langdon from New Hampshire met with the congress and agreed it "would be imprudent to enter into any decisive measure without the concurrence of the other New England colonies. . . ." [137] The next day the congress, by a vote of 96 of the 103 members present, resolved "it is necessary for this colony to make preparations for their security and defence, by raising and establishing an army," and to send dele-

[135] To John Adams, 4 April, Adams Papers, MHS.
[136] Spy to Gage, 11 April, French, *Informers*, 21–22. The number present on 30 March is given in Spy to Gage, 3 April, ibid. 18. JPCM, 135, gives the only recorded vote in the journals since the first congress.
[137] Spy to Gage, 9 April, French, *Informers*, 19–21.

gates to the other New England colonies to ask for their co-operation.

But that was as far as the majority would go. The congress did ask for a report on the number of men necessary "for the army proposed to be raised," but after a long debate it refused to consider exercising the minute men in battalions and paying them from the public treasury. It did authorize the committee of safety to form six companies of artillery to be in readiness "when an army shall be raised," but refused to consider the appointment of officers, although it did vote that the committee of safety should discover who would be willing to serve as officers "when an army shall be raised. . . ." "There was great division among the members of the congress," reported Gage's spy, "and great irresolution shown in the course of their debates this week." [138]

The day after Gage received this information, the congress adjourned until 10 May. Earlier the spy had reported that some members of congress wanted a recess to consult their constituents and he told Gage a recess could be easily brought about if Gage wanted it. He suggested that it would prevent the congress from taking "hasty steps" before Gage received his dispatches, and that "a sudden blow struck now or immediately on the arrival of the reinforcements from England, should they come within a fortnight, would overset all their plans." [139] As it turned out, the recess was obtained only with difficulty from the "apparent hazard" of leaving the colony without a council, but adjournment was finally agreed to because of the "impossibility of influencing the delegates to consent to an army taking the field" without the concurrence of the other New England colonies and "incontestable proof" of their support by supplying their quotas.[140]

Thus four days before Lexington and Concord, Massachusetts was left without any governing body except the committee of safety. The majority of the congress and General Gage agreed on one thing: neither wanted to start hostilities. Gage believed that British authority could not be re-established except by military force, but he had no intention of taking responsibility for starting what he knew would be a bitter war. Officials in London would have to send him orders before he would act. He got an official copy of such orders the day after the provincial congress adjourned. Three days later came the march to Lexington and Concord, and the country people of Massachusetts, who, unlike the quarrelling politicians, wanted to start a fight, showed that they could fight on 19 April 1775.

[138] Spy to Gage, 15 April, ibid. 23–24.   [139] Spy to Gage, 11 April, ibid. 22.
[140] Spy to Gage, 18 April, ibid. 27.

XXII

The Beginnings of a Civil War

The fighting between British soldiers and American farmers in April 1775 was looked upon by many men in both Britain and America as the beginning of a civil war. The ministers who proposed and the majorities of Parliament which adopted the measures concerning America during the winter of 1774–75 asserted that there was no middle ground between the absolute submission of America to Parliament and American independence. The opposition leaders in Britain argued that a middle ground between those extremes could be and should be found. They insisted that the measures adopted would lead to a civil war which might become a war for American independence. Such men had no power and the only satisfaction they derived was the bitter one of having their predictions proved right in little more than a year.

The ministers and the majority of Parliament ignored the arguments of the opposition. They ignored the fact, or refused to believe it if they knew it, that there were many influential leaders in America who, like the opposition leaders in England, believed that there was a middle ground and that it could be found. Those American leaders did not want independence and they opposed it with all their strength. At the same time they resolutely refused to yield to the demand for the absolute subjection of America to the will of Parliament. After the 19th of April 1775 they were convinced that Americans would have to oppose the force of the British army with the force of an American army; but they argued, and they were utterly sincere, that they were doing what Englishmen had done in the past: fighting to defend the rights of Englishmen. They hoped to the very end that the war would remain a civil war, and that reconciliation with the mother country could be achieved. There were some Americans who wanted independence after 19 April 1775, if not before, but they did not say so openly.

The *Newport Mercury* on 24 April 1775, in its report of the clash at Lexington and Concord, summed up what was probably the feeling of most American leaders when it said that the measures of the ministry and the readiness of a standing army to execute them "has commenced the *American Civil War* which shall hereafter fill an important page in history."

ह∾

Many months elapsed between the development of serious American resistance to the Intolerable Acts and the adoption of the measures in Britain that led to the outbreak of a civil war in Massachusetts. When Lord Dartmouth, secretary of state for America, sent the Massachusetts Government, the Administration of Justice, and the Quartering acts to Governor Gage early in June 1774, he assumed that trouble would soon be at an end. He expected the laws to "give vigor and activity to civil authority" and Gage to restore order by "a wise and discreet" use of the new power given him. Dartmouth was "willing to suppose that the people will quietly submit to the correction their ill conduct has brought upon them" and that the other colonies would not help. He predicted that "false hopes" might keep up "the spirit of the mob" for a while but that distress would soon bring the people to their senses. Late in August, Dartmouth told Gage that his conduct had given great satisfaction to the king and that he was entitled to the "highest encomiums" for the way he had withstood "the intemperate heat and prejudice" of some of the leading men of New England.[1] This was the last praise Gage ever received from his superiors.

English leaders remained unaware of the utter failure of the laws punishing Massachusetts as they turned their attention to a parliamentry election. Under the septennial act an election was not required until 1775, but the king suddenly dissolved Parliament at the end of September, perhaps because of America, and certainly to catch the opposition off guard. Most candidates and voters were unconcerned with either national or colonial issues although a few of the followers of John Wilkes proposed repeal of the Intolerable Acts as a part of their reform program. By mid-

[1] 3 June, 3, 23 Aug., Gage, *Corres.*, II, 163–67, 170–72.

November, Lord North reported to the king that the ministry had a comfortable majority in the new Parliament.[2]

By that time, however, the ministry was receiving anything but comfortable news from America. It got the first of many rude shocks just as the elections began. On 1 October, Governor Gage's letters of late August and early September reached London. They told of the "popular rage" that had swept over Massachusetts, Connecticut, and Rhode Island, the closing of the courts, the threat of the backcountry counties to attack his troops, and the assaults on the new royal councilors who had resigned or fled to Boston. In short, the Massachusetts Government Act was a total failure within a month of its receipt in the colony on 6 August.

Gage was blunt. The time for conciliation, moderation, and reasoning was over, and "nothing can be done but by forcible means." His analysis was sound. The people were *numerous, worked up to a fury, and not a Boston rabble but the freeholders and farmers of the country.*" Gage argued that he did not have enough troops to act decisively and that "a check anywhere would be fatal, and the first stroke will decide a great deal."[3]

The letters created a flurry of activity in London. The king suggested that two regiments be sent from Ireland, but Dartmouth insisted that it was too late in the year. The ministry did agree to send three guardships and ten companies of marines to Admiral Samuel Graves, who had taken command of the British navy at Boston in April and had been asking for reinforcements ever since. Reports that Americans were buying military stores in England and on the Continent led to an order in council prohibiting the shipment of military supplies from Britain without a license from the Privy Council. Naval vessels were sent to prevent the shipment of arms and ammunition to America from Dutch and other North Sea ports.[4]

After these measures had been taken, Dartmouth finally informed Gage that "the state of the kingdom" would not permit sending troops from England, and that while there were two regiments in Ireland, they could not be sent because of questions of policy and the lateness of the year. Dartmouth suggested that Gage might disarm the people of Massachusetts, Connecticut, and Rhode Island; he was sure there were "many friends to the constitution" whom Gage should encourage.[5]

---

[2] Donoughue, *British Politics*, chapter VIII.
[3] 27, 29, 31 Aug., 2 Sept., Gage, *Corres.*, I, 365–72. Italics mine.
[4] Donoughue, *British Politics*, 201–8.   [5] 17 Oct., Gage, *Corres.*, II, 173–75.

Meanwhile, the ministry was getting reports about and from the Congress in Philadelphia. On 28 October a ship brought the news of the adoption of the Suffolk Resolves on 18 September. Thomas Hutchinson described the vote as "more alarming than anything which has yet been done," and when he called on Dartmouth and John Pownall, he found that both men were "thunderstruck" by the news.[6] Ten days later word arrived of the vote of 22 September asking merchants to stop ordering goods from Britain until Congress decided upon a policy. Despite such news, Lord North told Hutchinson that no particular measures would be decided upon until "further was known of what was doing in Philadelphia."

The ministry had a reason for waiting, for it was receiving reports from a member of Congress. John Pownall told Hutchinson that "there was a private correspondence, and every step had been communicated." Later, William Lee informed his brother in Virginia that "Jay, one of the delegates from New York to the last Congress has by letter betrayed its secrets to administration here." This could not be proved, he said, because the letters could not be got at, but "the ministers have asserted it. . . ." Whoever the man was, the stories Pownall told Hutchinson of the disputes in the Congress indicate that the ministry was indeed receiving reports of its secret proceedings.[7]

While waiting to learn of the final outcome of the Congress, the ministry received more alarming news than ever from Gage. He told Dartmouth that if certain persons had been seized, as had been suggested, hostilities would have begun. He described how "the whole country was in arms" when the rumor spread that Boston had been shelled. The only way the coercive acts could be enforced was to conquer the New England colonies. The "disease" of rebellion might have been confined to Boston some time ago, "but now it's so universal there is no knowing where to apply a remedy."

Gage was far more specific in a letter to the secretary at war. The question, he said, is not "whether you shall quell disturbances in Boston, but whether those provinces shall be conquered. . . ." Tactlessly, he pointed out that people in England had been wrong in thinking that the punitive laws would concern only Massachusetts. The Massachusetts people had "contrived to get the rest of their brethren in every province to be as

---

[6] 28 Oct., 1 Nov., *Diary*, I, 272–74; JCC, I, 39.
[7] 10, 12, 19 Nov., *Diary*, I, 291–93, 296–97; William Lee to [F. L. Lee], 25 Feb. 1775, Arthur Lee Papers, HUL.

violent in their defense as themselves," and the country all the way to New York was "armed, training, and providing military stores." [8] Gage made one concrete proposal which he sent to Thomas Hutchinson: suspend the coercive acts and allow the colonies to send delegates to England. In the meantime Britain should prepare for the worst by hiring some Hessian and Hanoverian troops.

George III, at least, had made up his mind. In September he had declared that "the die is now cast, the colonies must either submit or triumph. . . ." Now he told Lord North that Gage's proposal for suspending the coercive acts was "most absurd." In fact he was glad that the "line of conduct seems now chalked out"; since New England was in "a state of rebellion, blows must decide whether they are to be subject to this country or independent. . . ." [9] The next day North, his spine stiffened for the moment by the king, "expressed himself in higher terms than ever" to Thomas Hutchinson. Massachusetts was in actual rebellion and must be subdued. Acts of Parliament could not be suspended and must be enforced.[10]

But North and the ministers preferred to retain their illusions rather than face the realities presented in the remarkably accurate reports from Gage. He must be wrong, or if not wrong, he must be responsible for permitting the conditions he described to develop. One official declared that Gage was "too far gone to be recovered" and should be replaced at once.[11] Others argued that a major general or two should be sent to help him. The king considered possibilities, remarking that "it is not a desirable commission." [12]

Then, as so many times in the past, the cabinet asked the solicitor and attorneys general if certain actions in Massachusetts were treasonable. The actions questioned were those of the mob at Worcester on 26 August that forced Timothy Paine to resign as councilor. This time the law officers agreed that the evidence was adequate. They reported that "J. Bigelow" and others were guilty of "levying war against His Majesty," and asked for instructions in drawing up a proclamation of rebellion.[13] The day the law officers replied, the proceedings of the First Continental Congress reached London. Lord Dartmouth told Thomas Hutchinson that every-

[8] To Dartmouth, 12, 25 Sept., and to Barrington, 25 Sept., Gage, Corres., I, 373–77; II, 654–55.
[9] To Lord North, 11 Sept., 18 Nov., Geo. III, Corres., III, 130–31, 153–54.
[10] 19 Nov., Diary, I, 296–97.   [11] Donoughue, British Politics, 212.
[12] To North, 18 Nov., Geo. III, Corres., III, 153.
[13] Donoughue, British Politics, 212–14. For Paine's resignation see Chapter XXI above.

one who had signed the Association was guilty of treason,[14] but he and the other ministers took no action. They decided to wait for further information from General Gage, and Dartmouth began indirect negotiations with Benjamin Franklin, which dragged on for weeks, in a futile attempt to find common grounds for reconciliation. Dartmouth also supported suggestions that commissioners be sent to America, but George III responded that he did not think much of commissioners. He did not want to drive the colonies "to despair but to submission," and commissioners would not make the colonies any more reasonable.[15]

Then on 18 December the ministers received further information from Gage. It was not information they wanted or liked, or perhaps even believed. Gage was blunter than ever: "if you would get the better of America in all your disputes, you must conquer her," and to do that "you should have an army near twenty thousand strong" composed of regulars, such irregulars as German huntsmen and Canadians, three or four regiments of light horse, and "good and sufficient field artillery." [16]

The immediate response, as before, was one of outrage. Gage's conduct, said one official, "seems devoid both of sense and spirit." [17] Lord North demanded that Gage be replaced, and in the meantime a major general be sent to help him. George III agreed that it would be "proper" to send a major general but he made the sensible suggestion that a "general plan" for America was necessary, that the ministry should stop acting "by detail" and should have "the whole digested before any step is taken." [18] The ministers who had been responding emotionally to news from America and acting "by detail" had no general plan nor could they form one, for they were taking off for the Christmas holidays as were the members of the new Parliament which had been in session since 29 November.

The ministry had not given Parliament any official information about America despite demands from some of its members. The king's speech told Parliament that "a most daring spirit of resistance and disobedience to the law" still prevailed in Massachusetts. The two houses replied that they abhorred and lamented the behavior of Massachusetts, applauded the

---

[14] 13, 14 Dec., *Diary*, I, 324.

[15] North to king, [?] Dec., and king to North, 15 Dec., Geo. III, *Corres.*, III, 158, 156; Donoughue, *British Politics*, 212–13. Franklin's account of the negotiations, written during his return voyage to America, is in a letter to his son, Sir William Franklin, 22 March, *Writings*(S), VI, 319–99.

[16] To Barrington, 3 Oct., Gage, *Corres.*, II, 656.

[17] Donoughue, *British Politics*, 217.

[18] North to king, 17 Dec., and king to North, 18 Dec., Geo. III, *Corres.*, III, 157; Donoughue, *British Politics*, 217.

king's activities in enforcing the laws, and promised their support for all
measures designed to maintain the dignity of the Crown and the supremacy of Parliament over the colonies. An attempt to amend the reply of the
House of Commons to call for caution and delicacy in dealing with the
American problem, and asking that no action be taken until full information was available, was roundly defeated, 264–73.[19]

By the time Parliament reassembled on 19 January 1775, the ministry
had at last worked out a "general plan." On 2 January more letters arrived
from Gage. They were more specific and even less satisfying. He told Dartmouth that he had 3000 men available, but that if it came to open war,
he should have 20,000 men to begin with. As usual his letters to Barrington
were more forceful. "If you think ten thousand men sufficient, send twenty;
if one million is thought enough, give two; you will save both blood and
treasure in the end. A large force will terrify, and engage many to join you,
a middling one will encourage resistance and gain no friends." [20] Gage was
right as usual, but the cabinet decided to send him only two regiments of
infantry, one of light cavalry, and 600 more marines.[21] The ministers then
turned to their favorite solution for the American problem: the replace-
ment of Gage with another general.

The man to send was Sir Jeffrey Amherst and George III conducted
the negotiations himself. He told Dartmouth that both the troops in America and the generals in Britain believed that if matters became more serious, a general with more "activity and decision" would be needed. However, the king thought well of Gage. He wanted "the affair treated with
all imaginable tenderness" and Gage permitted to keep his pay as commander in chief. The reason to be given for sending Amherst was that,
since all the ports of America were to be shut, the commander in chief
should be free to move from colony to colony, whereas Gage, as governor,
could not leave Massachusetts "where he conducts himself so well."

No one had bothered to consult Amherst, who had left America in 1764
and surrendered his lucrative governorship of Virginia rather than go back
to a land he detested. George III soon reported that "my negotiation
proved fruitless" and that he was "much hurt" at not succeeding. Amherst
insisted that "nothing but retreat would bring him to go again to America." We must do the next best thing, said the king: "leave the command
to Gage, [and] send the best generals that can be thought of to his assis-

[19] HCJ, XXXV, 8–9; PH, XVIII, 33–47.
[20] Gage to Dartmouth, 17, 30 Oct.; to Barrington, 2 Nov., Gage, Corres., I, 378–83;
II, 658–59.
[21] Donoughue, British Politics, 220–21.

tance. . . ." [22] Three days later major generals John Burgoyne, Henry Clinton, and William Howe were picked to go to America. Burgoyne called them a "triumvirate of reputation," but a London wit was closer to the mark concerning the future of the disastrous trio, as they departed in the *Cerberus,* when he wrote:

> Behold the *Cerberus* the Atlantic plough.
> Her precious cargo, Burgoyne, Clinton, Howe.
> Bow, wow, wow! [23]

Aside from sending reinforcements to America, the "general plan" consisted of an agreement to ask Parliament for a law confining the trade of the colonies to Britain, Ireland, and the West Indies, and stopping the New England colonies from fishing on the Newfoundland Banks. The cabinet agreed also to what came to be known as the "Olive Branch" resolution after Lord North proposed it on 20 February. The cabinet rejected a renewed plea from Dartmouth that commissioners be sent to America.[24]

When Parliament reassembled on 19 January, Lord North laid papers concerning America before the House of Commons. Among them were the petition to the king and other papers of the First Continental Congress. These had been sent to the colonial agents: Benjamin Franklin, agent for Massachusetts, New Jersey, and Pennsylvania; Arthur Lee and William Bollan for Massachusetts; Paul Wentworth for New Hampshire; Thomas Life for Connecticut; Edmund Burke for New York; and Charles Garth for South Carolina. The papers arrived shortly before Christmas, but Burke, Wentworth, and Life refused to have anything to do with them on the feeble grounds that their constituents had not instructed them and Garth was out of town. Franklin, Lee, and Bollan then took the papers to Dartmouth, who sent the petition to the king on to George III. Dartmouth reported that the king had received it "very graciously," but it contained matters of such importance that he would lay it before Parliament.[25]

But the petition to the king "came down among a great heap" of papers from America, "the last in the list, and was laid upon the table with them, undistinguished by any particular recommendation of it to the notice of either house. . . ." [26] When Edmund Burke asked if all the pa-

---

[22] King to Dartmouth, 28, 31 Jan., Historical Manuscripts Commission, *Thirteenth Report,* IV (London, 1902), 501.
[23] Quoted, Willard M. Wallace, *Appeal to Arms* (New York, 1951), 32.
[24] Donoughue, *British Politics,* 219–24.
[25] Franklin to Charles Thomson, 5 Feb., *Writings*(S), VI, 303–7.   [26] Idem.

pers from America had been laid before the house, Lord North confessed candidly that he had not read them.[27]

It soon became clear that the ministry intended to ride roughshod over all opposition. When Franklin, Arthur Lee, and William Bollan petitioned to be heard before the House of Commons in support of the petition to the king, their request was rejected, 218–68.[28] The petitions of London and Bristol merchants were given similar treatment. The Londoners outlined the complexities of colonial trade as they had at the time of the Stamp Act and asked that the whole question of commercial policy be reconsidered. The merchant petitions were not referred to the committee of the whole on American papers but to a different committee, which Edmund Burke called the "committee of oblivion." Three days later the Londoners petitioned again. They declared that the original connection between Britain and the colonies "was, and ought to be, of a commercial kind" and that the laws Americans complained of were inseparably connected with commerce. Therefore, their petition should be considered by the committee on American papers. Their request was denied, 250–89.[29] In the weeks that followed petitions came in from all over England demanding reconciliation with America on economic grounds.

The ministry's solid majority was not concerned with economic pleas but with punishing Americans and asserting the supremacy of Parliament. One member "spoke of the relation of parent and child that subsisted between the countries; he supposed ingratitude in the child and wished for its chastisement." Another "entertained no doubt that some resolutions for preserving the supremacy would answer every end of the merchants' petitions and restore trade." A third declared that American trade could not exist without a vigorous assertion of the supremacy of Parliament and the sovereignty of Britain, and "the merchants should forego their own interests for the sake of those permanent advantages which they would undoubtedly reap when the Americans were subdued, if, peradventure, a subduction, obtained by force, should be found expedient." [30]

Opposition speakers such as Edmund Burke and Charles James Fox were eloquent, and perceptive in predicting the future, but they spent almost as much effort in personal attacks on Lord North. He had been the target of Edmund Burke's wit from the day he took office. As early as the spring of 1770 an American newspaper reprinted an item from a London paper which said:

[27] PH, XVIII, 148.　　[28] HCJ, XXXV, 81.　　[29] Ibid., 70–71, 80.
[30] PH, XVIII, 186–87.

Lord North declared last week, that "All he had came unasked, quite freely and spontaneously to him," on which Mr. Edmund Burke compared him to an oyster which lay still, gaping for the tide, ready to receive it whether it came from the east, west, north, or south, and taking it in, however muddy, foul and dirty.[31]

By 1774 the attacks on North had become more vicious. Charles James Fox charged that North "had no system or plan of conduct, no knowledge of business," that he had brought the country to the brink of civil war, and that the present disputes with America were the result of his negligence and incapacity. "It was true, he said, the noble lord had often confessed his incapacity, and from a consciousness of it, pretended a willingness to resign; but the event had proved that whatever his consciousness might have been, his love of the emoluments of office had completely conquered it." [32]

The opposition groups simply could not muster the votes to match their skill at vituperation. They pled the cause of America eloquently and praised what the Americans had done. William Pitt, Earl of Chatham, told Arthur Lee that "the whole of your countrymen's conduct has manifested such wisdom, moderation, and manliness of character, as would have done honor to Greece and Rome in their best days." [33] Other opponents of the ministry's policies echoed his sentiments but they continued to distrust one another and made almost no effort to unite on policies. Chatham kept secret from all but one or two men his intention to move in the House of Lords on 20 January that the British troops be removed from Boston. He was supported by Shelburne, Rockingham, and a few others, but the prevailing opinion was that of Earl Gower, who declared that he was "well informed that the language now held by the Americans was the language of the rabble and a few factious leaders. . . ." Chatham's motion was defeated, 68–18.[34]

Ten days later, after hearing that "the doom against America is to be pronounced from the treasury bench, perhaps in a few hours," Chatham declared that no time was to be lost in "preventing a civil war, before it is inevitably fixed." [35] On 1 February he presented a provisional bill for settling the disputes with America. Chatham was as insistent as any member of the ministry that the Americans must recognize the supremacy of

31 PJ, 26 April 1770.   32 PH, XVIII, 191–93.
33 Arthur Lee to Richard Henry Lee, 22 Dec., R. H. Lee, *Memoir of the Life of Richard Henry Lee* . . . (2 vols., Philadelphia, 1825), I, 135–36; Chatham to Stephen Sayre, 22 Dec., Pitt, *Corres.*, IV, 368.
34 PH, XVIII, 149–68.   35 To Earl Stanhope, 31 Jan., Pitt, *Corres.*, IV, 388–91.

Parliament. However, he proposed the renunciation of military force, and a declaration that no taxes could be levied in America except by the consent of the colonial legislatures. The Second Continental Congress would be recognized as a lawful body and would be required to consider the grant of a perpetual revenue to the Crown and to assign quotas to each colony. The Intolerable Acts, the Quebec Act, and various other acts complained of by Americans would be suspended, and then repealed as soon as the colonies acknowledged the supreme authority of Parliament.[36]

Chatham told the House of Lords that the bill consisted of "crude materials" and he pled for the avoidance of prejudice, spleen, and blind predilection in discussing it. The plea was in vain. The bill, said Benjamin Franklin, was "treated with as much contempt as they could have shown to a ballad offered by a drunken porter." [37] Lord Dartmouth was willing to consider the bill, but his colleague in the ministry, Lord Sandwich, immediately moved to reject it. The Americans, he said, were not debating "about words but realities." Other lords denounced Chatham and virtually accused him of sanctioning the "traitorous" proceedings of the Congress.

When it came to invective, the onetime Great Commoner could take care of himself. He was neither surprised nor astonished, he said, that men who hated liberty opposed his bill, and that those who had no virtue would try to prosecute those who did. He could demonstrate that "the whole of your political conduct has been one continued series of weakness, temerity, despotism, ignorance, futility, negligence, blundering, and the most notorious servility, incapacity, and corruption." He told his opponents that they did have one merit: strict attention to their own interests. You would ruin, he told them, any plan of conciliation and oppose any measure "which must annihilate your power, deprive you of your emoluments, and at once reduce you to that state of insignificance for which God and Nature designed you." His bill was rejected, 61–32.[38]

The "doom against America" that Chatham feared was "pronounced" by Lord North. The ministry had won resounding victories in refusing to assign the merchants' and manufacturers' petitions to the committee of the whole on American papers, in refusing to consider the proceedings of the First Continental Congress, and in rejecting Chatham's proposals in the House of Lords. On 2 February Lord North declared that some of the colonies were in a state of rebellion, and that the supremacy of Parliament must be maintained. He said more military forces would be sent to Amer-

---

[36] PH, XVIII, 198–203.   [37] To Charles Thomson, 5 Feb., Writings(S), VI, 306.
[38] PH, XVIII, 198–215, for the bill and the debates.

ica and that the trade and fisheries of New England should be restrained. The issue "was simply whether we should abandon this claim, and at once give up every advantage arising both from the sovereignty and the commerce, or to ensure both? Or whether we should resort to the measures indispensably necessary on such an occasion?" He therefore proposed an address to the king asserting that "a rebellion at this time actually exists" within Massachusetts, and requesting the king to take the most effectual measures to enforce the authority of the supreme legislature.

An opposition speaker replied at once that "the Americans are not in rebellion" and that the tales of "riot, disorder, tumult, and sedition which the noble Lord has faithfully recounted from the newspapers, arises not from disobedience, treason, or rebellion, but is created by the conduct of those who are anxious to establish despotism; and whose views are manifestly directed to reduce America to the most abject state of servility, as a prelude to the realizing the same wicked system in the mother country." Samuel Adams could not have done better, and perhaps Joseph Dunning had been reading American newspapers. However, the dominant attitude was that of Colonel Grant, who said that he had served in America and knew Americans well. Americans would not fight. "They would never dare to face an English army, and did not possess any of the qualifications necessary to make a good soldier; he repeated many of their common place expressions, ridiculed their enthusiasm in matters of religion, and drew a disagreeable picture of their manners and ways of living."

Charles James Fox denounced the folly of the address and proposed an amendment declaring that all the evidence indicated that the measures of the ministry were tending to widen rather than heal the differences. Edmund Burke "painted the dreadful abyss into which the nation was going to be plunged," called upon the merchants to "rouse themselves at the open declaration of their approaching ruin," and warned the "landed interest" of the "fatal effects" that would reach them. Alexander Wedderburn replied that "there were points of greater importance to be settled and decided than those of commerce and manufacture" and that "the question was not now the importance of the American colonies, but the possession of the colonies at all." Fox's amendment was defeated, 304–105, and North's motion adopted, 298–106.

When an attempt was made to recommit the motion, John Wilkes supported the attempt in an eloquent speech in which he prophesied: "In the great scale of empire, you will decline, I fear, from the decision of this day; and the Americans will rise to independence, to power, to all the greatness of the most renowned states, for they build on the solid basis of general public liberty." Captain Harvey replied that the crisis was due not only to "some of those ungrateful subjects on the other side of the Atlantic, but to some no less restless ones on this side of it." Until "we put a stop to the sedition" blown from England, and "give a check to those incendiaries who dare breathe forth such inflammatory poison as every newspaper conveys," Britain could never "bring the wicked leaders of those deluded people" in America to a sense of their duty.

John Wilkes, now secure as the Lord Mayor of London, ignored this attack upon him. As the debate continued it ranged all the way from Roman history to responsibility for the Stamp Act. There were assertions that Americans were and were not in a state of rebellion. The debates made no difference. The House of Commons adopted the address to the king and the Lords agreed to it without change.[39] George III was pleased and told Lord North that "this language ought to open the eyes of the deluded Americans but if it does not, it must set every delicate man at liberty to avow the propriety of the most coercive measures." [40] The next day the king asked for an increase in the size of the army and navy and within a few days Parliament approved the request.[41]

On the day the king asked for increased military and naval forces, Lord North proposed a bill to restrain the commerce of the New England colonies. He said that since "the Americans had refused to trade with this kingdom, it was but just that we should not suffer them to trade with any other nation." It would be a temporary act and certain persons could be excepted if they received certificates of good behavior from their governors or took an oath acknowledging the supremacy of Parliament. Much of the debate again centered on whether or not a rebellion existed in Massachusetts, and the legal definition of rebellion. One member, after twitting the lawyers, suggested that the Americans were engaged in a "justifiable rebellion." The usual large majority voted that the bill be brought in.[42]

But Lord North was apparently worried about the opposition. Before the bill was taken up again he introduced the motion on reconciliation which the cabinet had agreed to before Parliament met. He explained to George III that he had "hopes for great utility (if not in America, at least on this side of the water)" and that the motion would "greatly facilitate" the passage of the bill restraining the commerce of New England. Further-

[39] Ibid. 221–96, for the debates in the House of Commons and the House of Lords.
[40] 8 Feb., Geo. III, Corres., III, 171.   [41] PH, XVIII, 298, 305–13, 316–17.
[42] Ibid., 299–305; HCJ, XXXV, 112.

more, he feared that the commerce of the other colonies must be restrained as well. The king approved the resolution, which "certainly will have a good effect in this country," and perhaps in some of the colonies.[43]

The purpose of Lord North's motion on reconciliation was thus fraudulent, at least so far as reconciliation was concerned. The motion, introduced on 20 February, proposed that when any colonial legislature provided its proper share of money for the common defense and gave the money to Parliament, and agreed to make provision for the support of civil government, and if the measures were approved by king and Parliament, then Parliament would not levy any taxes on that colony as long as it continued to provide the funds. The only duties levied would be those for the regulation of trade, with the net proceeds credited to the colony where they were collected.

Of all the actions of Parliament during the winter of 1774–75, this was probably the most futile, and the opposition recognized its fraudulent character. Fox charged Lord North with insincerity. "No one in this country, who is sincerely for peace, will trust the speciousness of his expressions and the Americans will reject them with disdain." Burke declared that the colonies were "to be held in durance by troops, fleets, and armies, until singly and separately they shall do—what? Until they shall offer to contribute to a service which they cannot know, in a proportion which they cannot guess, on a standard which they are so far from being able to ascertain, that Parliament which is to hold it, has not ventured to hint what it is they expect." [44]

Chatham denounced the resolution as "mere verbiage, a most puerile mockery," and he predicted that it would "be spurned in America, as well as laughed at here by the friends of America and by the unrelenting enemies of that noble country. Everything but justice and reason will . . . prove vain to men like the Americans, with principles of right in their minds and hearts, and with arms in their hands to assert those principles." [45] Americans in England were not deluded either. William Lee, the brother of Richard Henry Lee of Virginia, who had been elected a sheriff of London in 1773 and became an alderman of the city in 1775, reported that the only purpose of the motion was to help the passage of the bill "for starving the four New England governments." [46]

There were those in Parliament who thought the motion on reconcilia-

[43] 19 Feb., North to king and king to North, Geo. III, Corres., III, 176–77.
[44] PH, XVIII, 319–36.   [45] To Viscount Mahon, 20 Feb., Pitt, Corres., IV, 402–3.
[46] To [F. L. Lee], 25 Feb., Arthur Lee Papers, HUL.

tion too great a concession but it passed easily [47] and Lord Dartmouth sent it to the colonial governors to be laid before their legislatures.[48] The legislatures still in existence treated North's "Olive Branch" with the contempt that Burke and Chatham predicted they would.

As soon as the motion was agreed to, North went ahead with the New England Restraining Act. Opposition speakers painted a grim picture of the tens of thousands of Americans who would starve, and London merchants petitioned against the bill, but neither had any effect on the monolithic majority that supported the ministry.[49]

The bill passed the House of Commons on 8 March and the next day Lord North introduced a similar bill, except that the fisheries were not mentioned, to restrain the commerce of Pennsylvania, New Jersey, Maryland, Virginia, and South Carolina. New York, Delaware, North Carolina, and Georgia were exempted because, so the ministry believed, they were opposed to the proceedings of the Congress. Again heavy majorities bowled over the opposition. The king approved the New England act on 30 March and the second Restraining Act on 13 April.[50]

The opponents of the ministry made one last effort to change the direction of policy, although the hopelessness of the effort must have been obvious from the start. In the midst of the debates on the restraining acts, Edmund Burke said that he had been "a strenuous advocate for the superiority of this country; but I confess I grow less zealous when I see the use which is made of it. I love firm government; but I hate the tyranny which comes to the aid of a weak one." [51] On 22 March, Burke made his great speech on American reconciliation. He ranged widely over the whole history of the relationship between Britain and the colonies and argued that the policies of the ministry would lead to disaster. He concluded with a series of resolutions. Among other things he proposed that Parliament acknowledge the right of the colonies to raise and dispose of taxes, that the repeal of the Revenue Act of 1767, the Boston Port Act, and other acts be considered, and that changes be made in the colonial courts, the treason statute of Henry VIII, and the jurisdiction of admiralty courts. Burke's speech has lived to the present day, but it had no im-

[47] HCJ, XXXV, 161; PH, XVIII, 319–58.
[48] 3 March, C.O. 5/242; NYCD, VIII, 545–47.
[49] HCJ, XXXV, 129, 144, 152, 163–64, 174, 182, 220, 224–25, 231, 241; PH, XVIII, 379–99; Pickering, XXXI, 4–11.
[50] HCJ, XXXV, 182–83, 187, 192, 204, 259; PH, XVIII, 379–99; Pickering, XXXI, 37–43.
[51] To Richard Champion, 9 March, George H. Guttridge, ed., *The Correspondence of Edmund Burke*, III (Chicago, 1961), 132.

pact on the ministry and its majority. The first of his resolutions was over-whelmed, 270–78, and the rest suffered a similar fate.[52]

The addresses, resolutions, and laws adopted by such great majorities in Parliament in the session which lasted from 19 January to 26 May 1775 offered no solutions and had no effect except to alienate more Americans than ever. The ministers were blind to the realities across the Atlantic which they read about in the letters of General Gage. They agreed with George III that the colonies must submit to the absolute authority of Parliament, and be forced to do so by military power if necessary. Yet they refused to believe General Gage when he told them repeatedly that if they used force they must use enough of it to be effective.

Their attitude was summed up in a letter Lord Dartmouth wrote to Gage on 27 January. More troops were being sent and it was expected that Gage would play a "more active and determined part" instead of acting on the defensive as he had in the past. Dartmouth refused to be-lieve that Gage needed 20,000 troops. Gage had told the ministry that the acts of the people were not those of a rude rabble, but Dartmouth clearly believed that Gage was wrong. He said that the acts appeared to him to be those of "a rude rabble without plan, without concert, and without conduct," and that a smaller force would have more success than a great army. Gage should arrest "the principal actors and abettors in the provincial congress," and if he kept the plan secret, it could hardly fail and could probably be accomplished without bloodshed. In any case, the people would not be formidable in an encounter with regulars, and if hostilities did begin, as Gage had predicted, "it will surely be better that the conflict should be brought on, upon such ground, than in a riper state of rebellion." However, Dartmouth had no intention of taking responsi-bility: it was up to Gage's discretion to follow the suggestion or ignore it.[53] But the message of the letter was as plain as its abysmal lack of under-standing of conditions in America: the ministry expected Gage to act. And act he did, and thus began the civil war that soon widened into the war for American independence.

Nearly three months passed before Dartmouth's letter of 27 January got to Gage, for it did not leave London until after 22 February, and England until 13 March. Meanwhile, Gage's letters continued to make it clear that he expected orders to take the offensive but that if he got them

[52] PH, XVIII, 478–540.   [53] Gage, Corres., II, 179–81.

he needed adequate troops. In December he wrote: "I hope you will be firm and send me a sufficient force to command the country, by marching into it, and sending off large detachments to secure obedience thro' every part of it; affairs are at a crisis, and if you give way it is forever." Two months later he said that keeping the peace in Boston was no solution. "The troops must march into the country." [54]

Gage had no intention of taking the responsibility. His subordinate, Earl Percy, put Gage's policy simply. Boston might be attacked at any moment but the general "has received no account whatever from Europe so that [on] our side no steps of any kind can be taken as yet." Gage's soldiers called him an "old woman," but he would not move without orders.[55] A copy of Dartmouth's letter of 27 January reached Boston on 14 April, but Gage, with his usual caution, waited for the original letter, which he got two days later.[56]

Gage made no attempt to seize American leaders. The effort would have been futile, for with the exception of Joseph Warren, they had left Boston. Colonial governors, including Gage, complained endlessly that the Americans got secret information from London, and apparently they heard about Dartmouth's letter before Gage received it. After he returned to England, Gage explained that two vessels arrived at Marblehead on Sunday, 8 April, and at once "an unusual hurry and commotion was perceived among the disaffected." The "notorious rebel," Dr. Samuel Cooper, was presiding at the Brattle Square Church. He feigned illness and went home and "he with every other chief of the faction, left Boston before night, and never returned to it." The cause of their flight was unknown until the 14th when a vessel arrived with the government dispatches which "contained directions to seize the persons of certain notorious rebels. It was too late. They had received timely notice of their danger, and were fled." [57]

Gage was probably relieved for he had predicted that any attempt to seize the leaders would begin hostilities, but Dartmouth's letter made it plain that he had to do something. What he did was order a secret expedition to seize the military stores at Concord. He provided Lieutenant Colonel Francis Smith with a detailed description of the supplies and a

[54] To Barrington, 14 Dec. 1774, 10 Feb. 1775, Gage, Corres., II, 663, 669; John R. Alden, "Why the March to Concord?" AHR, XLIX (1944), 449–50.
[55] To Rev. Thomas Percy, April, C. K. Bolton, ed., Letters of Hugh Earl Percy (Boston, 1902), 48; John Andrews to William Barrell, [19?] March, MHSP, VIII, 401.
[56] Alden, AHR, XLIX.
[57] "Queries of George Chalmers, With the answers of General Gage . . . ," MHSC, 4 ser. IV, 371–72.

map showing the houses and barns where they were located, information provided by Dr. Benjamin Church.[58]

The troops began embarking about ten in the evening of 18 April, and were rowed across the Charles River to a point east of Cambridge. There they waded through a swamp and stood around in water for an hour or two waiting for provisions which they threw away when they got them. Between one and two in the morning they finally started for Concord.[59]

The march was one of the best publicized "secret expeditions" ever planned. Paul Revere and a group of mechanics had been watching the British for days and Dr. Joseph Warren was in Boston coordinating information. Gage had sent out mounted patrols on the afternoon of the 18th. The presence of the boats on the shore and the march of the troops to them could be seen by anyone in Boston. Even before the troops embarked, Earl Percy overheard street gossips say that the troops were going to Concord to seize the cannon there.

Just about the time the troops began embarking, Joseph Warren sent William Dawes to warn Samuel Adams and John Hancock at Lexington, and the people of Concord, that the British were coming. Dawes sneaked through the fortifications on Boston Neck and went on his way arousing the countryside. A little later, Warren sent Paul Revere on a similar mission. Revere had already arranged an alarm system: two lanterns were to be hung in the steeple of North Church to warn the people at Charlestown if the British marched—"one, if by land, and two, if by sea," as Longfellow said. Two friends rowed Revere across to Charlestown where he got a horse and started for Concord, arousing the people and escaping from two British officers on the way. Revere got to Lexington by midnight and warned Hancock and Adams to leave. Dawes, who had come by the longer route, arrived shortly thereafter. Accompanied by Dr. Samuel Prescott of Concord, who had been courting a girl at Lexington, they started for Concord, but ran into a mounted British patrol. Dawes escaped back to Lexington, and Prescott jumped his horse over a fence and carried the news to Concord. Paul Revere was captured and his horse was taken. He was released and walked back to Lexington. When the British arrived, he

[58] French, *Informers*, passim.
[59] There are many accounts of Lexington and Concord, none of which agree precisely as to the details. Among the best are Harold Murdock, *The Nineteenth of April 1775* (Boston, 1923); Allen French, *Day of Concord and Lexington* (Boston, 1925) and *General Gage's Informers*; and Arthur B. Tourtellot, *Lexington and Concord . . .* (New York, 1963). The last book, originally published as *William Diamond's Drum*, was written by a public-relations man. Although there are errors in detail, Tourtellot's approach is very stimulating indeed.

told the Reverend William Gordon, "he having nothing to defend himself with, ran into a wood where he halted, and heard the firing for about a quarter of an hour."

The British had marched to Lexington accompanied by the ringing of church bells, the firing of alarm guns, the beating of drums, and in sight of burning beacons. At Lexington, Captain John Parker and about seventy minutemen were drawn up on the village green when the British arrived about daybreak. The "shot heard round the world" was fired at Lexington, not at Concord, despite the poet, but who fired it will never be known. Both the Americans and the British insisted that the other side fired first and both produced witnesses to back up their claims. The one clear fact was that eight Americans and no British were killed. The affair was over within a few minutes. The Americans fled and the British resumed their march to Concord.

They got there about eight in the morning and occupied the town without opposition. Troops were sent here and there to seize military stores, although the Americans, forewarned, had removed some of them. The only firing took place at North Bridge. During the morning, between 300 and 400 Americans gathered beyond the bridge and then started toward it. When warning shots did not stop them, a British volley killed two Americans. The Americans fired back and killed three British soldiers and wounded several others. Both sides then stopped and the "battle" of North Bridge was over within a few moments. Thereafter Colonel Smith marched his men around aimlessly and did not start back to Boston until about noon.

By noon thousands of farmers from the surrounding countryside had gathered, and as the British marched the farmers fired at them from the woods and from behind stone walls. By the time the British neared Lexington they were almost out of ammunition and on the verge of panic. The arrival of reinforcements from Boston under the command of Earl Percy saved them. He escorted the battered troops back to Boston by way of Charlestown, harassed all the way by endless firing as new groups of Americans converged on the route.

It was a shattering experience for the British. Before the day was over between 1500 and 1800 of their troops had been involved, and their losses were 73 killed, 174 wounded, and 26 missing. Yet they were lucky, for if the thousands of leaderless farmers had had better guns, or had been better marksmen, the retreat might have been a complete disaster.

Percy, whose skill saved the day, did not like Americans, but he had come to respect them. The day after the retreat he wrote that "whoever looks upon them as an irregular mob, will find himself much mistaken." Among them were men who had been rangers against the Canadians and Indians and they knew how to fight in wooded and hilly country. "Nor are several of them void of a spirit of enthusiasm, as we experienced yesterday," for they advanced within ten yards to fire. They had had time to prepare, and "they are determined to go through with it, nor will the insurrection here turn out so despicable as it is perhaps imagined at home. For my part, I never believed, I confess, that they would have attacked the king's troops, or have the perseverance I found in them yesterday." [60]

The disorganized Americans lost nearly a hundred killed, wounded, and missing, but they had achieved what many thought impossible: they had attacked British regulars and driven them in a humiliating retreat back to Boston. But far more than that had been achieved, at least in the minds of some leaders. As Samuel Adams left Lexington, William Gordon wrote later, he exclaimed:" 'O! *what a glorious morning is this!'* in the belief that it would eventually liberate the colony from all subjection to Great Britain." And, added Gordon, "his companion did not penetrate his meaning, and thought the allusion was only to the aspect of the sky." Gordon despised Adams's companion, John Hancock.[61]

ॐ

A few days after Lexington and Concord, the two Adamses, John Hancock, and the other Massachusetts delegates to the Second Continental Congress set out for Philadelphia. Dr. Joseph Warren was left in charge and he was more than equal to the responsibility. He had escaped from Boston on the morning of 19 April and he and William Heath had provided what little leadership the Americans had had on that day. Warren was a popular hero as a result and he therefore had enormous influence.[62]

On the 20th of April, Warren sent out a circular superbly designed to arouse popular support throughout the colony.

> The barbarous murders committed upon our innocent brethren, on Wednesday, the 19th instant, have made it absolutely necessary, that we immediately raise an army to defend our wives and children from the butchering hands of an inhuman soldiery, who, incensed at the obstacles they meet with in their bloody progress, and enraged at be-

[60] To General Harvey, 20 April, *Letters of Percy,* 52–53.
[61] Gordon, *History,* I, 478–79, 485.
[62] John H. Cary, *Joseph Warren: Physician, Politician, Patriot* (Urbana, 1961), 185–87.

ing repulsed from the field of slaughter, will, without the least doubt, take the first opportunity in their power, to ravage this devoted country with fire and sword. We conjure you, therefore, by all that is sacred, that you give assistance in forming an army. Our all is at stake. Death and devastation are the certain consequences of delay. Every moment is infinitely precious. An hour lost may deluge your country in blood, and entail perpetual slavery upon the few of our posterity who may survive the carnage. We beg and entreat, as you will answer to your country, to your own consciences, and above all, as you will answer to GOD himself, that you will hasten and encourage by all possible means, the enlistment of men to form the army, and send them forward to headquarters at Cambridge, with that expedition, which the vast importance and instant urgency of the affair demands." [63]

A modern writer has described the circular as "a remarkably skillful document. There is not a single fact in it. There is not a place named, a detail revealed, a statistic given. There is not a military objective stated nor a military action reported. There is not an inkling of what happened, what was involved, what the outcome was—or even where. There is, indeed, not a single reference, beyond the general language of the opening phrase, to what happened." [64]

Its purpose was to win popular support for the creation of what the provincial congress had refused to create: a provincial army. On 21 April, Warren and the committee of safety voted to raise an army of 8000 men. The provincial congress reassembled the next day and on 23 April it ratified what Warren had done by voting that an army of 30,000 was needed and that Massachusetts's share should be 13,600. Then it elected Joseph Warren president.[65] As president of the congress and as chairman of the committee of safety, Warren was the dominant leader in Massachusetts in the weeks ahead.

One of Warren's major concerns was to present the American version of the 19th of April to the people of Britain. A committee was sent to collect depositions at Concord and Lexington, but Warren did not wait for the results. He wrote a letter to the people of Britain which declared that the British had marched secretly, that they had fired on the men at Lexington without provocation, and again at Concord. The letter admitted that more regulars than Americans had been killed, but the emphasis was on British atrocities.

To give a particular account of the ravages of the troops, as they retreated from Concord to Charlestown, would be very difficult if not

[63] JPCM, 518; Cary, *Warren*, 188–89.   [64] Tourtellot, *Lexington and Concord*, 216.
[65] JPCM, 520, 148–49.

impracticable. Let it suffice to say that a great number of houses on the road were plundered and rendered unfit for use; several were burnt; women in childbed were driven by the soldiery naked into the streets; old men, peaceably in their houses, were shot dead, and such scenes exhibited as would disgrace the annals of the most uncivilized nation.[66]

Warren's letter, the depositions collected at Concord and Lexington, and newspapers were sent to Britain. John Derby sailed from Salem on 28 April four days after General Gage had sent his official reports. Derby arrived at the Isle of Wight on 28 May, where he hid his vessel in a stream and then hastened to London. He took the papers to Arthur Lee, copies were made, and the originals given to John Wilkes for safekeeping. Within days English newspapers were filled with the American version of 19 April 1775. The ministry fumed and waited for nearly two weeks before Gage's reports arrived. They were dull things at best, and the newspapers hooted at them.[67]

Whatever the ministry might say, the Americans had won a second victory as a result of Joseph Warren's superb strategy. The British atrocities described by Warren and in the depositions could not be matched by the one American atrocity Gage had to report. As Ann Hulton told it, the troops on their return from Concord "found two or three of their people lying in the agonies of death, scalped, and their noses and ears cut off and eyes bored out, which exasperated the soldiers exceedingly." [68]

Within ten days after the event, a broadside presented a British version of the 19th of April. The broadside reported that the British soldiers had seen three of their fellows lying on the ground, "one of them scalped, his head much mangled, and his ears cut off, though not quite dead—a sight which struck the soldiers with horror." [69] A copy of the broadside, picked up in a Boston street, was sent to the provincial congress which first branded the story a lie and then procured a deposition to prove that it was. The two men who buried the soldiers swore that none of them had been scalped or had their ears cut off.[70]

The Reverend William Gordon, who had begun to gather material for what would become the first history of the American Revolution, undertook an investigation of what happened on the 19th of April. He said that

[66] Ibid. 26 April, 154–56; Cary, Warren, 190–91.
[67] Tourtellot, Lexington and Concord, 236–41.
[68] To Mrs. Adam Lightbody, [?] April, Letters, 77–80.
[69] "A Circumstantial Account . . . ," Force, 4 ser. II, 435. Gage sent a copy of the broadside to Governor Trumbull on 29 April, ibid., 434–35.
[70] Samuel Mather to [Joseph Warren], 8 May, ibid. 538; JPCM, 208, 211, 225, 677.

"soon after the affair, knowing what untruths are propagated by each party in matters of this nature, I concluded that I would ride to Concord, inquire for myself, and not rest upon the depositions that might be taken by others." Among the many people he talked to was the Reverend William Emerson, who had witnessed most of the day's events. After hearing Emerson's story, Gordon reported that "a boy coming over the bridge in order to join the country people, and seeing the soldier wounded and attempting to get up, [and] not being under the feelings of humanity, very barbarously broke his skull and let out his brains with a small axe (apprehend of the tomahawk kind), but as to his being scalped and having his ears cut off, there was nothing to it." [71] The people of Concord ignored the story for half a century while the British clung firmly to the belief that a scalp had been lifted.

The members of the provincial congress knew Gordon well, and probably heard his account, but they preferred the gravediggers' deposition. It was included as a part of the official "Narrative" which the congress ordered published on 22 May. Many more depositions had been collected since the first ones that had been sent to England, but they all told essentially the same story of arson and looting. Just how much looting took place is uncertain, but it is at least doubtful that the panic-stricken, exhausted soldiers, fleeing for their lives, had as much time to loot as the depositions claimed. And if they did have the time one wonders why the soldiers would have taken such an astonishing quantity of women's clothing (including lawn aprons) and bed linen, as well as knives and spoons, not to mention items such as two "moose skins." [72]

Long before the publication of narratives and depositions by either side, rumor had done a far more imaginative and effective job of stirring up popular opinion. The first stories were on the way before noon of 19 April. Committees of correspondence sent the news from town to town and colony to colony by express riders and ship captains and the newspapers were not far behind. On 21 April the *New Hampshire Gazette* published an account under the headline "BLOODY NEWS" and the *Salem Gazette* ran a long story the same day. A ship left Salem on 25 April with that day's *Essex Gazette* and arrived in Charleston, South Carolina on 8 May. Before the day was over the *South Carolina Gazette and Country Journal* appeared with the Salem newspaper's story.[73]

[71] Gordon to a Gentleman in England, Force, 4 ser. II, 630. See also Murdock, *Nineteenth of April*, 71–77, and French, *Informers*, 105–9.
[72] JPCM, 661–94.
[73] See Frank L. Mott, "The Newspaper Coverage of Lexington and Concord," NEQ, XVII (1944).

On 23 April a man in Wethersfield, Connecticut, wrote to New York that Paul Revere had supposedly been waylaid and slain, and that the British troops on the road to Concord had marked their way "with cruelties and barbarity, never equalled by the savages of America. In one house a woman and seven children were slaughtered. . . ." [74] "An American" told the inhabitants of New York that the British had fired at the men in Lexington without provocation and that on their way to Concord "they killed a man on horseback, and killed geese, hogs, cattle, and every living creature they came across. . . ." They searched the house where Adams and Hancock had stayed, and when they could not find the two men, "these barbarians killed the woman of the house and all the children in cool blood, and then set the house on fire." [75]

The Massachusetts newspapers were even more specific and equally imaginative. On 25 April the *Essex Gazette* told how the soldiers pillaged almost every house, destroying doors and windows, and stealing clothing and other valuables. "But the savage barbarity exercised upon the bodies of our unfortunate brethren who fell, is almost incredible: not contented with shooting down the unarmed, aged, and infirm, they disregarded the cries of the wounded, killing them without mercy, and mangling their bodies in the most shocking manner." But "our victorious militia" committed no cruelties. Instead, "listening to the merciful dictates of the Christian religion, they 'breathed higher sentiments of humanity.'"

Isaiah Thomas who had moved his newspaper, the *Massachusetts Spy*, from Boston published an account of the 19th of April in the first issue of his paper at Worcester on 3 May. He copied portions of the *Essex Gazette*'s story but he added embellishments. He told of the killings, burnings, and robberies by the British soldiers, "nor could the tears of defenceless women, some of them in the pains of childbirth, the cries of helpless babes, nor the prayers of old age, confined to beds of sickness, appease their thirst for blood, or divert them from their design of murder and robbery."

෫෨

Thousands of men had started for Boston on the spread of a rumor in September 1774, and within a few days after 19 April 1775, thousands penned up Gage and his troops on the tiny peninsula that was Boston. "The ardor of our people is such that they can't be kept back," reported the Connecticut committee of correspondence. Colonels of regiments were sending their best and most ready men as soon as possible, and the re-

[74] Force, 4 ser. II, 362.   [75] NYJ, 4 May.

mainder would be ready to march at a minute's warning.[76] On 23 April a man in Wethersfield wrote that "we are all in motion here" and 100 young men set out yesterday. "Our neighboring towns are all arming and moving" and "we shall, by night, have several thousands from this colony on their march." [77]

The governments of the New England colonies responded almost as quickly as their citizens. The Connecticut assembly met on 26 April and voted to create an army to be ready to go to Massachusetts if needed. But some of the leaders were cautious or opposed the creation of an army. The assembly sent a delegation to General Gage with a letter from Governor Jonathan Trumbull proposing a suspension of hostilities in the hope that peace could be restored.[78]

The letter created vast alarm in Massachusetts. Erastus Wolcott and Dr. Samuel Johnson showed the letter to the committee of safety, and Joseph Warren at once wrote Governor Trumbull that the proposal for a cessation of hostilities made them very uneasy and that the only solution was to drive Gage and his troops out of the country.[79] Trumbull replied that Connecticut would be firm but that he would like to have some "duly authenticated" evidence about what had really happened on the 19th of April.[80] When the Connecticut delegation returned from Boston with a letter from Gage to Trumbull, a committee of the Massachusetts congress tried to get them to open it, but they "thought it inconsistent with their honor, and the interests of the colonies" to do so. After an attempt to hold the Connecticut men in Massachusetts, they were allowed to return home.[81] The next day the congress sent a letter expressing alarm at the "unparalleled wickedness of our unnatural enemies" who had tried to persuade the people of Connecticut that the people of Massachusetts had started hostilities. To prove that the British had started them, the congress sent along copies of the depositions and the letter which had been sent to Britain. These were not to be published, however, until their effect in Britain could be known. As for General Gage, the letter implied that he was a scoundrel and a liar, and that the Connecticut mission to him was a naive if not dangerous venture. The only solution was to create a "powerful army." The Massachusetts congress sent the letter and other documents "with all possible speed" and ordered the messenger to stay there until he got a copy of Gage's letter.[82] The almost hysterical concern

[76] To John Hancock, 21 April, Force, 4 ser. II, 372–73.
[77] To a Gentleman in New York, ibid. 362.   [78] Ibid. 409–22.
[79] JPCM, 532–33.   [80] To Joseph Warren, 4 May, Force, 4 ser. II, 506.
[81] JPCM, 191.   [82] Ibid. 193–94, 198.

of the Massachusetts leaders was uncalled for. Connecticut's leaders were firm but they were cautious. They had had much experience in sorting out fact from fiction in the stream of stories coming from Massachusetts.

Rhode Island was as firm as Connecticut, but the leadership of the colony was far more sharply divided. Rhode Island had its annual election on 19 April. Joseph Wanton, the wealthy Newport merchant, had been governor ever since 1769 and he was re-elected despite charges of toryism against him and his son.

The legislature met at Providence on 25 April and voted to raise a 1500-man army. The upper house agreed, but a minority, led by Governor Wanton, Lieutenant Governor Darius Sessions, and two assistants, dissented. They argued that the raising of an army would endanger the colony's charter and lead to the horrors of civil war. When the assembly met again on 3 May, Governor Wanton did not attend to take the oath of office. He pled illness and sent a letter urging the assembly to adopt Lord North's "Olive Branch" resolution. He argued that Rhode Island's prosperity depended upon maintaining the connection with Britain and he urged the assembly to repeal the law creating an army, which, he said, would bankrupt the colony. The assembly responded by declaring that all his acts would be null and void until he took the oath. Before the end of the year the assembly voted the office of governor vacant and elected Nicholas Cooke. Meanwhile, the assembly authorized the secretary of the colony to commission the officers in Rhode Island's new army, which Governor Wanton had refused to do. That army had been authorized to march out of the colony, and after George Washington was named commanding general by the Continental Congress, the Rhode Island army was placed under his command.[83]

The colonies southwest of New England, with the one notable exception of Pennsylvania, reacted more in terms of patterns established by past events within their borders than of outrage at the shedding of American blood. There was an explosive reaction and a week of mob violence in New York City, but no one marched to Massachusetts. The upheaval was simply another incident in the continuing struggle between the popular leaders and the conservative merchants and politicians.

The news of Lexington and Concord got to New York Sunday afternoon, 23 April, and by four o'clock the committee of 60 had met and called

[83] Force, 4 ser. II, 389–90, 471–72; Lovejoy, *Rhode Island*, 179–84.

a mass meeting for the next day. Sunday night a mob broke into the armory, distributed arms and powder among the populace, and threatened to attack the British troops, about a hundred of whom still remained in the city. The city and colonial governments were paralyzed. On Monday, Governor Colden and the council confessed that they were helpless after the commander of the militia told them that he could provide "no aid from the militia for they were all liberty boys," and shortly thereafter the British commander asked permission to put his troops on board the naval vessel in the harbor. He said they were "fatigued with watching" for an attack on their barracks.[84]

Thousands of men went to the mass meeting Monday afternoon and voted to organize a militia and directed the committee of 60 to take the necessary steps to save the city. The committee decided that it had no authority except to enforce the Association, so on Wednesday it issued a call for the election on Friday of a committee of 100, and of delegates to a provincial congress. The committee then nominated a slate of 100 in an anonymous broadside. The popular leaders, once more calling themselves Sons of Liberty, nominated a slate of their own on Thursday. That afternoon, Isaac Sears and 360 armed men forced the collector of the port to surrender the keys to the customs house. William Smith reported that "the merchants are amazed and yet so humbled as only to sigh or to complain in whispers. They now dread Sears's train of armed men." The next morning Sears stopped the election. He "went with the pride of a dictator and forbid the polls, objecting to the list proposed by the committee. The better sort—Whigs and Tories are astonished and cry out for a committee." [85]

The committee of 60 pled for an end to disorder and confusion. It admitted that "many" on its slate of 100 were "objects of distrust and suspicion, and, perhaps, not without reason," but argued that they should not be rejected until they refused to help. In desperation the committee proposed that the election be put off until Monday, 1 May, and told the voters they could elect anyone they wanted. "What could be more fair?" At the same time the committee urged the counties to elect delegates to a new provincial congress to meet on 22 May.[86]

Friday afternoon some of New York's leaders narrowly escaped death after the arrival of a copy of Bradford's *Pennsylvania Journal* of 26 April. The newspaper reported that "authentic letters" from London proved that the "present hostile preparations against the American colonies" were the result of assurances from Oliver De Lancey, John Watts, Henry White,

[84] Smith, *Memoirs*, 221.   [85] Ibid. 222.   [86] Force, 4 ser. II, 427–28.

Myles Cooper, and Cadwallader Colden that New York would not join the other colonies and would submit to Britain, and that "De Lancey and his band of traitors" had asked that troops be sent to New York. The *Journal* declared: "you have unsheathed the sword of Britain, and pointed it against the bosom of your country. You have held up a signal for a civil war; and all the calamities of towns in flames, a desolated country, butchered fathers, and weeping widows and children now lay entirely at your door." American resentment could no longer be satisfied by "executions of villains in effigy," concluded the piece signed "Three Millions."

The New York mob gathered. "The populace rage[d]," said William Smith, and "meant to proceed to execute them immediately," but violence was finally prevented by calling a mass meeting for the following afternoon. The frightened men busily prepared affadavits swearing that they had not written letters asking for troops. James Duane and John Jay read De Lancey's letters and testified that the charge against him was false. Myles Cooper, president of King's College, fled to the British warship in the harbor.[87]

Friday night the committee of 60 hit upon a new device. It drafted an association which in ringing rhetoric expressed alarm at the ministry's design to raise a revenue, and great shock at "the bloody scene now acting in the Massachusetts Bay. . . ." The association resolved that New Yorkers would never become slaves and promised to abide by all the measures of the Continental Congress and of the forthcoming provincial congress. On Saturday, William Smith reported that "all parties ran this morning to sign the association at the Coffee House." That afternoon the frightened leaders turned out for the mass meeting and whigs and tories alike joined to support the committee.[88]

The slate of 100 proposed by the committee of 60 was elected without incident on Monday, 1 May. Thirty-eight of the committee of 100 had not served on either the committee of 51 or the committee of 60, but like the members of those committees, they represented the same wide diversity of opinion. Nine of the thirty-eight became loyalists but three of them were among the most radical of the popular leaders: John Morin Scott, John Lamb, and Daniel Dunscomb, chairman of the mechanics' committee. After the election, New York waited for the meeting of the provincial congress on 22 May, and seemingly forgot about Massachusetts.[89]

Pennsylvania's reaction to Lexington and Concord, unlike that of New

87 Ibid. 390, 445–46; Smith, *Memoirs*, 222–23.
88 Force, 4 ser. II, 471; Smith, *Memoirs*, 223.
89 For a detailed account of the week see Becker, *New York*, 193–99.

York, was colony-wide, and some Pennsylvanians had begun military preparations before the news of Lexington and Concord reached Philadelphia on Monday afternoon, 24 April. In frontier Bedford county, which had been created in 1771, the county committee made detailed plans for organizing militia companies in every township and providing the men with arms and ammunition when it heard that more British troops were being sent to America.[90] Reading, in Berks county, had organized two companies of troops by 26 April.[91]

The news from Massachusetts speeded up a movement already under way. The county committee of the western county of Cumberland met at Carlisle on 5 May. It reported that 3000 men had already associated and that they had 1500 stands of arms. The committee voted to draft 500 men for immediate service and levied a tax on the real and personal property of the county to pay the men and to provide them with arms.[92]

By the end of May, more than 3000 men were reported training in Lancaster county, "not only to defend themselves at home if attacked; but have solemnly engaged to leave all and march wheresoever and whensoever their assistance is needed." [93] So great was the enthusiasm, the story ran, that at Reading eighty Germans, all more than forty years old, organized an "Old Man's" company and drilled with great vigor. Their commander was ninety-seven and the drummer eighty-four.[94]

No one either within the colony or from other colonies expressed surprise at military preparations in the backcountry counties; what really astonished them was what happened in Philadelphia. Samuel Curwen fled to Philadelphia from Massachusetts after the 19th of April, "hoping to find an asylum amongst Quakers and Dutchmen, who I presume from former experience have too great a regard to ease and property to sacrifice either at this time of doubtful disputation on the altar of an unknown Goddess, or rather doubtful divinity." Instead, he found "the drums beating, colors flying, and detachments of newly raised militia parading the streets." [95]

A mass meeting of at least 8000 people met on 26 April and adopted the Philadelphia association by which they agreed to "associate for the

[90] Bedford county committee to Philadelphia committee, 9 May, Force, 4 ser. II, 542–43.
[91] Ibid. 400.   [92] Letter from Carlisle, 6 May, ibid. 516.
[93] William Bradford to James Madison, 2 June, Madison, *Papers*, I, 149.
[94] Force, 4 ser. II, 878.
[95] 4, 5 May, George A. Ward, ed., *Journal and Letters of the Late Samuel Curwen* (3rd ed., New York, 1845), 25–26.

purpose of learning the military exercise, and for defending our property and lives against all attempts to deprive us of them." [96] On Saturday, 29 April, the "Military Associators" organized the city. Each ward would have one or more companies, with the wards choosing their own officers. The organization of two troops of light horse, two companies of expert riflemen, and two companies of artillerymen was already under way. A newspaper account boasted: "In short, Mars has established his empire in this populous city; and it is not doubted but we shall have, in a few weeks from this date, four thousand men, well equipped, for our defense, or for the assistance of our neighbors." [97]

The retired druggist, Christopher Marshall, who was excommunicated by the Quakers for his sturdy support of the popular cause, noted gleefully in his diary: "it's admirable to see the alteration of the Tory class in this place since the account of the engagement in New England; their language is quite softened, and many of them have so far renounced their former sentiments as that they have taken up arms, and are joined in the association; nay, even many of the stiff Quakers" are ashamed of their proceedings.[98]

Two companies of Quakers were formed and drilled with the rest. John Lamb, who bewailed the many villains in New York who would take up arms against "us," was delighted with the spirit he found in Philadelphia and he expressed astonishment at Quakers drilling openly. In addition, he reported, many of them were doing military exercises privately "as they do not care to offend their parents, who are very rigid Quakers." [99]

When the Pennsylvania assembly met on 1 May it made no effort to control or guide the military fervor of the colony; instead, it showed great reluctance to act at all. It did reject Lord North's "Olive Branch" resolution as not being a reasonable or just basis for reconciliation, but most of the two-week session was spent in resisting requests for money. The "inhabitants" of the city and liberties of Philadelphia petitioned for a grant of £50,000 for defense, and the Philadelphia committee of 60 asked for legislative help in paying the debt it had contracted in behalf of "the public security." The legislature finally found that it had £2000 available to help out the committee of 60. Then, just before it adjourned, it made a feeble gesture. The assembly voted £5000 to buy military stores, but it had

---

[96] Force, 4 ser. II, 399–400.   [97] 3 May, ibid. 478.
[98] William Duane, ed., *Passages from the Diary of Christopher Marshall* (Philadelphia, 1849), 26.
[99] To Paul Revere, 21 May, Revere Papers, MHS; Curwen, *Journal*, 26.

no money and made no effort to raise any.[100] In the months to come the leaders of the assembly were ever more reluctant, and while they yielded to pressure from time to time, it was always slowly, and eventually too late to prevent a revolution in the government of Pennsylvania.

South Carolina was the only colony outside New England to organize for defense, as a colony, after the outbreak in Massachusetts and before the Continental Congress converted the cause of Massachusetts into the cause of America by appointing a "continental" general to command the motley crowd besieging Boston. The Carolinians had no thought of helping Masachusetts; their concern was with defending their own colony if British troops were sent, and above all, with the threat of a slave rebellion and of Indian attacks on the frontiers.[101]

The first concrete step was taken when news arrived of such British measures as the sending of more troops to Boston and the New England Restraining Act. In January the provincial congress had authorized its president, Charles Pinckney, to appoint a secret committee to provide supplies for the defense of the "interior parts" of the colony, and for "other necessary purposes." On 20 April he appointed William Henry Drayton and allowed him to pick the other four members. Drayton's attitude had changed radically since the days when he had denounced mechanics in politics and had been appointed to the royal council. In 1774–75 fellow councilors, who were also royal officials, attacked him for his support of the American cause and demanded his removal. On 1 March 1775, Governor Bull, Drayton's uncle, suspended him as a councilor. Thereafter Drayton was one of the most aggressive and effective leaders of the opposition to British policies in South Carolina.

One of the men he picked for the secret committee was equally aggressive and effective as a leader of the mechanics, Edward Weyman, an upholsterer. They demonstrated their abilities the day after they were appointed by organizing the seizure of the colony's entire supply of arms and powder. The most conspicuous storehouse was the State House in Charleston, and the committee had the help of such distinguished members of the legislature as Henry Laurens and Charles Pinckney, in breaking into

---

[100] Proceedings of the Assembly, 1–13 May, Force, 4 ser. II, 451–58.
[101] The best and most detailed account of this period of South Carolina history is in John Drayton, *Memoirs of the American Revolution* (2 vols., Charleston, 1821), which was based on a manuscript history left by his father, William Henry Drayton.

it. When Governor Bull asked the assembly to investigate the theft, the legislators blandly and unanimously replied that the persons who had taken the military supplies were unknown.

The legislators displayed no unanimity, however, when the delegates to the Second Continental Congress asked the assembly if it would provide the money if the delegates offered a contribution to the American cause after they got to Philadelphia. Men like Rawlins Lowndes argued that non-importation and non-exportation were adequate and that the delegates should be cautious and not go to extremes. Eventually the assembly agreed to provide money, but many legislators soon showed they were unwilling to do any more, no matter what the provocation.[102]

The Carolina delegates sailed on 3 May and immediately thereafter a letter from Arthur Lee in London raised anew a nightmare that haunted Carolinians. Lee reported that the ministry was considering a plan for starting a slave insurrection. What made the report even more alarming was that "it was already known" that the slaves "entertained ideas that the present contest was for obliging us to give them their liberty." The general committee of the colony, which had been created in the summer of 1774, at once appointed a special committee to prepare plans for defense, and the militia companies of Charleston were placed on round-the-clock duty. Then on 8 May the news of Lexington and Concord arrived on a ship from Salem, Massachusetts. The general committee immediately called the provincial congress to meet on 1 June, the day to which Governor Bull had adjourned the assembly because a new governor, Lord William Campbell, was expected to arrive shortly. Before the end of the day the special committee had prepared plans for the defense of Charleston and asked the members of the general committee to take an oath of secrecy before presenting it. The request was "like a stroke of thunder to several members. They thought that nothing less than an immediate revolution was to be ushered in" and they refused to take the oath. The special committee then withdrew its report. Two days later the committee proposed a defense association to be signed by all the inhabitants. The general committee debated it for seven hours and finally rejected the proposal by a vote of 25 to 23.

Despite such defeats, the special committee, of which Drayton was a key member, went ahead. It made plans for defending Charleston harbor and for raising and paying troops, for stopping the exportation of rice and

[102] Drayton, *Memoirs*, I, 218–30.

corn, and for a general association. There was strong opposition in the general committee, but the day before the provincial congress met, it ordered the chairman, Henry Laurens, to lay the plans before it.[103]

The legislature met the next day, but Governor Bull adjourned it to 19 June. Since most of its members were also members of the provincial congress, they continued in session as a congress. Charles Pinckney resigned as president, for Carolina had gone too far and too fast for him. Henry Laurens was elected in his place and at once explained why the congress had to meet. The attack of the British in Massachusetts was an attack on all the people of the continent; the colony was defenseless and had to prepare to defend itself; there was danger of a slave insurrection and of Indian attacks; and the reinforcement of the British troops in Boston made evident the plan of the British ministry "to quell the American troubles by the law of arms and not to quiet them by the laws of reason and justice." The only alternatives were "to submit to abject slavery, or appeal to the Lord of Hosts in defence of the common and unalienable rights peculiar to Englishmen."

The congress acted swiftly despite powerful opposition. An association was adopted declaring that Carolinians were justified in taking up arms to defend themselves until a reconciliation could be achieved upon constitutional principles, "an event which we ardently desire." The congress then organized two regiments, voted to issue one million pounds in paper money, and elected a council of safety with the power to manage the political and military affairs of the colony when the congress was not in session. The congress called for the election of delegates to a new congress to meet in December, or earlier if necessary. After an acid interchange with the new governor, who arrived while the congress was in session, the congress dissolved itself on 22 June.[104]

There was a scattered response in the other southern colonies to the outbreak in Massachusetts before the Continental Congress assumed direction of policy. The Georgians began a revolution and it was well under way by July. The sharply divided North Carolinians did not meet in another congress until August. The Virginians were in the midst of the uproar over Dunmore's seizure of the powder in Williamsburg, and once that subsided, they looked forward to the meeting of the House of Burgesses on 1 June.

In December 1774 the Maryland convention had called for the election of delegates to a convention to meet on 24 April. The first act of the new

[103] Ibid., 231, 246–50, 256.
[104] Ibid. 250–65; South Carolina Provincial Congress Journals, 33–67.

convention was to swear allegiance to George III, an oath to which many Maryland leaders subscribed with utter sincerity. The convention then elected delegates to the Continental Congress and told them that "this convention has nothing so much at heart as a happy reconciliation" between Britain and the colonies. The convention heard from the Philadelphia committee that the British were going to fortify New York and divide the colonies, so it sent a letter to Philadelphia asking if the story were true, and what Pennsylvania and New Jersey would do. The delegates declared that they had to get back to their counties and decided not to wait for an answer. The news of Lexington and Concord was published in Annapolis on 27 April while the convention was in session but the news was ignored, at least officially. The convention adjourned on 3 May to meet again on 22 May, but authorized the delegates to the Continental Congress to call it into session at either an earlier or a later date.[105]

The Maryland convention, like other conventions and legislatures that met during the spring of 1775, either explicitly or implicity agreed that the Second Continental Congress should propose measures and establish policies for all the colonies. As the delegates to the Congress converged on Philadelphia, no one really knew what those policies and measures would be. The Maryland convention was aware of the uncertainty when it told its delegates "that in the present state of public affairs, this convention is sensible that the measures to be adopted by the Continental Congress, must depend much upon events which may happen to arise. . . ."[106]

The policies and measures of the Continental Congress were indeed shaped by events which no one could foresee, but as the months passed its policies were debated more and more in terms of one fundamental issue: should the war be carried on until reconciliation with Britain could be achieved, or should it become a war for American independence?

[105] Proceedings of the Maryland Convention, 24 April–3 May, Force, 4 ser. II, 379–82.
[106] Ibid. 380.

XXIII

Revolution vs. Reconciliation: The American Dilemma

When the Second Continental Congress met on 10 May 1775, popular enthusiasm for fighting the British army was at a height it never again reached during eight long years of war. The thousands who marched on Boston and the many thousands more who passed resolutions, and practiced at soldiering, were stirred by the emotions of the moment, but as the months went by their enthusiasm declined. At times the American forces dwindled almost to the vanishing point, but enough men fought on to win what became the war for American independence.

Most of the American leaders saw that the future might be bleak, but there were almost as many opinions about what the future might be, and what Americans should do, as there were men capable of holding opinions. The facts of British policy were perfectly clear to all by 10 May 1775. Americans knew that Britain had treated the proceedings of the first Congress with contempt, that the trade of the colonies would be confined to the empire, and that military and naval power would be used to force Americans to submit to the absolute supremacy of Parliament. Henry Laurens put it very well in the South Carolina congress in June: the ministry had decided "to quell the American troubles by the law of arms and not to quiet them by the laws of reason and justice."

American leaders in 1775 were offered two simple choices: they could submit to the rule of a British army and to whatever decisions king and Parliament might make, or they could fight British force with American force in defense of the rights that most Americans insisted were theirs. In the spring of 1775 American leaders of every shade of political opinion, including some who eventually remained loyal to Britain, rejected the first choice and agreed, many of them reluctantly, that they must fight to maintain their rights. But they disagreed about what the outcome of that fight should be: reconciliation with Britain or independence. Americans divided into two broad groups in their attempt to resolve their dilemma, and each of these groups in turn contained men whose answers varied and shifted with the course of events.

One group was composed of those who were conservative by temperament and political conviction, or in the sense that they wanted to remain in the British Empire, but they believed that they had to fight until reconciliation was achieved. By the end of 1775 the recognized leader of this group was John Dickinson, who, when forced to choose, chose American independence rather than loyalty to Britain. Dickinson gave poignant expression to the plight of such Americans after Lexington and Concord. He said "that this most unnatural and inexpressibly cruel war began with the butchery of the unarmed Americans," that the people of the continent were preparing for vigorous resistance, and that "freedom or an honorable death are the only objects on which their souls are at present employed." Then he asked: "what topics of reconciliation are now left for men who think as I do, to address our countrymen? To recommend reverence for the monarch, or affection for the mother country? . . . No. While we revere and love our mother country, her sword is opening our veins." The future was dark, for Britain would retain her illusions until France and Spain fell upon her, and after defeating her, would turn upon America which would have to "wear their chains, or wade through seas of blood to a dear-bought and at best a frequently convulsed and precarious independence." [1]

There were many who thought like Dickinson that Lexington and Concord were examples of "butchery," and that they would have to meet force with force, but they insisted that the American army was created only for defense and that all they wanted was a reconciliation with the parent state on constitutional principles. They were utterly sincere, but those in power in Britain ignored them or refused to believe them. They fought a losing battle but they continued to hope for reconciliation until independence had been declared, and some still hoped for reconciliation afterward. Defeated though they were in the end, these men were a powerful force in the Congress and in their colonies during 1775–76.

Ranged in opposition to the conservative leaders were most of the men who had achieved fame as popular leaders during the preceding decade and who had won such a decisive triumph in the First Continental Congress.

[1] To Arthur Lee, 29 April, Force, 4 ser. II, 444–45.

Among the most important in this group were the Lees of Virginia and the Adamses of Massachusetts, who were soon to be known as the Lee-Adams junto. The popular leaders and their supporters were not a monolithic block but most of them did agree that reconciliation was hopeless and that independence would be the probable outcome of the dispute, although not all of them agreed that it would be a desirable outcome.

In 1775 the popular leaders did not admit they wanted independence, and they cannily avoided use of the word. They professed to want reconciliation but made it plain that they doubted it could be secured on terms acceptable to Americans. Their policy was to urge Congress to adopt measures that were in fact if not in name the acts of an independent state.

Their letters, like their policies, were implicit rather than explicit statements of their convictions. Thus when Richard Henry Lee got to Philadelphia, he wrote to his brother in London that Gage's wanton attack on unarmed people in Massachusetts had created such a union, such a military spirit, and so much resentment "against this savage ministry and their detestable agents, that now no doubt remains of their destruction with the establishment of American rights." [2] Samuel Adams wrote of "this important glorious crisis" and predicted that "the battle of Lexington will be famed in the history of this country." He said that the "spirit of patriotism" prevailed in the Congress but he lamented its slowness to act, although he realized that it was difficult for sixty men to all feel the same.[3] Most of his contemporaries believed that he wanted independence and suspected his every move. More than a half-century later the story was told that in 1775 he hoped fighting would start in Pennsylvania to make that colony more zealous in the cause. The Philadelphians had built some gunboats and it was known that a British vessel was down the river. One day when Adams was walking in the yard, he heard cannon shots. He rushed into the Congress and "skipping along, and snapping his fingers, exclaimed: 'the ball's begun, the ball's begun, thank God, the ball's begun.' " [4]

John Adams was, as usual, more direct. He said he was fond of reconciliation if it could be obtained but he doubted that it could. If Americans considered the education of British officials from the king on down, and how officials had been "trained and disciplined by corruption to the system

[2] To William Lee, 10 May, *Letters*, I, 134.
[3] To James Warren, 10 June, *Warren-Adams Letters*, I, 54–55.
[4] Timothy Pickering to Chief Justice John Marshall, 26 Dec., 1828, Pickering Papers, MHS. Pickering said he had heard the story from Thomas Willing about ten years earlier.

of the court, we shall be convinced that the cancer is too deeply rooted and too far spread to be cured by anything short of cutting it out entire." The hope of reconciliation prevented preparations for war "as it really is," and so far as he was concerned, "powder and artillery are the most efficacious, sure, and infallible conciliatory measures we can adopt." [5]

Adams recognized that the members of the second Congress were as suspicious of Massachusetts as they had been in the first Congress. He wrote his wife that "America is a great, unwieldy body. Its progress must be slow. It is like a large fleet sailing under convoy. The fleetest sailors must wait for the dullest and slowest." [6]

ᏄᏏ

Many delegates to the Continental Congress on 10 May 1775 were slow sailors, but they were not dull. They were men who believed in reconciliation or who wanted to go slowly. The "fleetest sailors" among the delegates fumed and fretted but they realized that Congress must present a united front to the world, and that if they insisted on immediate and drastic action the more conservative members might withdraw and the Congress collapse.

The Congress went into a committee of the whole to consider "the state of America" and began debating the nature of the policies to be adopted. During the first few weeks, Congress emerged from the committee only when events beyond its control forced it to act, and those events forced it to take one reluctant step after another in the direction of open warfare.

The Massachusetts delegates wanted action at once when the Congress met. They presented the letter to the people of Britain and the depositions taken at Lexington and Concord. Congress ordered them published, but ignored the rousing call for the creation of an American army in a letter from Joseph Warren. "A powerful army," he asserted, was "the only means left to stem the rapid progress of a tyrannical ministry." Without one "we must reasonably expect to become the victims of their relentless fury," but with an army we can put an end to "the inhuman ravages of mercenary troops. . . ." Congress referred the letter to the committee of the whole, where it lay buried for weeks. [7]

A few days later, Congress received a specific inquiry it could not ignore. The New York committee of 100 wanted to know what it should do if

[5] To Moses Gill, 10 June, *Works*, IX, 356–57.
[6] 17 June, Lyman H. Butterfield, ed., *Adams Family Correspondence* (Series II, 2 vols., Cambridge, 1963), I, 216.
[7] JCC, II, 24–25, 44.

British troops arrived in New York. Congress replied that the people should act only on the defensive. If the troops arrived they should be allowed to stay in barracks but should not be permitted to erect fortifications or cut off communications between city and country. The people were to repel force with force only if the troops committed hostilities or invaded private property. Meanwhile, military stores should be removed from the city. The New York delegates warned their fellow New Yorkers that Congress did not mean that they should seize and remove military stores belonging to the Crown.[8]

Congress had no sooner declared that people should act only on the defensive and respect the property of the Crown than it learned that a group of New Englanders had captured Fort Ticonderoga on Lake Champlain on 10 May, the day Congress had assembled. Among the supplies captured were cannon and other military stores that would be invaluable in a fight with the British. Of equal importance was the fact that Fort Ticonderoga, and Crown Point which was taken on 11 May, controlled the century-old invasion and trade route to and from Canada.

The capture of the two fortresses had been carried out by a diverse lot of people. A group of Connecticut men, without consulting the government, made plans to attack Ticonderoga. They sent word of their plans to Ethan Allen and asked his help. The Connecticut men started out, picked up additional recruits in western Massachusetts, joined forces with Allen and some of his Green Mountain Boys, and gave Allen command of the expedition. Meanwhile, Benedict Arnold of New Haven, Connecticut, had rushed to Massachusetts with part of his militia company. There he told Joseph Warren of the military supplies at Ticonderoga.

Warren and the committee of safety secretly gave Arnold a commission as a colonel, authorized him to enlist troops, and take the fortress. Arnold went ahead of his men and caught up with the expedition led by Allen. Arnold insisted that he should command, and bitter quarrels followed, although he and Allen stopped fighting long enough to take Ticonderoga. The British commander and his few men surrendered without firing a shot. Allen later said that he had ordered the commander to surrender in the name of "the great Jehovah and the Continental Congress," but at the time he was heard to call out: "Come out of there you damned rat."

The news of Ticonderoga spread rapidly and it threatened to create an intercolonial crisis, for the fort was within the boundaries of New York. Governor Trumbull of Connecticut assured New Yorkers that the raid had

[8] 15 May, ibid. 49, 52; LMCC, I, 91.

been carried out by "private persons" and that he hoped New York would not be offended. When the Massachusetts provincial congress heard the news, it praised Arnold and urged him to retain command, but asked Connecticut what it wished to do. Connecticut appointed a colonel to take command, and soon there were three "commanders" at Ticonderoga. Arnold insulted a committee from the Massachusetts congress when it arrived and he was suspended. Later the Massachusetts congress refused to reimburse him for his expenses.[9]

The Congress in Philadelphia displayed embarrassment rather than joy. Entirely apart from the effect the capture of the fortress might have on the hope of reconciliation, it had painful domestic implications. New York had offered a reward of £20 for the capture of Ethan Allen in 1771 and had raised the amount to £100 in 1774. Allen was one of the leaders in the region east of Lake Champlain that was claimed by both New York and New Hampshire, and both colonies had made overlapping land grants. New Hampshire had favored its own citizens and those of the other New England colonies. The Allens were from Connecticut and Ethan Allen was the hero of the "New Hampshire Grants" where he had organized the Green Mountain Boys in 1770 to fight off and drive out settlers with land grants from New York. New York had granted land to its own citizens, including speculators such as James Duane, a member of the Congress.

Congress was also aware of other intercolonial disputes over land. Connecticut had laid claim to the upper Susquehanna Valley in Pennsylvania and created a Connecticut county within the region. While the Congress was meeting, Pennsylvanians were shooting at Connecticut settlers and the settlers were shooting back. Pennsylvania and Virginia both claimed the region around Fort Pitt and both had created counties there. In May 1775 Virginia officials had the upper hand and had jailed Pennsylvania officials. The Virginians had also been struggling against a group of Pennsylvania and British speculators who had been trying to set up a new colony in the Kentucky region. In May 1775 the Virginia delegates were sitting in Congress with the man who had been the principal lobbyist in Britain for that colony—Benjamin Franklin—and neither he nor his allies had any intention of giving up their claims in an area claimed by Virginia.

It is not unlikely, therefore, that such inter-colonial rivalries were in the minds of members of Congress, and that they considered the domestic as

---

9 Willard M. Wallace, *Traitorous Hero: The Life and Fortunes of Benedict Arnold* (New York, 1954), contains a detailed account. Force, 4 ser. II, *passim*, contains much of the correspondence among the official bodies, committees, and the principal quarrelling antagonists.

well as the imperial implications of the capture of Ticonderoga. Congress tried to compromise. It asked the city committees of New York and Albany to move the military stores to the south end of Lake George and create a strong post there. Congress knew, however, that New York was so badly divided that it could do little, so it requested Connecticut to provide enough men and supplies to achieve the purpose. Then, with reconciliation in mind, Congress instructed the New York and Albany committees to make an "exact inventory" of the stores "in order that they may be safely returned when the restoration of the former harmony between Great Britain and these colonies, so ardently wished for," made it possible to do so.[10] Congress was also concerned about what the Canadians might think and spent time drafting a letter to the "oppressed" inhabitants of Canada expressing sympathy for their sad plight under the tyranny and slavery of the Quebec Act, and assuring them that the seizure of Ticonderoga was entirely for purposes of self-defense.[11]

The only time that Benedict Arnold and Ethan Allen ever agreed was when they heard of the order to remove the military stores from Ticonderoga to the southern end of Lake George. They both wrote to Congress opposing the move because it would leave hundreds of settlers open to attack from the north. They argued that Canada should be invaded at once while it was relatively defenseless, and many New Englanders agreed with them.[12] Before Congress received their letters, it heard from Arnold that a force of British regulars and Indians were planning to retake Ticonderoga. Congress at once reversed itself and told Arnold he could keep the cannon and other stores at Ticonderoga for the time being.[13] The next day the delegates solemnly resolved that "as this Congress has nothing more in view than the defence of the colonies," no colony or body of colonists should invade Canada.[14] Twenty-six days later Congress ordered the invasion of Canada.[15]

ह≈

While Congress had been responding erratically to the pressure of external events it had been debating a statement of policy and on 26 May it adopted a set of resolutions which were as contradictory as its actions, but which reflected the wide divergence of opinion among the delegates. The first two resolutions declared that the colonies were in a dangerous situa-

---

[10] JCC, II, 55–56.   [11] Ibid. 68–70.
[12] Allen to Congress and Arnold to Congress, 29 May, Force, 4 ser. II, 732–35.
[13] 31 May, JCC, II, 73–74. Arnold's letter was written 23 May.
[14] 1 June, ibid. 75.   [15] 27 June, ibid. 109–10.

tion because of the use of military force to impose the unconstitutional and oppressive acts of Parliament, and that the beginning of hostilities in Massachusetts and the sending of reinforcements made it necessary that "these colonies be immediately put into a state of defence." The third resolution insisted that the colonies wanted reconciliation and that a "humble and dutiful" petition should be presented to the king. The fourth stated that negotiations for reconciliation should be started at once and should be included in the petition to the king.

Those who were skeptical about reconciliation and petitions also had their way. They secured the adoption of a resolution which recommended that Congress "persevere the more vigorously in preparing for their defence, as it is very uncertain whether the earnest endeavors of the Congress to accommodate the unhappy differences between Great Britain and the colonies by conciliatory measures will be successful." [16]

The Congress moved comparatively rapidly after 26 May. The day before, it had recommended that the New York provincial congress, which had met on 22 May, should enlist militia and prepare to defend the city and the approaches to it. On 27 May, Congress appointed a committee on ways and means to secure military supplies. On 2 June, Congress received a letter from the Massachusetts congress requesting advice about the establishment of civil government and suggesting that since the army "now collecting from different colonies is for the general defence of the right of America" that Congress consider "taking the regulation and general direction of it, that the operations may more effectually answer the purposes designed." The next day Congress voted to borrow £6000 to buy powder and on 14 June finally committed itself to raising troops, and obliquely, to the creation of a "continental army." It voted that companies of riflemen should be raised in Virginia, Pennsylvania, and Maryland and sent to Boston. They were to enlist in "the American continental army" for one year and be paid by Congress. And Congress then appointed "Mr. Washington" head of a committee to prepare rules and regulations for the government of the army.[17] The next day Congress elected Mr. Washington General Washington "to command all the continental forces, raised, or to be raised, for the defence of American liberty." [18]

A few days later John Adams told James Warren that "nothing has given me more torment than the scuffle we have had in appointing the general officers." He had noted late in May that "Colonel Washington

[16] 26 May, ibid. 64–66.   [17] Ibid. 59–61, 67, 76–78, 79, 89–90.
[18] Ibid. 91.

appears at Congress in his uniform and, by his great experience and abilities in military matters, is of much service to us." [19]

He recalled later that the army around Boston was in desperate straits but in Congress "we were embarrassed with more than one difficulty. Not only the party in favor of the petition to the king, and the party who were jealous of independence, but a third party, which was a southern party against a northern and a jealousy against a New England army under the command of a New England general." It was clear that some of the southerners wanted Washington as commander. However, "Mr. Hancock himself had an ambition to be appointed commander in chief," and Adams discovered that the Virginia delegates disagreed because "the apostolical reasoning among themselves which should be greatest, were not less energetic among the saints of the ancient dominion than they were among us of New England."

One morning John Adams walked Samuel Adams up and down the yard telling him of the dangers they faced. Samuel Adams agreed but said no plan would ever be agreed to. John Adams replied that he was determined to force the members of Congress to "declare themselves for or against something," and that he intended to propose that Congress adopt the army and appoint Washington commander in chief. Samuel Adams said nothing.

When Congress opened John Adams moved that it adopt the army and then declared that he intended to nominate a general, "a gentleman from Virginia who was among us and very well known to all of us, a gentleman whose skill and experience as an officer, whose independent fortune, great talents and excellent universal character, would command the approbation of all America, and unite the cordial exertions of all the colonies better than any other person in the union." At that point Washington "darted into the library room."

Hancock, who had been elected president when Peyton Randolph had left for Virginia to preside over the House of Burgesses, listened with "visible pleasure" during the first part of John Adams's speech. "But," said Adams, "when I came to describe Washington for the commander, I never remarked a more sudden and sinking change of countenance. Mortification and resentment were expressed as forcibly as his face could exhibit them. Mr. Samuel Adams seconded the motion, and that did not soften the president's physiognomy at all."

[19] 20 June, *Warren-Adams Letters*, I, 61; to Abigail Adams, 29 May, *Family Corres.*, I, 207.

In the debate that followed some New Englanders argued for Artemas Ward who was in charge of the army around Boston. He was old and fat and enormously popular. There were a few southerners who wanted a New England general but most southerners insisted that a southerner be placed in command for they were fearful of New England's imperial ambitions.[20] The next day, Congress elected Washington unanimously and he understood as well as John Adams that his appointment was in part political. He wrote to a friend that he had not wanted the position but that the "partiality of the Congress, added to some political motives, left me without a choice." [21]

Washington in his speech accepting the appointment declared that "I do not feel myself equal to the command" and he wrote the same thing to his wife and friends. Congress had voted the commanding general $500 a month for pay and expenses, but Washington insisted that he would take only his expenses.[22] It was a superb political move, and it turned out to be a wise one economically, for his expenses averaged $20,000 a year during the eight years of war.[23]

The politics involved in the appointment of lesser officers caused John Adams and others even more "anxiety" and "distress." The colonies demanded commissions for their favorite sons, friends lobbied for friends, and many of the appointments demanded and made had nothing to do with either military experience or ability. To begin with, Congress decided there should be two major generals and five brigadier generals.[24] Washington insisted that two former British army officers living on half-pay in Virginia—Charles Lee and Horatio Gates—be given appointments. John and Samuel Adams worked for Lee even though they could not get the other Massachusetts delegates to vote for him, and John Adams at least was dubious, for New Englanders were attached to their own officers. He accepted Lee and Gates because of Washington's insistence and because of the "extreme attachment of many of our best friends in the southern colonies to them. . . ." [25] The New Englanders, however, managed to appoint Artemas Ward first major general and relegated Charles Lee to the

20 *Autobiography*, III, 321–23. There may be errors in Adams's recollections but it is the only account we have of Washington's appointment.
21 JCC, II, 91; Washington to Burwell Bassett, 19 June, *Writings*, III, 296–98.
22 JCC, II, 91–92.
23 "Accounts of G. Washington with the United States . . . ," Washington Papers, LC.
24 JCC, II, 93, and n. 2.
25 John Adams to Elbridge Gerry, 18 June, *Works*, IX, 358; to James Warren, 20 June, *Warren-Adams Letters*, I, 61.

position of second major general, which made that gentleman very unhappy indeed. Horatio Gates was content for the moment with an appointment as adjutant general with the rank of brigadier general.[26]

It was obvious that two major generals were not enough to satisfy the political demand. The New York delegates wrote their provincial congress early in June that general officers would probably be appointed in the near future and that it should send its recommendations to Philadelphia as soon as possible. The New York congress was so helpless that the Continental Congress told New York to ask Connecticut for troops to defend Manhattan Island, but the New Yorkers wanted New York generals nonetheless. They wrote glowing recommendations for Philip Schuyler as a major general and Richard Montgomery as a brigadier general.[27] It was obvious too that Connecticut had to be given appointments, for Congress depended upon it for help.

On 19 June Congress agreed it needed two more major generals. Philip Schuyler was elected third major general to "sweeten" and keep up the spirit of New York. Israel Putnam's "fame as a warrior" was so widespread that he was elected fourth major general "by universal voice," the only general aside from Washington so honored.[28] Two days later Congress agreed that it needed eight rather than five brigadier generals and gave three to Massachusetts, two to Connecticut, and one each to New York, New Hampshire, and Rhode Island.[29] Nathanael Greene of Rhode Island, whom Congress ranked eighth, turned out to be the ablest general of the lot. In the case of Israel Putnam, Congress gave him a rank superior to David Wooster and Joseph Spencer who were major generals in Connecticut. Both men were outraged. Wooster refused to accept a mere brigadier generalship from Congress, but at least stayed with his troops in Massachusetts, while Joseph Spencer was so angry that he left his troops and went home to Connecticut.[30] The war over rank and precedence between generals and lesser officers continued throughout the war for independence

---

[26] JCC, II, 97.

[27] New York Delegates to New York Provincial Congress, 3 June, LMCC, I, 110–11; JCC, II, 95; Provincial Congress to New York Delegates, 7 June, Force, 4 ser. II, 1281–82.

[28] JCC, II, 99; Eliphalet Dyer to Joseph Trumbull, 20 June, LMCC, I, 137.

[29] JCC, II, 103.

[30] Roger Sherman to David Wooster, 23 June, LMCC, I, 142 and n. 3; Silas Deane to Mrs. Deane [15 July], ibid. 164. L. C. Hatch, The Administration of the American Revolutionary Army (New York, 1904), is a useful account of such matters. On the disruptive political battles among generals, see Jonathan G. Rossie, The Politics of Command: The Continental Congress and Its Generals (Ph.D. Thesis, University of Wisconsin, 1966).

and it was sometimes as bitter as, and often fought more vigorously than, the war against the British.

Another source of dissension was the question of pay, and this too lasted throughout the war for independence. In 1775 the New Englanders and the delegates from other colonies, particularly from the South, were at odds. The southerners thought that Massachusetts paid privates too much and officers too little. They insisted on higher pay for officers and won out over the New Englanders. John Adams commented that "those ideas of equality, which are so agreeable to us natives of New England, are very disagreeable to many gentlemen in the other colonies." [31]

Despite the politics involved in the creation of a continental army, and politics were as inescapable as they were necessary to maintain and further the tenuous unity among the colonies, Congress made an irrevocable commitment to a war and to the direction of it. In addition to creating an American army, Congress made an equally irrevocable commitment to financing the war by voting to issue $2,000,000 in paper money.[32] Congress thus assumed two essential functions of a sovereign government although it lacked the power to tax and the power to coerce and was dependent upon the will of the individual colonies for its very existence. Congress, in fact, had no real power except the power to persuade Americans to support its policies.

႟⤺

While Congress was making fundamental commitments to carry on a war, for a purpose as yet undecided, it did not know that on 17 June the bloodiest battle of the eight-year war that lay ahead had been fought on Charlestown peninsula across the Charles River from Boston.

Major Generals Howe, Clinton, and Burgoyne arrived on the *Cerberus* on 25 May, eager for action and glory. They brought with them orders for General Gage. He was to occupy or destroy all garrisons or posts that might be useful to the rebels and to seize and secure all their military stores. All those guilty of treason and rebellion were to be arrested and imprisoned. The orders, which had been written on 15 April, had been irrelevant since the 19th of April. Gage was also told to issue a proclamation promising a royal pardon to those who submitted and took the oath of allegiance.[33] He duly issued a proclamation, written by the flamboyant Burgoyne, offering pardons to all except Samuel Adams and John Hancock.[34] The Americans

[31] To Elbridge Gerry, 18 June, Works, IX, 358.   [32] JCC, II, 105–6.
[33] Dartmouth to Gage, 15 April, Gage, Corres., II, 190–96.
[34] 12 June. Force, 4 ser. II, 968–70.

laughed at and denounced it. No rebel leaders surrendered, and Gage was no more able to arrest them than he was to follow his other orders.

Gage had received reinforcements, although not the numbers he wanted, and several naval vessels were stationed in the waters around Boston. Prodded by the three major generals who had come to help him, Gage decided to protect Boston by occupying Dorchester Heights to the south, and, when he received more troops, the hills of Charlestown peninsula to the north.

The decision was made on 12 June. The Americans learned of it almost at once, and the Massachusetts committee of safety ordered the occupation of Bunker Hill on Charlestown peninsula. On the night of 16 June American soldiers moved to the peninsula, but instead of following orders, they moved on to the much lower Breed's Hill, closer to Boston and to the guns of the British vessels in the Charles River. The men worked through the night digging a redoubt on Breed's Hill, and made some preparations on Bunker Hill as well, after prodding by Israel Putnam of Connecticut.

About four in the morning the sailors on a British warship saw what had happened during the night and began shelling the redoubt on Breed's Hill. The four generals debated what to do. Charlestown peninsula was connected to the mainland by a narrow neck of land which was sometimes covered with water at high tide. General Clinton proposed that he be given troops and naval help to land them on the neck, to cut off the possibility of an American escape. The suggestion was eminently sensible but General Howe was senior general and entitled to the glory which would come with victory. He proposed to achieve it in eighteenth-century style by making a frontal assault. By noon the British soldiers were parading on Boston Common in full battle equipment, including heavy packs, weighing between 75 and 125 pounds, and three days' rations. By one o'clock the soldiers had been landed on Charlestown peninsula directly across from Boston. General Howe spent an hour studying what lay before him and then sent back for reinforcements.

Colonel William Prescott and his men on Breed's Hill were thus able to continue with their preparations despite constant shelling by the British navy, and they erected a barrier consisting of stone walls and fences stuffed with hay, from the hill to the Mystic River on the east. During the morning Prescott, supported by Israel Putnam on Bunker Hill, demanded more reinforcements from General Artemas Ward at Cambridge, but the fat old general was afraid that Gage might attack his headquarters and did not send much help until ordered to do so by the Massachusetts committee of safety. Eventually the Americans probably had between 1400 and 1700 men and boys from Massachusetts, New Hampshire, and Connecticut awaiting the British attack.

By the time Howe was ready, about three in the afternoon, he had somewhere between 2200 and 2500 men and eight pieces of artillery. The artillery soon ran out of ammunition because someone had provided twelve-pound balls for cannon using six-pound balls, and grapeshot could not be used since the guns had been placed on marshy ground and had sunk into it so they could not be aimed. The British began their march up Breed's Hill and along the shore of the Mystic River, through tall grass and over fences, carrying their heavy packs and muskets. The Americans, except for a few understandably nervous ones, held their fire until they could "see the whites of their eyes," and then they poured murderous volleys at the magnificent targets in red and white coats, and the even-better targets of glittering ornaments worn by the officers. The British fell back. They regrouped and marched up a second time, and again the Americans held their fire until they could do the most damage. The British retreated a second time, leaving hundreds of dead and wounded behind. Howe decided to try a third time, and at last allowed his men to drop their heavy packs. This time the Americans waited until the British were within twenty yards, and once more they mowed down soldiers and officers. But the Americans ran out of powder and they could do nothing but retreat. Some of them were orderly and some panicked, but they escaped back across Charlestown Neck.

Clinton begged Howe to pursue the Americans. If he had done so he might have put an end to the rebellion, for while the Americans had men willing to fight and men to lead them on the battlefield, they lacked supplies and an adequate organization to back them up. They were, in fact, a potential not an actual army. But Howe refused to pursue them and returned to Boston.[35]

The 19th of April had been humiliating for the British, but their "victory" on 17 June was a shattering blow that reduced Gage's army to what it had been before he received reinforcements, and its morale was lower than ever. Nearly half of the officers and men who fought on 17 June were casualties: 226 killed and 828 wounded. Perhaps more officers were killed and wounded on that day than in all the remaining battles of the war. General Gage was a casualty, too, for he was recalled to England as soon as the

[35] The best among the many accounts of the events on 17 June is Allen French, *The First Year of the American Revolution* (Boston, 1934), chapters XV–XVI.

news of the battle got to London. He was replaced by William Howe who, until he was recalled in turn in 1778, was an even more cautious general than Gage had been.

The American losses were 140 killed, 271 wounded, and 30 captured, but because of the incompetence of the British generals the Americans escaped from a position they could not have held. They were lucky and they had achieved something of a victory. They had faced British regulars for a second time within two months and fought them to a standstill, until they ran out of powder. The belief in the invincibility of British regulars, which had been shaken at Lexington and Concord, was badly battered if not destroyed on Breed's Hill. Furthermore, after 17 June the British did not dare leave Boston peninsula. At the end of July, Earl Percy reported: "Here we are still cooped up, and now so surrounded with lines and works as not to be able to advance into the country without hazarding too much. For our army is so small that we cannot even afford a victory, if it is attended with any loss of men." [36]

At the same time that Americans achieved victory of a kind, their bitterness toward Britain increased. Some of them had long believed that Britain was bent on tyranny and the tales told of British brutality at Lexington and Concord confirmed them in their belief. The battle on Breed's Hill deepened their conviction, for tales of atrocities were told about it. Massachusetts lost a hero and one of its ablest leaders that day. Joseph Warren, like many popular leaders in other colonies, wanted to be a military leader as well. The Massachusetts congress had elected him a major general three days before; he was killed in the redoubt on Breed's Hill. The shock of his death was multiplied by a story that spread in the days that followed. As Abigail Adams told it, "the savage wretches called officers consulted together and agreed to sever his head from his body and carry it in triumph to Gage." [37]

The Congress in Philadelphia received the first news of the battle on 22 June, the day it elected eight brigadier generals and voted to issue $2,000,000 in paper money. The next day, Washington left to take command in Massachusetts, and Congress voted to take charge of the garrisons at Ticonderoga and Crown Point and to pay the men. It also made the extraordinary recommendation that New York raise an army and enlist the

[36] To General Harvey, 28 July, *Letters of Percy*, 58–59.
[37] To John Adams, 31 July, *Family Corres.*, I, 269.

Green Mountain Boys in it. On 27 June, Congress ordered General Schuyler to go to Ticonderoga and make preparations for the invasion of Canada, and on the 30th it adopted articles of war.[38]

In the midst of these preparations for war, Congress had been debating two documents that in many ways contradicted one another. On 23 June a committee had been appointed to draw up a declaration for Washington to read to the troops at Cambridge. John Dickinson and Thomas Jefferson, who arrived in Congress for the first time on 21 June, were largely responsible for the final form of the "Declaration of the Causes and Necessity of Taking up Arms" adopted on 6 July. Jefferson's version was far more aggressive while Dickinson's looked forward to reconciliation. The two versions as well as the final draft reflected the deeply divided views of the members of Congress, although in many ways the declaration anticipated the Declaration of Independence.[39]

Two days later Congress adopted the second petition to the king, which had been agreed upon late in May. The petition had been delayed from time to time because of strong opposition, but in the end John Dickinson won out because of his great prestige. He drafted the petition and Congress accepted it. The troubles were blamed on the king's ministers and the petition declared that Americans wanted to stop the shedding of blood. It argued that there was no inconsistency between the expression of loyalty and the use of force to oppose British troops, and beseeched the king to use his influence to end the conflict.[40]

The plea was heart-felt and sincere on the part of Dickinson and men who thought like him, but it infuriated John Adams. He was growing more and more angry at the New Yorkers and Pennsylvanians who were holding back. The day before the adoption of the petition to the king he wrote his wife that in every society there were men who were timid and "some who are selfish and avaricious, on whose callous hearts nothing but interest and money can make impression. There are some persons in New York and Philadelphia, to whom a ship is dearer than a city, and a few barrels of flour than a thousand lives—other men's lives I mean." [41]

Although Congress moved too slowly for John Adams, it did continue to prepare for war. Fearful that Britain would use Indians against Americans, Congress created three Indian departments to keep peace with the Indians.[42] It amended the Association to allow importers of military stores to

[38] JCC, II, 103–5, 109–10, 111–22.
[39] Julian Boyd, ed., *The Papers of Thomas Jefferson*, I (Princeton, 1950), 187–219, for a discussion of authorship and copies of the various drafts.
[40] JCC, II, 158–62. [41] To Abigail Adams, 7 July, *Family Corres.*, I, 242.
[42] 12 July, JCC, I, 174–77.

export produce of any kind in payment for them.[43] It recommended that all men in America between sixteen and fifty be enrolled in regular militia companies and urged the colonies to appoint committees of safety and provide means to protect their harbors and coastwise navigation.[44] It elected Franklin postmaster general for the "United Colonies" and rejected Lord North's "Olive Branch" resolution, as several colonies had already done.[45] In response to the acts restraining the trade of the colonies, Congress reconfirmed and made more explicit the non-exportation provisions of the Association, which were to go into effect on 10 September. Exportation would stop to every "island and settlement," British and foreign alike, between the southern boundary of Georgia and the equator.[46]

While those who wanted reconciliation agreed to such measures, however reluctantly, they defeated others which pointed far more directly toward independence. One such was a plan for articles of confederation which Benjamin Franklin presented to Congress on 21 July. Although the confederation, supposedly, would last only until reconciliation was achieved, it smacked too much of independence for some delegates and went too far in the creation of a centralized power to suit others. Congress relegated the plan to a pile of unfinished business.[47]

Benjamin Franklin was the best known, if not the best loved, American in Europe and America in 1775. He returned to Pennsylvania from England on 5 May after an eleven-year absence, and Pennsylvania elected him to Congress the next day. For weeks he remained silent, in Congress and out, and he was at once widely suspected of being a British spy. Some thought he was an agent for the minority in Parliament, others that he was an agent of the ministry, and in New York he was suspected of being a tool of Chatham. Richard Henry Lee of Virginia was reported "highly offended" and determined to find out if the gossip about Franklin was true.[48] When James Madison heard the tale he declared that "the bare suspicion of his guilt amounts very nearly to a proof of its reality."

It was indeed a time when men were suspicious of one another. The aged and respectable Richard Bland of Virginia was suspected of selling out for British gold,[49] and it was widely believed that many New York leaders had been bribed.[50]

Three days after Franklin returned he had written to a friend in Eng-

[43] Ibid. 184–85.   [44] 18 July, JCC, II, 187–90.

[45] 26, 31 July, ibid. 209, 224–34.   [46] Ibid. 238–39.   [47] Ibid. 195–99.

[48] William Bradford to James Madison, 2 June, Madison, *Papers*, I, 148–50; Smith, *Memoirs*, 224; Edward Shippen, Jr. to Jasper Yeates, 15 May, Shippen Papers, HSP.

[49] Madison to Bradford, 19 June, Madison, *Papers*, I, 151–53, 153n.

[50] For example see Eliphalet Dyer to Joseph Trumbull, 10 June, LMCC, I, 115.

land that a civil war had begun and that perhaps neither of them would live to see the end of it. He promised to send "authentic" intelligence from time to time and expected his friend to reciprocate.[51] He was a canny politician, and a Quaker had once asked: "Didst thee ever know Dr. Franklin to be in a minority?" [52] Franklin served quietly on various committees in Congress until he had made up his mind. By July he had apparently decided for independence,[53] and the news spread that "the suspicions against Dr. Franklin have died away: whatever was his design at coming over here, I believe he has now chosen his side, and favors our cause." [54]

On the same day that Franklin presented his plan of confederation, he and Richard Henry Lee offered Congress two versions of a virtual declaration of independence. They proposed that if the acts restraining American commerce were not repealed, the customs houses should be closed and the officers discharged. The ports of the colonies would then be declared open to the ships of foreign powers to bring in all except British goods duty free. The policy would be maintained for two years even if reconciliation were achieved. Congress rejected the proposal by putting it off to some "future day." [55] John Adams concluded that despite his detachment, Franklin was "a great and good man." [56]

Adams enthusiastically supported opening the ports, and the more he thought about the second petition to the king, and the refusal of Congress to consider confederation and opening the ports, the madder he got. He told his wife that when fifty or sixty men "have a constitution to form for a great empire," a country 1500 miles long to fortify, millions to arm and train, a navy to begin, commerce to regulate, Indians to negotiate with, and a standing army of 27,000 men to maintain, he pitied those men.[57] He wrote James Warren the same day that "a certain great fortune and piddling genius, whose fame has been trumpeted so loudly, has given a silly cast to our whole doings. We are between hawk and buzzard." After this tribute to John Dickinson he declared: "We ought to have had in our hands a month ago the whole legislative, executive, and judicial of the whole continent, and have completely modelled a constitution; to have raised a naval power, and opened all our ports wide; to have arrested every friend to government on the continent and held them as hostages for the

[51] To David Hartley, 8 May, Mason Franklin Collection, Yale Library.
[52] W. C. Bruce, *Benjamin Franklin Self-Revealed* (2 vols., New York, 1917), II, 98n.
[53] Van Doren, *Franklin*, 527–28.
[54] Bradford to Madison, [18 July], Madison, *Papers*, I, 158.
[55] 21 July, JCC, II, 200–202.
[56] To Abigail Adams, 23 July, *Family Corres.*, I, 252–53.
[57] 24 July, ibid. 255–56.

poor victims in Boston, and then opened the door as wide as possible for peace and reconciliation." He asked: "Is all this extravagant? Is it wild? Is it not the soundest policy?" [58]

The letters created a sensation, for the young man carrying them was caught by the British, who published them in the *Massachusetts Gazette* in Boston on 6 August. The letters convinced the British more than ever, and some Americans as well, that certain members of Congress were bent on independence. And when Congress reassembled in September, John Dickinson, the "piddling genius," refused to speak to John Adams.[59]

Early in the session the Second Continental Congress dealt with a question that was to loom ever larger in the months to come, one that some men believed to be as fundamental as that of the nature of the war to be fought. Should Americans establish new governments, and if the war for the defense of colonial rights became a revolutionary war for independence, would it be accompanied by a political revolution in America?

Men's responses were guided by their fears, hopes, and beliefs as they lived from day to day in the midst of upheaval and the collapse of the old order. Most of the courts were shut up and commerce was coming to a stop. Aside from Connecticut and Rhode Island, which retained their charters into the nineteenth century, only three colonial legislatures remained in existence, and their power was vanishing. The congresses and conventions and the host of uncontrolled local committees were dominating the daily lives of Americans as the old governments had never done. Accompanying the collapse of the old order were growing demands for political and other changes in American society that alarmed the more conservative colonial leaders, and many of the popular leaders as well.

No leaders in America were more appalled at what they had wrought than some of the popular leaders of eastern Massachusetts. For a decade they had been telling the people they had a right to govern themselves, a right based on the laws of God and nature as well as on colonial charters and the rights of Englishmen. They had appealed to and praised the virtues of "the people" as the only true defenders of American liberties, and called upon them for support in opposition to British policies and to Thomas Hutchinson and his political allies.

The praise of the virtues of the people began early. Thus a writer in the *Boston Gazette* in 1765 proclaimed that however "the tools of power"

[58] 24 July, *Warren-Adams Letters*, I, 88–89. [59] John Adams, *Diary*, 16 Sept.

might disparage the people and call them "Mob and rabble, they are the darlings of Providence; and in the eyes of their original author and continual preserver, of great estimation. They are the Lord's anointed. . . ." [60] Three years later the *Gazette* declared that "however meanly some people may think about the populace or mob of a country, it is certain that the power or strength of every FREE country depends entirely upon the populace. . . ." [61]

It was not surprising that, as Thomas Hutchinson wrote, "the spirit of liberty spread where it was not intended." In 1768, when Harvard tutors refused to accept any more excuses for not attending prayers, the students met and resolved in favor of liberty, declared the rule of the tutors unconstitutional, and threw bricks through the tutors' windows. When three or four rioters were expelled, the three junior classes threatened to leave the college. The senior class, within three months of graduation, asked the president for recommendations to "the college in Connecticut so that they might be admitted there." The overseers backed the president and tutors in expelling the rioters, and "a stop was put to the revolt." [62]

By the fall of 1774 the air was thick with chickens coming home to roost, for the abstract ideas the Massachusetts leaders had preached, and the political devices they had used, were being turned against them. They were faced with threatened revolt in the backcountry counties and in some eastern towns as well. The backcountry counties demanded that the "law of nature" be put into effect and they proposed to elect their own officials and govern themselves, and not be ruled by appointed officials as in the past.

The Massachusetts delegates in the First Continental Congress were soon getting letters about the demand for a political revolution at home. John Adams heard that the province was in a state of nature and that the people were eager to adopt the old charter of 1629 or some new form of government. He was asked: "What, tell us ye wise men, what is to be done?" [63] Dr. Thomas Young reported that "by all our advices from the westward the body of the people are for resuming the old charter" and were opposed to any compromise based on the charter of 1691. That charter would make it impossible to frustrate British machinations because under it "a party is so easily made of the most powerful men in every county, and even town, against the common people." [64]

The doctor was a bold revolutionary, ready to break with Britain at any

---

[60] 12 Aug.   [61] Ibid. 25 July 1768.   [62] Hutchinson, *History*, III, 135–36.
[63] William Tudor to John Adams, 3 Sept., Adams Papers, MHS.
[64] To Samuel Adams, 4 Sept., Samuel Adams Papers, NYPL.

time, but Joseph Warren was worried about the effect such a move would have on the other colonies. He told Samuel Adams that no matter how busy they were in Congress, nothing was more important than the subject of government. Almost all the people in the western counties and "many among us" wanted to resume the old charter but there were those in the east who thought it would be "trifling." They wanted to create a new government and make proposals for limited subjection to the king.[65] Such easterners, at least, wanted to stay in the empire whereas the westerners, and such men as Thomas Young, were ready to declare what amounted to independence.

The broad split between east and west was clear in the instructions the towns gave the delegates they elected to the first provincial congress. Eastern towns like Boston told their delegates to "adhere firmly" to the charter of 1691, and Topsfield told its delegate to secure the acknowledgment of George III "as our rightful sovereign." [66] But towns like Worcester were ready for revolution. Worcester told its delegate that if their rights under the charter of 1691 had not been confirmed by the time the provincial congress met, "you are to consider the people of this province . . . absolved . . . from the obligation therein contained and to all intents and purposes reduced to a state of nature. . . ." He was to exert all his efforts to raise from the old constitution, "as from the ashes of the Phenix, a new form wherein all officers shall be dependent on the suffrages of the people for their existence as such. . . ." [67]

The town of Leicester was even more eloquent. "Charters have become bubbles—empty shadows without any certain stability or security. . . ." Its delegate was to oppose any motions "for patching up" the charter of 1691. "And as we are without form, and void, and darkness seems to cover the face of the land," the delegate was to use his influence to establish a government suited to the circumstances.[68]

The eastern leaders had appealed to the First Continental Congress for help in heading off an attack by the country people on the British in Boston and they got the advice they needed and wanted: to act only on the defensive.[69] At the same time they hoped for advice to head off political revolution and they got that too when an alarmed Congress told them that if they could not secure justice under the charter of 1691, they should, in effect, do without government at all.[70]

---

[65] To Samuel Adams, 4, 12 Sept., Frothingham, Warren, 358, 375–76.
[66] BTR, XVIII, 191–92; G. F. Dow, ed., Town Records of Topsfield, Massachusetts (2 vols., Topsfield, 1917–20), II, 335–36.
[67] Worcester Town Records, 1753–83, 244.   [68] Washburn, Leicester, 451–54.
[69] See Chapters XIX and XXI above.   [70] JCC, I, 59–60. See Chapter XIX above.

John Adams was indignant, but he knew that the Congress in 1774 would not approve the assumption of government, even under the charter of 1691, for that would be an implicit declaration of independence.[71] Samuel Adams was disturbed by the split between the eastern and western counties and he suggested the formula which the Second Continental Congress agreed to in June 1775. He said that the assembly and the council elected in the spring of 1774 should meet, and if Gage did not attend, they should declare the governorship vacant. The council could then act as the executive. There must be unity, he said, and "you know there is a charm in the word 'constitutional.' " [72]

The advice from Philadelphia to submit to the suspension of justice, and of government, until the first Congress received a response from Britain, was accepted reluctantly by such towns as Worcester. That town demanded that the delegates to the Second Continental Congress be instructed to obtain advice concerning civil government as soon as possible. Worcester would abide by the decisions of the first Congress until the king replied to Congress's petition, unless hostilities began before then, and then its delegate was to endeavor to secure a government with the "best form possible . . . for the support of good order and the liberties of the people, which we think must and shall make every servant of the public dependent upon the suffrages of the people for their authority." [73]

James Warren was one easterner who was anxious for the assumption of civil government, and as he awaited the opening of the second provincial congress in January, he asked: "what reason can be given that the question for assuming and exercising government has not been stated and agitated in the public papers. Has any particular policy prevented?" [74]

The answer was that a group of men in Massachusetts were as opposed to the assumption of government as they were to the creation of an army and an attack upon the British troops in Boston. They blocked the westerners and such easterners as James and Joseph Warren during the winter, and while government was discussed from time to time, the provincial congresses deadlocked over the creation of a provincial army, a deadlock that was broken on the 19th of April 1775.

Early in May 1775 the issue of government came to the fore again (and remained there until long after the Declaration of Independence) when the committee of safety resolved that the public good of the colony required "that government in full form ought to be taken up immediately"

[71] To William Tudor, 29 Sept., *Works*, IX, 347–48.
[72] To Joseph Warren, 25 Sept., *Writings*, III, 156–57.
[73] *Worcester Town Records, 1753–83*, 252–53.
[74] To John Adams, 15 Jan., *Warren-Adams Letters*, I, 35–36.

and sent the resolution to the provincial congress sitting at Watertown.[75] On 1 April the congress had voted that if Gage issued writs for an election the towns should obey. On 4 May, after a "long and serious debate," 94 of the 107 men present agreed to reconsider. The next day the congress voted the 1 April decision null and void, declared that Gage was no longer fit to be governor, and called an election for a third congress to meet on 31 May. The towns and districts were to elect as many delegates as they wished. The congress then listened to the resolution of the committee of safety calling for the immediate adoption of a civil government, but it delayed consideration and turned to the question of what towns should send members, and how many members they should send to the next congress. A committee was appointed to consider the question of "equal representation." [76] "Equal representation," or representation by population, was a revolutionary idea that easterners seized upon for a counter-revolutionary purpose. They were alarmed by the aggressive westerners who demanded a revolution in government, and if they could substitute representation by population for representation by towns, the more populous east could control the new congress. The east failed in 1775, but in the spring of 1776 it won out.

The provincial congress ignored the call for the establishment of civil government as long as possible. On 12 May it delayed again by deciding to ask the Congress in Philadelphia for advice. An ingenuous letter said that since the question of civil government "equally affected our sister colonies," Massachusetts had declined to assume the reins of civil government without their advice and consent." But now "we tremble at having an army . . . without a civil power to provide for and control it." Therefore, Massachusetts wanted the "most explicit advice" and promised to abide by any "general plan" Congress might provide for the colonies, or to create for itself the best form of government possible.[77] Dr. Benjamin Church was elected to carry the letter to Philadelphia.[78]

The hope was that the Congress in Philadelphia would help the "moderate whigs" retain control. Warren's proposal for the immediate adoption of civil government early in May caused "some little uneasiness to the moderate whigs of the province" who argued that the provincial congress was an adequate government "until the Continental Congress had given their sanction to a form of government for us." [79]

[75] 3 May, JPCM, 536.   [76] Ibid. 190, 192–93, 195–96, 198.
[77] Ibid. 197, 207, 208, 219–20, 229–32.
[78] Church notified General Gage that he would not be able to send information while he was away. French, *Informers*, 155–57.
[79] David Cobb to Robert Treat Paine, 12 May, Paine Papers, MHS.

The "moderate whigs" were afraid of the ideas of such men as Joseph Warren, and of the people in the western counties who did not trust easterners any more than they trusted Englishmen. Worcester told its delegate to the third provincial congress that king and Parliament were "but a mere nose of wax turned and molded any and every way" by a despotic ministry intent on overthrowing the English constitution and plundering Americans of both liberty and property. And there were men in Massachusetts who were no different. The delegate was told that in granting public money, no man should be given more than adequate pay and that no person should "be allowed to live in luxury and idleness or become opulently rich at the public expense." Any community that allowed this would raise up another set of tyrants like those they were fighting against. Massachusetts should have a government in which all officers were "dependent on the suffrages of the people for their place and pay." [80]

Joseph Warren agreed with the westerners that certain Americans could not be trusted and he was opposed to the charter of 1691. He told Samuel Adams that he could not believe the Continental Congress would advise Massachusetts to assume government under it because it contained the seeds of despotism. What he wanted was a government in which "the only road to promotion may be through the affection of the people." Then the interest of the governor and the governed would be the same and "we shall no longer be plagued by a group of unprincipled villains, who have acted as though they thought they had a right to plunder and destroy their countrymen, as soon as they could obtain permission from Great Britain for doing it." [81]

Entirely apart from the form of government, Warren insisted that civil government must be established as soon as possible. If the southern colonies had any fears of the northern colonies, they certainly ought to realize that if there were no civil government to control an army taking the field, "a military government must certainly take place. . . ." [82]

Warren and others had reason for alarm. To prevent the members of congress from being seized by soldiers eagerly searching for traitors, the congress ordered 600 passes printed for its members as early as 1 May.[83] James Warren told John Adams that there was "such confusion" that he did not know where to begin or to end in describing it. Recommendations had to take the place of laws, and such "government" as there was, was "destitute of coercive power, exposed to the caprice of the people, and de-

[80] 29 May, *Worcester Town Records, 1753–83*, 264–66.
[81] To Samuel Adams, 14 May 1775, Frothingham, *Warren*, 483.
[82] To Samuel Adams, 17 May, ibid. 485.   [83] JPCM, 174.

pending entirely on their virtue for success." A little later he declared that government should have been created six months earlier and lamented that there was "a degree of timidity and slowness in our movements which my soul abominates." [84]

Conditions grew worse. At the end of May, Joseph Warren told Samuel Adams that the soldiers would get completely out of hand, and apparently some had done so. Warren said that "the least hint from the most unprincipled fellow, who has perhaps been reproved for some criminal behavior, is quite sufficient to expose the fairest character to insult and abuse among many; and it is with our countrymen as with all other men, when they are in arms, they think the military should be uppermost." Warren hoped that the Continental Congress would provide an immediate remedy, for "the infection is caught by every new corps that arrives." [85]

Despite the conviction of such men as the Warrens that there was an immediate and even desperate need for a civil government, the provincial congress waited to hear from Philadelphia although some members of it spelled out in ever more specific terms their fears of revolution. Elbridge Gerry, the wealthy Marblehead merchant who had supported Samuel Adams in opposition to Britain, was alarmed at the upsurge of popular feeling and demands for change, and he outlined precisely how it had come about. Government could not be adopted too soon, for "the people are fully possessed of their dignity from the frequent delineation of their rights, which have been published to defeat the ministerial party. . . . They now feel rather too much their own importance, and it requires great skill to produce such subordination as is necessary." This was evident, "principally in the army," and civil government and a "regular general" were needed to discipline it.[86]

Nearly a month after the provincial congress sent its appeal for advice to Philadelphia, a group of men prepared a second appeal which had a note of hysteria about it. (If the word "communist" had been current at the time, the appeal would have used it.) It asserted that because of the lack of civil government "there are, in many parts of this colony, alarming symptoms of the abatement of the sense, in the minds of some people, of the sacredness of private property, which is plainly assignable to the want of civil government; and your honors must be fully sensible, that a com-

---

[84] To John Adams, 7 May, and to Mercy Warren, 18 May, *Warren-Adams Letters*, I, 46–50.
[85] To Samuel Adams, 26 May, Frothingham, *Warren*, 495–96.
[86] To the Massachusetts Delegates in Congress, 4 June, Force, 4 ser. II, 905. Gerry suggested that Washington would be an acceptable general.

munity of goods and estate, will soon be followed with the utter waste and destruction of the goods themselves. . . ." [87] Joseph Hawley, who helped prepare the appeal, felt that it had not gone far enough in expressing the "irrepressible disadvantage" resulting from the lack of government.[88]

The Congress in Philadelphia voted on 9 June that Massachusetts need not obey the government act of 1774, and that in order "to conform, as near as may be, to the spirit and substance of the charter," the provincial congress should call upon the towns to elect representatives to the assembly. The assembly should then elect a council and the two houses could govern the colony until a governor appointed by the king "will consent to govern the colony according to its charter." [89] "Your government was the best we could obtain for you," John Adams told James Warren.[90]

The advice was a bold step forward for the Continental Congress, which had refused to give such advice in the fall of 1774, and it was welcome advice for the "moderate whigs" in Massachusetts who looked backward to the restoration of the old order. The provincial congress at once issued broadsides directing the towns to hold elections for an assembly to meet on 19 July, to observe the property qualifications for voting, and to elect only the number of delegates the old law entitled them to.[91]

The advice did not please James Warren, who was elected president of the congress to succeed Joseph Warren who had been killed on Breed's Hill the day the advice was received. He told Samuel Adams that while they were grateful, "we could only have wished you had suffered us to have embraced so good an opportunity to form for ourselves a constitution worthy of freemen." The day after he was chosen speaker of the newly elected assembly, he bewailed that "so much moderation and timidity still prevail here that there is no doing without them," and that he almost wished that "we were again reduced to a congress till we had a constitution worth contending for." As the months went by he was more and more opposed to the semi-restoration of the old order and many people of the backcountry counties agreed. Furthermore, he called for independence. He made his attitude toward the mother country clear in a comment: "No news from England. What the old squaw is about we can't conjecture and don't much care. I hope she is raising troops to subdue America." [92]

[87] 11 June, JPCM, 318–20.
[88] To Robert Treat Paine, 12 June, Paine Papers, MHS.
[89] JCC, II, 83–84.   [90] 27 June, Warren-Adams Letters, I, 67.
[91] JPCM, 358–60.
[92] To Samuel Adams, 21 June, 20 July, 4 Aug., Warren-Adams Letters, II, 413, 415–16, 418.

When he heard of the king's proclamation in August declaring the existence of a state of rebellion, he hoped that it would put an end to petitioning and that he expected such actions as "a declaration of independency,
treaties with foreign powers" and the like from Congress, actions which
"may now perhaps be considered by even piddling genius as not exceeding
the line of moderation." He agreed with his wife, Mercy Warren, who told
him to tell John Adams that he "should no longer piddle at the threshold.
It is time to leap into the theater, to unlock the bars, and open every gate
that impedes the rise and growth of the American republic. . . ." [93]

The Warrens were a minority, and leaders in other colonies, as well as in
Massachusetts, were resisting the idea of independence. Their resistance
was based in part on loyalty to Britain—a loyalty that had many roots—
and in part on their fear of the consequences of the "rise of the people."

When Elbridge Gerry told the Massachusetts delegates in Congress that
"the people are fully possessed of their dignity from the frequent delineation of their rights, which have been published to defeat the ministerial
party" and that "they now feel rather too much their own importance, and
it requires great skill to produce such subordination as is necessary," he was
describing a process and a result that had taken place in every colony, and
the problem facing those who feared that independence might mean a
revolution at home.

South Carolina was no more exempt than Massachusetts from the consequences of appeals to the people for support. William Henry Drayton
published a newspaper statement in 1769 asserting that while illiterate men
might know how to cut up meat, cobble shoes, and build necessary houses,
"nature never intended that such men should be profound politicians or
able statesmen. . . ." The Charleston mechanics were openly contemptuous in their reply. They could not see that his "liberal education" had produced "good fruits" in either his public or private life, and his language,
despite his use of Latin tags, was better suited to the "high-bred dames" of
Billingsgate and Drury Lane. The mechanics, at least, had common sense
and could tell right from wrong, and they loved their country, whereas
Drayton had shown that "an attachment of this sort is not one of his ruling passions." Drayton had inherited and married money whereas the
mechanics worked with their hands and were "the most useful people in a
community. . . ." If Drayton had to earn a living with either his head or

93 To Samuel Adams, 12 Nov., and John Adams, 14 Nov., ibid. II, 426; I, 184.

his hands, the mechanics doubted that he was qualified for any business that required either knowledge or skill.[94]

The gentry were not accustomed to such replies, and they found the mechanics had power. When a clergyman in South Carolina in 1774 denounced "every silly clown, and illiterate mechanic" who undertook to censure "his prince or governor," and told such men to keep to their own rank, the mechanics demanded that he be fired and he was.[95] The tale was told throughout America. A Virginia newspaper picked it up from a Rhode Island newspaper with the comment that "all such divines should be taught to know that mechanics and country clowns (infamously so called) are the real and absolute masters of king, lords, commons, and priests; though (with shame be it spoken) they too often suffer their servants to get upon their backs and ride them most barbarously." [96]

During the Tea Act crisis a perceptive Philadelphian described the danger of using the people for political ends. He said that "unless internal peace is speedily settled, our most wise and sensible citizens dread the anarchy and confusion that must ensue." Philadelphia had been peaceable with no mobs, no insults to individuals, no injury to private property, but "the frequent appeals to the people must in time occasion a change, and we every day perceive it more and more difficult to repress the rising spirit of the people." [97]

By 1774 it was evident that the sovereignty of the people, in practice if not in theory, had reared what was to some its ugly head. What this might mean for the old order was well put by Gouverneur Morris, who attended a New York mass meeting called in May 1774 to discuss an answer to Boston's plea for the stoppage of trade. He reported that both the "people of property" and the populace appeared, and that in addition to talking about Boston they debated "about the future forms of our government, whether it should be founded upon aristocratic or democratic principles." "The mob began to think and reason. Poor reptiles! It is with them a vernal morning . . . and ere noon they will bite, depend upon it." Morris predicted that if the disputes with Britain continued, "farewell aristocracy . . . we shall be under the worst of all possible dominions; we shall be under the domination of a riotous mob." The solution, he said, was "reunion with the parent state." [98]

With less rhetoric but with equal clarity Lieutenant Governor William

---

[94] SCG(T), 21 Sept., 5 Oct. 1769.
[95] Walsh, *Charleston's Sons of Liberty*, 71.   [96] VG(P), 13 Oct. 1774.
[97] Joseph Reed to Dartmouth, 27 Dec. 1773, Reed, *Life*, I, 55.
[98] To [John] Penn, 20 May, EHD, IX, 861–62.

Bull commented on the rise of the power of the people in South Carolina. "The men of property," he said, "begin at length to see that the many-headed power the people, who have hitherto been obediently made use of by their numbers and occasional riots to support the claims set up in America, have discovered their own strength and importance, and are not now so easily governed by their former leaders." [99]

A New Jersey councilor expressed the same feeling when he asked: "what then have men of property not to fear and apprehend" if they are known to differ "in sentiment from the generality? They become a mark at once for popular fury" and are not even allowed to remain neutral. Governor Franklin sent the letter to England with the comment that none of the "gentlemen of the country" would draw their swords to support taxation by Parliament, but they would support the supremacy of Parliament in other respects. "There is indeed a dread in the minds of many here, that some of the leaders of the people are aiming to establish a republic. . . ." [100]

The dilemma of those Americans who denied the right of Parliament to tax America, but who opposed independence and were fearful of an internal revolution, was summed up by Sir William Tryon, governor of New York. He returned from England on the same day that General George Washington passed through New York en route to Massachusetts.[101] Tryon pointed out that "independency is shooting from the root of the present contest" but that he would be doing a "great injustice to America were I to hold up an idea that the bulk of its inhabitants wishes an independency." He was positive that "a very large majority" of New York was opposed to independence but that "the great affliction is, the American friends of government in general consider themselves between Scylla and Charybdis, that is the dread of parliamentary taxation and the tyranny of their present masters." [102]

While most Americans probably opposed the right of Parliament to tax the colonies, and her use of military force, some Americans dreaded even more the "tyranny of their present masters." It was a dread that grew and it drove them to abandon principle and cling to Britain to save them from what seemed to be a far more immediate and pressing danger. They hoped that the Second Continental Congress would block a declaration of inde-

[99] To SS, 28 March 1775, quoted in Rogers, W. L. Smith, 78.
[100] Daniel Coxe to Cortland Skinner, 4 July, and Franklin to SS, 2 Aug. 1775, N.J. Ar., 1 ser. X, 652–55.
[101] Smith, Memoirs, 228c.   [102] To SS, 7 Aug. 1775, NYCD, VIII, 603–4.

pendence if it were proposed, and they hoped that Britain would offer terms that would make a reconciliation possible. They hoped in vain because Britain adopted measure after measure during the winter of 1775–76 that justified the contentions of those Americans who insisted that reconciliation was impossible, and that the only alternative to absolute submission was a declaration of American independence.

XXIV

The Dream of Reconciliation and the
Drive for Independence 1775–1776

The question of independence loomed ever larger after the Continental Congress re-assembled in mid-September 1775. To begin with, however, the delegates had to deal with a host of problems arising from their decision to create a continental army and to finance a war. Congress had no administrative staff except for the secretary, Charles Thomson, and two treasurers who were appointed after the vote to issue paper money in July. Congress therefore appointed one committee after another as problems arose, and the delegates worked from early morning to late at night, acting as accountants, clerks, and secretaries, as well as members of Congress. Special committees were elected from time to time to visit the army, Ticonderoga, and Canada. By the end of the year another series of committees had evolved into the "Naval Committee" which wrote "Rules for the Regulation of the Navy of the United Colonies" and created a continental navy of four small armed vessels. In November, Congress established a committee of correspondence soon known as the "Secret Committee of Correspondence," and then in 1777 the Committee for Foreign Affairs.[1]

One of the first, and one of the most important and controversial, committees was created on 18 September to buy military supplies as secretly as possible.[2] In a short time it too was known as the "Secret Committee," and it was in trouble almost at once. According to certain outraged members of Congress it made a contract with Robert Morris for gunpowder

[1] See JCC, III, passim, for the evolution of the many committees and their work. Congress soon began to hire clerks but the burden remained on the members of Congress.
[2] JCC, II, 253–54.

by which he was to be paid £14 a barrel if he delivered the powder, and if it were seized by British naval vessels or customs officers he would still receive £14 a barrel. He would make a profit of £12,000 no matter what happened. Thomas Willing, Morris's partner, said he knew nothing of the contract but extolled his partner's character, and merchant members of Congress argued that it was a good contract because Morris could sell powder to Philadelphia at £19 a barrel. The problem, as one Virginian saw it, was: "The contract is made and the money paid. How can we get it back?"[3] Whether or not Congress got either the money or the powder is unknown. As for Robert Morris, Pennsylvania soon elected him to Congress, and before the end of the year he was chairman of the Secret Committee. Between then and 1777 the committee received about $2,000,000 from Congress to buy supplies and nearly one-fourth of it went to the firm of Willing and Morris. Throughout the war there were charges of profiteering and corruption (and they were true) which embittered political life during the war and long after it.[4]

A far more immediate issue facing Congress in the fall of 1775 arose from the fact that the non-exportation provision of the Association went into effect on 10 September. The delegates from New York, Delaware, North Carolina, and Georgia, which had been exempted from the acts restraining the trade of other colonies, offered all sorts of ingenious arguments to prove that all America would benefit if the Association was broken and their merchants continued to export. The delegates from the colonies whose trade was restrained were unimpressed. After a protracted debate Congress strengthened the Association. It thanked the four colonies for not taking advantage of the Restraining Act in the past, and then ordered that no produce be exported until 1 March 1775 without the permission of Congress. The only exception was the exportation of produce to pay for arms and ammunition.[5]

No problems were more harassing than those involving the army. The difficulties in electing generals during the summer were the merest foretaste of what was to come. When Congress re-assembled in September it was presented with letters demanding medicine, powder, more money to

<hr />

[3] John Adams, Notes of Debates, 24 Sept., *Diary*, II, 183–84.
[4] E. James Ferguson, "Business, Government, and Congressional Investigation in the Revolution," WMQ, 3 ser. XVI (1959).
[5] 1 Nov., JCC, III, 313–14.

pay the soldiers, and the like. Even more important were the letters from the commander in chief.

General George Washington was shaken by what he found in Massachusetts. There were generals without regiments and field officers without companies, and the regiments and companies from different colonies were of different sizes. Washington was appalled by the scarcity of powder, the cowardice of some officers, and the frauds committed by others.

He was utterly contemptuous of the people of Massachusetts but, fortunately for himself, he confined his remarks to private letters. He told one of his relatives that the people of Massachusetts "have obtained a character which they by no means deserved; their officers, generally speaking, are the most indifferent kind of people I ever saw." The men might fight well if properly officered "although they are an exceeding dirty and nasty people," and if they had been properly led at Bunker Hill the British would have "met with a shameful defeat" and lost more than 1057 killed and wounded. Washington told Richard Henry Lee that there was "an unaccountable kind of stupidity in the lower class of these people which, believe me, prevails but too generally among the officers of the Massachusetts part of the army who are nearly of the same kidney with the privates. . . ." He reported that he had cashiered some officers for corruption and that he had "made a pretty good slam among such kind of officers as the Massachusetts abound in since I came to this camp, having broke one colonel and two captains for cowardly behavior in the action on Bunker Hill. . . ." The British who fought the Americans on that day had far more respect for them. General Burgoyne reported that "their defense was well-conceived and obstinately maintained. Their retreat was no flight; it was covered with bravery, and even military skill. . . ." [6] The fact was that the "dirty and nasty people" of New England had delivered a devastating blow to the British, one that Washington was unable to equal after he took command.

Washington, like many another southerner, was shocked at the independence and the "democracy" that prevailed among the New Englanders. One of his aides, Joseph Reed, explained that the attempt to introduce discipline and subordination into a new army was always difficult, "but where the principles of democracy so universally prevail, where so great an equality and so thorough a levelling spirit predominates," either no discipline can be established or the one who tries to do so becomes odious

[6] To Lund Washington, 20 Aug., and Richard Henry Lee, 29 Aug., Writings, III, 433, 450–51; Abstract from letter of Burgoyne, 25 June, Geo. III, Corres., III, 224–25.

and detestable. As an example of the equality between officers and men he reported that "a captain of horse, who attends the General, from Connecticut, was seen shaving one of his men on the parade near the house." [7] The New Englanders, who elected their own officers, could not see why the town barber should stop work merely because he had been elected a captain, but southerners could not understand such a point of view.

Congress did not act until 29 September when it received a letter from Washington declaring that unless something was done in a hurry "the army must absolutely break up." The Connecticut and Rhode Island troops were enlisted only until 1 December and no troops at all were enlisted beyond the end of the year. The men were naked or soon would be. They had not been paid and were on the point of mutiny. There were quarrels about rank and differences in pay. And there was an appalling lack of distinction between officers and privates where there ought to be proper subordination and discipline.[8]

Congress elected a committee, none of whom were New Englanders, to talk to Washington and New England officials.[9] It then prepared instructions for the committee which showed that Congress was at least as interested in saving money as it was alarmed by the horrendous account in Washington's letter. The committee was to tell Washington that it was the "sense" of Congress that the British should be driven from Boston before the end of the year. If he could not do so, then it was the "wish" of Congress that he reduce the number of soldiers for the rest of the winter, and reduce the pay of those who remained to five dollars a month. However, the committee was to talk to Washington about raising a "continental army" for the year 1776.[10]

When the committee returned to Philadelphia from its trip to New England, it proposed that Washington be given everything he asked for, and Congress agreed. A "new army" of more than 20,000 men would be enlisted to serve until the end of 1776. The size of regiments and companies was standardized. The pay of captains, lieutenants, and ensigns was raised. The articles of war were amended to give Washington sweeping powers of punishment. Penalties ranged from seven days of bread and water for soldiers away without leave to thirty-nine lashes for drunkenness

[7] To Mrs. Reed, 11 Oct., Reed, *Life*, I, 243.
[8] To the President of Congress, 21 Sept., *Writings*, III, 505-13.
[9] JCC, III, 265-66. Benjamin Franklin (Pa.), Benjamin Harrison (Va.), and Thomas Lynch (S.C.) were the committee.
[10] Ibid. 270-71.

and theft, and to death for cowardice, sedition, and desertion to the enemy.[11] Thomas Lynch of South Carolina, a member of the committee, told Washington: "The articles of war has all the amendments we reported. You will enforce them. You will not now suffer your officers to sweep the parade [with] the skirts of their coats or bottoms of their trousers, to cheat or to mess with their men, to skulk in battle or sneak in quarters, in short being now paid they must do their duty and look as well as act like gentlemen." [12]

Despite his new powers, Washington continued to complain. He declared "such a dearth of public spirit, and want of virtue, such stockjobbing, and fertility in all the low arts to obtain advantages of one kind or another, in this great change of military arrangement, I never saw before, and pray God I may never be witness to again." By the end of November he had managed to enlist only 3500 men and to get that many he had to give furloughs to as many as fifty men in a regiment. He declared that "such a dirty, mercenary spirit pervades the whole" that he would not be surprised at any disaster. By the last of the month the lines would be so weak that he would have to call in the minute men and militia to defend them and this would "destroy the little subordination" he had achieved. "Could I have foreseen what I have, and am likely to experience, no consideration upon earth should have induced me to accept this command." [13]

On New Year's Day 1776, Washington issued a general order proclaiming the "commencement to the new army, which, in every point of view, is entirely continental," and recommended "a laudable spirit of emulation" without which very few officers ever achieved much of a reputation. As for the privates, he asserted that "subordination and discipline" were "the life and soul of an army" and that without them an army was no better than a "commissioned mob." [14]

Despite the proclamation, recruiting went no better than it had, and Washington's letters continued to tell of an army without adequate supplies, money, and discipline despite all his efforts. Washington's difficulties were partly the result of his attitude and that of southerners in general, who did not like New Englanders or their "democracy." They preferred to retain their prejudices and had power enough in Congress to enforce them.

The idea of a continental army itself was offensive to many New

[11] 4, 7 Nov., ibid. 321–24, 330–34.   [12] 13 Nov., LMCC, I, 253–54.
[13] To Joseph Reed, 28 Nov., Writings, IV, 124–25.   [14] Writings, IV, 202–4.

Englanders, as Samuel Ward of Rhode Island tried to explain to Congress. The attempt to create a "wholly continental" army had "induced so many alterations disgusting to both officers and men" that recruiting was difficult. Nevertheless, the southerners insisted on detaching both officers and men from their own colonies and making them "look up to the continent at large for their support or promotion." [15]

The dispute over pay was equally important. Joseph Hawley warned that the southerners in the army had a "strange mistaken opinion" that the pay of privates was too high and that of officers too low, and warned that unless Congress did more for the privates "you will have no winter army." He insisted that there must be a small enlistment bounty.[16]

There would be no bounty, replied John Adams, and the forty shillings a month for privates was obtained only after "much altercation" and many an anxious day and night of effort. It was simply impossible to suddenly alter the "temper, principles, opinions, or prejudices of men. The characters of gentlemen in the four New England colonies differ as much from those in the others, as that of the common people differs; that is, as much as several distinct nations almost." There were far fewer gentlemen "of sense or any kind of education" in the other colonies than in New England. They had "large plantations of slaves, and the common people among them are very ignorant and very poor. These gentlemen are accustomed, habituated to higher notions of themselves, and the distinction between them and the common people, than we are."

But Adams was a realist and he was convinced that however ignorant and arrogant southern gentlemen might be, New England had to have their support. He begged Hawley: "for God's sake, therefore, reconcile our people to what has been done" for nothing more could be expected from Congress.[17]

Despite exhortations many New Englanders refused to be reconciled and enlist in the new army. Men who had been electing their own officers disliked the arrogance of gentlemen and would-be gentlemen from other colonies, and the brutality of some of them. Flogging was the customary way of enforcing discipline in European armies but the attempt to flog New England farmers and artisans into the "subordination" Washington demanded was probably disastrous. This was not the kind of "freedom" many New Englanders were willing to fight for. Nevertheless, Congress

---

[15] To Henry Ward, 21 Nov., LMCC, I, 256.
[16] To John Adams, 14 Nov., Adams, *Works*, IX, 364.
[17] To Hawley, 25 Nov., ibid. 366-67.

had approved up to thirty-nine lashes for various breaches of regulations such as drunkenness and theft in November 1775, and raised the maximum to a hundred lashes in September 1776.[18] And that maximum could be made even more effective by spreading it over two days and then washing the man with salt and water, as was done to a would-be deserter in 1778.[19]

There were of course some men who did enlist in the continental army, but Washington could not raise the army he wanted. Of the more than 20,000-man army that had been planned, by mid-February he had enlisted only 8797 privates fit for duty, and another 1040 that could be called to camp.[20]

In time a continental army of professional quality was created, but it was never large enough to free itself from dependence upon the state militias in times of emergency. The militiamen sometimes fought well and sometimes ran away to fight another day, but however much they were despised by Washington and his officers, they too played a role in the winning of the war for independence.

In creating a continental army, Congress had taken a major step toward the final break with Britain although few if any delegates seemed to realize it as they squabbled over pay, rank, and the like. Furthermore, the delegates struggled to cope with such a mountain of detail from day to day that it was often difficult to keep larger issues in mind. Thus, after the committee on claims had approved a bill for $22 from Timothy Matlack for wood supplied to Congress, the entire Congress had to vote that it be paid.[21] Likewise the Congress had to vote that soldiers in barracks near Philadelphia should be supplied with forty iron pots.[22] It turned from such petty matters on one day to resolving the next day that if Washington thought he could make a successful attack on the British in Boston, "he do it in any manner he may think expedient, notwithstanding the town and the property in it may thereby be destroyed." [23]

The Congress was also beset by quarrels between colonies and within colonies. The Connecticut delegates told Congress that they had been unable to agree with the Pennsylvania delegates about the Susquehanna Valley, that the people of the two colonies in the valley "had proceeded

[18] JCC, V, 806.   [19] General Orders, 25 March, Washington, *Writings*, XI, 143.
[20] French, *First Year of the Revolution*, chapter XXXI.   [21] JCC, III, 310.
[22] Ibid. 441.   [23] Ibid. 445.

to bloodshed," and asked Congress to appoint a committee. Congress repeatedly appealed to the two colonies to stop the hostilities.[24] They refused and the disruptive quarrel lasted until after the end of the war. Equally disruptive were internal quarrels in South and North Carolina, where many former Regulators were inclined to remain loyal to Britain, and the Scottish Highlanders who had settled in the Carolina back-country after 1745 were not only loyal, but were skilled fighters as well. South Carolina was able to handle its problem without outside help, but North Carolina was so divided that it appealed to Congress. Congress urged other colonies to supply North Carolina with gunpowder, promised to pay two battalions to be raised in North Carolina, and agreed to give forty dollars a month to each of "two ministers of the gospel" to go "amongst the regulators and highlanders in the colony of North Carolina for the purpose of informing them of the nature of the present dispute between Great Britain and the colonies. . . ."[25]

Congress was rocked when it learned in October that Dr. Benjamin Church had been caught corresponding with the enemy.[26] Church's old associates, the two Adamses, were stunned. "Our pride is sorely mortified," wrote Samuel Adams, "when there are grounds to suspect that so eminent a countryman is become a traitor. The fool will say in his heart, there is no such thing in the world as public spirit" and the "most virtuous citizen" will be suspected and "the brightest examples will lose their influence."[27] "There is a fatality attends our province," said John Adams. "It seems destined to fall into contempt."[28]

Such matters were only a few among the many that came before Congress during the fall of 1775. They tended at times to obscure the overriding issue of the purpose of the war. But when that fundamental question was brought before Congress, it was clear at once that the division of opinion so evident during the summer was sharper than ever. New Hampshire requested advice about government on 18 October. The initiative had come from New Hampshire delegates in Philadelphia who had urged the provincial congress to send a petition insisting that a formal government was needed in order to tax, otherwise paper money would ruin the colony.[29] All the delegates got was an instruction to ask advice, and they

---

[24] Ibid. 295, 321, 439–40 for examples.   [25] Ibid. 387–88.
[26] French, *Informers*, chapter V.
[27] To James Warren, 13 Oct., *Warren-Adams Letters*, I, 140–41.
[28] To James Warren, 18 Oct., ibid. 143.
[29] Josiah Bartlett and John Langdon to Matthew Thornton, 2 Oct., LMCC, I, 213.

did so. John Adams recalled later that he had "embraced with joy the opportunity of haranguing on the subject at large," and of urging Congress to call on all the colonies to create regular governments. The "opposition was still inveterate," but finally on 26 October Congress appointed a committee· with John Rutledge as chairman and John Adams, Samuel Ward, Roger Sherman, and Richard Henry Lee as members. The committee was "as well disposed to encourage the enterprise" as could be found in Congress but it could not agree to a report until 3 November. By that time, Adams said, he mortally hated the words "province," "colonies," "mother country," and strove to get them out of the report. All he managed to eliminate were the words "mother country." "Nevertheless, I thought this resolution a triumph and a most important point gained." [30]

The report was indeed a great step beyond the advice given to Massachusetts in June. It recommended that the New Hampshire convention "call a full and free representation of the people, and that the representatives, if they think it necessary, establish such a form of government, as, in their judgment, will best produce the happiness of the people" and secure peace and good order during the continuance of the "present dispute between Great Britain and the Colonies." [31]

The New Hampshire delegates reported that "the arguments on this matter (being the first of the kind, as we had no charter) were truly Ciceronial. . . ." They pointed out that "the government is limited to the present contest. To ease the minds of some few persons who were fearful of independence, we thought it advisable not to oppose that part too much. . . ." The delegates rejoiced at the "groundwork" and "hope by the blessing of divine providence never to return to our former despotic state." [32] The next day John Rutledge asked for and received the same advice for South Carolina. [33]

The two Adamses were delighted. Samuel Adams declared that the time was near "when the most timid will see the absolute necessity of every one of the colonies setting up a government within itself." "We live in a most important age. . . . It is the Age of George the Third; and to do justice to our most gracious king, I will affirm it as my opinion that his councils and administration will necessarily produce the grandest revolu-

---

[30] *Autobiography*, III, 354–57.   [31] JCC, III, 319.
[32] To Matthew Thornton, 3 Nov., LMCC, I, 246–47.
[33] JCC, III, 326–27. Virginia was given similar advice on 4 December after Dunmore declared martial law in November. Ibid. 403–4.

tions the world has ever yet seen. The wheels of providence seem to be in their swiftest motion." Samuel Adams was one who helped keep those wheels going, although he professed to believe he should be recalled, for "men of moderate abilities, especially when weakened by age, are not fit to be employed in founding empires." [34] John Adams asked rhetorically: "who expected to live to see the principles of liberty spread and prevail so rapidly, human nature exerting her whole rights, unshackled by priests, or kings or nobles, pulling down tyrannies like Samson, and building up what governments the people think best framed for human felicity?" [35]

Happiness with the advice to New Hampshire and South Carolina was far from universal. James Warren in Massachusetts congratulated the two colonies and bewailed the plight of Massachusetts, surrounded by governments founded on proper principles "and constituted to promote the free and equal liberty of mankind." "I hate the name of our charter, which fascinates and shackles us. I hate the monarchical part of our government," and he assured John Adams that he would too if he knew "our present monarchs." Warren was bitter about the council which demanded all the powers of a royal governor. "They have got a whirl in their brains, imagine themselves kings, and have assumed every air and pomp of royalty but the crown and scepter." [36]

Some people in New Hampshire were alarmed. Petitions from Portsmouth and several other towns protested that the assumption of government would be a step in the direction of independence. Despite the protests, the provincial congress declared itself a house of representatives on 5 January 1776 and elected a council while maintaining that "we never sought to throw off our dependence upon Great Britain" and "we shall rejoice" if the Continental Congress achieves reconciliation.[37]

No one was more alarmed than John Dickinson, and six days after Congress advised New Hampshire to create a government to secure "the happiness of the people," he began a campaign to prevent adoption of a declaration of independence, if one were proposed. The Pennsylvania assembly instructed its new delegation in Congress: "we strictly enjoin you, that you, in behalf of this colony, dissent from and utterly reject any propositions, should such be made, that may cause or lead to a separation from our mother country, or a change of the form of this government." [38]

[34] To James Warren, 4 Nov., *Warren-Adams Letters*, I, 170-71.
[35] To James Warren, 5 Nov., ibid. 175.
[36] To John Adams, 14 Nov., ibid. 181-82.
[37] Force, 4 ser. V, 1-3; ibid. IV, 459-60.   [38] 9 Nov., Force, 4 ser. III, 1792-93.

The instructions were attacked at once. One newspaper writer asserted that the delegates to the Congress were the delegates of the people, not of the assembly, and that the giving of instructions was the sacred right of the people at election time.[39] When another newspaper writer denied that there was any danger of independence, "Independent Whig" replied that the only solution was independence.[40]

Delaware, the "three lower counties" of Pennsylvania, was likewise opposed to independence. When the assembly elected delegates to the Second Continental Congress it had told them to "studiously avoid . . . everything disrespectful or offensive to our most gracious sovereign, or in any measure invasive of his just rights and prerogative."[41]

New Jersey followed Pennsylvania's lead when the assembly met in November. Several petitions were presented urging that it discourage any attempt to promote independence, and it was Governor William Franklin's opinion that the majority of the people were opposed to independence. The assembly declared that "reports of independence" were groundless, but it instructed the New Jersey delegates in Congress to reject any proposition "that may separate this colony from the mother country, or change the form of government thereof." The assembly also voted to petition the king to intervene to prevent bloodshed, but gave it up when an agitated Congress in Philadelphia sent a delegation to persuade the assembly to maintain the "union" of the colonies. Ironically, two opponents of independence, John Dickinson and John Jay, were members of the congressional delegation.[42] The colonial assembly of New Jersey never met again.

Despite the fact that Maryland had been governed by a revolutionary convention ever since 1774, no colony was more adamantly opposed to independence. On 11 January it told its delegates that they were not to consent to independence, alliances with any foreign power, or any union or confederation of the colonies unless a majority of them thought it absolutely necessary. However, if the Continental Congress should go against the judgment of the Maryland delegates and declare independence or take any actions that might lead to it, the Maryland delegates were to return to the convention to report. The Maryland convention "will not hold this province bound by such majority in Congress until the representative body of the province, in convention, assent thereto." A few days

[39] PJ, 22 Nov.   [40] Ibid. 29 Nov.   [41] 29 March 1775, Force, 4 ser. II, 129.
[42] Governor Franklin to SS, 5 Jan. 1776, N.J. Ar. 1 ser. X, 676–78; Force, 4 ser. III, 1851–65, 1874–75.

later the Maryland convention made its position even clearer after it learned of the king's speech to Parliament in October in which he declared that the rebellion in America was being waged to win independence. The convention declared that "the people of this province . . . being thoroughly convinced that to be free subjects of the king of Great Britain, with all its consequences, is to be the freest members of any civil society in the known world, never did, nor do entertain any views or desires of independency." [43] Most of the Maryland delegates agreed with the convention. One of them reported that he showed the instructions in confidence to "the Pennsylvania Farmer" and others, who said that "they breathe that spirit, which ought to govern all public bodies, firmness tempered with moderation." [44]

John Dickinson's campaign to block independence and a revolution in the government of Pennsylvania, in the hope that reconciliation could be achieved, received its first setback on the day the Pennsylvania legislature adopted the instructions Dickinson wrote for himself and the other Pennsylvania delegates to Congress. On 9 November, Congress listened to a letter from Richard Penn and Arthur Lee who reported that the king had scorned the second petition to him by refusing to receive it "on the throne," and therefore no answer would be given.[45] Earlier, Congress heard of the royal proclamation in August, which declared that many Americans were "engaged in open and avowed rebellion," and that those people in England who were corresponding with or aiding and abetting the Americans, should be brought to "condign punishment." [46]

The rejection of the second petition to the king, and the news that Britain was sending still more troops, confirmed the belief of those who were convinced that reconciliation was impossible.[47] Even some of those who wanted reconciliation, like Joseph Hewes of North Carolina, confessed that "we have scarcely a dawn of hope" that it can be achieved.[48]

Their hopes were also being destroyed by events in America as well as by news from England, and notably by the actions of some of the colonial governors. Governor Josiah Martin of North Carolina urged a royal pardon for the Regulators and fled to a British warship in July. He assured British officials that if they would send him arms and ammunition

[43] Proceedings of the Maryland Convention, 11, 18 Jan. 1776, Force, 4 ser. IV, 738–40.
[44] Robert Alexander to the Maryland Council of Safety, 30 Jan., LMCC, I, 334.
[45] JCC, III, 343 and n.
[46] 23 Aug., EHD, IX, 850–51. For Congress's answer see JCC, III, 409–12.
[47] Samuel Ward to Henry Ward, 11 Nov., LMCC, I, 251–52.
[48] To Samuel Johnston, 9 Nov., LMCC, I, 251.

he could regain control of North Carolina with the help of Scottish Highlanders and former Regulators in the backcountry.[49]

The new governor of South Carolina, Lord William Campbell, arrived in Charleston in June. He refused to recognize the provincial congress and called the legislature to meet on 10 July. He sent messages to it denouncing "outrageous," "illegal," and "barbarous" acts, and finally declared that he and his family were unsafe.

The assembly replied that it was not surprised that the people had been driven to extremities and had adopted measures not warranted by written law. So far as the assembly was concerned those acts were more "justifiable and constitutional than many of the late acts of the British administration." As for the governor's safety, the assembly told him that "in times like the present . . . it is not in our power . . . to prescribe limits to popular fury." The governor dissolved the assembly on 30 August, and like the governor of North Carolina, fled to a British warship. He too assured British officials that with troops, and the help of loyal backcountrymen, he could regain control of his colony.[50]

Virginia's leaders made an effort to carry on government as usual when the House of Burgesses met in June 1775. The burgesses rejected Lord North's motion on reconciliation in one of the most eloquent statements of the American position written during the era. The burgesses had not met for a year and they tried to take care of the normal business of a session. But Dunmore refused to co-operate. He declared that he was unsafe on land and remained on board a British warship. He insisted that the burgesses must meet him there. They replied that it would be a breach of their privileges to do so. The wrangle continued until 24 June, when the oldest legislature in the New World died a reluctant death by adjourning itself.[51]

The leaders of the burgesses then turned to a convention in an attempt to regain control of Virginia. The convention in July and August levied taxes, issued paper money, created two Virginia regiments, and elected a committee of safety to serve as an executive body.

As in other colonies, the creation of the regiments involved politics. Patrick Henry's followers elected him colonel of the first regiment to the anguish of men who thought that Henry had too much popularity as it

[49] Martin to SS, 16 May, 30 June, 16 July, 30 Aug., NCCR, IX, 1257–58, X, 96–98, 41–50, 230–37.
[50] SCHJ, 10 July–30 Aug. See Lord North to George III, 15 Oct., Geo. III, Corres., III, 265–66, for a summary of letters from the governors of the southern colonies.
[51] JHB (1773–76), 173–283.

was. Such men controlled the committee of safety, however, and it controlled the movement of troops. Edmund Pendleton, its chairman, had been Henry's political enemy for a decade, and he saw to it that Henry had no chance to lead his regiment to glory. Pendleton, like other conservative Virginia leaders, wanted reconciliation if possible, and still looked upon Dunmore as the legal, if wayward, governor of Virginia.[52]

Unfortunately for the conservatives, the governor destroyed their hopes. He raised troops from among loyal Virginians, and he had a few British regulars and some British naval vessels. Then on 7 November he did more to convert many Virginians to the idea of independence than all the acts of Parliament since the founding of the colonies. He issued a proclamation offering freedom to all the slaves who would join his forces and fight their former masters!

Reluctantly the committee of safety decided that it must use force, but it kept Patrick Henry behind and sent the second regiment to oppose Dunmore. Its commander proceeded cautiously, and after a few skirmishes he finally occupied Norfolk with the help of some volunteers from North Carolina. On New Year's Day 1776, Dunmore ordered the town shelled. The shelling did some damage, but much more was done by the Virginia and North Carolina soldiers who raided grog shops and began pillaging and burning. By the end of the next day two-thirds of Norfolk had been destroyed.[53] All the blame was placed on Dunmore, and that, added to his proclamation offering freedom to the slaves, did much to destroy the hopes of those Virginians who wanted reconciliation.

And yet there were still Americans who continued to hope for reconciliation as the year 1775 came to an end, not knowing that Britain was taking more drastic measures than ever, measures which would justify those who soon insisted openly that Americans must declare their independence.

ॐ

Parliament had adjourned on 26 May 1775, the day before the American version of Lexington and Concord reached England. There was some excitement but, because it was an American version, the ministry assumed that the report must be unreliable. General Gage's account reached London on 10 June. It was far less lurid than the report of Joseph Warren, but the essential facts were the same, except that Gage said the Americans

[52] Virginia Convention Proceedings, Force, 4 ser. III, 365–430. Mays, *Pendleton*, II, 32–65, contains a detailed account of the politics involved in the command of the Virginia regiments.
[53] Mays, *Pendleton*, II, 66–85.

fired first. Most of the ministers relaxed but they could not ignore the news which reached London on 25 July of the decimation of British troops on Breed's Hill on 17 June.[54]

The next day Lord North told the king that the war in America "must be treated as a foreign war" and the cabinet decided that 20,000 troops should be sent by April 1776. George III agreed that reinforcements could not be sent until the next spring.[55] Two days later, he ordered that General Gage, who had been asking for 20,000 troops for months, should "instantly" return to England.[56]

Where could Britain raise 20,000 troops? Recruiting went so slowly that within a month Lord North reported that not more than 5000 or 6000 troops could be raised by the spring of 1776. North recommended that several men who had volunteered to raise troops be allowed to do so. The king flatly refused. He would not give commissions to "every young man that pretends he can soon complete them," for such troops had been no good in the past and would not be in the future. The thing to do was to fill the vacancies in regular regiments rather than recruit new corps.[57]

Earlier Dartmouth had told Sir Guy Johnson, the heir of Sir William Johnson, to persuade the Indians "to take up the hatchet against his Majesty's rebellious subjects in America"; [58] but Indians were at best uncertain allies. The only solution was to hire foreign troops. By 1 August, George III, who was Elector of Hanover as well as King of Great Britain, had arranged for more than 2000 Hanoverian soldiers to be sent to Gibraltar and Minorca. The troops there could then be sent to Ireland to replace men sent from Ireland to America.[59]

There had been talk of hiring 20,000 Russian troops as early as June, and George III wrote a personal letter to the Empress of Russia asking for Russian soldiers. He was indignant at the reply from Catherine the Great. She sent back a "clear refusal and not in so genteel a manner," and she did not have the civility "to answer in her own hand and has thrown out some expressions that may be civil to a Russian ear but certainly not to more civilized ones." [60]

---

[54] Hutchinson, *Diary*, I, 494.
[55] North to king, and king to North, 26 July, Geo. III, *Corres.*, III, 234–35; Donoughue, *British Politics*, 277.
[56] To North, 28 July, Geo. III, *Corres.*, III, 236–37.
[57] North to king, 25 Aug., and king to North, 26 Aug., ibid. 249–51.
[58] 24 July, NYCD, VIII, 596. Johnson had fled to Canada and got a promise for Indian support before he heard from Dartmouth. Johnson, "Journal," ibid. 658–82.
[59] King to North, 1 Aug., Geo. III, *Corres.*, III, 237–38.
[60] King to North, 3 Nov., ibid. 275–76; Donoughue, *British Politics*, 274.

The king and cabinet then agreed to approach some of the petty German states which had soldiers for hire.[61] Negotiations proceeded rapidly and treaties were signed with Brunswick for 4000 men on 9 January 1776; with Hesse Cassel for 12,500 men on 15 January; and with Hesse Hanau for 900 men on 5 February.[62]

Officials were on the watch meanwhile to secure information about plots and suspected plots by Britons friendly to America. Post-office officials opened private letters to and from America and passed them along to the ministry. Spies were sent among disaffected shipwrights who had been discharged for petitioning the king. It was rumored that William Lee and other Americans were providing money to send them to America. A man from "Scots Yard" reported that he had prevented a merchants' meeting and would prevent others for fear that "they would only tend to introduce sedition in the whole commercial line." A suggestion came from Scotland that the heavy emigration of Highland Scots to America should be stopped. They might forget their duty "when exposed to the insidious arts and falsehoods of American agents" who were recruiting them to go to America in every bay and creek along the Scottish coast.[63]

The result of concern with such matters was the royal proclamation of 23 August 1775 declaring there was open rebellion in parts of America and that it "hath been much promoted and encouraged by the traitorous correspondence, counsels, and comfort of divers wicked and desperate persons within this realm. . . ." Henceforth all people within the realm were bound by law to aid in suppressing the rebellion and to provide information concerning "traitorous conspiracies in order to bring to condign punishment the authors, perpetrators, and abettors of such traitorous designs."[64]

The actions taken by the ministry and other officials during the summer and fall of 1775 demonstrated that they believed their policies were right and should not be changed. At first they had refused to believe General Gage when he insisted that American opposition was serious. They had then come to realize that it was serious but still underestimated it, and most of them had only contempt for Americans.

After the war was over Benjamin Franklin recalled that in 1774 he had

---

[61] North to king, 12 Nov., and king to North, 18 Nov., Geo. III, *Corres.*, III, 289–90, 293–94.

[62] Max von Eelking, *The German Allied Troops in the North American War of Independence, 1776–1783* (translated and abridged by J. G. Rosengarten, Albany, 1893), 15–20.

[63] CHOP, IV, 353, 384, 398.   [64] EHD, IX, 850–51.

heard a British general assert that he could solve the problem of America. With a thousand British grenadiers "he would undertake to go from one end of America to the other, and geld all the males, partly by force, and partly by a little coaxing. It is plain he took us for a species of animals very little superior to brutes." The "Yankee was understood to be a sort of Yahoo, and the Parliament did not think the petitions of such creatures were fit to be received and read in so wise an assembly." [65]

Franklin did not exaggerate in his summing up of an attitude of many political and military leaders, and of lesser bureaucrats such as Henry Hulton, who had been in America since 1767 as one of the America board of customs commissioners. In reporting the battle on Breed's Hill, Hulton commented that the "rascally patriot and apothecary," James Warren, "happily was killed. . . . You may judge what the herd must be when such a one is their leader." He lamented that in the British army there were "many of noble family, many very respectable, virtuous, and amiable characters, and it grieves one, that gentlemen, brave British soldiers, should fall by the hands of such despicable wretches as compose the banditti of the country; amongst whom there is not one who has the least pretension to be called a gentleman. They are a most rude, depraved, degenerate race, and it is a mortification to us that they speak English, and can trace themselves from that stock." [66]

Soldiers were as contemptuous as the bureaucrat and deplored the lack of gentlemen among their opponents. General Clinton's aide, Lord Rawdon, said he had hoped to be able to prove his worth "against a more reputable enemy" and that he would soon have done "with these scoundrels, for one only dirties one's fingers by meddling with them." [67] General James Murray assured Lord George Germain that "the native American is an effeminate thing, very unfit for and very impatient of war." [68] After the Battle of Long Island in August 1776, his nephew commented that Americans in that action were "the poorest mean spirited scoundrels that ever surely pretended to the dignity of rebellion." [69]

If further evidence was needed to prove that Americans were cowards and lacking the qualities of gentlemen, it was supplied by their practice of aiming at officers. Horace Walpole reported that they "do not picque

[65] To William Strahan, 19 Aug. 1784, *Writings*(S), IX, 261.
[66] H. H. [Henry Hulton] to ————, 20 June, Hulton, *Letters*, 99–100.
[67] Quoted in Eric Robson, ed., *Letters from America 1773 to 1780* (New York, [1951]), xxiv.
[68] 27 Aug. 1776, ibid. 18, n.1.
[69] General James Murray to Mrs. Smyth, 31 Aug., ibid. 36.

themselves upon modern good breeding, but level only at the officers, of whom they have slain a vast number. We are a little disappointed indeed, at their fighting at all, which was not in our calculation." [70] The Reverend Richard Price, who defended Americans, was excluded from the salon of Mrs. Elizabeth Montagu when she learned "that the Americans in battle take aim at our officers which makes the service very dangerous. . . ." [71]

There were exceptions like Chatham and Shelburne among the politicians and General Gage and Earl Percy among military men, but they had no influence on policy as Parliament met on 26 October. The king's speech was, in effect, an answer to the second petition to him from the Continental Congress. It had insisted that Americans were fighting to maintain their rights as Englishmen, and that their great hope was to remain within the British Empire. The king's speech asserted flatly that "the rebellious war now levied is become more general, and is manifestly carried on for the purpose of establishing an independent empire." A speedy end would be put to the disorders by the most decisive exertions. The navy had been increased and the army greatly augmented and there had been "friendly offers" of foreign assistance. When the "unhappy and deluded multitude against whom this force will be directed, shall become sensible of their error," the king would be ready to receive the "misled with tenderness and mercy." [72] Majorities in both houses of Parliament promised support for the policies of the ministry despite the eloquent speeches of the opposition. [73]

No one had anything new to say; it had all been said in previous sessions of Parliament. There was bitter opposition to the use of Hanoverian troops within the realm without the consent of Parliament, but the opposition achieved no more success in this than in any of the other tactics it tried.

The ministry proposed only one law relating to America: the American Prohibitory Act. Lord North introduced it on 20 November. He proposed the repeal of the Boston Port Act, and of the two restraining acts passed in the spring of 1775. The new act would put a complete stop to the commerce of the American colonies until they submitted, and it would authorize the king to appoint commissioners to receive their submission. As usual the opposition speakers made remarkably acute predictions about

[70] To Sir Horace Mann, 3 Aug., ibid. 18, n.2.
[71] Quoted in Carl B. Cone, *Torchbearer of Freedom* . . . (Lexington, Ky., 1952), 58.
[72] PH, XVIII, 695-98.
[73] Debate in Lords, ibid. 705-29; debate in Commons, ibid. 730-98.

what would happen. They called the bill a "declaration of war" on America, but the ministry hurried the bill through Parliament with remarkable speed, and George III signed it into law on 22 December.[74]

The American Prohibitory Act quite simply declared that all vessels and cargoes belonging to Americans were forfeited to the Crown "as if the same were the ships and effects of open enemies" and shall be so adjudged in any court. Naval commanders, sailors, marines, and soldiers on board naval vessels were declared to "have the sole interest and property" of all such ships and their cargoes.[75]

The Americans were thus declared enemies and outlaws and the royal navy turned loose upon them to engage in legalized piracy. It was the most drastic act concerning America ever passed by Parliament—and the most disastrous. In the course of the debate about it Charles James Fox made the one completely relevant comment when he said: "it is a bill which should be entitled, a Bill for carrying more effectually into execution the resolves of the Congress." [76]

ৡ

The Congress across the Atlantic began the year 1776 as it had ended the old one: paying petty bills, ordering supplies, electing officers, exhorting colonial conventions to greater efforts, denouncing those inimical to the "cause," listening to the reading of endless letters and petitions, and worrying about mounting expenses. The advice to New Hampshire, South Carolina, and Virginia to establish governments, and its implications, was temporarily forgotten as the delegates struggled with the mass of detail that threatened to overwhelm them.

There were those like Samuel Adams, however, who had larger issues always in mind. On 7 January he wrote to James Warren: "You ask me 'when you are to hear of our Confederation?' I answer, when some gentlemen (to use an expression of a Tory) shall 'feel more bold.'" Adams, who was usually more cautious, suggested that certain members of Congress had such characteristics as "the vanity of the ape, the tameness of the ox, or the stupid servility of the ass. . . ." Confederation "is not dead but sleepeth," but he did not despair "since our enemies themselves are hastening it." As he was writing he heard of the attack on Norfolk and was pleased. "This will prevail more than a long train of reasoning to accom-

---

[74] Debate in Commons, ibid. 992–1000, 1028–42, 1056–65, 1103–6; debate in Lords, ibid. 1065–1103.
[75] 16 Geo. III. c.5, Pickering, XXXI. 135–54.   [76] PH, XVIII, 1059.

plish a Confederation and other matters, which I know your heart as well as mine is much set upon." [77]

The next day a copy of the king's speech asserting that Americans were fighting for independence arrived in Philadelphia.[78] Samuel Adams denounced the speech and the king and said he hoped that Americans would "act the part which the great Law of Nature points out" and declare American independence.[79]

The majority of Congress did not agree. On 9 January, the day after the speech arrived, James Wilson moved that "the Congress . . . expressly declare to their constituents and the world their present intentions respecting an independency, observing that the king's speech directly charged us with that design." Wilson was "strongly supported," although some members said that they would be for independence if foreign troops were sent to America.[80] Samuel Adams was much alarmed by the motion for fear it might get Congress "upon dangerous ground," and he and others managed to get it postponed. But they could not prevent the assignment of a day to consider it. Adams was even worried about the Portsmouth, New Hampshire, instructions against independence, which if adopted by that colony, "would wholly defeat a design, which, I confess, I have much at heart."

Adams, with the help of Franklin and George Wythe, counterattacked by proposing that a day be set to consider Franklin's plan of confederation, which had been relegated to a pile of unfinished business in July 1775. Outside Congress it was reported that "Judas Iscariot," as Samuel Adams was called by his enemies, had made the motion. Congress, led by John Dickinson, defeated the proposal, for they recognized it for what it was: a gesture toward independence.[81]

On 24 January Dickinson had his turn. Congress elected a committee of five staunch opponents of independence—John Dickinson, James Wilson, James Duane, Robert Alexander, and William Hooper—to prepare the address to the people that Wilson had proposed on 9 January. Congress debated the issue most of the day and in the course of it "much was said about independency and the mode and propriety of stating our dependence on the king." [82]

[77] Warren-Adams Letters, I, 199–200.   [78] Marshall, Diary, 62.
[79] To James Sullivan, 12 Jan., and to John Pitts, 21 Jan., Writings, III, 255–58.
[80] Smith, Diary, LMCC, I, 304.
[81] To John Adams, 15 Jan., Writings, III, 258–60; Smith, Diary, LMCC, I, 311–13; Edward Tilghman to his father, 4 Feb., Charles J. Stillé, The Life and Times of John Dickinson (Philadelphia, 1891), 174.
[82] JCC, IV, 87; Smith, Diary, LMCC, I, 326.

Early in February an outsider reported that the majority in Congress were believed to be in favor of reconciliation and "abhorrent from independency." The New Englanders, except for the evenly divided Rhode Island delegation, and the Virginians were reported to "hang very much together. They are what we call violent, and suspected of independency." All the other colonies "breathe reconciliation" except Delaware which was sometimes divided because of the absence of George Read or Caesar Rodney, whereas Thomas McKean "is a true Presbyterian and joins the violents." The "violents" were a minority but they "are indefatigable, try all schemes in all shapes, act in concert, and thereby have a considerable advantage over the others, who are by no means so closely united." [83]

By the time Wilson presented his address against independency on 13 February, the minority had become a majority as a result of a shift in the membership of Congress. No shift was more dramatic or important than that in the Massachusetts delegation, a majority of which had voted for Wilson's original motion.

The Massachusetts delegates had been at odds from the start and by the end of 1775 they were close to an open break. Thomas Cushing was opposed to independence and Robert Treat Paine followed his lead. John Hancock, who had no perceptible principles, had opposed John and Samuel Adams ever since they had nominated Washington as commanding general in June. The Adamses in turn despised Hancock for various reasons, including his refusal to surrender the presidency of Congress to Peyton Randolph after he returned from Virginia in the fall.

As early as July 1775 John Adams lamented "the unfortunate and fatal divisions" among the Massachusetts delegates "which have lost us reputation, as well as many great advantages which we might otherwise have obtained for our colony," and his letters thereafter continued to hint that a change would be welcome. The hints had their effect but the Massachusetts legislature became so embattled over the issue that in November 1775 it was unable to elect a delegation to Congress for 1776. It extended the terms of the 1775 delegates to the end of January, and the deadlock was not broken until 15 December. John Adams, Samuel Adams, Hancock, and Paine were re-elected, but the latter only by the bare minimum of votes needed. Thomas Cushing was replaced by Elbridge Gerry. James Warren, who had carried on the fight for his friends, the Adamses, told Samuel Adams that Cushing's absence from Massachusetts "could not

[83] Edward Tilghman to his father, 4 Feb., Stillé, *Dickinson*, 173–74.

longer be dispensed with!"[84] Cushing was furious and he formed a political alliance with Hancock and Paine, an alliance aimed at the Adamses and James Warren. Cushing told Paine: "it seems we are not men to suit them. We are not subservient enough. We do not pay an implicit obedience to their sovereign dictates."[85]

The implications for the future of Massachusetts politics were important, but they were of more immediate significance in Congress. John Adams returned to Philadelphia on 9 February, and with him was Elbridge Gerry. The majority of the Massachusetts delegation was now for independence, and while Hancock, as president of Congress, tried to block the Adamses, he could not stop them or control the vote of the Massachusetts delegation.

When Wilson presented his address on 13 February one delegate described it as "very long, badly written, and full against independency." Congress ordered it "to lie on the table" and there it remained.[86] The men who believed in independence at once began an offensive. Samuel Chase, who differed with the other Maryland delegates, announced that the next day he would move that the little American navy be ordered to seize British vessels and that the colonies be encouraged to fit out privateers to prey on British commerce.[87] On 16 February, in the course of a debate over opening the ports of the colonies, George Wythe, whose colony of Virginia had opened its ports to the trade of the world on 20 January, declared that "we must declare ourselves a free people" and proposed that the colonies had the right "to contract alliances with foreign powers." There was opposition because this involved "independency," but Congress turned the proposition over to the committee of the whole by a vote of seven colonies to five.[88]

A few days later the issue of independence was raised once more, but in a quite different way. Congress had learned by the middle of January of the death of General Richard Montgomery and the wounding of Benedict Arnold before Quebec on 31 December 1775. Hooper of North Carolina

---

[84] John Adams to James Warren, 23 July; Warren to John Adams, 14 Nov., and to Samuel Adams, 19 Dec., *Warren-Adams Letters*, I, 85–88, 56–57, 183, II, 430. For an account of Massachusetts politics during the winter of 1775–76, see Patterson, *Political Parties in Massachusetts*, chapter VI.
[85] 13 Feb. 1776, Robert Treat Paine Papers, MHS.
[86] Smith, Diary, 13 Feb., LMCC, I, 348; JCC, IV, 146.
[87] Smith, Diary, 13 Feb., LMCC, I, 348.
[88] John Adams, Notes of Debates, 16 Feb., *Diary*, II, 229–30; Smith, Diary, LMCC, I, 350–51.

at once moved that Congress wear crape armbands for a month and that a sermon be preached, while Lynch of South Carolina proposed that a monument be built to the first general (and one of the few) killed during the war. Samuel Ward of Rhode Island protested that "Courts" did not wear armbands upon such occasions, and so a committee was appointed. A month later Congress and the Pennsylvania assembly listened to an oration by the Reverend Dr. William Smith in praise of Montgomery. William Livingston proposed a vote of thanks to Smith and the printing of his oration. He was supported by James Duane, James Wilson, Thomas Willing, all opponents of independence. John Adams, George Wythe, Edward Rutledge, Oliver Wolcott, and Roger Sherman led those opposed, and forced Livingston to withdraw the motion. The reason for their opposition was that "the Doctor declared the sentiments of the Congress to continue in a dependency on Great Britain, which doctrine this Congress can not now approve." Oliver Wolcott commented that Smith claimed lands in the Wyoming Valley and disliked New Englanders.[89]

The squabble was petty but the outcome was the first clear victory for the forces of independence, and on the last day of February Congress debated "declaring our independency on Great Britain. . . ." The debate ended "when it appeared that five or six colonies have instructed their delegates not to agree to an independency till they, the principals, are consulted." [90] The colonies opposed to independence were now in a minority, but John Dickinson's strategy of securing instructions against independence served the purpose of those who opposed it, or at least hoped to delay it as long as possible. Led by John Dickinson, they fought skillfully and they fought hard. But time and events were on the side of those who believed that reconciliation was a futile dream and that independence was inevitable.

One of the events was the publication of *Common Sense* on 9 January, the day James Wilson proposed that Congress answer the king's speech by denying that it wanted independence.[91] But it took far more than pamphlets to convert the opponents of independence, and people like the Adamses and the Lees did not need conversion. What they expected was some further action on the part of Britain to prove that their cause was

[89] Smith, Diary, 18 Jan., 19, 21 Feb. and Oliver Wolcott to Mrs. Wolcott, 19 March, LMCC, I, 318, 356, 359, 399.
[90] Smith, Diary, 29 Feb., ibid. 369.
[91] For a discussion of *Common Sense* see Chapter XXV below.

just and their predictions right. They were not disappointed. On 26 February, Robert Morris laid before Congress a copy of the American Prohibitory Act and letters from England reporting that an army of 25,000 would be sent, part of it to the southern colonies, and also that commissioners would come to treat with the colonies. "The bill is very long and cruel," Richard Smith of New Jersey noted in his diary.[92]

The Prohibitory Act, as Charles James Fox had predicted, served the purposes of at least some members of Congress. John Adams called the act an "act of independency" and was glad that it had come from Parliament rather than Congress. He thought it "very odd that Americans should hesitate at accepting such a gift from them." [93] Richard Henry Lee commented that it was "curious to observe that whilst people here are disputing and hesitating about independency, the court by one bold act of Parliament . . . have already put the two countries asunder." [94]

Those who hoped for reconciliation were stunned. Robert Alexander of Maryland said he did not know what Congress would do but "with me every idea of reconciliation is precluded by the conduct of Great Britain, and the only alternative, absolute slavery or independency. The latter I have often reprobated both in public and private, but am now almost convinced the measure is right and can be justified by necessity." [95]

Yet many still clung to the hope of reconciliation and grasped at the section of the Prohibitory Act authorizing the king to appoint commissioners to come to America. They did not know when commissioners would come, or what their powers would be, but they continued to oppose every measure that might lead to independence, and insisted that Congress must wait for their arrival. James Duane declared that he was unwilling to take an "irrevocable measure [to] tie up our hands" while "commissioners are daily looked for. . . ." [96] In April, Robert Morris cried: "where the plague are these commissioners, if they are to come what is it that detains them?" The time had come to know whether the liberties of America could be established by reconciliation, or whether we must renounce our connection with Britain "and fight our way to a total independence." [97] Thomas Stone of Maryland was equally anxious for reconciliation and asserted that the "proper way to effect this is not to

[92] LMCC, I, 366.   [93] To Horatio Gates, 23 March, LMCC, I, 406.
[94] To Landon Carter, 1 April, *Letters*, I, 173.
[95] To the Maryland Council of Safety, 27 Feb., LMCC, I, 366.
[96] To Robert R. Livingston, 20 March, E. P. Alexander, *A Revolutionary Conservative: James Duane of New York* (New York, 1938), 114-15.
[97] To ———, [9 Dec. 1775] and to Horatio Gates, 6 April 1776, LMCC, I, 271, 416.

move too quick." At the same time he declared that "anything is preferable to a surrender of our rights." [98]

A young Pennsylvanian reported to Washington that notwithstanding the Prohibitory Act and a "thousand other proofs of a bitter and irreconcilable spirit, there is a strange reluctance in the minds of many to cut the knot which ties us to Great Britain," especially in Pennsylvania and the southern colonies. Joseph Reed told Washington that he was infinitely more afraid of commissioners than he was of British generals and armies, for "if their propositions are plausible, and behavior artful, I am apprehensive they will divide us." [99]

Congress was already divided, and bitterly so. Joseph Hewes of North Carolina did not want independence but he despaired of reconciliation. Members of Congress, he said, no longer treated one another with decency. "Jealousies, ill-natured observations and recriminations take place of reason and argument." There were those who argued "for independency and eternal separation, others wish to wait a little longer. . . ." [100]

Those who did not want to wait were growing more and more impatient, including army officers. A Pennsylvania colonel asked in January: "Shall we never leave off debating and *boldly declare independency?*" [101] When Washington sent General Charles Lee with two Connecticut regiments to New York to prepare that city for a possible British invasion, he found the city supplying British warships in the harbor on orders from the provincial congress. It had also released certain tories on Long Island whom the Congress in Philadelphia had ordered disarmed and held. Their release, Lee said, "must and ought to be considered an act of absolute idiotism, as reconciliation and reunion with Great Britain is now as much of a chimera as incorporation with the people of Tibet." He predicted that if he and his troops left, the provincial congress and the people would allow any British troops that arrived to "take quiet possession of the place." [102]

Among other things, Lee stopped shipment of supplies to the British warships in the harbor and insisted that the inhabitants take a loyalty oath. There were outraged cries at military interference with civil power and the provincial congress demanded control of Lee and his troops.[103]

---

[98] To Daniel of St. Thomas Jenifer, 24 April, ibid. 431–32.
[99] 3, 15 March, Reed, *Life,* I, 163–64, 173.
[100] To Samuel Johnston, 20 March, LMCC, I, 401.
[101] Colonel Moylan to Joseph Reed, 30 Jan., Reed, *Life,* I, 160.
[102] To Joseph Reed, 28 Feb., ibid. 160–61.
[103] Becker, *New York,* chapter X, contains an account of the strong loyalist stand of New York.

When Lee was sent to command in the South, the New Yorkers resumed their profitable supply business and kept it up until they got a blistering letter from General Washington. He moved his headquarters to New York in April after the British evacuation of Boston in March. He was as shocked as Lee by the behavior of New Yorkers. He told the committee of safety that supplying the British vessels was a "glaring absurdity" and injurious to the common cause. "We are to consider ourselves either in a state of peace or war with Great Britain. If the former, why are our ports shut up, our trade destroyed, our property seized, our towns burnt, and our worthy and valuable citizens led into captivity and suffering the most cruel hardships? If the latter, my imagination is not fertile enough to suggest a reason in support of the intercourse." [104]

At the end of January, George Washington had declared that a few more "flaming arguments" such as the burning of Norfolk, "added to the sound doctrine and unanswerable reasoning contained in the pamphlet *Common Sense* will not leave numbers at a loss to decide upon the propriety of a separation." [105] In mid-April he asserted that the British would never offer acceptable terms of reconciliation. His main concern was with the divisions in Congress and the southern colonies "on the score of independence." [106] When he visited Philadelphia at the end of May he said that the idea of sending commissioners had been to deceive Americans and that it had succeeded all too well. He found that many members of Congress, and even whole delegations, "are still feeding themselves upon the dainty food of reconciliation," whereas the only commissioners that would ever be sent were Hessians and other foreigners.[107]

More and more members of Congress were just as impatient as the army officers but they had to deal with political reality. In the summer of 1775 John Adams had dreaded "like death" the proposal for negotiations included in the second petition to the king. But it had to be included for "discord and total disunion" would have been the result of a refusal to petition and negotiate. James Warren had replied that he dreaded smallpox in the army but he dreaded even more "proposals of a conciliatory nature from England." [108]

In April 1776 John Adams explained that "we continue still between

[104] To New York Committee of Safety, 17 April, *Writings*, IV, 486–87.
[105] To Joseph Reed, 31 Jan., ibid. IV, 297.
[106] 15 April, to John Adams and to Joseph Reed, ibid. 482–84.
[107] To John Augustine Washington, 31 May, ibid. V, 91–92.
[108] Adams to Warren, 6 [July] and Warren to Adams, 20 July, *Warren-Adams Letters*, I, 74–75, 84.

hawk and buzzard. Some people yet expect commissioners, to treat with Congress, and to offer a Chart Blanc." The management of so "complicated and mighty a machine, as the united colonies, requires the meekness of Moses, the patience of Job, the wisdom of Solomon, added to the valor of David." John Adams was neither meek nor patient but he had considerable wisdom and much valor. He told Warren that they were advancing slowly but surely "to that mighty revolution which you and I have expected for some time." But any attempt to "accelerate" the colonies "would have been attended with discontent and perhaps convulsions." [109]

When Benjamin Franklin was asked why Congress had not "by general consent" formed a supreme legislature, opened the ports, and the like, he replied that the only thing lacking was "general consent." "The novelty of the thing deters some, the doubt of success others, the vain hope of reconciliation, many." But like the Adamses, Franklin pointed out that "our enemies" were removing the obstacles day by day "so that there is a rapid increase of the formerly small party, who were for an independent government." [110]

The supporters of independence followed the policy which Samuel Adams stated so well: "We cannot make events. Our business is wisely to improve them." "Mankind," he said, "are governed more by their feelings than by reason. Events which excite those feelings will produce wonderful effects." He cited as examples the Boston Port Act, Lexington and Concord, and the burning of Norfolk, and he hoped that British troops would soon arrive in the South for "one battle would do more towards a declaration of independency than a long chain of conclusive arguments in a provincial convention or the Continental Congress." [111]

The believers in independence had been seeking "wisely to improve" events from the beginning of the Congress. John Adams had argued for closing the customs houses, setting up local governments and a confederation, and opening the ports to the trade of the world ever since the summer of 1775.[112] By the end of 1775 it was obvious that the Association had not forced Britain to yield and Congress began a debate about opening the ports on 1 March 1776.[113]

[109] To James Warren, 2 April, LMCC, I, 413 and 22 April, Warren-Adams Letters, I, 232.
[110] To Josiah Quincy, 15 April, Writings(S), VI, 446.
[111] To Samuel Cooper, 30 April, Writings, III, 284–85.
[112] To James Warren, 6, 23 July, Warren-Adams Letters, I, 75, 87–88.
[113] 26 Dec., JCC, III, 457.

The debate went on and on during the early weeks of the year 1776. By the beginning of February, Congress had agreed that the colonies would carry on trade with every part of the world except Britain, Ireland, and the British West Indies, but the delegates could not agree when it should be done or under what conditions.[114] The reconciliationists were opposed because it smacked of independence, and their opponents demanded it because it did.[115]

When the news of the Prohibitory Act arrived at the end of February "a large number of Philadelphians" at once applied to Congress to issue letters of marque so they could seize British ships. Congress wrangled about the request off and on during the first three weeks of March. On 18 March the four New England colonies, New York, Virginia, and North Carolina voted for granting letters to privateers while Pennsylvania and Maryland voted against it. Only the ships of Britain itself would be subject to seizure, while Ireland and the other British dominions would be exempt.

A few days later independence was in the open again. George Wythe reported a preamble to the privateering act, and he and Richard Henry Lee proposed an amendment "wherein the king was made the author of our miseries instead of the ministry." John Jay, James Wilson, and Thomas Johnson opposed the amendment "on supposition that this was effectually severing the king from us forever," and at the end of a four-hour debate, Maryland "interposed its veto" and the vote was put off until the following day.[116]

The opponents of independence had their way. A long and eloquent preamble was adopted but it did not blame the king as the author of American miseries.[117] John Adams agreed with General Gates that "in politics the middle way is none at all," and if Americans failed, it would be because they bewildered themselves "in groping after this middle way. We have hitherto conducted half a war, acted upon the line of defence, etc., etc. But you will see by tomorrow's paper, that for the future we are likely to wage three-quarters of a war." [118] At last, on 6 April, Congress declared Americans could export all goods except staves and empty casks to any place in the world except the British dominions, and could import goods from any place in the world except the British dominions. However, two items could not be imported: East India tea and slaves.[119]

[114] Oliver Wolcott to Samuel Lyman, 3, 19 Feb., LMCC, I, 338–39, 355–56.
[115] Smith, Diary, 29 Feb., ibid. 368–69.
[116] Smith, Diary, ibid. 371, 386, 395, 398, 402, 404.
[117] JCC, IV, 229–32.   [118] 23 March, LMCC, I, 405–6.
[119] JCC, IV, 257–59.

Before the ports were opened John Adams warned that when it was done, "take care that you don't call it, or think it, independency. No such matter. Independency is a hobgoblin of so frightful mien that it would throw a delicate person into fits to look it in the face." [120]

࢝

The reasons for opposition to independence were many and varied, and when forced to choose, some Americans chose loyalty to the new nation, and others chose loyalty to the mother country. Whatever the final choice, men's reasons for opposing independence were much the same and differed only in the emphasis individuals placed upon them.[121]

Simple loyalty to the mother country was a real if intangible and unweighable force that shaped opinion. Britain was "home," even to some Americans who had never crossed the Atlantic to study law or medicine, or to trade, or to visit. There was also a loyalty born of the understandable self-interest of officeholders who had achieved status and power within the governmental machinery of the British Empire. They saw membership in the empire as the guarantee of stability and good order as well as of their own positions, and departure from it, in their eyes, would be a long and perhaps fatal step in the direction of anarchy.

Their feeling was shared by many American merchants. They objected to British measures, but they knew that as part of the empire, Americans belonged to the greatest protected trading area in the world, and merchants found it difficult to conceive of carrying on trade outside its boundaries. Nor could merchants, accustomed to crossing and circling the Atlantic Ocean in search of markets and of profits, conceive of a future without a government to protect and guide their ocean-borne commerce. Men like Joseph Galloway and James Duane made that clear in the First Continental Congress, and despite the Prohibitory Act, there were merchants who still felt that way in the spring of 1776.

There was another kind of opposition to independence which was based on a "realistic" appraisal of the chances of winning a war against the greatest naval power and manufacturing nation in the world. How could two and a half million people, nearly 20 per cent of whom were slaves, fight a nation of eight million people, a nation which only a few years

---

[120] To Horatio Gates, 23 March, LMCC, I, 406.
[121] For two recent and quite different accounts of those opponents of independence who remained loyal to Great Britain, see William H. Nelson, *The American Tory* (Oxford, 1961), and Wallace Brown, *The King's Friends* (Providence, R.I., 1966). The latter book contains a useful bibliography.

earlier had achieved the pinnacle of world power in the Seven Years War?

Another form of loyalty to Britain was born of past experience with certain American leaders. The backcountry farmers of North and South Carolina, whether they had been Regulators or not, were suspicious of the low-county leaders. The tenant farmers in New York who had rebelled against their landlords had no more reason to trust them and the Sons of Liberty in 1776 than they had in 1766. And since the Regulators and tenant farmers had been granted royal pardons, it was natural enough for them to be more loyal to a king who might be as evil as some Americans were saying, but who was a more distant evil than some of the American leaders near at hand who had shot them, hanged them, and ordered them drawn and quartered.

The fear of civil war between colonies over land claims was a powerful source of opposition to independence. Joseph Galloway predicted such civil war in 1774 and John Dickinson pointed to it in his final speech against independence in July 1776. The fear was based on the simple fact that a form of civil war had existed for several years, and by 1776 the danger seemed greater than ever. New Yorkers and the inhabitants of the New Hampshire Grants, who declared themselves the independent state of Vermont in 1777, had been brawling for years. Sporadic fighting continued between the Connecticut settlers in the Wyoming Valley and Pennsylvanians who were trying to get rid of them. The quarrel between Virginia and Pennsylvania over the region around Fort Pitt was erupting in violence from time to time.

In addition, there were the speculative land companies like the Indiana, Wabash, Illinois, and Transylvania companies which were trying to carve out claims within the boundaries of Virginia. Since members of those companies such as Benjamin Franklin, Robert Morris, James Wilson, Samuel Chase, and others were also members of Congress, they were in a position where they could try to benefit themselves and their partners. And they did try.[122] The quarrel between them and Virginia was so bitter and prolonged that it delayed the ratification of the first constitution of the United States, the Articles of Confederation, until the war for independence was nearly over.[123]

Among the reasons given by a Virginia planter for opposing independence were the many bitter unsettled disputes over rival land claims. "And

122 Abernethy, *Western Lands and the American Revolution*, passim.
123 Merrill Jensen, *The Articles of Confederation: An Interpretation of the Social-Constitutional History of the American Revolution, 1774–1781* (Madison, 1940), passim.

yet without any adjustment of those disputes and a variety of other matters, some are for lugging us into independence." [124] And John Adams,
who was one of those doing the "lugging," decried "that avarice of land
which has made upon this Continent so many votaries to Mammon, that
I sometimes dread the consequences." [125]

Of all the sources of opposition to independence the most pervasive
was the conviction that independence might bring with it a political, and
even a social, revolution, and some men believed that a revolution was
well under way by the beginning of 1776. In June 1775 the New York
provincial congress adopted a "Plan of Accommodation between Great
Britain and America." The plan was sent to the New York delegates in
Congress with a letter summing up in classic form the feelings of those
who feared a revolution in America. "We must now repeat to you the
common and just observation, that contests for liberty, fostered in their
infancy by the virtuous and wise, become sources of power to wicked and
designing men; from whence it follows, that such controversies as we are
now engaged in frequently end in the demolition of those rights and
privileges which they were instituted to defend. We pray you, therefore,
to use every effort for the compromising of this unnatural quarrel between
the parent and child. . . ." [126]

The same conviction was equally powerful in Pennsylvania. James Allen,
son of the former chief justice and proprietary leader, noted in his diary in
July 1775 that many people thought that America had seen its best days,
and that even if there were a victorious peace, it would be difficult to
restore order. Yet, he wrote, the eyes of Europe are upon us and "if we
fall, liberty no longer continues an inhabitant of this globe." In October
1775 he joined the Associators in Philadelphia and carried a musket for "a
man is suspected who does not," and because "I believe discreet people
mixing with them may keep them in order." The times, he said, were
dreadful. By March 1776 he reported "thinking people uneasy, irresolute,
and inactive. The mobility triumphant." Congress was in a state of equi-
librium about independence. "I love the cause of liberty; but cannot
heartily join in the prosecution of measures totally foreign to the original
plan of resistance. The madness of the multitude is but one degree better
than submission to the Tea Act." [127]

Virginia planters accustomed to deference from the "lower orders" were
shocked when men they looked upon as ambitious, ignorant, and inexperienced appeared in the Virginia convention in the spring of 1776.

[124] Carter Braxton to Landon Carter, 14 April, LMCC, I, 421.
[125] To Horatio Gates, 23 March, ibid. 406.   [126] 28 June, Force, 4 ser. II, 1329.
[127] 26 July, 14 Oct. 1775, 6 March 1776, PMHB, IX, 184–86.

Landon Carter told George Washington that "I need only tell you of one definition that I heard of independency. It was expected to be a form of government that, by being independent of the rich men, every man would then be able to do as he pleased. And it was with this expectation they [the voters] sent the men they did, in hopes they would plan such a form." Carter heard one of the delegates object to the patrolling law "because a poor man was made to pay for keeping a rich man's slaves in order." Carter reported that "I shamed the fool so much for it that he slunk away, but he got elected by it." Another delegate, "in a most seditious manner," objected to drafting the militia by lot, and he too was elected. Formerly, "such rascals would have been turned out; but now it is not to be supposed that a dog will eat a dog." From such origins, said Carter, it seems that our independence is to arise. Papers were circulating everywhere "for poor ignorant creatures to sign, as directions to their delegates to endeavor at an independency." [128]

Thomas Stone of Maryland put the same feeling very simply when he said that if commissioners did not come soon, a separation would take place and then all governors and officers would have to quit their posts "and New Men must be placed in the Saddle of Power." [129]

Men like Richard Henry Lee and John Adams were as aware as any opponent of independence that "new men" might attain power. Lee urged Virginia to create a government in the spring of 1776 for "how long popular commotions may be suppressed without it, and anarchy be prevented, deserves intense consideration." Only by creating "a wise and free government" could the "numerous evils to be apprehended from popular rage and license" be avoided in Virginia.[130]

Years later John Adams remembered as vividly as if it had happened the day before, that when he went home from Congress in the fall of 1775, he met with a "common horse jockey" whom he had often defended in the courts. The man approached and said: "Oh! Mr. Adams, what great things have you and your colleagues done for us! We can never be grateful enough to you. There are no courts of justice now in this province, and I hope there never will be another!"

Adams rode on "without any answer to this wretch," and as he rode he asked himself: "is this the object for which I have been contending?" "Are these the sentiments of such people? And how many are there in the country? Half the nation for what I know; for half the nation are debtors if not more, and these have been in all countries the sentiments of debtors.

[128] 9 May, Force, 4 ser. VI, 390-91.
[129] To Daniel of St. Thomas Jenifer, 24 April, LMCC, I, 431-32.
[130] To Robert Carter Nicholas, 30 April, *Letters*, I, 184.

If the power of the country should get into such hands, and there is great danger that it will, to what purpose have we sacrificed our time, health, and everything else?" [131]

Adams's memory did not play him false. In 1776 he inveighed with all the fervor of a Landon Carter in Virginia against "that rage for innovation which appears in so many wild shapes in our province." The proposals for reforms in government in Massachusetts were "founded in narrow notions, sordid stinginess, and profound ignorance, and tend directly to barbarism." [132] And the day after Congress voted American independence, Adams told his wife: "the people will have unbounded power. And the people are extremely addicted to corruption and venality, as well as the great. I am not without apprehensions from this quarter. But I must submit all my hopes and fears, to an overruling Providence, in which, unfashionable as the faith may be, I firmly believe." [133]

Many Americans did not have Adams's faith in Providence, but his explanations of why they opposed independence were very much like the reasons they offered themselves. In March 1776 he declared that "all our misfortunes arise from a single source—the reluctance of the southern colonies to republican government." The Prohibitory Act had "declared" Americans independent, but Americans refused to accept it. The big difficulty was in forming constitutions for each colony and in creating a "Continental Constitution." "This can be done only on popular principles and maxims which are so abhorrent to the inclinations of the Barons of the South, and the proprietary interests of the middle colonies. . . ." [134]

There were leaders in the South, and in New York and Pennsylvania as well, who were indeed reluctant to accept "republican" government, for to them it meant "democracy," and they suspected that the New Englanders wanted to spread their "democracy" throughout America. Carter Braxton explained that the New England colonies did not want reconciliation because two of them had governments "purely democratical, the nature and principle of which, both civil and religious, are so totally incompatible with monarchy, that they have ever lived in a restless state under it." "The best opportunity in the world being now offered them to throw off all subjection and embrace their darling democracy, they are determined to accept it." [135]

---

[131] *Autobiography*, III, 326.
[132] To John Winthrop, 23 June, MHSC, 5 ser. IV, 310.
[133] 3 July, *Family Corres.*, II, 28.
[134] To Horatio Gates, 23 March, LMCC, I, 406.
[135] To Landon Carter, 15 April, ibid. 420–21.

When Braxton read John Adams's *Thoughts on Government*, which proposed the establishment of governments modelled on that of Massachusetts, he considered it a dangerously democratic model. Adams's plan was being circulated in Virginia with enthusiastic support from Richard Henry Lee and Patrick Henry, and Braxton wrote an address to the Virginia convention attacking it and all other "democratic" schemes.

He admitted that independence was necessary but he wanted Virginia to adopt a government as near a limited monarchy as possible. He told the convention that "the systems recommended to the colonies seem to accord with the temper of the times, and are fraught with all the tumult and riot incident to simple democracy; systems which many think it their interest to support, and without doubt will be industriously propagated among you. The best of these systems exist only in theory, and were never confirmed by the experience, even of those who recommend them." If such a government were adopted, it was inevitable that the poor would divide all property equally among themselves.[136]

"This contemptible little tract," said Richard Henry Lee, "betrays the little knot or junto from whence it proceeded. Confusion of ideas, aristocratic pride, contradictory reasoning, with evident ill design, put it out of danger of doing harm. . . ."[137] Patrick Henry explained to John Adams that "there is among most of our opulent families a strong bias to aristocracy," and he hoped that Adams's *Thoughts* would do some good.[138] Adams was not surprised. He replied that "the dons, the bashaws, the grandees, the patricians, the sachems, the nabobs, call them by what name you please, sigh, and groan, and fret, and sometimes stamp, and foam, and curse, but all in vain. The decree is gone forth, and it cannot be recalled, that a more equal liberty than has prevailed in other parts of the earth, must be established in America. That exuberance of pride which has produced an insolent domination in a few, a very few, opulent, monopolizing families, will be brought down nearer to the confines of reason and moderation, than they have been used to."[139]

ꝑ❧

When John Adams asserted early in June 1776 that "the decree is gone forth," he was pointing to the achievement of the men who wanted

---

[136] "Address to the Convention of . . . Virginia, on the Subject of Government . . . ," Force, 4 ser. VI, 748-54.
[137] To Edmund Pendleton, 12 May, *Letters*, I, 190.
[138] 20 May, Adams, *Works*, IV, 201.
[139] To Henry, 3 June, ibid. IX, 387-88.

independence but who had been blocked for so long by the men who opposed it. The Lees and the Adamses could say over and over again that British acts had declared independence for Americans, but the political obstacles that had to be overcome were the instructions of several colonies to their delegates in Congress to vote against independence. And no matter what Britain might do, those colonies showed no intention of changing their instructions in the spring of 1776.

To break the deadlock the men for independence adopted two strategies: they sought positive instructions from their own colonies to vote for independence, and they helped bring about a political revolution in those colonies where it was needed to break the hold of the opponents of independence on their governments. The success of those two strategies, and the steady growth of popular support, at last made a declaration of independence possible.

XXV

The Founding of a Nation: "The Unanimous Declaration of the Thirteen United States of America"

During the spring of 1776 while the members of Congress engaged in intricate political maneuvers to further or hinder the cause of independence, the public debate grew more and more intense. Some newspaper writers had argued for independence at least as early as 1773, but it was the publication of *Common Sense* on 9 January 1776 that set "a terrible wordy war waging on the subject of independence." [1]

Thomas Paine had come to Pennsylvania from England in the fall of 1774 with a letter of introduction from Benjamin Franklin whom he had met in London. The ideas in *Common Sense* were not new, for most of them had appeared in dozens of newspapers and pamphlets. What was different about *Common Sense* was its stirring prose, so unlike most of the ponderous political writings of the times. It "poured forth a style hitherto unknown on this side of the Atlantic" and it was "pregnant with the most captivating figures of speech," Edmund Randolph wrote admiringly after independence had been won.[2]

Paine proclaimed that "the cause of America is in a great measure the cause of all mankind." "Every spot of the old world is overrun with oppression. Freedom hath been hunted round the globe. Asia and Africa have long expelled her. Europe regards her like a stranger, and England hath given her warning to depart. O! receive the fugitive, and prepare in time an asylum for mankind." Government, at its best, was "but a necessary evil," for "government like dress is the badge of lost innocence; the palaces of kings are built on the ruins of the bowers of paradise."

[1] Joseph Reed to [Charles] Pettit, 30 March, Reed, *Life*, I, 182.
[2] "Essay on the Revolutionary History of Virginia," *Virginia Magazine of History and Biography*, XLIII (1935), 306.

England had had a few good monarchs but most of them were a bad lot, all the way from William the Conqueror, "a French Bastard," to George III, that "hardened, sullen-tempered Pharaoh" who was not the father of his people but "the Royal Brute of Great Britain." "Of more worth," declared Paine, "is one honest man to society and in the sight of God, than all the crowned ruffians that ever lived."

Government in America would be a simple thing and law would be king. There would be equality of representation and annually elected assemblies. The business of the assemblies would be purely domestic; all other matters would be left to the Continental Congress. Paine called for a constitutional convention to draft an American Magna Charta "fixing the number and manner of choosing members of Congress, members of assembly, with their date of sitting, and drawing the line of business and jurisdiction between them" and "securing freedom and property to all men, and above all things, the free exercise of religion, according to the dictates of conscience. . . ." [3]

The pamphlet delighted the supporters of independence. Samuel Adams told James Warren that it "has fretted some folks here more than a little." [4] Before Warren saw a copy he reported back that the "sentiments, the principles, and the whole book are prodigiously admired here by the best judges." He, Joseph Hawley, and John Winthrop were ready to vote for independence at once and he wondered why Congress was hesitating to do so.[5] Even so cautious a man as James Bowdoin, who borrowed a copy of *Common Sense* from Mercy Warren, declared that he and his "dear Rib" had been confirmed in their belief in independence by reading it.[6]

Other men were shocked by the pamphlet and by the slashing attack on monarchy. Americans had lived all their lives under monarchical government and many of their political leaders had long believed that the English constitution, in its ideal form, represented the best balance among the contending forces in society. The pamphlet was denounced by newspaper writers such as the Reverend William Smith, whose "Cato" articles appeared in the *Pennsylvania Gazette*. A pamphlet attacking *Common Sense* was printed in New York, but the mechanics committee, with the help of Isaac Sears, destroyed it before it could be sold.[7]

The major pamphlet published in reply was *Plain Truth* by James Chalmers, a Maryland landowner who later became a loyalist. As "Candi-

[3] Jensen, *Tracts*, 400–446.   [4] 13 Jan., *Warren-Adams Letters*, I, 204.
[5] 14 Feb., ibid. II, 434–35.   [6] To Mercy Warren, 28 Feb., ibid. I, 208–9.
[7] Becker, *New York*, 252, n. 153.

dus" he attacked the author of *Common Sense* as a "political quack" and defended monarchy and the English constitution. He charged, like many another opponent of independence, that without the control of the Crown, "our constitution would immediately degenerate into democracy" and that the history of "democratical or popular governments" was a history of warfare, internal rebellion, and of constant oppression of the rich by the poor.[8]

Common Sense was enormously popular. Within three months after it first appeared 120,000 copies were sold. How many persons it converted to independence is unknown, but contemporaries agreed that its impact was great. Edmund Randolph wrote that "this pamphlet put the torch to combustibles," and that because of *Common Sense* perhaps a majority of Virginia counties instructed their delegates to the Virginia convention in May to vote for independence.[9]

In David Ramsay's judgment, Thomas Paine "held the most distinguished rank" among the writers for independence, and his pamphlet, "in union with the feelings and sentiments of the people . . . produced surprising effects. Many thousands were convinced, and were led to approve and long for a separation from the Mother Country. Though that measure, a few months before, was not only foreign from their wishes, but the object of their abhorrence, the current suddenly became so strong in its favor, that it bore down all opposition. The multitude was hurried down the stream. . . ."[10]

It took more, however, than pamphlets and newspaper essays to convert enough people to a belief in independence to make it possible. Looking back from the vantage point of 1789, Ramsay concluded that despite British acts, and even Lexington and Concord, the idea of independence did not "preponderate" until early in 1776. The Prohibitory Act "proved that the colonists might constitutionally declare themselves independent, but the hiring of foreign troops to make war upon them, demonstrated the necessity of their doing it immediately."[11] The Prohibitory Act had an immediate impact on those involved in ocean-borne commerce, but popular opinion was probably swayed more by the news of the hiring of foreign troops. Samuel Adams, with his uncanny ability to sense what Britain might do, predicted in October 1775, before the king and cabinet had decided to begin negotiations, that Britain would hire 16,000 Hessians.[12]

---

[8] *Plain Truth* is reprinted in Jensen, *Tracts*, 447–88.
[9] "Essay," *Virginia Magazine of History and Biography*, XLIII, 306–7.
[10] *History*, I, 338–39. See also Gordon, *History*, II, 275.   [11] *History*, I, 335–37.
[12] To James Warren, 7 Oct., *Warren-Adams Letters*, I, 129.

Congress learned in mid-March 1776 that Britain had tried and failed to hire Russian troops, but it was not until 21 May that Congress received copies of the treaties hiring almost the exact number of German troops Samuel Adams had predicted. An American rifleman captured at Quebec had been taken to England and put in jail in London. Lord Mayor Sawbridge released him and sent him to Bristol, where a "number of gentlemen" provided his passage to Halifax, Nova Scotia. There he was searched several times, but eventually he arrived in Philadelphia with the treaties, newspapers, and other documents sewn in his clothing.[13] The next day translations of the treaties were published in the *Pennsylvania Journal*. "The clouds grow very dark," wrote William Smith, Jr. "My hopes of a conciliatory negotiation almost fail me. . . ." [14]

Popular support for independence was growing before the news of the hiring of foreign troops reached America, growing so fast in fact that members of Congress were warned that Congress was lagging too far behind popular opinion. Joseph Hawley told Samuel Adams that it was within the realm of possibility that "the army or a great mob made up partly of your own army and partly of others" would descend upon Congress, disperse it, and appoint others from among themselves to "dictate for the whole continent. . . . The people are now ahead of you and the only way to prevent discord and indiscretion is to strike while the iron is hot. The people's blood is so hot as not to admit of delays. . . ."

Robert Morris got the same kind of warning from General Charles Lee in Virginia who asked: "For God's sake why does your Congress continue in this horrible, nonsensical manner? Why not at once take the step you must take soon?" If you do not "you will force at last the people to attempt it without you—which must produce a noble anarchy." Hawley in Massachusetts, where demands for radical changes in government were frightening many men, was even more pointed. He begged Samuel Adams: "for God's sake make the best constitution you can and give it out, or the Lord only knows who we shall have for our leaders." [15]

ટેટ

But the members of Congress who wanted independence faced practical problems in turning popular feeling into political reality. How could they get the colonies that had instructed their delegates to vote against inde-

---

[13] LMCC, I, 458 n.5, 462; JCC, IV, 369.   [14] 8 June, *Memoirs*, 271.
[15] Hawley to Adams, 1 April, Adams Papers, NYPL; Lee to Morris, 16 April, *Lee Papers*, I, NYHSC (1871), 426.

pendence to change their instructions? One device hit upon by the Adamses and the Lees was to ask their own colonies to give them positive instructions to work for independence.

When General Charles Lee arrived in Virginia he congratulated Richard Henry Lee on the evacuation of Boston. But, he said, it appeared "that as our affairs grow more prosperous, the namby pambys of the senatorial part of the continent (great and small) grow more timid and hysterical," and that certain members of the Virginia committee of safety were among that group. He asked: "For God's sake, why do you dawdle in the Congress so strangely? Why do you not at once declare yourself a separate independent state?" [16]

Richard Henry Lee replied that Congress was "heavily clogged with instructions from these shamefully interested proprietary people" and that this would continue until "Virginia sets the example of taking up government, and sending peremptory orders to their delegates to pursue the most effectual measures for the security of America." Then the people of the proprietary colonies would "force the same measure, after which adieu to proprietary influence and timid senseless politics." [17]

Two days earlier Richard Henry Lee had sent Patrick Henry an urgent plea for action. Virginia, he said, had led in the past and should act now to arouse America from "the fatal lethargy" into which she had been thrown by the proprietary governments. Virginia should take up government immediately "for the preservation of society," and "above all," to set an example for North Carolina, Maryland, Pennsylvania, and New York. There was danger that Britain might divide up America among foreign powers as the price of help from them. America would need foreign alliances, but no foreign power would help America "until we take rank as an independent people." [18]

The Massachusetts delegates began trying to secure positive instructions in favor of independence late in March when Elbridge Gerry asked James Warren to "originate instructions" from the legislature "in favor of independency." It would turn many doubtful minds and "produce a reversal of the contrary instructions adopted by some assemblies." But, since some "timid minds are terrified at the word independence," Warren could call it something else if need be.[19] Two weeks later, after John Adams heard from Warren that "sighs for independence are universal," and moderation and timidity were at an end, Adams refused to believe it. He asked: "Why

[16] 5 April, *Lee Papers*, I, 378–80.   [17] 22 April, *Letters*, I, 182–83.
[18] 20 April, ibid. 176–80.   [19] 26 March, LMCC, I, 410.

don't your honors of the General Court, if you are so unanimous in this, give positive instructions to your own delegates to promote independency." [20] A few days later John Adams reported that South Carolina had assumed government, that North Carolina would repeal its instructions against independence, and that the cry throughout Virginia was for "Common Sense and Independence." He said that if North Carolina and Virginia followed South Carolina's example, "it will spread through all the rest of the colonies like electric fire." He repeated that if Massachusetts were so unanimous for independence, "now is the proper time for you to instruct your delegates to that effect." [21]

Despite such pleas the Massachusetts legislature never adopted instructions for independence, or even approved the idea until after independence had been declared. Certain leaders in the colony, such as James Warren and Joseph Hawley, wanted independence, and agreed that instructions would be a good thing, but they did little or nothing to secure them. James Warren complained to Samuel Adams that the legislature was too busy with minor matters to concern itself with "the grand question," and a little later he explained that he had tried to get instructions but that he had been ill. Hawley, who was constantly telling the delegates in Congress that independence should be declared as soon as possible, delayed action in Massachusetts by deciding that the legislature should consult the towns.[22]

Massachusetts did nothing because there was strong opposition to independence in the colony, but above all, because most of the legislators were so concerned with the struggle for power within the colony that they had no time to consider events outside its borders. The struggle began in 1774 when the backcountry counties, and some rural areas in the east, overthrew the county courts and demanded a revolution in government. The eastern leaders of the colony had appealed to the Continental Congress for help in 1774, and again in 1775 when they secured advice to assume government under the charter of 1691.[23]

In July 1775, when government was established according to the advice, the House of Representatives elected a council as it had done before the Government Act of 1774. Because the governor was "absent," the council functioned as the executive as well as the upper house of the legislature. The council was dominated by easterners and it at once set about trying to re-establish the court system. It appointed justices of the peace and judges,

[20] 16 April, *Warren-Adams Letters*, I, 227–28.
[21] To James Warren, 20, 22 April, ibid. 230–34.
[22] To Samuel Adams, 2 May, and to John Adams, 8 May, ibid. II, 437 and I, 240.
[23] See Chapter XXI above.

and it claimed the royal governor's power of appointing militia officers.

By the end of 1775 the council was under full-scale attack. The House of Representatives was clearly far more radical than the council which it had elected in July. The house insisted that it, as the representative of the people, should appoint militia officers. The council appealed to the Massachusetts delegates in Congress, who could not agree upon a joint reply. John and Samuel Adams told the council that it should follow the resolution of Congress in July 1775 recommending that "assemblies" elect militia officers. John Hancock and Thomas Cushing sided with the council but reluctantly advised it to yield. Cushing's stand helped prevent his reelection to Congress while the reputation of John and Samuel Adams went up. The council caved in and agreed that the house should appoint militia officers, although it claimed the right to veto appointments.

The attempt to re-establish the old court system met with powerful opposition in the western counties and in some areas in the east as well. They refused to accept a government based on the charter of 1691. In mid-December 1775 a Berkshire county convention resolved that the people should not support government under the charter, and should have the right to nominate their own justices of the peace and other civil officers. There were some dissenters at the convention who declared that the resolutions tended "to dissolve all government and introduce dissension, anarchy, and confusion among the people," but they did not represent majority opinion.[24]

A few days later the town of Pittsfield in the same county sent an eloquent petition to the legislature. It was written by the Reverend Thomas Allen, the leader of the "Berkshire Constitutionalists." He was a Congregational minister who had absorbed the more radical theories of the times and who used them to justify the political demands of his constituents. The petition declared that Berkshire county had been ruled "for many years past with a rod of iron," and that it was again in danger of returning to a "yoke of oppression which we are no longer able to bear." The old government with "its various sluices of corruption and oppression," and "the dangerous effects of nominating to office by those in power," was the "most defective, discordant, and ruinous system of government of any that has come under our observation."

The petition demanded the "privilege of electing our civil and military officers" and the popular election of a governor and lieutenant governor.

24 Resolves of the Stockbridge Convention, 15 Dec., reprinted in Robert J. Taylor, ed., *Massachusetts, Colony to Commonwealth* (Chapel Hill, 1961), 16–17.

"If the right of nominating to office is not invested in the people we are indifferent who assumes it, whether any particular persons on this or the other side of the water."

The petition declared that the people of Berkshire county would continue to govern themselves by committees as they had for the past sixteen months unless they got what they wanted. What they wanted was a government "de novo," and that in "the establishment of such a new constitution regard will be had for such a broad basis of civil and religious liberty as no length of time will corrupt, and which will endure as long as the sun and moon shall endure." [25]

In the spring of 1776 Pittsfield summed up the western demand for a new government and the theoretical basis upon which it should be founded. The petition asserted that "the people are the fountain of power," and that ever since the dissolution of the power of Britain over the colonies "they have fallen into a state of nature." The first step in the creation of civil government was to form a "fundamental constitution" which must have the approval of the "majority of the people" to "give life and being to it. That then and not 'til then is the foundation laid for legislation." A representative body may form "but cannot impose said fundamental constitution upon a people. They being but servants of the people cannot be greater than their masters, and must be responsible to them." [26]

Such ideas were shocking to many easterners who looked upon them as leading to utter anarchy, although many of those easterners had used the same ideas to oppose Britain. One correspondent of Samuel Adams declared flatly that "the people of this province . . . have not virtue enough to set up and maintain that democracy they almost universally and most ardently desire and are now aiming at." They are so opposed to monarchy that "they are not aware of the danger of the most popular kind of government that was ever thought of." [27]

Even more shocking than the ideas were the policies of the House of Representatives which was controlled by westerners, or at least by men who sympathized with them, during the winter of 1775-76. The first victory of the house came during the struggle over the appointment of militia officers. The second came with the suspension of some of the courts. The westerners refused to allow courts to operate unless they elected their own justices, and they stopped the courts from sitting. In

[25] Pittsfield Petition, 26 Dec., ibid. 14, 17-19.
[26] Pittsfield Petition, May 1776, ibid. 26-29.
[27] Benjamin Kent to Samuel Adams, 24 May 1776, Adams Papers, NYPL.

January the legislature issued a feeble proclamation, which had been written by the council, pleading for law and order. Two days later the house
resolved that the courts should be closed temporarily until a new list of
fees could be prepared. The house then stalled until April when it adjourned the superior court of Middlesex county until October. A few days
later it adjourned the courts of Hampshire, Worcester, Plymouth, and
Barnstable counties. The house then began the preparation of a list of fees
which was so low that James Warren told John Adams it would "drive
every man of interest and ability out of office." Warren, who had been
bitterly opposed to government based on the charter of 1691, now wailed:
"I dread the consequences of the levelling spirit, encouraged and drove to
such lengths as it is." [28] A majority of the council was opposed to low fees
but the house insisted, and if it could not "worry them out," it planned to
wait until after the election in May, and then it would elect a "more
pliant" council.[29]

The threat that the May elections might be followed by the election of a
council as radical as the house, inspired certain eastern leaders to stage a
brilliant counter-revolution which demonstrated that revolutionary ideas
could be used for anti-revolutionary purposes. Salem and Marblehead
called an Essex county convention to meet on 25 April at Ipswich. In a
series of resolutions, that convention appealed to the legislature for equality of representation. It declared that if "representation is equal, it is
perfect; as far as it deviates from this equality, so far it is imperfect and
approaches to that state of slavery; and the want of a just weight in
representation is an evil nearly akin to being totally destitute of it." Unequal representation of the worst kind existed in Massachusetts, whether
one considered population or property as the basis for it. There were
thirty towns and districts which paid no more taxes than any single town
in Essex county. The county paid a sixth of the colony's taxes but it did
not have one-tenth of the representation in the legislature. There were
eight western towns that sent ten representatives, yet the town of Ipswich,
with the same amount of property and the same population as the eight,
could send but two representatives. Whatever method the legislature
used, the convention would be satisfied with an "equality of representation"
based on numbers or property, or a combination of the two.[30]

The resolutions were presented to the legislature on 2 May and by
6 May a bill for "equal representation" had been passed. It was late in the

---

[28] 3 April, *Warren-Adams Letters*, I, 219.
[29] William Stearns to John Adams, 1 May, Adams Papers, MHS.
[30] Resolutions of an Essex County Convention, 25 April, Taylor, *Massachusetts*, 38–39.

session, and presumably the members from the more distant parts of the colony had left for home, thus making it possible for the easterners to get what they wanted. The popular party had used the technique many times during the past decade in its battles with Bernard and Hutchinson, and it was still a viable procedure. Representation by towns was not abolished and no towns lost representatives, but now towns with 220 freeholders could elect three representatives, those with 320 could elect four, and so on up. Boston's representation was raised from four to twelve, and Salem's from two to seven. James Warren, who was not concerned with the theoretical basis of the act but with political reality, put it quite simply: "Being threatened to be overrun from the frontiers, the county of Essex stirred themselves and sent a petition well supported for a more equal representation." [31]

The elections in May were to be a triumph for the east. The three eastern counties of Suffolk, Essex, and Middlesex increased their representation from 77 in July 1775 to 125 in May 1776, while the three western counties of Berkshire, Hampshire, and Worcester increased their representation from 70 to 72.[32]

It was not until 9 May, the day before the legislature dissolved prior to the annual election, that it at last took up the question of independence. The house resolved that the inhabitants of each town ought to advise the men they chose to represent them whether or not they would support Congress if it declared independence.[33] Even this was too much for the council, which, led by Thomas Cushing, rejected the resolution. The house then sent it to the *Boston Gazette* where it was published.[34]

Worcester voted unanimously for independence on 23 May.[35] Pittsfield was as usual both pointed and eloquent. Its representative was instructed "on no pretence whatever [to] favor a union with Great Britain" and to encourage the House of Representatives to tell Congress "that this whole province are waiting for the important moment which they in their great wisdom shall appoint for the declaration of independence and a free republic." [36] But many towns took no action. On 7 June the legislature decided that the notice in the *Boston Gazette* had probably not reached them and

[31] To John Adams, 8 May, *Warren-Adams Letters*, I, 241.
[32] See Patterson, Political Parties in Revolutionary Massachusetts, chapter VI, for a detailed account of the history of events in Massachusetts in 1775–76. My account, where not otherwise documented, is based on this chapter.
[33] MHJ, 10 May.
[34] Samuel Cooper to Samuel Adams, 13 May, Adams Papers, NYPL; BG, 13 May.
[35] *Worcester Town Records*, 1753–1783, 278.
[36] Force, 4 ser. VI, 649.

ordered the publication of a handbill asking the towns for their views. The reasoning was specious since towns in western Berkshire had known about the request and voted for independence. It was the eastern towns that had been slow to act. Boston, for instance, told its delegates to agree to independence if Congress voted it, but spent most of its instructions in defending the new representation act, to which there was growing objection. Of the sixteen Essex county towns for which there is any record, only one supported independence unequivocally.[37] Finally on 3 July the House of Representatives agreed to appoint a committee to prepare a letter to the Massachusetts delegates in Philadelphia telling them that if the Congress "should think it proper to declare the colonies independent of the kingdom of Great Britain, this house will approve of the measure." [38]

The day before in Philadelphia, the Continental Congress had voted for independence, thanks in part to the unceasing labors of the Massachusetts delegates who had waited in vain for instructions from their own colony.

ᘒᕋ

The failure of Massachusetts to lead the movement for independence was a source of anguish to her delegates in Philadelphia. In mid-April, John Adams said bluntly that "the southern colonies say you are afraid," and two weeks later Elbridge Gerry commented acidly that unless Massachusetts sent some of its "cool patriots" to Virginia, that colony might declare independence before Congress was ready for it.[39]

However, South Carolina rather than Virginia took the first although indirect step toward independence in the southern colonies. When the second provincial congress reassembled early in February, it at once appointed a committee to consider the Continental Congress's resolution advising South Carolina to form a government if one were necessary. On 10 February the committee reported that a new government was necessary, but there were immediate objections. Some delegates wanted to delay the question, others were unprepared "for so decisive a measure," and still others argued that their constituents had not vested them with the power to write a constitution. Christopher Gadsden, who had returned from Philadelphia with the first copy of Common Sense to reach South Carolina, then "boldly declared himself, not only in favor of the form of gov-

[37] Patterson, Political Parties, 426–28.   [38] MHJ, 3 July.
[39] Adams to Warren, 16 April, Warren-Adams Letters, I, 228; Gerry to Warren, 1 May, LMCC, I, 438.

ernment, but for the absolute independence of America." His declaration was "like an explosion of thunder upon the members of congress," for the resolution of the Continental Congress had not led them to expect "so decisive a step; neither had the majority of the members at that time, any thoughts of aspiring at independence." "Even the few who wished for independence" thought Gadsden had been imprudent in suddenly presenting a matter of such great importance to a house unprepared to consider it.

The subject of independence was dropped, but the congress agreed to appoint a committee to write a constitution. There was sturdy and continuing resistance to the proposed constitution until 21 March when the news of the American Prohibitory Act reached Charleston. Two days later the congress authorized its delegates in the Continental Congress to join with the majority in every measure judged "necessary for the defence, security, interest, or welfare of this colony in particular, and of America in general," and on 26 March it adopted the constitution and declared itself "the general assembly." In order that the constitution "might not strike in too glaring a light the apprehensions of timid or weak minds," the preamble stated that the government was necessary until an accommodation with Great Britain could be obtained.[40]

The Georgia congress acted next. On 5 April it informed its delegates to the Continental Congress that it was so remote "from the seat of power and arms" that it was ignorant of the ultimate designs of Congress. Therefore it would not give its delegates "any particular instructions" except to remind them of the peculiar situation of Georgians, with Indians at their backs "together with our blacks and tories within us." But the delegates were to remember too "that the great and righteous cause in which we are engaged is not provincial but Continental." When the two Georgia delegates arrived on 20 May their instructions were widely regarded as allowing them to support independence, and they did.[41]

The North Carolina provincial congress was the first colonial body anywhere to approve independence by name. In September 1775 the congress had ordered its delegates in the Continental Congress not to agree to a confederation without consulting the provincial congress, an order re-

[40] South Carolina Provincial Congress *Journals*, 184–85, 223, 227–28, 248, 254–63; Drayton, *Memoirs*, II, 172–73, 175–81. John Drayton's account is based on the narrative and papers left by his father William Henry Drayton who was president of the provincial congress.
[41] Archibald Bulloch to the Georgia Delegates, 5 April, JCC, IV, 367, n.1.

garded as being an instruction against independence. The congress reversed itself on 12 April 1776 when it unanimously empowered its delegates to "concur with the delegates of the other colonies in declaring independency, and forming foreign alliances," but reserving to the colony the "sole and exclusive right" to form a constitution and laws for the colony. The next day it elected a committee to prepare a temporary constitution.[42] Unanimity disappeared at once and it was not until December 1776 that North Carolina was able to create a constitution for the new state.

The Rhode Islanders acted next. As usual they ignored what Congress or their neighbors might or might not do. Rhode Island had been represented in Congress by its once-embattled former governors, Stephen Hopkins and Samuel Ward. Hopkins dragged his heels on independence, but Ward was committed to it by the fall of 1775 and worked closely with the Adamses and the Lees. He died of smallpox in March 1776, to the great grief of the Adamses. But his colony went ahead. There was a strong loyalist element in Rhode Island, but after the spring elections in 1776 the legislature balked at requiring the elected officers to take the usual oath of allegiance to the king, and on 4 May declared Rhode Island's independence. George III had broken the compact, and "entirely departing from the duties and character of a good king, instead of protecting, is endeavoring to destroy the good people of this colony, and all the united colonies by sending fleets and armies to America. . . ." The act requiring an oath to the king was repealed and the king's name dropped from all commissions and writs and replaced by "the name and authority of the governor and company of this colony. . . ." Courts of law would no longer be considered king's courts nor would any piece of public or private writing mention the year of the king's reign. On the same day Rhode Island gave its delegates in Congress sweeping authority to unite with the other colonies in any measures necessary "to annoy the common enemy" and to secure American rights and liberties.[43]

So far no colony had ordered its delegates to move for independence, and, except for North Carolina, none had used the word. Such orders came from the Virginia convention which met on 6 May. Virginians were no more united on the subject of independence than the people of the other colonies. Carter Braxton wrote from Philadelphia to his uncle Landon Carter, only three weeks before the Virginia convention met, that inde-

[42] NCCR, X, 192, 512, 515.
[43] RICR, VII, 522–23, 526; Lovejoy, *Rhode Island*, 191–93.

pendence was "in truth a delusive bait which men inconsiderately snatch at, without knowing the hook to which it is affixed." He agreed that it was an object to be desired if it could be obtained with safety and honor but he was firmly convinced that the time had not yet arrived. His uncle in turn looked upon independence as little more than a lower-class uprising, but both men accepted independence when it was declared.[44] Other prominent Virginians such as Attorney General John Randolph, brother of Peyton Randolph, did not, yet his son Edmund Randolph chose the American side. The Randolph family was by no means the only family in Virginia or in other colonies to be split in 1776.

Probably half the Virginia counties instructed their delegates to vote for independence when they went to the convention in May, and apparently the backcountry counties were overwhelmingly in favor of it. When Thomas Jefferson returned to the Continental Congress in May, he reported back to Thomas Nelson that he took great pains while at home to inquire into the sentiments of the people about independence, and that "in the upper counties I think I may safely say nine out of ten are for it." He urged Nelson "to bring on as early as you can in convention the great question of the session." [45]

When the convention met on 6 May the drive for independence was led by Nelson and by Patrick Henry, who had resigned his military commission in disgust and returned to politics. The two men agreed, after "the disposition of the people, as exhibited by their representatives, could not be mistaken," that Nelson "should introduce the question of independence, and that Henry should enforce it." Nelson was no orator. He did not emphasize the difficulties that would be involved but argued for independence on the grounds that Americans were oppressed, that their appeals for a redress of grievances "had been refused with insult; and that to return from battle against the sovereign, with the cordiality of subjects, was absurd."

Henry followed Nelson and at first talked without committing himself, "but after some time he appeared in an element for which he was born." His reasoning was not subtle "but was roused by the now apparent spirit of the people, as a pillar of fire" and "he inflamed, and was followed by the convention." The vote was unanimous except for Robert Carter Nicholas, who promised, nevertheless, to "rise and fall" with his country. "The

[44] Braxton to Carter, 14 April, LMCC, I, 420; Carter to George Washington, 9 May, Force, 4 ser. VI, 390–91.
[45] 16 May, Papers, I, 292.

principles of Paine's pamphlet," said Edmund Randolph, "now stalked in triumph under the sanction of the most extensive, richest, and most commanding colony in America." [46]

There were some members of the convention who thought Virginia should declare its own independence, but the final outcome was the resolution of 15 May instructing the Virginia delegates in Congress "to propose to that respectable body to declare the United Colonies free and independent States, absolved from all allegiance to, or dependence upon the Crown or Parliament of Great Britain," and giving advance approval to any measures for forming foreign alliances and a confederation that Congress might adopt.[47] Patrick Henry told John Adams "I put up with it in the present form for the sake of unanimity. 'Tis not quite so pointed as I could wish." He also told Adams that a confederation and an alliance with France ought to precede "an open declaration of independency," for he was afraid that France might aid Britain.

His major concern, however, was with the kind of government that Virginia would adopt. As soon as the convention had voted for independence it appointed a committee to draft a bill of rights and a constitution. Henry told both John Adams and Richard Henry Lee that the "opulent" had a "bias" to aristocracy, and to Lee he wrote: "I own myself a democrat on the plan of our admired friend, J. Adams, whose pamphlet I read with great pleasure." [48]

Patrick Henry, like every other American leader in 1776, was concerned with the shape of the future that independence would bring, and much of that concern was with the nature of the new governments to be created. Some men were proposing radical alterations while others clung to the political structure of the past. No group of political leaders held to the past with more tenacity than most of the older leaders of Pennsylvania, who feared that independence would destroy the "constitution" that guaranteed their political power.

ह﹅

After the "war" had been won, Elbridge Gerry, who had come to Congress in February 1776, said that ever since his arrival "the New England

[46] Edmund Randolph, "Essay," *Virginia Magazine of History and Biography*, XLIV, 41–43. Randolph was a member of the convention and his account is as close to an eye-witness account as we have.
[47] Force, 4 ser. VI, 1524. For two different accounts see Eckenrode, *Revolution in Virginia*, 157–62, and Mays, *Pendleton*, II, 106–7.
[48] To John Adams, 20 May, Adams, *Works*, IV, 201–2; to Lee, 20 May, Henry, *Henry*, I, 411.

delegates have been in a continual war with the advocates of proprietary interest in Congress and this colony." [49]

In the spring of 1776 the political agencies representing the middle colonies were still opposed to independence. It did not matter whether they were the revolutionary bodies of New York, New Jersey, and Maryland, or the old colonial legislatures of Pennsylvania and Delaware; they showed no intention of repealing the instructions which prevented their delegates in Congress from voting for independence. Among these colonies, Pennsylvania was looked upon as the biggest obstacle, and the supporters of independence did not dare go ahead without one of the richest colonies and the largest city in America. It was assumed that if Pennsylvania would vote for independence, the neighboring colonies would follow her example.

Most of the older leaders of the proprietary and Quaker parties had buried their enmities and joined forces to oppose independence, which they feared would destroy what they repeatedly called "our excellent constitution." With John Dickinson as their leader, both in the assembly and in Congress, they refused to change the instructions of November 1775 forbidding the Pennsylvania delegates in Congress to vote for independence.

By 1776 a new group of popular leaders had risen in Philadelphia, men almost unknown before 1774. In February they got control of the Philadelphia committee of inspection of which John Dickinson had once been chairman. Such men as Timothy Matlack, James Cannon, David Rittenhouse, Dr. Benjamin Rush, and Christopher Marshall had various reasons for wanting independence, but they saw eye to eye with the Adamses, Thomas Paine, and Dr. Thomas Young, who proved to be as adept an agitator in Philadelphia as he had been in Boston. These men met together constantly to plan means of reversing the Pennsylvania instructions against independence, and eventually, for overthrowing the assembly itself.[50]

Late in February the Philadelphia committee decided to call a convention to meet in April, and followed it with a petition to the assembly for more adequate representation. For years the assembly had rejected all appeals for additional representation from the western counties, but in March 1776, in a desperate effort to retain control and to head off a convention, the assembly voted to authorize seventeen additional representatives and called an election for 1 May to fill the new seats.[51] The

[49] To James Warren, 25 June, LMCC, I, 508.
[50] Christopher Marshall's *Diary* lists almost daily meetings among these men.
[51] Assembly Proceedings, 8, 13, 14 March, Force, 4 ser. V, 679, 683–84.

Philadelphia committee agreed to suspend the call for a convention and await the outcome of the election.[52] John Adams took some of the credit for "this maneuver" and he predicted that the new representatives "will give a finishing blow to the Quaker interest in this city—at least its ascendancy. It will strip it of all that unjust and unequal power which it formerly had over the balance of the province." [53]

A few days after the Philadelphia committee forced the assembly to grant more representation by threatening to call a convention, the committee asked the assembly to rescind its instructions against independence. This time the assembly defied the popular leaders. It was willing to vote paper money to buy military supplies, to levy additional taxes on those who would not join the military associations, and for other defense measures, but it would not vote for independence. On 6 April "after a debate of considerable length" it rejected alteration of the instructions to the delegates in Congress "by a great majority." [54]

Attention then turned to the election on 1 May. The Philadelphia committee prepared a slate of four candidates for the new seats awarded the city and so did "the moderates" who wanted reconciliation with Britain.[55] That the issue in the election was independence was understood by everyone. A South Carolina doctor noted soon after he arrived that "the body of the people were for independency. The proprietary, [Governor] John Penn, and most of the gentlemen of the city . . . were against it lest the form of government should be changed. . . ." [56]

The opponents of independence turned out in force at the election and won a stunning victory. They captured three of the four new city seats with a ticket headed by Andrew Allen, an outspoken opponent of independence. Most of the backcountry counties elected supporters of independence, although James Allen won one of the two new seats in Northampton county. Christopher Marshall commented bitterly that "the Quakers, Papists, Church, Allen family, with all the proprietary party, were never seemingly so happily united as at this election, notwithstanding [the] Friends' former protestation and declaration of never joining with that party. . . ." [57]

The attempt to capture the assembly by legal means had failed, and opponents of independence still retained a majority in it. There would

---

[52] Marshall, *Diary*, 69.
[53] To James Warren, 21 March, *Warren-Adams Letters*, I, 213–14.
[54] Marshall, *Diary*, 72; 4–6 April, Force, 4 ser. V, 695–716.
[55] Marshall, *Diary*, 75–76.
[56] "Diary of James Clitherall," 13 May, PMHB, XXII (1898), 469.
[57] 1 May, *Diary*, 77; Thayer, *Pennsylvania*, 178–79.

have to be a revolution overthrowing the assembly if the Pennsylvania instructions against independence were to be reversed. John Adams, with the help of Richard Henry Lee, undertook to provide a justification for such a revolution, and to make it respectable. On 10 May Congress adopted a resolution which John Adams had introduced some days earlier. It "recommended to the respective assemblies and conventions of the United Colonies, where no government sufficient to the exigencies of their affairs have been hitherto established, to adopt such government as shall, in the opinion of the representatives of the people, best conduce to the happiness and safety of their constituents in particular, and America in general." [58]

It was passed with "remarkable unanimity," in part because John Dickinson agreed to it. John Adams commented that gentlemen were being converted every day to sentiments and measures which he had supported for ten months, and that "Mr. Dickinson himself is now an advocate for colony governments and continental confederation." Dickinson assumed, apparently, that the resolution of 10 May did not apply to Pennsylvania which, from his point of view, had a perfectly adequate government. But he underestimated John Adams and made the mistake of leaving for Delaware.[59]

The resolution of 10 May needed a preamble and Congress appointed John Adams, Richard Henry Lee, and Edward Rutledge to prepare one. The preamble John Adams wrote provided the theoretical foundation for revolution which Jefferson was to elaborate in the Declaration of Independence a few weeks later, but its immediate purpose was to justify a revolution in Pennsylvania. All governments deriving their authority from the Crown, said Adams, "should be totally suppressed, and all the powers of government exerted, under the authority of the people of the colonies. . . ." [60]

No member of Congress could mistake either the long-range or immediate purpose of the preamble. James Duane of New York insisted that the instructions of the New York delegation to work for reconciliation be read, and then declared Congress had no more right to pass such a preamble than Parliament had, for Congress had no power over the internal affairs of

[58] JCC, IV, 342.
[59] John Adams to James Warren, 12 May, *Warren-Adams Letters*, I, 242, and to John Winthrop, 12 May, MHSC, 5 ser. IV, 302. For Dickinson's trip to Delaware, see Thomas Rodney to Caesar Rodney, 19 May, G. H. Ryden, ed., *Letters To and From Caesar Rodney, 1756–1784* (Philadelphia, 1933), 82.
[60] 15 May, JCC, IV, 357–58.

the colonies. He insisted that commissioners would come from England and asked: "Why all this haste? Why this urging? Why this driving?" "I do protest against this piece of mechanism, this preamble," but, he concluded bitterly, "I suppose the votes have been numbered and there is to be a majority."

James Wilson pled for the old order in Pennsylvania, and as he was to do many times in the years to come, he used revolutionary ideas in an effort to prevent revolutionary action. He began by agreeing that "all government originates with the people. We are servants of the people sent here to act under a delegated authority. If we exceed it, voluntarily, we deserve neither excuse nor justification." Wilson's hearers knew that his main concern was to defend the position of the assembly and to block the wishes of those people in Pennsylvania who wanted independence. He got to the heart of the matter when he declared that "in this province, if that preamble passes, there will be an immediate dissolution of every kind of authority. The people will instantly be in a state of nature." [61]

The votes had been counted, as Duane had guessed, but the victory was a narrow one. Apparently six colonies voted for the preamble while four voted against it. Furthermore, the Maryland delegates walked out after declaring that they would not be bound by any actions of Congress until they received instructions from their convention. Nevertheless, John Adams rightly treated the vote as a great victory. He wrote in triumph: "this day the Congress has passed the most important resolution that ever was taken in America." [62] He looked upon the preamble as a declaration of independence. Britain had driven America to the last step, "a complete separation from her, a total absolute independence, not only of her Parliament but of her Crown, for such is the amount of the resolve of the 15th." Many another member of Congress agreed with him, as did people "out of doors." [63]

Pennsylvanians of all shades of opinion understood exactly what the preamble meant. The day it passed James Allen noted that the assembly probably would not agree to change the constitution, and then there would be a convention. "A convention chosen by the people will consist of the most fiery independents; they will have the whole executive and legislative authority in their hands." [64] The Philadelphia leaders did not wait to see

61 John Adams, Notes of Debates, 13–15 May.
62 Carter Braxton to Landon Carter, 17 May, LMCC, I, 454; John Adams to James Warren, Warren-Adams Letters, I, 245.
63 To Abigail Adams, 17 May, Family Corres., I, 410. See also LMCC, I, 453–55.
64 "Diary," PMHB, IX, 186–87.

what the assembly would do. On the evening of 15 May the Philadelphia committee met to discuss the action of Congress and the next day a number of persons met and decided "to call a convention with speed," and to protest against the assembly doing any business until "the sense of the province was taken" in such a convention. On the 18th, the Philadelphia committee decided, with only five dissenting votes, to call a mass meeting on 20 May "to take the sense of the people" concerning the resolve and the preamble of Congress.[65]

The mass meeting voted that the assembly's instructions against independence should be rescinded, that the assembly had no authority to form a new government, and that a convention, with members chosen by the people, be called to write a constitution.[66] The next day the Philadelphia committee sent a letter to the county committees throughout the colony asking them to send representatives to a provincial conference on 18 June to make plans for calling a convention. The convention would be for the "express purpose of forming and establishing a new government on the authority of the people only" according to the recommendations of the Continental Congress.[67]

The Pennsylvania assembly met on 20 May, the day of the Philadelphia mass meeting, and made a desperate effort to retain control. But whenever it tried to act, enough members stayed away to prevent a quorum. It tried and failed to get control of the movement to write a new constitution.[68] Finally, when the Virginia instructions for independence were laid before the assembly on 5 June, it appointed a committee to write new instructions to the Pennsylvania delegates in Congress. Among the committee's members were two of those delegates, John Dickinson and Robert Morris, and both of them were opposed to independence.[69]

The committee reported back the next day but it was not until Saturday, 8 June, that the assembly finally agreed to withdraw the instructions, only to put off final action until the next week, after a member offered amendments. On Monday, 10 June, the *Pennsylvania Packet* reported that the instructions had been withdrawn, but the assembly, which no longer could obtain a quorum, quibbled the rest of the week. Finally, on Friday the 14th the speaker signed a statement withdrawing the instructions against

---

[65] Marshall, *Diary*, 80–81, 82.   [66] PG, 22 May.
[67] Philadelphia committee to the county committees, 21 May, J. E. Gibson, "The Pennsylvania Provincial Conference of 1776," PMHB, LVIII (1934), 335–37.
[68] Assembly Proceedings, 22, 24 May, Force, 4 ser. VI, 847–49.
[69] Ibid. 857.

independence and the assembly adjourned until August, but it never met again.[70]

Four days later the provincial conference met and laid plans for the constitutional convention that wrote a constitution exemplifying all that the men who had controlled the colonial assembly looked upon as evil in government. John Adams, whose ideas about government were far closer to those of the leaders of the colonial assembly than to those of the men who wrote the Pennslyvania constitution of 1776, explained why the colonial leaders had lost power. "The timid and trimming politics of some men of large property here have almost done their business for them. They have lost their influence and grown obnoxious. The Quakers and proprietarians together have little weight."[71]

They had lost because they had abdicated leadership in their blind resistance to independence and to any change in government. In most other colonies, enough established political leaders and men of large property had the wit or the wisdom to remain a part of the popular movement, however much they deplored it, and were able to exercise a measure of influence in shaping the political future of their states. Thus in New York, Robert R. Livingston pointed to "the propriety of swimming with a stream which it is impossible to stem." He said that he had advised the Pennsylvania leaders "that they should yield to the torrent if they hoped to direct its course—you know nothing but well-timed delays, indefatigable industry, and a minute attention to every favorable circumstance, could have prevented our being exactly in their situation."[72]

ළ

The day the Philadelphia mass meeting set in motion the events that destroyed the Pennsylvania assembly, John Adams wrote gleefully: "Every post and every day rolls in upon us independence like a torrent." Georgia, South Carolina, and North Carolina were "firm" and "this day's post has brought a multitude of letters from Virginia, all of which breathe the same spirit."[73]

The North Carolina and Virginia delegations laid their instructions concerning independence before Congress on 27 May, but ten days elapsed before the Virginia delegates acted.[74] Congress began the morning of

[70] Ibid. 859, 860, 862–63.   [71] To William Tudor, 24 June, Works, IX, 411.
[72] To James Duer, 12 June 1777, quoted in Alfred F. Young, The Democratic Republicans of New York: The Origins 1763–1783 (Chapel Hill, 1967), 15.
[73] To James Warren, 20 May, Warren-Adams Letters, I, 249.   [74] JCC, IV, 397.

7 June as usual. It voted to pay damages to a Charles Walker of New Providence whose sloop, with a cargo of four tons of lignum vitae and 100 cedar posts, had been seized by Commodore Esek Hopkins of the Continental Navy. The governor of Connecticut was asked to appoint "judicious and indifferent" persons to estimate the value of the vessel and the goods at the time they were seized. Congress then debated and recommitted a report on resolutions of the South Carolina congress respecting battalions of troops raised in that colony. It next turned to a complaint about defective powder manufactured by Mr. Oswald Eve, and appointed a committee to investigate and to take measures to remedy the defect.

Richard Henry Lee then rose and offered three resolutions:

> That these United Colonies are, and of right ought to be, free and independent States, that they are absolved from all allegiance to the British Crown, and that all political connection between them and the State of Great Britain is, and ought to be, totally dissolved.
>
> That it is expedient forthwith to take the most effectual measures for forming foreign Alliances.
>
> That a plan of confederation be prepared and transmitted to the respective Colonies for their consideration and approbation.

It was entirely fitting that John Adams seconded the resolutions offered by his friend and co-worker. Congress agreed to consider the resolutions at ten o'clock the next day and then turned to a committee report about a woman in New Jersey who, with the help of her husband, had counterfeited Continental paper money, and had been caught and jailed.[75]

Congress began the great debate on independence on Saturday morning, 8 June, and at the end of the day it agreed to renew the debate on Monday, 10 June. That night Edward Rutledge of South Carolina wrote to John Jay in New York that "the sensible part of the house" opposed Lee's motion and that the only reason offered for declaring independence was "the reason of every madman, a show of our spirit." The "sensible part" did not object to a confederation or to planning treaties with foreign powers. One would have to have, said Rutledge, "the impudence of a New Englander to propose, in our present disjointed state, any treaty (honorable to us) to a nation now at peace." He reported that the argument on one side was carried by Robert R. Livingston, James Wilson, John Dickinson, and himself, and "by the power of all New England, Virginia, and Georgia at the other."[76] The next day John Adams wrote confidently: "we

[75] Ibid. V, 424–26.   [76] LMCC, I, 476–77.

are in the very midst of revolution, the most complete, unexpected, and remarkable of any in the history of nations." [77]

By Monday morning no minds had been changed. The men who opposed independence admitted that it was inevitable, but argued that it should not be adopted at that time. As in the past, Congress should wait "till the voice of the people drove us into it." The people of the middle colonies were not "ripe" for independence, but were "fast ripening," and in a short time "would join in the general voice of America." They argued that the ferment created in the middle colonies by the preamble Congress adopted on 15 May proved that they were not ready for independence. Furthermore, some of the colonies had forbidden their delegates to vote for independence, and others had given no instructions and therefore their delegates had no power. The speakers who demanded delay then threatened to walk out if Congress voted for independence: "if such a declaration should now be agreed to, these delegates must now retire and possibly their colonies might secede the Union."

The threat was real, but John Adams, Richard Henry Lee, and George Wythe asserted bluntly that it was the representatives of the people, rather than the people, who were opposed to independence. The only question before Congress was whether or not to "declare a fact which already exists." America had always been independent of the people and Parliament of Britain, and the king had dissolved the bond between the Crown and the colonies by agreeing to the Prohibitory Act. The people were waiting for Congress to lead the way and "they are in favor of the measure, though the instructions given by some of their representatives are not." The "voice of the representatives is not always consonant with the voice of the people, and . . . this is remarkably the case in these middle colonies."

As for the preamble of 15 May, the independents asserted that it "called forth the opposing voice of the freer part of the people" in Pennsylvania and Maryland "and proved them to be the majority, even in these colonies." The backwardness of the two colonies was not to be blamed on the people but on "the influence of proprietary power and connections, and partly to their having not yet been attacked by the enemy."

In the heat of the argument, someone delivered a low, and possibly accurate blow, when he charged that there was "reason to suspect" that some colonies had lagged behind from the beginning so "that their particular prospect might be better, even in the worst event." But it was necessary for the colonies who had hazarded their all from the start to come forward

[77] To William Cushing, 9 June, *Works,* IX, 390.

again "and put all again to their own hazard." The history of the Dutch revolution proved that "the secession of some colonies would not be so dangerous as some apprehended." In any event, it would be useless to wait "either weeks or months for perfect unanimity, since it was impossible that all men should ever become of one sentiment on any question."

A part of the debate centered on the possibility of securing foreign aid and, like many a debate on "foreign policy" since then, it consisted more of assertions based on hope than of statements based on fact. Those who wanted to delay independence as long as possible insisted that if Congress declared independence and their colonies seceded, foreign powers would either refuse to help or demand hard terms. France and Spain would probably not help, for they were jealous of that rising power "which would one day certainly strip them of all their American possessions." They would be more likely to ally with Britain who would return Canada to France and the Floridas to Spain in return for their help. In any case Congress should wait for a report from the agent who had been sent to Paris. If his report were favorable, and the next military campaign successful, Americans could expect better terms. Furthermore, Americans ought to agree to the terms of an alliance before agreeing to enter into one. If all such matters could be settled, then it would be time to consider a declaration of independence.

The supporters of independence replied that foreign powers would never help Americans unless they first declared their independence. France and Spain might be jealous of America, but it was to their interest to prevent a coalition between America and Britain; in any case, Americans would never know about foreign help unless they tried to get it, and they should try at once. The coming military campaign might not turn out well and it would be better to propose an alliance while American affairs looked hopeful. Congress should not waste time talking about the terms of an alliance before deciding whether it wanted an alliance or not.

Despite all the argument and counter-argument, the one controlling factor that prevented a decision on independence on 10 June was the threat of certain delegates to walk out if Congress approved Richard Henry Lee's motion. The outcome was a compromise. The vote was not delayed to some indefinite future as some delegates wanted, nor was there a showdown as other delegates insisted there should be. When it appeared, wrote Jefferson, "in the course of these debates that the colonies of New York, New Jersey, Pennsylvania, Delaware, Maryland, and South Carolina were not yet matured for falling off from the parent stem, but that they were fast advancing to that state, it was thought most prudent to wait a while for them, and to postpone the final decision to July 1." The vote was seven to five.[78]

In order to avoid delay, a committee consisting of Thomas Jefferson, John Adams, Benjamin Franklin, Roger Sherman, and Robert R. Livingston were appointed "to prepare a declaration of independence." A second committee, with John Dickinson as chairman, was appointed to draft articles of confederation, and a third committee to make plans for foreign alliances.[79]

Various delegates appealed to their home colonies for instructions and Congress resumed its consideration of the day-to-day problems of running a war. The new committees began their work and within a few days, one of the most concerned members predicted that they would report in a week or two, "and then the last finishing strokes will be given to the politics of this revolution. Nothing after that will remain but war." [80]

ॐ

Within days after the congressional debate on 10 June, independence received widespread support. In Philadelphia nearly 2000 men in four battalions of the military associators met and voted. Two battalions were unanimous for independence. Only two privates in one battalion and four officers and twenty-three privates in another had the courage to vote against the overwhelming opinion of their fellows.[81] When the Pennsylvania provincial conference met on 18 June, the delegates were unanimous for independence, and many of them produced instructions from their constituents to vote for it. The conference adopted a "declaration on the subject of independence" promising to concur in independence when it was voted by Congress.[82]

On 14 June the Connecticut Assembly, as the Virginia convention had done, specifically instructed its delegates in Congress to propose that Congress "declare the United American Colonies free and independent

[78] All that we know about the debates on 8 and 10 June, aside from the letter of Rutledge to Jay, comes from the notes taken by Thomas Jefferson. These, with a superb introduction by Julian Boyd, are in Jefferson, *Papers*, I, 299–313. The vote is given in Maryland delegates to Maryland Committee of Safety, 11 June, LMCC, I, 485–86.
[79] JCC, V, 428–29, 431, 432.
[80] John Adams to John Winthrop, 23 June, *Works*, IX, 410.
[81] *Pennsylvania Evening Post*, 11 June 1776.
[82] PMHB, LVIII (1934), 335–37; John Adams to Samuel Chase, 24 June, *Works*, IX, 413.

states. . . ." [83] The New Hampshire delegates asked for instructions as soon as the Virginians laid their instructions before Congress, and described independence as "this necessary step." [84] On 15 June the New Hampshire House of Representatives unanimously instructed its delegates to join with the other colonies in declaring independence.[85]

Delaware yielded on the same day as New Hampshire. Thomas McKean returned from Congress and laid the congressional resolution of 10 May and preamble of 15 May before the assembly on 14 June. The assembly approved unanimously and the next day voted to continue all officeholders in office until a new government could be created. The assembly then authorized its delegates in Congress to concur in forming further compacts among the colonies, to make treaties with foreign nations, and to adopt "such other measures" as were necessary for "promoting the liberty, safety, and interests of America. . . ." The assembly could not bring itself to mention the word independence.[86]

A provincial congress had taken over the government of New Jersey in January 1776. Benjamin Franklin's son, Sir William Franklin, had been an able governor but he opposed the policies of Congress. He lost much of his popularity but was allowed to remain in the colony. The provincial congress had not, however, made any effort to reverse the instructions against independence adopted by the colonial legislature in November 1775.

A newly elected provincial congress met for the first time on 10 June 1776. The Virginia instructions were "read, and ordered to be filed" on 12 June, and two days later the congress turned on Governor Franklin, who had called the assembly to meet. The congress voted 38-11 that his call should not be obeyed, and the next day it resolved 48-10 that he was "an enemy to the liberties of this country" and ought to be arrested. The decision seems to have been the turning point. Jonathan Sergeant, who had left Congress, wrote back to John Adams that day: "we are passing the Rubicon and our delegates in Congress on the first of July will vote plump." [87] On 21 June, Governor Franklin was brought before the provincial congress. He refused to answer questions and flatly denied the authority of the congress to ask them. It then declared him a "virulent enemy to this country, and a person that may prove dangerous," and

---

[83] Force, 4 ser. VI, 868.
[84] To the President of New Hampshire, 28 May, LMCC, I, 466–67.
[85] Nathaniel Bouton, ed., Documents and Records . . . State of New Hampshire . . . 1776 to 1783, VIII (Concord, 1874), 149–50.
[86] Resolutions of the Delaware Assembly, 14–15 June, Rodney, Letters, 91–92.
[87] 15 June, Adams Papers, MHS.

resolved unanimously that he should be confined wherever the Continental Congress might decide.

The provincial congress then turned to the questions of government and independence. It voted to approve the 15 May preamble of the Continental Congress, and the next day it elected a new delegation and gave it the power to join with the other colonies in declaring independence and entering into a confederation with them.[88]

By the 25th of June, Elbridge Gerry could report that only New York and Maryland stood in the way of independence, and he was convinced that the people in those colonies were for independence and would support it even if their conventions and their delegates voted against it.[89]

The Maryland convention denied that it and "the people" of Maryland wanted independence in January 1776, and when it adjourned that month, several of its leaders held a secret meeting with Governor Robert Eden to discuss means of bringing about reconciliation with Britain. Eden assured the secretary of state that they were sincere in their "abhorrence" of independence. By spring, however, such men as Charles Carroll of Carrollton were shaken by the Prohibitory Act and were coming to the reluctant conclusion that independence must be the outcome.

At the same time Maryland's leaders were alarmed at, and at times almost paralyzed by, the fear of popular uprisings. The *Peggy Stewart* had been burned at Annapolis in the fall of 1774 because some extremist political leaders insisted upon it, and it was done under the threat of mob reprisal. By the end of 1775 debtors were refusing to pay debts and freeing other debtors from jails, and armed bands were roaming the colony attacking tax collectors.

Most horrifying of all was the fear of a rebellion on the eastern shore, where poor whites and slaves were threatening to combine in an attack on the planters. In May 1775 the Dorchester county court took a deposition from James Mullineaux who had talked to a wheelwright whom he found fishing. He asked the man if he was going to the militia muster at Cambridge the next Monday. The man replied that he was going, but not to the muster. He said that he understood "that the gentlemen were intending to make us all fight for their lands and Negroes, and then said, damn them (meaning the gentlemen) if I had a few more white people to join me, I could get all the Negroes in the country to back us, and they would do more good in the night than the white people could do in the day. . . ." The wheelwright said he knew where he could get ammunition

[88] Force, 4 ser. VI, 1627.   [89] To James Warren, LMCC, I, 508.

and that "if all the gentlemen were killed we should have the best of the land to tend, and besides could get money enough while they were about it as they have got all the money in their hands."

Governor Dunmore's proclamation in November 1775 offering freedom to the slaves of Virginia who would fight for him was as frightening to Maryland leaders as it was to Virginians. Turmoil continued on the eastern shore. The Dorchester county committee of inspection disarmed some slaves and reported that "the malicious and imprudent speeches of some among the lower classes of whites have induced them to believe that their freedom depended on the success of the king's troops. We cannot be too vigilant nor too rigorous with those who promote and encourage this disposition in our slaves." [90]

The fear that their society would disintegrate completely if they made the leap to independence, helps to explain, in part at least, why many of Maryland's leaders clung so long to the hope of reconciliation. When Congress adopted the preamble of 15 May asking that governments be based on the will of the people, the Maryland delegates withdrew from Congress, announcing that they would not be bound by its actions until they reported to the Maryland convention and had received instructions as to how to act "upon this alarming occasion." [91]

The Maryland convention received the preamble on 20 May, and the next day agreed unanimously and flatly that the convention had ample power, and that it was not necessary that all authority of the Crown should be suppressed in Maryland or that all powers of government should be exercised under the people. It re-elected its delegates to Congress and resolved unanimously that a reunion with Britain "on constitutional principles would most effectually secure the rights and liberties, and increase the strength and promote the happiness of the whole empire. . . ." The delegates were told to govern themselves by the instructions against independence which had been adopted on 11 January.

The convention did make a few gestures. It requested Governor Eden to leave the colony for the sake of its public quiet and safety, but declared that he had full liberty to leave peaceably with his effects. The convention also established an admiralty court according to the recommendations of Congress, and it resolved that the prayers for the king in the book of common prayer were to be omitted in all churches "until our unhappy

[90] For the above information I am indebted to Ronald Hoffman who is writing a doctoral thesis on Maryland during the Revolution under my direction.
[91] Carter Braxton to Landon Carter, 17 May, LMCC, I, 453–54.

differences are ended." On 25 May the convention adjourned to meet again in August unless called together earlier by the committee of safety.[92]

John Adams snorted that "Maryland has passed a few eccentric resolves, but these are only flashes which will soon expire";[93] but the Marylanders showed no intention of doing anything further until after the debate on 10 June. The next day the Maryland delegates told the Maryland committee of safety the convention should meet as soon as possible, and suggested that it would be well if the delegates to the convention were directed to "collect the opinion of the people at large, in some manner or other" previous to the meeting.[94] Samuel Chase and Charles Carroll arrived in Philadelphia from their mission to Canada on 11 June and they soon left for Maryland. Chase, who had worked with the Adamses since the first Continental Congress, began stirring up support for independence. He left Philadelphia on 14 June and on the 21st he wrote back to John Adams that he was almost angry with him, and insisted that he write constantly. "I am almost resolved not to inform you," said Chase, "that a general dissatisfaction prevails here with our convention. Read the papers and be assured Frederick [county] speaks the sense of many counties. I have not been idle. I have appealed *in writing* to the people. County after county is instructing."[95]

Chase wrote on the first day the convention reassembled, but far from voting in favor of independence, it at once ordered the Maryland delegates in Philadelphia to attend the convention, but told them not to leave Congress without first obtaining a guarantee that it would not discuss "questions of independence, foreign alliance, and a further confederation of the colonies" until the Maryland delegates returned to Philadelphia.[96]

Congress responded by voting that the "great questions" would not be postponed because "it is now become public in the colonies that those questions are to be brought on the 1st of July."[97] On 17 June John Adams had written Chase that Pennsylvania, Delaware, and New Jersey had agreed to independence and that "Maryland now stands alone. I presume she will soon join company; if not, she must be left alone."[98]

Adams's letters were handed to Chase in the Maryland convention. At

[92] Proceedings of the Maryland Convention, 20–25 May (Early State Records, Microfilm).
[93] John Adams to Benjamin Hichborn, 29 May, *Works*, IX, 379.
[94] 11 June, LMCC, I, 485.   [95] Adams Papers, MHS.
[96] Force, 4 ser. VI, 1485.
[97] John Adams to Samuel Chase, 24 June, *Works*, IX, 413–14. The journals do not record this vote.
[98] Ibid. 396–98. The letter is misdated by the editor of Adams's *Works*.

nine o'clock Friday evening 28 June, Chase left the convention to find an express rider to send the news to Adams that the Maryland convention had voted unanimously for independence. You can see, he told Adams, "the glorious effects of county instructions. Our people have fire if not smothered." He concluded his hasty note with *"Now for a Government."* [99]

Chase's emphasizing of his statement about government reflected the desperation of Maryland's leaders. By the end of June they were far more worried about threats to the internal stability of the colony than they were about the implications of independence from Britain. The convention spent most of 28 June, not in debating independence but in making plans to send troops to the eastern shore to suppress a threatened rebellion against the planters by poor whites, slaves, and loyalists. And a few days later the convention voted for fitting out armed vessels to cruise along the eastern shore.[100]

The leaders of New York were as opposed to independence as the leaders of Maryland, but the provincial congress, controlled by the Livingston faction, seemed paralyzed. The old leaders of the Sons of Liberty who had pushed and shoved the Livingstons into opposition to British policies were no longer united. Alexander McDougall, always more conservative than the other leaders, and always loyal to the Livingstons, acquiesced in their hope of reconciliation. John Lamb joined the army as an artilleryman and was captured before Quebec in December 1775. Isaac Sears became so disgusted with the vacillation of the Livingstons that he left for Connecticut in August 1775, although he returned twice. He came back with a hundred Connecticut men in November 1775, and destroyed James Rivington's press, and then in February 1776 as a deputy of General Charles Lee.

The mechanics in New York City, which had been the center of agitation for a decade, did not have the talents of the leaders who had deserted them. Thus there was no effective popular pressure on the provincial congress. Most of the Livingston faction, and John Jay, James Duane, and Robert R. Livingston, who were its principal representatives in Philadelphia, no more wanted independence than did the De Lanceys, who had sunk with the royal government they had clung to. Furthermore, whether

[99] Adams Papers, MHS. The Maryland resolution for independence is in Force, 4 ser. VI, 1491.
[100] Force, 4 ser. VI, 1490–91, 1496.

independence came or not, they hoped to maintain the power of the aristocracy within New York, and to fend off demands for a more democratic society. John Jay, who deplored "the tenderness shown to some wild people" in New York, soon became the leader of the Livingston faction in its effort to maintain the old order. Their strategy, as Robert R. Livingston explained it, consisted of "well-timed delays, indefatigable industry, and a minute attention to every favorable circumstance. . . ." [101]

The preamble adopted by the Continental Congress on 15 May calling for the creation of governments based on the power of the people presented New York's leaders with a problem. They accepted the theory of the sovereignty of the people but they had no intention of implementing it. To avoid doing so, the provincial congress finally agreed on an ambiguous report which was the work of John Jay's wily mind, and was obviously designed to befuddle the voters. Government by the congress and committees had been intended to end with reconciliation, but reconciliation now seemed remote and uncertain. Such government was inadequate and therefore the voters were to authorize their delegates in congress to consider the matter, or to elect new delegates. Then, if a majority of counties in the congress decided to create a new government, it would remain in force "until a future peace with Great Britain shall render the same unnecessary." The voters should act promptly so the congress could consider the question of a new government after the second Monday in July. [102]

There was no mention of independence but it could not be ignored. On 4 June representatives of the "General Committee of Mechanics in Union" appeared at the doors of the congress with a "humble address" stating that it would give the mechanics the "highest satisfaction" if New York's delegates in the Continental Congress were instructed to use their "utmost endeavors . . . to cause these united colonies to become independent of Great Britain. . . ." The congress replied blandly that it looked upon the "Mechanics in Union" as a voluntary committee "warmly attached to the cause of liberty," but one without any authority whatsoever in public matters. As for independence, the "Continental Congress alone have that enlarged view of our political circumstances, which will enable them to decide upon those measures which are necessary for the general welfare." The provincial congress would not "presume" to instruct New York's dele-

[101] To Alexander McDougall, 23 March, H. P. Johnston, ed., *The Correspondence and Public Papers of John Jay* (4 vols., New York, 1890–93), I, 49–50; Young, *Democratic Republicans*, 15.
[102] 31 May, Force, 4 ser. VI, 1351–52.

gates about independence until the question had been brought before the Continental Congress, and the New York congress was asked for the "sense" of New York.[103]

But New York's leaders had no intention of trying to discover the "sense" of the people. On the first day of the debate over Richard Henry Lee's motion for independence, the New York delegates in Philadelphia sent an urgent letter asking for instructions. "The matter will admit of no delay," they said.[104] The letter got to New York on 10 June where the congress discussed and then postponed an answer. The next day John Jay offered some extraordinary resolutions "on the subject of independence." The main points were that the "good people" of New York had not authorized either the congress or the delegates in Philadelphia to vote on independence; that it was inconvenient to recur to the people at large on every great question; that the people should give the provincial congress unlimited power to do anything it thought best for the colony; and finally, that the people should inform their delegates in congress "of their sentiments relative to the great question of independency. . . ."

The congress adopted the resolutions and then voted at once not to publish them until *after* the election of deputies with the power to form a new government.[105] John Jay then wrote a letter to the delegates in Philadelphia telling them that they did not have the power to vote on independence, that the constituents of the members of the provincial congress had not given the congress the power to decide, and that the congress did not intend to ask the people for the power. It would be "imprudent" to ask the people "lest it should create division" and have an unhappy influence upon the creation of a new government for New York.[106]

New York's leaders, like those of Maryland, were frightened by demands for a political revolution in New York, but were saved from a confrontation with those who made such demands by the British army and navy. The occupation of New York City by the British destroyed that center of radical activity as a political force in New York and allowed the Livingstons and their allies to write a state constitution with only minimal regard for popular participation.

But their artful dodging could not avoid independence, and it left the New York delegates in the Continental Congress powerless to vote either yes or no during the first and second days of July 1776 while the delegates

103 Ibid. 1362–63. The mechanics' address, dated 29 May, was widely reprinted in newspapers. It is reprinted ibid. 614–15.
104 8 June, LMCC, I, 477.   105 Force, 4 ser. VI, 1395–96.
106 11 June, ibid. 814.

of the other twelve colonies transformed the colonies into independent states as the "United States of America."

By the first of July 1776, the "embarrassing opposition" which had forced certain members of Congress "to do the work of the Lord deceitfully" had almost vanished.[107] However, there were men who still opposed independence, or at the very least, hoped to delay it. Before Congress resumed the debate on Richard Henry Lee's resolution, Edward Rutledge begged John Jay to return to Philadelphia. A declaration of independence, a confederation of the colonies, and a plan for foreign treaties would be laid before Congress on Monday 1 July. "Whether we shall be able effectually to oppose the first and infuse wisdom into the others will depend in a great measure upon the exertions of the honest and sensible part of the members."[108]

"This morning is assigned for the greatest debate of all," wrote John Adams early on Monday. "May Heaven prosper the new-born republic, and make it more glorious than any former republics have been."[109] Just as the debate began, Maryland's unanimous vote for independence was given to Congress, to the joy of John Adams, but at the end of the day he reported that the debate "was an idle mispence of time for nothing was said but what had been repeated and hackneyed in that room before, a hundred times, for six months past."[110]

John Dickinson began the debate with an eloquent speech against a declaration of independence at that time. He foresaw a dark and uncertain future without foreign aid, and he did not expect that such aid would be forthcoming. He could see no advantages to a declaration until after many problems had been solved. The colonies should first make sure of foreign help; they should settle bitter rivalries over land claims; establish settled governments; and above all, agree upon a constitution uniting the colonies. The committee drafting articles of confederation, of which he was chairman, was disputing almost every article so strongly that "some of us totally despair of any reasonable terms of Confederation." He would be glad, he said, "to read a little more in the Doomsday Book of America—Not all— that like the Book of Fate might be too dreadful." He feared civil war and the breakup of "this Commonwealth of Colonies" within twenty or thirty

107 John Adams to Samuel Chase, 24 June, *Works,* IX, 413.
108 29 June, LMCC, I, 517.   109 To Archibald Bulloch, *Works,* IX, 414.
110 To Samuel Chase, 1 July, ibid. 415–16.

years.[111] John Adams replied to Dickinson, but he kept no notes, and years later could not recall what he had said.[112]

The speeches were finished and the vote on Lee's resolution was called for. Nine colonies voted yes: New Hampshire, Connecticut, Massachusetts, Rhode Island, New Jersey, Maryland, Virginia, North Carolina, and Georgia. Two colonies—Pennsylvania and South Carolina—voted no. Delaware had no vote because Thomas McKean voted yes and George Read voted no. The New York delegates did not vote. They said that as individuals they were for independence, and believed their constituents were for it, but their instructions forbade them to consider anything but reconciliation with Great Britain.

Could nine colonies go ahead and proclaim independence? Congress was saved from that decision by Edward Rutledge of South Carolina. He suggested that the final vote be put off until the next day. He and his colleagues of the South Carolina delegation were opposed to Lee's resolution, but he believed that they "would then join in it for the sake of unanimity." "The ultimate question" was then postponed.

The next day the question was again moved and South Carolina voted for independence. So did Delaware. Thomas McKean had sent a messenger to Caesar Rodney, who, "tho detained by thunder and rain," arrived in time to break the tie in the Delaware delegation.[113] Pennsylvania changed its vote. On 1 July three of its delegation—Franklin, John Morton, and James Wilson—had voted for Lee's motion, but John Dickinson, Robert Morris, Thomas Willing, and Charles Humphreys voted against it. On 2 July Dickinson and Morris abstained. Thus Pennsylvania voted for independence, three votes to two.[114]

During the day, before the final vote was taken, Elbridge Gerry wrote James Warren that since "the facts are as well known at the Coffee Houses of the city as in Congress," he could tell him that independence had been carried the day before by the vote of nine colonies.[115] Philadelphians, at least, were therefore not surprised on 3 July when the *Pennsylvania Gazette* announced that "Yesterday the Continental Congress declared the United Colonies Free and Independent states."

What came to be known as the "Declaration of Independence" was

[111] J. H. Powell, ed., "Speech of John Dickinson Opposing the Declaration of Independence, 1 July 1776," PMHB, LXV (1941).
[112] *Autobiography*, III, 396–97.
[113] Caesar Rodney to Thomas Rodney, 4 July, LMCC, I, 528.
[114] Thomas McKean to A. J. Dallas, 26 Sept. 1796, LMCC, I, 533–34. Thomas Jefferson's Notes of Proceedings are the most complete account of the actions in Congress on 1 and 2 July. Jefferson, *Papers*, I, 314–15.
[115] LMCC, I, 526.

largely the work of Thomas Jefferson to whom the committee appointed early in June had delegated the task of preparation. His draft was presented to Congress on Friday, 28 June, when it was read and then ordered "to lie on the table." [116] At least one delegate thought the document "a pretty good one. I hope it will not be spoiled by canvassing in Congress." [117] Other members disagreed and they began arguing about Jefferson's draft after the vote for independence on 2 July, and kept at it off and on until the evening of 4 July. Jefferson was indignant because the "pusillanimous idea" that Americans still had friends in England led Congress to strike out censures of the people of England. Struck out too was an attack on slavery in "complaisance" to South Carolina and Georgia, which wanted to continue importing slaves, and also because the "northern brethren . . . felt a little tender" since they had been involved in the slave trade.[118]

The members of Congress finally finished revising Jefferson's work on the evening of 4 July and ordered that "the declaration be authenticated and printed." [119] It was not until 19 July that a busy Congress got around to giving the document an official title. On that day it ordered "the Declaration passed on the 4th, be fairly engrossed on parchment, with the title and style of 'The unanimous Declaration of the thirteen united States of America,' and that the same, when engrossed, be signed by every member of Congress." [120]

३৯

The American people did not have to wait to read the Declaration until it had been engrossed on parchment and signed by the members of Congress—a process that took months, if not longer.[121] As soon as the delegates agreed to the final draft on 4 July, Congress ordered it printed and distributed throughout America.[122] The *Pennsylvania Evening Post* published the Declaration on Saturday, 6 July, and public celebrations began of what most Americans at once called "The Declaration of Independence."

Monday noon, 8 July, "the Declaration of Independence was pro-

[116] JCC, V, 491.
[117] Josiah Bartlett to John Langdon, 1 July, Force, 4 ser., VI, 1195.
[118] Jefferson, Notes of Proceedings, *Papers*, I, 314–15.   [119] JCC, V, 516.
[120] Ibid. 590–91. The capitalization of the title above is that of the engrossed copy rather than that used by the editor of the *Journals*.
[121] The engrossed copy was ready for signing on 2 August. For discussions of the signing of the Declaration of Independence see Edmund C. Burnett's note, LMCC, I, 528–32 and Julian Boyd, "Editorial Note," Jefferson, *Papers*, I, 299–308.
[122] JCC, V, 516.

claimed at the State House in this city, in the presence of many thousand spectators who testified their approbation by repeated acclamations." [123] John Adams who watched the celebration in Philadelphia reported that "three cheers rended the welkin. The battalions paraded on the Common, and gave us the *feu de joie*, notwithstanding the scarcity of powder. The bells rang all day and almost all night. Even the chimers chimed away." [124] That same day at Trenton, New Jersey, "the Declaration was this day proclaimed, together with the new constitution of the colony," and the proceedings "were received with loud acclamations." [125]

On the afternoon of 10 July "the Declaration of Independence was read at the head of each brigade of the Continental Army posted at and in the vicinity of New York. It was received everywhere with loud huzzas, and the utmost demonstrations of joy. . . ." That night the equestrian statue of George III was "by the Sons of Freedom . . . laid prostrate in the dirt—the just desert of an ungrateful tyrant. The lead wherewith the monument was made is to be run into bullets to assimilate the brains of our infatuated adversaries, who to gain a peppercorn, have lost an empire." [126]

While the people celebrated joyously, thoughtful men were taking stock of what had been done, and trying to peer into the future. The "sensible" and "moderate" men who had opposed independence calculated the odds and very sensibly concluded that the Americans could never win a war against one of the greatest powers in Europe. They knew that tens of thousands of Americans were not "unanimous" for independence, and that states, communities, and even families were divided on the issue. They knew that there were bitter, unsettled quarrels among the states and that independence would leave Americans with no umpire to turn to. The Continental Congress was no substitute for the government of Great Britain. It did not have the power to tax, to regulate trade, to control finance, or to settle interstate disputes. All that gave force to the recommendations of the Congress was the fickle support of public opinion. Joseph Galloway raised such questions in the First Continental Congress and John Dickinson raised them anew in his last speech against independence on 1 July 1776.

Some of the men who thus assessed the problems that would arise from independence remained loyal to Britain. Others accepted independence, although some of them continued to hope for reconciliation, as did Robert Morris.

---

[123] PG, 10 July. [124] To Samuel Chase, 9 July, *Works*, IX, 420–21.
[125] PJ, 17 July. [126] Ibid.

For months some Americans hoped that commissioners would come from Britain with proposals that would make reconciliation possible, but it was not until the week after Congress voted for independence that Admiral Richard Howe arrived with authority for him and his brother, General William Howe, to act as "peace commissioners." The admiral also brought with him the greatest fleet and army that had ever come to America, and his brother, the general, landed his army on Staten Island on 2 July. Before Americans learned that the two brothers did not have the power to offer acceptable terms, hopes of reconciliation rose anew. Robert Morris was sorry that "there are some amongst us, that cannot bear the thought of reconciliation on any terms." If the commissioners had any propositions to offer, Americans should listen to them. "I have," said Morris, "uniformly voted against and opposed the Declaration of Independence, because, in my poor opinion, it was an improper time, and will neither promote the interest nor redound to the honor of America; for it has caused division when we wanted union. . . ." [127]

What such men could not understand was the attitude of the men who believed in independence. They could not comprehend the calm optimism of a Samuel Adams who said that it had taken time and patience "to remove old prejudices, to instruct the unenlightened, to convince the doubting, and fortify the timid" as Americans had moved step by step "till at length we are arrived to perfection . . . in a Declaration of Independence. Was there ever a Revolution brought about, especially so important as this, without great internal tumults and violent convulsions!" [128]

Nor could practical men understand the faith of those people who looked ahead to a bright future as an independent nation at the same time that they realized the road to that future would be dark and beset by peril. Yet it was that faith, combined with the knowledge that the way would be hard, that enabled enough Americans to carry on through years of defeat and despair until they at last forced the world to recognize the new nation they hopefully named the United States of America.

No one summed up better both the faith in the future and the obstacles on the way to it than the man who did as much to bring about independence as any man in America—John Adams. The day after Congress voted for independence he wrote two letters to his wife. In the first letter he said: "Yesterday the greatest question was decided, which ever was debated in America, and a greater perhaps, never was or will be decided among men."

[127] To Joseph Reed, 20 July, Reed, *Reed*, I, 200–201.
[128] To Benjamin Kent, 27 July, *Writings*, III, 304–5.

It was the will of Heaven that the two countries should be separated forever and "it may be the will of Heaven that America shall suffer calamities still more wasting and distresses yet more dreadful. If this is to be the case, it will have this good effect, at least: it will inspire us with many virtues, which we have not, and correct many errors, follies, and vices, which threaten to disturb, dishonor, and destroy us. The furnace of affliction produces refinement, in states as well as individuals. And the new governments we are assuming, in every part, will require a purification from our vices, and an augmentation of our virtues or they will be no blessings. The people will have unbounded power. And the people are extremely addicted to corruption and venality, as well as the great. I am not without apprehensions from this quarter. But I must submit all my hopes and fears, to an overruling Providence, in which, unfashionable as the faith may be, I firmly believe."

His second letter that day concluded with an eloquent reaffirmation of his faith:

"The second day of July 1776, will be the most memorable epocha in the history of America. I am apt to believe that it will be celebrated, by succeeding generations, as the great anniversary festival. It ought to be commemorated as the Day of Deliverance by solemn acts of devotion to God Almighty. It ought to be solemnized with pomp and parade, with shows, games, sports, guns, bells, bonfires, and illuminations from one end of this continent to the other from this time forward forever more.

"You will think me transported with Enthusiasm but I am not. I am well aware of the toil and blood and treasure, that it will cost us to maintain this Declaration, and support and defend these States. Yet through all the gloom I can see the rays of ravishing light and glory. I can see that the end is more than worth all the means. And that posterity will triumph in that day's transaction, even although we should rue it, which I trust in God we shall not." [129]

[129] To Abigail Adams, 3 July, *Family Corres.*, II, 27–31.

Table of Symbols

HCJ	House of Commons *Journals*	II, n.16
HEHL	Henry E. Huntington Library	II, n.13
HSP	Historical Society of Pennsylvania	II, n.36
HUL	Harvard University Library	IV, n.14
JCC	*Journals of the Continental Congress*	XIX, n.27
JHB	*Journals of the House of Burgesses*	III, n.48
JPCM	*Journals of Each Provincial Congress of Massa-chusetts*	XXI, n.63
LC	Library of Congress	I, n.20
LMCC	*Letters of the Members of the Continental Congress*	XIX, n.1
Mass. Ar.	*Massachusetts Archives*	VII, n.16
Md. Ar.	*Maryland Archives*	IX, n.97
MdG	*Maryland Gazette*	IV, n.2
MG	*Massachusetts Gazette*	IV, n.27
MHJ	Massachusetts House *Journals*	III, n.35
MHS	Massachusetts Historical Society	V, n.54
MHSC	Massachusetts Historical Society *Collections*	III, n.20
MHSP	Massachusetts Historical Society *Proceedings*	VI, n.59
MVHR	*Mississippi Valley Historical Review*	XV, n.43
NCCR	*Colonial Records of North Carolina*	VII, n.24
NEQ	*New England Quarterly*	III, n.17
NHG	*New Hampshire Gazette*	III, n.3
N.J.Ar.	*New Jersey Archives*	VII, n.23
NM	*Newport Mercury*	III, n.2
NYAJ	New York Assembly *Journals*	III, n.27
NYCD	*Documents Relative to the Colonial History of the State of New York*	III, n.45
NYDH	*Documentary History of New York*	XIII, n.35
NYG	*New York Gazette*	III, n.9
NYHSC	New York Historical Society *Collections*	V, n.7
NYHSQ	New York Historical Society *Quarterly*	V, n.73
NYJ	*New York Journal*	IV, n.36
NYM	*New York Mercury*	III, n.13
NYPL	New York Public Library	III, n.32
Pa.Ar.	*Pennsylvania Archives*	III, n.29
PC	*Pennsylvania Chronicle*	IX, n.16
PG	*Pennsylvania Gazette*	IV, n.29
PH	*Parliamentary History of England*	VI, n.25
Pickering	Pickering, *Statutes at Large*	II, n.8

PJ	*Pennsylvania Journal*	V, n.42
PMHB	*Pennsylvania Magazine of History and Biography*	I, n.3
PrG	*Providence Gazette*	III, n.9
PRO	Public Record Office	II, n.9
RICR	*Records of the Colony of Rhode Island*	III, n.24
RNYG	*Rivington's New York Gazetteer*	XVII, n.44
SCG	*South Carolina Gazette*	IV, n.1
SCG(C)	*South Carolina Gazette and Country Journal* (Crouch)	V, n.3
SCG(T)	*South Carolina Gazette* (Timothy)	IV, n.1
SCHJ	South Carolina Commons House of Assembly Journals	IV, n.46
SS	Secretary of State	II, n.9
VG(DH)	*Virginia Gazette* (Dixon and Hunter)	XX, n.27
VG(P)	*Virginia Gazette* (Purdie)	V, n.34
VG(PD)	*Virginia Gazette* (Purdie and Dixon)	I, n.22
VG(Py)	*Virginia Gazette* (Pinkney)	XX, n.29
VG(R)	*Virginia Gazette* (Rind)	V, n.37
WMQ	*William and Mary Quarterly*	I, n.8
Writings(S)	*The Writings of Benjamin Franklin*, Smyth edition	IV, n.35

Index

Incidental references to individuals, places, events, and institutions are not included in this index.

296; tries to force Shelburne to resign, 315-16; and Wilkes affair, 317-20; rejects Hillsborough's American policy, 322-23; supports North ministry, 328; and East India Company, 434, 436; approves sending troops to colonies and opposes peace commission, 570, 572-73, 580; approves North's "Olive Branch" resolutions, 580-81; rejects petition of First Congress, 643; hires Hessians, 646-47; proclaims colonies in rebellion, 647, 649; speech to Parliament (1775), 649

Georgia, 8-9, 14-15, 58, 61, 117, 123, 128, 138, 152, 192, 233, 308-9, 312, 370, 582, 600, 633, 687-88, 700-701; and Stamp Act, 117, 123, 138, 152, 231; non-importation in, 312; legislature, 322, 518; and Intolerable Acts, 477; and the Association (1774), 516, 518; counties, 518; provincial congresses and conventions, 518, 678; and independence, 678, 700

Gerry, Elbridge, 415-16; on *Gaspée* incident, 429; and preparations for war, 559; fears social revolution in Massachusetts, 626-28; replaces Cushing in Second Congress, 652-53; requests instructions to vote for independence, 671

Gill, John (publisher, *Boston Gazette*), 128, 246, 254-55, 360, 368, 411

Glasgow, 163, 171

Goddard, William: *The Partnership*, 400; on Thomas Wharton, 442

Gordon, Rev. William: on colonial mobs, 145-46; on Boston Tea Party, 452; on colonial disunity (1774), 515; on Lexington and Concord, 586-87, 589-90; on John Hancock, 587

Government, structure of in colonies, 19-30, 35, 75, 92-94, 98, 118, 227; legislatures, 5, 20-26, 35, 157, 227; qualifications for voting, 12, 22-26, 55, 62, 99, 157, 259, 479, 481, 522, 561, 627; courts, 20-24, 26; governors, 21-23, 227; councils, 21-24, 505, 508; local governments, 21-28, 30-31, 49; parties, nature of, 148, 153, 191-92, 373-76. *See also: individual colonies.*

Governors, colonial. *See:* Governments,

structure of; Francis Bernard (Mass.); Thomas Boone (S.C.); Lord Botetourt (Va.); William Bull (S.C.); Lord William Campbell (S.C.); Guy Carleton (Que.), Cadwallader Colden (N.Y.); Robert Dinwiddie (Va.); Lord Dunmore (Va.); Robert Eden (Md.); Francis Fauquier (Va.); Thomas Fitch (Conn.); Sir William Franklin (N.J.); Thomas Gage (Mass.); Stephen Hopkins (R.I.); Thomas Hutchinson (Mass.); Josiah Martin (N.C.); Lord Charles Montagu (S.C.); Sir Henry Moore (N.Y.); John Penn (Pa.); Thomas Pownall (Mass.); William Shirley (Mass); Jonathan Trumbull (Conn.); Sir William Tryon (N.C. and N.Y.); Joseph Wanton (R.I.); Samuel Ward (R.I.); John Wentworth (N.H.); William Wright (Ga.).

Grafton, Duke of, 163, 290; attacks Rockingham ministry, 215; heads Pitt ministry, 217, 315; creates secretary of state for colonies, 315-16; agrees to station troops in Boston, 322; replaced by Lord North, 325

Gray vs. Paxton, 76

Great Britain: colonial policies: pre-1763 policies, 5, 19-21, 42-45, 51-53, 55-59; origins of post-1763 policies, 35, 41-48, 52-55, 59-60, 66; 1763–76 policies, Chapters II, VI, VIII, XII and pages 252-54, 288-91, 296-301, 395-97, 434-39, 453-60, 569-583, 645-50

Great Britain: politics: character of in 1760, 36-38; role of monarchy in, 37-38; political changes in 1762–63, 39-40; impact of American opposition on, 180-81, 221-23, 297-99, 326-29, 438-39, 453-60, 569-70, 573-83, 649; political changes after 1763, 215-19, 223, 225, 314-15, 316, 325. *See also:* William Beckford; Duke of Bedford; Edmund Burke; Lord Camden; Henry Conway; George III; Duke of Grafton; George Grenville; Lord Hillsborough; "King's Friends"; Lord North; William Pitt; Marquis of Rockingham; Lord Sandwich; Earl of Shelburne; Earl Temple; Charles Townshend; John